Sally S. Kimball
1108 Tacoma St.,
Port Orchard, Wa.

June 13, 1968

W9-BFB-164

SECOND EDITION

GREGG

► TYPEWRITING

► FOR

► COLLEGES

ALAN C. LLOYD, Ph.D.
Director, Gregg Typing Instructional Service
Gregg Division, McGraw-Hill Book Company

JOHN L. ROWE, Ed.D.
Chairman, Department of Business Education
College of Education, University of North Dakota

FRED E. WINGER, Ed.D.
Professor of Secretarial Science and Business Education
Oregon State University

COMPLETE COURSE

GREGG DIVISION

McGraw-Hill Book Company

NEW YORK   CHICAGO   DALLAS   SAN FRANCISCO   TORONTO   LONDON

Copyright © 1964, 1957, by McGraw-Hill, Inc.
All Rights Reserved. This book, or parts thereof, may not be
reproduced in any form without permission of the publishers.

Library of Congress Catalog Card Number 63-17340

    5 6 7 8 9 RRD-64 2 1 0 9 8 7

38199

Printed in the United States of America

Contents

CONTENTS

INDEX

OVERVIEW

This book focuses on three goals—

Gregg Typewriting for Colleges, Second Edition, has been developed, tested, and published—

A. To help you become a *rapid, accurate touch operator* of the typewriter.

B. To make you proficient in the *production* of letters, reports, tables, documents, forms, and manuscripts.

C. To help you master the *rules* that govern word division, paragraphing, correspondence courtesies, and similar typewriting technicalities.

Millions of trainees achieved these goals via the preceding edition of this book. To help *you* achieve them, too, but even more quickly and easily, this edition features a number of notable aids:

A. To help you become a skillful typist

1. *Selective Practice.* You will learn how to analyze and select drills so that you may (*a*) focus mainly on those that will help *you* most and (*b*) practice them in the way that will most surely help *you.*

2. *Massed Drill.* Skill comes from drill. This book contains more drills than any other book of similar length. More than a fourth of the lessons concentrate solely on skill boosting, and every lesson contains some drills for sustaining and extending your skill.

3. *Copy Control.* Your drill needs will change as you improve; to be sure the drills are right for you at each stage, every drill and exercise has been controlled for word length, vocabulary, repetition, and other factors basic to rapid growth.

B. To help you become a production expert

4. *Power Cycles.* You will learn to use your typing power even while you increase it, for this book is organized in a spiral. After the introductory first Part, each Part is a 25-lesson cycle:

6 lessons on skill extension
6 lessons on correspondence typing
6 lessons on tables or business forms
6 lessons on manuscripts and reports
1 lesson that is a test on the others

Each cycle boosts your typing power and then gives you production assignments geared to your new level of power.

5. *Picture-Page Approach.* So that you may develop full understanding of production typing, every new step in each area of production begins with studying, then copying, an annotated model. This book has more models than any similar book.

6. *Production Count.* The production exercises are accompanied by a special "production word count" that will enable you to use identical material for both building skill and applying it—a procedure that will enable you to attain much higher production rates and to achieve them much sooner.

7. *Practical Procedures.* The typing shortcuts introduced in the first edition and now standard in all books are continued; and new ones are provided for letter placement, ZIP-coding, balance-lining, and error-absorbing.

C. To help you master typing technicalities

8. *Learning Guides.* Pioneering in the direction of programmed instruction, this book introduces in its companion workbooks "Learning Guides" that you will use in your typewriter (making a "teaching machine" of it). By providing instant confirmation of your answers to questions, the Learning Guides will give you greater mastery, faster. These aids cover such technical areas as margin determination, word division, number expression, footnoting, punctuating, and related areas that the informed typist is expected to master.

9. *Copy Editing.* Most rules about technicalities are presented, also, in intensive summaries that you will reproduce as reports (and keep for permanent reference) and then apply to the kinds of unedited material with which most typists work.   THE AUTHORS

1 THE TYPEWRITER · THE ALPHABET
AND THE NUMBER KEYS

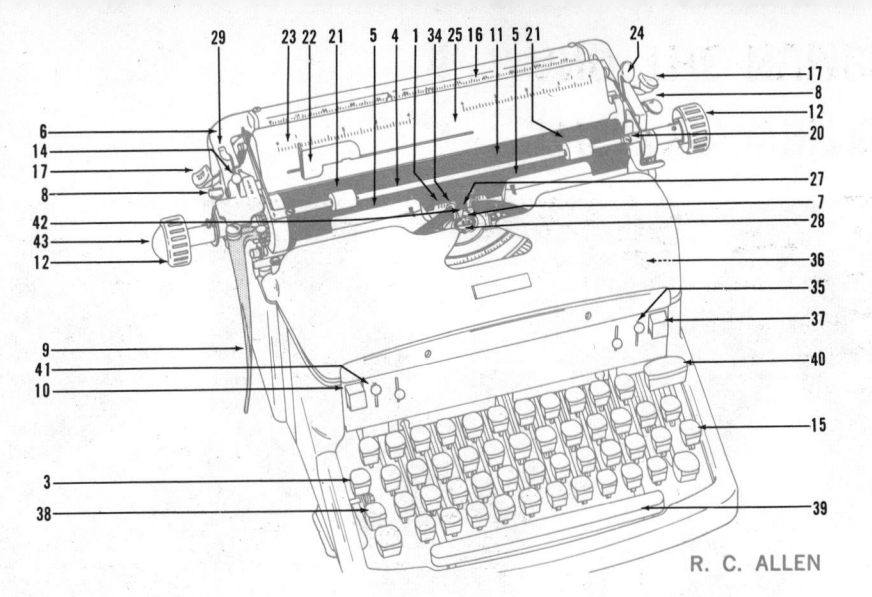

R. C. ALLEN

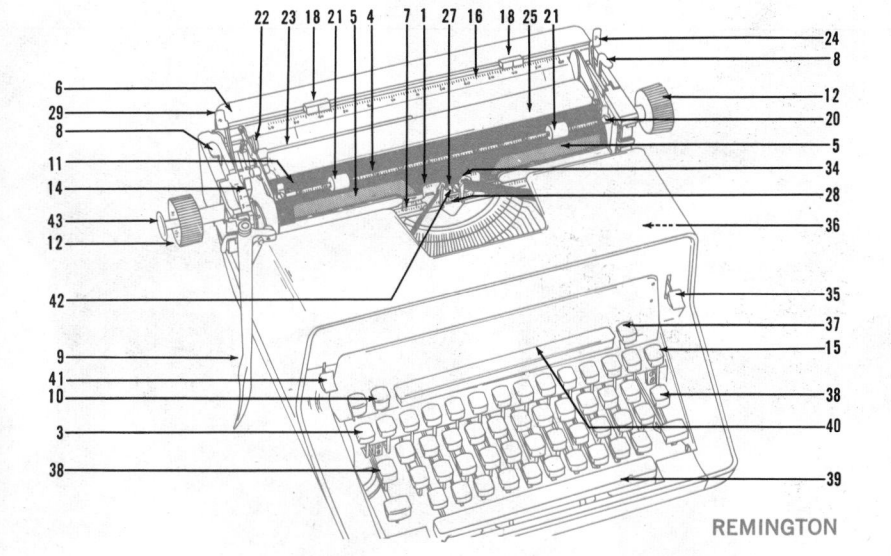

REMINGTON

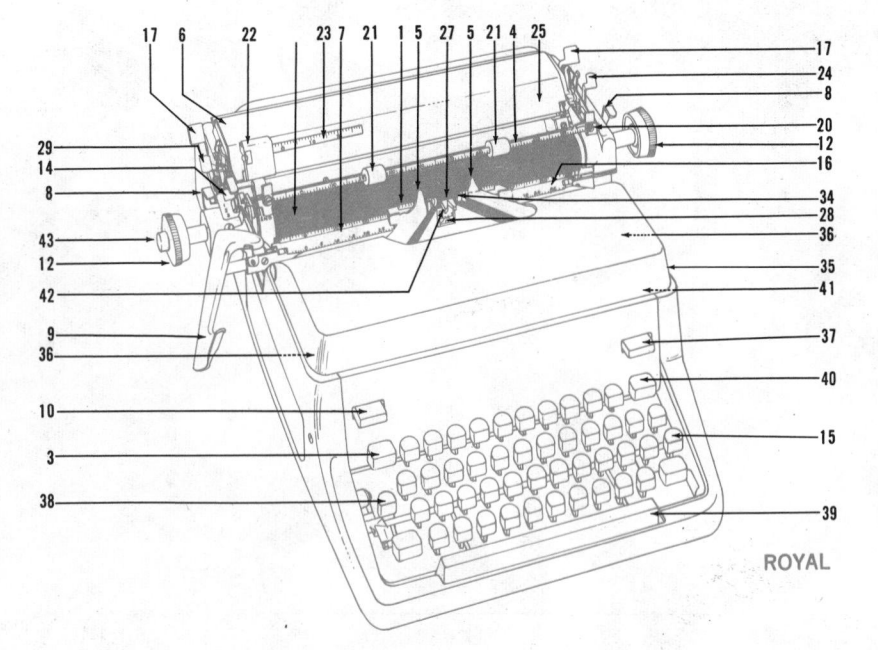

ROYAL

1. Aligning Scale
2. All Clear (lever)
3. Backspacer (key)
4. Bail Scale
5. Card Holders
6. Carriage
7. Carriage-Position Scale
8. Carriage Releases (levers)
9. Carriage Return (lever)
10. Clear Key (for tab stops)
11. Cylinder
12. Cylinder Knobs
5. Envelope Guides
14. Linespace Regulator
9. Linespacer (lever)
15. Margin Release (key)
16. Margin Scale
17. Margin Set (key)
18. Margin Stops
20. Paper Bail
21. Paper-Bail Rolls
4. Paper-Bail Scale
22. Paper Guide
23. Paper-Guide Scale
24. Paper Release (lever)
25. Paper Rest
11. Platen (Cylinder)
27. Printing Point
28. Printing-Point Indicator
29. Ratchet Release (lever)

Continues below

2

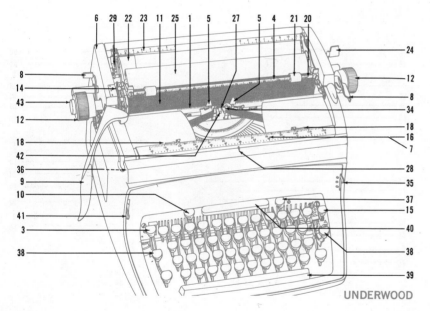

SMITH-CORONA

UNDERWOOD

Continued from above

34. Ribbon Carrier
35. Ribbon Control (lever)
36. Ribbon Reverse (lever)
17. Set Keys (for margins)
37. Set Key (for tab stops)
38. Shift Locks (keys)
39. Space Bar
10. Tab Clear (key)
37. Tab Set (key)
2. Tab Total Clear (lever)
40. Tabulator (key or bar)
41. Touch Control (lever)
42. Typebar Guide
43. Variable Linespacer

*Parts you need to know
for the first lessons*

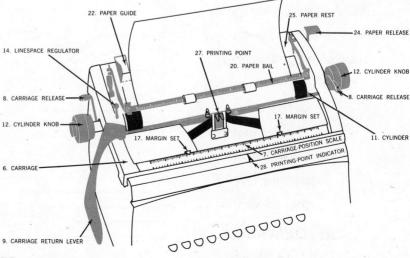

22. PAPER GUIDE
25. PAPER REST
24. PAPER RELEASE
14. LINESPACE REGULATOR
27. PRINTING POINT
20. PAPER BAIL
12. CYLINDER KNOB
8. CARRIAGE RELEASE
8. CARRIAGE RELEASE
12. CYLINDER KNOB
17. MARGIN SET
11. CYLINDER
17. MARGIN SET
7. CARRIAGE-POSITION SCALE
6. CARRIAGE
28. PRINTING-POINT INDICATOR
9. CARRIAGE RETURN LEVER

REFERENCE • MANUAL TYPEWRITERS

3

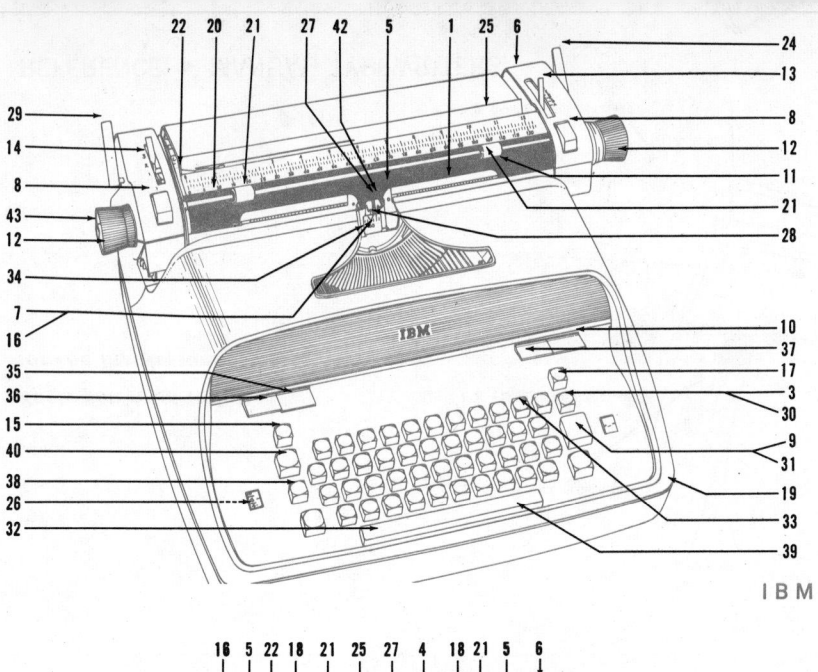

IBM

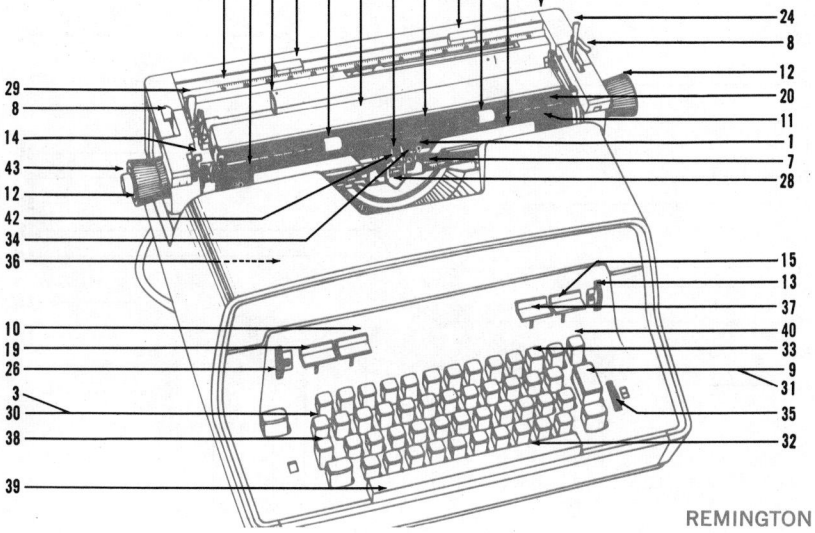

REMINGTON

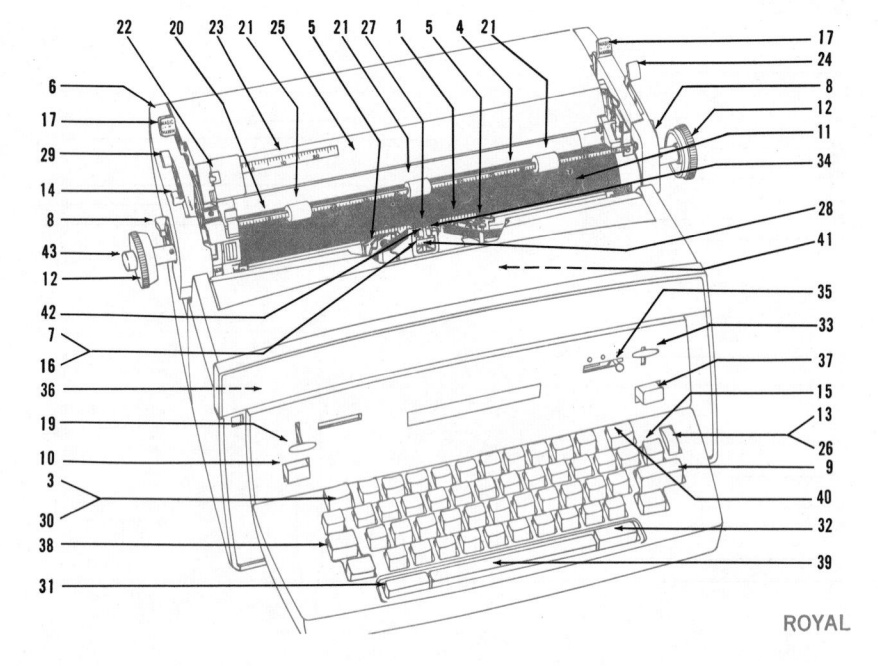

ROYAL

B. PRINCIPAL PARTS OF ELECTRIC TYPEWRITERS

1. Aligning Scale
2. All Clear (lever)
3. Backspacer (key)
4. Bail Scale
5. Card Holders
6. Carriage
7. Carriage-Position Scale
8. Carriage Releases (levers)
9. Carriage Return (key)
10. Clear Key (for tab stops)
11. Cylinder
12. Cylinder Knobs
5. Envelope Guides
13. Impression Regulator (carbons)
14. Linespace Regulator
9. Linespacer (key)
15. Margin Release (key)
16. Margin Scale
17. Margin Set (key)
18. Margin Stops
19. Off-On Switch
20. Paper Bail
21. Paper-Bail Rolls
4. Paper-Bail Scale
22. Paper Guide
23. Paper-Guide Scale
24. Paper Release (lever)
25. Paper Rest
11. Platen (Cylinder)
19. Power Switch
26. Pressure Regulator

Continues below

4

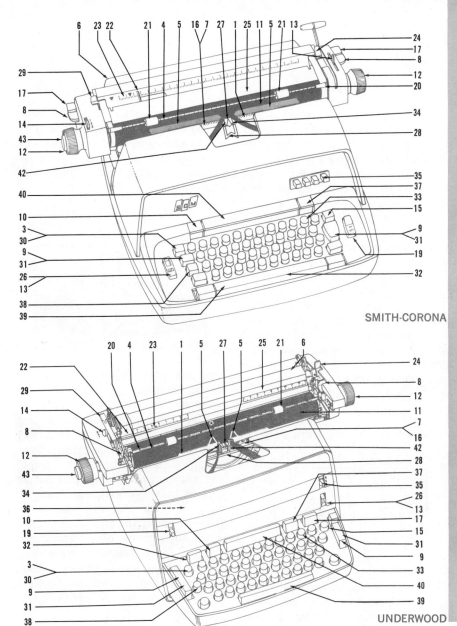

SMITH-CORONA

UNDERWOOD

Continued from above

27. Printing Point
28. Printing-Point Indicator
29. Ratchet Release (lever)
30. Repeat Backspacer
31. Repeat Carriage Return
32. Repeat Forward Spacer
33. Repeat Underscore
34. Ribbon Carrier
35. Ribbon Control (lever)
36. Ribbon Reverse (lever)
17. Set Keys (for margins)
37. Set Key (for tab stops)
38. Shift Locks (keys)
39. Space Bar
10. Tab Clear (key)
37. Tab Set (key)
 2. Tab Total Clear (lever)
40. Tabulator (key or bar)
41. Touch Control (lever)
42. Typebar Guide
43. Variable Linespacer

Parts you need to know
for the first lessons

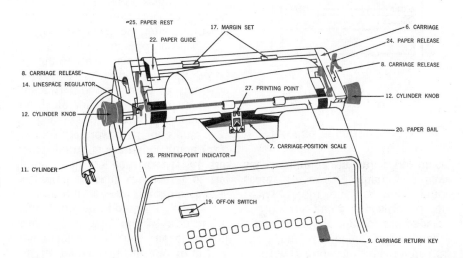

C. HORIZONTAL SPACING

1. Counting the spaces

Each time a key or the space bar is tapped, the carriage (6) moves one space to the left. Each tap moves the carriage exactly one space.

Remember: Typewriters space uniformly, as though printing on graph paper. Each space is the same size.

The quick brown fox jumped over Tom's Lazy dog.

The spaces can be counted. Every typewriter has a carriage-position scale (7) that marks off the spaces. The scale numbers every fifth or tenth space, too, so that the typist may know the number of each space across the carriage.

Every machine has some kind of arrowhead, line, or other marker, called the printing-point indicator (28), that points to the space on the scale at which the carriage is positioned and at which the machine is ready to print. When the carriage is at the 50th space, for example, the marker points at 50.

2. Finding the center space

A typist is expected to center across the paper almost everything he types—that is, he arranges what he types so that half appears on each side of the center of the paper. Such centering requires the typist to know at what point on the carriage-position scale the center of the paper will fall and to adjust his machine so that the center of the paper will always appear at that centering point.

The part of the machine that is adjusted so that the center of the paper will be consistently at the same point is the paper guide (22). It may be moved left or right. The typist selects the centering point he wishes to use and then adjusts the paper guide so that the center of the paper will always be at the point he has selected.

Which point should be selected? Recommended: 50. This number is easy to remember, easy to find on the carriage-position scale, and easy to add to and subtract from in planning margin settings. Remember: For efficiency, adjust the paper guide so that the center of the paper will fall at 50.

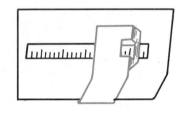

3. Adjusting the paper guide

To adjust the paper guide so the center of the paper will always be at 50 [or whatever point may be selected], seven steps are involved. They need to be taken only once; after that, the typist knows where the guide belongs and does not need to repeat the steps.

STEP 1. Set the carriage at 50 [or other selected point].

STEP 2. At the top of a sheet of paper, mark the center by a pencil mark or by a crease.

STEP 3. Insert the paper.

STEP 4. Depress the paper release (24), so the paper will be loose and can be slid left or right.

STEP 5. Keeping the paper straight, slide it left or right until the center crease or mark is squarely at the printing point (27).

STEP 6. Restore the paper release to its normal position.

STEP 7. Slide the paper guide (22) to bring its blade edge snugly against the left edge of the paper. Now the guide is positioned correctly. Note on the paper-guide scale (23) exactly where you have set the guide; remember the place.

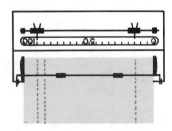

4. Planning margin settings

STEP 1. Determine what length of writing line is to be used.

The line length for drills is given in the lesson headings. For example, LINE: 40 means "set margins for a 40-space line." The line length for letters, reports, and other work is something to be learned as an aspect of producing such work [see Index, page iv].

STEP 2. Plan the setting for the left margin stop. From the center of the paper, subtract half the desired line length and set the stop at the resulting number.

STEP 3. Plan the setting for the right margin stop. To the center of the paper, add half the desired line length plus 5 extra spaces [to provide for the warning signal of the bell] and set the stop at the resulting number.

EXAMPLE: Settings for a 40-space line would be $50-20=30$ for the left margin stop and $50+20+5=75$ for the right margin stop.

LINE DESIRED	LEFT MARGIN STOP AT	RIGHT MARGIN STOP AT
COMMON MARGIN SETTINGS (With the Paper Centered at 50)		
40 spaces	$50-20=30$	$50+20+5=75$
50 spaces	$50-25=25$	$50+25+5=80$
60 spaces	$50-30=20$	$50+30+5=85$
70 spaces	$50-35=15$	$50+35+5=90$

5. Setting the margin stops

Procedures vary for different makes and models of typewriters.

SPRING-SET MACHINES. Royals, Smith-Coronas, and some R. C. Allens have a margin-set key (17) at each end of the carriage. To set the left stop: Press the left margin-set key, move the carriage to the desired scale point, and release the set key. To set the right stop: Press right margin-set key, move carriage to desired scale point, and release set key.

HAND-SET MACHINES. The margin stops (18) of Underwoods, IBM Selectrics, Remingtons, and some R. C. Allens are adjustable by hand, without use of a set key. Adjust each margin stop separately: Press 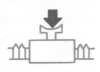 down the top of the margin stop, slide the stop left or right to desired scale point, and release stop.

HOOK-ON MACHINES. Electric Underwoods, standard IBMs, and some Remingtons have hook-on margin stops (18). To set the left margin stop: Move the carriage to the left margin, hook onto the left margin stop by holding down firmly the margin-set key (17) on the keyboard, move the carriage to the desired scale point, and release the set key. To set the right margin stop: Move the carriage to the right margin, hook onto the right stop by holding down firmly the set key (same key you used for left margin), move carriage to desired scale point, and release margin-set key.

6. Pica and elite spacing

Typewriters are usually equipped with either of two sizes of type: pica [pronounced *pie*-ka] and elite [pronounced ay-*leet*].

Pica type, the larger, prints 10 letters to an inch; elite prints 12 letters to an inch. On standard typing paper, 8½ inches wide, a pica machine can type 10 x 8½ = 85 characters; and an elite machine can type 12 x 8½ = 102 characters.

To determine whether a machine is pica or elite, type a series of periods and compare them with the ones printed here:

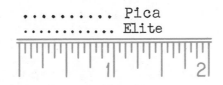

The distinction between pica and elite sizes is unimportant in typing forms, tables, and drills but becomes important when typing letters and reports, whose placement guides are usually expressed in terms of inches. When planning the margins for letters and reports, the typist must convert *inches* into *spaces* (and for elite machines, he must also "round off" the figures), as shown in this table:

INCHES TO SPACES
When Planning Margin-Stop Settings

	4″	5″	6″
Number inches in the line	4″	5″	6″
Pica spaces (10 per inch)	40	50	60
Elite spaces (12 per inch)	48	60	72
Elite line, "rounded off"	50	60	70

7. Indenting with the tabulator

For use in indenting paragraphs and other operations in which the typist wishes to spring the carriage to an assigned point without repeatedly striking the space bar, all machines have a "tabulator" mechanism. It has three controls on, or slightly above, the keyboard:

TAB-SET KEY (37) is used to set a pin, known as a "tab stop," at the point where it is desired that the carriage stop automatically.

TAB-CLEAR KEY (10) is used to clear, or eliminate, an individual tab stop that was previously set. Some machines have an ALL-CLEAR KEY (2) to eliminate simultaneously all stops that are already set.

TAB KEY OR BAR (40) is used to free the carriage from its regular

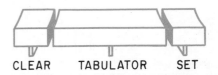

spacing so that it may spring to the point where a tab stop is set.

The use of these controls is illustrated by the steps involved in preparing for paragraph indenting:

STEP 1. Confirm margin settings.

STEP 2. Clear any tab stops already set: Press the all-clear key (2) or move the carriage to the right margin and then return it while pressing the clear key (10).

STEP 3. Set a tab stop at the point to which the carriage is to spring: Space in from the margin (standard indention: 5 spaces) and press the tab-set key (37).

STEP 4. Test the setting: draw the carriage back to the margin; then firmly press the tab bar or key (40). The carriage should hop to the point where the stop is set.

8. Centering a word or line

To center a word or group of words (title of an essay, for example), three steps are involved:

STEP 1. Set the carriage at the centering point.

STEP 2. Say *in pairs* the strokes (letters *and* spaces) in the material to be centered, depressing the backspacer (3) once for each pair of strokes. If an odd, leftover letter remains after calling the pairs, do *not* backspace for it.

STEP 3. Beginning at the point to which the carriage has been backspaced, type the material; it will be centered horizontally.

If several lines are to be centered, centering the carriage for each line is simplified by setting a tab stop at the center. The typist then tabulates (indents) to that point instead of positioning the carriage manually.

D. VERTICAL SPACING

9. Controlling the spacing

The amount of blank space between lines of typing is controlled by the linespace regulator (14), which may be set at "1" for single spacing and which provides *no* blank space between typed lines; at "2" for double spacing, which provides *one* blank line be-tween lines of typing; and at "3" for triple spacing, which provide *two* blank lines between lines of typing. Examples:

```
single ——— double ——— triple
double ——— single
single
double ——— single
single ——— triple
```

Some machines *also* have 1½ spacing (midway between single and double) and 2½ spacing (midway between double and triple); but even on such machines, most work is typed in standard single and double spacing.

10. Inserting extra blank lines

To leave *extra* space between some lines of typing, advance the paper one line more than the number of lines that are to be left blank. For example, to leave a blank line be-tween two sets of drills, advance

```
ddd kkk kkk ddd kkk dd kk dd k
ddd kkk kkk ddd kkk dd kk dd k
ddd kkk kkk ddd kkk dd kk dd k

fff jjj jjj fff jjj jj ff jj f j
fff jjj jjj fff jjj jj ff jj f j
fff jjj jjj fff jjj jj ff jj f j
```

the paper *two* lines (by returning the carriage twice instead of once), one to be the blank line and one to be the next line on which to type.

Remember: Always advance the paper one more line than the num-ber of lines to be left blank.

This book occasionally displays an arrow and a number to signal how many lines to advance the paper, to solve a special arrangement problem. An arrow-3, for example, does not mean to leave three blank lines but to leave two blank lines by advancing the paper three lines.

The typist must always be aware of the spacing for which his type-writer is set. Advancing the paper three lines when the machine is set for single spacing, for example, simply requires three carriage re-turns. But advancing the paper the same three lines when the machine is set for *double* spacing requires a single carriage return (two lines) and one line turned up by hand.

Sometimes the instructions are to "Leave 1 inch space." Most ma-chines provide 6 lines of space to a vertical inch. To leave 6 blank lines, advance the paper 7 lines—6 for the blank inch and 1 to reach the line of typing.

```
Line 1
Line 2
Line 3
Line 4
Line 5
Line 6
```

11. Centering material vertically

Standard typing paper (11 inches long) provides 11 x 6 = 66 possible lines of space to a page. To center lines within these 66 lines:

STEP 1. Count the lines (includ-ing blank ones) the material fills.

STEP 2. Subtract the number of lines needed from the 66 available (or from 33, on a half sheet).

STEP 3. Divide the remainder by 2 (count a fraction as a whole) to get the number of the line, counting from the top, on which to begin.

[NOTE: For material to *look* cen-tered, the bottom margin should be a little wider than the top one; the three steps above provide for this desirable difference.]

EXAMPLE. A 21-line display would be 66−21=45; and 45÷2=22½ or 23, the line on which to begin. This provides a top margin of 22 lines and a bottom one of 23 lines.

E. CARE OF THE TYPEWRITER

12. Keeping a machine in trim

DAILY CARE. Brush the printing faces of the typebars. Dust inside the machine with a long-handled brush. Wipe adjacent desk surfaces and under the machine. Keep ma-chine covered when not in use.

WEEKLY CARE. Using a cloth moistened with oil, wipe the rails on which the carriage moves.

BIWEEKLY CARE. Using a cloth dampened with alcohol, wipe the cylinder (11) and paper-ball rolls (21).

CONSTANT CARE. Return carriage briskly but without a *bang!* Untan-gle jammed keys carefully—never *pull* typebars, lest they be bent.

13. Putting on a new ribbon

STEP 1. Before removing the old ribbon, note how it is threaded and which of these winding arrangements is used to approach the spool:

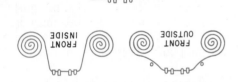

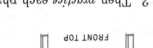

FRONT OUTSIDE   FRONT INSIDE   FRONT TOP

STEP 2. Then *practice* each phase of the ribbon change—lift out a spool, put it back; unthread the carrier, rethread it; and so on.

STEP 3. Wind the old ribbon on one spool; detach the end, noting how it was hooked to the spool. Discard old spool and ribbon.

STEP 4. Fasten end of the new ribbon on the empty spool. Place both spools in their sockets.

STEP 5. Thread the new ribbon into place. (Depressing the shift lock makes it easier to thread the ribbon through the carrier.) Check that the ribbon reverses properly.

F. STEPS WHEN PREPARING TO TYPE

1. Arrange the table

Machine, even with front of table. Book at right, turned and tilted. Extra paper, left of machine.

2. Check the paper guide

Paper guide should be adjusted so center of paper will be at 50. Review §8 on page 6.

3. Set the linespace regulator

Instructions at the start of each lesson say whether to set machine for single or double linespacing.

4. Set the margin stops

LINE: 40

Instructions at the start of each lesson state for what line length you are to set the margins. Review §4, page 6; and §5, page 7.

5. Move paper bail away

So the paper bail will not interfere with the paper insertion, pull the bail toward you. (If it will not pull forward on your typewriter, lift the bail straight upright.)

6. Grasp and insert paper

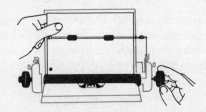

Left hand grasps paper and puts it behind cylinder, against paper guide. Right hand turns cylinder knob, to draw paper into machine. Turn up 4 or 5 inches of paper.

7. Straighten the paper

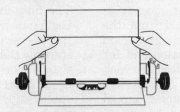

The left side of the paper should align, top and bottom, at the paper guide. If the alignment is not correct, loosen paper (use paper release) and straighten it.

8. Reset the paper bail

Adjust rolls to divide paper approximately into thirds; then place the bail snugly against the paper.

9. Provide for top margin

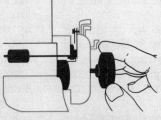

If preparing to type drills: Turn paper down (use cylinder knob) until only a quarter inch or so of paper shows above the top of the bail.

If preparing for production work: Before resetting paper bail, turn paper down until its top edge is even with aligning scale (1) and then advance the paper for the assigned depth of top margin. *Then* reset the paper bail in clamping position.

10. Check typing posture

Head erect, turned to face the book

Back straight, elbows relaxed

Body centered opposite J key, leaning forward

Feet apart and firmly set

11. Check hand position

Position finger tips on home keys:
Left hand on A S D and F
Right hand on J K L and Semicolon

ON MANUAL MACHINE, curve fingers *tightly* (as though to pull an iron bar) and let them rest lightly *on* home keys, without pressure.

ON ELECTRIC MACHINE, curve fingers *slightly* and hold them as close to home keys as you can without quite touching them (as though they were too hot to touch).

Rules For Typewriting Contests

The following rules are given for the convenience of teachers and students who wish to observe contest rules in marking papers or in conducting competitions. *These are the rules commonly used in calculating scores on employment tests.* The rules are based on those issued by the late James N. Kimball, official judge of the International Typewriting Contests for 25 years.

Rules for correcting papers

1. General Rule. Every word (including its following punctuation and spacing) omitted, inserted, misspelled, or changed in any way from the test copy must be penalized. BUT NOTE: Only *one* error may be charged against any one word.

2. Errors in Printed Copy. Any error in the printed test copy may be copied exactly or corrected.

3. Punctuation and Horizontal Spacing. A word that is otherwise correct must be marked as an error if its following punctuation mark or spacing is omitted, incorrectly made, or changed from the copy. NOTE: Contest authorities should agree upon definite rules for sequence of punctuation and for spacing and describe them in detail. Require each contestant's work to be consistent.

4. Erasing. Erasing is not allowed, unless agreed upon prior to a specific test.

5. Transposition. Any transposition in any word or group of characters constitutes an error. Single words or groups of words that are transposed are penalized one error for the transposition plus one error for each mistake in the transposed matter.

6. Rewritten Matter. Rewritten words, groups of words, or characters are charged one error for the rewriting, plus an error for each mistake in the rewritten matter.

7. Last Word. An error made in the last word typed, whether the word is completed or not, must be charged.

8. Crowding, Piling, and Misspacing. No word shall occupy other than its proper number of spaces. If a portion of one character overlaps a portion of another character or extends into the space between words so that it would overlap a portion of any character that might be in that space, an error is charged.

9. Word Division. A word incorrectly divided at the end of a line is penalized. NOTE: Contest authorities should identify acceptable guides.

10. Faulty Shifting and Lightly Struck Characters. Unless the complete character is discernible, an error is charged.

11. Left-Hand Margin and Paragraph Indention. The first character on all lines, except those that begin paragraphs, must appear at the same point on the line scale—at the left margin. Each line not starting thus and each paragraph indented other than 5 spaces will constitute errors.

12. Short and Long Lines. Except when using special copy designed and declared for shorter lines, the last character typed on each line (other than the last line of a paragraph or of the test) must rest on some space between the 61st and 76th, inclusive, considering the left margin as space No. 1. Every shorter or longer line is an error.

13. Short Pages. Any page, except the last, containing fewer than 33 lines (on 13-inch paper) or 27 lines (on 11-inch paper) is a short page and constitutes an error.

14. Line Spacing. Double spacing is required. Each line irregularly spaced is penalized one error.

15. Cut Characters. If any part of a character or a word is cut off at the edge of the paper, it is charged as an error.

16. Other Questions. Interpretations of the rules and any question not described in them shall be subject to final decision by the contest manager.

Calculation of test results

17. Gross Strokes. Strokes are counted correctly by considering the entire copy as having been typed in *one continuous line.* Each character or space in such a line counts as one stroke.

18. Gross Words. The total gross words are the total gross strokes typed, divided by 5. Do not add strokes in repeated matter or subtract strokes in omitted matter. NOTE: The count given with most test copy is the cumulative gross word count (strokes ÷ 5).

19. Penalty. For each error charged under these rules, *10 words* must be deducted from the gross words.

20. Net Words. After deducting the penalty from the gross words, the remainder represents the *total net words.* The typist's *net rate* (words a minute—wam) is computed by dividing his total net words by the number of minutes he typed. Fractions of .500 or less are discarded; fractions over .500 are credited to the next whole number.

EXAMPLE: A typist writes 5,808 gross strokes with 8 errors in 15 minutes—

$5{,}808 \div 5 = 1{,}161.6$ or $1{,}162$ gross words

$8(\text{errors}) \times 10 = 80$ (penalty)

$1{,}162 - 80 = 1{,}082$ net words

$1{,}082 \div 15$ (minutes) $= 72.1$ net words a minute

Home Keys

Space Bar . . . Right thumb

LINE: 40 (SEE PAGE 9)
SPACING: SINGLE
GOAL: CONTROL SPACE
  BAR AND HOME KEYS
STRESS: BOUNCE-OFF
  KEY STROKES

Adjust the machine and position your hands as illustrated on page 9.

1-A. With all fingers held motionless in the home position, poise your right thumb about a quarter of an inch above the space bar. Now sharply tap the space bar in its center—bounce your thumb off it. Repeat until you hear the margin bell ring.

1-A. Practice striking the space bar

Space once [TAP THE SPACE BAR ONCE] . . . twice [TAP THE SPACE BAR TWICE] . . . once . . . once . . . twice . . . once . . . twice . . . once . . . twice . . . twice . . . once . . . once . . . Repeat

1-B. Practice returning the carriage

1-B. Practice returning the carriage (including getting your hand back to home position) until you can do so with confidence and without raising your eyes from the book. Then repeat the drill until you can return the carriage without raising your eyes from the printed words.

MANUAL MACHINE. In one continuous sweep of the left hand, (a) place the forefinger and next two fingers against the return lever; (b) *flip* the lever with a toss of the wrist, returning the carriage to the margin; and (c) dart your left hand back to its home-key position.

ELECTRIC MACHINE. In a quick, stabbing motion, (a) extend the little finger of your right hand to the adjacent carriage-return key; (b) lightly flick—press—the return key, causing the carriage to return automatically; and (c) *zip* the finger back to its home-key position.

Space once . . . twice . . . once . . . twice . . . Ready to return
[MOVE HAND TO RETURN LEVER OR FINGER TO RETURN KEY]
—Carriage! [RETURN IT] . . . Home! [FINGERS ON HOME KEYS] . . . Repeat

1-C. Practice striking the forefinger keys

1-C. Using the right-hand thumb and the forefingers (with all other fingers kept in home position), type these three lines experimentally to determine how much force is needed to make each key print clearly and cleanly. On a manual machine, use a very sharp, "biting" stroke; on an electric machine, just "tap" the keys lightly.

Left forefinger on *F* key
Right thumb on space bar   }   fff fff ff ff f f ff ff f f

Right forefinger on *J* key
Right thumb on space bar   }   jjj jjj jj jj j j jj jj j j

Left forefinger on *F* key
Right forefinger on *J* key
Right thumb on space bar   }   fff jjj ff jj f j ff jj f j

5-MINUTE SPEED WITHIN 2 ERRORS OR 10-MINUTE SPEED WITHIN 5 ERRORS			
45-49	50-59	60-64	65-Up
D	C	B	A

Spacing: double
Paragraphs: tab 5
Line: 70 (lines
  will align)
SI: 1.49—fairly
  difficult

1 | 2 | 3 | 4 | 5 | 6 | 7 | 8 | 9 | 10 | 11 | 12 | 13 | 14

As long as the memory of man goes back, the people living in the   14
British Isles have thought of the English Channel as a veritable moat   28
that kept enemy invaders from their shores; and the enemy thought the   42
same. Half the conquerors of Europe have floundered in their efforts   56
to ford that 30 miles or so of turbulent water that make the Channel.   70

So for whole centuries the British have thwarted every proposal,   84
rejected every plan, denied all consideration of any of the ideas for   98
building a bridge over the Channel or constructing a tunnel under it.   112
It is said that some Britons still shudder when a historian refers to   126
the plans that Napoleon was shaping for tunneling to England in 1802.   141

But the age of airplanes and missiles has dried up the moat, you   155
might say, so that the Channel is just a nuisance that handicaps both   169
the British and their neighbors in both trade and vacation ambitions.   183
All concerned want to build an easy route across the Channel, and the   197
number of speculators who are anxious to make a fortune by financing,   211
through stock purchases, the construction of a bridge or a tunnel has   225
no limit; the argument is not about "whether" but only about "which."   239

At the moment the odds seem to favor a "chunnel," as the channel   253
tunnel is called in Britain; but there is room for debate. Those who   267
prefer a bridge, possibly one made on anchored pontoons, point up the   281
economy of such construction; a tunnel would cost infinitely more, of   295
course. Those who favor the tunnel, however, point out the hazard of   309
the weather and scornfully claim that one earnest Channel storm would   323
spread the bridge over or under the whole North Sea; whereas, there'd   337
be no weather in a tunnel but only a steady stream of toll dividends.   351

Many fine engineers have given great study to the tunnel design.   365
It is envisioned as no scant mining shaft but rather as a multilevel,   379
gigantic tube that would carry trains and trucks and automobiles both   393
directions in their own lanes. One plan calls for having automobiles   407
ride piggyback on trains built for the purpose; this would be faster,   421
they say, and a lot safer. It would sure cut down on the collisions!   436

The point of leapfrogging the Channel is only in part the factor   450
of time; a bridge or tunnel would reduce the trip only from about two   464
hours to forty or so minutes. The big thing is the facility; ferries can   478
carry only a thousand autos a day, but a bridge or a tunnel could carry   492
three thousand vehicles each way across the Channel every hour!   506

1 | 2 | 3 | 4 | 5 | 6 | 7 | 8 | 9 | 10 | 11 | 12 | 13 | 14

RIGHT HAND

J .... Forefinger
K .... Second finger
L .... Third finger
; ...... Little finger

Space Bar ... Right thumb

1-D. Use forefingers on F and J keys. Keep other fingers motionless in home position. Tap the space bar with the thumb of your right hand.

1-D. Practice the F and J keys

1
```
fff fff jjj jjj fff jjj ff jj ff jj f j
fff fff jjj jjj fff jjj ff jj ff jj f j
fff fff jjj jjj fff jjj ff jj ff jj f j
```

Leave a blank line (return carriage twice) before you start a new drill.

1-E. Use second fingers. The forefingers may rise slightly; other fingers should remain motionless in their home positions.

1-E. Practice the D and K keys

2
```
ddd ddd kkk kkk ddd kkk dd kk dd kk d k
ddd ddd kkk kkk ddd kkk dd kk dd kk d k
ddd ddd kkk kkk ddd kkk dd kk dd kk d k
```

1-F. Use third fingers. Little fingers should be kept anchored in home position. Your other fingers may rise slightly.

1-F. Practice the S and L keys

3
```
sss sss lll lll sss lll ss ll ss ll s l
sss sss lll lll sss lll ss ll ss ll s l
sss sss lll lll sss lll ss ll ss ll s l
```

Return the carriage without looking up.

1-G. Use fourth fingers. Keep forefingers anchored in home position. Other fingers may rise slightly.

1-G. Practice the A and ; keys

4
```
aaa aaa ;;; ;;; aaa ;;; aa ;; aa ;; a ;
aaa aaa ;;; ;;; aaa ;;; aa ;; aa ;; a ;
aaa aaa ;;; ;;; aaa ;;; aa ;; aa ;; a ;
```

1-H. Note the pattern of each drill line; then type lines 5-7 two times each (plus an extra time if the line is difficult for you).

1-H. Build some words

5
```
aaa ddd add add|aaa lll all all|add all
```

6
```
aaa sss kkk ask|jjj aaa lll jal|ask jal
```

7
```
ddd aaa ddd dad|lll aaa ddd lad|dad lad
```

1-I. Notice the change in the drill pattern here from that in lines 5-7; then type lines 8-10 two or three times each.

1-I. Build a few longer words

8
```
a as ask asks asks; f fa fal fall falls
```

9
```
a al ala alas alas; f fl fla flas flask
```

10
```
a ad add adds adds; s sa sal sala salad
```

1-J. Type line 11 twice. GOAL: To finish both of the copies in 1 minute.

1-J. Measure your progress

11
```
a sad fad; a lass falls; dad asks a lad
```

Space once after semicolon.

Manuscript 82

2-PAGE REPORT
WITH FOOTNOTES

Paper: workbook 445-446
Spacing: double
Line: 6 inches, centered
Grade: as marked on copy,
   for 30 minutes' work

MAKING CORRECTIONS
By (Your Name)

There is no such thing as a perfect typist;
so we must all learn to correct mistakes.
This report is intended as a guide for making corrections. It is a digest of information
to be found in books by Rowe[1] and by
Gavin and Hutchinson.[2]

TECHNIQUE 1: ERASING

A. Be sure your hands and eraser are
clean. (To clean an eraser, rub it briskly
on paper or on fine-grained sandpaper.)

B. Move the carriage as far as possible
to one side so that erasure crumbs cannot
fall into the machine.

C. Roll the paper so that the error to be
corrected is on top of the cylinder. Hold the
paper firmly by pressing it against the cylinder with the tips of your fingers.

D. Erase with light, short, circular motions, blowing very lightly to keep the dust
out of the machine.   (Grade: D)

E. Return the paper to writing position
and type the correction. Tap the key lightly. Tap it repeatedly until the corrected
letter is as dark as the other letters on the
page.

---

1. John L. Rowe, *et al., Gregg Typing,
191 Series, Book One* (New York: McGraw-Hill, 1962), page 129.

2. Ruth E. Gavin and E. Lillian Hutchinson, *Reference Manual for Stenographers
and Typists,* Third Edition (New York:
McGraw-Hill, 1961), page 5 ff.

TECHNIQUE 2: REALIGNING   (Grade: C)

If an error is detected after the paper
has been removed, erase the error and reinsert the paper for typing a correction:

A. Insert the paper and roll it up so that
the line on which the correction is to be
made is above the aligning scale.

B. Depress the paper release and adjust
the paper so that (1) the line is straight, (2)
the line is the same distance above the scale
as in normal typing, and (3) the white lines
on the scale point exactly to the center of
the letter i or l.

C. Set the carriage at the point of correction.   (Grade: B)

D. Type the correction very, very lightly—so lightly that you can barely see it—to
check the accuracy of your aligning.

E. Improve the aligning, if necessary.

TECHNIQUE 3: WORD SHIFTING

When an extra letter is to be typed in a
correction, the whole word is erased and
retyped a half space to the left of its original position. If one less letter is to be
typed, the word is erased and retyped a
half space to the right.

Shifting the word may be accomplished
by moving the paper or by holding the carriage in half-space position as each letter is
typed. Rowe[3] suggests using the backspace
key to hold the carriage in half position.
The carriage can also be held by hand or,
on some machines, by holding down the
space bar.

---

3. Rowe, *op. cit.,* page 129.   (Grade: A)

New Keys

LINE: 40
SPACING: SINGLE
GOAL: CONTROL E, U,
  G, AND RIGHT SHIFT
STRESS: KEEPING
  FEET FLAT ON FLOOR

On charts like this, keys already practiced appear in color. New keys to be mastered in the lesson are shown in black and white.

2-A. Type lines 1 and 2 twice each. Leave 1 blank line (return the carriage twice) after the second copy of each of the lines.

2-B. Use D-finger. Try the ded reach (keep A-finger in home position, to guide D-finger back after it has struck E key); then type lines 3-6 three times.

2-C. Use J-finger. Try the juj reach (keep Sem-L-K-fingers in home position, to guide J-finger back after striking U key); type lines 7-10 three times. Speed up on repetitions.

2-D. Use F-finger. Try the fgf reach (keep your A-S-D fingers at home; move only the F-finger); then type lines 11-14 three times.

2-E. To capitalize any letter that is on the left half of the keyboard:

(1) Keeping J-finger home, press and hold down right shift key with Sem-finger.

(2) Strike the letter key.

(3) Release the shift key and return all fingers to their home-key position.

Type lines 15-18 three or more times each.

2-A. Review the keys you know

1   fff jjj ddd kkk sss lll aaa ;;; fff jjj

2   sss aaa ddd sad sad aaa sss kkk ask ask

2-B. Practice the **E** key

3   ddd ded eee ddd ded eee ddd ded eee ded

4   ded see see ded fee fee ded lee lee ded

5   ded led led ded fed fed ded fee fee ded

6   ded sea sea ded elk elk ded elf elf ded

Dotted lines are to spotlight the reach-path you are practicing.

2-C. Practice the **U** key

7   jjj juj uuu jjj juj uuu jjj juj uuu juj

8   juj dud dud juj due due juj sue sue juj

9   juj us; us; juj use use juj uke uke juj

10   juj due due juj sue sue juj use use juj

2-D. Practice the **G** key

11   fff fgf ggg fff fgf ggg fff fgf ggg fgf

12   fgf lag lag fgf jag jag fgf sag sag fgf

13   fgf dug dug fgf lug lug fgf jug jug fgf

14   fgf leg leg fgf keg keg fgf egg egg fgf

2-E. Practice the right **SHIFT** key

15   ;;; A;; A;; ;;; S;; S;; ;;; D;; D;; ;;;

16   ;;; Ask Ask ;;; Alf Alf ;;; Ada Ada ;;;

17   ;;; See See ;;; Sal Sal ;;; Del Del ;;;

18   ;;; Elk Elk ;;; Fae Fae ;;; Gae Gae ;;;

Table 76

OPEN TABLE

Paper: workbook 443, Center in top half
Spacing: single
Special: arrange alphabetically by first column

STANDARD REFERENCE BOOKS

Information	*Source Book (Title)*
Financial ratings	Moody's Manuals; Poor's Manuals
Advertising rates	Standard Rate & Data
Credit ratings	Dun & Bradstreet Ratings
Congress	Congressional Directory
Churches	Yearbook of American Churches
Postal	U. S. Official Postal Guide
Hotels	Official Hotel Red Book
Books	United States Catalogue
Banks	The Banker's Blue Book
People	Who's Who in America

Table 77

OPEN TABLE

Paper: workbook 443, Center in bottom half
Spacing: single, with 3-line groupings

NAMES OF THE MONTHS IN FOUR LANGUAGES
(Note the Capitalization)

ENGLISH: January, February, March, April, May, June, July, August, September, October, November, December. FRENCH: janvier, fevrier, mars, avril, mai, juin, juillet, aout, septembre, octobre, novembre, decembre. GERMAN: Januar, Februar, Marz, April, Mai, Juni, Juli, August, September, Oktober, November, Dezember. SPANISH: enero, febrero, marzo, abril, mayo, junio, julio, agosto, septiembre, octubre, noviembre, diciembre.

Table 78

RULED TABLE

Paper: workbook 444, Center in top half
Spacing: double

COMPARATIVE EARNINGS STATEMENT
(Years Ending December 31)

Item	Last Year	This Year
Operating Revenues..............	$65,605,838	$81,960,327
Operating Charges..............	53,283,067	61,011,682
Net Income before Taxes........	$12,322,771	$20,948,645
Federal and State Taxes.......	3,207,610	6,960,400
NET INCOME	$9,115,161	$13,988,245

Table 79

BOXED TABLE

Paper: workbook 444, Center in bottom half
Spacing: as marked

INVENTORY OF OFFICE EQUIPMENT
> Knoxville Office, ~~August 31~~ today & year

ITEMS	# Condition: Good	Fair	Poor	TOTAL
Chairs, Executive	2 ✓	8 ✓	4 ✓	14 ✓
Chairs, Guest	10 ~~12~~	8 ~~10~~	8 ~~3~~	25 ✓
# > Chairs, Stenographic	8 ~~9~~	7 ~~8~~	13 ~~11~~	28 ✓
# > Desks	10 ✓	20 ~~24~~	13 ~~8~~	43 ~~42~~
# > Electric Fans	4 ~~5~~	7 ~~9~~	4 ~~1~~	15 ✓
Files, 3-Drawer	8 ~~6~~	0 ✓	0 ✓	8 ~~6~~
Files, 4-Drawer	24 ✓	11 ✓	12 ✓	47 ✓
# > Mimeograph Machines	1 ~~2~~	2 ~~1~~	0 ✓	3 ✓

2-F. Build some word families

2-F. Note the pattern of each line; then type lines 19-21 twice each. Speed up and sustain an even pace on the repetitions.

19 Dell fell jell ell; fads gads lads dads

20 Flag slag skag lag; fuse uses used use;

21 Gale kale sale ale; full dull gull lull

2-G. Measure your progress

2-G. Type line 22 twice. GOAL: To finish both of the copies in 1 minute.

22 Sue fed a sad lad a salad; Ask a judge;

LINE: 40
SPACING: SINGLE
GOAL: CONTROL R,
PERIOD, H, AND
LEFT SHIFT
STRESS: BOUNCE-OFF
SPACE-BAR STROKES

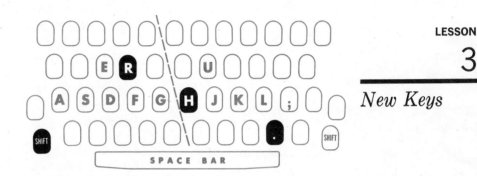

LESSON
3

New Keys

3-A. Review the keys you know

3-A. Type lines 1 and 2 twice—evenly and rapidly.

1 aaa ;;; sss lll ddd kkk fff jjj aaa ;;;

2 ded led fed fgf leg keg juj jug lug dug

3-B. Practice the R key

3-B. Use F-finger. Try the frf reach (keep the A-S-D-fingers at home; move only the F-finger); then type lines 3-6 three times. You should be able to type each of the lines rapidly.

3 fff frf rrr fff frf rrr fff frf rrr frf

4 frf fur fur frf far far frf jar jar frf

5 frf err err frf ere ere frf are are frf

6 frf red red frf rug rug frf rag rag frf

3-C. Practice the . key

3-C. Use L-finger. Try the l.l reach (keep Sem-finger anchored in home position, to guide L-finger back); then type lines 7-10 three times. Keep arms still!

7 lll l.l ... lll l.l ... lll l.l ... l.l

8 l.l dr. dr. l.l sr. sr. l.l fr. fr. l.l

9 l.l Dr. Dr. l.l Sr. Sr. l.l Fr. Fr. l.l

10 Dad fed us. See us. See Al. Ask Red.

Space once after a period following an abbreviation, and twice after a period at end of sentence.

Scoring 30 Minutes' Production Output	
7 acceptable . . . . . . A	5 acceptable C
6 acceptable . . . . . . B	4 acceptable . . . . . . D

Forms Test

Paper: workbook 439

Form 90
VOUCHER CHECK

Voucher check No. 240, to Edward L. Hastings, 831 Warner Building, Washington, D. C., 22013, for $53.67 in payment of travel expenses on trip to Chicago on the sixth of last month.

Paper: workbook 439

Form 91
RECEIPT

Receipt for $98.75, paid on account, by Mrs. Esther K. Stouffer.

Paper: workbook 439

Form 92
PROMISSORY NOTE

Note No. 273: Alexander Wilson promises to pay the sum of $500 at the First National Bank of Chicago to the order of the International Supply Company, Inc., within 30 days. Be sure Mr. Wilson's name is typed beneath the line for his signature.

Paper: workbook 440

Form 93
PURCHASE REQUISITION

Mr. Hazleton requisitions (No. AD-8-H) 10 new venetian blinds (green metal, with white tapes), to measure 3 by 7 feet, to replace those now in the Advertising Department offices. The blinds are needed next Monday. Mr. Gibson approves the requisition.

Paper: workbook 440

Form 94
PURCHASE ORDER

Mr. W. P. Busk authorizes the purchases of the blinds for Mr. Hazleton from Martin Miller & Sons, 58 Broad Street, Atlanta, Georgia, 30303. Each blind (Cat. No. 392-WG-7) costs $10.00. The purchase order is No. J-18803.

Paper: workbook 441

Form 95
TELEGRAM

Fred T. Dixon, of Martin Miller & Sons, wires W. P. Busk, Purchasing Manager, International Supply Company, Inc., 463 North LaSalle Street, Chicago, Illinois: "Delivery your order J-18803 delayed ten days because size of blinds is irregular."

Paper: workbook 441

Form 96
INVOICE

Martin Miller & Sons sends invoice No. 3013 for Mr. Hazleton's blinds, at $10 each, less 2% in the net amount for payment within 30 days, plus delivery charges (by railway express) of $8.68. The invoice is addressed (and delivery is the same) to the International Supply Company, Inc., 463 North LaSalle Street, Chicago, Illinois, 60607. There was no salesman involved in the transaction for which this invoice is the bill.

Scoring 30 Minutes' Production Output	
4 acceptable . . . . . . A	2 acceptable C
3 acceptable . . . . . . B	1 acceptable . . . . . . D

Tables Test

CAUTION! It is natural to make typing errors at this stage. It is better to risk some errors than to slow down, or break rhythm, or look away from the line you are copying. Sail right in and type every line vigorously!

If you forget where a key is located, fight off the temptation to look at your fingers; look at this keyboard chart instead.

3-D. Use J-finger. Try the jhj reach (anchor K-L-Sem fingers in home position); then race through lines 11-14 three times each.

3-D. Practice the H key

11   jjj jhj hhh jjj jhj hhh jjj jhj hhh jhj

12   jhj had had jhj hag hag jhj has has jhj

13   jhj he; he; jhj she she jhj her her jhj

14   jhj ash ash jhj hue hue jhj hug hug jhj   SMOOTHLY!

3-E. To capitalize any letter that is on the right half of the keyboard:

(1) Keeping F-finger home, press and hold down left shift key with A-finger.

(2) Strike the letter key.

(3) Release the shift key and return all fingers to their home key position.

Type lines 15-18 three or more times each.

3-E. Practice the left SHIFT key

15   aaa Jaa Jaa aaa Kaa Kaa aaa Laa Laa aaa

16   aaa Jed Jed aaa Lea Lea aaa Hal Hal aaa

17   aaa Her Her aaa Has Has aaa Had Had aaa

18   aaa Use Use aaa Led Led aaa Les Les aaa

3-F. Analyze pattern of each line; then type it twice. GOAL: To finish both copies of line 22 in 1 minute. Keep eyes very firmly on copy. Can you?

3-F. Measure your progress

19   Hear dear gear ear; hues rues sues dues

20   Hare dare fare are; reed reel reek reef

21   Rash sash hash ash; Jake lake fake sake

22   Jed has a glue jar; Alf has a red desk.

3-G. This routine should be followed at the end of each practice period— but note: your instructor may not wish you to cover the machine at the end of each period during the day.

3-G. Clean up your table

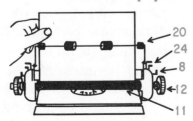

1. Remove your paper: depress paper-release lever (24); draw out paper; release the lever.
2. Place bail (20) against cylinder (11).
3. Center the carriage: holding the right cylinder knob (12), press carriage release (8); move carriage to middle; release the lever.
4. Cover the typewriter; put away your work.

Scoring 30 Minutes' Production Output			
4 mailable . . . . A		2 mailable C	
3 mailable . . . . B		1 mailable . . . . D	

Letter Test

Letter 118
FULL-BLOCKED LETTER

Paper: standard size,
workbook page 435
Production words: 334
SI: 1.48—fairly difficult

The letter below is from John R. Powell, training director. Type it in full-blocked form. Address it to Herbert ("Dear Herb:") J. Mullen, 521 Aldine Drive West, Chicago, Illinois, 60607.

Letter 119
BLOCKED LETTER

Paper: official size,
workbook page 436
Production words: 291
SI: 1.48—fairly difficult

Retype the letter, this time addressing it to L. Richard Shields, personnel manager, Scott-Williams Company, 1657 East Nadeau Street, Los Angeles, California, 90052. Omit paragraph 3 and arrange the three items in paragraph 2 as an enumeration.

Letter 120
SEMIBLOCKED LETTER

Paper: monarch size,
workbook page 437
Production words: 221
SI: 1.58—difficult

Retype the letter, omitting paragraphs 2 and 3 but inserting a subject line, *Some Ideas, Please!* Address: Mrs. Eunice F. Markham, executive secretary, Legal Secretaries Association, 4216 Wabash Avenue, Chicago, 60609. A carbon copy is to go to Mr. Kling.

Letter 121
BLOCKED LETTER

Paper: baronial size,
workbook page 438
Production words: 157
SI: 1.58—difficult

Use only paragraph 4, divided into three paragraphs. Address the letter to Executives Association, Quaker State Building, Erie, Pennsylvania, 16501, *Attention Training Director*. After the word *observance*, add the phrase *of Secretary's Day*.

(1) you will be interested to learn...i am sure...that one of the groups to which i belong...the national personnel club... will soon take steps to boost the Secretary's Day sponsored each spring by the national secretaries association... 7 15 23 32 41 46

(2) we feel that this special day is most worthwhile and that our support of it will achieve several goals: first...it is sure to give us a chance to publicize the merits of office work in general and of the secretarial career in particular...secondly...the publicity should attract the interest of more bright young men and women to this career field...thirdly...the publicity may revive ambition in our present staffs... 54 63 72 81 90 98 107 115 124 130

(3) the npc thinks so highly of the value of this observance that...as a part of the 139 147

campaign...member firms will be asked to show an orchid and a statement of tribute to secretaries in advertisements that are scheduled to appear on that day...april 27 ...this request will be for both the local and national levels... 155 164 172 181 189 193

(4) as a member of a special committee for my chapter of npc...i'm looking for things we can ask local firms to do to boost the observance...do you have any suggestions...the best that our committee has come up with yet is to suggest that employers give their secretaries a gift of candy or flowers or perhaps take them to lunch... but we know that a great many employers would be unreceptive to this sort of personal gesture...if you have any suggestions ...we should be grateful to have them. 201 209 218 226 234 241 251 259 267 275 284 292

| 1 | 2 | 3 | 4 | 5 | 6 | 7 | 8 |

New Keys

LINE: 40
SPACING: SINGLE
GOAL: CONTROL I,
O, AND T
STRESS: KEEPING A-
AND SEM-FINGERS
ANCHORED AT HOME

4-A. Type lines 1 and 2
twice each, stressing an
even and rapid pace.

4-A. Review the keys you know

1 aaa ;;; sss lll ddd kkk fff jjj fgf jhj

2 a;a ded l.l frf juj fgf jhj a;a Les Sue

4-B. Use K-finger. Try the
kik reach (keep Sem- and
L-fingers anchored on the
home keys, grazing but not
pressing them); then type
lines 3-6 three times.

4-B. Practice the I key

3 kkk kik iii kkk kik iii kkk kik iii kik

4 kik air air kik fir fir kik sir sir kik

5 kik kid kid kik did did kik rid rid kik

6 kik dig dig kik jig jig kik rig rig kik

4-C. Use L-finger. Try the
lol reach (keep J-finger
or Sem-finger, whichever
is easier for you, in the
home position); then type
lines 7-10 three times.

4-C. Practice the O key

7 lll lol ooo lll lol ooo lll lol ooo lol

8 lol log log lol jog jog lol dog dog lol

9 lol off off lol odd odd lol old old lol

10 lol oar oar lol our our lol oil oil lol

4-D. Use F-finger. Try the
ftf reach (keep the A-S-D-
fingers at home); then
type lines 11-14 three
times each. Return the
carriage without looking
up even once as you do so.

4-D. Practice the T key

11 fff ftf ttt fff ftf ttt fff ftf ttt ftf

12 ftf aft aft ftf its its ftf hat hat ftf

13 ftf too too ftf toe toe ftf the the ftf

14 ftf let let ftf lot lot ftf got got ftf

4-E. Analyze the pattern
of each line; then type
lines 15-18 twice each,
without hesitating and
without looking up once.

4-E. Build skill on word families

15 to toe tog tot too; it sit fit hit kit;

16 ut jut hut rut out; ot got rot lot hot;

17 ig fig dig rig jig; et let jet set get;

18 at sat hat fat eat; ir ire sir fir air;

UNIT 1

LESSON 4

15

Unit 36. Final Tests

Could you do a typist's work, hold down a typist's job? Do you know enough; have you skill enough? This unit contains six tests to help answer these questions—to answer them *now*, while you still have time in which to fill in any gaps you unveil.

You are allotted the time of seven lessons (Lessons 219-225) in which to preview and take the six tests. This schedule permits one period (Lesson 219) in which to preview the tests and to verify any details of which you are uncertain, plus one period for each of the six tests to be taken.

You are encouraged to preview, to study, *even to practice* these tests before you take them. Reason: If the tests are to succeed in measuring your capacity as an office typist, you should be just as familiar with the vocabulary, arrangement patterns, phrasing of directions, and so on, as the office typist is familiar with these characteristics of *his* work. But note: do not use or mark your workbook pages for the tests until you take the tests officially, under your instructor's direction.

The production tests may be taken in either of two ways, as your instructor may direct.

1. Your instructor may time you for exactly 30 minutes, permitting you to correct a reasonable number of errors; then you proofread your work and grade it (standards are given with each test) on the quantity of acceptable work you have produced.

2. Your instructor may permit you as much time as you need (within reason!) to complete all the assignments in a test, *without* correcting errors; then you would proofread your work, grade *each page* of work on the basis of the penalty-point table below, and then average the page grades to arrive at a mark for that test. The grading table:

Deduct 3 points for each major error (wrong top margin, line length, linespacing, form, etc.).

Deduct 2 points for each minor error (each instance of incorrect blocking, aligning, centering, indenting, pivoting, and similar technicalities.

Deduct 1 point for each typographical error.

Grade the total penalty points of each page:

10	9	8	7	6	5	4	3	2	1	0
D	D	D	C	C	C	B	B	A	A	A

A 120-question test covering general typing information (word division, typing terminology, language usage, error detection, etc.) is provided on workbook pages 431-434. Detach these pages and bring them to class. Fill in the answers under the supervision of your instructor when he directs you to do so.

Note that the office typist does not have time to ponder answers to the kind of questions that are included in this test, nor does he have an opportunity to change his mind. To simulate the same conditions, (1) you are to complete all 120 questions in 30 minutes, maximum time; and (2) you are not to erase on this test—each page of questions has been printed with fine dots so that (as on a bank check) any mark or erasure will be seen immediately.

When you preview this test, therefore, be very careful not to place any marks on the test pages, for you will not be able to remove any marks.

Checking your answers against the list provided to your instructor, grade your work on the number of incorrect answers (use the same scale as in the panel above): 10-9-8 incorrect answers, *D;* 7-6-5 incorrect answers, *C;* 4-3 incorrect answers, *B;* and 2-1-0 incorrect answers, *A.*

Compare this typing with lines 19-21 below.

4-F. Learn how errors are marked and counted

4-F. Making errors is natural for all beginning typists. Errors should not alarm you; instead, they should guide you.

Too many errors, for example, show that you may be pushing too hard or too carelessly for speed; too few errors mean the opposite.

Errors tell what kind of practice will help you most, whether to slow down or to speed up, and much other helpful information.

On sentence and on paragraph work, draw a circle around each error after you complete the whole page of work. Don't circle errors on drills unless your instructor tells you to do so.

The red (shue) is (his,) It is a good (fit .)
The red shoe is his. It is a good fit.

All of us (l ke) Sue; she has (good) taste.
All of us like Sue; she has good taste.

Ask to (to) see that all of (get us) to go.
Ask (Al) to see that all of us (fgrt)to go.

As indicated in the examples above, *count it an error* when—

1. Any stroke is incorrect.
2. The punctuation, if any, after a word is incorrect or is omitted.
3. The spacing after a word or after its punctuation is incorrect.
4. Any stroke is so light that it does not show clearly.
5. A stroke is made over another.

6. A word is omitted.
7. A word is repeated.
8. Words are transposed.
9. A direction about spacing, indenting, etc., is violated.
10. A word contains a capital that does not print completely.

Note that (11) only one error is charged to any one word, no matter how many errors it may contain.

4-G. Build skill on short sentences

4-G. Each line twice, without stopping or looking up. One blank line after each pair. Mark and count your errors, if any.

19 The red shoe is his. It is a good fit.

20 All of us like Sue; she has good taste.

21 Ask Al to see that all of us get to go.

4-H. Check your progress

4-H. Type this two-line paragraph twice and mark errors. GOAL: To type a copy of both lines in 1 minute.

22 Joe fell off a ladder; he hurt his leg.

He asked Dr. Todd to take a look at it.

LINE: 40
SPACING: SINGLE
GOAL: REVIEW KEYS YOU KNOW
STRESS: KEEPING EYES ON COPY

LESSON

5

Review

5-A. Review the keys you know

5-A. Each line twice, setting a good pace on easy line 1 and holding it on harder lines 2 and 3.

1 aaa sss ddd fff fgf jhj jjj kkk lll ;;;

2 ded lol frf kik ftf juj fgf jhj ded l.l

3 Alf Sue Del Flo Gae Joe Kit Lil Ted Her

Manuscript 81
MAGAZINE ARTICLE

Paper: plain, full
Carbons: file only
Review: page 150
Spacing: double

The material in 217-B, including the centered subheadings, is the revision to which Mr. Fairbanks referred in his letter to Mr. Spooner. Type this material on a 50-character line, identifying it as pages 14 and 15. Use 3-space paragraph indentions.

Forms 88-89
VOUCHER CHECKS

Paper: workbook 429

1. To spooner & moran...inc....1258 delaware avenue...buffalo...new york...14205... for $100 in payment of consultation fee for november...per agreement of may 1.

2. To mr. tracy r spooner...same address ...for $85.10 in payment of traveling expenses to new york city...per memorandum received from him on december 6.

Table 75
RULED 2-PAGE TABLE

Paper: plain, full
Carbons: two

"This table," says Mr. Fairbanks as he gives you the two-page table shown below, "is so important that I want it typed more attractively. Please retype it with normal spacing between the columns and a full space above and below each horizontal ruled line. Arrange it on two, face-to-face pages. And put today's date somewhere on it, too."

SALES ESTIMATES OF

Eastern Division

Quarter	Chicago	New Orleans	New York	Totals
1	12,000	8,000	10,000	30,000
2	14,000	12,000	15,000	41,000
3	18,000	15,000	15,000	48,000
4	20,000	12,000	12,000	44,000
First Year	64,000	47,000	52,000	163,000
1	20,000	12,000	15,000	47,000
2	24,000	18,000	24,000	66,000
3	30,000	24,000	32,000	86,000
4	33,000	27,000	35,000	95,000
Second Year	107,000	81,000	106,000	294,000
1	30,000	25,000	30,000	85,000
2	36,000	30,000	35,000	101,000
3	42,000	36,000	40,000	118,000
4	40,000	25,000	38,000	103,000
Third Year	148,000	116,000	143,000	407,000
THREE YEARS	319,000	244,000	301,000	864,000

PREFABRICATED HOUSES

Western Division

Quarter	San Fran	Denver	Totals	NATIONAL TOTALS
1	7,000	5,000	12,000	42,000
2	10,000	8,000	18,000	59,000
3	12,000	12,500	24,500	72,500
4	10,000	10,000	20,000	64,000
First Year	39,000	35,500	74,500	237,500
1	12,000	10,000	22,000	69,000
2	15,000	11,000	26,000	92,000
3	20,000	12,000	32,000	118,000
4	20,000	10,000	30,000	125,000
Second Year	67,000	43,000	110,000	404,000
1	17,000	10,000	27,000	112,000
2	20,000	12,500	32,500	133,500
3	25,000	15,000	40,000	158,000
4	20,000	12,500	32,500	135,500
Third Year	82,000	50,000	132,000	539,000
THREE YEARS	188,000	128,500	316,500	1,180,500

5-B. Strengthen control of the home-row keys

5-B. Note the pattern (one letter changes from word to word in each group); then type lines 4-8 two times. Speed up and keep a steady, smooth pace on each of the repetitions.

4 Ada ade are art aft|;;; to; so; do; go;
5 Sal sat set sit sir|Lou lot log lug lag
6 Dee due dug dog dig|Kit elk ilk irk ark
7 Fil fir far fur for|Joe jog jag jug jig
8 Go; got get gat gag|Hal hat hit hut hot

5-C. Strengthen control of the other keys you know

5-C. The pattern is like that in 5-B. Type lines 9-12 two times, increasing your speed but keeping the pace steady as you repeat each of the drill lines.

9   Ira ire irk ilk ill|Tat hat oat eat fat
10 Rue rug rut rot rod|Era ere err ear eat
11 Our oar oat out oft|1.1 Jr. Sr. Dr. Fr.
12 Ted tee toe tie the|Usa use uke ute ure

5-D. Learn how typing speed is measured

5-D. It is helpful to time some of your efforts, so that you may know exactly how rapidly you can type.

If you record your error score and your speed score in each lesson, you can note your progress. Such scores also tell you if you should press more for accuracy improvement or if you should press more for an increase in speed.

1. Type for an exact number of minutes while someone times you.

2. Find how many words you typed. Every 5 strokes count as 1 word, as marked off by the horizontal scales and, in paragraph copy, as cumulatively totaled after each line. The first example below contains

$(8+8+4=)$ 20 words. The second example contains $(24+4=)$ 28 words.

3. Divide the words typed by the minutes typed. If you type 28 words in 2 minutes, for example, you type $(28 \div 2 =)$ 14 *wam* (words a minute); or in 1 minute, $(28 \div 1 =)$ 28 *wam*; or in ½ minute, $(28 \div .5 =)$ 56 *wam*.

```
Ask Ted or Louis to go out to see Kirk.
Ask Ted or Louis to go out to see Kirk.
Ask Ted or Louis to
 1 | 2 | 3 | 4 | 5 | 6 | 7 | 8
```
Compare with line 15.

```
The goal for this task is to do it just
as fast as is safe.  Look out for a lot
of errors if too great a rush is tried.
The goal for this
 1 | 2 | 3 | 4 | 5 | 6 | 7 | 8
```
Compare with paragraph 16.

5-E. Build skill on sentences

5-E. Type lines 13-15 two times (or take a 1-minute writing on each line, so that you can figure your typing speed); then mark and count your errors.

13 The girls tried to get out to the lake.
14 Gail has a fur; her dad got it for her.
15 Ask Ted or Louis to go out to see Kirk.

```
 1  |  2  |  3  |  4  |  5  |  6  |  7  |  8      = 5-stroke words
```

5-F. Build skill on a paragraph

5-F. Type this paragraph twice (or take three 1-minute writings on it); then circle any errors.

CUMULATIVE WORDS

16 The goal for this task is to do it just   8
    as fast as is safe. Look out for a lot   16
    of errors if too great a rush is tried.   24

```
 1  |  2  |  3  |  4  |  5  |  6  |  7  |  8
```

5-G. Measure your progress

5-G. Type the paragraph two times. GOAL: To type it once in 1-minute.

17 The three of us took a good ride out to   8
    the lake to fish. Jake got us a trout.   16

```
 1  |  2  |  3  |  4  |  5  |  6  |  7  |  8
```

Assume the date is DECEMBER 10. You work for Mr. Fairbanks, of International, in New York City. He prefers blocked letter style and this closing arrangement:

```
            Sincerely yours,

            INTERNATIONAL ENGINEERING
            AND CONSTRUCTION COMPANY


            Richard Ellington Fairbanks
            Executive Vice-President
```

Letter 116
2-PAGE, BLOCKED

Paper: workbook 425
Carbons: file, 1 cc, 2 bcc
SI 1.67—difficult

mr duncan j pomeroy...secretary...east- 15
ern association of architects...525 park 23
avenue...new york...new york...10017... 30

we appreciate very much the interest in 44
our plans for developing prefabricated 52
homes expressed by your letter of inquiry 60
...we certainly have no objection to your 68
publishing in *the eastern architect* any com- 84
mentary you wish about our plans... 91

as i intimated to you some time ago, we 100
have no idea whatsoever of displacing 107
architects by this process of building low- 116
and medium-priced homes...our prefabri- 124
cated materials are in a form that permits 132
of infinite variation...especially for interior 142
construction...sufficient leeway exists in 150
the choice of materials for the exterior of 159
homes to enable an architect to construct 168
two homes of the same materials side by 176
side...yet with enough difference in ap- 183
pearance to satisfy most homeowners...as 191
a matter of fact...we are counting on archi- 200
tects to help us avoid the sameness that is 209
the bane of the prefabricating industry. 217

within the next two or three months... 225
we expect to issue a booklet prepared espe- 234
cially for architects...it is being prepared 243
with the counsel of tracy r spooner...whom 251
i believe you know...once the publication 260
date of the booklet is firmed...we shall 268

take space in your and other trade journals 277
to announce its availability. 283

if there are more particulars you may 291
wish spelled out...i should be happy to tell 300
you what you wish...perhaps you would 308
prefer to write to mr spooner...whose ad- 343
dress is below...since he is the one person 351
who is completely familiar with the tech- 359
nical nature of our plans. 365

cc mr tracy r spooner...spooner & moran 410
...inc...1258 delaware avenue...buffalo 417
...new york 14205...bcc TTJ and RBW. 435

Letter 117
BLOCKED LETTER

Paper: workbook 427
Carbons: file, 2 bcc
SI 1.50—fairly difficult

dear tracy...*spooner, that is*...a letter i 33
have just received from duncan pomeroy 41
indicates that "the cat is out of the bag" 49
and that word has got around about our 57
prefab plans...this is what he wrote: 65

the ominous news that your organ- 73
ization is planning to enter and develop 82
the prefabrication field has come to my 91
attention...can you tell me whether 100
it is true? 102

if it is true...can you tell me any- 112
thing about the scope and nature of 120
your plans...for release to *the eastern* 134
architect magazine? 142

i think...tracy...that it would be wise 150
for you to write to him without waiting 158
for him to write to you...give him enough 167
information to stir his curiosity and per- 175
haps to stimulate some degree of enthusi- 183
asm...if you do write to him...be kind 190
enough to send me carbons of your letters 199
...will you...please? 203

ps i have gone over part one of your ar- 257
ticle series and think it is wonderful...i 266
felt...however...that page 14 and the first 274
part of page 15 were a bit negative...i am 283
enclosing for your consideration a revision 292
of that portion of your manuscript. 317

Clinic Review

LINE: 40
SPACING: SINGLE
GOAL: INCREASE
    KEYBOARD CONTROL
STRESS: KEEPING
    EYES ON COPY

6-A. Type lines 1-3 twice each, with a blank line after each repetition. The lines are very easy; get off to a racing start!

6-B. To reveal weaknesses, type straight through lines 4-7 once. Press for speed and do not look up. Each key you know is used at least eight times here.

6-C. Proofread your copy of lines 4-7 very carefully and make a list of all the letters typed incorrectly. Then, take these steps:

(1) Note the four letters you incorrectly typed most often. Then, in lines 8-22, find the drills for the four letters and type each of the drills twice.

(2) Then type lines 8-22 straight through once, but pause to rest briefly after typing lines 12 and 17.

(3) Finally, retype lines 4-7 as a retest. You should do much better this time.

6-D. Type the complete sentence twice. GOAL: To finish the sentence easily in 1 minute or less.

6-A. Review the keys you know

1   aaa ;;; sss lll ddd kkk fff jjj ggg hhh
2   lol ded kik frf juj ftf jhj fgf l.l aaa
3   a d e f g h i j k l o r s t u . ; a d e

6-B. Measure your control of keys

4   self jail late just good felt dogs joke
5   huge took dust jade tiff hulk flag jigs
6   tuft jerk high furl drag judo ajar kite
7   lake fork held risk hair fish jugs hard

EYES ON
THE COPY!

6-C. Reinforce your skill selectively

8   aa alas aa ajar aa area aa gala aa data
9   dd deed dd died dd dude dd duds dd dead
10   ee seek ee free ee feel ee flee ee edge
11   ff ruff ff gaff ff doff ff guff ff huff
12   gg eggs gg flag gg gags gg gift gg grog

13   hh high hh hush hh hath hh hoot hh hash
14   ii idea ii irks ii ills ii idol ii idle
15   jj jell jj joss jj just jj jolt jj jilt
16   kk kale kk kill kk silk kk disk kk talk
17   ll loll ll doll ll lilt ll sell ll lull

18   oo food oo hood oo odor oo door oo oleo
19   rr roar rr errs rr rare rr risk rr rear
20   ss sees ss sits ss sirs ss toss ss sets
21   tt trot tt taut tt tuft tt that tt test
22   uu used uu dull uu uses uu full uu true

6-D. Measure your progress

WORDS

23   Jud is to go to the edge of the lake to   8
     see if the old oak tree is still there.   16

     1 | 2 | 3 | 4 | 5 | 6 | 7 | 8

LINE: 60
TAB: 5
SPACING: DOUBLE
DRILLS: THREE TIMES
GOAL: DO AN HOUR'S
   WORK IN AN HOUR!
STRESS: USABLE COPY
   ON FIRST ATTEMPT

217-A. Three copies of
each paragraph, or a
1-minute writing on
each and a 2-minute
writing on the group.
Repeat in Lesson 218.

217-A. Tune up on these easy review lines

1   One way the man can get the job and get the pay for it   12
is to show that he can do the work as well as we can do it.   24

2   Margie filled four or five dozen jars with jam, sealed   36
them with liquid wax, and packed them away on a back shelf.   48

3   We were told that the answer to question 10 on page 56   60
was to be found on pages 28, 39, or 47; I couldn't find it.   72

   1 | 2 | 3 | 4 | 5 | 6 | 7 | 8 | 9 | 10 | 11 | 12

217-B. Change margins
to 70 spaces, plus a
tab-5 indention (lines
should align at right).

How long should it take
you to type these 322
words of straight copy?
At 40 wam, about 8 or
so minutes; at 50, an
estimated 6 minutes; at
60, about 5 minutes.
Test your power:

Type the selection,
pausing to correct any
errors you are conscious
of making; and then
compute your speed.

Or, take two 7-minute
writings, with rests
after each minute in
the first writing but
none in the second.

SI 1.44—average

217-B. Sustain your skill on production copy

4 One of the factors that encourage those who work in the field of   14
prefabricates is the increasing interest that architects are showing.   28
Suddenly, many of the best are responding to the challenge of prefab.   43

Illustrious Origins

The past reluctance of some architects to use prefabricates is a   57
perplexing thing, for prefabs are as American as is American history.   71

The first prefab on this continent, we believe, was a log cabin.   85
Consider: For a log cabin, trees of a uniform size had to be located   99
and cut down; and then the logs had to be trimmed to a uniform length   113
and girth. Only when uniform units were ready did building commence.   127

Or if you reject that instance, then think of "house raising" of a   142
slightly later day. The walls of a house were built on the ground, and   156
then the men of the community together raised the walls and bound   169
them together; and the jeering that exploded when two of the prebuilt   183
walls did not adjoin evenly has a sturdy echo that still rings today.   197

American? Indeed, there are some who say that the first man who   211
made a mold in which to press straw and clay and so evolve a brick is   225
the person to whom the whole industry of prefabs should offer homage.   240

The Enduring Shadow

The prejudice against prefabs finds its main root, I believe, in the   254
long rows of callously identical houses that were the curse of so many   269
mill and mining towns at the turn of the century and in too many of   282
the housing developments spawned in support of the war industries.   296
I think that all of us rebelled against the dull sameness and against   310
some of the shoddy pretenses of distinction which some builders used.   324

   1 | 2 | 3 | 4 | 5 | 6 | 7 | 8 | 9 | 10 | 11 | 12 | 13 | 14

Manuscript 81

MAGAZINE ARTICLE
See page 337

217/218-C. Apply your skill to an integrated typing project

New Keys

LINE: 40
SPACING: SINGLE
GOAL: CONTROL COMMA,
C, M, AND COLON
STRESS: KEEPING
WRISTS CLOSE
TOGETHER

7-A. Type lines 1 and 2 twice, leaving a blank line between each of the pairs. Keep your fingers going!

7-A. Review the keys you know

1 if it is; to go to; or to us; or if it.

2 Joe is; Kit is; Let us; For Al; His dog

7-B. Use K-finger. Try the k,k reach (keep Sem- and L-fingers at home; curl K-finger, to ease reach to Comma key). Then, type lines 3-6 three times.

7-B. Practice the , key

3 kkk k,k ,,, kkk k,k ,,, kkk k,k ,,, k,k

4 k,k as, as, k,k is, is, k,k us, us, k,k

5 k,k to, to, k,k do, do, k,k so, so, k,k

6 k,k of, of, k,k if, if, k,k it, it, k,k

7-C. Use D-finger. Try the dcd reach (keep your A- and S-fingers anchored on home keys; curl D-finger, to make reach to C easier). Then type lines 7-10 three or more times each.

7-C. Practice the C key

7 ddd dcd ccc ddd dcd ccc ddd dcd ccc dcd

8 dcd cad cad dcd cod cod dcd cud cud dcd

9 dcd ice ice dcd ace ace dcd act act dcd

10 dcd cue cue dcd cut cut dcd cur cur dcd

7-D. Can you complete a copy of the sentence in 1 minute? Type it twice, concentrating on the C's.

Note: 1 space after Comma.

7-D. Measure your progress

WORDS

11 Get Carol, Charles, or Cathie to act as   8

a guide; the others are to check coats.   16

1 | 2 | 3 | 4 | 5 | 6 | 7 | 8

7-E. Use J-finger. Try the jmj reach (keep K-L-Sem-fingers anchored at home). Type lines 12-15 three times each, speeding up on each of the repetitions.

7-E. Practice the M key

12 jjj jmj mmm jjj jmj mmm jjj jmj mmm jmj

13 jmj jam jam jmj ham ham jmj him him jmj

14 jmj mar mar jmj mat mat jmj mad mad jmj

15 jmj sum sum jmj gum gum jmj hum hum jmj

pects them to score their papers by the 'net' method that is explained in this bulletin. Please type enough copies to have a carbon for each young lady. We will use your original copy as a guide for having the

bulletin duplicated. You can almost copy this line for line."

"May I make a copy for myself?" you ask.

"Certainly, if you wish," he replies.

SCORING THE TESTS

TYPING TESTS / 2   3

                                                          5

printed

You copy simple essay material from a ∧leaflet for the 10   19
minutes. You listen for the warning bell; you do not copy line 39
for line as the material is printed. You use a 70-space line   65
and double spacing. *You indent the paragraphs 5 spaces.*   77

Scoring ~~involves~~ *takes* four steps. First, you proof read the work 95
and ∧encircle the errors. Second, you find the total number of 108
words typed. Third, from that total you subtract 10 for each er- 120
ror. Fourth, you divide what is left by 10 (the number of minutes) 134
to get your "net" words a minute. ~~This is your score~~.   154

For example, in 10 minutes you type 575 words and ~~you~~ make 5 167
errors. You subtract 50 from 575, to get 525; and you divide the 180
525 by 10, ~~(minutes)~~, to get 52.5 net words a minute as your score. 192
In effect, you lose 1 wam for each error. Accuracy pays(!)   216

                                                          218

PREPPING FOR THE TEST   222

Don't make the mistake of practicing 10-minute writings one 260
after another. If you do, you will get tired and ~~simply~~ drill 276
yourself in ~~typing with~~ poor posture, poor stroking, etc. In- 286
stead, take one 10-minute writing a day, preceding this practice 303
by short writings in which you get the feel of a pace that you 316
can manage to sustain for 10 minutes. (*for five or six days*) 321

Don't make the mistake of pushing for speed. If you do, you 353
invite errors; at ~~fifty~~ *50*∧strokes each, they cost ~~you~~ too much. 364

Do practice changing the paper quickly. With practice, you 393
can get it down to 2 or 3 seconds.   400

Do sharpen your proofreading. A paper with ~~even just one~~ *an* 423
unmarked error is likely to stamp you as unreliable and to end in 436
the wastebasket, along with all your application papers(!)   448

If you can type ∧at a net rate of 50.0 or ~~more~~ *higher* for 10 minutes, 469
let us know. We will test you to confirm your score and arrange 482
for your placement interview and ~~official~~ test ~~by the employer~~. 489

WHAT TO DO RIGHT NOW   —Richard E. Longley 497

December 9, 19—   502

Idea: Find your "net" 10-minute rate; use page 278.

Final Page of a Manuscript Typed in News-Bulletin Form

UNIT 35   LESSON 216   334

7-F. The Colon (:) is the shift of Sem. Practice ;:; several times, keeping the J-K-L fingers anchored on home keys. Type lines 16-19 three times each.

Note: 1 space after Period used with an abbreviation; 2 spaces after the Colon.

7-F. Practice the : key

16 ;;; ;:; ::: ;;; ;:; ::: ;;; ;:; ::: ;;;

17 Dear Al: Dear Jo: Dear Lu: Dear Sir:

18 Mr. Em: Dr. Doe: Miss Ree: Mrs. Mor:

19 To Mr. Ulm: To Mrs. Ulm: To Miss Ulm:

7-G. Measure your progress

WORDS

20 Dear Mack: I heard that Carl, Jack, or   8
    Cedric might come to see our last game.   16

21 Dear Harold: Either Cora or Jack is to   24
    go home for the game. Dick is too ill.   32

    1 | 2 | 3 | 4 | 5 | 6 | 7 | 8

LESSON

8

New Keys

8-A. Review the keys you know

1 aaa ;;; sss lll ddd kkk fff jjj fgf jhj

2 lol ded kik frf juj ftf jmj dcd k,k l.l

8-B. Practice the W key

3 sss sws www sss sws www sss sws www sws

4 sws sow sow sws sew sew sws saw saw sws

5 sws low low sws mow mow sws wow wow sws

6 sws we, we, sws who who sws was was sws

Dotted lines are to spotlight the reach you are practicing.

8-C. Practice the Y key

7 jjj jyj yyy jjj jyj yyy jjj jyj yyy jyj

8 jyj sly sly jyj shy shy jyj sky sky jyj

9 jyj yes yes jyj yet yet jyj you you jyj

10 jyj jay jay jyj way way jyj may may jyj

Paper: plain, full
Copies: five
SI: 1.54—fairly hard

"We must have a copy of this bulletin, which I have just finished, for each of the four young ladies we are sending to Mr. Fudenske," says Mr. Stevens. "He always tests applicants; and when he does, he ex-

TAKING TEN—MINUTE TYPEWRITING TESTS   21

22

"Block center":
center longest
line, set tab,
align other
lines at tab.

Fred C. Stevens   38
Stevens Secretarial Service   46
Wheeling, West Virginia   54

December 9, 19—   58

BULLETIN TO CLIENTS   63
                West Coast
    A large⌃ firm, extending its operations to the _east_, is open-   79
ing a district office in Wheeling next month. <u>Needed: about 325</u>   97
<u>office workers within three months</u>.   121
            top-drawer   _will_
    To attract ~~superior~~ talent, the firm ~~plans to~~ pay 5 to 10   134
per⌃cent above present rates in this city. So: <u>There will be</u>   152
<u>stiff competition for these ~~attractive~~ positions</u>.   175

177

CAUTION   178

    Applicants for typing positions in most ~~of our~~ Wheeling   190
firms are given <u>a qualifying test</u>. Usual base: ✱60 words a min- 210
ute, 5 minutes, 3 or fewer errors, better of 2 efforts.   221
                                              return
    But the new office, to get a better staff in ~~exchange~~ for   234
better pay, plans to use <u>a competitive test</u>, not a qualifying   254
test. The test will be for 10 minutes. Speed will be charged   266
50 strokes (10 words) for each error. <u>Those who make the top</u>   288
<u>scores will get ~~the~~ first consideration for the jobs</u>.   317
                                      better
    If you hope to land one of these ~~superior~~ jobs, <u>learn how</u>   334
<u>to take and to score</u> a ~~ten~~-minute typewriting test: 352

354

TAKING THE TEST   357
                            of the paper.   _about_
    You start 9 or 10 lines from the top⌃ You stop typing⌃an   374
inch or so from the bottom of the sheet, change paper quickly,   387
and continue on another sheet.   393

    (To speed up paper change: Make a double crease about an   407
inch and a half from the bottom of the paper; your typing will   420
sound ~~a lot~~ different when you reach the creases. Do not use   431
the paper bail. Use two sheets of paper; when you remove the   443
       move
two, ~~shove~~ them straight back across the top of the cylinder and   456
reinsert both, bringing the clean paper up in ~~the~~ front.)   467

First Page of a Manuscript Typed in News-Bulletin Form

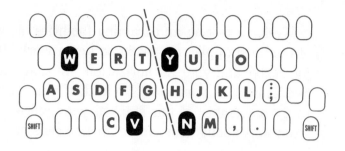

By curling your finger under whenever reaching downward, like d-to-c and j-to-m, you can make such reaches without moving your hands at all. Result: accuracy; greater speed.

Spacing reminder: Space once after a comma, semicolon, or a period following an abbreviation.

Space twice after a sentence and after a colon.

8-D. Type this note twice, concentrating on the W's and Y's. GOAL: To finish a copy in 1 minute or less.

8-D. Measure your progress

WORDS

```
11  Dear Mary:   We wish you would tell Judy      8
    how to get her team to work like yours.      16
     1  |  2  |  3  |  4  |  5  |  6  |  7  |  8
```

8-E. Typists who keep their wrists low and hold their right thumb well above the space bar make few spacing errors. The thumb should be bent so that its tip points toward and nearly touches the B key.

8-E. Check your space-bar technique

SPACE BAR

Q: *Sometimes I leave out a space. Sometimes I get extra spaces. What am I doing wrong?*

A: Probably letting your thumb rest on the space bar or your palm lean on the machine. Hold your thumb a half inch above the bar, so you can get a sharp, *bounce-off* space stroke.

8-F. Use F-finger. Try the fvf reach (keep the A-S-D-fingers anchored at home). Then type lines 12-15 three times. Can you make the fvf reach without moving any finger except the F?

8-F. Practice the V key

```
12  fff fvf vvv fff fvf vvv fff fvf vvv fvf
13  fvf vie vie fvf vim vim fvf via via fvf
14  fvf vet vet fvf vat vat fvf eve eve fvf
15  fvf velvet, fvf valves, fvf vividly fvf
```

8-G. Use J-finger. Try the jnj reach (K-L-Sem-fingers should be anchored in home position). Type lines 16-19 three times. Move only J-finger as you reach for the N key. Speed up on each of the repetitions.

8-G. Practice the N key

```
16  jjj jnj nnn jjj jnj nnn jjj jnj nnn jnj
17  jnj nun nun jnj run run jnj sun sun jnj
18  jnj not not jnj now now jnj nor nor jnj
19  jnj and and jnj one one jnj can can jnj
```

8-H. Measure your control of all keys that you have learned so far by typing each note at least twice. GOAL: To finish each note in 1 minute or less and to finish both in 2 minutes.

8-H. Measure your progress

WORDS

```
20  Dear Vic:   When we see Jay, we will ask     8
    him to give Wally a list of five names.     16

21  Dear Roy:   I may have to see Amy today;     24
    if so, I will try to run over at seven.     32
     1  |  2  |  3  |  4  |  5  |  6  |  7  |  8
```

We have testing and training facilities, as well as an extensive file 339
of qualified applicants ready to begin work. If you will send us your 353
job roster and your authorization, we shall embark at once upon the 367
recruitment of your staff. Indeed, if you wish, we would be pleased 381
to fly a member of our staff to your office in order that precise in- 394
structions about your employment needs and policies could be given 407
us. 408

| 1 | 2 | 3 | 4 | 5 | 6 | 7 | 8 | 9 | 10 | 11 | 12 | 13 | 14 |

215/216-C. Apply your skill to an integrated typing project

Assume the date is DECEMBER 9. You work for Fred C. Stevens, owner-manager of Stevens Secretarial Service, in Wheeling, West Virginia. He prefers the standard blocked letter arrangement.

Letter 115
2-PAGE, BLOCKED

Paper: workbook 417
Carbons: 1 bcc, 1 file
Review: page 203
SI: 1.51—fairly difficult

"First," says Mr. Stevens, giving you the letter in 215-B, "this letter to Mr. J. Harrison Law, Director of Personnel, Matthews and Carter, Inc., Cactus Sight Road, Van Nuys, California, 91408. Also, send a bcc copy to Bob (that is, Robert L.) Foods, at the Chamber of Commerce, with the note: *Wouldn't it be wonderful IF.*"

Form 83
FILL-IN RECORD

Paper: workbook 419
Spacing: double

"Here is the record [below] of the tests that Catherine Quincy gave today," says Mr. Stevens. "Please type it on a clean sheet for the files."

Paper: workbook 421-424

Forms 84-87
INTRODUCTION CARDS

"There are two openings at Perry-Willis," says Mr. Stevens. "Let's send the four women who typed 60 and better over tomorrow for interviews by Frank Fudenske. Schedule them alphabetically, the first at 9:30, then one every 30 minutes after that."

Table 74
ORIGINAL TABLE

Paper: plain, full
Carbons: file only

"Prepare for the first applicant to take to Mr. Fudenske, but in a sealed envelope, the *List of Applicants from Stevens Secretarial Service To Be Interviewed December 10,*" says Mr. Stevens.

"Arrange them in the sequence of their appointments, of course; and indicate the *Hour*, the *Name*, and *10-Minute Typing Score.* You know, even though the scores were made on straight paragraph copy, they are pretty good, aren't they? I wonder, now, are their scores better than *yours* would be?"

	APPLICANT	TYPEWRITING			TRANSCRIPTION			FILING				
No.	Name	Mins	Gross	Error	Mins	Speed	Rate	Alph	Num	Subj	Geog	
1291	Marotskey, Alice Anne	10	63	2	3	100	31	Yes	No	Yes	Yes	
1292	Beemes, Norma Jean	10	48	9	—	—	—	Yes	No	No	No	
1293	Tannen, Roger L.	10	61	3	—	—	—	Yes	No	Yes	Yes	
1294	Priness, Mary Agnes	10	67	0	3	120	30	Yes	Yes	Yes	Yes	
1295	Korbin, Betty C.	10	62	3	3	100	19	Yes	No	Yes	No	
1296	Belham, Ruth P.	10	66	1	3	120	28	Yes	No	No	Yes	

Administrator

Catherine

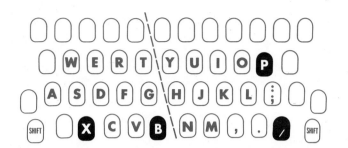

New Keys

LINE: 40
SPACING: SINGLE
GOAL: CONTROL X, P,
  B, AND DIAGONAL
STRESS: KEEPING
  ELBOWS IN

9-A. Type lines 1-2 twice each, trying to double your speed on each repetition. Leave a blank line between each pair of drill lines.

9-A. Review the keys you know

1 led vet ice due kit rim jay aft fan jam

2 for how joy fog cod sow gum jug sum log

9-B. Use S-finger. Try the sxs reach (keep A-finger or F-finger anchored in home position, whichever is easier for you). Then type lines 3-6 three times. Speed up on repetitions.

9-B. Practice the X key

3 sss sxs xxx sss sxs xxx sss sxs xxx sxs

4 sxs six six sxs nix nix sxs fix fix sxs

5 sxs wax wax sxs tax tax sxs lax lax sxs

6 sxs fox fox sxs sox sox sxs axe axe sxs

9-C. Use Sem-finger. Try the ;p; reach (anchor your J-K-L-fingers close to the home keys and keep elbows in, motionless). Then type lines 7-10 three times.

9-C. Practice the P key

7 ;;; ;p; ppp ;;; ;p; ppp ;;; ;p; ppp ;p;

8 ;p; lap lap ;p; nap nap ;p; map map ;p;

9 ;p; pin pin ;p; pen pen ;p; pan pan ;p;

10 ;p; pox pox ;p; pot pot ;p; put put ;p;

9-D. Type the note twice. GOAL: A copy in 1 minute. Concentrate on P's and X's.

9-D. Measure your progress

WORDS

11 Dear Rex: Please pay Max for the sixty   8

    papers I lost; I can pay you next week.   16

    1 | 2 | 3 | 4 | 5 | 6 | 7 | 8

9-E. Use F-finger. Try the fbf reach, keeping your A- and S-fingers at home (D-finger, too, if you can!). Type lines 12-15 three or more times. Speeding up?

9-E. Practice the B key

12 fff fbf bbb fff fbf bbb fff fbf bbb fbf

13 fbf fob fob fbf job job fbf rob rob fbf

14 fbf bud bud fbf but but fbf bug bug fbf

15 fbf be, be, fbf box box fbf by, by, fbf

9-F. Use Sem-finger. Try the ;/; reach (keep your J-finger at home—and your K-L-fingers, too, if you can). Type lines 16 and 17 three times. Gradually speed up on repetitions.

9-F. Practice the / (diagonal) key

16 ;;; ;/; /// ;;; ;/; /// ;;; ;/; /// ;/;

17 ;/; his/her ;/; him/her ;/; we/they ;/;

LINE: 60
TAB: 5
SPACING: DOUBLE
DRILLS: THREE TIMES
GOAL: DO AN HOUR'S
  WORK IN AN HOUR!
STRESS: CLEAN COPY

215-A. Three copies of each paragraph, or a 1-minute writing on each and a 2-minute writing on the group.

215-A. Tune up on these easy review lines

1   The old log was too big for the saw the men had found, 12
and the oak was too much for the axe the men had with them. 24

2   When he worked as agent for a jazz band, Dixie had one 36
battle after another. He proved to be quite lucky in most. 48

3   The answers ranged from 1910 to 1956, but most writers 60
picked out 1928, 1939, and 1947 as the most critical years. 72

   1 | 2 | 3 | 4 | 5 | 6 | 7 | 8 | 9 | 10 | 11 | 12

215-B. Sustain your skill on production copy

215-B. Confirm margins and tab stop (the lines should always align).

How long should it take you to type this letter body of 408 words? At 40 wam, about 10 or so minutes; at 50, about 8; at 60, less than 7. Make this a test situation:

Type the entire body (it continues on page 332), pausing to correct any errors you know that you make; and then compute your "output" speed.

Or, take two 7-minute writings, with rests after each minute in the first writing but with no rests in the second.

SI 1.48—fairly difficult

4   Dear Mr. Law: Thank you for your letter of December 5 and the 14
exciting news that it contains. The thought that a famous firm such 27
as Matthews and Carter may establish headquarters in Wheeling is 40
a most welcome one; you may be sure that all services of the com- 53
munity stand ready to help you. 60

You may also be sure that most of the employees needed for your 74
new installation will be available locally. There is no lack of trained 88
talent for your office staff, for the local schools and colleges have strong 104
and popular programs of office training. Indeed, there is even a surplus 118
in the office labor force, one that is so strong that leaders here have 133
been concerned about the number who have been going to Pittsburgh, 146
and elsewhere, in their search for office work. 156

There is also a strong force of skilled technicians to man your plant. 171
As you are undoubtedly aware, the foundry, steel, and other heavy 185
industries have long maintained huge installations here in Wheeling, 198
a fact that has led schools to offer wide, effective programs of training 213
for industry. 216

Moreover, the automating of most plants has created an excess 229
supply of skilled labor. In their responsibility to the community, 243
local firms have tried to spread employment, principally by reducing 256
the number of turns a week that the men report for work. These firms 270
would welcome an employer who would share the labor force and so 283
bolster our economy. 288

This agency is concerned solely with the recruiting of office em- 302
ployees. If you so authorize us, we should gladly undertake the task 316
of assembling the office force you need.   [Turn page.] 324

   1 | 2 | 3 | 4 | 5 | 6 | 7 | 8 | 9 | 10 | 11 | 12 | 13 | 14

Letter 115

2-PAGE, BLOCKED
See page 332

9-F, continued. Type lines 18-19 three times. Keep elbows in close and eyes on the copy at all times.

18 Two kinds of current: the a/c and d/c.

19 There is no charge.   Mark the bill n/c.

9-G. Measure your progress

9-G. Measure your control of keys you have practiced so far by typing each of the notes twice. GOAL: A copy of note 20 or 21 in 1 minute and a copy of both notes in 2 minutes.

WORDS

20 Dear Bill: We will plan on your taking   8
   five or six boys to the game on Friday.   16

21 Dear Pat: My car may be in the garage;   24
   so I will get Jack to bring those boys.   32

   1 | 2 | 3 | 4 | 5 | 6 | 7 | 8

LINE: 40
SPACING: SINGLE
GOAL: CONTROL ?, Z, Q, AND HYPHEN
STRESS: KEEPING ELBOWS IN

LESSON
10

New Keys

10-A. Review the keys you know

10-A. Type lines 1, 2, 3 twice, both times as evenly and unhesitantly as though keeping time to music.

1 ask lad met sue jam dig rub hog sir boy

2 fog the jet six ice cup gum now via sow

3 Rex Ned Von Kay Alf Joe Con Jan Gay Pam

10-B. Practice the ? key

10-B. The Question Mark is shift of the Diagonal, controlled by Sem-finger. Practice the ;/; and ;?; reaches. Then type lines 4-7 three or more times.

4 ; ; ;   ;/;   ;/?;   ;??;   ; ; ;   ;/;   ;/?;   ;??;   ;?;

5 ;/;   ;?;   who?   who?   ;/;   ;?;   how?   how?   ;?;

6 ;/;   ;?;   why?   why?   ;/;   ;?;   you?   you?   ;?;

7 ;?;   Who is there?   ;?;   Will you see?   ;?;

10-C. Practice the Z key

10-C. Use A-finger. Try the aza reach (keep F-finger at home; curve A-finger tightly, to make the reach to Z easy). Type lines 8-11 three times, keeping your elbows motionless.

8 aaa aza zzz aaa aza zzz aaa aza zzz aza

9 aza zip zip aza zig zig aza zag zag aza

10 aza zoo zoo aza zed zed aza zee zee aza

11 aza buzzers aza zestful aza dizzily aza

between columns, thus providing ample room for the vertical lines you will need to draw; and to leave one blank line of space at each point where you will need to draw a horizontal ruled line.

| Table 73 | Paper: plain, full |
| LONG BOXED TABLE | Carbons: enough for all attending conference |

"At our conference," says Mr. Gibbs, "I want to propose that we group our states in a different way, making six districts instead of four. The six districts would be—" He gives you a slip:

Dist. 1		#2		#3	
Alaska	7	Idaho	12	Calif.	26
Oregon	12	Mont	10	Hawaii	7
Wash	12	Nev.	4		33
	31	Wyo.	7		
			33		
#4		#5		#6	
Ariz	7	Kansas	12	Okla.	9
Col	13	Neb	10	Texas	22
N.M.	7	N.D.	6		31
Utah	5	S.D.	5		
	32		33		

"Now, type another table, *arranged exactly like that last one*, but grouping the states as I have shown on this listing. Let's call this table *Proposed District Organization*. You can copy all the 1950, 1960, and 1970 data off the first table."

| Letters 113-114 | Paper: baronial size, workbook page 415 |
| BLOCKED LETTERS | Copies: you decide |

dr edward h swensen...school of business 15
...utah state university...logan...utah 22
...84321...i shall be at the hotel utah in 36
salt lake city on december 13...14...and 44
15...is there any possibility that you and 53
mrs swensen could drive down to have din- 61
ner with me on december 12...please drop 70
a line to me at the hotel to let me know. 98

　mr kenneth fairpoint...president... 14
fairpoint & greeves...1200 timpanogos av- 21
enue...salt lake city 84102...by a wonder- 36
ful stroke of luck...i shall be in salt lake 45

city on december 14 and...therefore... 52
will be able to attend your dinner and re- 61
ception for senator martin...thank you 69
very much for inviting me...please express 78
my appreciation...also...to mrs fairpoint. 106

| Manuscript 79 | Paper: plain, full |
| TRIP ITINERARY | Copies: three |

i t i n e r a r y...december 13-15...tuesday 28
...december 13...7:00 a.m. depart san 37
francisco on united air lines 352...9:29 a.m. 45
arrive salt lake city...10:15 a.m. check in 56
hotel utah and confirm facilities for con- 65
ference; arrange lunch in suite...12:00 73
noon luncheon in suite to open conference; 83
distribute agenda and discuss it in broad 92
terms...1:30 p.m. begin discussion of topic 102
one..."dealerships"...idea: see whether 111
edward vargen...salt lake city dealer... 120
would join this part of the discussion... 128
5:00 p.m. adjourn for the day...6:30 p.m. 138
open for dinner with dr and mrs swensen... 146
utah state university...if they accept the 156
invitation. 158

　wednesday...december 14...9:00 a.m. 169
breakfast in suite...10:00 a.m. resume con- 178
ference...probably start topic two..."dis- 187
trict organization"...distribute copies of 196
"proposed organization"...12:30 p.m. 205
lunch in suite...2:00 p.m. resume confer- 213
ence...try to wind up "organization"... 221
5:00 p.m. adjourn for the day...6:30 p.m. 230
dinner at home of kenneth fairpoint... 237
president of fairpoint & greeves. 245

　thursday...december 15...9:00 a.m. 256
breakfast with mr prince in suite...10:00 264
a.m. resume conference...probably start 273
topic three..."incentive pay"...12:00 noon 283
end of conference...12:30 lunch with mr 292
vargen if he wishes...5:00 limousine to salt 303
lake city airport...6:05 depart salt lake 314
city on western airlines 75...6:35 p.m. ar- 322
rive san francisco...met by mrs gibbs. 330

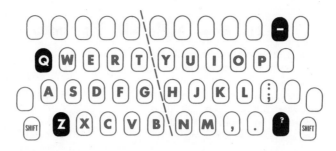

Note in 10-H that Hyphen is typed without a space when used as follows:

(1) To indicate any word division (as in line 21).

(2) To join words in a compound (as in line 22).

(3) To indicate a dash, which is made with two hyphens (as in line 23).

10-D. Type the note twice. GOAL: A copy in 1 minute.

10-D. Measure your progress

WORDS

12 Dear Blaze: Would you and/or Buzz like 8
    to hear our new jazz records? Tonight? 16

    1 | 2 | 3 | 4 | 5 | 6 | 7 | 8

10-E. Check your elbow control

Q: Is it all right to swing out the elbows for keys like Q, -, and Z?

A: No. If you do, your hands will be out of position for striking the next keys. REMEMBER: Keep your elbows in close, hanging loosely by your sides. Keep your shoulders down and your fingers well curved.

10-F. Use Sem finger. Try ;-; reach, keeping the J-finger at home. Your K-L-fingers spread and rock forward as Sem-finger straightens for long reach to Hyphen. Then type lines 13-16 three times each.

10-F. Practice the ▬ (hyphen) key

13 ;;; ;p; ;p-; ;--; ;;; ;p; ;p-; ;--; ;-;
14 ;p- ;-; blue-gray ;p- ;-; one-third ;-;
15 ;p- ;-; one-fifth ;p- ;-; part-time ;-;
16 ;p- ;-; left-hand ;p- ;-; one-sixth ;-;

10-G. Use A-finger. Try the aqa reach (keep your F-finger anchored and lift your D-S-fingers only slightly; A-finger stays curled). Then type lines 17-20 three times each.

10-G. Practice the Q key

17 aaa aqa aqqa aqqa aaa aqa aqqa aqqa aqa
18 aqa aqa quit quit aqa aqa quip quip aqa
19 aqa aqa quiz quiz aqa aqa quay quay aqa
20 aqa quick quickly aqa quiet quietly aqa

10-H. Type each note twice. GOAL: A copy of each note in 1 minute and a copy of any two in 2 minutes.

If time permits, take a 2-minute timing: begin with the first note and type straight through the others as far as you can get in 2 minutes. Proofread your work carefully. Do errors indicate that you need special practice typing?

10-H. Measure your progress

WORDS

21 Dear Jacqueline: Do you know the equa- 8
    tion Mr. Zelt quoted? Is it a new one? 16

22 Dear Zoe: My family is planning for an 24
    eight-day trip to Zion Park next month. 32

23 Dear Buzz: Was the quiz--the one about 40
    the mazes--very hard? Were you amazed? 48

    1 | 2 | 3 | 4 | 5 | 6 | 7 | 8

213/214-C. Apply skill to an integrated typing project

Assume the date is DECEMBER 8. You are secretary to Mr. J. T. Gibbs, general manager of Western States Corporation, with the headquarters in San Francisco and with branch offices in Portland, Denver, and Albuquerque. The president of the firm, Paul V. Prince, has asked Mr. Gibbs to set up a conference, and it is with this that you will be busy. Mr. Gibbs prefers standard blocked letter form and this closing to his letters:

Cordially yours,

John T. Gibbs
General Manager

Forms 79-82

TELEGRAMS

Paper: workbook 411, 413
Note that one is a full-rate telegram and three are night letters

"Send a telegram for me," says Mr. Gibbs, "to the Hotel Utah." He continues speaking and dictating as indicated in 213-B, page 328. He adds, "Make a folder for me to take on this conference trip; include copies of *everything* in it."

Manuscript 78

MEETING AGENDA

Paper: plain, full
Carbons: enough for all attending conference

agenda...salt lake city management con- 28
ference...december 13-15...topic one: the 54
dealership development program...ques- 60
tion 1...are new dealerships developing on 70
the schedule made at our sun valley meet- 80
ing...question 2...do the previous esti- 87
mates for 1970 look good...what is the 96
substantiating evidence...question 3...is 104
it time to move eastward to the next tier of 113
states...minnesota to louisiana...question 122
4...are dealers gratified with their present 131
rate and amount of compensation... 140
    topic two: the district organization 150
...question 1...are our present districts 158
too large for good supervision by the dis- 168
trict managers...question 2...would the 175
company interest be served best by adding 184
assistant managers or by creating more 193
districts, each with its own district man- 204

ager...question 3...if we have more dis- 211
tricts, how would the states be grouped 221
in the new plan of organization... 227
    topic 3: incentive pay for field repre- 238
sentatives...question 1...in general...how 246
much of an increase in compensation is 256
needed to attract top personnel...question 263
2...is it better to provide an increase in 272
base salary or to provide for incentive com- 283
pensation... 285

Table 72

LONG BOXED TABLE

Paper: plain, full
Carbons: enough for all attending conference

DISTRICT ORGANIZATION
Western States Corporation

District	States	number of Dealerships		
		1950	1960	1970
1	Alaska	2	4	7
	Idaho	4	8	12
	Montana	3	7	10
	Oregon	3	7	12
	Washington	4	8	12
	Wyoming	2	4	7
	TOTAL	18	38	60
2	California	12	18	26
	Hawaii	0	4	7
	Nevada	1	2	4
	Utah	0	3	5
	TOTAL	13	27	42
3	Colorado	4	8	13
	Kansas	3	7	12
	Nebraska	4	6	10
	North Dakota	0	3	6
	South Dakota	0	2	5
	TOTAL	11	26	46
4	Arizona	2	4	7
	New Mexico	2	4	7
	Oklahoma	0	4	9
	Texas	0	14	22
	TOTAL	4	26	45

"Please type this, including the figures I have added for 1970," says Mr. Gibbs, "but spread it so it will look good on a full sheet of paper." You plan carefully: You decide to leave the standard six spaces

Review

**LINE: 40
SPACING: SINGLE
GOAL: STRENGTHEN
CONTROL
STRESS: SHARP,
BOUNCE-OFF STROKES**

11-A. Type each line twice. Stress sharp, even strokes.

11-A. Review the alphabet keys

1 kit lid mad net vie why yet zoo aim tax
2 bow fit hug icy jig orb pit quo sir use

11-B. Type each line twice, followed by a blank line (return carriage twice).

If you break rhythm, look up, or jam keys on second typing of any line, type that line once more.

Try to maintain a very even, steady pace and to keep your arms and wrists almost motionless—to make reaches FINGER motions, not arm motions.

The dotted lines remind you of the reach-path that you are practicing.

11-B. Build accuracy on reach-stroke words

Downward reaches

3 aza azure aza amaze ;/? ball? ;/? hall?
4 sxs taxes sxs sixes 1.1 mall. 1.1 call.
5 dcd coded dcd decoy k,k mask, k,k bank,
6 fvf favor fvf fives jmj major jmj James

Inward reaches

7 fbf abaft fbf fable jnj joins jnj junks
8 fgf fight fgf flags jhj rajah jhj John;
9 ftf after ftf swift jyj delay jyj enjoy

Upward reaches

10 aqa quail aqa quake ;p; prop; ;p; shop;
11 sws sweet sws swipe lol loose lol slope
12 ded deeds ded delay kik skill kik kilts
13 frf fresh frf fruit juj judge juj juror

11-C. Apply the directions given for 11-B, above.

The vertical lines guide your eyes for grouping the words in phrases. Do not pause when you reach any words in phrases; do not pause when you reach any vertical line.

Lines 14-24 are extremely easy, so easy that you run the risk of jamming keys unless you strike them very sharply. If typebars do jam, untangle them very carefully—never yank!

11-C. Build speed on phrase sequences

Twos

14 if he|if he|if he is|if he is|if he is
15 is to|is to|he is to|he is to|he is to
16 to go|to go|is to go|is to go|is to go
17 or do|or do|or do so|or do so|or do so

Threes

18 and for|and for|and for the|and for the
19 got the|got the|and got the|and got the
20 has had|has had|has had the|has had the
21 the man|the man|the man may|the man may

Fours

22 with them|with them both|with them both
23 will have|will have them|will have them
24 came from|came from them|came from them

1 | 2 | 3 | 4 | 5 | 6 | 7 | 8

Unit 35. Secretarial Projects

LINE: 60
TAB: 5
SPACING: DOUBLE
DRILLS: THREE TIMES
GOAL: DO AN HOUR'S
WORK IN AN HOUR!
STRESS: RUSH OUTPUT

213-A. Three copies of each paragraph; or a 1-minute writing on each and a 2-minute writing on the group.

Repeat in Lesson 214.

213-A. Tune up on these easy review lines

1 The two men had the boy get out the old red box. Then 12
the men put the key in the box and had the boy put it back. 24

2 Vic took from their waxy bags the dozen or so jugs you 36
had purchased in Iraq; we thought they were very beautiful. 48

3 There were a lot of 10¢ and 28¢ items for sale, but it 60
seemed that those for 39¢ or 47¢ or 56¢ were put out first. 72

1 | 2 | 3 | 4 | 5 | 6 | 7 | 8 | 9 | 10 | 11 | 12

213-B. Make errorless copy of each paragraph or take two 5-minute writings, with rests after the minutes in the first writing but no rests in the second.

GOAL: 60 or more words a minute with two or fewer typing mistakes.

SI 1.39—normal

213-B. Sustain your skill on production copy

4 Send a telegram for me, J. T. Gibbs, of Western States 12
Corporation, to the Hotel Utah. It is on Temple Avenue, in 24
Salt Lake City. Say "Please reserve a suite of three rooms 36
plus three single rooms for December 13 through 15. Please 48
wire confirmation." Oh, can you cut that down to 15 words? 60

5 Now send a telegram to our branch manager in Portland, 72
Oregon. He is Mr. F. I. Beauchamp, and the address for him 84
is our office at 800 Fourth Street West. Say, "Paul Prince 96
has called meeting of branch managers at Hotel Utah in Salt 108
Lake City for noon, December 13, through noon, December 15. 120
Your room has been reserved. Bring full data on dealership 132
plans for your territory." That message is a night letter. 144

6 Now we must send a similar night letter to our manager 156
in Denver. He is Bob Ferris, and his address is our office 168
in the Brown Palace Hotel. The message is exactly the same 180
as the one I gave you to send to Mr. Beauchamp. Have that? 192

7 One more night letter, then we are through. It is for 204
the manager of our office in Albuquerque, but he is away on 216
his vacation. Well, we can reach him in Houston, where the 228
gentleman is visiting his relatives. So send this message, 240
please, to Gerald T. Foster, care of Mr. Tellman Foster, at 252
3928 Ruskin Street, in Houston: "Regret to break into your 264
vacation, but Paul Prince" and so on. Thank you very much. 276

1 | 2 | 3 | 4 | 5 | 6 | 7 | 8 | 9 | 10 | 11 | 12

Forms 79-82

TELEGRAMS
See page 329

11-D. Learn how to indicate a new paragraph

When a paragraph is double spaced, indent the first word 5 spaces. Use the tabulator for this indention. Review (page 7) the steps for using the tabulator mechanism.

When a paragraph is single spaced, precede it with 1 blank line. The first word may be either indented 5 spaces or blocked at the margin. Summary of possibilities:

Dear Mr. Hale:

    I do appreciate very much

your help in tracking down the

list of customers in Iowa.

    If there is ever a chance

that I can repay the favor, do

give me a chance to do so.

Double spaced, indented

Dear Mr. Hale:

    I do appreciate very much
your help in tracking down the
list of customers in Iowa.

    If there is ever a chance
that I can repay the favor, do
give me a chance to do so.

    I think that your company
will be rather pleased to know
that your bid got our order.

Single spaced, indented

Dear Mr. Hale:

I do appreciate very much your
help in tracking down the list
of customers in Iowa.

If there is ever a chance that
I can repay the favor, do give
me a chance to do so.

I think that your company will
be rather pleased to know that
your bid got our order.

Single spaced, blocked

11-E. Boost and measure your progress

WORDS

Dear Mr. Jackson:	4
5➡ Our club is quite grateful to you,	12
sir, for what you have done to help us.	20
5➡ In the next few days we shall send	28
you a gift, very small in size but very	36
big in what it means.	40

1 | 2 | 3 | 4 | 5 | 6 | 7 | 8

Clinic Review

12-A. Review the alphabet keys

1   move back quit pond girl waxy fish jazz

2   vows joke foxy quiz calm drab nigh tops

12-B. Measure your keyboard control

WORDS

My dear Mr. Baker:	4
5➡ I had to stop in the office on the	12
sixth floor today; I saw Mr. Jay there.	20
He told me he had changed his mind	28
and does not plan to give a quiz at the	36
end of the course.	40

1 | 2 | 3 | 4 | 5 | 6 | 7 | 8

Side margin notes

Setting a tab stop:
1. Clear machine.
2. Space in 5 from left margin setting.
3. Press "tab set."
4. Test setting.

Word-count credit: The word counts in this book credit you 1 word (5 strokes) for each of the indentions and each of the EXTRA carriage returns you must make in timings.

11-E. Three steps:
1. Measure your skill; type a double-spaced copy and proofread it.

2. Improve your skill: If you made 5 or more errors in 11-E, repeat 11-B once; but if you made 4 or fewer errors, then repeat 11-C once.

3. Test your skill: Retype the letter once. GOAL: A complete copy in 2 minutes or less.

LINE: 40
TAB: 5
SPACING: SINGLE
GOAL: REVIEW KEYS; CORRECT WEAKNESSES
STRESS: EYES ON COPY

12-A. Type each of these lines twice. Eyes on copy!

12-B. Measure your skill and then increase it:

1. Using double spacing and tab-5 indention, type and proofread a copy of 12-B. Count your errors.

2. If you make 5 or more errors, type lines 4-12 (page 27) twice each and lines 13-21 once each.

3. If you make 4 or fewer errors, type lines 4-12 (page 27) once each and lines 13-21 twice each.

3. our local borough council passed an ordinance in february against unnecessary noise in general and noise from faulty mufflers in particular...as a result...we have enjoyed some added business.

These are the figures:

ANALYSIS OF MUFFLER SALES		
Period Ending November 30, 19--		
	This Year	Same Period
Make	To Date	Last Year
Buick	162	190
Chevrolet	278	264
Chrysler	193	167
Ford	315	290
Mercury	198	173
Plymouth	246	237
Pontiac	192	168
Studebaker	131	102
Oldsmobile	201	139
TOTALS	1,916	1,730

part four: miscellaneous matters...this month...mr vance...there are two matters about which i should like your opinion:

1. until recently there was a small coffee shop adjacent to our store...where customers often went while waiting for us to install seat covers...seat belts...or mufflers...now the customers stand around and impatiently wait as they watch every move of our men...might we have permission to install a coffee and candy canteen... we would put it at the garage entrance... around back...and maintain it exclusively for waiting customers and our staff.

2. i have been dismayed at the dismal ...even macabre...nature of our promotion for the wonderful corey roll-up seat belt...i think we would sell a great many more of these belts if our advertisements were cheerier...to illustrate what i mean ...i enclose a sample...if you feel it has any merit...would you pass it along to the appropriate agency...please?

respectfully submitted...and so on.

20
29
37
46
52
..
..
74
96
116
124
147
153
160
165
171
178
185
191
198
215
244
252
260
270
278
287
294
302
310
318
327
335
343
351
361
367
376
384
419
428
436
444
450
495

Paper: plain, full
Review: pages 305, 306

Manuscript 76
ADVERTISING DISPLAY

Giving you the display below, Mr. Horne says, "This is the 'sample' to which I referred. Please type it as attractively as you can."

BUTTONS...   2" x 1" picture of a child's hand pushing down the button of a door lock.

'n' BELTS...   2" x 1" picture of a child fastening a Corey seat belt around himself.

COREY ROLL-UP SEAT BELTS
Aren't seat belts wonderful! They make driving so much safer. At least, they do when they are as sturdily web-anchored as those strain-tested

COREY ROLL-UP SEAT BELTS
And aren't you glad that someone perfected that idea of having the belts "drawn in" by a button spring! It keeps the seat straps out of your way when you don't want them, but right in reach when you do. And the handiest belts of all are

COREY ROLL-UP SEAT BELTS

Paper: plain, half sheet
Arrangement: you decide
Review: pages 305, 306

Manuscript 77
BULLETIN DISPLAY

"Finally," says Mr. Horne, "prepare a bulletin announcement to say—" and he dictates:

to the staff...in order that you may make your holiday plans...i am pleased to tell you that...in view of the fact that both christmas and new year's day fall on sunday this year ...our store will close at five on saturday and remain closed until nine on tuesday morning ...let me add the best wishes of the corey stores and of myself for the holiday season ...my name.

12-C. Using single spacing, type each line twice if you made 5 or more errors in 12-B, but only once if you made 4 or fewer typing errors in 12-B (page 26).

The drills are designed to help you keep your wrists and arms almost motionless (most of the words bring your fingers back to their home-key positions).

Any time you want a drill to sharpen stroking, turn to this page and retype lines 6, 9, and 12.

12-C. Build accuracy on tight motions

4	calls backs chalk flax mass balk baa zag	Rows 1&2
5	glass flask shall slag dash glad ask all	Row 2
6	equal plush yells risk owls wish oil was	Rows 2&3
7	bands smash naval jabs sank ball cad bag	Rows 1&2
8	flags flash halls sash alas gala sag ash	Row 2
9	usual heels pulls talk desk poll rag ail	Rows 2&3
10	lacks gnash banks mask sank labs van bad	Rows 1&2
11	slags slash salad flag lash shag lag has	Row 2
12	toils speak swish rush yolk wail era old	Rows 2&3

12-D. Using single spacing, type each line twice if you made 4 or fewer errors in 12-B, but only once if you made 5 or more errors in 12-B (on page 26).

Do not pause when you come to the vertical lines —they are simply guides to help you read the copy by grouping words for you.

12-D. Build speed on phrase sequences

13	if it|if it|if it is|if it is|if it is	Twos
14	or if|or if|or if it|or if it|or if it	
15	if we|if we|if we do|if we do|if we do	
16	are not|are not|are not yet|are not yet	Threes
17	ask him|ask him|ask him for|ask him for	
18	get the|get the|get the one|get the one	
19	they said|they said that|they said that	Fours
20	with this|with this form|with this form	
21	they wish|they wish that|they wish that	

```
    1  |  2  |  3  |  4  |  5  |  6  |  7  |  8
```

12-E. Set tab stops at the points indicated on the scale; using the tab by touch, type lines 22-23 three times. Don't look up!

12-E. Sharpen proficiency in tab-indenting

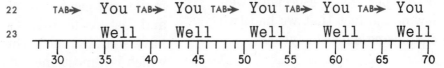

```
22  TAB➜ You TAB➜ You TAB➜ You TAB➜ You TAB➜ You
23       Well      Well      Well      Well      Well
    ╫╫╫╫╫╫╫╫╫╫╫╫╫╫╫╫╫╫╫╫╫╫╫╫╫╫╫╫╫╫╫╫╫╫╫╫╫╫╫╫╫╫╫
    30    35    40    45    50    55    60    65    70
```

12-F. To measure progress, type 12-F twice. Use a tab-5 indention and double spacing. GOAL: A complete copy in 2 minutes or less, with 4 or fewer errors.

Remember to tab-indent the paragraphs without looking up from the book once.

12-F. Measure your progress

WORDS

24	Dear Mr. Lovejoy:	4
5➜	You asked me to try to get you two	12
	tickets for the next World Series.	19
	Well, sir, I was quite lucky.	26
	Two prize seats are yours, back of	34
	third base, for the opener.	40

```
    1  |  2  |  3  |  4  |  5  |  6  |  7  |  8
```

Assume the date is DECEMBER 3. You work for Norton Horne, manager of the Fort Pierce, Florida, store of the Corey chain of stores. He expects you to type these few tasks in about an hour. He prefers semiblocked letter style with this closing arrangement:

Sincerely yours,

C O R E Y ,   I N C .

Norton Horne, Manager
Fort Pierce Branch

Letter 112

SEMIBLOCKED LETTER

Paper: workbook 405
SI: 1.47—fairly hard
Review: bcc, page 247
Carbons: you decide

"This letter," says Mr. Horne, "is in answer to one we received today from the sales manager of the *Fort Pierce Daily Press.*" He continues speaking and dictates the letter, as in 211-C, page 325.

Form 78
Tables 69-71

INTERBRANCH REPORT

Paper: workbook 407-410
If you lack workbook forms, type report as a four-page semiblocked letter; use the ruled form for the tables

monthly report to kenneth p vance...district sales manager...corey stores inc... 128 worth street...west palm beach...florida...33401...part one: financial summary ...i am pleased to report a net profit of 3,500 dollars, a gain of 300 dollars over the corresponding figure for last year... this gain of 8.6 percent is especially welcome in view of the fact that we had two fewer merchandising days this year.

| 13 |
| 21 |
| 28 |
| 57 |
| 67 |
| 73 |
| 81 |
| 89 |
| 97 |
| 105 |

SUMMARY OF OPERATIONS
Month Ending November 30,19--

Item	This Year	Last Year	
Total Sales	$24,600	$23,800	190
(Mdse) cost	− 6,500	− 6,300	200
Gross profit	$18,100	$17,500	220
Fixed expenses	−14,600	−14,300	229
Net before taxes	$ 3,500	$ 3,200	250

| 125 |
| 147 |
| 166 |
| 230 |

part two: staff performance...members of the sales staff averaged 3,280 dollars sales during the month...which is an average 53 dollars higher than last month and accounts for the increase in sales...mr brody and mr rheems continue in their race for first place...with mr rheems still ahead for the year but mr brody passing him slightly for the month...note particularly that mr holman...who joined our staff only two weeks ago...got off to an excellent start.

| 285 |
| 293 |
| 301 |
| 308 |
| 350 |
| 358 |
| 366 |
| 375 |
| 383 |
| 390 |
| 398 |
| 402 |

ANALYSIS OF SALES PERFORMANCE
Period Ending November 30, 19--

Name	Month	Year to Date	
Brody, J.B.	$3,750	$39,200	486
Dodds, Edward	3,150	33,175	495
Holman, William	1,500	1,500 ᵃ	506
Jackson, Thomas	2,780	31,250	515
Lewis, Frank T.	3,225	30,685	524
Norris, Parker	3,320	12,940 ᵇ	534
Rheems, Jorge	3,700	40,350	544
Klein, Robert	3,175	32,600	554
TOTALS	$24,600	$221,700	573
a. from 11/14	b. from 9/1		592

part three: directed analysis...in accordance with the directive in your staff bulletin dated november 21...i have made a study to compare sales of mufflers for the makes we carried in stock both this year and last...the analysis indicates that we have sold 186 more this year than last... which is almost one a day...for a 10.8 percent increase...i would attribute this gratifying increase to three causes:

| 618 |
| 626 |
| 634 |
| 643 |
| 652 |
| 660 |
| 668 |
| 676 |
| 685 |
| 691 |

1. we have included display reference to our muffler installation service in all advertisements...along with the specific makes of cars we can serve without delay.

| 701 |
| 710 |
| 718 |
| 726 |

2. we now have a competitor within half a block...he advertises...also...and so motorists come to both stores to "shop" ...because our prices are lower...we gain.

| 736 |
| 744 |
| 752 |
| 760 |

Unit 3. Skill Development

Skill Drive

LINE: 50
TAB: 5
SPACING: SINGLE
GOAL: LEARN TO
    CENTER HORIZONTALLY
STRESS: TOUCH
    CONTROL

13-A. Type each line twice, as smoothly as you can.

13-A. Review the alphabet keys

1 back dent high joke melt hope quiz rust vows foxy

2 Jack Dave Ruth John Mell Hope Quen Russ Vera Ford

13-B. To select practice goals, type and proofread a copy. Use single spacing and a tab-5 indention.

Note that the word count credits you with 1 word (5 strokes) for each extra carriage return (for the blank line before each of the paragraphs) and for each paragraph indention.

13-B. Measure and improve your keyboard control

WORDS

3 Jeff King: 2

) double space

    The next time you are out this way, try   12
to drop in at our plant.) double space   17

    We are quite worried about our accident   27
rate and hope you will help us look over the   36
hazards to our men.   40

   1 | 2 | 3 | 4 | 5 | 6 | 7 | 8 | 9

13-C. To boost accuracy, type lines 4-7 three times if you made 5 or more errors in 13-B, but each line twice if you made 4 or fewer errors. Keep your hands from bouncing!

13-C. Build accuracy on one-hand words

4 wade join free milk fact look face hull dare hill

5 fare jump stew link wave pull vase hoop rate pink

6 best mill east pony raft hulk ease puny fast lump

7 date only test pump afar oily fads upon draw poll

13-D. To increase speed, type lines 8-11 three times if you made 4 or fewer errors in 13-B, but each line twice if you made 5 or more errors. Always tap keys sharply, to keep the typebars from jamming.

13-D. Build speed on alternate-hand words

8 chapel bushel endow angle they lend for the it is

9 profit formal bugle right work duty vow rib or if

10 height dismay their gland than when owl pan do so

11 handle mangle handy giant coal mend lay cut ox of

13-E. To synchronize the capital-shift motions and eliminate "flying caps," type lines 12-13 three or more times each. Increase speed on repetitions.

13-E. Increase efficiency in capitalizing

12 Drew Earl Evan Carl Fred June Kirk Lois Jill Lola

13 Cora Dick Bill Rita Anne Paul Jane Hank Nate Irma

13-F. To boost and to measure your skill, type 13-F twice, line for line. GOAL: A complete copy in 2 minutes or less, with 4 or fewer typing errors.

13-F. Measure your progress

WORDS

14 Miss Gray: 2

    As soon as you can, please find out for   12
us the exact steps in the new Ozite process.   21

    What I have read about it seems to show   31
it may be just what we require for our work.   40

   1 | 2 | 3 | 4 | 5 | 6 | 7 | 8 | 9

LINE: 60
TAB: 5
SPACING: DOUBLE
DRILLS: THREE TIMES
GOAL: DO AN HOUR'S
    WORK IN AN HOUR!
STRESS: WORK THAT
    IS MAILABLE

211-A. Three copies of
each paragraph; or a
1-minute writing on
each, plus a 2-minute
writing on the group.

211-A. Tune up on these review lines

1   When will Miss Hall come from the bank with that cash?   12
They said that the young lady left the bank some while ago.   24

2   The log jam broke up with a quiver and crash after the   36
logger used his oversize ax to hack and slash the key logs.   48

3   We were ahead 39 to 28 at the half, but then the other   60
team ran up 10 straight and then finally took us, 56 to 47.   72
    1 | 2 | 3 | 4 | 5 | 6 | 7 | 8 | 9 | 10 | 11 | 12

211-B. Type to your need.

ACCURACY: Lines 4-5
as a paragraph four or
more times; then lines
6-7 as a paragraph two
or more times.

SPEED: Each line three
consecutive times.

211-B. Sharpen skill by selective preview practice

4   unauthorized manifestly, appreciate immediate December June
5   advertising, responsible repetition attention contract West
    1 | 2 | 3 | 4 | 5 | 6 | 7 | 8 | 9 | 10 | 11 | 12
6   feel that|will note|ask you|one of|for it|but it|and not to
7   to one|of the|to pay|if you|to our|to the|do not|we had not

211-C. Confirm margins
are for 60-space line
(lines will align if you
observe bell correctly).

Type one complete copy
or take two 5-minute
writings, with rests
after each minute in
the first writing but
no rests in the second.

GOAL: 60 or more words
a minute with no more
than 2 typing mistakes.

SI 1.39—normal

211-C. Sustain skill on production copy

	C	D
This letter is in answer to one we received today from the sales	14	9
manager of the Fort Pierce Daily Press. We reach him at Post	26	17
Office Box 882 in Fort Pierce, Florida. He has repeated one of our	40	24
ads without our telling him to, and now he wants us to pay for it.	54	..
Well, we're not going to do so.	60	..
Dear Sir: I am returning for correction the statement you	73	39
mailed to this office on December 1. If you will refer to our space	87	54
contract, dated June 19 of this year, you will note that you are	100	67
authorized to run our advertisements only according to the exact	113	80
schedule we provide on the first day of each month. We provided	126	93
you such a schedule last month.	132	100
Although we appreciate the value of extra advertising, we do	146	114
not feel that we are responsible for the unauthorized repetition	159	127
on November 21 of the display we had run the day previous.	171	139
Manifestly, it is not our fault that the display was repeated in	184	152
error. We ask you for a revised statement, and we assure you we	197	167
shall give it our immediate attention.	205	175
Sincerely yours, and so on, and send a blind carbon of that to	218	204
Mr. Vance, in West Palm Beach. On his copy, please add a	230	222
comment: "You told me this would happen, and it has; I really	242	234
think, however, that the error was an honest one."	252	244

    1 | 2 | 3 | 4 | 5 | 6 | 7 | 8 | 9 | 10 | 11 | 12

Letter 112

SEMIBLOCKED LETTER
See page 326

<table>
</table>

Shortcut to save time in centering the carriage: Before you begin to backspace, set the stop at the centering point; then you can tabulate to that point to center the carriage.

If you correctly center the names in the exercise, the letter B in each name will align vertically.

LINE: 50
TAB: 5 AND CENTER
SPACING: SINGLE
GOAL: LEARN TO CENTER HORIZONTALLY
STRESS: TOUCH CONTROL

14-A. Type each line twice; keep eyes on the copy.

14-B. To define practice goals, type and proofread a copy of this letter.

Note that you must tab twice in succession to reach the center, where you begin the name "Jeff King." The double tab—make it without looking up!—counts as 2 words.

14-C. To boost accuracy, type lines 4-7 three times each if you made 5 or more errors in 14-B, but twice each if you made 4 or less typing errors in 14-B.

14-D. To increase speed, type lines 8-11 three or more times each if you had 4 or fewer errors in 14-B, but twice each if you had 5 or more errors in 14-B.

13-G. Learn to center horizontally

To center words across the page:

1. Set the carriage at the center point of the paper.

2. Find the backspace key in the upper left or right of the keyboard. This key is ordinarily controlled by the nearest little finger; but, *on a manual machine,* it is better to use the *thumb* on the backspace key *when using it for centering.*

3. Say the letters and spaces of the words in pairs, pressing and releasing the backspace key one time after you say each pair of strokes.

Caution: You will often have a letter left over after calling the pairs; do *not* backspace for this letter.

4. Type the words. They should appear in the middle of the paper.

PRACTICE. Center these names.

Ralph Tolberts
Helen Debolt
Kathryn Robinson
Mary Lee Busch
Joseph F. Bentley
John Thomas Philbertson, Jr.

Check: The letter "B" lines up.

LESSON
14
Skill Drive

olympic college
[Bremerton, Washington

14-A. Review the alphabet keys

1 tab vow lag zip fox ham bed irk joy quo act an so
2 jobs vary zone flax lone milk crew quit digs help

14-B. Measure and improve your keyboard control

WORDS

3 Mr. Queen: 2
                                                     3
      Thank you for inviting me to stop in at   12
your plant. I expect to be able to do so on   21
Monday and will do my best to see what risks   30
or hazards I can detect.   35
                                                     36
                          Jeff King   40

→TAB →TAB
1 | 2 | 3 | 4 | 5 | 6 | 7 | 8 | 9

14-C. Build accuracy on double-letter words

4 grammarian succeeds powwows apples radii burr add
5 assistants quitters vacuums suffer guess ebbs baa
6 bookkeeper withhold flivver jammed dizzy eggs inn
7 staggering possible process supper fluff been odd

14-D. Build speed on phrase sequences

8 to see|to see|to see him|to see him|to see him at
9 are you|are you free|are you free|are you free to
10 to show|to show us|show us their|to show us their
11 have been|been able|have been able|have been able
   1 | 2 | 3 | 4 | 5 | 6 | 7 | 8 | 9 | 10

UNIT 3   LESSON 14   29

the broadcast; so make enough carbons! On each person's copy, underscore *his* cues in colored pencil, as I marked the 'Husband' cue lines."

"Do I mark the 'sound' and 'music' cue lines, also?" you ask Mr. Lawrence.

"Yes, please do," he replies.

<table>
<tr><td colspan="3" align="center">WMAQ & NET</td><td align="right">6</td></tr>
</table>

Manuscript 75
RADIO SCRIPT

	WMAQ & NET	6
	Station Break Commercial	23
	KINLEY ELECTRONICS COMPANY	41
	Saturday, December 6, 19—	58
	7:29–7:30 P.#M. CST	72
		73

SOUND	CLATTER OF DISHES BEING WASHED.	82
<u>HUSBAND</u>	HUMMING...STOPS HUMMING AND SPEAKS SOLICITOUSLY. Darling,	97
	you take care of those hands of yours! The old boy doesn't	110
	mind doing ~~up those~~ dishes. Matter of fact, might show you	121
	a thing or two!	126
WIFE	*Thanks, Dear⊙ I don't like to ask you!*	136
MUSIC	SPRIGHTLY VERSION OF "PRISONER'S SONG"...STAB...UP...UNDER.	151
ANNCR	Good old Jonesy. It's Saturday, and this businessman is at	166
	home. Doesn't mind doing the dishes. Not at all!	178
MUSIC	SWEEP IN, SLIGHTLY SLOWER "PRISONER'S SONG"...FADE OUT.	192
<u>HUSBAND</u>	Hands still bad, Trudie? *Okay,* ~~Well~~, I'll do ~~the dishes.~~ *them⊙*	205
SOUND	CLATTER OF DISHES BEING WASHED.	214
ANNCR	Good old Jonesy! He's a trooper! He doesn't mind doing the	229
	dishes...once in a while. But, day after day?	240
MUSIC	SWEEP IN WITH HEAVY, SLOW "PRISONER'S SONG"...FADE OUT.	254
<u>HUSBAND</u>	Honest to goodness, Tru, the boys in the office are accusing	270
	me of having dishpan hands!	276
WIFE	You know, Dear, they are starting to look like mine.	290
<u>HUSBAND</u>	Didn't anyone ever invent a machine for this job?	303
ANNCR	BREAKS IN. You bet someone did, Mr. Jones! It's the famous	319
	Kinley dishwasher—Kinley! Mr. Jones...Mr. Jones?	350
WIFE	He's gone. To the Kinley dealer. *I hope!*	362
MUSIC	SWELL IN WITH SWING VERSION OF "PRISONER'S SONG"... *STAB* ~~FADE~~ OUT.	377

SOUND BANG OF A DOOR AND RUNNING FEET⊙
ANNCR CALLING ANXIOUSLY⊙

14-E. To sharpen your carriage returns, type each word on a separate line; repeat the drill, this time indenting each word 5 spaces. If your machine is manual, type line 13 before line 12.

12   will bill Jake Joan Mark Kaye Dell Sara Rita They

13   pour miss Dana Walt Bill Ford Miss Jory Mrs. Lane

14-F. Measure your progress

14-F. To increase and to measure your typing skill, type this letter twice.

GOAL: A complete copy in 2 minutes or less, with 4 or fewer typing errors.

Remember to double-tab to the name of the writer.

		WORDS
14	Mr. Glenn:	2
		3
	I have been able to make a date for the	12
	man from the Ozite firm to show us their new	21
	process. Are you free to see him at a quar-	30
	ter to four next Monday?	35
		36
→TAB →TAB	Jane Gray	40

1 | 2 | 3 | 4 | 5 | 6 | 7 | 8 | 9

14-G. Learn to type all capitals

14-G. Centering and "all capping" are two display techniques that all typists use. If you type the lines correctly, the letter E will align vertically, Use the tab to recenter the carriage; double space.

LOCK

SHIFT LOCK

To type all the letters of a word or group of words in capitals:

   1. Press the shift lock. It is above one or both shift keys.

   2. Type the word or words.

   3. Release the lock by touching the opposite shift key.

   CAUTION. Do not forget to release the lock whenever a stroke that cannot be typed in capitals (a hyphen,

for example) appears among the capitalized letters. Why?

   PRACTICE. Center horizontally:

```
A Report by Earl Carr on the
OZITE PROCESS
Newly Developed by the
OZITE-PARKER CORPORATION
of Cleveland, Ohio
```

LINE: 50
TAB: 5 AND CENTER
SPACING: SINGLE
GOAL: IMPROVE SKILL AND CENTERING
STRESS: TOUCH CONTROL

LESSON
15

Skill Drive

15-A. Review the alphabet keys

15-A. Each line twice, with almost perfect rhythm.

1   ply jam keg cot big her fox sat zoo que vied know

2   many spur wove back quit hazy deft exit high jolt

15-B. Measure and improve your keyboard control

15-B. To pinpoint your practice goals, type and proofread a copy of 15-B.

Remember to double-tab to the signature position.

If you do complete this letter in 2 minutes, what is your average speed?

		WORDS
3	Dear Dean Case:	3
		4
	I wish to express my thanks now for the	13
	time you gave me on Thursday. I realize how	22
	busy you are, sir; and I am grateful for the	31
	quarter hour that you gave me.	37
		38
	Jay White	42

1 | 2 | 3 | 4 | 5 | 6 | 7 | 8 | 9

209/210-C. Apply skill to an integrated typing project

Assume the date is DECEMBER 2. You work for A. T. Lawrence, advertising manager of Kinley Electronics Company, of Milwaukee. He expects you to accomplish the following tasks in about an hour. He uses baronial (5½ by 8½) stationery. He prefers the full-blocked arrangement and this closing arrangement in letters:

> Sincerely yours,
>
> Advertising Manager
> Kinley Electronics

Form 75
Manuscript 74
NEWS RELEASE

Paper: workbook 399
Review: pages 147, 148
Material: page 322
Arrangement: you decide
SI: 1.45—fairly difficult

Giving you the material in 209-B, page 322, Mr. Lawrence says, "Please arrange this copy as a news release. Note that it is dated December 16, not today. Send the news release—"

Form 76
Table 68
MEMO INCLUDING A DICTATED TABLE

Paper: workbook 401
Table: decide whether to type it separately or in the memorandum
SI: 1.58—difficult

"—to our Executive Vice-President, Mark B. 14
Kinley, along with this memorandum." 28

i am enclosing for your approval a copy 36
of the news release we plan to issue at 44
the december 16 r/t congress...we will 52
take immediate steps to have the release 60
processed...something that will require a 68
week or so...as soon as we have your ap- 76
proval...the campaign...as i have worked 85
it up with pratt & wilson...includes the 93
following schedule or calendar: 99

date dec 10 responsibility mr gershwin 159
advertising plates to trade magazines 170

date dec 11 responsibility miss bonner 176
bulk mailing of circulars to dealers 186

date dec 12...mr young..."what's up at 195
kinley" news teaser to the wire services 207

date dec 13...miss bonner...mailing of 217
picture mats and "hold for action" note 229
to all newspapers with TV news columns 238

date dec 15...mr young..."sneak pre- 247
view" for milwaukee newspapermen 255

date dec 16...my job...the big news 264
conference at the r/t congress 278

you will be pleased to know...also... 299
that we have changed the commercial in 307
the dishwasher campaign as you suggested. 331

Form 77
TELEGRAM

Paper: workbook 403

richard k young...pratt & wilson...inc 30
...418 south dearborn street...chicago... 37
60607...cancel script for saturday...de- 47
cember 6...new script mailed today will 55
require same personnel and sound effects. 75

Letter 111
FULL-BLOCKED LETTER

Paper: workbook 401
SI: 1.54—difficult

"Now this letter to confirm that telegram," says Mr. Lawrence. He dictates:

dear mr young...in confirmation of the 37
telegram i sent you today...a copy of 44
which is attached...i am enclosing the new 53
script for use on wmaq and the net in the 61
december 6 try-out...although the possi- 70
bility of changing the script is one that 78
you had forecast...i suspect that you will 86
be relieved to know that the changes are 95
modest and the personnel the same...mark 103
kinley thought the original script was a 111
bit implausible and suggested the changes 120
...if there are any difficulties with the 129
studio...do not hesitate to phone me. 157

Manuscript 75
RADIO SCRIPT

Paper: plain, full
Caution: study directions very, very carefully
SI: 1.48—fairly difficult

Giving you the script shown on the next page, Mr. Lawrence says, "In addition to a file copy, we shall need a copy of this for each of the participants in

15-C. Build accuracy on double-reach words

15-C. To strengthen your accuracy, type lines 4-7 three times if you made 5 or more errors in 15-B, but twice each if you made 4 or fewer mistakes.

4 gr groan grown growl grope grape grade graze gray
5 hu hurry hurts hubby hush, hunts hulks human hull
6 rt smart heart chart start quart darts apart cart
7 my enemy hammy Sammy dummy rummy gummy tummy army

15-D. Build speed on rock-reach words

15-D. To speed up your key stroking, type lines 8-11 twice each if you made 5 or more errors in 15-B, but three times if you made 4 or fewer typing errors.

8 at plate crate orate float that flat neat pat hat
9 ly dully fully sully silly July only lily sly fly
10 ag again snags flags stage cage crag slag jag lag
11 py happy nippy wispy pylon copy pyro pyre pyx spy

15-E. Increase efficiency in using space bar

15-E. To develop sharper space-bar strokes, type lines 12-14 three times— once very slowly and then twice more, to pick up a faster and faster stroke.

12 b c d e f g h i j k l m n o p q r s t u v w x y z
13 We are to go to the shop as soon as we can do so.
14 He tried . . . tried very hard . . . but he lost.

15-F. Measure your progress

15-F. To increase and to measure your skill, type this letter twice. GOAL: A copy in 2 minutes or less, with 4 or fewer errors.

WORDS

15 Dear Vic: 2
                                                                     3
       Our group will meet at a quarter to six   12
on Monday to plan the kind and size of proj—   21
ect the club will do this year. I hope that   30
you will plan to be there with us.   37
                                                                    38
                        Bob Grant   42

   1 | 2 | 3 | 4 | 5 | 6 | 7 | 8 | 9

15-G. Learn to center vertically

15-G. There are 11 x 6 = 66 lines on a full sheet of paper. There are 33 lines on a half sheet.

Line 1
Line 2
Line 3
Line 4
Line 5
Line 6

If you have not already done so, study the section on "Vertical Spacing" on page 8.

PROBLEMS. On what line of a *full* page of paper would you begin typing to center: (*a*) 26 single-spaced lines? (*b*) 25 single-spaced lines? (*c*) 12 double-spaced lines?

On what line of a *half* page would you begin typing to center: (*d*) 21 single-spaced lines? (*e*) 18 single-spaced lines? (*f*) 12 double-spaced lines? (*g*) 8 triple-spaced lines?

PRACTICE. Center this display on a half sheet of paper. Center each line horizontally. Use double spacing.

"CENTER" CHECK: To see whether you correctly center the work vertically, fold the paper, top to bottom, and make a crease across the center. The crease should come close to the point indicated by the arrow. Does it?

16   The Next Meeting of
17   THE WOODLAWN BUSINESS CLUB
18   Will Be Held
CENTER➤
19   OCTOBER SIX :: THREE—THIRTY :: ROOM NINE
20   Members Only

LINE: 60
TAB: 5
SPACING: DOUBLE
DRILLS: THREE TIMES
GOAL: DO AN HOUR'S
    WORK IN AN HOUR!
STRESS: COMPLETELY
    MAILABLE WORK

209-A. Three copies of
each paragraph, or a
1-minute writing on
each and a 2-minute
writing on the group.

209-A. Tune up on these review lines

When they send Miss Hall over with cash from the bank,   12
make very sure that they have paid what they owed our firm.   24

Jim acquired poor typing habits because he was so lazy   36
that he never faced up to the extra work that was required.   48

It's one thing to pay $10 or $28 for a jacket, but $39   60
or $47 or $56 is too much to pay for a light spring topper.   72

    1 | 2 | 3 | 4 | 5 | 6 | 7 | 8 | 9 | 10 | 11 | 12

209-B. Adjust margins
to 55-space line.

Type one complete copy
or take two 5-minute
writings, with rests
after each minute in
the first writing but
no rests in the second.

GOAL: 60 or more words
a minute with two or
fewer typing mistakes.

SI 1.44—normal

209-B. Sustain your skill on production copy

KINLEY DEVELOPS MIRROR TV   15
16

MILWAUKEE, Dec. 16—Would you like your TV screen   27
the size of a bedroom mirror? One that was only three   38
inches deep? One that really IS a mirror when the set   49
is not turned on? One that you can hang above a piano   60
in the living room, or over a chest of drawers in your   71
bedroom, or on the wall of the family playroom or den?   82

Well, you can have it. It is here. It is great.   93
You put it where you want it, like hanging a painting.   104

Today the Kinley Electronics Company unveiled its   115
spectacular new TV Mirror in a news conference here in   126
Milwaukee in conjunction with the opening of the Radio   137
and Television Congress, meeting at the Hotel Denkler.   148

"It's the biggest development since the invention   159
of color television," said Paul Kinley, KEC president,   170
as he commented upon the research behind the new sets.   181

The TV Mirror is composed of two units. One, the   192
size of a small end table, contains the basic receiver   203
of the set. It may be placed anywhere, even in a dif-   214
ferent room. It connects to the second unit, which is   225
the mirror screen, by a slim wire cable. The "screen"   236
really is a mirror. At its base is the Kinley cathode   247
tube, core of the new development. The tube is shaped   258
like a fluorescent light and is as long as the mirror.   269
It projects onto the mirror the pictures received from   280
the other unit. Speakers are mounted at both sides of   291
the mirror, which has "touch controls" along its base.   302

Price of the Kinley TV Mirror will be competitive   313
with standard color TV sets. Sets in a broad range of   324
sizes and decor will be displayed by dealers tomorrow.   335

    1 | 2 | 3 | 4 | 5 | 6 | 7 | 8 | 9 | 10 | 11

Form 75
Manuscript 74

NEWS RELEASE

See page 323
Review: pages 147-148

Skill Drive

LINE: 50
TAB: CENTER
SPACING: SINGLE
GOAL: EXTEND
  CENTERING SKILL
STRESS: TOUCH
  CONTROL

16-A. Type each line twice; use very sharp strokes.

16-B. To target practice goals, type and proofread a copy on a 40-space line.

16-C-D. To reinforce skill, type lines 4-7 three times each and lines 8-11 twice each if you made 5 or more errors in 16-B; but if you made 4 or fewer errors, then type lines 4-7 twice each and lines 8-11 three times each. Eyes on copy!

16-E. To improve your touch control of the shift lock and release, type lines 12-13 three times.

16-F. To improve and to measure your skill, type two copies on a 40-space line. GOAL: A complete copy in 2 minutes (start with carriage centered) with 4 or fewer mistakes.

Remember to tab-indent to the center to position the name of the writer.

16-A. Review the alphabet keys

1 the lap vex bag ask wig car jet qua fed zoo no my

2 silk whim quiz five lock jade oxen cafe type brig

16-B. Measure and improve your keyboard control

WORDS

3 CARL VANCE   6

will explain the unique new Ozite chalk   15
process in the Board Room at three next   23
Friday. All those who wish to hear his   31
talk are free to plan to do so.   37

TAB➤   Kane Glenn, Jr.   42

1 | 2 | 3 | 4 | 5 | 6 | 7 | 8

16-C. Build accuracy on double-stroke words

4 sw sweep sweet sweat swear swap swat swab swim sw

5 lo loose lords longs lower loaf load lore love lo

6 de delay demon dense delve deny desk deal dent de

7 ki kinds kilts kitty kings kits kite kick kiln ki

16-D. Build speed on alternate-hand words

8 such they hand half soap held mane naps dusk amen

9 firm clan diem when pair with down roam curl girl

10 rich hang clay wish paid lake land fork fuel make

11 duty coal clam disk fish cork dock flap duel cozy

16-E. Increase efficiency in using the shift lock

12 The TWO men from HILL-AGE want two MORE meetings.

13 Get ANOTHER jar of HI-SPEED, the SHINE-UP powder.

16-F. Measure your progress

WORDS

14 WE REGRET   6

to tell you that Carl Vance was injured   15
quite badly when a box of Ozite blew up   23
in his car en route to see us. We will   31
not plan a new meeting date.   37

TAB➤   Kane Glenn, Jr.   42

1 | 2 | 3 | 4 | 5 | 6 | 7 | 8

Table 67

REVISED RULED TABLE
See page 320

William Blake & Sons Company
⌐OVERDUE ACCOUNTS

~~October 31, 19—~~ *NOVEMBER 30, 19—*

Account	30 Days Overdue	60 Days Overdue	Total Overdue
Mr. Harry Pepper, Treasurer Consumers' Cooperative Assn. 3123 Washington Avenue Racine, Wisconsin 53401	($1,210.45)	————————	$1,210.45
~~Mr. R. N. Maxwell, Manager Central Wabash Association 322 Arcade Building Fort Wayne, Indiana 46802~~	————————	~~$ 68.75~~	~~68.75~~
Mrs. Mark E. Smythe, Manager The Danville Farmers League 616 North Jackson Street Oak Park, Illinois 60301	(294.75)	~~1,130.60~~	*294.75* ~~1,425.35~~
~~Mr. M. M. Zimmerman, Manager Consumers' Exchange, Inc. 217 United Farmers Building Flint, Michigan 48502~~	~~1,704.90~~	————————	~~1,704.90~~
~~Miss Evangeline C. Springer Manager, Elkhart Association 3197 West 14 Street Elkhart, Indiana 46514~~	~~811.38~~	~~438.44~~	~~1,249.82~~
Miss Ella Q. Wilcox, Manager Michigan Cooperative Assn. 314 Phoenix Building Bay City, Michigan 48706	*162.75* ~~149.68~~	————————	*162.75* ~~149.68~~
TOTALS	~~$4,171.16~~ ?	~~$1,637.79~~ ?	~~$5,808.95~~ ?

*MR. JAMES T. BECKMAN, MGR.
KALAMAZOO CITIZENS' LEAGUE
623 SECOND AVENUE
KALAMAZOO, MICH. 49001*   *$1,125.73*   ------   *$1,125.73*

17
18
37
38
48
63
64
72
84
99
100
105
111
116
130
↓
131
136
142
147
161
↓
162
168
173
178
192
↓
237
238
249
263
193
199
204
208
223 ↑

IDEA: To save time and paper, crease a sheet of paper across the center, side to side. Type Practice 1 on the top half of one side, for practice in centering on half sheets; and type Practice 2 on the opposite full side, for practice in centering on a full sheet of paper.

In Practice 2, remember to count 1 blank line between the double-spaced lines.

16-G. Learn to center paragraph copy

Announcements to be circulated a-mong a staff or posted on a bulletin board are usually centered both ver-tically *and* horizontally.

1. Vertical centering is by steps you know: (*a*) Count the lines the display will fill, (*b*) subtract them from the lines available on the pap-er, and (*c*) split the difference. To center the single-spaced display in 16-F on a half sheet, for example: $33 - 8 = 25$; and $25 \div 2 = 12\frac{1}{2}$, or 13, the line where typing begins.

2. Horizontal centering: To deter-mine where to set the left margin stop, select an average-length line and backspace from the middle of the paper enough to center that line.

PRACTICE 1. Center on a *half* sheet the announcement in 16-B. Use *single* spacing. Leave 1 blank line before and after the body of the display.

PRACTICE 2. Center on a *full* sheet the announcement in 16-F. Use *double* spacing. Leave 2 blank lines before and after the body of the display.

LINE: 50
TAB: CENTER
SPACING: SINGLE
GOAL: EXTEND SKILL
STRESS: ARM CONTROL

LESSON

17

Skill Drive

17-A. Type lines 1 and 2 twice, with smooth-as-music rhythm each time.

17-A. Review the alphabet keys

1 joy irk quo ham bed lag fox zip vow bat act no so

2 zone vary jobs help quit digs crew milk lone flax

17-B. To increase skill and to target your practice goals, type and proofread a copy of this letter. Try to finish it in 2 minutes.

17-B. Measure and improve your keyboard control

WORDS

3 Dear Mr. Vance: 3
                                                       4
We are glad to learn that you have recovered   13
from the explosion and will be in to see us.   22
However, our interest in Ozite cannot be re-   31
vived by all the eloquence in the world.   39
                                                       40
TAB➤   Kane Glenn, Jr.   44

   1 | 2 | 3 | 4 | 5 | 6 | 7 | 8 | 9

17-C. Boost your accuracy by typing lines 4-7 three times each if you made 5 or more errors in 17-B or twice each if you made only 4 or fewer errors.

17-C. Build accuracy on outside reaches

4 az blaze amaze craze fazed lazy daze gaze haze az

5 l; nail; bail; fail; mail; ail; oil; ill; all; l;

6 qa quart quack quail quake quay quad aqua Iraq qa

7 op opera opens chops slope hope mope stop shop op

17-D. Increase speed by typing lines 8-11 three times each if you made 4 or fewer errors in 17-B or twice each if you made 5 or more typing errors.

17-D. Build speed on different phrase rhythms

8 he did| he and| he put| he may| he saw| he got| he told

9 can he| may he| and he| for he| did he| say he| for him

10 he will| he says| he gave| he said| he took| he is the

11 when he| that he| wish he| sure he| then he| for he is

207/208-C. Apply skill to an integrated typing project

Assume the date is DECEMBER 1. You work for Layne I. Collyer, assistant manager of the Credit Department of William Blake & Sons Company. Before beginning any of the work in this one-hour project, review all of it so you may determine how many carbons to make of each task. Looking in the files, you see that Mr. Collyer prefers blocked letter style and this closing arrangement:

Yours sincerely,

WILLIAM BLAKE & SONS COMPANY

Assistant Manager
Credit Department

Layne I. Collyer/urs

Table 67
REVISED RULED TABLE

Giving you the revised table on the next page, Mr. Collyer says, "I have brought up to date our list of overdue accounts. Please type the list with a file copy and a working copy for next month's report."

You notice that he did not compute the new totals figures. You will do this.

Form 74
INTEROFFICE MEMO

Paper: workbook 389
SI: 1.51—fairly difficult

"Send the original of the table to Mr. Busk—that is William P. Busk, the credit manager—on the eighth floor," says Mr. Collyer, "with this memorandum."

i have attached the december 1 listing 38
of overdue accounts...you will be pleased 47
to note that the number is down to four 55
...the lowest we have had for some time... 63

you will be interested to note...also 71
...that consumers' exchange has finally 79
squared away its account...a letter from 87
the firm explained that the recent election of 96
new officers led to litigation in which the 105
exchange's treasury was tied up for three 113
months...now that that matter is cleared 122
...the exchange has moved swiftly to meet 130
its obligations... 133

there is only one new account on the 142
overdue list...it is that of the kalamazoo 150

citizens' league...i was surprised to see 159
this...for they have always paid their 166
bills promptly in the past... 172

we shall dispatch the usual notices to 181
all the current overdue accounts. 196

Letters 107-110
BLOCKED FORM LETTERS

Paper: workbook 391 ff.
Enclosure: Manus. 73
SI: 1.57—difficult

"Next," says Mr. Collyer, "as soon as that memo is on its way to Mr. Busk, please send a copy of the credit-policy statement [Manuscript 73, page 319] and this letter to each of the overdue accounts."

your account shows a balance of (*insert* 41
the correct amount)...which is now (*insert* 46
the correct number days, written in figures) 47
days overdue... 50

you are undoubtedly aware that...with 58
the exception of such organizations as the 67
one you represent...our terms are cash 74
only...our splendid service and low prices 83
are based on our ability to dispense with 91
an expensive credit and accounting organi- 100
zation... 101

we appreciate that many associations 110
like yours find they must extend credit 118
to their members...since our position and 126
policies are so well known...however... 134
we feel that you should have made some 142
arrangement to liquidate this account 149
within the usual 30-day period... 156

(*Insert this next paragraph only in the* ..
"60 days overdue" letters.) since your ac- 159
count is now more than 60 days overdue 167
...we are compelled to call your attention 175
to our policy of shipping c.o.d. any goods 184
you may order in the future until you remit 193
the (*insert the balance due*) that is now so 199
long overdue... 202

we hope that you will find some way to 210
clear up this matter shortly...in the mean- 219
time...we shall continue to serve you both 227
promptly and well. 287

17-E. Increase attention by a concentration drill

17-E. To increase your concentration power: Omitting the word "no" wherever it occurs, type each line twice. All lines should end up at exactly the same point.

12   is if it in no at ax as am ah aw ad no by my me no
13   pa ma ha no ok oh or ow ox of on no el em et en no
14   be me he we re no us up pi no do so lo ho go to no

17-F. Measure your progress

17-F. To encourage and to measure your skill, type this letter twice. GOAL: A complete copy in 2 minutes or less, with 4 or fewer typing errors in your copy.

	WORDS
15 Dear Mr. Vance:	3
	4
I admit that I am quite impressed by the way	13
you refuse to give up on Ozite. You are one	22
exceptional salesman. How would you like to	31
join OUR staff and sell OUR products?	39
	40
Kane Glenn, Jr.	44

1 | 2 | 3 | 4 | 5 | 6 | 7 | 8 | 9

17-G. Learn to block-center a group of lines

When several lines or words are to be listed, center them as a block: (*a*) Pick the longest item; (*b*) backspace to center that item and set the margin stop at the point to which you backspace; and (*c*) type the list, with each word beginning at the margin stop.

PRACTICE 1. Block-center the adjacent display on a half sheet of paper. Use single spacing. Leave 2 blank lines below the title.

PRACTICE 2. Block-center the adjacent display on a full sheet of paper. Use double spacing. Leave 2 blank lines below the title.

```
METHODS OF DISPLAY TYPING

   Aligning
   Block Centering
   Blocking
   Capitalizing
   Extra Spacing
   Horizontal Centering
   Indenting
   Pivoting
   Spread Centering
   Typing All Capitals
   Underscoring
```

at home set margin and finish

Centering a block of lines is much like centering a paragraph. The difference:

To center a block, you center the longest line in the block; but to center a paragraph, you center the average full line instead of the longest line. The difference may matter.

Could each line in a list be centered individually? Yes, but doing so takes about three times as long as it does to block-center the same group of lines.

LINE: 50
TAB: 5 AND CENTER
SPACING: SINGLE
GOAL: INCREASE SKILL
STRESS: TOUCH
   CONTROL

18-A. Review the alphabet keys

18-A. Type lines 1-3 two times, as smoothly as you can each time. Set a good pace on easy line 1; then try to sustain it on the harder lines that follow.

1   pox him beg jot zip via sin ask fed cry qua lo we
2   part view frog next dime just quit cabs yolk haze
3   Quickly pick up the box with five dozen gum jars.

1 | 2 | 3 | 4 | 5 | 6 | 7 | 8 | 9 | 10

Unit 34. Secretarial Projects

LINE: 60
TAB: 5
SPACING: DOUBLE
DRILLS: THREE OR MORE
GOAL: DO AN HOUR'S
WORK IN AN HOUR!
STRESS: MAILABLE,
COMPLETE WORK

207-A. Three copies of each paragraph, or a 1-minute writing on each and a 2-minute writing on the group.

207-A. Tune up on these review lines

1   They said that they will have paid what they owed when   12
they send over Miss Hall with some more cash from the bank.   24

2   I know that Mr. Bank became a florist, specializing in   36
violets and jonquils; he moves about sixty dozen every day.   48

3   The firm used to be at 10 East 28 Street; but now it's   60
moved to 3947 West 56 Street, which is near Seventh Avenue.   72

  1 | 2 | 3 | 4 | 5 | 6 | 7 | 8 | 9 | 10 | 11 | 12

207-B. Confirm margins for 60-space line (the lines will align).

Type one complete copy with all corrections made; save your paper for reference use when you type Manuscript 73.

Or, take two 5-minute writings, with rests after each minute in the first writing but with no rests in the second. GOAL: 60 or more words a minute with two or fewer typing mistakes.

SI 1.51—fairly difficult

207-B. Sustain your skill on production copy

4   Credit Policy   8

  9

    The firm of (Wm.) Blake & Sons was founded ~~about~~ *MORE THAN* a quar-   22
ter century a~~ɡo~~ on the worthy principa̶l̶ *LE* of giving ~~our cus-~~   32
~~tomers~~ the maximum quality and service with *THE* minimum cost.   43
Through the years, this principle has brought growth and   55
success to the *FIRM* ~~company~~ and satisfaction to its ~~whole~~ great   65
family of customers.   69

          (*COST OF COLLECTING*)

¶ Basic to the factor of minimum cost, of course, is the need   82
for keeping down the ~~collection costs for~~ the moneys due   93
the firm for its goods and service. William Blake & sons,   105
therefore, has always held to a policy of cash dealing with   117
~~with~~ all its customers. Some 80 per cent of these *CUSTOMERS* send   129
payment with their orders; Most of the remaining 20 per   140
cent remit within seven days after receiving delivery.   152

no ¶ It is an uncommon thing for William Blake & Sons to   162
request payment.   167

    An exception to the *CREDIT* policy has been made in *A* the case of   179
co~~-~~operative organizations because the officers of these   191
groups may have to hold payment until the expenditure is   202
approved at a group meeting, ~~and so~~ a period of 30 days   212
CREDIT ~~grace~~ has been and is allowed such accounts. New orders   224
received from them when they are in arrears, however, maybe   236
shipped only C.O.D. or on receipt of cash with ~~the new~~   245
order. (It's) unjust to our ɡreat family of *CASH* customer~~s~~   257
to raise the *in* prices ~~to them~~ and thus to require them, ~~in~~   267
~~effect~~ to subsidize the ~~extension of~~ credit *of* others.   274

                     James Blake, president   289

TODAY'S DATE   293

  1 | 2 | 3 | 4 | 5 | 6 | 7 | 8 | 9 | 10 | 11 | 12

Manuscript 73

CENTERED DISPLAY
Paper: plain, full
Carbons: Enclosures,
  Letters 107-110
Line: 60
Spacing: double
SI: 1.51—fairly difficult

skip

18-B. Measure and improve your keyboard control

18-B. To define practice goals, type and proofread a copy. Remember to tab once for the paragraph indentation and twice for the writer's signature.

WORDS

4   Dear Miss Queen: 3

4

     It was kind of you to correct the index   13
to our club handbook for us. The job needed   22
to be done. All the men realize what a fine   31
task you did and are very grateful.   38

39

                    Paul J. West   44

1 | 2 | 3 | 4 | 5 | 6 | 7 | 8 | 9

18-C. Build accuracy on alphabetic word lines

18-C. To boost accuracy, type lines 5-8 three times each if you made 5 or more errors in 18-B, but only twice each if you made 4 or fewer errors in 18-B.

5   five high worm quid back lazy boys axle join port
6   mink dove taxi jump bowl size figs hour quit clay
7   silk daze hymn upon text rave flag wick aqua jobs
8   band gave rest quip lazy joke from axis what race

18-D. Build speed on alternate-hand words

18-D. To boost your speed, type lines 9-12 three times each if you made 4 or less errors in 18-B, but twice each if you made 5 or more typing errors in 18-B.

9   work such them city dial hand pans maid held pays
10   both than make with keys duel soap form half dusk
11   when mane town maps form lake roam dorm lamb then
12   down firm turn duty auto wish goal paid half rush

18-E. Increase efficiency in the hyphen reach

18-E. To improve your control of the hyphen, type lines 13 and 14 two times each—by touch!

13   The blue-green mat is the most up-to-date design.
14   The shadow--that of a man, I believe--faded away.

18-F. Measure your progress

18-F. To increase and to measure your skill, type this note twice. GOAL: A complete copy, with 4 or fewer errors, in 2 minutes or less. How many times will you use the tab?

WORDS

15   Dear Miss Queen: 3

4

     The men in the club believe they should   13
extend more than just thanks to you for fix-   22
ing the index for us. So, by way of a bonus   31
prize, a little gift is on its way.   38

39

                    Paul J. West   44

1 | 2 | 3 | 4 | 5 | 6 | 7 | 8 | 9

18-G. Learn to center spread-out words

The shortcut method of centering works because it is really the same as the regular method—except for saying "space" after each letter (or space between the words) to make a pair of strokes for which you then backspace one time. If you do the practice exercises correctly, the letter E aligns vertically.

To spread words for extra display impact, leave 1 space between letters and 3 spaces between words. To center a spread line, use the standard backspace-centering method (13-G) *or use this shortcut:* From the center, backspace once for each space *except the last* that the line would occupy if it were *not* spread out.

PRACTICE 1. Using the standard method, spread-center these lines.

PRACTICE 2. Using the shortcut method, spread-center these lines.

A T T E N T I O N
S P E C I A L
S U P P E R   M E N U
T H E   E N D

206-A. Repeat 205-A for a quick tuneup

206-B. Measure your skill on weighted technical copy

206-B. Steps to follow:

STEP 1. Make one copy of paragraph 13 without pausing or looking up.

STEP 2. Proofread very carefully. If you erred on a $, ", or ', place a check mark beside the appropriate paragraph following (14, 15, 16).

STEP 3. Type paragraphs 14, 15, and 16 twice each plus once more if you checkmarked it.

STEP 4. Finally, repeat paragraph 13 until you have an errorless copy.

13   "Okay," says Sergeant; "whose money is this?" He   11
counts it out, "$10, $28, $39, $47, $56. Wow!" Bob's   22
face "reds up" a bit, but we're "mum." Sergeant says,   33
"Well, if it ain't nobody's, it's mine!" That's that.   44

   1 | 2 | 3 | 4 | 5 | 6 | 7 | 8 | 9 | 10 | 11

14   Joe cleared $10 on Monday, $28 on Tuesday, $39 on   11 55
Wednesday, $47 on Thursday, and $56 on Friday morning.   22 66

15   How do you "start" a "timed writing"? Some call,   11 77
"Three, two, one, type"; others call, "Ready? Begin."   22 88

16   It's Joe's dog we see, blinkin' at us and yawnin'   11 99
in the sun. Joe's dog! That means Joe's around, too!   22 110

   1 | 2 | 3 | 4 | 5 | 6 | 7 | 8 | 9 | 10 | 11

206-C. Measure your skill on more weighted technical copy

206-C. As in 206-B.

17   When I checked Invoice #3829 from Dubbs & Miller,   11 121
I saw it was discounted 28% only for the first 10# and   22 132
then 39% for the rest. Invoice #3928 from Coe & Clark   33 143
was right: 28%, the first 100#; and 39% for the rest.   44 154

   1 | 2 | 3 | 4 | 5 | 6 | 7 | 8 | 9 | 10 | 11

18   We find 10% discounts common, but those of 28% or   11 165
39% are just as irregular as discounts of 47% and 56%.   22 176

19   You sent them 10# of #10, 28# of #28, 39# of #39,   11 187
47# of #47, and 56# of #56, to total at 180# of candy.   22 198

20   I did business with Hall & Hill until Hall & Hill   11 209
were merged with Karen & Kole, or was it Kole & Karen?   22 220

   1 | 2 | 3 | 4 | 5 | 6 | 7 | 8 | 9 | 10 | 11

206-D. Measure your skill on more weighted technical copy

206-D. As in 206-B.

21   In summary, _our_ analysis of the 30 vacancies gave   12 232
(1) 10 stenographers, 20 typists; (2) 10 women, 8 men,   23 243
12 either men or women; and (3) 10 with _no_ experience,   35 255
9 _with_ experience, plus 11 _with or without_ experience.   54 274

   1 | 2 | 3 | 4 | 5 | 6 | 7 | 8 | 9 | 10 | 11

22   We need someone who can (a) sell at the counters,   11 285
(b) arrange window displays, and (c) keep sales books.   22 296

23   _First_, take the crate apart; _second_, remove scale   15 311
from wrappings; and _last_, mount the legs on the scale.   28 324

   1 | 2 | 3 | 4 | 5 | 6 | 7 | 8 | 9 | 10 | 11

206-E. Measure your sustained skill on technical copy

206-E. Make a complete copy of the typewriting on this page or take a 5-minute writing on it.

Unit 4. The Number Keys

19-A. Review the alphabet keys

1 Few men can say the lazy boy can run his car far.

2 John will keep the six dogs very quiet this week.

19-B. Practice the ❶ key

3 aqla aqla alla alla alal alal all lll and lll,lll

4 ll arts ll axes ll aims ll alms ll aces 1.11 1:11

5 We need ll pairs of size ll shoes for the ll men.

19-C. Practice the ❷ key

6 sw2s sw2s s22s s22s s2s2 s2s2 all 222 and 112,122

7 22 sons 22 sums 22 seas 22 sips 22 suns 2.22 2:22

8 The 12 men and the 22 boys played 122 full games.

19-D. Measure your progress

9 Of the 122 who paid, only ll or l2 were children.

10 About ll2 caught the 12:12 train on Track No. 21.

| 1 | 2 | 3 | 4 | 5 | 6 | 7 | 8 | 9 | 10 |

19-E. Practice the ❸ key

11 de3d de3d d33d d33d d3d3 d3d3 all 333 and 123,123

12 33 dads 33 dips 33 dues 33 dots 33 dogs 3.13 3:13

13 Did the 3 men catch 31 or 33 fish in the 13 days?

19-F. Practice the ❹ key

14 fr4f fr4f f44f f44f f4f4 f4f4 all 444 and 123,441

15 44 furs 44 fins 44 fish 44 fell 44 flew 4.14 4:14

16 The 44 boys lost only 14 of their 144 golf games.

Side notes:

LINE: 50
SPACING: SINGLE
GOAL: CONTROL 1, 2, 3, AND 4
STRESS: ANCHOR KEYS

Some machines have a "1" key on the top row, which is controlled by A-finger.

On other typewriters, the small letter L is used as the "1" and is controlled by L-finger, of course.

19-A. Type each line twice. Set a fast pace on line 1; hold the pace on line 2.

19-B. If you have a 1 key on your machine, control it with A-finger (keep F-finger anchored). If not, use the small letter L as the 1. Type lines 3-5 three or more times each.

19-C. Use S-finger. Try the sw2s reach (keep your F-finger at home). Type lines 6-8 three times.

19-D. Type lines 9-10 two times. GOAL: A complete copy of both lines in 1 minute, with eyes kept on copy and with no errors.

19-E. Use D-finger. Try the de3d reach (keep your A- or F-finger at home—which is easier?). Type lines 11-13 three times.

19-F. Use F-finger. Try the fr4f reach (keep your A-finger at home). Type lines 14-16 three times.

LINE: 60
TAB: 5
SPACING: DRILLS SINGLE,
    PARAGRAPHS DOUBLE
DRILLS: THREE OR MORE
GOAL: STRENGTHEN
    NUMBER CONTROLS
STRESS: TYPE BY TOUCH!

205-A. Race through the three drills three times without pausing, without looking up even once. Repeat in Lesson 206.

205-A. Tune up on these review lines

1 Both of the men paid us for the visit to the island chapel.
2 Bennie won five major prizes equal to your six good checks.
3 If it isn't on pages 10, 28, or 39, look on pages 47 or 56.

   1 | 2 | 3 | 4 | 5 | 6 | 7 | 8 | 9 | 10 | 11 | 12

205-B. Type four copies, being sure that at least one is error free. GOAL: A copy per minute.

SI 1.29—fairly easy IF you know your numbers

205-B. Measure your skill on technical material

4 At the start of the 1900's, gliding had become quite a hobby. 14
Orville and Wilbur Wright built and flew gliders in 1900, 1901, 26
and 1902; their biplane glider set all kinds of records in 1902. In 40
1903, they built a motor and propellor for their glider and, on 53
December 17 of that year, flew it. 60

   1 | 2 | 3 | 4 | 5 | 6 | 7 | 8 | 9 | 10 | 11 | 12

205-C. Three times each. Type slowly on the first copy and seek to speed up on every repetition. Do not type the underscores.

205-C. Increase number fluency via "we 23" drills

5 we 23 24 25 you 697 698 699 tow 592 593 594 rut 475 476 477
6 or 94 95 96 wit 285 286 287 wry 246 247 248 tri 548 549 550
7 to 59 60 61 rye 463 464 465 wet 235 236 237 pry 046 047 048

205-D. Type another copy of 205-B and then three copies of paragraph 8; be sure at least one copy is completely error free.

SI 1.30—fairly easy IF you know your numbers

205-D. Measure your skill again on technical material

8 Orville made the first of four successful flights that day; it was 14 74
for 120 feet and lasted 12 seconds. Wilbur was pilot on the last 28 88
and longest flight; it lasted 59 seconds, and he flew 852 feet from 41 101
the upskid to the downskid marks. Thus, December 17, 1903, is 54 114
the birthdate of all airplanes. 60 120

   1 | 2 | 3 | 4 | 5 | 6 | 7 | 8 | 9 | 10 | 11 | 12

205-E. Three times each. Speed up on repetitions.

205-E. Increase number fluency on number-sequence sentences

9   They have their main offices on 17th, 18th, or 19th Street.
10 Lt. Coe was at sea during 1941, 1942, 1943, 1944, and 1945.
11 The firm did well in 1955 and 1956 but not in 1957 or 1958.

   1 | 2 | 3 | 4 | 5 | 6 | 7 | 8 | 9 | 10 | 11 | 12

205-F. Type one copy of 205-B and of 205-D and then two copies of this. Be sure one copy of this is error free. Remember: Keep eyes on the copy!

SI 1.30—fairly easy IF you know your numbers

205-F. Measure your skill again on technical material

12 During 1904 and 1905, the Wrights constructed many new 12 132
planes; and they flew a craft for 38 minutes in 1905. They were 25 145
then awarded patents, in 1906, and won the interest of the War 38 158
Department, which requested bids in 1907, looked at models in 50 170
1908, and gave them their first contract in 1909. 60 180

   1 | 2 | 3 | 4 | 5 | 6 | 7 | 8 | 9 | 10 | 11 | 12

19-G. With machine set for double spacing, type each of the lines twice. GOAL: To retype all lines once each in 2 minutes or less, with 4 or fewer errors, and without looking up.

19-G. Measure your progress

17 1. Of the 43 persons attending, 34 placed orders.

18 2. The orders of the 34 came to about 112 pounds.

19 3. Of the 34 persons, 12 ordered 2 or more boxes.

20 4. About 12 of the 34 asked us to ship the candy.

    1 | 2 | 3 | 4 | 5 | 6 | 7 | 8 | 9 | 10

LINE: 50
TAB: 5 AND CENTER
SPACING: SINGLE
GOAL: INCREASE
    CONTROL OF 1, 2,
    3, AND 4
STRESS: TOUCH
    CONTROL

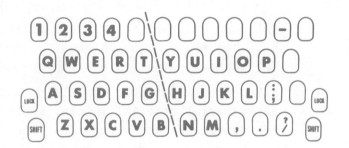

LESSON

20

Number Review

20-A. Type lines 1-3 two times; then repeat line 3 until you can type it without pausing once.

20-A. Review the keys you know

1 Joe and the six new men may now quit for the day.

2 Eve will come back when they play that maze game.

3 To get 111, add up 1 and 11 and 22 and 33 and 44.

20-B. To improve and test your control of numbers you now know, type a copy, line for line and double spaced, and proofread it.

Use the tab for indenting and positioning the name of the writer. Remember: each use of the tabulator is counted as 1 word.

20-B. Measure and improve your keyboard control

WORDS

4 Dear Mr. Quigley: 4

      If we could get the six crews in train-   13

ing by May 3 or 4 instead of June 1 or 2, we   22

might have a chance to take first prize this   31

year. Does May 3 or 4 seem to be too early?   40

                Ed Steele   44

    1 | 2 | 3 | 4 | 5 | 6 | 7 | 8 | 9

20-C-D-E. To improve skill, type lines 5-13 (continuing on page 38) twice each.

Then repeat twice more each one of the following:

(a) Lines 5-7 if you made any number error in 20-B.

(b) Lines 8-10 if you made more than 4 errors in 20-B.

(c) Lines 11-13 if you made no figure errors and had 4 or fewer errors in 20-B.

20-C. Build accuracy on the number keys

5 May 11 and 12, May 12 and 13, then May 13 and 14.

6 May 21 and 22, May 22 and 23, then May 23 and 24.

7 May 11 and 22, May 12 and 23, then May 13 and 24.

20-D. Build accuracy on the alphabet keys

8 prize might quite jury deft loan back fix saw eve

9 exact dozen quart evil upon whom jack say beg fun

10 every seize equip echo bang next walk job mud for

204-A. Repeat 203-A for a quick tuneup

204-B. Inventory your present skill on difficult copy

204-C. Improve stroking on 3-letter word endings

204-B. Type the last three paragraphs, page 315; or take a 5-minute writing on them. GOAL: 50 or more wam with 2 or fewer mistakes. If you make more than two errors, your goal is ACCURACY; if you make fewer, then your goal should be SPEED.

25 ING speaking thinking getting sending meeting typing having
26 AGE mortgage coverage package postage average garage damage
27 ITY priority activity quality ability charity rarity parity

28 UAL punctual habitual gradual unusual factual actual annual
29 EST interest greatest highest largest nearest finest nicest
30 IFY identify simplify clarify specify qualify modify notify

31 BLE probable portable visible capable taxable enable double
32 IAL material official initial special cordial burial social
33 FUL faithful grateful tactful fearful careful sinful useful
     1 | 2 | 3 | 4 | 5 | 6 | 7 | 8 | 9 | 10 | 11 | 12

204-C-D. Type to goal determined in 204-B.

ACCURACY: Type each three-line group, as a paragraph, three times.

SPEED: Type each line three consecutive times.

204-D. Improve stroking on 4-letter word endings

34 TENT penitents competent impotent penitent existent content
35 ABLE honorable insurable payables portable syllable capable
36 IBLE invisible inedibles credible sensible possible visible

37 TION education objection deletion fraction relation section
38 TION exemption rejection question position notation mention
39 TION condition dictation creation ambition adoption station

40 MENT apartment implement pavement basement tenement torment
41 MENT deferment equipment judgment shipment document element
42 MENT allotment sentiment argument sediment bailment ailment

43 TIAL essential impartial initials partials official initial
44 TIVE defective executive relative positive elective festive
45 TURE departure miniature immature puncture fracture fixture
     1 | 2 | 3 | 4 | 5 | 6 | 7 | 8 | 9 | 10 | 11 | 12

204-E. Regain stride on very easy sentences

204-E. Take a series of 1-minute writings to regain peak fluency.

ACCURACY: Use the three-line groups as a solid paragraph.

SPEED: Take each timing on a separate line.

SI 1.00—very easy

46 It is a shame that you did not buy some of the stock today.
47 The form they sent you is a good one and will help our job.
48 They both think the man should spend more time at his work.
     1 | 2 | 3 | 4 | 5 | 6 | 7 | 8 | 9 | 10 | 11 | 12
49 The time from six to nine is the right one for such a plan.
50 We do not wish to have as much stock as you ask us to take.
51 Both of them paid more than they should have for a new car.

204-F. Repeat 204-B to measure your progress

20-E. Build speed on alternate-hand words

20-E. Note directions on page 37. Try to hold your typing at a steady pace, though words get longer.

11 it for map fuel they pane wish forms panel chapel
12 of aid but also body form hand spend works visual
13 by men she paid vial then odor visit handy usurps

20-F. Measure your progress

WORDS

20-F. To bolster and to measure your typing skill (on numbers particularly), type the letter twice, line for line and double spaced. GOAL: A complete copy in 2 minutes or less, with 4 or fewer errors.

14 Dear Ed: 2

    I think that May 3 or 4 is a bit early,   11
but perhaps the six crews could begin indoor   20
work then and strike the water about May 21,   29
22, or 23. The prize idea sounds very good.   38

            J. Fred Quigley   43

LINE: 50
TAB: 5 AND CENTER
SPACING: SINGLE
GOAL: CONTROL 7, 8, 9, AND 0
STRESS: TOUCH CONTROL

Number Keys

21-A. Review the keys you know

21-A. Type lines twice; speed up on second copy.

1 Zoe can pay you the new tax but may ask for help.
2 Only four boys got done when Joel gave that quiz.
3 To get 123, add up 1 and 44 and 23 and 34 and 21.

21-B. Practice the 7 key

21-B. Use J-finger. Try the ju7j reach (L-Sem-fingers anchored); type lines 4-6 three times. Note use of / in making a fraction (in line 5).

4 ju7j ju7j j77j j77j j7j7 j7j7 you 777 for 123,477
5 77 jugs 77 jars 77 jigs 77 jets 77 jogs 7/17 7:17
6 On June 7, the 7 men left Camp 7 on the 7:17 bus.

21-C. Practice the 8 key

21-C. Use K-finger. Try the ki8k reach (with Sem-finger anchored); type lines 7-9 three times. Note no space after the period between small-letter initials (in line 9).

7 ki8k ki8k k88k k88k k8k8 k8k8 irk 888 for 123,478
8 88 kits 88 keys 88 kids 88 inks 88 inns 8/18 8:18
9 Train No. 188 departs at 11:18 a.m. or 12:18 p.m.

21-D. Measure your progress

21-D. Type each line twice. GOAL: A complete copy of both lines in 1 minute or less, without looking up.

10 Of the 178 who paid, only 37 or 38 were children.
11 About 187 caught the 12:47 train on Track No. 18.

   1 | 2 | 3 | 4 | 5 | 6 | 7 | 8 | 9 | 10

LINE: 70
SPACING: DOUBLE
TAB: 5
SI: 1.57—difficult

The paper used in our paper money is just about the most precise   14
product of the whole paper industry. You can hardly believe what the   28
Treasury Department requires. The paper has to be so very tough that   42
it's next to impossible to tear it, it has to weigh a certain amount, it must   58
be only the right size, and its quality must be so definitely superior that   73
it cannot possibly be duplicated. That's asking a lot!   84

One concern, an outstanding paper company, has held the contract   98
for manufacturing this special paper for nearly a century. The other   112
firms try to compete for the current order, but the standards for the   126
paper are so high that other manufacturers cannot meet them. You can   140
get some insight into the manufacturing problem when you realize that   154
this paper has to be able to withstand 4,000 foldings and unfoldings.   168
Even so, a new one-dollar bill is expected to last only about a year; the   183
monthly wear-out rate today is approximately 250 million dollars.   196

Currency paper is produced in sheets rather than in rolls. Each   210
sheet permits the printing of 32 bills. Once approved, the paper for   224
a new shipment is escorted to Washington, where it is guarded no less   238
carefully before the printing operation than after it. Even the mill that   253
produces the special paper is under surveillance 24 hours a day.   266

LINE: 70
SPACING: DOUBLE
TAB: 5
SI: 1.64—very difficult

Only the finest materials go into the making of currency papers.   14   280
The percentage of rag content is extraordinarily high, and the fibers   28   294
used are not from old, discarded, junk-style rags but are exclusively   42   308
new cotton and linen cuttings from cloth mills and tailor industries.   56   322
Among the fibers are unique red and blue ones that are characteristic   70   336
of our currency; these fibers, by law, can be used in no other paper.   84   350

The actual production process is quite interesting, based mostly on   99   365
the original Chinese formula for paper making, although cotton and   112   378
linen have replaced the silk the Chinese used. The secret formula of the   127   393
Chinese was guarded closely for centuries and did not arrive here until   141   407
1690. The ancient manufacturers would recognize the steps that the   155   421
paper undergoes, but they would be amazed at the huge boilers and   168   434
giant mixing vats and tremendous drying cylinders we are using today.   182   448

The newest money entering circulation is the new Federal Reserve   196   462
series, which augments the Silver Certificate series that has been in   210   476
dominance since World War II. Behind the new issuance lies the great   224   490
demand for more currency for everyday use by our swelling population,   238   504
on the one hand, in the face of diminishing silver stocks and growing   252   518
prices for it, on the other hand. The bullion released by the recent   266   532
Federal Reserve series will thus be available for new silver coinage.   280   546

IN ABBREVIATIONS:
No space after the period between small letters: a.m., p.m., c.o.d., f.o.b., etc.

One space after the period between capital letters: A. M., P. M., U. S. A., etc.

21-E. Use L-finger. Try the lo9l reach (keep the J-finger anchored). Type lines 12-14 three times. In line 13, note use of / in making a fraction.

21-F. Use Sem-finger. Try the ;p0; reach (J-finger anchored). Type lines 15-17 three times each. In line 17, note spacing between capital letters.

21-G. To increase and to measure your skill (on the numbers particularly), type the letter twice, line for line and double spaced. GOAL: A complete copy in 2 minutes or less, with 4 or fewer errors.

21-H. This assignment is optional but worth doing, for it reviews four things that are required in the test on pages 44 and 45:

(1) Spread centering.
(2) Horizontal centering.
(3) Vertical centering.
(4) Block centering (if you are wise and do not center names individually).

Center this announcement on a half sheet of paper; use single spacing. Leave 2 blank lines under the all-capitals title.

21-E. Practice the 9 key

12   lo9l lo9l 1991 1991 1919 1919 all 999 for 234,789
13   99 lots 99 lids 99 laws 99 logs 99 less 9/19 9:19
14   In 1919, there were 199 men in each of 19 lodges.

21-F. Practice the 0 key

15   ;p0; ;p0; ;00; ;00; ;0;0 ;0;0 dip 000 for 347,890
16   10 pegs 10 pins 10 play 10 paid 10 push 1/10 1:10
17   Meet them at 10:00 A. M. or 1:00 P. M. for lunch.

21-G. Measure your progress

                                                                                          WORDS
18   Dear Mr. Quigley: 4

        I have arranged for the six crews to do   13
     indoor drills from May 4 until May 17 or 18,   22
     with May 19 or 20 for hitting the lake; they   31
     will be ready for the prize meet on July 23.   40

                                   Ed Steele   44

     1 | 2 | 3 | 4 | 5 | 6 | 7 | 8 | 9

21-H. Optional review of centering

19   A N N O U N C E M E N T

     The Annual Banquet of The Business Club
     will be held on December 10 at 7:00 p.m.
     in the Silver Room of the Hotel Statler.

     Tickets are four dollars each and may be
     obtained from these committee members:

                  John King, Chairman
                   Maxwell Gilbert
                  Holly Anne Parker

     Reservations should be made on or before
     November 24. Members are urged to make
     their reservations as early as possible.

LINE: 60
TAB: 5
SPACING: DRILLS, SIN-
GLE; PARAGRAPHS,
DOUBLE
DRILLS: THREE TIMES
GOAL: BOOST SKILL
STRESS: STEADY PACE

203-A. Type each line in
"pyramid" style, like:
Their
Their firm
Their firm is

203-B. Type the first
three paragraphs, page
315, or take a 5-minute
timed writing on them.

GOAL: 50 words a
minute, 0-1-2 errors.

If you make more than
two errors, your goal
in Lesson 203 must be
for accuracy; fewer,
the goal is speed.

203-C-D-E. Type to the
goal found in 203-B.

ACCURACY: Each three-
line group three times
as though a paragraph.

SPEED: Each line three
consecutive times.

SUGGESTION: These
drills will be easy if
you type very smoothly.
Do not press for speed;
let the repetitions and
downhill momentum bring
a speed upsurge to you.

203-A. Tune up on these review lines

1 Their firm is paid to visit the towns for the eighth audit.
2 Five extra-bright boys could work now to pass a major quiz.
3 We looked at Models 2810, 2839, 2847, and 2856 at the shop.
   1 | 2 | 3 | 4 | 5 | 6 | 7 | 8 | 9 | 10 | 11 | 12

203-B. Inventory your present skill

203-C. Improve stroking on 2-letter word beginnings

4 RE request regards receipt record really rebate refer react
5 AL almonds already altered alloys almost always allow album
6 DE deposit details depends demand decide deduct delay defer
7 EX expense explain express excess expect except extra exact
8 UN unusual untried unknown unpaid unless unable until under
9 IM improve imagine impress import impose impact imbue imply
   1 | 2 | 3 | 4 | 5 | 6 | 7 | 8 | 9 | 10 | 11 | 12

203-D. Improve stroking on 3-letter word beginnings

10 COM complete commence compete company comment common coming
11 PRO progress provided project produce proceed proper profit
12 SUB subtract sublease sublime subways subject submit sublet
13 OUT outcomes outright outlook outline outside output outfit
14 CAN canteens canopies candies candles canvass cannot candid
15 PRE prepared previous precede premium prevent prepay prefer
16 SUR surfaces surmount surpass surplus survive surtax survey
17 PER perspire personal persist perfect perhaps person permit
18 CEN centered censured century central censure census center
19 DIS district distance discuss dislike display disown dispel
20 SUP supplied supplant suppers suppose support supple supply
21 CON contract consider conduct contain concern concur confer
    1 | 2 | 3 | 4 | 5 | 6 | 7 | 8 | 9 | 10 | 11 | 12

203-E. Improve stroking on 4-letter word beginnings

22 WITH withdrew withdraw withers without withal wither within
23 POST postpone postmark postman postage posted postal poster
24 FORE forebear foremost forearm foreman forest foredo forego
    1 | 2 | 3 | 4 | 5 | 6 | 7 | 8 | 9 | 10 | 11 | 12

203-F. Repeat 203-B to mark your progress

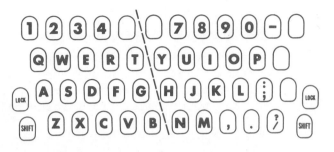

Number Review

LINE: 50
TAB: 5 AND CENTER
SPACING: SINGLE
GOAL: INCREASE
   CONTROL OF 7, 8,
   9, AND 0
STRESS: TOUCH
   CONTROL; CORRECT
   POSTURE

22-A. Review the keys you know

22-A. Type each line twice; then repeat once more if you break rhythm on any line. Sitting properly?

1   Mel and his boy may get our back pay for one day.
2   That next quiz will have just five more new jobs.
3   The 23 men and 40 boys ate 90 apples and 78 pies.

22-B. Measure and improve your keyboard control

22-B. To inventory your controls (particularly of numbers), type a double-spaced copy; proofread it.

Before starting, locate the three points where you use the tabulator—by touch!

WORDS

4   Dear Jim: 2

It may be November 27 or 28 before I am   11

sure of the exact number of dinners to order   20

for the banquet. The size of the group will   29

be between 190 and 200, I believe, as it was   38

last year.   40

John King   44

1 | 2 | 3 | 4 | 5 | 6 | 7 | 8 | 9

22-C. Build accuracy on the number keys

22-C-D-E. To improve skill, type lines 5-16 twice each. Then repeat twice more one of the following:

(a) Lines 5-7 if you made any figure error in 22-B.

(b) Lines 8-11 if you made more than 4 errors in 22-B.

(c) Lines 12-16 if you made no figure errors and had 4 or fewer errors in 22-B.

5   November 27, 28, 29, or 30 and December 13 or 14.
6   Look for Invoices No. 3900, 3977, 3988, and 3999.
7   We must read pages 171–178, 181–189, and 191–200.

22-D. Build accuracy on one-hand words

8   aware imply extra holy acre loom case hip bad ill
9   great union trade polo gave kink save joy car you
10   refer knoll after milk draw only safe non age mum
11   grade jolly exact upon area join data ink tax him

22-E. Build speed on alternate-hand words

Do you find it difficult to concentrate? Then, try this: Retype lines 12-16, typing the words in reverse order —last word, next-to-last, etc. Makes you alert!

12   an cot due city form gown idle their firms social
13   is fit got keys mane risk work goals audit profit
14   us hem bit yams duty fuel sign fight usual bushel
15   do jam key busy with down them gowns widow formal
16   if own sue born span diem town theme shame lament

202-D. Improve stroking on horizontal reaches

39   attends purse agree water lunge save puff army once put ate
40   attempt slate lunch about ounce late page able purr ago wag
41   hollows blade gaily trace trail hope talk game ball ram pat
42   barging upper basal frail value gale shop hoop hump tan gas

202-E. Repeat 202-B to mark your improvement

202-F. Now set a record on this smooth, easy copy

202-F. Use single spacing, a 50-space line, and tab-5 indention for paragraphs.

Type one fluent copy with no pauses except a brief rest after each paragraph. Or, take two 5-minute writings, the first with a rest after each minute and the second solidly.

Strive for near-perfect rhythm and error-free copy.

SI 1.22—easy

```
    1  |  2  |  3  |  4  |  5  | 6  |  7  |  8  |  9  |  10
```

43   The first and quickest step to take, for the   10
person who wants to win the title of The Pest, is   20
to become the ear of the head of the office. Run   30
to him with every tidbit of news you can. He may   40
not seem grateful, and it is hardly surprising to   50
learn that your fellow workers will be unhappy to   60
have you do this; but there is no doubt that they   70
will know who you are. This is a sure method for   80
becoming well known, even if not very well liked.   90

44   Another big, sure step, and it is not a very   100
hard one for most of us, is to become the one who   110
knows all the answers, right or wrong. If you do   120
not know an answer, invent one. Don't hold back;   130
speak up. When a group in the office is talking,   140
barge in and have your say. There is probably no   150
better way to break up office cliques and prevent   160
wasteful use of office time. It also keeps other   170
folks from talking about you, something that they   180
will be prone to do if you take this simple step.   190

45   A third step that you can take if you desire   200
more direct action in winning the title is to ask   210
for help from all the others. Make it clear your   220
work load is heavier than that of the others, and   230
much more important, too, and that the least they   240
can do is lend a hand. Now, you cannot make much   250
headway in this realm unless you persist; plan to   260
grab at least two helpers a day. And watch them,   270
too, so you can be sure to criticize what they do   280
for you. They will concede your title very soon.   290

46   There are, of course, many other tricks that   300
one can do to become The Pest. You can always be   310
late, you can make mistakes and pass the blame on   320
to others, you can wear strange clothing and talk   330
about it a lot, you can tell others to make phone   340
calls for you, and so on; but the truly effective   350
steps are the three outlined above. And when you   360
have won the title, cherish it; for, you will not   370
be there long enough to make very much use of it.   380

```
    1  |  2  |  3  |  4  |  5  | 6  |  7  |  8  |  9  |  10
```

22-F. To increase and to measure your skill, type this letter twice. GOAL: A copy in 2 minutes, with 4 or fewer typing errors. It is permissible to practice any troublesome words between timings.

LINE: 50
SPACING: SINGLE
GOAL: CONTROL ½, ¼, 5, AND 6
STRESS: TOUCH CONTROL

23-A. Type each line twice; then repeat once more if you falter (break rhythm, lose place in copy, stall) in the second typing.

*23-B. Use Sem-finger. Try the ;½; reach (with your J-finger anchored and the other fingers spreading). Type lines 4-6 three times.

*23-C. The ¼ is shift of ½ and is controlled by Sem-finger. Try the ;½ ¼; reach. Then type lines 7-9 three times, steadily not rapidly.

*23-D. Type the sentences twice each—once straight through and once with this GOAL: To finish each of the sentences in 1 minute, with no number errors.

*NOTE: If your machine does not have a ½-¼ key, you must construct the fractions (see note at top of page 42).

22-F. Measure your progress

WORDS

18   Dear John: 2

Mr. Blazer tells me that we can have up   11
to December 7 for an exact count on the ban-   20
quet, with final figures on December 8. Can   29
we, I hope, push sales over the 200 mark to,   38
say, about 210?   41

Jim   44

1 | 2 | 3 | 4 | 5 | 6 | 7 | 8 | 9

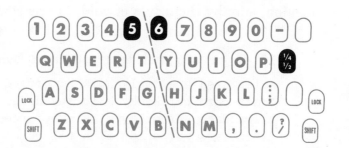

Number Keys

23-A. Review the keys you know

1   Max did not run for our team but did get his cup.

2   Jack told them that your last quiz was very hard.

3   Adding 13 and 43 and 10 and 78 and 90 totals 234.

23-B. Practice the ½ key

4   ;$\frac{1}{2}\frac{1}{2}$; ;$\frac{1}{2}\frac{1}{2}$; ;$\frac{1}{2}$;$\frac{1}{2}$;$\frac{1}{2}$;$\frac{1}{2}$ $\frac{1}{2}$ pay; $\frac{1}{2}$ mile; $\frac{1}{2}$ hour; $\frac{1}{2}$ week

5   Yes, 4 is $\frac{1}{2}$ of 8, $4\frac{1}{2}$ is $\frac{1}{2}$ of 9, and 7 is $\frac{1}{2}$ of 14.

6   He worked $10\frac{1}{2}$ hours in May and $11\frac{1}{2}$ hours in June.

23-C. Practice the ¼ key

7   ;$\frac{1}{2}\frac{1}{4}$; ;$\frac{1}{2}\frac{1}{4}$; ;$\frac{1}{4}$;$\frac{1}{4}$;$\frac{1}{4}$;$\frac{1}{4}$ $\frac{1}{4}$ pay; $\frac{1}{4}$ mile; $\frac{1}{4}$ hour; $\frac{1}{4}$ week

8   Yes, 2 is $\frac{1}{4}$ of 8, $2\frac{1}{4}$ is $\frac{1}{4}$ of 9, and 7 is $\frac{1}{4}$ of 28.

9   We gave $\frac{1}{2}$ to him and $\frac{1}{4}$ to her; I got the other $\frac{1}{4}$.

23-D. Measure your progress

10   Please order 10 more of size $10\frac{1}{2}$, 28 more of size $28\frac{1}{2}$, 39 more of size $39\frac{1}{2}$, and 4 more of size $47\frac{1}{2}$.

11   Then ask for 10 more of size $10\frac{1}{4}$, 28 more of size $28\frac{1}{4}$, 39 more of size $39\frac{1}{4}$, and 7 more of size $47\frac{1}{4}$.

1 | 2 | 3 | 4 | 5 | 6 | 7 | 8 | 9 | 10

201-F. Type one copy to mark your rate and set your goal for 201-G.

If you make more than one error, your goal must be for accuracy; one or no errors, then it is speed.

SI 1.27—fairly easy IF you have mastered control of one-hand sequences.

201-F. Measure your skill on one-hand-loaded text

23 Once upon a time, it was a treat to look upon the vast herds of   14
skinny cattle that lanky cowboys, feet in stirrups and seat in saddle,   28
drove off the grasslands to the market. The great drives were uphill   42
going, likely, and were a test of man and beast. The cattle were far   56
from the plump breed we enjoy now; but the reward for millions of   69
steers was raw cash, cash pumped willy-nilly East to West. In my   82
opinion, only by the drives of wild, jumpy steers did the West grow.   96

1 | 2 | 3 | 4 | 5 | 6 | 7 | 8 | 9 | 10 | 11 | 12 | 13 | 14

201-G. Type to the goal you set by your 201-F.

ACCURACY: Each group of five lines three times, as though a paragraph.

SPEED: Each individual line three quick times.

CAUTION: Sit erect; do not sway. Shoulders and arms must stay level.

201-G. Improve stroking on one-hand words

24 after area are imply hulk hip freed best bet jumpy join ink
25 craft card car kinky kiln joy defer date dad lumpy noun lip
26 extra ease ear milky mink mum farce gave set nylon upon kin
27 great fare get onion lion oil react read red pupil yolk ply
28 state save web phony only him waste were few union p.m. mop

29 seated pinion better uphill treats hominy crate lymph after
30 aware pylon grade knoll exact plump deter holly water mommy
31 acre holy base jump case kink draw lily edge mill fact noon
32 age hum bad ill car nip err ohm fad pun gas yon sew hop vex
33 at on as no we in be my ad up ax un ex ho de pi re oh be no

201-H. Errorless, now?

201-H. Repeat 201-F to mark your improvement

202-A. This time, each line three quick times.

202-A. Repeat 201-A for a quick tune-up

202-B. Type one copy to mark your rate and set your goal for 202-C.

If you make more than one error, your goal must be for accuracy; one or no errors, then it is speed.

SI 1.57—difficult

202-B. Measure your skill on long-reach-loaded text

34 The cultivation of our coffee requires limitless care, and five pains-   15
taking years are required to develop a mature product. The snowy   28
and fragrant blossoms turn into red and green cherries; they cannot be   42
harvested by machinery. The beans are the pits from the coffee   55
cherries. Approximately 2,000 of these are necessary for a pound of   69
roasted coffee. Beans require a long drying process before they are   83
hulled, graded, and shipped out to be tested, blended, and roasted.   96

1 | 2 | 3 | 4 | 5 | 6 | 7 | 8 | 9 | 10 | 11 | 12 | 13 | 14

202-C. Type to the goal you set by your 202-B.

ACCURACY: The group of four lines three times, as though a paragraph.

SPEED: Each individual line three quick times.

202-C. Improve stroking on vertical reaches

35 borrow chance enemy bran boat bore mush mutt cue may but my
36 models creams noisy veer note crow vest bent mix cry vow be
37 axioms lesson gowns poem webs room iron town web pin won on
38 loaned convex items next oxen owns pins upon ebb ton one in

NOTE in line 14:
In a mixed number, leave 1 space between the whole number and the fraction when the fraction is made with a diagonal. If one fraction must be made with a diagonal, use a diagonal with all fractions that are in the same sentence.

23-E. Use F-finger. Try the f5f reach (with the A-finger anchored); type lines 12-14 three times. See note above concerning fractions in line 14.

23-E. Practice the 5 key

12   f55f f55f f5f5 f5f5 5 falls 5 fires 5 folks 5 red

13   55 fell 55 find 55 fewer 55 fix 55 fuss 5/55 5:55

14   The answer to No. 155 is either 55 1/2 or 55 2/5.

23-F. Use J-finger. Try the jy6j reach (with Sem-finger at home); then type lines 15-17 three times. Can you make reach to 6 without moving your arm?

23-F. Practice the 6 key

15   jy6j jy6j j66j j6j6 6 jays 6 jumps 6 jugs 6 jades

16   66 join 66 jump 66 more 66 must 66 have 1/66 1:16

17   We shall need 36 pencils or 6 pens for the 6 men.

23-G. Type a complete copy with this GOAL: To finish in 2 minutes or less, with no number errors and not more than 4 other errors. Then center a copy on a half sheet of paper.

NOTE: When you type any enumeration, the periods after the numbers must line up. The typist must remember to check whether the enumeration includes two-digit numbers; if it does, one-digit numbers must be indented 1 space.

23-G. Measure your progress   WORDS

18   WAYS TO DISPLAY TYPING   5

To align the periods, space in once before typing numbers 1 through 9.

        1. Aligning   8
        2. Block Centering   12
        3. Blocking   15
        4. Capitalizing   18
        5. Extra Spacing   22
        6. Horizontal Centering   27
        7. Indenting   30
        8. Pivoting   32
        9. Spread Centering   36
       10. Typing All Capitals   41
       11. Underscoring   44

LINE: 50
TAB: 5 AND CENTER
SPACING: SINGLE
GOAL: INCREASE NUMBER CONTROL
STRESS: KEY-STROKE PRECISION

24-A. Type each line twice. You should easily finish each line in ½ minute.

LESSON

24

Number Review

24-A. Review the keys you know

1   She may quit her job the day you get her new car.

2   Buzz will pack your five bags when her taxi goes.

3   I dialed rooms 10, 28, and 39; he rang 47 and 56.

     1 | 2 | 3 | 4 | 5 | 6 | 7 | 8 | 9 | 10

LINE: 60
TAB: 5
SPACING: DRILLS, SIN-
  GLE; PARAGRAPHS,
  DOUBLE
DRILLS: THREE TIMES
GOAL: BOOST SKILL
STRESS: LEVEL HANDS

Unit 33. Skill Development

201-A. Type each line in
  "pyramid" style, like:
  The
  The chairman
  The chairman of

201-A. Tune up on these review lines

1   The chairman of the panel paid us for a visit to the dorms.
2   Zeke buys exquisite jewels and gives them for a prize copy.
3   For 2 for 23 for 234 for 2345 for 6 for 67 for 678 for 7890
      1 | 2 | 3 | 4 | 5 | 6 | 7 | 8 | 9 | 10 | 11 | 12

201-B. Type one copy. If
you stall, circle the word.

If you make more than one
  error, your goal must be
  for accuracy; one or no
  error, the goal is speed.

  SI 1.53—rough, tough,
  and alphabetic!

201-B. Measure your skill on double-letter-loaded text

4   All sorts of goods, needs, and supplies are offered in vending ma-   14
chines. A traveler buys sweet-smelling perfumes, a toothbrush and   27
toothpaste, hairdressing, and other common traveling needs. Such   40
supplies as books, booklets, writing paper, boxes of cards, puzzles,   54
and hobby goods help pass a few hours. Hungry people have access to   68
all manner of food matter. One buys apples, coffee, eggs, jellies, bot-   82
tles of liquids, butter, rolls, berries, cheeses, and allied foods.   96
      1 | 2 | 3 | 4 | 5 | 6 | 7 | 8 | 9 | 10 | 11 | 12 | 13 | 14

201-C-D. Type to goal you
  ascertained in 201-B.

ACCURACY: Each group of
  lines as a paragraph at
  least three steady times.

SPEED: Each individual
line three or more times.

  If the drill is for any
  letter you missed or on
  which you paused in
  201-B, type the line two
  or three extra times.

201-C. Improve stroking on double-letter words

5   EE veneered between upkeep seems green breed been sees feel
6   OO overlook foolish cooler looks goods flood pool soon good
7   SS possible express excess dress asset class toss pass miss
8   LL followed million fellow spell hilly drill mill full ball
9   TT attempts matters bitter attic witty putty mutt putt mitt
10 FF effected differs effort stuff offer cliff miff buff cuff
11 MM commands commerce immense grammar mammoth hammers common
12 CC accepted accuracy accused success account accents occurs
13 PP happened equipped appeals dropped clipper support apples
14 ZZ dazzling puzzling puzzles fizzled muzzles fuzzily nuzzle
15 BB pebbling cribbage cabbage cribbed jobbers ribbons abbeys
16 NN connects channels manners pennies annexed annuals canned
17 GG suggests struggle begging baggage logging diggers bigger
18 OO moonshot bloodily coolant toolbox schools boodles stools
19 RR surround borrowed stirred correct arrived borrows errors

201-D. If you can be
  timed, take 1-minute
  writings on each line
  (speed) or the group of
  lines (accuracy) rather
  than as directed in
  "201-C-D" preceding.

201-D. Regain stride on alternate-hand speed sentences

20 The eight men may make their bid for the big fight by then.
21 Hang the fur cowls by the big chair; then sit down with us.
22 The men paid us for six pans, but did they pay us for soap?
      1 | 2 | 3 | 4 | 5 | 6 | 7 | 8 | 9 | 10 | 11 | 12

Errorless copy, please!

201-E. Repeat 201-B to mark your improvement

24-B. To define practice goals, type and proofread a double-spaced copy. See whether you can complete it in 2 minutes or less.

24-B. Measure and improve your keyboard control

WORDS

4   Dear Jim: 2

As of December 3, our ticket sales come   11
to 187. Holly Anne has 14 or 15 requests on   20
hand, and Max has 6 or 7 more. These add up   29
to 207 or 209. The 210 victory goal will be   38
realized.   40

John King   44

1 | 2 | 3 | 4 | 5 | 6 | 7 | 8 | 9

24-C-D-E. To reinforce your skill, type lines 5-13 twice each; repeat twice more each one (or more) of the following:

(a) Lines 5-7 if you made any figure error in 24-B.

(b) Lines 8-10, if you made more than 4 errors in 24-B.

(c) Lines 11-13 if you made no figure errors and had 4 or fewer errors in 24-B.

24-C. Build accuracy on the number keys

5   The total of 10, 28, 39, 47, and 56 is about 180.
6   Now, please total 10 and 28 and 39 and 47 and 56.
7   The sum of 10, 28, 39, 47, and 56 is exactly 180.

24-D. Build accuracy on alphabetic word lines

8   only view drag back taxi jump left helm size quip
9   hazy quit junk very flax grab clip spot weed mane
10 next bowl limp zero vice hunk good quay from just

24-E. Build speed on fluent, rhythmic phrases

11 have firm|goal will|for you|add our|as of|up to a
12 sure wish|make this|and has|did you|or if|to be a
13 have sold|when they|ask the|you get|if it|is to a

24-F. To increase and to measure your skill, type this letter twice—double spaced. Do not look up as you type it. GOAL: A copy in 2 minutes or less, with 4 or fewer typing errors.

24-F. Measure your progress

WORDS

14 Dear Jim: 2

We have sold 194 tickets and have firm,   11
extra requests for 15, to total 209. I sure   20
wish we could tell Mr. Blazer to make up the   29
210 you wished. Say, Chum, did you get YOUR   38
tickets?   40

John King   44

1 | 2 | 3 | 4 | 5 | 6 | 7 | 8 | 9

24-G. Center a double-spaced copy vertically and horizontally on a half sheet of paper. Line 15 is to be spread. Use this year's date, not 196-.

24-G. Review centering

15   A D M I T   O N E
16   To the Annual Banquet of
17   THE BUSINESS CLUB
18   December 10, 196-, at 7:00 p.m.
19   SILVER ROOM : : HOTEL STATLER

9 SKILL BUILDING • SECRETARIAL
PROJECTS • INVENTORY TESTS

Progress Test on Part One

Test 1

Test 1-A

2-MINUTE WRITING
ON PARAGRAPHS
Paper: workbook page 44,
    or plain
Line: 50
Tab: 5
Spacing: double
Start: machine set;
    carriage at margin
Grade: box below
SI: 1.19—easy

The group of us stood by the small twig fire   10

and wished we could be dry, even if just for five   20

minutes. Max pushed a wet stick into the flames;   30

it squeaked and sizzled and then started smoking.   40

With a yell of dismay, we jumped back from a   50

gust of smoke. Max stood there, quietly laughing   60

at us. I looked at the heavy clouds; they seemed   70

to promise that the drizzle would last all night.   80

1 | 2 | 3 | 4 | 5 | 6 | 7 | 8 | 9 | 10

2-MINUTE SPEED
WITHIN 4 ERRORS*

40-up wam . . . . . . A
35-39 wam . . . . . . B
25-34 wam C
20-24 wam . . . . . . D
* If more than 4 errors
are made, compute the
speed on what is typed
before the fifth error.

Dear Jim: 2

Now that the banquet is all over and all the   12

money is in, let me report: 18

1. Max Gilbert sold 87 tickets.   26

2. Holly Anne Parker sold 56 tickets.   34

→ 3. I sold 76 tickets, including the one that   44

you almost forgot to buy.   50

4. Altogether we sold 219 tickets.   58

I am sure that you take as much pride in the   68

record we set as my committee does.   76

John King   80

1 | 2 | 3 | 4 | 5 | 6 | 7 | 8 | 9 | 10

Test 1-B

2-MINUTE WRITING ON
AN ENUMERATION
Paper: workbook page 44,
    or plain
Line: 50
Tab: 5, center
Spacing: double
Start: machine set;
    carriage at margin
Grade: box above
SI: 1.31—fairly easy

If preferred, Tests 8-B, 8-C, and 8-D may by typed completely (maximum time: 15 minutes for each) and be graded on this penalty scale.

PENALTY SCALE

—3 for each major error (top margin, line length, line-spacing, general correctness of form, etc.)
—2 for each minor error (blocking, aligning, centering, indenting, etc., of individual parts of the job)
—1 for each typographical error

GRADING SCALE

0-1 PENALTY	A
2-3 PENALTY	B
4-6 PENALTY	C
7-8 PENALTY	D

Test 8-C
Letter 106
TIMED WRITING ON DICTATED LETTER

Paper: workbook 385
Style: blocked
Grade: panel above or page 308 box
Body: 245 words
SI: 1.35—easy-normal

Test 8-D
Table 66
TIMED WRITING ON DICTATED TABLE

Paper: workbook 386
Style: ruled table
Grade: panel above or page 308 box
Start: plan made and machine adjusted

james e flaherty...392 harvard street... 16
albany...new york...12001...dear jim... 24

i am more than delighted to learn of 33
your quick recovery from your accident 41
...it does not seem possible that you are 49
ready to come back to work already...but 57
...of course...i am extremely happy that 64
you are...i hope that you will not overdo 73
things at the start...take it easy for a 81
while...jim...please do not try to step 89
back into full harness right away... 96

i suspect that the visit to harding-hill 105
company will be the first thing you will 113
wish to confirm...i found mr thompson... 121
our contact at harding-hill...to be a very 130
congenial man who really knows what the 138
score is...he was promoted up from the 145
ranks...he has been an operator of most 153
kinds of office machines and is now in 161
charge of the mailroom production work 169
for his firm...he knows exactly what he 177
wants and how he will use whatever equip- 185
ment is purchased for him... 191

mr thompson is almost certain to requi- 199
sition a battery of eight or nine of our 208
model 19's...but he also wants a folder 215
that will handle a special paper stock... 224
the factory is now completing this spe- 231
cial folder and will have it in your hands 240
within a week...i have been told... 247

if you can...jim...write him two or 254
three days before you call to see him... 262
and when you do...tell him that you will 270
be bringing the special folding machine 278
for which he asked...cordially *and so* 290
on...theodore wilson...sales manager 301

This is table 16, "secretarial impact on 28
supply purchases," compiled by you... 34
we will have the rank of each item, the 52
name of the item, and its percent. 82

rank 1 is carbon paper, 60% 90
rank 2 is typewriter ribbons, 59% 97
rank 3 is erasers, 55% 103
rank 4 is filing materials, 53% 109

rank 5 is typewriter cleaners, 50% 118
rank 6 is typewriting paper, 49% 124
rank 7 is electric typewriters, 48% 132
rank 8 is manual typewriters, 47% 139

rank 9 is posture chairs, 46% 146
rank 10 is desk staplers, 45% 152
rank 11 is writing ink, 43% 158
rank 12 is duplicating stencils, 41% 165

rank 13 is duplicating masters, 40% 173
rank 14 is copyholders, 39% 178
rank 15 is desk pen sets, 38% 184
rank 16 is dictation notebooks, 37% 192

rank 17 is boxed paper clips, 36% 199
rank 18 is boxed ball pencils, 34% 208
rank 19 is office desks, 32% 214
rank 20 is dictation machines, 31% 221

rank 21 is engagement calendars, 30% 230
rank 22 is scissors, blades, 29% 236
rank 23 is postal meters, 28% 242
rank 24 is duplicating machines, 27% 250

rank 25 is boxed lead pencils, 26% 257
rank 26 is adding machines, 24% 263
rank 27 is filing cabinets, 22% 269
rank 28 is photocopy equipment, 16% 277
.........Average is 34% 293

PENALTY SCALE

—3 for each major error (top margin, line length, line-spacing, general correctness of form, etc.)
—2 for each minor error (blocking, aligning, centering, indenting, etc., of individual parts of the job)
—1 for each typographical error

GRADING SCALE

0-1 PENALTY	. . . .	A
2-3 PENALTY	. . . .	B
4-6 PENALTY	. . . .	C
7-8 PENALTY	. . . .	D

Test 1-C

2-MINUTE WRITING,
GROUP CENTERING
Paper: workbook
 page 22; or plain
Line: clear out
Tab: center
Spacing: single
Start: carriage
 centered
Grade: box below
SI: 1.65—difficult

2-MINUTE SPEED
WITHIN 4 ERRORS*

40-up wam	. . . . . .	A
35-39 wam	. . . . . .	B
25-34 wam	. . . . . .	C
20-24 wam	. . . . . .	D

* If more than 4 errors are made, compute the speed on what is typed before the fifth error.

Test 1-D

2-MINUTE WRITING,
LINE CENTERING
Paper: workbook
 page 22; or plain
Line: clear out
Tab: center (for
 recentering carriage
 for each line)
Spacing: double
Centering: each
 line separately
Start: carriage
 centered
Grade: box above
SI: 1.67—difficult

TYPEWRITING DISPLAY TECHNIQUES

	18
	19
	20
1. Align lines	33
2. Block lines	36
3. Capitalize words	40
4. Center a group of lines	46
5. Center horizontally	51
6. Center vertically	55
7. Indent paragraphs	59
8. Pivot from margin	64
9. Spread and center	68
10. Type in all capitals	73
11. Underscore	76
12. Use extra spacings	81

CENTER →

TRAINEES

	5
	6
Richard I. Edwards	18
Alvin Dwight Smith	30
Quintin Dark	38
Aloysius Witt	47
Henry Ira Brown	58
Dominic Wirt	66
J. Gilbert	73
Emil Lisle Park	83

CENTER →

Check: The
letter "i"
lines up.

PART ONE TEST

LESSON 25

45

Progress Test on Part Eight

Test 8-A

TIMED WRITING ON
PARAGRAPH COPY

Paper: workbook 383
Line: 70 spaces
Tab: paragraph 5
Spacing: single
Length: 5 min. (2)
 or 10 min. (1)
Grade: box below
SI: 1.42—normal

Training Bulletin 23:   THE TELEPHONE

	8-B
	8-A	22

When a customer or other friend of the company reaches one of us   14   36
on the telephone, we are the company to that caller. If we are quick   28   50
to answer the phone, the company seems wide awake. If we are   40   62
helpful and sympathetic, the company seems to be that way, too. If   54   76
our voice is zestful, if our manner is friendly, the caller will associate   69   91
such cheerfulness and friendliness with the whole company. These   82   104
examples are obvious. The reverse is also obvious, is it not?   95   117

Anything that we can do, therefore, to improve our techniques of   109   131
telephoning will be to the good. The purpose of this bulletin is not   123   145
to criticize any department or person but simply to review some basic   137   159
things that make a difference in the image we create with the public.   151   173

     WHEN WE ANSWER   1. We Are Prompt.   186

As already intimated, few things are quite as critical as is the   165   200
promptness of our picking up the phone when it rings. It should be a   179   214
general rule that we answer between the first and second ring, surely   193   228
before the third. This means that all of us should make arrangements   207   242
with someone to answer our phone when we are not there.   219   254

     2. We Identify Ourselves.   269

The first words we speak are also keenly significant. We should   233   283
express a word of greeting appropriate to the hour of the day and   246   296
add a word or two that will assure the caller that he has the right   259   309
party or department. A secretary says, "Good morning, Mr.   271   321
Wilson's office; Miss Smith speaking. May I help you?" If she then   285   335
connects the call to Mr. Wilson, he says, "Good morning; Mr.   297   347
Wilson speaking," or "Good morning; this is George Wilson." A call   311   361
to a department should bring the reply, "Good morning, Credit   323   373
Department; Miss Hall speaking. May I help you?" The person who   335   385
simply says, "Hello," doesn't play fair!   344   394

     3. We Smile As We Speak.   408

There is a middle ground we should seek between being too sugary   358   422
and too crisp. The middle ground seems to come best if we smile   371   435
when we reach for the phone and hold the smile as we express our   384   448
greeting. It is very hard, thank goodness, to smile and grumble   397   461
simultaneously.   400   464

     4. We Really Try to Help.   479

When someone calls us, it is for a reason; if we can satisfy his   414   493
purpose, he is indebted and impressed and grateful. We serve   428   507
company interest best if, within the limits of our authority, we try   440   519
our best to help him fulfill his purpose.   448   527

1 | 2 | 3 | 4 | 5 | 6 | 7 | 8 | 9 | 10 | 11 | 12 | 13

5-MINUTE SPEED
WITHIN 2 ERRORS
10-MINUTE SPEED
WITHIN 5 ERRORS

60-up	. . . .	A
55-59	. . . .	B
45-54	. . . .	C
40-44	. . . .	D

If you make excessive
errors, base speed on
what you type prior to
first excessive error.

Test 8-B

Manuscript 72

TIMED WRITING ON
SPACE-SAVER REPORT

Paper: workbook 384
Line: 6½ inches
Top margin: 1 inch
Style: page 299
Grade: box above or
 page 309 panel
SI: 1.42—normal

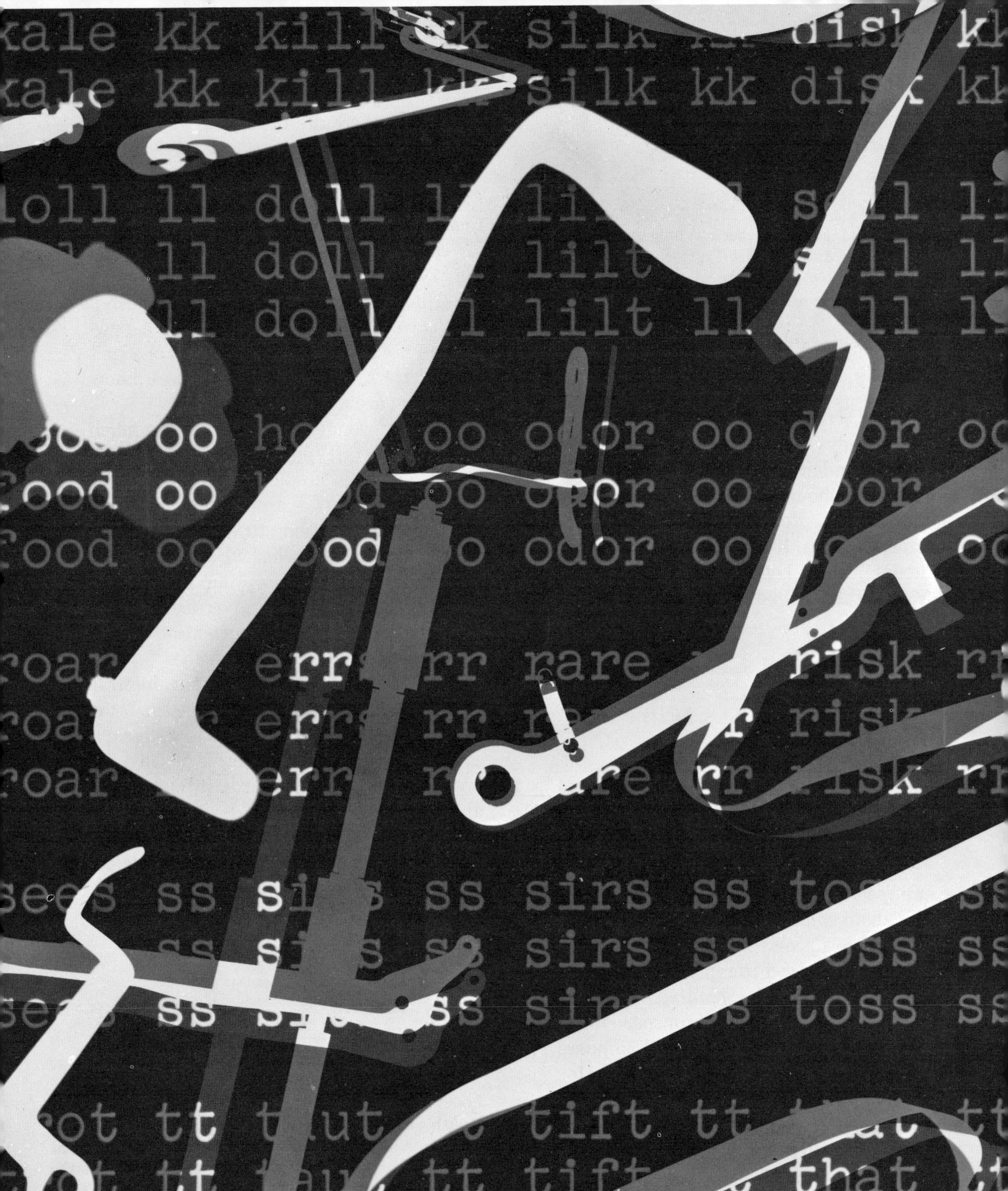

2 SKILL BUILDING • BASIC LETTERS, TABLES, AND MANUSCRIPTS

Table 64	Paper: full, plain
	Carbons: file only
DICTATED TABLE	Style: ruled form

The material you have been typing [pages 299-305] has been for Miss Priscilla Trotter, director of training. She dictates a table to you, which is to be an enclosure for the next letter.

Entitle this table "Distribution of Training Time," subtitled "Portland Products Company." We have three columns, to be headed "Activity," "Hours," and "Percent." Ready? 18 / 29 / 33 / 48 / 50

Correspondence, 40 hours, 28.6%. Skill building, 30 hours, 21.4%. Tabulation, 25 hours, 17.8%. Reports, 23 hours, 16.5%. Forms, 15 hours, 10.7%. Company policies, 5 hours, 3.5%. Display typing, 2 hours, 1.5%. Totals, 140 hours, 100.0% 67 / 77 / 84 / 93 / 101 / 128

Letter 104	Paper: workbook 377
	Carbons: file only
	Review: page 203
2-PAGE LETTER,	Body: 291 words
DICTATED; BLOCKED	SI: 1.46—fairly hard

"This letter," says Miss Trotter, "is a reply to one from Miss Jane T. Brown, Department of Personnel, Martin Miller & Sons, 50 Broad Street, Atlanta, Georgia, 30303. Ready for dictation? 4 / 15 / 24 / 34

we feel very much flattered by your inquiry about some of the details of our training program for new members of our office staff...i am pleased to reply to your questions...*Please center a heading, "1. Time Allotment"*...our program for new office employees lasts for four weeks of 35 hours each...giving us a total of 140 hours for the program...the hours are distributed as indicated on the enclosed table...*paragraph* ...you will wish to note that the program is for persons who have already had basic training in school...the program is focused on orienting the new worker to our (*underscore "our"*) policies...for example...you 42 / 51 / 59 / 67 / 78 / 94 / 102 / 120 / 129 / 136 / 145 / 153 / 162 / 170 / 176

know that there are dozens of ways to arrange letters...in our program we deal only with the one (*underscored*) way we (*underscored*) arrange our (*underscored*) letters... *Center a heading, "2. Display Typing"*... 184 / 192 / 198 / 204 / 223

yes...we do give much attention to display typing...of the 140 hours...we schedule 2 hours for what might be considered art (*quote "art"*) typing...we teach newcomers to justify lines and to construct large letters...few new employees know how these are done...*paragraph*... 232 / 240 / 248 / 253 / 261 / 269 / 273

you may wonder why we give this much attention to artyping (*quote "artyping"*) ...the answer is simple...many of our employees are typists...and we find that they give more attention to announcements when they are embellished with signs of real typing craft...also...our firm makes great use of duplicated advertisements... these...too...get more attention when they are given deft art touches...*paragraph*...i am enclosing for your interest two of our current training bulletins that deal with display typing...as well as a sample of the kind of attractive displays we post on the bulletin boards in our offices and lounges...you would be surprised by some of the fine work that our typists are able to create. *Fine. Please enumerate the four enclosures.* 282 / 287 / 294 / 303 / 311 / 319 / 327 / 335 / 342 / 349 / 382 / 390 / 398 / 407 / 416 / 424 / 432 / 439 / 451

Letter 105	Paper: workbook 379
	Carbons: file only
Table 65	Body: 317 words
	SI: 1.47—fairly hard
LETTER WITH TABLE	

Looking at your work, Miss Trotter says, "It seems foolish—especially for a training director!—to put the table on a separate page when it is short enough to fit in the letter. Please retype the letter and insert the table—without the title and subtitle, of course—after the second paragraph. Change the lead-in to *hours are distributed as follows.*" With a grin, she adds, "Now that will change the enclosure listing, too, won't it?"

Unit 5. Skill Development

P. 41 - 55

LINE: 50
TAB: 5
SPACING: SINGLE
GOAL: INCREASE SKILL
STRESS: WRISTS LOW,
    FINGERS CURVED

26-A. Ripple through lines 1-3, typing each at least twice. Use these lines as the warmup for Lesson 27.

26-A. Tune up on these easy lines

1   a; sl a;sl dk a;sldk fj a;sldkfj gh a;sldkfjgh a;

2   and the in so do to is it if ox or go do by an am

3   work wish they lazy quit cove oak six jam pay own

26-B. To define your goal for Lesson 26, type and proofread a double-spaced copy of this paragraph. If you make 4 or fewer errors, your goal is SPEED; but if you make more than 4, your goal must be ACCURACY.

    SI 1.19—easy copy*

26-B. Measure and improve your keyboard control

WORDS

4   Typing skill grows best in two steps: First   10
the typist drills on copy that is so easy that he   20
is sure to type at a good speed and with very few   30
errors; in this way he gets the feel of typing at   40
a better pace. Then he must seek to hold the new   50
rate as he works on copy that, while not hard, is   60
not easy. In this book the booster step is taken   70
in the first unit of the four units in each part,   80
and the second is taken in the other three units.   90

  1 | 2 | 3 | 4 | 5 | 6 | 7 | 8 | 9 | 10

*NOTE: SI (the syllabic intensity—average number of syllables per word) indicates the approximate difficulty of the copy:

SI 1.00-1.15 ... very easy
SI 1.15-1.25 .... easy
SI 1.25-1.35 .. fairly easy
SI 1.35-1.45 ..... normal
SI 1.45-1.55 .. fairly hard
SI 1.55-up ...... difficult

26-C. Improve skill on patterned word drills

5   po po post pour poem pore port pods pout poll pot
6   as as asks ashy task mask dash lash last past ash
7   oi oi toil soil boil coil foil coin join loin oil

8   th th thou thud thug thus than them they then the
9   fo fo fore folk fold fort foam fork form fowl for
10   sl sl slat slow sled slot slag slay slap slam sly
11   bu bu bulb bulk burr buff busy bury burn bush bud

26-C. Target on your goal.

  ACCURACY: Type lines 5-7 three times each and lines 8-11 two times each.

  SPEED: Type lines 5-7 two times each and lines 8-11 three times each.

26-D. Improve skill on patterned sentence drills

12   Quietly pack more new boxes with five dozen jugs.
13   Quietly pick up the box with five dozen gum jars.
14   Quickly pack the box with five dozen modern jugs.

    1 | 2 | 3 | 4 | 5 | 6 | 7 | 8 | 9 | 10

15   It is their duty to pay for the six fuel signals.
16   He is busy with the big social but may come down.
17   The form she got for them may work also for this.
18   She may go to the city for a visit with the girl.

26-D. Target on your goal.

  ACCURACY: Type lines 12-14 three times each and lines 15-18 two times each.

  SPEED: Type lines 12-14 two times each and lines 15-18 three times each.

Manuscript 70

LETTERED DISPLAY

Paper: plain
Carbons: file
Spacing: optional
Style: as shown

Training Bulletin 22:   DISPLAY LETTERING

The most useful form of artistic lettering in display typing
is the style shown in the alphabet below. It is constructed
of small m's, arrayed with half spacing. The easiest way to
make such letters is to type
all the m's that will appear   machine to half-line spacing
on the regular single-spaced   so you may insert the needed
lines. Next, you adjust the   parts of each letter. Thus:

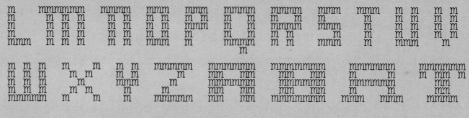

Manuscript 71

**LETTERED AND
JUSTIFIED DISPLAY**

Paper: plain
Carbons: file

*Be sure to justify
all the lines!*

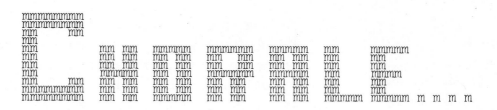

Members of the Portland Products Company Chorale will meet,

speak, sing, recite, enact, and in general have a wonderful

time this evening at eight o'clock in the auditorium. New#

members are welcome. There are no dues. All you need is##

a standard speaking voice. Come one, come all! Have fun##

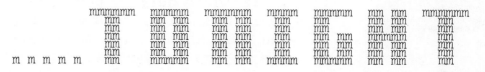

26-E. Improve skill on special paragraph copy

19 As soon as you know that you are to go up to   10
the camp, be sure to tell me so that I can plan a   20
trip up there, too. I would like to be with you,   30
if I can, when it is time to cast the first line.   40

   1 | 2 | 3 | 4 | 5 | 6 | 7 | 8 | 9 | 10

20 There is one sure way that we can get from a   10
job what we should like to get, and that is to be   20
sure to look in the job for some of the things we   30
know that we can do well and like to do that way.   40

   1 | 2 | 3 | 4 | 5 | 6 | 7 | 8 | 9 | 10

21 The path that goes past our house is the one   10
that goes down to the lake. The fish down there,   20
they say, are so quick to bite that you must hide   30
in a bush or climb a tree when you bait the hook.   40

26-F. Make an interim progress check

27-A. Learn to respond to the margin bell

Sometimes you cannot copy material line for line, but must yourself decide where to end lines. To help you in making line-ending decisions without looking up from your copy, your machine has a bell that rings when the carriage is 7 or 8 spaces from the right margin stop. For example, if you wish lines to end at 75 and have therefore set the margin stop at 80, the bell rings when the carriage reaches 72 or 73, to warn you that the carriage is only 2 or 3 spaces from 75. When the bell rings, plan to end the line as near the desired ending point as you conveniently can (preferably without dividing a word). If your typewriter gives a 3-space warning, for example, here are typical line-ending decisions you would face and make:

	DESIRED ENDING		RETURN CARRIAGE AFTER TYPING
	BELL	LOCK	

I now realize these *realize*

Somehow, we must be *we*

The possibility she *possibility*

He is philosophical *philo-*

27-B. Improve skill on patterned word drills

22 qu qu quote quilt quill quart quip quiz quad quit
23 up up upper group croup super coup soup cups upon
24 cr cr cruel crown cross crush crux crib crow crop
25 um um crumb flume strum humid dumb jump chum drum

26 oo oo stood floor crook proof book soon good look
27 ss ss gross issue guess cross loss boss less miss
28 ll ll shall skill stall droll will full sell tell
29 ee ee speed sheer trees creed need been feel keep

UNIT 5   LESSONS 26-27   48

Side notes:

26-E. Target on your goal.

ACCURACY: Type each of the three paragraphs twice.

SPEED: Type each of the paragraphs once; then type whichever paragraph seems easiest three times.

26-F. To confirm your goal for Lesson 26 and to set your goal for Lesson 27, retype the 26-B paragraph.

If you make 4 or fewer errors this time, your goal is SPEED; but if you make more than 4 errors, your goal is ACCURACY.

27-A. The correspondence in Unit 6 often requires your making line-ending decisions; learn now how to do so. In addition to the information here, use the Learning Guide (pages 25-26 of your workbook) to assure your responding to the margin bell correctly.

How many strokes can you make on your typewriter after the bell rings and before the margin locks?

27-B. Target on your goal for Lesson 27 (see 26-F).

ACCURACY: Type lines 22-25 three times each and lines 26-29 two times each.

SPEED: Type lines 22-25 two times each and lines 26-29 three times each.

Always speed up when you repeat a drill line. Are your fingers well curved?

198-C. Adjust machine for double spacing, 70-space line (lines will align), and a tab-5 indention.

In Lesson 198, type the first paragraph three times with no more than one error in each copy or until you have a copy that is errorless. Type the second paragraph in this way in Lesson 199.

SI 1.28—easy-normal

7 Once in a while a typist has a task that is important enough for   14
him to take extraordinary pains in making it look professional. When   28
that occasion comes up, the typist who can make every line end evenly   42
with the others and can design big display letters to use in headings   56
will see that he has a big jump over other typists. Such specialized   70
skills require a bit of practice, but they are easy and fun after you   84
have got the knack of them. They are not skills for a beginner; they   98
demand that the typist be a true master of the machine and its parts.   112

8 When you wish to justify a group of lines (that is, make all the   126
lines end at the same point), you start by typing a first draft. You   140
set the margins for the length of line you want to fill; and then you   154
type the material, making every line come as close as you can to your   168
desired point of line ending. In general, it is better to have lines   182
too short than to have them too long. Scrutinize the draft carefully   196
and note exactly how many spaces have to be saved or inserted to   209
make the lines end evenly; most typists fill out the lines with the   223
number sign, to show how many spaces will be needed. Finally you   236
retype the copy, making all the adjustments you need—if you miss   249
one, look out!   252

1 | 2 | 3 | 4 | 5 | 6 | 7 | 8 | 9 | 10 | 11 | 12 | 13 | 14

198/199-D. Apply your skill to display production

Training Bulletin 21:   LINE JUSTIFYING   23

25

When there is occasion to give material special display, try   37
the artistic touch of line justifying; here is how to do it: 49

50

Manuscript 69

JUSTIFIED DISPLAY
Paper: plain, full
Carbons: file
Spacing: optional
Style: as shown

To justify lines (that is,   63
to make them end evenly),### two steps are required: 76 87

1. Type the copy, ending## each line as near to the de-   99
sired ending point as you### can. Except for paragraph## endings,   112 124 137
fill in short lines with # signs to show how#### many spaces each line needs.   150 162 175

2. Type the final draft,## inserting all the necessary# spaces to spread the lines.#   188 200 213
Scatter the spaces so that## they do not occur together.   226 238

To justify lines (that is,   63
to make them end evenly),   76
two steps are required: 87

1. Type the copy, ending   99
each line as near to the de-   112
sired ending point as you   124
can. Except for paragraph   137
endings, fill in short lines   150
with # signs to show how   162
many spaces each line needs.   175

2. Type the final draft,   188
inserting all the necessary   200
spaces to spread the lines.   213
Scatter the spaces so that   226
they do not occur together.   238

239

This technique would not be used in correspondence but would   252
be very fine in typewritten announcements or advertisements.   264

27-C. Improve skill on patterned sentence drills

30 I was quite crushed when he had to quit the crew.
31 Lum was quoted saying it was dumb to crib a quiz.
32 My group went to the quad and got quarts of soup.
33 His chum jumped across a flume by the upper crib.

   1 | 2 | 3 | 4 | 5 | 6 | 7 | 8 | 9 | 10

34 Dee will collect all the needed bookkeeping fees.
35 Ross needs a better broom for glossing the floor.
36 Bess will miss her book and will need to call us.
37 Bill took three weeks to sell all his good books.

27-D. Target on your goal.

  ACCURACY: Lines 38-41,
  three times; 42-45, twice.

  SPEED: Lines 38-41, two
  times; 42-45, three times.

  One-hand words:

  Troublesome words:

  Troublesome words:

  Double letters:

  Speed phrases:

  Speed phrases:

  Speed phrases:

  Alternate-hand words:

27-D. Improve skill on preview words and phrases

38 million feed are you eat few on we no at in be up
39 excellence present, typists realize powder typing
40 although, invention fingers learned beaten though
41 classroom million offices dollars shall pill feed

42 those who|pick up|stop at|able to|come to|that no
43 know that|glad to|nice to|more in|take to|kind of
44 stop to|if you|to pay|no one|is not|to eat|we did
45 handy such they rich rush did pay box to do so if

27-E. To measure your
skill achievement, type 1
copy. GOAL: To finish
this 150-word alphabetic
paragraph in 5 minutes,
with 4 or fewer mistakes.

27-E. Measure your progress in sustained writing

                                                 WORDS

46 If you would like to become a rich person in   10
a rush, just invent some kind of pill or tonic or   20
powder a typist could take to double his skill in   30
typing. Do you realize that there are about nine   40
million typists in offices and some three million   50
more in classrooms who would be glad to pay a few   60
dollars for such a quick route to excellence? It   70
is so. It is nice to know that no one has beaten   80
you to the invention yet; although, come to think   90
about it, it would be handy to be able to stop at   100
a shop and pick up a box of words a minute, would   110
it not? For the present, though, just like those   120
who learned to type before we did, we shall drill   130
and drill our fingers until at last they learn to   140
eat up the word meals that our eyes feed to them.   150

   1 | 2 | 3 | 4 | 5 | 6 | 7 | 8 | 9 | 10

IDEA: Type 27-E as a 5-
minute timed writing and
record your scores on the
timed-writing scoreboard
on workbook page 47. If
you complete the copy
before the 5 minutes are
up, start it over.

SI 1.21—easy copy

```
;'; ''' ;'; Al's car isn't as new as he'd like us to think!    13
;'" """ ;"; "Welcome home," I said.   "When did you arrive?"    31
k8* *** k*k The asterisk (*) is on the 8 on some electrics.    50
j6¢ ¢¢¢ j¢j Jim bought 14 for 5¢, 21 for 6¢, and 18 for 7¢.    68
s2@ @@@ s@s The gloves sell @ 26¢ a pair, not @ 62¢ a pair.    86
```

22. POWER DRILLS. Repeat each of these lines until you can do so   100
without one pause or one error.   107

```
Jack quietly moved up front and seized the big cask of wax.    125
Jinx gave back the prize money she won for her quaint doll.    143
Ask her for the big rig she had the two men get out for us.    161
Jan got the forms for the firm and may also work with them.    179
```

A FINAL SUGGESTION   189

Some typists expect their speed to soar the moment they begin to   208
work on an electric machine. Please note that your speed will *not*   223
soar. It might creep up slightly, but not much. It is like having a new   237
pair of fine shoes: you have to break them in; then you can walk more   251
comfortably and with less fatigue, but your habits of walking will   264
probably keep you from walking faster than you did before.   276

It takes about three days on an electric before the manual typist is   291
fully at home with his new machine. On the first of these three days,   305
aim for about half your former speed; on the second day, for about   319
three-fourths your speed; on the third day, get back to your normal   332
pace. *Then* perhaps you can speed up a bit!   343

If you use the same
space-savers you did
on pages 299 and 300,
you will complete
"Bulletin 20" fully
in three typed pages.

LINE: 60
SPACING: SINGLE
DRILLS: THREE TIMES
GOAL: TO LEARN ABOUT
  DISPLAY ARTYPING
STRESS: EVEN STROKING

198-A. Each line three
  times or a 1-minute
  timed writing on it.
  Repeat in Lesson 199.

198-A. Tune up on these review lines

```
1   Both the town and city may make the firm fix both big oaks.
2   Roxie picked off the amazing yellow jonquils by the cavern.
3   She lost checks #10, #28, #39, #47, and #56 along the road.
    1 | 2 | 3 | 4 | 5 | 6 | 7 | 8 | 9 | 10 | 11 | 12
```

198-B. Type to your need.
  ACCURACY: The three
  lines as a paragraph
  three or more times.
  SPEED: Each three times.

198-B. Regain full skill on preview words

```
4   extraordinary important headings justify squeeze pains look
5   professional carefully indicate occasion finally other jump
6   specialized scrutinize inserted material require draft long
```

Skill Drive

LINE: 50
TAB: 5
SPACING: SINGLE
DRILLS: TWICE OR MORE
GOAL: INCREASE SKILL
STRESS: POSTURE

28-A. Type each line twice. Don't sag on the numbers! Use these lines for the warmup in Lesson 29, too.

28-B. To define your goal for Lesson 28, type and proofread a double-spaced copy of this paragraph. If you make 4 or fewer errors, your goal is SPEED; but if you make more than 4, your goal is ACCURACY.

SI 1.23—easy copy

28-A. Tune up on these review lines

1 a;sldkfjghfjdksla; a;sldkfjghfjdksla;sldkfjghfjdk
2 cab yet fed zoo ask jig not lax him row eve quips
3 Read pages 10—28, then pages 39—47, then page 56.

28-B. Measure and improve your keyboard control

WORDS

4 The oceans of the world are huge; they cover 10
more than 70 percent of its surface and, in a few 20
spots, are so deep that a mountain the size of an 30
Everest would be lost in them. The oceans play a 40
major role in shaping the weather. They serve as 50
a source of food, as an exciting playground, as a 60
means of travel. The oceans touch on the life of 70
each of us, and frequently at that. Yet, in some 80
regards, man knows more about the distant planets 90
than he does about the seas that lie at his feet. 100

  1 | 2 | 3 | 4 | 5 | 6 | 7 | 8 | 9 | 10

28-C. Target on your goal.

ACCURACY: Lines 5-8, three times; 9-12, twice.

SPEED: Lines 5-8 two times; 9-12, three times.

28-C. Improve skill on patterned word drills

5 op op open hope rope lope crop flop stop shop top
6 sa sa same sail sank sang salt safe sash sane say
7 ew ew blew flew slew view crew brew drew stew hew
8 ly ly only duly ably lily oily ally July illy fly
9 di di dish disk dire dine dime dial dice dirk did
10 le le lend lent leap lean left lest leak less led
11 co co cork coat cone come colt corn coal coke cot
12 na na name nail nape nays navy naps snap gnaw nab

28-D. Target on your goal.

ACCURACY: Lines 13-15, three times; 16-19, twice.

SPEED: Lines 13-15, two times; 16-19, three times.

28-D. Improve skill on patterned sentence drills

13 Joe quietly picked six razors from the woven bag.
14 The quick brown fox jumps over all the lazy dogs.
15 Jack Farmer was quite vexed by such lazy plowing.
   1 | 2 | 3 | 4 | 5 | 6 | 7 | 8 | 9 | 10
16 He may go to the club and work with the chairman.
17 The man may endow the chapel with an ivory panel.
18 She is apt to laugh when I go to the city social.
19 Eight of the girls do wish to go to the big lake.

For extra practice, have someone time your work; then take a series of 1-minute timings until you achieve your GOAL:

ACCURACY: Line 13 typed three times in 1 minute or less; Lines 13-15 typed once in 1 minute or less, with 2 or fewer mistakes.

SPEED: Line 16 finished four times in 1 minute or less; lines 16-19 typed in 1 minute or less, with 2 or fewer typing errors.

aa ;; ss ll dd kk ff jj gg hh ff jj dd kk ss ll aa ;; ss ll   13

aqqa ;pp; swws lool deed kiik frrf juuj fttf jyyj fggf jhhj   31

azza ;//; sxxs l..l dccd k,,k fvvf jmmj fbbf jnnj fghj jhgf   49

Leave a blank half-space above each line of drill and a full blank line after each set of drills. Use tab-5 on each drill.

15. SPACING. Get the thumb off the space bar quickly. Keep your   64
wrists low. Emphasize a straight, sharp, up-and-down tap stroke. Do   78
not let your thumb swerve inward or outward.   87

z y x w v u t s r q p o n m l k j i h g f e d c b a ; : , .   105

a b c d e f g h i j k l m n o p q r s t u v w x y z . , / ?   123

16. CARRIAGE OR CARRIER RETURN. After each of these words,   136
return the carriage or carrier by a single quick jab of the little finger.   151

waist seize farms exits stirs shall silky doily quick whist   169

payer minor order hunts handy leash moron pearl match knock   187

17. CAPITALS. Get every letter squarely on the line of writing. Hold   202
the shift key down long enough—but not too long. In the last line,   216
capitalize each letter separately; do not use the shift lock.   228

aAa bBb cCc dDd eEe fFf gGg hHh iIi jJj kKk lLl mMm nNn oOo   246

pPp qQq rRr sSs tTt uUu vVv wWw xXx yYy zZz ;:; ,,, ... ;/?   265

Fran Dale Carl Stan Drew Bess Anne Cora Ruth Vick Alan Dora   283

Lyle Jinx Lisa Nora Linc Mina Jack Hall Nate Hank Jane Paul   301

A NEIGHBOR MAY WISH TO MAKE A VISIT TO THE CHAPELS WITH US.   319

18. TAB CONTROL. Clear any stops that may already be set and set   333
new ones 13, 28, 38, and 50 spaces from the left margin.   344

Leave 6 spaces between these "columns."

Abcdefg	Hijklmnop	Qrst	Uvwxyz	Alphabets	362
Buffalo	Cleveland	Lina	Moscow	Baltimore	380
Phoenix	Ford City	Cody	Dallas	Corvallis	398

19. REPEAT UNDERSCORE. Use the same tab stops as in No. 18.   412
Avoid "running over" with the repeat underscore. You will need to   426
look at the paper as you do this practice with the repeat underscore.   440

| Atlanta | St. Louis | York | Denver | Lynchburg | 472 |
| ——— | ——— | —— | ——— | ———— | 490 |

20. BACKSPACER AND SHIFT LOCK. Clear the tab stops from No. 19   503
and set a new stop at the center. Center each of these lines; if you do   518
so correctly, the letter E should align.   526

Leave 4 spaces between these groups of words.

Come One   Come ALL   To the Finest   Junior–Senior Ball   545

21. NEW KEYS. Type the drills appropriate for the key relocations   560
on your new machine.   564

Hermes Electric

Olympia Electric

28-E. Improve skill on special paragraph copy

WORDS

20   With a whoop and a shout, the gang rushed to   10
the truck and piled in, just the way your dad and   20
I and our friends did a score of years back, when   30
each fall of snow would bring out the old sleigh.   40

   1 | 2 | 3 | 4 | 5 | 6 | 7 | 8 | 9 | 10

21   It is said that we can see the soul of a man   10
in the books that he keeps in his own room, and I   20
think that this is so. They show what he dreams,   30
what he likes to think of, and where his mind is.   40

   1 | 2 | 3 | 4 | 5 | 6 | 7 | 8 | 9 | 10

22   When I was a child, it was a grand old tree;   10
but it was hit by a bolt from the sky which split   20
it, and then the rain and snow and wind got in to   30
strip it down to the rough, old trunk we now see.   40

28-F. Make an interim progress check

29-A. Learn when NOT to divide words

1. Don't divide if you can get within 3 strokes, plus or minus, of a desired margin without dividing.

2. Don't divide any word with fewer than 6 strokes (but a 5-letter word followed by a punctuation mark may be divided, such as *six- ty*, or *uni- fy*; or *mix- er!*).

3. Don't divide a word pronounced as one syllable, like *shipped*.

4. Don't divide a contraction, like *couldn't, shouldn't, mustn't*.

5. Don't divide an abbreviation, like UNESCO or U. S. N. R.

6. Don't divide a word unless you can leave at least a 2-letter syllable (and hyphen) on the upper line.

7. Don't divide a word unless you can carry at least 3 strokes (the third may be a punctuation mark) to the next line.

8. Don't divide a number unless it fills 10 or more spaces (in which case you may divide after a comma).

NOTE. These rules are for typists, not printers. Because their lines must end evenly, printers use a different set of word-division rules.

29-B. Improve skill on patterned word drills

23 rt rt short court inert forth port hurt fort dirt
24 ou ou could bough tough touch bout sour rout ours
25 af af chafe shaft after draft safe cafe deaf raft
26 in in train incur pains inner rain find gain inch

27 bb bb blabber rubber bubble babble abbot abbey bb
28 mm mm trimmed summer gummed dimmer rummy dummy mm
29 tt tt buttons kitten bottle gotten ditto petty tt
30 pp pp shopper happen pepper supper apple upper pp

28-E. Target on your goal.

ACCURACY: Type the three paragraphs twice each.

SPEED: Type the three paragraphs once each; type three times whichever paragraph seems easiest.

SI 1.00—very easy

28-F. To confirm your goal for Lesson 28 and to set your goal for Lesson 29, retype the 28-B paragraph.

If you make 4 errors or fewer in this retyping, your goal for Lesson 29 is SPEED; but if you make more than 4 errors, your goal must be ACCURACY.

29-A. Of the eight rules, the most vital is rule 1— as you will find when you type 29-D and 29-F, both of which require you to make line-ending decisions.

In addition to studying the eight rules here, use the Learning Guide on workbook pages 27-28 to reinforce your learning when not to divide words in typed copy.

29-B. Target on your goal for Lesson 29 (see 28-F).

ACCURACY: Lines 23-26, three times; 27-30, twice. Stress very even cadence; avoid any speed spurts.

SPEED: Lines 23-26, two times; 27-30, three times. Start slowly; then steadily increase speed. Avoid all temptations to slow down.

IBM Selectric has a

printing head instead of type bars and carriage.

Adler Electric

Facit Electric

1. How to release the carriage (or carrier) by hand so that you may reposition it; practice moving it back and forth. 14 25

2. How to know at what point the carriage (or carrier) is now set; move the carriage to 40, to 75, and so on, noting where the space scale, the print-point indicator, and so on, are located. 39 52 64

3. How to adjust the paper guide; set it to center your paper at 50 or 60 or some other point that is easy to find and remember. 78 91

4. How to set the margin stops; set them for a 60-space line. 105

5. How to adjust the spacing; set it for single spacing. 117

6. How to adjust the ribbon; set for the top, black, position. 131

STAGE TWO: THE NEW 141

Because the typewriter is electric, it has some parts you do not have on a manual. Locate and use these parts: 161 169

7. *The pressure regulator* adjusts the impact of the typebars on the paper; move it from lowest to highest, then back to midway. 193 205

8. *The carbon impression regulator* moves the cylinder back to provide room for thick carbon packs; adjust the regulator across its full range and then set it at its lowest (forward) position. 231 246 257

9. *The power switch* turns the motor on and off; turn it on. 277

10. *The space bar* may have two positions: a shallow one for normal spacing and a deep one for continuous spacing. Try both a heavy and a light stroke on your space bar—any difference? 296 310 320

11. *The carriage or carrier return* is an oversize key at the right side of the keyboard (if there is one on the left side, too, ignore it). It is controlled by the little finger of the right hand. This key, too, may have two positions: a shallow one for a single return, a deep one for repeated returns. Test yours. 347 362 376 390 396

12. Most electrics have some "repeat keys" that continue to repeat their function so long as you hold them depressed. Check your machine for a repeat space bar, a repeat carriage or carrier return, a repeat underscore, and a repeat backspace key. 411 425 439 447

13. Confirm whether your machine has relocated its apostrophe, quotation, underscore, cent, per, and asterisk keys. 460 471

STAGE THREE: BUILD CONTROL 482

The thing to avoid in becoming used to your electric machine is any effort to press for speed in the first hour of using it. Instead, type each of the following drill lines three or more times. 502 517 527

14. STROKING. Use short *tap* strokes, just miniatures of the firm strokes you use on a manual. Keep hands in home position, but *above*, not *on*, the home keys. Say "and" to yourself before each key stroke. 542 556 570

29-C. Improve skill on patterned sentence drills

31 I doubt that a train could gain one hour in four.
32 The staff quit after your craft was safe in port.
   1 | 2 | 3 | 4 | 5 | 6 | 7 | 8 | 9 | 10
33 Mr. Abbott has written that he is getting better.
34 The yellow bottle was crammed in a supply closet.

29-D. Use double spacing, a 50-space line, and a tab-5 indention. Make a complete copy of this material, trying to finish it within 4 or fewer minutes and with 4 or fewer errors. Proofread your copy and then repeat for either:

ACCURACY: Type straight through the copy twice.

SPEED: Type two copies of each paragraph.

SI 1.00—very easy

29-D. Improve skill on special paragraph copy

WORDS

35 The need for food, which the sea gives up to those who   12
have both the stout heart and the sheer strength it takes to   24
fight for it, has led to new thought of what is to be found   36
in the dark deeps.   40

36 Far down in the silt in the beds of the sea, there are big   53
fields of ore; and lakes of oil are trapped in the thick folds of 66
rock that crust the world and serve as the strong shell of our 79
globe.   80

37 And in the sea, too, are the things that the streams of the 93
earth have squeezed from the soil, gouged from their banks,   106
and dragged on for miles through hill and vale to sink at   117
last in the sea.   120
   1 | 2 | 3 | 4 | 5 | 6 | 7 | 8 | 9 | 10 | 11 | 12

29-E. Improve skill on preview words

38 streams indeed on great in start up reefs no seas
39 naught island field their then map own men got to

29-F. To measure your skill achievement, type a copy, using a 50-space line and double spacing, and alertly listening for the bell.

GOAL: To complete these two alphabetic paragraphs in 5 minutes or less, with 4 or fewer errors. All Lines should end evenly.

SI 1.24—easy copy

29-F. Measure your skill in sustained writing

WORDS

40 Men have long traveled the seas without much knowledge   12
of them. They made a few charts of the coastal bays and is-   24
lands, but they knew naught of currents and depths. Indeed,   36
one of the first to explore this field of science was our own   48
amazing Benjamin Franklin, who asked sailors a great many   60
questions and then put their answers on a map, to fashion the   72
first crude chart of the Gulf Stream.   80

41 In the years that followed this start, other inquirers have 93
mapped the sea streams. But ocean science as men now know   105
it got its start when the submarine came on the scene. Since   117
then, mapping currents and reefs and depths has led the   128
experts through a maze of research that is judged just as   140
urgent as what other men are doing up in the sky.   150
   1 | 2 | 3 | 4 | 5 | 6 | 7 | 8 | 9 | 10 | 11 | 12

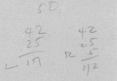

LINE: 60
SPACING: SINGLE
DRILLS: THREE TIMES
GOAL: LEARN ABOUT
 ELECTRICS
STRESS: CONTINUITY

196-A. Each line three
times or a 1-minute
timed writing on it.
Repeat in Lesson 197.

196-A. Tune up on these easy review lines

1 A neighbor may wish to make a visit to the chapels with us.
2 Jack quietly moved up front and seized the big cask of wax.
3 The different log lengths were 10", 28", 39", 47", and 56".
   1 | 2 | 3 | 4 | 5 | 6 | 7 | 8 | 9 | 10 | 11 | 12

196-B. Adjust margins
for 6½-inch line; set
for tab-5 indention.
Allow 1-inch top margin
and plan for half-inch
to 1 inch bottom margin.

Read the copy and note
where you will need to
half-space. This is to
be arranged in space-
saver style, as you used
on pages 299 and 300.

If possible, start by
taking a 5-minute timing
on this page, then con-
tinue the manuscript.

SI, this page 1.62—difficult

196-B. Apply skill to sustained production

Training Bulletin 20: ELECTRIC TYPING   23

GENERAL PURPOSE   32

   The purpose of this bulletin is to provide help and guidance for   51
manual typists who convert to the use of electric typewriters. As in 65
the rest of the business community, about half our machines are al-   78
ready electric; we look forward to a complete transfer away from the 92
manual machine within the next six to ten years.   102

GENERAL ORIENTATION   112

   There are many kinds of electric typewriters. Manufactured in the 131
United States are the IBM, the Remington, the Royal, the Smith-   144
Corona, and the Underwood. Brought in from Europe are the Adler,   157
the Facit, and the Olympia.   163

   Two manufacturers produce machines with proportional spacing   176
(that is, the machines allow more space for wide letters and less space 191
for narrow letters); these machines are the IBM "Executive" model   204
and the Underwood "Raphael" model.   211

   One manufacturer also produces a machine, the IBM "Selectric"   224
model, with no typebars and no carriage. It has a "printing head" the 239
size and shape of a golf ball that whirls and tilts to strike the paper. 253
The printing head is mounted in a carrier that spaces across the paper. 268
Except that one returns the carrier instead of a carriage, the machine 282
is operated like most other electrics.   290

   The Smith-Corona electric is available in three sizes: the full-size 305
"400" model, a portable, and a mid-size "250" model.   316

   When you receive your machine, orient yourself to it in three   329
stages: find the known; find the new; then build control.   341

STAGE ONE: THE KNOWN   351

   All machines must have certain basic controls. Start on your new 371
machine by learning the controls for these operations: 382
   1 | 2 | 3 | 4 | 5 | 6 | 7 | 8 | 9 | 10 | 11 | 12 | 13 | 14

Illustrations: standard
American electrics, pages
4-5; "Selectric" and the
European, pages 302-303.

Manuscript 68

LONG MANUSCRIPT IN
SPACE-SAVER FORM
Paper: plain, full
Carbons: one, for
 you to retain
Line: 6½ inches
Style: page 299-300
Spacing: single with
 half-space blanks

LINE: 50
TAB: 5 AND CENTER
SPACING: SINGLE
DRILLS: TWICE OR MORE
GOAL: BOOST SKILL
STRESS: TOUCH
CONTROL

30-A. Type each line twice (extra drill on line 3?). Repeat in Lesson 31, too.

30-B. To define your goal for Lesson 30, type and proofread a copy of this letter (reset margins for a 40-space line).

(a) Your goal is NUMBERS if you mistype any of the numbers in the paragraph.

(b) If you made no number errors and had 4 or fewer other errors, your goal in Lesson 30 is SPEED.

(c) If you made no number errors and had 5 or more other errors, your goal in Lesson 30 is ACCURACY.

SI 1.19—easy (if you know your numbers!)

30-A. Tune up on these review lines

1 asdfghjkl; asdfghjkl; asdfghjkl; asdfghjkl; asdfg
2 jag ask new zip ray six cob vim led for his quite
3 Order 10 red, 28 tan, 39 blue, 47 gray, 56 white.

30-B. Measure and improve your keyboard control

WORDS

4   Dear Mr. Keezer: 4

5

5   It is a pleasure to hear from you after 13
    so long a time. I guess it was back in 21
    October, 1963, that you last wrote. 28

29

6   Yes, the club still meets once a month; 37
    our next meeting will be on Friday, the 45
    24th. There will be about 17 or 18 who 53
    attend; it would be quite a happy event 61
    if you could join us. 66

67

7   I shall be driving to this next meeting 75
    and would be more than pleased to drive 83
    by your office and pick you up at, say, 91
    5:30 or 5:45. Shall I do so? 97

98

8   Cordially yours, 103

  1 | 2 | 3 | 4 | 5 | 6 | 7 | 8

30-C-D. To increase skill, type lines 9-20 twice each and repeat twice more whichever fits your goal—

NUMBERS: Lines 9-11.
ACCURACY: Lines 13-16.
SPEED: Lines 17-20.

NOTE: In lines 9-12, the words and numbers appear in pairs: each word and following number are typed with the same fingers and in the same sequence. Such drills, called "we-23 drills," are especially good for developing your number-typing fluency.

30-C. Improve skill on patterned number drills

9 we 23 you 697 two 529 rip 480 wore 2943 pipe 0803
10 it 85 yet 635 put 075 rut 475 pity 0856 wiry 2846
11 or 94 wet 235 our 974 eye 363 your 6974 type 5603
12 up 70 tie 583 pit 085 owe 923 tory 5946 pier 0834

30-D. Improve skill on patterned word drills

13 ef ef chief brief cleft grief chef deft left beef
14 ok ok choke broke stoke poker book took joke coke
15 ar ar arrow heart clear charm harm year mare tear
16 lu lu glued lurid blunt clues flue lurk blue plum

17 fi fi first field fined final firm fish fist five
18 je je jeans jelly jeers jewel jerk jest jeep jets
19 sh sh shall crash blush shave ship dash rush bush
20 oz oz dozed froze dozen ozone ooze doze doz. cozy

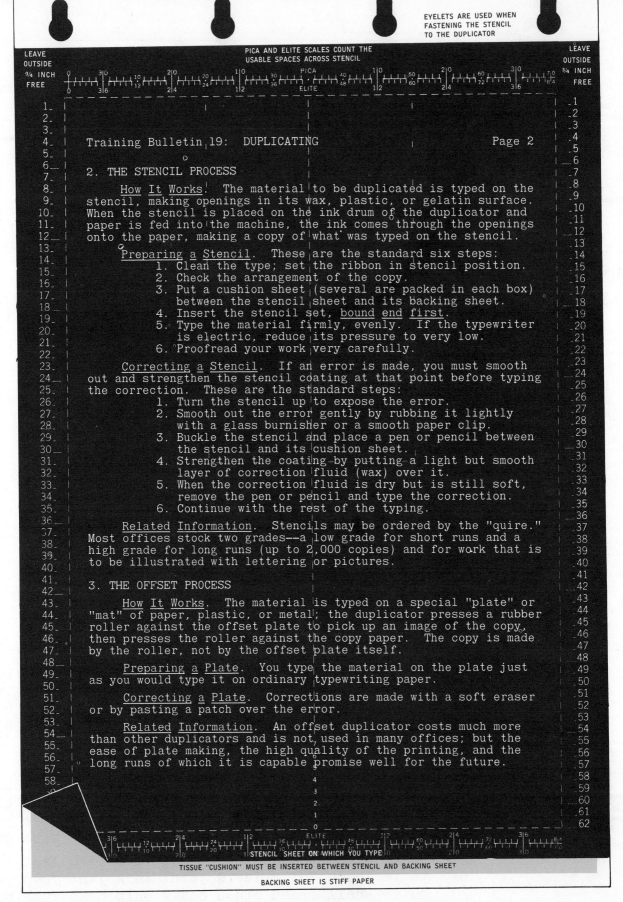

LEAVE
OUTSIDE
¾ INCH
FREE

PICA AND ELITE SCALES COUNT THE
USABLE SPACES ACROSS STENCIL

LEAVE
OUTSIDE
¾ INCH
FREE

Training Bulletin 19: DUPLICATING   Page 2

2. THE STENCIL PROCESS

How It Works. The material to be duplicated is typed on the
stencil, making openings in its wax, plastic, or gelatin surface.
When the stencil is placed on the ink drum of the duplicator and
paper is fed into the machine, the ink comes through the openings
onto the paper, making a copy of what was typed on the stencil.

Preparing a Stencil. These are the standard six steps:
    1. Clean the type; set the ribbon in stencil position.
    2. Check the arrangement of the copy.
    3. Put a cushion sheet (several are packed in each box)
       between the stencil sheet and its backing sheet.
    4. Insert the stencil set, bound end first.
    5. Type the material firmly, evenly. If the typewriter
       is electric, reduce its pressure to very low.
    6. Proofread your work very carefully.

Correcting a Stencil. If an error is made, you must smooth
out and strengthen the stencil coating at that point before typing
the correction. These are the standard steps:
    1. Turn the stencil up to expose the error.
    2. Smooth out the error gently by rubbing it lightly
       with a glass burnisher or a smooth paper clip.
    3. Buckle the stencil and place a pen or pencil between
       the stencil and its cushion sheet.
    4. Strengthen the coating by putting a light but smooth
       layer of correction fluid (wax) over it.
    5. When the correction fluid is dry but is still soft,
       remove the pen or pencil and type the correction.
    6. Continue with the rest of the typing.

Related Information. Stencils may be ordered by the "quire."
Most offices stock two grades--a low grade for short runs and a
high grade for long runs (up to 2,000 copies) and for work that is
to be illustrated with lettering or pictures.

3. THE OFFSET PROCESS

How It Works. The material is typed on a special "plate" or
"mat" of paper, plastic, or metal; the duplicator presses a rubber
roller against the offset plate to pick up an image of the copy,
then presses the roller against the copy paper. The copy is made
by the roller, not by the offset plate itself.

Preparing a Plate. You type the material on the plate just
as you would type it on ordinary typewriting paper.

Correcting a Plate. Corrections are made with a soft eraser
or by pasting a patch over the error.

Related Information. An offset duplicator costs much more
than other duplicators and is not used in many offices; but the
ease of plate making, the high quality of the printing, and the
long runs of which it is capable promise well for the future.

STENCIL SHEET ON WHICH YOU TYPE

TISSUE "CUSHION" MUST BE INSERTED BETWEEN STENCIL AND BACKING SHEET

BACKING SHEET IS STIFF PAPER

Manuscript 67: Space-Saver Arrangement (Pica) on a Duplicating Stencil

30-E. Improve skill on special paragraph copy

30-E. Type each paragraph once; repeat twice more whichever paragraph fits your improvement goal—

NUMBERS: Paragraph 21.

ACCURACY: Paragraph 22.

SPEED: Paragraph 23.

SI 1.00—very easy (if you have touch control and can respond instantly to the sound of the margin bell.)

21   We won the game by a score of 32 to 28. The strange thing   13
is that we hoped to win by 15 or 16 points, and at times we   25
led by 10, by 9, and by 7 points; but we won the cup by just   37
4 thin points.   (All the numerals)   40

1 | 2 | 3 | 4 | 5 | 6 | 7 | 8 | 9 | 10 | 11 | 12

22   When Mr. Bruce said we would have a quiz, we thought he   12
meant a brief one; but, sad to say, it turned out to have six   25
parts and took at least an hour to write. I got done just as   37
the bell rang.   (All the letters)   40

1 | 2 | 3 | 4 | 5 | 6 | 7 | 8 | 9 | 10 | 11 | 12

23   If the two men are to get paid for their day off next week,   13
they will have to ask one of us to sign on their time slips to   26
show on the slip that the day off is one for which they are to   38
be paid.   (Common words)   40

30-F. To confirm your goal for Lesson 30 and to set your goal for Lesson 31, retype the 30-B letter. Use the same guides (30-B) to define your goal for the practice in Lesson 31.

30-F. Make an interim progress check

31-A. Learn how to divide words correctly

31-A. Besides studying the six rules here (continued from 29-A, page 51), use the Learning Guide (pages 29-30 in the workbook) to reinforce your knowledge of the word-division rules.

The only intricate rule is rule 13. As a suggestion, make it your own private rule never to "lop off" a -ble ending; either finish the word at the risk of an overlong line or divide it at some other point.

9. Divide only between whole syllables. If uncertain about syllabic structure, consult a dictionary. Examples: *prod- uct*, not *pro- duct* and *knowl- edge*, not *know- ledge*.

10. Divide near the middle of the word if there is an option. Thus: *pictur- esque*, not *pic- turesque*.

11. Divide after, not within, any prefix. (A prefix is a combination of letters put before a root word to change meaning; thus, in *foreman*, *fore-* is the prefix and *-man* is the root. Common prefixes include *anti-, ante-, be-, con-, de-, ex-, fore-, in-, intro-*, etc.) You may write *intro- duce*, but not *in- troduce*.

12. Divide before, not within, a suffix. (A suffix is a combination of letters put after a root word to change meaning; thus, in *leading*, the root is *lead-* and the suffix is *-ing*. Common suffixes include *-able, -fully, -ible, -icle, -ing, -sion, -tion, -tive*, etc.) You may write *wonder- fully*, but not *wonderful- ly*.

13. Divide after a one-letter syllable in the middle of a word *unless the syllable is part of a suffix*. Thus: *sepa- rate*, not *sep- arate*. But: *vis- ible*, not *visi- ble*.

14. When two strongly-accented vowels appear together, divide between them (even though the second may be a one-letter syllable). Thus: *radi- ator*, not *radia- tor*.

31-B. Improve skill on patterned word drills

31-B-C. To increase skill, type lines 24-35 (see page 55, too) twice each. Then repeat twice more those lines that fit your goal—

ACCURACY: Lines 24-27.

SPEED: Lines 28-31.

NUMBERS: Lines 32-35.

24   be be below berth bench bells bent belt lobe tube
25   no no noble north known snort snow none know note
26   ag ag again stage pages brags slag flag agog rage
27   pu pu punch purge purse putty pure puts push punt

28   ic ic icing stick which quick rich nice pica tick
29   em em ember remit tempt lemon gems memo hems stem
30   os os those gloss hosts whose lost most post pose
31   wh wh while whale wheel white what when whim whip

                Training Bulletin 19:   DUPLICATING ↓2½   11
                                                                         17
GENERAL POLICY ↓1½   27

     As recommended in most books on office procedure, it is our   40
policy to duplicate copies by stencil when 200 or more are needed   69
or when the copies are to be sent outside our office and to use   89
the spirit process on all other occasions. This office does not   102
have an offset duplicator (but it is discussed in this bulletin). ↓2   117
                                                                         118
1. THE SPIRIT PROCESS ↓1½   127

     How It Works. A "master" is made on a sheet of coated paper   145
against which is placed a sheet of special carbon (it contains a   158
reproducing dye). The coated paper and carbon sheet are fastened   171
at the bottom and called a "master set." Typing on the master   184
set creates a carbon copy on the reverse side of the master.   196
     When the master is put on the duplicator, the machine dampens   210
the copy paper with a chemical fluid, which is the "spirit," then   223
presses the damp paper against the dye on the back of the master.   236
Some of the dye transfers to the paper, making a copy on it. ↓1½   254

          Preparing the Master. Six steps are involved. They are: 279
               1. Clean the typewriter type.   287
               2. Check the arrangement of the material.   297
               3. Remove the protective packing sheet from the set.   310
               4. Insert the master set, open end first.   326
               5. Type the material firmly, evenly. If the typewriter   340
                  is electric, reduce its pressure to very low.   352
               6. Proofread your typing with great care.   362

          Correcting a Master. Making a correction is just a matter of 387
removing the carbon of the error and replacing it with the carbon   400
of the correction, a process that can be executed in many ways.   413
          To correct a simple typing error: 421
               1. Roll the paper up and bend the master back to expose   434
                  the carbon of the error.   442
               2. Using a knife or dull razor, lightly scrape off the   455
                  carbon containing the error.   464
               3. Place a slip of unused carbon (cut from a top corner) 477
                  at the point where the correction is to be typed.   490
               4. Roll the paper back to typing position and type the   503
                  correction. It appears on the front as a strikeover. 517
               5. Remove the carbon slip; then continue typing.   529

          Related Information. Reproducing carbon is available in red, 554
green, blue, black, and purple colors. Of these, only the purple   567
serves for long runs (up to 200) of vivid copies, which explains   580
why most spirit copies one sees are purple. The other colors are   593
used for illustrating, ruling, and other special art effects.   606
     When writing, drawing, or tracing on a master, use a ball pen   619
with a very fine tip or a hard, sharp pencil.   627

Manuscript 66: Space-Saver Arrangement (Pica) on a Spirit Duplicating Master

31-C. See the directions on the preceding page.

31-C. Improve skill on patterned number sentences

32 The sum of 10 and 28 and 39 and 47 and 56 is 180.
33 I need 10 of Blue 28, 39 of White 47, and 56 Red.
34 Add up 10 and 28 and 39 and 47 and 56 to get 180.
35 Ship it May 10 to 2938 West 47 Street, Newark 56.

   1 | 2 | 3 | 4 | 5 | 6 | 7 | 8 | 9 | 10

31-D. For more practice in responding to the bell and making correct line-ending decisions without taking your eyes off the copy, type a double-spaced copy of each paragraph (use a 50-space line and a tab-5 indention). Then repeat twice more the paragraph that targets your goal—

SPEED: Paragraph 36.
ACCURACY: Paragraph 38.
NUMBERS: Paragraph 38.

SI 1.07—very easy

31-D. Improve skill on special paragraph copy
WORDS

36   The wheel is a great help to man, and he who thought of it   13
in the first place should have deep thanks from all of us. But   26
it now looks a bit as though the end of the wheel may well   37
be in sight.   (SI 1.00)   40

37   Come to take the place of a wheel is what is called an air   53
cushion. You get in your car. You switch on a fan, and it   65
pushes air under the car; the car lifts up, and now you are   77
off the ground.   (SI 1.09)   80

38   You turn on the next jet, and air shoves you forward. Off   93
you go, getting up to a speed of 70 miles an hour in a minute   105
or so and whizzing with equal ease over road or field or marsh   118
or stream.   (SI 1.14)   120

   1 | 2 | 3 | 4 | 5 | 6 | 7 | 8 | 9 | 10 | 11 | 12

31-E. Improve skill on preview words

31-E. Target on your goal.

ACCURACY: Lines 39-40, three times; 41-42, twice.

SPEED: Lines 39-40, two times; 41-42, three times.

39 adjustable hydrofoils stabilize waterbug exciting
40 faster waters jump bear look fast hull test 70 80
41 world giant shape work lake when rush down air go
42 one is use of and to on and on to our as it in an

31-F. Measure your skill in sustained writing
WORDS

31-F. To measure your skill achievement, type a copy, using a 50-space line and double spacing and alertly listening for the bell.

GOAL: To complete these two alphabetic paragraphs in 5 minutes or less, with 4 or fewer errors. Lines should end evenly, without need for dividing words.

SI 1.24—easy

43   A new kind of work boat has come to our lake and coastal   12
waters. It looks like any small boat when it glides along slowly   26
and lazily. But when it jumps up its speed in quiet water,   38
it rises on stilts to skim above the water, for all the world   50
like a giant waterbug, except that this one roars as it scoots on   63
and on at 70 to 80 miles an hour.   70

44   This new boat required two special points of design. One   83
is the use of adjustable fins, known as hydrofoils, to lift and to   96
stabilize the boat. The other is the shape of the hull, which is   109
made to trap air under it in an air cushion that lifts the boat   122
so that it can go faster and bear bigger loads while taking less   135
water. This is exciting, for the boat is seen as a kind of truck   148
that will rush heavy loads up and down even shallow rivers.   160

   1 | 2 | 3 | 4 | 5 | 6 | 7 | 8 | 9 | 10 | 11 | 12

Unit 32. Manuscripts

LINE: 60
TAB: 5
SPACING: SINGLE
DRILLS: THREE TIMES
GOAL: LEARN ABOUT
    DUPLICATING
STRESS: JUDGMENT

194-A. Each line three times or a 1-minute timed writing on it. Repeat in Lesson 195.

194-B. See whether you can produce this:

$\frac{1}{2}$ 1 $1\frac{1}{2}$

mmm mmm mmm
mmm mmm
mmm mmm mmm
mmm mmm
mmm mmm mmm
mmm
mmm mmm mmm

194-A. Tune up on these easy review lines

1 When they got to the lake, the men paid for the oak panels.
2 Joe quietly picked six razor blades from the old woven bag.
3 Did he move from 1028 39th Street or from 4756 39th Street?
   1 | 2 | 3 | 4 | 5 | 6 | 7 | 8 | 9 | 10 | 11 | 12

194-B. Learn to half-space vertically

To delete half a line of space: [1] press the variable spacer (button in left cylinder knob) as you [2] turn down the paper *half a line* (until the tops of the short letters disappear under the aligning scale); then [3] release the variable spacer and [4] return the carriage as usual.

194-C. Sustain skill on manuscript production copy

194-C. Confirm machine settings: 60-space line, tab-5; change to double spacing. Lines align.

Type two copies (one in Lesson 194, one in 195) or take two 5-minute writings, the first with 10-second rests after each minute, the second solidly, without rests.

SI 1.27—fairly easy

4 When a report must be duplicated so that copies may be given to   14
many persons or departments, the typist must study its length so he   27
can decide how many "space savers" to use.   36
    There are dozens of ways to save space. You might use single   50
spacing. You might use run-in headings instead of a style that calls   64
for headings on separate lines. You might leave only one blank line   77
where you would otherwise provide two, and only half a blank line, or 91
perhaps none at all, at points where you would usually leave one.   105
Paragraphs could be indented less than five spaces, and the margins   119
could be cut a half inch to get more, and longer, lines on the page.   132
    Why bother? Well, a great deal more than space itself is saved. The 147
report will take fewer stencils, less paper, and less time for running 161
and collating the copies; postage will be less for the mailed copies; 175
less file space will be used in the files of all concerned. A great deal is 191
saved! It will be saved, that is, if the typist saves a whole page and not 206
just a fraction of a page; cutting a report of five pages to four and a 220
half does not save much paper, does it?   228
   1 | 2 | 3 | 4 | 5 | 6 | 7 | 8 | 9 | 10 | 11 | 12 | 13 | 14

Manuscript 65

EXPERIMENTATION
Paper: 2, plain
Line: 60
Copies: 2
Copy 1: 1½ spacing
Copy 2: 2½ spacing
Title: Space Savers
By-Line: yours

194/195-D. Apply skill to manuscript production

After typing the two forms of Manuscript 65 to master the technique of half-spacing, type Manuscripts 66 and 67 in the space-saver form shown, *using a 6½-inch line.* If possible, type Manuscript 66 on a spirit master and Manuscript 67 on a stencil, using the techniques they describe.

LINE: 50
TAB: CENTER
SPACING: SINGLE
DRILLS: TWICE OR MORE
GOAL: START LETTER
   PRODUCTION
STRESS: ALERTNESS TO
   DETAILS

Unit 6. Correspondence

32-A. Tune up on these review lines

32-A. Type each line twice. Hold on lines 2 and 3 the pace you set on line 1. Repeat in Lesson 33.

1   The new man did not get pay for the day he had off.

2   g H i J k L m N o P q R s T u V w X y Z a B c D e F

3   10 28 39 47 56 we 23 or 94 tip 580 you 697 rue 473.

32-B. Learn how to "pivot"

32-B. Pivoting is an important technique you will use in positioning the date line of letters, as a glance at pages 57 and 58 will show you.

To pivot a line (make it *end* at a preselected point):

STEP 1. Set the carriage at the first space *after* that point.

STEP 2. Backspace once for each space the typed line will occupy.

STEP 3. Type the line; the final stroke will be in the desired space.

In timed writings, each stroke of pivoted copy counts as 3 strokes.

PRACTICE. Pivot these lines so that each ends at 70 on the scale.

Richard Montrose   Use your name;
Period 4   class period;
October 16, 196-   today's date.

32-C. Learn three symbol keys you will need today

32-C. NEW KEYS.

Parentheses are the shift of the 9 and 0 keys, controlled respectively by the L- and Sem-fingers.

Ampersand (&), meaning "and," is the shift of the 7 key, controlled by the J-finger. Type lines 4-9 two times each.

4   191 1(1 191 1(1 and ;0; ;); ;0; ;); (1) (10) (11)

5   The captain (John, that is) caught the long pass.

6   Bob is (1) tall, (2) dark, and (3) very handsome.

7   They need (a) six invoices and (b) six envelopes.

8   j7j j&j j7j j&j Jones & Sons buy from Brown & Co.

9   Write to Dodd & Co., Hess & Park, and Wold & Son.

32-D. Build skill for production power

32-D. Type the letter once, trying to finish it within 3 minutes, with 4 or fewer errors; or take a 3-minute writing on it to see whether you can hold on this production copy the best pace you developed in Unit 5.

The letter is shown in elite type (12 spaces to an inch), so you may contrast it with the pica type (10 spaces to an inch) in the drill lines above it.

SI 1.31—fairly easy

10   Dear Mr. Jones: 3

   4

It was a real pleasure to receive your order this   14

morning, for it has been too long (six months, at   24

least) since we have had one from Jones & Frazer.   34

   35

The goods that you requested are in stock and are   45

scheduled to be delivered to you (we have our own   55

truck now) in the morning or at noon, October 23.   65

   66

Thanks again, Mr. Jones, for your order. We hope   76

that it will mark the renewal of frequent service   86

to our old friends and customers, Jones & Frazer.   96

   97

       Yours truly,   100

1 | 2 | 3 | 4 | 5 | 6 | 7 | 8 | 9 | 10

IMPORTANT EMPLOYMENT ANNIVERSARIES			
Week of February 16			
Employee	Department	Date	Year
Chicago Branch			
Mr. Ulysses Hunter	Warehouse	February 16	10th
Mr. Norton McCall	Mail Sales	February 20	15th
Miss Georgia Tyrone	Accounting	February 18	10th
Miss Helen T. Ki	Advertising	February 19	10th
New York Branch			
Mr. Stephen Kloss	Jewelry	February 17	10th
Miss Margaret Carte	Personnel	February 20	10th

Horizontal rules are used to subdivide a ruled table.

Table 62

ABSTRACTED TABLE

Paper: plain, full
Carbons: file and 3
Special: clip table draft
　　　to typewritten table

Mr. Hildreth says, "Each week our computer tells us which employees will be observing their tenth and fifteenth anniversaries the following week. Here is the report for the week of the fourteenth."

```
ANNIVS 10 & 15 WEEK 14TH 20TH INCL

ARTMAN JOAN - CHI - PERSNL - 14TH - 15
DODDS ALICE - SF - ACCTG - 17TH - 10
EASTMAN HAROLD - NY - WAREHS - 15TH - 10
FRENCH BENJ F - CHI - BLDG - 16TH - 10
JORDAN WM - NY - EXEC - 18TH - 15
JUSTIN FAITH - CHI - DRUGS - 19TH - 10
MANN BITHA W - NY - JEWELRY - 16TH - 15
MASSEY EDNA L - SF - RETAIL - 16TH - 10
STRUTH O D - NY - ADVER - 20TH - 10
TOLBER RICHARD - SF - WAREHS - 19TH - 15
```

Computer data is usually highly abbreviated.

"You notice," he continues, "that it includes the employee's name, the branch and department where he works, the date of the anniversary, and whether the anniversary is the tenth or fifteenth. Please make three copies of the data, typed in proper, *un-abbreviated* form, *and subdivided by branches*, for us to send to our branch managers."

Letter 102

DICTATED MEMO

Paper: plain, full
Carbons: file and 3
Enclosure: Table 62

"Now please prepare the following memo for our Director of Personnel, Mr. Dixon, to send to *Branch Managers.* Use my initials in the reference line."

Subject...employment anniversaries...week of june 14...we are pleased to send you on the enclosed page the usual data about employee anniversaries for next week...the list is shorter this year...i believe...than it was a year ago and a great deal shorter than the last two or three lists we sent to you...you will wish to note that personnel bulletin no. 17-J concerning proper observance of anniversaries becomes effective with this group of celebrants... russell p dixon.

Table 63

Letter 103

MEMO CONTAINING AN
ABSTRACTED TABLE

Paper: plain, full
Carbons: file only

"Our next task," says Mr. Hildreth, "is to send this same information to the editor of the *News Bulletin*, our employees' paper. So take a memo, please:"

i am pleased to provide you with the data about the employees whose tenth and fifteenth anniversaries will be observed next week...

Insert the table, please, but arrange it with the Fifteenth Year people first, followed by the Tenth Year people.

there are two newsworthy aspects in this release above and beyond the usual credit and honor to the employees named...first...the fifteen-year people are the first to benefit by the new policy of awarding an extra week's vacation to these employees...and secondly...bill jordan ...i mean william jordan...assistant manager of the new york office...whose fifteenth anniversary is to be observed...was a war hero who received the congressional medal of honor in world war ii...the human-interest side of that honor might enable you to build quite a story in connection with his fifteen years with the company.

"Is this memorandum from you or from Mr. Dixon?" you ask. "From me," he replies, "in my role of Personnel Statistician."

32-E. Learn to identify the basic parts of a business letter

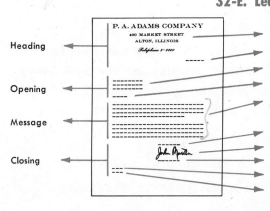

Heading

Opening

Message

Closing

Letterhead . . . printed name and address of the company.
Date line . . . month, day, and year the letter is written.
Inside address . . . address of the party to whom you are writing.
Salutation . . . opening greeting, such as "Dear Miss Smith."
Body . . . text of the letter, usually single spaced, with 1 blank line between the paragraphs.
Complimentary closing . . . closing farewell, such as "Yours truly."
Signature . . . handwritten signature of the writer.
Writer's identification . . . his typed name, or title, or both.
Reference symbols . . . initials of dictator and/or typist.
Enclosure reminder . . . used if something accompanies letter.

32-F. Learn the steps in producing a business letter

STEP 1. Insert paper. Estimate number of words in *body* of letter and set appropriate margins:

WORDS	LENGTH OF WRITING LINE
Under 100	4 inches (40 pica, 50 elite)
100 - 200	5 inches (50 pica, 60 elite)
Above 200	6 inches (60 pica, 70 elite)

STEP 2. Type *today's date* on line 15. Estimate position, or pivot, so date will end at margin.

STEP 3. Drop down 5 lines and type the inside address; continue through the letter, leaving 1 blank line before the salutation, each paragraph, and the complimentary closing. After typing the compli-

mentary closing, *pause to judge the placement*. If the letter appears to be well placed (bottom margin will be a little wider than the side margins), finish it: drop 4 lines and type the signer's identification; then drop 2 more lines and type the reference initials. BUT:

STEP 4A. If the letter is *high*, spread the closing lines: allow extra space for the signature (up to 6 blank lines) and before typing the initials (up to 4 blank lines). OR:

STEP 4B. If the letter is *low*, condense the closing lines: allow less signature space (as few as 2 blank lines) and, if necessary, raise the initials (may be level with the identification line).

32/33-G. Practice the production of business letters

GOAL: To finish each letter, pages 58-59, within 4 errors and 5 minutes from the time the paper is at the date line and the carriage is at the margin, ready for you to backspace-pivot the date. Use workbook letterheads or plain paper on which you crease a

line 1½ inches from the top to represent a letterhead's depth. Note whether each letter is shown in the type size you have on your machine; if the size is different, you must set margins correctly and listen carefully for the warning bell.

LINE: 60
TAB: 5
SPACING: SINGLE
DRILLS: THREE TIMES
GOAL: HANDLE TABLES
  LIKE A SECRETARY
STRESS: SUSTAINED
  PRODUCTION

192-A. Type lines 2-3 in cadence with someone who sets a good but steady pace on line 1. Repeat in Lesson 193.

192-A. Tune up on these review lines

1 Why did the man say the box was for him and was not for me?
2 Five or six big jet planes zoomed quickly by the new tower.
3 He gave us 10% plus 28% for 39%. He gave them 47% for 56%.
   1 | 2 | 3 | 4 | 5 | 6 | 7 | 8 | 9 | 10 | 11 | 12

192-B. Adjust machine for double spacing; confirm 60-space line (lines are aligned) and the tab-5.

Read each paragraph very closely, looking for any words that you remember have been troublesome; practice these words by typing a line of each. Then type each paragraph until you have produced a copy with 1 or 0 errors.

SI 1.32—fluently easy

192-B. Regain full stride on easy alphabetic paragraphs

4 There is an old, old saying to the general effect that   12
there is more than one way to skin a cat. It is difficult,   24
indeed, to imagine any kind of work where the adage applies   36
more truly than in typewriting. Think, for example, of the   48
many ways to set up a letter. Think of tables; you can fix   60
them up with rules or without rules. Think of reports; you   72
can type them with wide margins or thin ones, equal ones or   84
odd sizes. Just think of all the options that you can use!   96
   1 | 2 | 3 | 4 | 5 | 6 | 7 | 8 | 9 | 10 | 11 | 12

5 Now, some typists lament the options. They wish there   108
were just one way to do each different thing, not realizing   120
that each option was invented to solve some unique problem;   132
thus, knowing the options gives you a kit of ways to settle   144
most problems. For example, suppose you have a letter with   156
a table in it; and suppose further that it is a very wicked   168
table—too wide to stay within the letter margins, perhaps;   180
or so long it spoils the letter placement. What do you do?   192
   1 | 2 | 3 | 4 | 5 | 6 | 7 | 8 | 9 | 10 | 11 | 12

Alternate plan: Take two 5-minute writings, the first with a rest after each minute, the second with no rest whatsoever.

6 The obvious thing to do, of course, is to lift out the   204
table and type it on a separate sheet as an enclosure; then   216
you say "on the enclosed table" or something like that when   228
you come to the spot where the table should be. Or, if you   240
wish, you can squeeze the columns together, putting four or   252
two spaces between them instead of six. And you can always   264
inject a subtitle that might save space, too, or change the   276
phrasing of your column headings. Yes, options are useful!   288

NOTE: The solution here is the one you will use in Lessons 192 and 193.

192/193-C. Apply skill to secretarial production

BLOCKED LETTER STYLE

Letter 1

BLOCKED LETTER
Shown: in pica
Body: 90 words
Line: 4 inches
Tab: center
Date: today's,
  on line 15
Paper: letterhead
SI: 1.31—fairly
  easy

October 15, 19-- ↓5

12
13
14
15
16

Mr. Alexander F. Jones
Jones & Frazer Company
1200 West Parke Street
Bangor, Maine   04401

21
25
30
34
35

Space three
times after
state before
typing postal
ZIP number.

Dear Mr. Jones:

38
39

When we talked at the Kiwanis meeting last
Tuesday, I promised to send you a letter
in blocked form. Well, sir, here it is.

48
56
65
66

All lines begin at the left margin except
the date (it is typed at the right margin)
and the principal closing lines (they are
begun at the center). The typist usually
sets a tab stop at the center to use when
he positions the closing lines.

74
83
91
99
108
114
115

Standard
punctuation:
colon after
salutation,
comma after
closing line.

If there is anything else that you would
like me to explain, I should be pleased
to try to do so.

124
132
135
136

Cordially yours, ↓4 or 5

141
142
143
144

If the dictator's name is
typed under his signature,
type only your initials
(instead of URS). If his
name is not typed, type
his initials, a colon, and
your initials as shown here.

Training Director

HIS:URS

148
149
150

If you take a timed writing on
production copy and end with an
incomplete line, count 1 word
credit for each 5 strokes and
for each use of the tabulator
in that final incomplete line.

Business Letter in Blocked Style

UNIT 6   LESSON 32   58

Table 12

**WHERE OUR EMPLOYEES WENT FOR VACATIONS
AND WHAT THEY SPENT EACH DAY AWAY**

(Summer, 19—)

In a 2-line title make first line longer than second.

Place	Percent Employees	Daily Expense
Metropolitan city	38%	$14.00
Seaside resort	32%	19.00
Mountain resort	23%	11.50
Motor trip	20%	14.00
Lake resort	9%	12.50
Miscellaneous	18%*	11.75
AVERAGES	23%	$13.80

* That is, 18 percent of employees collectively had other kinds of vacations.

Display the column headings by centering each above its column. Align the headings at bottom.

Arrange sequence in some definite pattern. Here, items are by percentages. A miscellaneous item is always put last.

Block any summary word like "Totals" or "Averages."

Arrange as shown here any footnote with more than one line.

Tables in series are numbered, the numbers displayed as shown here.

To get 1 blank line above and below a ruled line, single space before typing the line and double space after typing it.

Repeat % sign after each percent number; the % sign is not typed just once, then discontinued (as a $ sign is). It is wise to use the % sign, even though the column heading says "percent," if other columns have numbers that are not percent figures.

Summary of Guides for Arranging a Ruled Table

25. Department D has 19 often, 10 sometimes, 4 never, to total 33. Department E has 13 often, 9 sometimes, 3 never, for a total of 25. Department F has 20 often, 4 sometimes, and 10 never, to total 34. The column totals are 98 often, 70 sometimes, 34 never, and 200 as the final total.

Table 60

DICTATED TABLE

Paper: plain, full
Carbons: file, draft
Special: clip the written table to the typed one

Table 2 is entitled, in two lines, *Do Our Supervisors Recommend That a Coffee Break Be Authorized?* Again, five columns, to be headed *Dept., Yes, Indifferent, No, Total.* Department A scores 2 - 1 - 1 - 4. Department B scores 4 - 1 - 0 - 5. Department C scores 4 - 0 - 0 - 4. Department D scores 3 - 0 - 0 - 3. Department E, 3 - 0 - 1 - 4. Department F scores 3 - 1 - 1 - 5. The bottom totals are 19 yes, 3 indifferent, 3 no, for a grand total of 25.

Table 61

DICTATED TABLE

Paper: plain, full
Carbons: file, draft
Special: clip the written table to the typed one

Table 3 is entitled, in two lines, *What 382 Large Firms Have Found Upon Introducing Coffee Breaks, Serviced by a Caterer.* There are four columns; head them *Question, Yes, Perhaps,* and *No.* The question *Has it been popular* scored 95% yes, 3% perhaps, 2% no. The question *Has it improved morale?* got 80% yes, 15% perhaps, 5% no. The question *Has it reduced tardiness?* got 72% yes, 18% perhaps, 10% no. The question *Has it saved time?* got 60% yes, 30% perhaps, 10% no. The question *Has it been convenient?* got 60% yes, 25% perhaps, 15% no. The question *Has it been inexpensive?* got 50% yes, 0% perhaps, 50% no. The question *Has it reduced absenteeism?* got 40% yes, 36% perhaps, 24% no. Question *Would you recommend it?* got 80% yes, 12% perhaps, 8% no. There are no total figures at the bottom.

Letter 2

BLOCKED LETTER
Shown: in elite
Body: 89 words
Line: 4 inches
Tab: center
Date: line 15
Paper: letterhead
SI: 1.34—fairly easy

October 16, 19—— ↓5   12
                        16

Mr. Paul J. Thorne   20
Thorne & Clark, Inc.   24
220 North Canal Street   29
Waco, Texas   76701   33
                                                34

Dear Mr. Thorne: 37
                                                38

Mr. Wilcox and I are glad to approve the layouts   48
and the artwork for the two ads. We believe you   58
have done a fine job.   62
                                                    63

We shall need to check the wording of the copy very   74
closely, of course. (Ever since that trouble last   84
year, we have been very wary about using the super-   94
lative degree.)   97
                                                       98

I should like to have a conference with you about   108
the ads next Monday. Will you plan to be here at   118
noon and have lunch with me? This would save time   129
for both of us.   132
                                                      133

Sincerely yours, ↓4 or 5   137
                            140

Benjamin I. Foster   145
Sales Manager   149
                            150

URS   151

SPECIAL NOTES:

1. If a signer's name and title are long, type the name first and align the title below it.

2. If a signer's name is typed below his signature, omit his initials in the reference position.

Letter 3

BLOCKED LETTER
Shown: unarranged
Body: 83 words
Line: ? inches
Tab: set at ?
Paper: letterhead
SI: 1.40—normal

Current date ↓? | Miss Lee Anne Smith | Apartment 14-C   23
| 56 North Flynne Street | Akron, Ohio   44316 | Dear Miss   36
Smith: 37

We were pleased to receive the letter in which you asked   48
whether we might have any vacancy for which you could apply.   61

In about two weeks, we shall have open a position for an ac-   73
countant who would do tax work and cost breakdowns. Would   85
you be able to do the work of this position?   94

If you would like us to consider you for this fine opening,   107
please call Miss Wells (my assistant); she will arrange for your   120
interview and a review of your credentials. | Very cordially   135
yours, ↓? | Frank L. Tressler | Director of Personnel | *Initials*   150

Letter 4

BLOCKED LETTER
Shown: unarranged
Body: 87 words
Paper: letterhead
SI: 1.37—normal

Current date ↓? | [Type the letter in 32-D, page 56, using the inside address and closing lines that appear on page 58. The total production word count is 145 words.]

Table 55
ORIGINAL TABLE

Paper: plain, full
Carbons: file, draft
Special: make new tally,
 type it as a table,
 clip tally to table

Mr. Hildreth says, "Here's the first of three reports to prepare for Mr. Dixon. This one reports the *monthly* employment record of *each branch*. I made a tally—" He shows you this tally:

NUMBER OF NEW EMPLOYEES (By Month and Branch) January 1 Through May 30				
Month	Chi	N.Y.	S.F.	Total
Jan	|||	||	||	7
Feb	|||	|||			7
Mar	HHT |||					10
Apr			||	||||	8
May	|||	||	||	8
Total	19 ⊗	11 ⊗	10	40

"—but it is incorrect; Chicago, I know, should be 18, not 19. Please do it over and type it."

"No memo?" you ask.

"No," he replies. "Center the table on a page."

Table 56
ORIGINAL TABLE

Paper: plain, full
Carbons: file, draft
Special: make tally, type it,
 clip tally to the table

"The next job is easier but requires your making another tally," says Mr. Hildreth. "Mr. Dixon wants the score on the respective numbers of men and women employed by each branch. You'll have four columns: *Branch, Men, Women,* and *Total*."

You ask, "Center it on the page?" Yes. The tally sheet you draft shapes up like this:

NUMBER OF NEW EMPLOYEES (By Branch and Sex) January 1 Through May 30			
Branch	Men	Women	Total
Chi			
NY			
SF			
Total			

Table 57
ORIGINAL TABLE

Paper: plain, full
Carbons: file, draft
Special: work on draft
 of Table 56; attach
 it to Table 57

"Next," says Mr. Hildreth, "type again that same table [Table 56], but convert it to percents. For example, the Chicago tally is 12 - 6. In percentages, that would be 66.7% and 33.3%. You won't need a totals *column*, of course, although you *will* need a totals line at the bottom."

Table 58
ORIGINAL TABLE

Paper: plain, full
Carbons: file, draft
Special: make the tally,
 type it, attach tally
 to the typed table

"Now, for the last table in this series," says Mr. Hildreth, "prepare for Mr. Dixon an analysis by *departments* and *branches*. You will have five columns: *Department, Chicago, New York, San Francisco,* and *Total*. You'll have to tally the scores."

You say, "Let's see: The title will be *Number of New Employees* with two subtitles, (*By Departments and Branches*) and *January 1 Through May 30*. Right?"

"Right."

Table 59
DICTATED TABLE

Paper: plain, full
Carbons: file, draft
Special: clip your written
 table to the one you type

As you finish Table 58, Mr. Hildreth says, "Now we are starting a new project, an investigation I have been making for Mr. Dixon. My report consists of three tables; you'll find them interesting."

He gives you the table shown at the top of the next page. "This is the *form* I wish you to use," he says. "Ruled. Double spaced. Columns a half inch [six spaces] apart. One of the three titles will go on a single line, but the other two will take two lines, as shown in this sample table."

You make a note to study the sample table *very* closely; you are *not* to type *it*. Mr. Hildreth begins to dictate the first table:

Table 1 is entitled *Do Our Employees Take a Coffee Break?* It has five columns, to be headed *Dept., Often, Sometimes, Never,* and *Total*. Department A has 12 often, 18 sometimes, 3 never, to total 33. Department B has 18 often, 21 sometimes, 11 never, to total 50. Department C has 16 often, 6 sometimes, 3 never, to total

LINE: 50
TAB: CENTER
SPACING: SINGLE
DRILLS: TWICE OR MORE
GOAL: LEARN ', ", AND !
STRESS: EVEN TYPE
  IMPRESSIONS.

34-A. Type each line twice. In line 2, keep capitals on the line. In line 3, speed up slowly! Repeat these lines in Lesson 35.

34-A. Tune up on these review lines

1. Why did the new man get no pay for his one day off?

2. j K l M n O p Q r S t U v W x Y Z A b C d E f G h I

3. we (23) up (70) to (59) or (94) it (85) your (6974)

34-B. Type each line twice.

Manual   Electric

MANUAL: Apostrophe is the shift of 8 key. Quotation mark is shift of 2 key. Omit lines 4E and 7E.

ELECTRIC: Apostrophe is the key beside Sem key, controlled by Sem-finger. Quotation mark is shift of the Apostrophe key. Omit drill lines 4M and 7M.

NOTE: Exclamation point in line 4 is typed this way:
(1) Period.
(2) Backspace.
(3) Apostrophe.

34-B. Practice two symbol keys you will need today

4M. k8k k'k k8k k'k It's John's job to get Dad's car.

4E. ;'; ''' ;'; ''' It's John's job to get Dad's car.

5. We can't find Johnny's cap. Help us look for it!

6. A dog's bark isn't as bad as his growl, I'm told.

7M. s2s s"s s2s s"s "Well," he said. "Hello, again."

7E. ;'; ;"; ;'; ;"; "Well," he said. "Hello, again."

8. Joe "hurried"; so did I. He "mewed": "Who, me?"

9. I called, "Help!" Did he "beg"? How he "cried"!

34-C. Reinforce your study of the rules by doing the Learning Guide exercises on workbook pages 45-46.

34-C. Learn about quotation mark sequences

Rules to remember about punctuation sequences at the end of a quotation:

1. A quotation mark is typed *after* a comma or period, but *before* a colon or a semicolon. *Always*.

2. A quotation mark is typed *after* a question mark or exclamation mark *if the quotation asks a question or makes an exclamation;* otherwise, the quotation mark is typed *before* the question mark or exclamation mark.

Find an example of each possible punctuation sequence in lines 7, 8, and 9 above.

34-D. Set margins for a 55-space line, so that you can copy line for line.

Type the letter once; try to finish it in 3 minutes, with 4 or fewer errors.

OR, take a 3-minute timing to see if you can type the letter at a record rate.

Hold a steady pace when you type the apostrophes, the quotation marks, and the parentheses. Can you?

SI 1.37—normal

34-D. Build skill on production power practice

10. Dear Mr. Wood: 3
                                                               4

I should like to authorize you to sublet the apartment   15
for the months of December and January. I shall leave   26
here on the last day of November, and I expect to move   37
back in on or about the first of February.   46
                                                               47
To protect all the "belongings," I request that a bond   58
be posted (but I'm sure you'll have no trouble on this   69
score, Mr. Wood).   72
                                                               73
Please feel free to bring people to see the apartment,   84
Mr. Wood, any time you have someone who wishes to look   95
at it; I don't need to be there, you know!   104

    1 | 2 | 3 | 4 | 5 | 6 | 7 | 8 | 9 | 10 | 11

LINE: 60, THEN 70
SPACING: SINGLE
DRILLS: THREE TIMES
GOAL: EDIT TABLES
  LIKE A SECRETARY
STRESS: PLANNING
  BEFORE TYPING

190-A. Type lines 2-3 in cadence with someone who sets a good pace on easy line 1, if you can. Repeat in Lesson 191.

190-A. Tune up on these review lines

1   Joe and Bob did not get the day off but got the pay for it.

2   Jane gave my excited boy quite a prize for his clever work.

3   He asked for 47% and 56% but instead got 10%, 28%, and 39%.

    1 | 2 | 3 | 4 | 5 | 6 | 7 | 8 | 9 | 10 | 11 | 12

190-B. Type to your need.

ACCURACY: Type lines 4-6 four times as a paragraph and then lines 7-9 two times as a paragraph.

SPEED: Type each line three consecutive times.

190-B. Improve skill by selective preview practice

4   parentheses horizontal designing feasible titles nouns data

5   expedients, mentioning subtitles majority reader "all" kept

6   indifferent frequently adjective vertical column equal trim

    1 | 2 | 3 | 4 | 5 | 6 | 7 | 8 | 9 | 10 | 11 | 12

7   came from used most both the one more but not has to an aid

8   date line trim down they are the size aid for are in or the

9   also used they must line for and your use the out of to any

190-C. Adjust machine for double spacing, 70-space line (lines will align), and tab-5 indention.

In Lesson 190, type the first paragraph three times with no more than one error in each or until you have a copy that is errorless. In Lesson 191, similarly do the second paragraph.

SI 1.38—normal

190-C. Build skill on alphabetic paragraphs

10 One more guide well worth mentioning as an aid for designing new   14
tables concerns headings. There are three kinds of them: titles and   28
subtitles and column headings. Every tabulation has to have a title,   42
of course; but not all tables justify both the others. Use the other   56
two as expedients to trim down the size of a table or make it clearer   70
for your reader. The subtitle is used most frequently as a date line   84
for a table. It is also used, with parentheses, to explain where the   98
data came from or what units of measure are used, like: "All figures   112
are hundreds of bushels" or "All figures are in millions of dollars."   126

    1 | 2 | 3 | 4 | 5 | 6 | 7 | 8 | 9 | 10 | 11 | 12 | 13 | 14

11 Column headings are, of course, the most useful expedients; they   140
are frequently the chief part of the table. They must be kept brief,   154
concise, and clear. A group of such headings should be, if possible,   168
phrased in similar terms—don't use nouns for some and adjectives for   182
others unless there is no other way out of the problem. If feasible,   196
keep equal headings to the same number of lines; but if some are long   210
and some are short, at least make sure that all end on the same line.   224
What about rules? The majority of firms like horizontal rules, which   238
make any table look better, but are indifferent about vertical lines.   252

Alternate plan: Take two 5-minute writings, the first with a rest after each minute, the second with no rest whatsoever.

MINIMUM GOAL: to complete the paragraphs in 5 or fewer minutes with 2 or fewer errors.

190/191. Apply skill to unarranged tables

34/35-G. Practice the production of business letters

See how many of the letters below and on page 62 you can produce in the time allotted for typing Lessons 34-35. Type the letters on *plain* paper.

GOAL: To finish each letter (a) with 4 or fewer errors and (b) within 5 minutes, counting from the time when the paper is inserted to line 13 (where the return address should be begun) and the carriage is at the margin, ready for you to backspace-pivot the longest line of the return address. Read Letter 5 before typing it.

Pivot the longest line

Pivot first line; when you return carriage for other two lines, draw it back only to this same starting point. (If using an electric, set a tab stop to use in repositioning carriage to this point.)

Letter 5

BLOCKED LETTER
Shown: in elite
Body: 89 words
Line: 4 inches
Tab: center
Paper: plain
Start: line 13, so date will fall on line 15
SI: 1.30—fairly easy

REMEMBER: Space three times after state before typing postal ZIP number.

Use no reference initials in letters that you type for yourself.

1108 Tacoma

```
                        3928 South Park Street          13
                        Troy, New York   12180          19
                        October 17, 19---  5            23
```
Port Orchard, Wa. 98366   24
25
July 12, 1968   26
27

```
Mr. Edward Whitman                                      31
Smith & Whitman, Inc.                                   35
1047 Fifth Avenue                                       39
New York, New York   10028                              43
                                                        44
Dear Mr. Whitman:                                       48
                                                        49
This letter shows how to use the "blocked style" in     59
one's personal business letters, typed on ordinary     70
plain paper.                                            72
                                                        73
You should type your address in two lines above the    84
date, with the number and street on the first line     94
and the city, state, and ZIP number on the second;    104
start these two lines and the date at the point       114
reached by pivoting for the longest line.             122
                                                        122
You must always be sure to type your name below the   133
space where you will sign the letter.                 140
                                                        141
                        Yours sincerely,   4 or 5     146

                                                        149

                        J. Henry Hale                 152
```
S. T. Kimball

Personal Business Letter in Blocked Style

Table 51

See page 291

NEW EMPLOYEES—ALL BRANCHES

January 1 Through May 30

Name	Branch	Dept.	Position	Date	
					16
					33
					47
					60
					75
Adams, Yvonne	San Fran	Music	Clerk	Jan 20	88
Allison, Allan	Chicago	Advertising	Layouts	Mar 10	102
Baker, Alexander	Chicago	Drugs	Buyer	Mar 12	115
Boer, Willard	New York	Drugs	Clerk	Apr 2	127
Brown, Jerome	Chicago	Boy's Wear	Buyer	Jan 18	141
Burton, Frederick	San Fran	Executive	Asst Mgr	Jan 2	156
Chinnock, Susan	New York	Executive	Secy	Apr 19	169
Counts, Edward	Chicago	Advertising	Photog	May 27	183
Doyle, Richard	New York	Off Eqt	Salesman	May 15	197
Drury, Caroline	Chicago	Jewelry	Clerk	Feb 8	210
Edwards, John	Chicago	Off Eqt	Salesman	Mar 10	224
Everett, Polly	New York	Shipping	Steno	Jan 18	237
Farmer, Paul S.	New York	Furniture	Buyer	Jan 25	251
Farmer, Ralph	New York	Furniture	Clerk	Feb 8	264
Esuark, Ruthetta	Chicago	Personnel	Director	Mar 18	278
Fein, Henrietta	Chicago	Boys' Wear	Asst Buyer	May 16	294
French, Mary	Chicago	Jewelry	Buyer	May 23	306
Gordon, Howard	New York	Advertising	Writer	Apr 19	320
Graham, Ruppert	Chicago	Drugs	Clerk	Mar 25	332
Hamilton, Wilma	San Fran	Boys' Wear	Buyer	Feb 1	346
Harper, Jerry	Chicago	Off Eqt	Asst Mgr	Mar 17	360
Harrison, Joe	Chicago	Building	Porter	Feb 15	373
Jones, Jeremiah	New York	Executive	~~Steno~~ Secy	Apr 12	387
Kenwood, Martin	Chicago	Shipping	Wrapper	Apr 19	400
Kliptok, Virginia	New York	Mail Sales	Supervisor	May 18	415
Llewelyn, Inez	San Fran	Mail Sales	Asst Mgr	Apr 25	430
Morrison, Joanne	New York	Building	Elev Op	Feb 8	444
Norton, Willard	San Fran	Shipping	Supervisor	Mar 19	459
Olivia, Sarah	San Fran	Personnel	Recep	May 15	472
Parker, Josephine	Chicago	Accounting	Clerk	Jan 2	486
Potter, Alice	San Fran	Drugs	Clerk	May 29	499
Quincy, Jason	San Fran	Mail Sales	Clerk	Apr 2	513
Rawlson, Robert	New York	Building	Porter	Feb 8	526
Reilly, Patrick	New York	Executive	Vice-Pres	Mar 15	541
Rowe, Howard	San Fran	Accounting	Asst Mgr	Apr 12	554
Sullivan, Anne	Chicago	Furniture	Asst Buyer	Feb 3	570
Stone, Freeman	Chicago	Accounting	Clerk	Jan 2	583
Rarranti, Angelo	Chicago	Personnel	Interviews	Mar 11	597
Tomlinson, Bertha	San Fran	Shipping	Steno	May 18	611
Wilhelms, Francis	Chicago	Music	Buyer	Mar 25	624

3928 South Park Street   13
Troy, New York   12180   19
Current date ▼ 5   23
                                27

Letter 6

BLOCKED LETTER
Shown: unarranged
Body: 86 words
Paper: plain
Line: 4 inches
Tab: center
SI: 1.36—normal

Mr. John Green, Editor | Journal of Home Living | 270 Madi-   38
son Avenue | New York, New York   10016 | Dear Mr.   47
Green: 49

The last time we met, you said, "Let me know whenever you   62
get a unique idea for a different kind of magazine article." 74

In about three weeks, I shall leave for a two-month trip   87
through France and England. Would you like an article on   98
places where Americans abroad can get a meal (or at least a 110
cup of coffee!) to their taste?   117

What day next week could we have lunch to talk over the   129
idea or a much better one that you might have? | Cordially   143
yours, ▼ 4 or 5 | J. Henry Hale   150

Letter 7

BLOCKED LETTER
Body: 91 words
Paper: plain
SI: 1.28—fairly
   easy

Foreign Department | First National Bank | ·1000 Eighth   37
Avenue | New York, New York   10019 | Gentlemen: 45

I have read that you have "a new plan" for issuing letters of 58
credit to persons who take a trip to a nation in which your 70
firm has a branch office.   76

I shall leave in about three weeks for a long trip through   89
France and England. I shall be gone nine weeks or more,   100
spending nearly all my time in Paris and in London.   111

If you have branches in these cities, I should be pleased to 124
learn all the details of your new plan. Might I hear from you 136
soon? | Yours very truly, ▼ 4 or 5 | J. Henry Hale   150

Letter 8

BLOCKED LETTER
Body: 83 words
Paper: plain
SI: 1.31—fairly
   easy

Customer Service Agent | Trans World Airlines | Kennedy Air- 37
port | Jamaica, New York   11430 | Dear Sir: 46

I wish to fly to Paris, then to London, then back to New   58
York. Do you have any tourist-rate flights for such a trip? 71

If you do, please let me have complete information about the 84
flight schedules, the fare, the luggage weight permitted, and 96
the steps I must take to get the passport that I shall need. 109

If you do not have "tourist flights" this season, please let 122
me know which airline does have them; I shall be most grateful 134
for your advice. | Yours very truly, ▼ ? | J. Henry Hale   150

Letter 9

BLOCKED LETTER
Body: 96 words
Paper: plain
SI: 1.37—normal

Mr. George Wood, Manager | Colfax & Mills Agency | 3900   36
South Park Street | Troy, New York   12180 | Dear Mr. Wood: 48

The body of this letter is given as 34-D, page 60. | Cordially 152
yours, ▼ ? | J. Henry Hale   162

You work for John Hildreth, senior statistician in Personnel. Most of his work is compiling data for company executives. Your work is to type the data (which may be in his writing, or be in rough draft, or be dictated to you) as tables within memos or as tables centered on full pages and accompanied by memos. You use only the ruled form for tables (review page 139). Always make a file carbon and one spare to use in drafting an additional problem.

Table 51

RULED TABLE

Paper: plain, full
Carbons: 4 or 5 to use
    in subsequent tasks

Mr. Hildreth gives you the rough draft shown on the next page. "Please type this," he says. "Make several carbons for us to use."

"Why so many copies, Mr. Hildreth?" you ask.

"Well," he replies, "we have to prepare a number of reports that consist of parts of this master table. It will be easier for us if we have copies we can use as work sheets—we can simply cross out what we *don't* use and then copy what is left."

You study the job, noting:

1. The page looks crowded. You decide to put just 4 spaces between the columns. Grouping the lines in 5-line groups will help, too.

2. The year was overlooked; you will add it.

3. Unpunctuated abbreviations are shown; this is satisfactory on the work sheet you are to prepare but would not be satisfactory for reports to be sent to anyone outside the Personnel Department.

Table 52

Letter 99

MEMO CONTAINING AN
ABSTRACTED TABLE

Paper: plain, full
Carbons: file, draft
Special: group names
    in 4-name groups
Special: clip the marked
    worksheet to your work

"Evangeline Prescott is president of the company Women's Club," says Mr. Hildreth. "She has asked for a list of the women who have joined the company since January 1. Please prepare a table of the *names*, *branches*, and *departments* for her."

You realize this will be easy. You will use a copy of Table 51, crossing off the last two columns and all the lines about the men. Then you will type what is left as the table. There will be 16 names, which group handily in 4-name groups.

Mr. Hildreth continues, "Take a memo, please."

To evangeline prescott...billing department ...(president...women's club)...*from me*, john hildreth...personnel department...*dated today, of course*...*subject*...names of new women employees...last week...miss prescott...you asked for the names of the women who have joined the company since january 1...here are the names: *Insert the table here, then wind up:* please note that this table overlaps a similar one that we sent to you two months ago...have a good year!

Table 53

Letter 100

MEMO CONTAINING AN
ABSTRACTED TABLE

Paper: plain, full
Carbons: file, draft
Special: group names
Special: clip the marked
    worksheet to your work

"Let's make the same kind of report for the Men's Club," says Mr. Hildreth, "even though the request has not yet come in. The name of the president is George Montgomery, in accounting. The memo—"

someone in the men's club always asks for a list of the spring crop of new men employees along about this time...george...but this time i am beating you to it! here it is:

Table 54

Letter 101

MEMO CONTAINING AN
ABSTRACTED TABLE

Paper: plain, full
Carbons: file, draft
Special: group names
Special: clip the marked
    worksheet to your work

"Please make a copy of all parts of the master table concerning employees who joined our staff on *April 1 or later*," says Mr. Hildreth, "for us to send to Mr. Dixon, Director of Personnel, in this memo:"

we are pleased to provide you...mr dixon... the identification of the 16 employees who have joined the staff since april 1...you will wish to note that the disproportionately large number in san francisco is due to the expansion of the retail facilities there...*The table; since it is to someone within the same department, you may use the abbreviated form*...if there are other data you would like to have, we should be very much pleased to provide them.

LINE: 50
TAB: 5 AND CENTER
SPACING: SINGLE
DRILLS: TWICE OR MORE
GOAL: INCREASED
PRODUCTION POWER
STRESS: EVEN STROKES

36-A. Type lines 1-3 two or more times, as evenly as though typing to music. Repeat them in Lesson 37.

36-B. Type each line twice, as smoothly and evenly as a clock ticking. Pause and check your work after each repetition; if you made any error or if you recall faltering, repeat the line.

Manual typists omit 4E and 6-E; electric typists omit drill lines 4M and 6M.

36-C. Type each paragraph once. GOAL: To finish both paragraphs in 2 minutes, with 3 or fewer errors.

Repeat paragraph 8 twice if you made more than 3 errors; repeat paragraph 9 if you had fewer than 3.

SI 1.12/1.06—both easy

36-D. Take these steps in practicing this selection:

(1) Read the article and compare what it says with the letter on page 64.

(2) Scan the copy once more, selecting and typing from two to four times any word you wish in each line.

(3) Type a double-spaced copy, trying to finish it in 5 minutes or less, with 4 or fewer errors. OR, take a 5-minute timing on it and record your score.

SI 1.42—normal

36-A. Tune up on these review lines

1 The men may go to the city or the island with us.
2 a A ; : s S l L d D k K f F j J g G h H / ? , , .
3 "we" 23 "our" 974 "rut" 475 "pit" 085 "type" 5603

36-B. Reinforce control of the symbol keys

4M ki8' ki8' ki8' ki8' It's Richard's car, isn't it!
4E ;''; ;''; ;''; ;''; It's Richard's car, isn't it!
5   ju7& ju7& ju7& ju7& He works for Sears & Roebuck.
6M sw2" sw2" sw2" sw2" "So," he said, "Here we are!"
6E ;'"; ;'"; ;'"; ;'"; "So," he said, "Here we are!"
7   lo9(lo9(;p0) ;p0) He is (a) short and (b) slim.

36-C. Improve skill on special paragraph copy

8 The next time I have a note to type, I shall   10
make sure I use paper that is just the right size   20
and quality; I know that both of these do matter.   30
9 Bob has such fine work habits that he may be   40
one of the first to get his work done. If so, it   50
is then his duty to ask for some more work to do.   60

1 | 2 | 3 | 4 | 5 | 6 | 7 | 8 | 9 | 10

36-D. Measure your skill in sustained writing

10 Now and then the typist must write a message   10
for which a standard business letter may not seem   20
adequate. One would not wish a "commercial" look   30
for a letter of condolence, for example, which an   40
employer might send to a customer or for a letter   50
of thanks or regret that a typist might write for   60
himself. The form that is used on such occasions   70
is the one that is known as "formal" arrangement.   80
To make a letter "formal," the typist writes   90
the inside address at the end of the letter. The   100
writer's name may or may not be typed beneath his   110
signature; the absence of a typed name means that   120
the writer is claiming to be a personal friend of   130
the addressee, and so the name is typed when that   140
claim should not be made or would be presumptive.   150
The models that follow contrast the "formal"   160
design with two of the standard business designs.   170

1 | 2 | 3 | 4 | 5 | 6 | 7 | 8 | 9 | 10

Unit 31. Tabulation

LINE: 60, THEN 70
SPACING: SINGLE
DRILLS: THREE TIMES
GOAL: EDIT TABLES
  LIKE A SECRETARY
STRESS: TYPE FIGURES
  WHOLLY BY TOUCH

188-A. Tune up on these review lines

188-A. See whether you can type difficult lines 2 and 3 in cadence with someone who sets a fast pace on easy line 1! Repeat in Lesson 189.

1 The two men got the big saw and cut the old oak log for us.

2 Professor Charlton was quite vexed by Jimmy's buzzing talk.

3 My answers are: 10%, 28%, 39%, 47%, and 56%; what are his?
    1 | 2 | 3 | 4 | 5 | 6 | 7 | 8 | 9 | 10 | 11 | 12

188-B. Improve skill by selective preview practice

188-B. Type to your need.

ACCURACY: Type lines 4-6 four times as a paragraph and lines 7-9 two times as a solid paragraph.

SPEED: Type each line three consecutive times.

4 surrounding considered experience mystery series often felt

5 information tabulation adjusting, exactly that's table size

6 interesting emphasize, unarranged version guides typed down
    1 | 2 | 3 | 4 | 5 | 6 | 7 | 8 | 9 | 10 | 11 | 12

7 long time this kind know why has been for the out of is one

8 read over take time when you the most you can air of do not

9 felt that look like that you not hard try the one of is not

188-C. Build skill on alphabetic paragraphs

188-C. Adjust machine for double spacing, 70-space line (lines will align), and tab-5 indention.

In Lesson 188, type the first paragraph three times with no more than one error in each or until you have one copy that is errorless. In Lesson 189, similarly do the second paragraph.

SI 1.33—easy-normal

10 For a long time there has been an air of mystery surrounding the   14
most interesting aspect of typing: designing a table from unarranged   28
information. I do not know why this should be considered hard. Yes,   42
this kind of work takes time; but I should like to emphasize the fact   56
that planning is not hard. It takes a little experience, that's all.   70
Nine times out of ten, the grouping of the data is quite obvious when   84
you read over the information; for the tenth instance, the files will   98
probably have a precise model that you can follow. I have often felt   112
that planning a table is not as hard as adjusting the machine for it.   126
    1 | 2 | 3 | 4 | 5 | 6 | 7 | 8 | 9 | 10 | 11 | 12 | 13 | 14

Alternate plan: Take two 5-minute writings, the first with a rest after each minute and then the second without a rest.

MINIMUM GOAL: To complete the paragraphs in 5 or fewer minutes with 2 or fewer errors.

11 There are several guides that could be kept in mind when you are   140
planning a table. The first guide: If the table is one of a series, then   155
it should be made to look and read exactly like the others; this applies   170
not only to tables in a report or thesis but equally to those that you   184
type in business, where most tabulations are just the newest version   198
of the tables you typed last month. The second guide: Where you can,   212
make a table longer than it is wide; try to make its general size in the   227
same shape as the sheet of paper. A third guide: If you can, get the   241
totals figures typed down at the bottoms of the columns.   252

188/189-D. Apply skill to statistical tabulation

...roduce a letter summary: ...l); on pages 48, 49, and 50, ...arrangements:

ASSIGNMENTS	ARRANGEMENTS	SPECIAL INSTRUCTIONS	WORDS
Letter 10	Blocked form, formal (personal) arrangement	Arrange as shown... ...address	152
Letter 11	Blocked form, personal business arrangement	...ation in arrangement shown on page 61.	147
Letter 12	Blocked form, standard business arrangement	Omit return address; type inside address above salutation; add initials.	142

Letter 10

BLOCKED LETTER
Shown: in elite
Body: 89 words
Tab: center
Line: 4 inches
SI: 1.34—fairly
 easy

3947 Frank Street   10
Ames, Iowa   50010   15
October 20, 19— ↓5   19

     23

Dear Doctor Brown: 27
     28

Thank you very, very much for giving me so much of   38
your time yesterday morning. I did follow up your   48
suggestion; and, I am happy to report, I got the   58
position for which you recommended me. I begin my   68
work this coming Friday, at three.   76
     77

Getting this weekend job means that I shall be able   87
to go on with my program and, at the same time, get   97
experience that should prove a help in my studies   107
and my career. I do not know how I can thank you   117
enough.   119
     120

Respectfully yours, ↓4 or 5   125
     126
     127
     128

George C. Mills ↓2 to 5   132

     136

Dr. Lee K. Brown   140
Institute of Commerce   144
1900 Eighth Street   148
Des Moines, Iowa   50308   152

The typed signature is usually omitted in letters between persons who know each other well. The inside address may be raised or lowered to give visual balance to the letter.

Formal Letter in Blocked Style

```
To:       Theodore Wilson, Sales
From:     Jay Trayne, Advertising
Date:     October 14, 19—
Subject:  Conference on Publicity for Portland Folder

          Thanks to your suggestion, Ted, we will hold a staff
meeting to discuss publicity possibilities for the Folder:
          1. We will meet next Monday, 9:30 to 11:00, in the
Fourth Floor conference room. My entire staff will be there.
          2. An agenda for the discussion is attached.
          We are delighted that you suggested having this con-
ference and even happier to know that you can attend it.
                                          J. T.
CJW
Enclosure:  Agenda
```

A Style of Interoffice Memo Typed on Plain Paper

Letter 97	Paper: plain, full
DICTATED MEMO	Line: 60 Tab: 10
	Carbons: file only
	SI: 1.42—normal

First, a memo to jay trayne *in* advertising   7
on specimen letter for the trade journals...   30
after our staff conference about means of   40
getting the folder mentioned in more news   49
columns...i drafted a sample letter...a   56
copy is attached...i should like your re-   64
actions: (1) would such a letter get the re-   75
sults for which we hope...namely...a   82
picture and a news report? (2) you are the   93
advertising man whom the magazine is   100
eager to please...accordingly...would it   108
be better if such a letter were signed by you   118
...not by me? (3) if we send review clippings   129
...an editor might think our folder is not   137
"news" any longer...therefore...would it   144
be better *not* to send the clippings? if you   155
will think the matter through and then see   164
me about it...maybe we can get the snow-   172
ball rolling!... *Now for the—*   183

Letter 98	Paper: plain, full
DICTATED LETTER	Carbons: file only
	Body: 149 + display
	SI: 1.39—easy-normal

—sample letter we mention in the memo. Just
draft it, please, on plain paper to journal of   10
office supplies...375 east sixth street...   18

newark...new jersey...07102...attention   26
new products editor...as i have received   38
each recent issue of the *journal of office sup-*   56
plies...i have looked closely for some men-   66
tion of the new portland folding machine   74
in your column about new products...to   82
this point...alas...no mention of it has   90
been made...when i was wondering why   97
it has not been mentioned...i realized that   106
we may not have sent you the material you   114
would need for the column...therefore...i   122
am sending you: (1) a large photograph of   132
the machine (2) a brochure that tells how it   142
works (3) copies of the photographs that   151
we used in the brochure (4) some clippings   162
from other reviews...if there is any other   171
aid we can provide...i should be happy to   179
send it...or...if you would like to see a   187
demonstration of the way the machine   195
works...i should be most happy to arrange   203
one for your office.   227
I think Jay will like that!

Forms 72-73	Forms: workbook 375
DICTATED TELEGRAMS	Carbons (plain): file
	Review: page 109

Telegram, please to the general manager *of*   22
our factory at 5720 touhy avenue *in* chicago   35
...how much advance notice would you   42
require to deliver 500 model 19 folders to   51
birmingham?   67

Day letter to that fellow thompson *up in*   24
syracuse [Letter 88]: our representative   46
...james flaherty...was injured in auto   54
accident en route syracuse and will be laid   62
up at least a month...may i send one mod-   70
el 19 portland folder for your trial use...i   79
will gamble that it will pay for itself so   88
quickly that you will decide to keep it.   110

Unit 7. Tabulation

LINE: 50
TAB: 5
SPACING: SINGLE
DRILLS: TWICE OR MORE
GOAL: LEARN TO
  ARRANGE TABLES
STRESS: ATTENTION TO
  TECHNICAL DETAILS

38-A. Type lines 1-3 two times. Repeat in Lesson 39.

38-A. Tune up on these review lines

1 They will wish this plan done over one more time.

2 We vexed Jack by quietly helping a dozen farmers.

3 "Is the room 28' 10" long or is it 39' 10" long?"

38-B. Type each line twice (manual typists omit 10E; electric typists omit 10M).

Number/pounds sign is the shift of the 3 key. Percent sign is the shift of the 5 key.

6 OR -

Underscore* is shift of the 6 key (manual) or of the hyphen key (electric).

38-B. Practice three symbol keys you will need soon

4 d3d d#d d3d d#d d3#d Order #3 needs 13# of nails.

5 Pack them in lots of 10#, 28#, 39#, 47#, and 56#.

6 Give orders #10, #28, #39, #47, and #56 to Frank.

7 f5f f%f f5f f%f f5%f We want 5% and 15% and 155%.

8 Try to get a 4.5% stock or some 5% bonds for her.

9 She wanted 15% interest, but I would pay only 5%.

10M j6j j_j j6j j_j He <u>did</u> say he would <u>not</u> ask Paul.

10E ;-; ;_; ;-; ;_; He <u>did</u> say he would <u>not</u> ask Paul.

11 I have <u>not</u> read that new book, <u>Paying for Supper</u>.*

12 Remember, <u>he is not to help us</u> solve the problem.*

38-C. Each line: Backspace to center the line; set the left margin at the point to which you backspace; then type the line three times.

In lines 15 and 16, allow 6 spaces between words; set tab stops to help align the words when line is repeated.

38-C. Review horizontal centering

13   South Philadelphia, Pennsylvania

14   Petrified Forest National Park

15   Oldsmobiles 6→ Cadillacs

16   Coffee 6→ Milk 6→ Tea

38-D. See whether you can type both paragraphs in 4 minutes or less, with 4 or fewer typing mistakes.

SI 1.30—fairly easy

38-D. Build sustained skill on paragraph copy

17 One of the more challenging kinds of work in   10
the office is that of typing data in column form.   20
Known as <u>tabulation</u>, this kind of typing requires   34*
more thought and judgment than do other tasks and   44
so is a welcome break from routine kinds of work.   54

When you stop to analyze how a table is pro-   65
duced, you will see that it is mostly a matter of   75
centering. You pick out the longest item in each   85
column, then back up from the middle of the paper   95
enough to center all those items and to leave six   105
blank spaces between them. You set tab stops, to   115
make it easy to line up the items in each column.   125

1 | 2 | 3 | 4 | 5 | 6 | 7 | 8 | 9 | 10

* Underscore solidly (line 11) unless each word is to be stressed separately (as in line 12). Type the words to be underscored, backspace (if 5 or fewer strokes) or draw the carriage back by hand, and then underscore.

Word count includes triple credit for all underscored material in timed writings.

LINE: 60
TAB: 3, 6
SPACING: SINGLE
DRILLS: THREE TIMES
GOAL: EDIT AND TYPE
LIKE A SECRETARY
STRESS: SMOOTH-AS-
MUSIC RHYTHM

186-A. Type lines 2-3 in cadence with someone who sets a good pace on the first line, if possible. Repeat in Lesson 185.

186-A. Tune up on these review lines

1 When your boys must win, then they find that they know how.
2 The very next question emphasized the growing lack of jobs.
3 They give discounts of $10\frac{1}{2}$, $28\frac{1}{4}$, $39\frac{1}{2}$, $47\frac{1}{4}$, and $56\frac{1}{2}$ percent.

1 | 2 | 3 | 4 | 5 | 6 | 7 | 8 | 9 | 10 | 11 | 12

186-B. Type the lines slowly to pinpoint any awkward parts; practice those parts. Then type each line three times.

186-B. Sustain rhythm on difficult preview words

4 conjunction expressions semicolon paragraph events left out
5 explanation independent connected separate clauses hire him
6 enumeration commodities adverbial contains between save $5.

186-C. Type a complete copy or take two timed writings for 5 minutes, the first with 10-second rests after the minutes and the second with no rests during the effort.

Be sure to leave a blank line before each rule.

SI 1.42—normal

186-C. Sustain full pace on technical copy

1. Use the semicolon to separate two independent clauses if   12
   there isn't any conjunction between them: 22
   a. There may be a big crowd; we can handle it all right.   34
   b. He tried hard for the order; his best was not enough.   47

2. Use the semicolon between two independent clauses if the   60
   clauses are connected by adverbial connectives: 71
   a. We need a new man; however, we must not hire him yet.   83
   b. They did not write us; therefore, it is not my fault.   96

3. Use the semicolon between two independent clauses if the   109
   first clause contains one or more commas: 118
   a. Yes, we lost it, Mr. Smith; but we really tried hard.   131
   b. We had one until March, 1964; and then it was stolen.   144

4. Use the semicolon before any term that introduces an ex-   156
   planation or enumeration; a comma comes after that term: 169
   a. We picked three men; namely, Frank, Lloyd, and Blake.   182
   b. It is a good bargain; that is, you can save $5 on it.   194

5. Use the semicolon to set off groups of items, like names   207
   and addresses, dates and events, commodities and prices,   220
   persons and offices, and so on, if they're in a sentence   232
   form; use the comma to separate the items within groups: 245
   a. The new officers are Ralph Haynes, president; William   257
      Brown, treasurer; and Clyde Hall, secretary.   268
   b. New members of the team include Mr. Frost, East Lynn;   280
      Mr. White, West Lynn; and Mr. Keene, Partch.   291

1 | 2 | 3 | 4 | 5 | 6 | 7 | 8 | 9 | 10 | 11 | 12

NOTE: To reinforce your control of these rules, which you must apply in lessons 186 and 187, do the Learning Guide on workbook pages 373-374.

186/187-D. Apply skill to communication production

38-E. Learn to identify the basic parts of a table

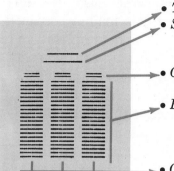

- *Title* . . . identifies table; is centered and typed in all capitals.
- *Subtitle* . . . gives more information about table; is centered a double space below title, with principal words capitalized; is not always used; may be arranged on more than one line (if more, the lines are single spaced).
- *Column heads* . . . tell what is in columns; are centered above columns; are preceded by 2 blank lines and followed by 1 blank line.
- *Body* . . . consists of the columns; is centered horizontally, usually with 6 spaces between columns; is commonly single spaced, but may be double spaced or arranged with lines in groups that facilitate horizontal reading of the table.
- *Column* . . . is a listing in a table, including the column head; is considered as wide as the longest item in the column (body *or* head); word columns align at left; number columns align at right.

38-F. Learn basic steps in arranging a simple table

PRELIMINARY STEP. CLEAR THE MACHINE:

Eliminate all tab stops that may already be set and move margin stops to ends of the carriage.

STEP 1. SELECT THE "KEY LINE":

It consists of the longest item in each column, plus 6 spaces for each between-column open area.

STEP 2. SET LEFT MARGIN STOP:

From the middle of the paper, backspace to center the key line; set left margin stop at the point to which you backspace. The backspace-centering is easiest if you backspace for the blank areas first— simply backspace 3 times (half of 6 spaces) for each blank area—and *then* backspace for the pairs of letters in all the longest items combined.

STEP 3. SET TAB STOPS:

Using the space bar, space across the paper to set a tab stop at the start of each new column.

STEP 4. COMPUTE TOP MARGIN AND INSERT PAPER:

Figure the top margin necessary to center the table vertically. Insert the paper to the appropriate starting line and center the carriage.

Now you are ready to type the table. You backspace-center the title and type it in all capitals, drop down 3 lines, and type the body of the table. To avoid confusion in spacing after heading lines, leave the machine set for single spacing until you are ready to type the body; *then* adjust for double spacing.

PRACTICE 1. Type this short table, centering it in double spacing on a half sheet. Can you complete it correctly in 5 or fewer minutes?

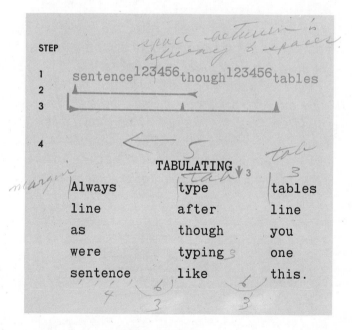

38/39-G. Practice the production of simple tables

GOAL: To finish each table on page 67 in 6 minutes (3 for making machine adjustments and 3 for typing the table) or less, with *no* arrangement errors and with not more than 3 typographical errors.

For each table, use a full sheet of plain paper. Type the title in all capitals and follow it with 2 blank lines. Double space the body. Tabulate from column to column wholly by *touch* control.

When you type any table as a timed writing, note (1) that you start with the carriage centered, ready to backspace-center the title; (2) that you triple space and start over if you finish the copy before time is called; and (3) that the word count credits you with 1 word for each use of the tabulator (as, between columns) and each extra carriage return (as, after a heading line).

Letter 94
DICTATED DOUBLE CARD

Card: workbook 369
Carbons (plain paper):
file and Mr. Brinks

Type another sample double card for me, please. Use the same two addresses that you typed on the first double card, but arrange the message to say: 70

dear dealer...you will be pleased to 78 know that the new model portland folding 97 machine...concerning which you have re- 104 ceived a number of announcements in the 112 past few weeks...has come off the assem- 120 bly line...has been introduced with great 128 [*please put "great" in all-caps*] success at the 131 new orleans show of business machines... 142 and is now ready [*please put "now ready" in* 145 *all-caps*] for prompt delivery...please re- 151 turn the attached card to let us know how 160 many to deliver to you...delivery will be 168 made within two weeks after we receive 176 your card...portland products company 186 [*in all-caps, clear to the right, please*]...

Then arrange the return message like the .. *other one, except that the message between the* .. *salutation and the address lines should be:* .. Send _____ portland folding machines to 199 us...on our usual credit terms...at the ad- 207 dress below *and use a colon after "address."* 255

Letter 95
DICTATED LETTER

Paper: plain, full
Carbons: you decide
Body: 190 + display
SI: 1.39—normal
Review: page 170

Please make this letter attractive. We may .. *eventually duplicate it, so please use plain* .. *paper and center our name and address at the* 52 *top. Address it:* to all office managers | who 61 worry about costs | in handling mailings | 69 dear friends... 73

this letter was printed on a duplicator 82 ...folded by a folding machine...placed 90 in its envelope by an inserting machine... 98

and then sealed and stamped by a mailing 106 machine...each of the machines did its 114 part in preparing this mailing...which is 122 of 7,500 pieces...in an hour or less...a real 131 accomplishment, that!...can you do as 138 well with your staff and equipment? 146

if your answer is "no, i cannot," 154 then it is time to take a look at 161 the line of portland machines. 168

the newest member of the portland line 176 of mailing machines is the portland folder 185 ...which will fold any paper that can be 193 run through a duplicating machine...it 201 can give you 1, 2, 3, or 4 folds on any sheet 210 of paper from 4 to 9 inches wide and from 218 4 to 14 inches long...you ought to see how 227 fast it works! 230

there's an idea: see how fast the 238 portland folder works! write us to 246 arrange a demonstration for you. 253

and when your friendly portland man is 262 there for the demonstration...ask him for 270 more details about the whole line of port- 278 land machines. *Use the company signature* 294 *and my name and title, please.* 306

Letter 96
DICTATED LETTER

Paper: workbook 371
Carbons: file only
Body: 93
SI: 1.43—normal

mr lester d brinks...c/o mr tauro kimoto 16 ...post office box 20...miyakojima, osaka 24 ...japan...this is just a quick report... 36 mr brinks...to let you know that the port- 45 land folder is off to a wonderful start... 54 taking top honors at the new orleans show 62 ...the campaign in the trade journals is a 71 great success...just as you predicted... 78 we are working now on the direct-mail 86 plans...copies of which are enclosed for 94 your interest...all of us hope you are en- 103 joying your visit with mr kimoto...to 111 whom i hope you will give my regards... 118 and his family...we are looking forward to 127 your return. *Oh, leave my title off this one.* 147

Table 1

3-COLUMN TABLE
Paper: full sheet
Spacing: double
Tab stops: 2

TRANSPORTATION TERMS ↓3

airline	collision	dunnage	12
automobile	commutation	embargo	13
backhaul	compartments	excursion	14
			21
baggage	consignee	f.o.b.	30
CENTER→			38
(See page 31) boxcar	consignor	freightage	45
carload	demurrage	gondola	53
carrier	destination	hangars	60
coastwise	drayage	helicopter	68
			76

automobile123456compartments123456freightage ←Key Line

Table 2

4-COLUMN TABLE

TRANSPORTATION TERMS ↓3

airline	carrier	consignor	excursion	12
				13
automobile	coastwise	demurrage	f.o.b.	14
backhaul	collision	destination	freightage	24
baggage	commutation	drayage	gondola	35
boxcar	compartments	dunnage	hangars	46
carload	consignee	embargo	helicopter	56
				67
				77

CENTER→

automobile123456compartments123456destination123456freightage ←Key

Table 3

3-COLUMN TABLE

AVAILABLE BOND ISSUES ↓

Cleveland, City of	5.0%	25 years	13
			14
			15
Grand Rapids, City of	4.5%	18 years	23
Hawaii, State of	4.8%	20 years	33
			41
Pittsburgh, City of	5.0%	25 years	52
Pittsburgh, School District of	4.8%	20 years	71
San Francisco, City of	4.7%	19 years	80

CENTER→

Pittsburgh, School District of123456 5.0%123456 25 years ←Key

Note in column 2 that the % sign is always repeated.

184/185-C. Apply skill to correspondence production

Letter 92
DICTATED LETTER

Paper: workbook 367
Carbons: file, 1 cc
Body: 156 + display
SI: 1.27—easy

mr. james l. marsh, young & gaul, inc., 12   16
west fifty-first street, new york, new york,   23
10020. *Oh, in this project, make a copy of*   25
everything for Mr. Brinks. Subject line: drafts   41
of mailing pieces.   51

here are the drafts...about which i   59
phoned you today...of the mailing pieces   67
for the next campaign: (1) the postal card   77
you developed and which...with apologies   87
to the author...i have revised...it would   96
do the job on our mailing to List B...(2) my   106
own design for another postal card...which   114

is based on yours...of course...i think that   124
it would be right for mailing to the new list   134
c...(3) a display letter...which is based on   144
the one we used when we brought out the   153
new duplicator...to mail with a circular to   163
the master list a...what I like about all   172
three pieces is that they can be prepared on   181
our own machines...a fact that will save us   190
both time and money...i think...however   198
...we should test each of the pieces before   206
we nail them down...do you agree...if so   214
...how soon do we start? *That's it.*   242

Letter 93
DOUBLE POSTAL CARD

Card: workbook 369
Carbons (plain paper):
  file and Mr. Brinks
Material: below

Dear *mr.* Stationer:

Two weeks ago, the great new Portland Folder *ing* Machine was ~~introduced~~ *unveiled* at the business machines show in New Orleans. It was an instant~~aneous~~ success--the ~~c~~ hit of the show! If you would like one or more *of these* machines on consignment, we could deliver an order to you within ~~two or~~ three weeks. Be the first in your community with this timesaver! Just fill in the card attached and return it to us. ACT NOW!

PORTLAND PRODUCTS COMPANY)⟶‖

wonderful   *center top and bottom*

THIS SIDE OF CARD IS FOR ADDRESS

Mr. Theodore Wilson
Sales Manager
Portland Products Company
3 Park Avenue
New York, New York   10016

FRONT SIDE: MESSAGE AND RETURN ADDRESS

THIS SIDE OF CARD IS FOR ADDRESS

\# ⟩ Manager, Stahl's Stationery
\# ⟩ 352 West Eighth Avenue   *15121*
     Homestead, Pennsylvania   ~~00000~~

Dear Mr. Wilson: *the*   *my*
YES! I want to be first in ~~this~~ community to
show--~~AND~~ SELL--your new folding machine!

Send _____ machines on consignment to:

Address: _____
   X _____
   X _____
   X _____
   X _____
Signed: _____ X
        ~~Authorized Signature~~

BACK SIDE: ORIGINAL ADDRESS AND REPLY

Double Postal Card

LINE: 50
TAB: 5
SPACING: SINGLE
DRILLS: TWICE OR MORE
GOAL: LEARN TO USE
COLUMN HEADINGS
STRESS: TOUCH
CONTROL

40-A. Type each line two times. Repeat in Lesson 41.

40-B. Type each line twice (manual typists omit lines 7E and 10E; electric typists omit lines 7M and 10M).

Dollar sign ($) is shift of 4 key (manual and electric).

 OR

MANUAL   ELECTRIC

Cent (¢) key is beside Sem on a manual machine or the shift of 6 on an electric.

Per (or "at") sign is shift of ¢ key (manual) or shift of 2 key (electric).

40-C. Two ways to reinforce the information given here:

(1) Use the Learning Guide on workbook pages 53-54.

(2) Study each column in the tables on pages 69-70.

Then center each column head above the longest item in its column.

40-D. After slow, arduous drills like those above, it is always wise for you to type something easy "to get back in stride." So:

(1) Preview by practicing any one word in each line.

(2) Type the paragraph twice. On the second copy, see if you can finish it in 3 or fewer minutes, with not more than 3 typing errors.

SI 1.21—easy

40-A. Tune up on these review lines

1 He may go by bus to visit the firm on the island.

2 Jack Mixbye had a powerful zest for quiet living.

3 Orders #10 and #28 made up over 39% of the total.

40-B. Practice three symbol keys you need soon

4 f4f f$f f4f f$f f4$f Pay $4 or $14 or $41 or $44.

5 Buy him the gift for $4 or $5, not for $9 or $10.

6 May thought that $14 was about $4 or $5 too much.

7M ;;; ;¢; ;;; ;¢j ;¢j Pay up to 16¢ or 16½¢ or 17¢.

7E j6j j¢j j6j j¢; j¢; Pay up to 16¢ or 16½¢ or 17¢.

8 We got 6 orders at 16¢, 6 at 16½¢, and 12 at 17¢.

9 Prices were 10¢, 28¢, 39¢, 47¢, and 56¢ per item.

10M ;¢; ;¢@ ;@; ;¢; ;@; We got 12 @ 16¢ and 12 @ 19¢.

10E s2s s2@ s@s s2s s@s We got 12 @ 16¢ and 12 @ 19¢.

11 Order 12 boxes @ 86¢ and another 12 boxes at 87¢.

12 Try to get 10 @ 28¢, 39 @ 47¢, and 56 @ 56¢ each.

40-C. Learn to center a heading above a column

To center a heading over its column, (*a*) note the difference between the length of the heading and the length of the longest item in its column; then (*b*) divide the difference by 2, ignoring fractions, to find how much to indent the shorter line from the start of the longer line. Example:

Juniors12345   12Juniors345
Alice Weller   Alice Weller

If the column includes a $ sign, it may be counted or ignored, whichever makes the centering easier. Example:

Amount   Amount
$100 $75

40-D. Renew typing fluency on this easy material

13   If you would like to cut down the errors you   10
make, check first on your posture. It is amazing   20
how much the way you sit alters the way you type.   30
Control is what you have when each finger goes up   40
and down the same path, exactly the same path, to   50
jab the key or keys assigned to it; if you change   60
posture, so that the angle of the path is not the   70
same, then the finger gets off the path and makes   80
an error. The majority of mistakes can be traced   90
to moments when you squirmed in your seat, or let 100
your wrists or shoulders sag, or did something to 110
change the pathway your fingers expected to take. 120

1 | 2 | 3 | 4 | 5 | 6 | 7 | 8 | 9 | 10

LINE: 60
TAB: 3
SPACING: SINGLE
DRILLS: THREE TIMES
GOAL: EDIT AND TYPE
   LIKE A SECRETARY
STRESS: CLEAR-CARBON
   STROKING

184-A. Type lines 2 and 3 in cadence with someone who sets a pace on the first line, if possible. Repeat in Lesson 185.

184-A. Tune up on these review lines

1   They will have much that they must save when they sell out.
2   Six or seven quickly jumped off with Frank for a big pizza.
3   The postage dues this week are .10, .28, .39, .47, and .56.

    1 | 2 | 3 | 4 | 5 | 6 | 7 | 8 | 9 | 10 | 11 | 12

184-B. Type a complete copy or take two timed writings for 5 minutes, the first with 10-second rests after the minutes and the second with no rests in the effort.

Be sure to leave a blank line before each rule.

SI 1.27—easy

184-B. Sustain your pace on technical copy

1. Use a comma before a conjunction in a compound sentence: 12
   The store will open today, and we expect a big crowd.   24
   We have worked here for a week, but we are resigning.   36

2. Use a comma before a conjunction that connects the final   49
   two parts of a series of words, phrases, or clauses: 61
   Should Doctor Smith go by plane, by train, or by car?   73
   You took first place, Joe got second, and I got last.   85

3. Use a comma to set off a dependent clause or long phrase   98
   that precedes the main clause of a sentence: 108
   If you have a good record, you will get a better job.   120
   In answer to your request, we are sending a new list.   132

4. Use a comma to set off a nonrestrictive clause (one that   145
   gives facts about the antecedent but that can be omitted   157
   without changing the meaning of the main clause):   169
   Mr. French, whom you met today, is a credit customer.   181
   Her fine gold watch, which was a gift, has been lost.   193

5. Use a comma to set off also a nonrestrictive participial   206
   phrase, which may or may not start the sentence: 217
   Being her close friend, Jan would not talk about her.   229
   Ralph quit that job, believing that it had no future.   241

6. Use a comma to set off a word, phrase, or clause that is   254
   parenthetic (not needed for the sense of the sentence):   266
   We may find we must, therefore, mail them their bill.   278
   Both of us, as you might guess, were pleased with it.   290

7. Use a comma to set off a word, phrase, or clause that is   303
   introductory to the main part of the sentence: 314
   Of course, there is still a chance to get that order.   326
   If you wish, we can get a man to take it over to you.   338

8. Use a comma to set off expressions that are in contrast: 351
   It was Smith, not Stern, who got us the big contract.   363

9. Use a comma to set off a word, phrase, or clause that is   376
   in apposition to other words, phrases, or clauses: 387
   Last June, the month of our annual sale, we did well.   399
   The new rule, that we get Saturdays off, now applies.   411

    1 | 2 | 3 | 4 | 5 | 6 | 7 | 8 | 9 | 10 | 11 | 12

NOTE: To reinforce your control of these rules, which you must apply in Lessons 184 and 185, do the Learning Guide on workbook pages 365-366.

40-E. Learn how to produce a table with column heads

A table with column heads is produced almost like simpler tables (as described on page 66):

STEP 1. Select the key line (but note: the longest item in a column may be the column head; if so, the column head is used in the key line).

STEP 2. Backspace-center to set left margin.

STEP 3. Space across to set column tab stops.

STEP 4. Compute top margin and insert paper.

But you must pause *between Steps 3 and 4* to note how many spaces to indent each column head from the start of its column (or, if the column head is wider than its column, to note how many spaces to indent the column from the start of the head). Writing lightly, pencil in each indention reminder, right on the problem copy, so you cannot possibly forget to make each indention. As you type the table and reach the point where each reminder applies, space in accordingly. Study this table:

Table 4

3-COLUMN TABLE
Paper: full sheet
Spacing: double
Tab stops: 2

		A	ACE BOX COMPANY	9

Branch	Manager	Years with the Company	
			10
			18
			37
Albuquerque	Irwin F. Massey	12	39
			50
Atlanta	Earl Lane Simpson	10	58
Dallas	Richard Miller, Jr.	15	66
Detroit	Gertrude Slattery	7	73
Los Angeles	Robert Wellerton	13	82
Miami	Harold H. O'Brian	24	89

Albuquerque 123456 Richard Miller, Jr. 123456 the Company

THIS TABLE ILLUSTRATES THE FOLLOWING TECHNICALITIES

A. TITLE: Centered, typed in all capitals.

B. COLUMN HEADS: Centered, underscored, capitalized, preceded by 2 blank lines, followed by 1 blank line.

C. ANNOTATIONS: Typist marks on problem copy his reminders of indentions for centering.

D. TWO-LINE COLUMN HEAD: Aligned with other headings at bottom, underscored completely (both lines) and solidly, preceded by 1 blank line if it "clears" the title (by 2 blank lines if it fell under title).

E. TAB SHIFT: When typist reaches start of a narrow column, he clears the heading tab stop and sets a stop at point appropriate to center the column.

F. LINESPACING: Typist uses single spacing through headings; shifts to double spacing for body.

G. NUMBERS: Always aligned at right side; typist spaces in to align shorter number.

40/41-G. Practice production of tables with column heads

GOAL: To produce Tables 4-7 in 6 minutes each (3 for setting margin and tab stops, 3 for typing the table) or less, with *no* arrangement errors and with not more than 3 typographical errors. Center each table on a full sheet, the body double spaced.

When you type any table as a timed writing, note that the word count credits you with 5 strokes (1 word) for each use of the tabulator, each clearing and each resetting of a tab stop, each extra carriage return, and each linespace adjustment. As in other kinds of copy, material that must be underscored or centered is given a triple count.

i am beginning to wonder whether there 96
might be someone in that office who, for 105
reasons of his own, is *deliberately* tampering 114
with the equipment. the last two times you 123
visited mm&s, remember, you noted that 130
the motor governors on both the duplicator 139
and the postal meter had been tampered 147
with and "cleaned." i simply cannot believe 156
that the same thing could go wrong with 164
each of the five pieces of equipment that 172
we have installed. 176

in any case, gene, if you cannot find the 186
answer when you see them again, please 193
yank out the installation and replace it; 202
itemize the whole cost of doing this and 210
send it to me as a charge for special serv- 219
ices, which i shall have credited to your 227
account. we would rather take a loss on 235
this department than jeopardize our con- 243
siderable volume with the rest of mm&s. 251

Cordially yours and so on; oh, add a post- 270
script, please: i would like us to exhibit in 272
the atlanta business show, gene, but the 281
prices are wholly out of line. i have written 290
to kling (carbon copy is enclosed) in the 298
hope we can pressure him into a more real- 307
istic view of the situation. want to follow 316
up for us? 328

Letter 90	Paper: workbook 361
DICTATED LETTER	Carbons: file, Letter 89
	Body: 153
	SI: 1.57—difficult

mr. thomas j. simmons, martin miller & 8
sons, 58 broad street, atlanta, georgia, 15
30303, with a carbon to gene. 22

thank you for your letter about the un- 30
satisfactory service that you are getting 39
from your portland duplicator. i am deeply 47
concerned about the situation and am ask- 55
ing our atlanta dealer, mr. gordon, to see 64
you about it. 67

this latest breakdown is the fifth you 76
have had with as many machines, isn't it? 84

how annoying it must be to you! we are, 93
naturally, disturbed about this record; we 101
have had a few machines get out of order 109
before, but we have never had so many col- 118
lapse in one installation. most of our cus- 126
tomers have never had even one service 134
call, let alone any need for the replacement 143
of our equipment. moreover, no other in- 151
stallation has ever had the drum of the 159
duplicator "run backwards," as you said 167
was the case this time. 172

i am writing to mr. gordon, giving him full 182
authority to settle the matter. your friends 191
in this company appreciate your patience. 200
That ought to do it! 221

Letter 91	Paper: workbook 363
DICTATED LETTER	Carbons: file, Letter 89
	Body: 119 + display
	SI: 1.59—difficult

atlanta business show, inc., attention mr. 14
kenneth w. kling, national bank building, 18
peachtree street, atlanta, 30304. 37

we appreciate very much your invitation 46
to exhibit in the business show you will 54
sponsor next month. we have read your 62
prospectus with interest but, for the fol- 70
lowing reasons, have decided not to reserve 79
space for an exhibit: (1) your space rates 90
are much higher than for shows that draw 99
much larger crowds. (2) your conference 109
activities are to be held away from the ex- 119
hibit hall, thus drawing away prospective 128
viewers. (3) the innumerable extra fees for 139
labor and facilities, which are a part of the 149
flat exhibit fee in other shows, have priced 159
your space beyond its value, in our opinion. 169
if there occurs a basic change in the admin- 179
istration of these three items, we may be 187
interested. 190

Remember to make a "bcc" for gene. Add 206
this note on his copy: what we really object 229
to, gene, is the third item. If they corrected 239
that, we'd be interested.—TW *Be sure that* 245
note is on the file, too.

Table 5

3-COLUMN TABLE
Paper: full sheet
Spacing: double
Tab stops: 2

Note the use of a colon to separate the minutes and seconds in elapsed time.

Table 6

3-COLUMN TABLE

Note the two places where tab stops should be reset.

Note that $ sign is not repeated, but that space is left as though it were.

Table 7

3-COLUMN TABLE

* Count assumes the four make-ready steps (page 66) are taken: stops set, paper inserted to starting line, carriage centered, etc.

SIX RECORDS FOR RUNNING A MILE

Record	Runner	Country
3:54.4	Peter Snell	New Zealand
3:54.5	Herb Elliot	Australia
3:55.9	Merv Lincoln	Australia
3:57.2	Derek Ibbotson	England
3:57.5	Ron Delaney	Ireland
3:57.5	Murray Halburg	New Zealand

YEARBOOK BIDS

November 3, 19—

Company	Quantity and Rate	Amount
Atlas Printing	2,000 @ $1.50	$3,000
Haber & Haber	2,500 @ 1.40	3,500
Jackson, Inc.	2,000 @ 1.35	2,700
Phillips Printing	2,000 @ 1.38	2,760
Rogers & Sons	2,500 @ 1.30	3,250

DUTY ROSTER, OCTOBER 24

Watch	Officer of the Deck	Junior Officer of the Deck
0000	Lt Martin	Ens Hughes
0400	Lcdr Greene	Ens Shaw
0800	Lt Foster	Ltjg Carews
1200	Ltjg Young	Ens Krell
1600	Lt Martin	Ens Hughes
2000	Lcdr Greene	Ens Shaw

UNIT 7

LESSONS 40-41

70

182/183-D. Apply skill to correspondence production

You work for Theodore Wilson, sales manager, Portland Products Company. He prefers blocked letter form. He dictates the following letters, expecting you—when necessary—to paragraph them (page 207), capitalize them (page 282), and provide correct salutations and closings (page 208) and the appropriate carbons and annotations.

Letter 87
DICTATED LETTER

Paper: workbook 355
Carbons: file only
Body: 185 words
SI: 1.44—normal

This letter is to my friend Jim Flaherty. 5
That's james e. flaherty, *at* 392 harvard 16
street, albany, new york, 12201. 25

as you will see from the letter i am en- 34
closing, we have a strong prospect in the 43
harding-hill corporation, in syracuse. your 52
itinerary indicates that you will be in syra- 60
cuse about the end of next week. could you 69
get there a day or two ahead of schedule 77
and give the firm some time? i am partic- 86
ularly anxious to land this deal because, 94
if i may judge by the number of h-h circu- 112
lars that come to my desk, this prospect 120
will need not one but several of the ma- 128
chines. 130

i checked on the weight of paper stock 139
that h-h is using; it varies, but none of it 148
is too heavy for our machine. h-h has ap- 156
parently standardized on No. 10 envelopes 164
and two folds. it would be good strategy 173
to have the machine ready. 178

i should not bother to go into the me- 187
chanics of the machine's operation, if i 195
were you, jim. i think this customer is in- 204
terested in only one thing: economy. i 212
suspect that this is the line to follow. let 220
me know whether you visit the company, 228
jim, and how you make out. 233

cordially yours, theodore wilson, sales 247
manager, *and so on.* 252

Letter 88
DICTATED LETTER

Paper: workbook 357
Carbons: file, letter 87
Body: 140 words
SI: 1.46—fairly hard

Now, this is the letter I was telling Jim about. ..
It's to marvin j. thompson, production 15
manager, harding-hill corporation, 1067 22
south clinton street, syracuse, new york, 30
13201. 37

we appreciate very much your inquiry 45
about our new folding machine. i assure 54
you that it will fold all the standard sizes 63
of paper used in duplicating machines. as 71
a matter of fact, it will fold papers as small 81
as 4 inches square and as large as 9 by 14 88
inches. 90

our representative for upper new york, 99
mr. james e. flaherty, to whom i am send- 107
ing a copy of this letter, will be in your city 117
in about ten days. i believe that he will be 126
able to stop in to see you when he arrives 134
in syracuse. he has a model of the folding 143
machine and can let you see for yourself 151
how efficient it is. 156

i am enclosing literature about the new 165
machine. if there is any other help i can 173
give, mr. thompson, please let me know. 202

Letter 89
DICTATED LETTER

Paper: workbook 359
Carbons: file only
Body and PS: 251
SI: 1.47—fairly hard

This letter is to eugene r. gordon, 818 13
rhodes-haverty building, 1200 conway bou- 21
levard, atlanta, 30307. dear gene: 31

we seem to be having another tussle with 40
your friend simmons at martin miller & 48
sons, as you can tell from the enclosed copy 57
of my current letter to him. i don't know 65
why we have had so much trouble with the 74
installation in his department. do you have 83
any thoughts on the subject? [CONTINUED] 89

Review

LINE: 60
TAB: 5
SPACING: DOUBLE
DRILLS: TWICE OR MORE
GOAL: REFRESH SKILL
 AND REVIEW LETTERS,
 TABLES

42-A. Type each line twice, hitting the keys sharply. Repeat lines in Lesson 43.

42-A. Tune up on these review lines

1 She may make the girls do the theme for their eighth panel.
2 Poor Jack was vexed about my long and quite hazy falsehood.
3 We bought the $47 bracelet for $28 and the $56 pin for $39.

42-B. Type paragraph 9 once, within 2 minutes; proofread the copy. Then:

(1) If you made more than 3 errors, type lines 4-5 three times each; then type 6-7 two times each.

(2) If you made 3 or fewer errors, type lines 4-5 two times each; then type lines 6-7 three times each.

42-B. Improve skill on patterned sentence drills

4 Zoe was given pay for that queer black box of jade markers.
5 Kay reviewed the subject before giving Max and Paul a quiz.
   1 | 2 | 3 | 4 | 5 | 6 | 7 | 8 | 9 | 10 | 11 | 12
6 He paid for the world maps and then cut them for the girls.
7 When may Mr. Melvor make the sights for the six new rifles?

42-C. First, scan your copy to satisfy your curiosity about it. Second, practice three or four times each any ONE word in each line.

Then, center a copy on a full sheet OR take two 5-minute writings. GOAL: 35 or more words a minute, with 4 or fewer errors.

SI 1.35—near normal

42-C. Measure and build your sustained typing skill

8   For more than a year now, it has been my pleasure each   12
morning to study the window of a fine jewelry store that is   24
located at the corner where I get my bus. I arrive there a   36
little before eight each morning and have six or seven min-   48
utes to wait before the bus is due. While I wait for it, I   60
study the big display of clocks in the window; it is really   72
quite something to see, with clocks of all sizes and kinds.   84
There are several timepieces that always amaze me. You see   96
no moving parts whatsoever, just the oval faces and pointed   108
hands, somehow suspended in the front corner of the window.   120

9   I have never seen so many clocks in different sizes or   132
shapes as appear there in the display at the jewelry store.   144
You see shelves of small, squatty alarm clocks and two rows   156
of small, slim china clocks shaped exactly like spires of a   168
church. There is a very big display of wrist watches, too.   180

10   One particular clock (a sign explains) is wound by the   192
changes in the weather. That one dumbfounds me, and I have   204
some very real doubts about it. Deep inside I nurture some   216
quiet little prayers that the expert who built that job for   228
us lazy folks must, surely, have put a winding key in some—   240
where as insurance on days when the weather stays the same.   252
   1 | 2 | 3 | 4 | 5 | 6 | 7 | 8 | 9 | 10 | 11 | 12

SUGGESTION: When you are typing line after line of steady copy, concentrate on evenness instead of pushing hard for speed.

A high speed score comes from not losing time. The most common speed cutters are losing the place (from looking up) in the copy and key jams.

Unit 30. Correspondence

LINE: 60
TAB: 5
SPACING: DRILLS SINGLE,
   PARAGRAPHS DOUBLE
DRILLS: THREE TIMES
GOAL: EDIT AND TYPE
   SECRETARIAL LETTERS
STRESS: GOOD POSTURE,
   VIGOROUS STROKING

182-A. Tune up on these review lines

182-A. If you can, type lines 2 and 3 in cadence with someone who sets a pace by typing line 1. Repeat in Lesson 183.

1 Many find that they must have more cash when they dine out.
2 Zeke quietly placed five new jumping beans in the gray box.
3 We need the discount signs for 10%, 28%, 39%, 47%, and 56%.

　　1 | 2 | 3 | 4 | 5 | 6 | 7 | 8 | 9 | 10 | 11 | 12

182-B. Sharpen skill on an alphabetic preview

182-B. Type to your need.

ACCURACY: Lines 4-7 as a paragraph, three times.

SPEED: Each line three times consecutively.

4 AA aims BB been CC capital DD said EE needed FF for GG gaps
5 HH whom II bit JJ major KK clerk LL skill MM most NN carbon
6 OO ought PP proper QQ quickly RR rules SS secretary TT that
7 UU must VV have WW knowledge XX exception YY likely ZZ hazy

182-C. Hold your best pace on normal paragraph copy

182-C. One errorless copy of each paragraph or two 5-minute writings—one with a 10-second rest after each minute and one without such rests.

GOAL: To complete the selection within two errors and five minutes.

SI 1.42—normal

8 As has been said before, the man who dictates a letter must decide   14
when he must send out a letter and what he must say in it. He leaves   28
to his secretary, whom he employs for this purpose, the details of   42
typing the letter, deciding on the carbon copies needed, and so on.   56
Among the "and so on" items is the responsibility for editing the   69
letter so it is proper in language, in punctuation, and in use of capitals. 84

This means that the typist who aims at the secretarial desk must   98
know the rules that concern these matters. It is important that he   112
know them, for his skill in applying such rules is one of the two things 126
that distinguish a secretary from a clerk typist. (The other factor is 141
the knowledge of shorthand.) Most persons have gaps in their control   155
of the laws of writing; let us be sure that you are the exception.   168

Of all the categories of rules that you ought to know, the first one   183
is the set of rules about using capitals. It may also be the most im-   197
portant set; for while a businessman may be a bit hazy about the   210
distinction between a comma and a semicolon, he is likely to be   223
familiar with all the major proprieties of capitals. He will spot your 237
oversights more quickly in this regard than in others. So, know the   251
rules!   252

　1 | 2 | 3 | 4 | 5 | 6 | 7 | 8 | 9 | 10 | 11 | 12 | 13 | 14

182-D. Review the business uses of capitals

182-D. To reinforce your control of these rules, review page 151 and then do the Learning Guide on workbook pages 353-354.

In business letters, capitalize—
1. The start of any sentence.
2. Personal titles (like *Miss*).
3. Business titles *preceding* names and in addresses and signatures.

4. Names of persons, places, companies, and trade-named products.
5. First and all major words in attention and subject lines, salutations, and titles of publications.

42/43-D. Speed up production of letters and tables

Letters 13-14. Review letter typing, pages 57-58; then type Letters 13-14 on workbook letterheads (or plain paper with a line or crease 1½ inches from the top, to represent a letterhead). GOAL: To finish each letter in 5 minutes or less, with 4 or fewer errors.

Tables 8-9. Review table typing, pages 66-70; then center these two tables on full sheets. Use double spacing for the bodies; arrange the columns 6 spaces apart. GOAL: To finish each table in 6 minutes (2-3 for adjustments, 3-4 for typing) with 3 or fewer errors.

Letter 13

BLOCKED LETTER
Paper: letterhead
Body: 90 words
Line: 4 inches
Tab: center
SI: 1.37—normal

NOTE: When something is to be mailed with a letter, type "Enclosure" below your initials as a reminder.

Date | Miss Florence Stahl | Apartment 12-C | 3928 Lakeview Drive | Detroit, Michigan   48213 | Dear Miss Stahl: | 24 / 36

Thank you for the recent letter in which you asked about the plays for which you might still be able to obtain tickets for a show in the first week of December. | 48 / 61 / 69

We are enclosing a list of such plays. | 78

If you wish us to reserve seats for you, please let us know within the next week. It is necessary for you to make a deposit of $1 on each ticket you wish to reserve; we will then hold the ticket or tickets until 24 hours prior to curtain time. | Yours sincerely, | John Clark Williams | Ticket Reservations | URS | Enclosure | 91 / 104 / 117 / 131 / 148 / 150

Letter 14

BLOCKED LETTER

Date | Mr. John R. Jackson | Hotel Parkview | 4756 East 28 Street | St. Louis, Missouri   63155 | Dear Mr. Jackson: | 24 / 36

[Repeat the body and closing of the letter above.] | 150

Table 8

3-COLUMN TABLE
Paper: full sheet
Spacing: double

THEATER TICKETS AVAILABLE
For Week of December 3

Play	Star	Price Range	
			15
			31
			49
Shadowed Rainbow	Nancy Reeves	$2.40 to $6.80	62
Seventh Son	Gloria Langley	2.20 to 7.50	75
Inherit a Plew	Paul Montrose	2.20 to 8.80	85
Holly Ann, Dear	Ross Willard	4.40 to 8.80	96
Comedy of Errors	Victor Bennett	1.60 to 4.40	107
Regretfully So	Janis Prellis	2.20 to 5.50	117

Table 9

4-COLUMN TABLE
Paper: full sheet
Spacing: double

SUMMARY OF ORDERS
Received on November 18

Cat. Item	Quantity and Rate	Billing	Company	
				10
				26
				30
				55
376	160 boxes @ 42¢	$67.20	Phelps, Inc.	71
376	200 boxes @ 42¢	84.00	Harris & Sons	84
394	100 units @ 37¢	37.00	Dale-Acme	94
416	144 boxes @ 46¢	66.24	Stephens Bros.	105
739	100 reams @ 71¢	71.00	Akron Schools	116

181-A. Tune up by repeating 180-A, page 280

181-B. Inventory your present symbol-typing skill

181-B. Without looking up or pausing even once, type one double-spaced copy. As you proofread, put a light checkmark beside the drill below for each key that you have typed incorrectly.

18   Invoice #3311 was addressed to Smith & Hart, Inc. (now   12
Hart & Sons, Inc.) and was for 1,000# of #12 filings (15.5%   24
steel) @ 11¢ a pound, for a total of $110.00, less discount   38
(5% on whole 100's); so the "amount due" is $105.00.   Their   53
credit is "good" as Smith & Hart but "poor" as Hart & Sons.   65
      1 | 2 | 3 | 4 | 5 | 6 | 7 | 8 | 9 | 10 | 11 | 12

181-C. Improve control of the #, $, %, () and & keys

181-C. Each line three times, plus another time if you missed the key when you typed 181-B.

19   dd ## Box #333 contained 3.3# of blue labels, the #33 size.
20   jj && We get Lord & Howe ties at Swiss & Sons or Cole & Co.
21   ff $$ The suit cost $75; the shoes, $20; and the coat, $90.
22   ll ((;;)) He looked for (10), (28), (39), (47), and (56).
23   ff %% She says that 5% of 5% is .25%, but 10% of 10% is 1%.
      1 | 2 | 3 | 4 | 5 | 6 | 7 | 8 | 9 | 10 | 11 | 12

181-D. Repeat 181-B to confirm your progress

181-E. Improve control of the ¢, @, ", ', and __ keys

181-E. Each line three times, plus another time if you missed the key when you typed 181-D.

24   ;; ¢¢ jj ¢¢ The pamphlets cost 10¢, 28¢, 39¢, 47¢, and 56¢.
25   ;; @@ ss @@ Please order 100 @ 28¢, 39 @ 47¢, and 10 @ 56¢.
26   kk '' ;; '' It's Tim's or Bob's cap; it's not Vi's or Jo's!
27   ss "" ;; "" "Average" is "good" but "superior" is "better."
28   jj __ ;; __ They are not to know what cherchez la femme is!
      1 | 2 | 3 | 4 | 5 | 6 | 7 | 8 | 9 | 10 | 11 | 12

181-F. Repeat 181-B to confirm your progress

181-G. Regain fluency with pair-pattern sentences

181-G. If you made any number-key error when typing 181-B-D-F, type 29-31 three times as a paragraph; otherwise, type each line three times consecutively.

29   They assigned us Rooms 10, 28, 39, 47, and 56 for seminars.
30   Put Group 10 in Room 28, Group 39 in 47, the others in 156.
31   Check lockers 10, 28, and 39 for books numbered 56 and 147.
      1 | 2 | 3 | 4 | 5 | 6 | 7 | 8 | 9 | 10 | 11 | 12

181-H. Repeat 181-B to confirm your progress

181-I. Regain full stride on an alphabetic paragraph

181-I. Type three rapid copies at full stride. If time permits, take a wrap-up 5-minute writing on the page 278 copy.

SI 1.36—easy-normal

32   Did you ever wait for a bus in a big station and spend   12
your time watching other people?   Some quietly relax.   Some   24
visit with friends or doze.   Some pass the time just watch-   36
ing others.   A great many go over to the magazine stand and   48
look sideways at the daring covers of books they won't buy.   60
      1 | 2 | 3 | 4 | 5 | 6 | 7 | 8 | 9 | 10 | 11 | 12

LINE: 60
TAB: 5
SPACING: SINGLE
DRILLS: TWICE OR MORE
GOAL: COMPLETE
  SYMBOL KEYS, LEARN
  BASICS OF
  MANUSCRIPT TYPING
STRESS: CORRECT
  POSTURE

44-A. Type each line twice. Repeat them in Lesson 45.

44-B. Each line twice. If necessary, construct the symbols that you need.

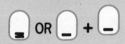

44-C. To get back in full stride and maybe pick up some extra speed, type each paragraph twice. Or, even better, make two attempts to finish each paragraph in 2 minutes or less within 3 errors, followed by a 5-minute writing in which you set a new speed record (but do it within 4 errors!).

SI 1.00—very easy

Unit 8. Manuscripts

44-A. Tune up on these review lines

1 They paid for the pen and the box, so I paid for the chair.
2 Pack my five boxes in with the dozen jugs of brown lacquer.
3 I phoned rooms 10, 28, 39, and 47 before he phoned room 56.

44-B. Practice the rest of the symbol keys

1. Exclamation. If your machine has a top-row *1* key, ! is its shift. Use A-finger to drill *ala!* with F-finger anchored. If you have no *1* key, make the ! by typing a period, backspacing, and typing an apostrophe.

4 alala ala!a a!a!a Vote for Jones! Vote for Jones! Hurrah!
5 They counted the seconds: Five! Four! Three! Two! One!

2. Equals. Some machines have = key at the top right of the keyboard, controlled by Sem-finger: ;=;=;. On other machines, make = by typing a hyphen, backspacing, and typing another hyphen with the cylinder turned up slightly.

6 ;=; ;=; ;=; F = 25, A = 30, S = 40, E = 45 (for 3 minutes).

3. Plus. On machines with = key, + is shift of =. Drill: ;=;+;. On other machines, make + by typing a hyphen, backspacing, and intersecting the hyphen with an apostrophe or diagonal (whichever gives the better result).

7 ;=; ;+; ;+; He said to total a + b, then b + c, then c + d.
8 if a + b = 25 and b + c = 45, could a = 10, b = 15, c = 30?

4. Asterisk. The asterisk (*) is the shift of either the hyphen (drill: ;-;*;) or of the 8 key (drill: *k8k*k*), depending on the make of machine.

9 John Wilson* used an asterisk (*) in a number of footnotes.

44-C. Regain fluency on easy paragraph material

10 All through the lunch hour, we sat there and played an   12
old quiz game that Mike had found in a box of junk that his   24
dad had thrown out. The game was a lot of fun, too; but we   36
got tired of that, of course. The rain kept on. Dave came   48
up with a game he had found in some old book; we tried this   60
one for a while, too. We were glad to see the sun at last.   72

   1 | 2 | 3 | 4 | 5 | 6 | 7 | 8 | 9 | 10 | 11 | 12

11 Once in a blue moon, it is good to get up at the crack   12
of dawn and watch the world wake up. You see the sun break   24
through the shades and mist of night and gleam on the drops   36
of dew that weigh down the leaves and the grass; and as you   48
look, the leaves lift up and the grass turns straight while   60
the dew fades and dries in the first soft breath of breeze.   72

LINE: 60
SPACING: DOUBLE FOR
(B), OTHERS SINGLE
DRILLS: THREE OR MORE
GOAL: STRENGTHEN
TOP-ROW CONTROLS
STRESS: EYES ON COPY

180-A. Race through each drill three times without pausing and without looking up. Repeat in Lesson 181.

180-A. Tune up on these review lines

1 They may wish to work with the social chairman of the firm.
2 Kay bought five or six cans to award as equal major prizes.
3 Type 1 and 2 and 3 and 4 and 5 and 6 and 7 and 8 [Continue to 50]

   1 | 2 | 3 | 4 | 5 | 6 | 7 | 8 | 9 | 10 | 11 | 12

180-B. Without looking up or pausing even once, type one double-spaced copy. As you proofread, put a light checkmark beside the drill below for each key that you have typed incorrectly.

180-B. Inventory your present number-typing skill

4 7601 2702 2603 6804 2805 4906 1607 7308 3809 8010 4711 9512

8013 2914 7815 5016 9617 6718 5719 3620 1821 1922 9823 4624

9425 1926 9827 4028 9029 5630 8531 8932 9633 8334 7035 2936

6737 4838 6439 2040 6941 3042 7543 8744 5945 9146 5847 8348

6349 9750 6151 8652 7253 1054 1755 3756 7457 6258 7959 6760

   1 | 2 | 3 | 4 | 5 | 6 | 7 | 8 | 9 | 10 | 11 | 12

180-C. Each line three times, plus another time if you missed the key when you typed 180-B.

180-C. Improve control on number keys 1-5

5 aa 11 The 11 teams from 11 schools had 11 games in 11 days.
6 ss 22 I sold 22 cars in 22 days to 22 people from 22 towns.
7 dd 33 The 33 groups sent 33 books to the 33 men in tier 33.
8 ff 44 Seat 44 in row 44 was 44 rows up and 44 seats inward.
9 ff 55 Car 55 traveled 55 laps in 55 minutes and 55 seconds.

   1 | 2 | 3 | 4 | 5 | 6 | 7 | 8 | 9 | 10 | 11 | 12

180-D. Repeat 180-B to confirm your progress

180-E. Each line three times, plus another time if you missed the key when you typed 180-D.

180-E. Improve control on number keys 6-0

10 jj 66 Route 66 is 66 miles west of 66th Street on U. S. 66.
11 jj 77 The 77 workers in Plant 77 average 77 dollars weekly.
12 kk 88 The 88 teams from District 88 won the first 88 games.
13 ll 99 The 99th division handles 99 items for 99 cents each.
14 ;; 00 If you add 00 or 000 or 0000 to 00, you still have 0.

   1 | 2 | 3 | 4 | 5 | 6 | 7 | 8 | 9 | 10 | 11 | 12

180-F. Repeat 180-B to confirm your progress

180-G. If you made any error in 180-F, type 15-17 three times as a paragraph; otherwise, type each line three times consecutively.

180-G. Increase fluency by typing "we 23" drills

15 we 23 24 25 toe 593 594 595 owe 923 924 925 rye 463 464 465
16 ty 56 57 58 pry 046 047 048 try 546 547 548 toy 596 597 598
17 it 85 86 87 wit 285 286 287 pit 085 086 087 out 975 976 977

   1 | 2 | 3 | 4 | 5 | 6 | 7 | 8 | 9 | 10 | 11 | 12

180-H. Repeat 180-B to confirm your progress

44-D. Learn to identify the basic parts of a short manuscript

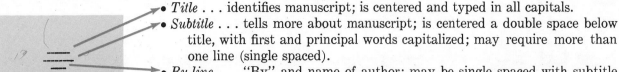

- *Title* . . . identifies manuscript; is centered and typed in all capitals.
- *Subtitle* . . . tells more about manuscript; is centered a double space below title, with first and principal words capitalized; may require more than one line (single spaced).
- *By-line* . . . "By" and name of author; may be single spaced with subtitle lines or may be displayed separately, preceded by 1 blank line.
- *Body* . . . separated from heading by 2 blank lines; 5-space indentions.
- *Subheading* . . . principal subdivision; centered and underscored, with first and principal words capitalized; preceded by 2 blank lines.
- *Sideheading* . . . important subdivision; may be underscored capital and small letters, but usually all caps; preceded by 2 blank lines.
- *Balance line* . . . something (date, reference, etc.) added at bottom to stretch manuscript when it is too short or too high on the page.

44-E. Learn basic procedures in positioning short manuscripts

MECHANICAL OPERATIONS

Tab stops. Always set two—one for the standard 5-space paragraph indention and one for use in repositioning the carriage for centering lines.

Spacing. As when typing tabulations, set the machine for single spacing until you begin the body.

Extraspacing. To leave one additional blank line when the machine is set for double spacing, turn up the paper one line by hand (turn the right cylinder knob) *before* returning the carriage.

Bottom guard. Typists usually pencil two very light lines (later erased) near the bottom of the paper: one to mark where the last line of typing could go and a cautionary signal an inch higher. Or, they use a *visual guide*—a sheet on which the four margins are ruled; placed under the paper on which you will type, the ruled lines show through to guide you visually in margin observance. Your workbook has a visual guide to use in this unit.

Placement plans. The two common ways of positioning material are *by centering* and *by formula.*

1. PLACEMENT BY CENTERING

The final typing of a short manuscript is usually a *retyping* of a preliminary draft; with the draft at hand for use as the basis of figuring, the typist can readily center it just as he centers any block of lines: He counts lines and computes the appropriate top margin; then he selects an *average full-length line* and backspace-centers this line to determine where to set the margins.

2. PLACEMENT BY FORMULA

When a manuscript is composed directly at the machine or when the preliminary draft is inadequate for centering (if written by hand, for example), the typist follows this formula:

Top margin, 2 inches (he starts on line 13).

Line length and spacing depend on the amount of material in the manuscript:

    Under 200 words: 5-inch line; double space
    200 - 300 words: 6-inch line; double space
    Above 300 words: 6-inch line; single space

Bottom margin, 2 inches when a 5-inch line is used, 1½ inches when a 6-inch line is used. *If the copy is too long,* continue it on another page or retype it higher on the page. *If the copy is too short* (too high on the page), type a "balance line" (date, assignment number, etc.) near the bottom to give the page proper balance.

44/45-F. Practice the production of short manuscripts

GOAL: To finish each manuscript on pages 75-76 in 10 minutes (3-4 for studying the problem and making machine adjustments, 6-7 for typing the work) or less, with *no* arrangement errors, and with not more than 4 typographical errors.

Note that each manuscript is to be typed twice: first by formula, *including a balance line* about 2 inches from the bottom, with the use of the visual guides, workbook pages 59-60; and then by centering, *without a balance line*, using your first copy for figuring the centering adjustments. Use plain paper and appropriate line length and spacing.

The word count credits you fully for all centering, indenting, and other required operations.

179-A. Tune up by repeating 178-A, page 277

179-B. Inventory your present skill

179-C. Improve skill via selective practice

179-B. Adjust machine to double spacing, 70-space line, tab-5 indention. Copy the bottom three paragraphs on page 278.

If you make more than 2 errors, your goal for Lesson 179 is accuracy; 2 or fewer, then speed.

28 McMann member mimic madam hammy maim memo mums harm mom May
29 Norton ninety noons linen ninth neon none nine nuns one Nan
30 Olivio orator odors polio solos onto oboe polo oleo too Ona
31 Pepper people poppy pipes paper prop pulp pipe pups pop Pat
32 Quincy quoted equip query quart quad quiz quit aqua quo Que

    1 | 2 | 3 | 4 | 5 | 6 | 7 | 8 | 9 | 10 | 11 | 12

33 problem lament curls visit tight dusk sigh idle map fit eye
34 torment wieldy bugle shake handy gown bury worm sob ham fog
35 auditor bushel ivory widow shelf lane pane worn tie lap oak
36 apricot social fight chair spend risk half snap box foe aid

179-D. Improve skill via more selective practice

179-C-D-E. Type to goal determined in 179-B.

ACCURACY: The group of alphabetic-control lines as a paragraph three times plus once more if include one you missed the letters drilled on in 179-B; then type the alternate-hand drills twice as a paragraph.

SPEED: Each alphabetic-control line twice, then each alternate-hand line four or more times.

37 Reigor repair refer recur error purr rare roar rear err Ron
38 Sister senses suits sizes sales sees sirs uses says sis Sue
39 Tootle traits trout truth total tent trot that tact tot Ted
40 Ushers unused usurp usury usual true unto upon unit but Una
41 Velvet vivify verve vivid valve vote view have very vow Van

    1 | 2 | 3 | 4 | 5 | 6 | 7 | 8 | 9 | 10 | 11 | 12

42 ancient theory world shame laugh paid when turn lay row sit
43 chapels visual shape panel eight soap rush body bid pen key
44 antique eighty giant blame right form worn lame dog cow due
45 visitor profit title throw their with both them fur rod sir

179-E. Improve skill via still more selective practice

CAUTION: If you start to jam keys, you will know you are pushing much too hard for speed.

46 Wislow window which where widow whew what when with owe Wes
47 Xavier deluxe proxy exact toxin exit text next taxi fix Tex
48 Youngs yearly slyly study shyly your duty year city fly You
49 Zinzer puzzle dozen dizzy dozed zone zero jazz lazy zip Zoe

    1 | 2 | 3 | 4 | 5 | 6 | 7 | 8 | 9 | 10 | 11 | 12

50 turkeys mantle docks rocks blend lair tidy sock rye jam hay
51 sleighs pajama soaps autos turns cork duel urns bit fig tub
52 dismays icicle tucks dog's toxic alto idle jamb fox pry woe
53 bushels enrich virus roams socks also firm name rug sow cue

179-F. Speed up your spacebar stroke

179-F. Type to your goal.

ACCURACY: Lines 54-56 three times, typed as though a paragraph.

SPEED: Type each line three consecutive times.

54 hand duck kept torn name ends slow wish held disk keys soft
55 tool look keen nook keep peer room mood deer roll loop pool
56 let two one end dry yet the elf for rim may yes sit tug gem

    1 | 2 | 3 · | 4 | 5 | 6 | 7 | 8 | 9 | 10 | 11 | 12

179-G. Repeat 179-B to confirm your progress

Manuscript 1
Manuscript 2

ONE-PAGE REPORT
Shown: in pica
Body: 109 words
SI: 1.41—normal
Copies: 2 (directions,
    page 74)

NOTE: Substitute your teacher's
name for "Mr. Strang" and your
name for "Jean L. Worth."

ONE–PAGE REPORTS   ◄TITLE   10

11

A Report to Mr. Strang   ◄SUBTITLE   26
By Jean L. Worth ▼3   ◄BY-LINE   38

40

    This report is designed to show how a one–page   51
report should be arranged. ▼3   57

58

SIDEHEADING►   HEADINGS   60

    Business asks that a report be identified by a   70
heading (what, to whom, by whom) and by sideheadings   81
that classify the contents at a glance.   89

90

MARGINS AND SPACING   94

    The top margin is 2 inches (but can be less).   104
The common line lengths are: 110

    Under 200 words: 5 inches, double spaced   121
    200 – 300 words: 6 inches, double spaced   130
    Above 300 words: 6 inches, single spaced   140

142

BALANCE LINE   145

    If a report is so short that it looks high on   155
the page, the typist writes something (date, for in-   166
stance) 2 inches from the bottom at either margin. ▼₂   176

177

BALANCE LINE►   November 15, 19––   180

1 | 2 | 3 | 4 | 5 | 6 | 7 | 8 | 9 | 10

One-Page Report with Sideheadings

1 | 2 | 3 | 4 | 5 | 6 | 7 | 8 | 9 | 10 | 11 | 12 | 13 | 14

The annual vacation is one outing to which families look forward   14
all year long. Most families plan for a week or two or more for this 28
big affair. The youngsters hardly realize, of course, how many exact 42
plans have to be made—how cash for the sojourn must be set aside and   56
frozen there, how the wardrobe of each member of the family has to be 70
designed for the square inches per suitcase, and other such problems. 84

And problems they are, and they must be settled; but whether the   98
problems are fun or troublesome to solve depends on how a family goes 112
about them. Our family tackles the plans together, with the juvenile 126
members pulling an oar with the rest of us; you would be quite amazed 140
at the soundness of most of their suggestions, and it is mighty smart 154
to hear the ideas expressed before the vacation instead of during it. 168

The first step is picking the dates for the excursion, something   182
that is not much of a problem to wage earners. If you have a cottage 196
and a boat waiting for you, deciding where to go is not a tough deal, 210
either. It's the options that make vacation planning hard, you know. 224
Then you have to contemplate the kind of junket you'll take, the size 238
of your luggage load, and a hundred or two questions along that line. 252

1 | 2 | 3 | 4 | 5 | 6 | 7 | 8 | 9 | 10 | 11 | 12 | 13 | 14

There are some of us who seize this one chance a year to get new   14 266
experience. We go to a different part of the country, or we make the 28 280
journey by some different means of transportation, or we rough it the 42 294
camping way instead of living in hotel luxury. Thus, you see, option 56 308
there is; and this means discussion, a few squabbles, and finally The 70 322
Great Decision. After that, we enjoy a gradually growing excitement. 84 336

Two summers ago our family followed one of the historical trails   98 350
and took our chances on lodging; that was some experience, a new one, 112 364
all right. It is amazing how suddenly there aren't any motels except 126 378
ones that have just one bank vault left. The next summer we equipped 140 392
ourselves with camping gear; this was an experience, too, in which we 154 406
never did learn the basic thing in camping: how to cook in the rain. 168 420

So this summer, the family council has decided, we will take our   182 434
comfort with us: we are going to rent a trailer. We shall scorn the 196 448
hotels and motels and camping sites. We shall laugh at the rain. We 210 462
shall be cozy, living as poshly as a railroad czar. We shall drive a 224 476
thousand—mile jaunt up the coast, stopping as long as we wish at each 238 490
quaint or beautiful place we see. If only I can keep it on the road! 252 504

1 | 2 | 3 | 4 | 5 | 6 | 7 | 8 | 9 | 10 | 11 | 12 | 13 | 14

Manuscript 3
Manuscript 4
ONE-PAGE REPORT
Shown: in elite
Body: 137 words
SI: 1.34—fairly easy
Copies: 2 (directions,
   page 74)

CHANGING THE LENGTH | 12

A Report to Mr. Strang | 13 / 28

By Jean L. Worth | 40

| 42

It is possible for the typist to make a report look long | 55

or look short. It is a matter of using headings that do or | 67

do not take extra space. | 72

| 73

TO STRETCH A REPORT | 77

To make a report look long, the typist may use sidehead- | 89

ings or centered subheadings. Each of these occupies a line, | 102

is preceded by two blank lines, and is followed by one blank | 114

line—four lines in all. | 119

| 120

TO CONDENSE A REPORT | 124

To make a report look short, the typist will change to | 136

"paragraph headings," which take no extra space at all, as | 148

shown in these two: | 152

PARAGRAPH
HEADINGS

Point 1. Paragraph headings are indented the same five | 167

spaces as other paragraphs. | 173

Point 2. To make them stand out clearly, such headings | 188

are underscored. | 192

November 16, 19— | 197

1 | 2 | 3 | 4 | 5 | 6 | 7 | 8 | 9 | 10 | 11 | 12

One-Page Report with Paragraph Headings

LINE: 60
SPACING: DRILLS
  SINGLE, PARAGRAPHS
  DOUBLE
DRILLS: THREE OR
  MORE
GOAL: BOOST SKILL FOR
  FIVE MINUTES
STRESS: EVEN CADENCE,
  STEADY INCREASE

178-A. Each line three
times or for a minute.
Repeat in Lesson 179.

178-B. Adjust machine to
double spacing, 70-space
line, tab-5 indention.
Copy the first three
paragraphs on page 278.

If you make more than 2
errors, your goal for
Lesson 178 is accuracy;
2 or fewer, then speed.

178-C-D-E. Type exactly
for the goal determined
by your 178-B results.

ACCURACY: The four
alphabetic-control lines
as a paragraph three
times plus once more if
the letters drilled on
include one you missed
when you typed 178-B;
then type the alternate-
hand lines two times as
an easy paragraph.

SPEED: Each alphabetic-
control line twice, then
each alternate-hand line
four consecutive times.

178-A. Tune up on these review lines

1 If he and Al go to town, they may visit with the neighbors.
2 Judge Flynn was very much puzzled by Alex's quick thinking.
3 Type 7 and 14 and 21 and 28 and 35 and 42 and 49 [Continue to 100]
   1 | 2 | 3 | 4 | 5 | 6 | 7 | 8 | 9 | 10 | 11 | 12

178-B. Inventory your present skill

178-C. Improve skill via selective practice

4 Addams banana salad mania again alas data aqua saga any Ada
5 Bobbit bubble bobby bible abbey blob blab balm barb bib Bob
6 Church cancel check chuck click city nice each came can Cas
7 Druids deduct deeds daddy dried duds dude dyed adds did Don
   1 | 2 | 3 | 4 | 5 | 6 | 7 | 8 | 9 | 10 | 11 | 12
8 neighbor socials icicle burnt audit neigh malt slap and dig
9 quantity divisor quench amend slang title vial coal for the
10 chairman rituals height shape cycle visor mane dusk she own
11 downtown bushels ensign rocks whale throb curl diem big did

178-D. Improve skill via more selective practice

12 Elders degree level every exert ease else even edge fee Eve
13 French buffer fluff fifty fifth cuff tiff muff fife oft Flo
14 Grange groggy aging going gauge gags gang agog eggs ago Gus
15 Heathe hurrah harsh humph hunch hush hath hash high had Hal
   1 | 2 | 3 | 4 | 5 | 6 | 7 | 8 | 9 | 10 | 11 | 12
16 ornament element shaken forks laity quake clan dial but man
17 rhapsody suspend thrown works rifle soaks turn such may cut
18 problems visible author angle theme sighs pair soak got six
19 fieldmen ensigns handle shape vigor field tock disk fix end

178-E. Improve skill via still more selective practice

20 Inslip invite visit limit livid hide bite item five irk Ida
21 Jaguar jacket major enjoy judge join jury ajar just job Joe
22 Kelley kicker knock knack khaki milk know kick kink ask Kim
23 Leslie little local loyal lilac tall lilt loll lily all Les
   1 | 2 | 3 | 4 | 5 | 6 | 7 | 8 | 9 | 10 | 11 | 12
24 vigoroso enamels turkey forms turns dorms girl tick hem nap
25 sorority bicycle dismal sight throw elbow lame cozy pay men
26 rifleman signals island slept usual gowns dusk wish icy wit
27 Manfield sleighs chapel rigid signs ducks iris owls bow pan

178-F. Repeat 178-B to confirm your progress

PROFESSIONAL TIP:

To keep drill repetition
from becoming
monotonous, give your
mind something to think
about: make a game of
seeing how evenly you
can type. Keep saying
"Smoothly, smoothly!" to
yourself, as you type.

UNIT 29   LESSON 178

LINE: 60
TAB: 5
SPACING: SINGLE
DRILLS: TWICE OR MORE
GOAL: TYPE
 ENUMERATIONS BY
 TABULAR TOUCH
STRESS: EYES ON COPY

46-A. Each line two or more times. Repeat in Lesson 47.

46-B. Type an experimental copy of each example; then, each three times on a line.

"times":

"equals":

"minus":

"divided by":

"plus":

"degrees":

superior figures:

inferior figures:

military "zero":

"brackets":

roman numerals:

46-C. Type each line two times; then type all lines straight through once more.

OR, take five consecutive 1-minute writings (that is, a 5-minute writing with a 10-second rest after every minute); and then take one unbroken 5-minute writing (but with each minute called off so you can see if you are keeping up with the pace set previously).

GOAL: To set new speed record within 4 errors.

SI 1.00—very easy

46-A. Tune up on these review lines

1 Pamela works for us but may wish to work for the city firm.
2 Paul said Buzz and Jack might quit five or six weeks early.
3 If you add 10, 28, 39, 47, and 56, the total should be 180.

46-B. Learn to construct special characters

4 What is 2 x 2? ....expressed by small letter x.
5 12 x 12 = 144. ...two hyphens, one below the other (*turn roll by hand*).
6 106 − 14 = 92. ....a single hyphen or a raised underscore.
7 144 ÷ 12 = 12. ....hyphen intersected by the colon.
8 92 + 14 = 106. ....hyphen intersected by one or more apostrophes.
9 Freeze at 32°. ....small letter o, raised slightly (*turn roll by hand*).
10 4^3 x 5^2 = 39^a. ....type number or letter above line (*turn roll by hand*).
11 H_2O is liquid. ....type number or letter below line (*turn roll by hand*).
12 Leave at 1800. ....0, intersected by a diagonal.
13 He /Williams/. ....diagonals, with underscores facing inside.
14 Chapter XLVII. ....capitals of I, V, X, L, C, and M.

46-C. Renew typing fluency on these speed sentences

15 When can we two men find time to see those four firms? 11
16 I do not seem to have done my share at the old school. 22
17 He may call him back and ask him to work with us soon. 33
18 Both the men we met on the street came here to see us. 44
19 We should ask him to come to the club for a golf game. 55
20 One rich man said he would come down here if he could. 66
21 It is time for us and the right men to leave for town. 77
22 I could make it to class if I could get back by eight. 88
23 Both of us would like to roam by the side of the lake. 99
24 I was to have been there at one, but got there at two. 110
25 We might get the stuff out on time if we work all day. 121
26 One of them should be here to help you with the sales. 132
27 You ought to pay the state tax by check on the eighth. 143
28 How much do you plan to pay me for the desk and chair? 154

177-C. Improve control on one-hand-run preview words

30 multiplying standard targets letter starts think loose junk
31 sarcastic millions sandbags ponders create quill wages case
32 excellent protested formula success revamp idiom frank only

   1 | 2 | 3 | 4 | 5 | 6 | 7 | 8 | 9 | 10 | 11 | 12

177-D. Improve control on preview words on rows 2 and 3

33 qualities judged really tailor tossed adjust wages high out
34 protested spiral target dipped itself squirt prior halt use
35 writers stirred whether effort people dilute first read how

177-E. Improve control on preview words stressing row 1

36 excellent ancient having mixes began lack than lamb dab an,
37 exciting obvious dozens; pains alas, land make lick can am,
38 exchange really, revamps dizzy basic back curb each man and

   1 | 2 | 3 | 4 | 5 | 6 | 7 | 8 | 9 | 10 | 11 | 12

177-F. Improve control on alternate-hand-run preview words

39 qualities problem handle, mighty when firm with both men if
40 onslaught produce ancient chaos, they halt such than did do
41 quantity eloquent whether might, turn them work lend bit of

177-G. Sharpen attention on a concentration paragraph

42   D—ar Mr. W—lliams: I sh—ll b— pl—as—d to h—lp y—u and   12
yo—r st—ff s—t up a n—w f—ling syst—m. As y—u kn—w, I h—v—   24
b——n d—ing m—ch —f th—s k—nd —f w—rk r—c—ntly. If y—u w—ll   36
not—fy m— wh—n to b—g—n, I sh—ll b— th—r—. C—rd—lly y——rs   48

   1 | 2 | 3 | 4 | 5 | 6 | 7 | 8 | 9 | 10 | 11 | 12

177-H. Now inventory your skill again!

43 There is no obvious way to halt the onslaught of trite letters. If   15
you have dozens to produce in the hour, you do not tailor them; you   28
squirt them out of a formula gun. You do not have time to review   41
and revamp, to chop out boastful words and replace them with proud   55
ones, to dilute the sugar with a bit of frank honesty, to toss in an   69
eloquent turn of words in place of the standard idioms, or to curb or   83
adjust an ironic expression that proves more sarcastic than witty.   96
Still, wouldn't it be exciting if each writer did take time and pains to   111
write one excellent, inspired letter each day? The injection of such a   125
letter from each of the millions of correspondents might at least revive   140
the ancient qualities.   144

   1 | 2 | 3 | 4 | 5 | 6 | 7 | 8 | 9 | 10 | 11 | 12 | 13 | 14

177-C-D. For your goal:

ACCURACY: Type 177-C three times and 177-D two times, typing the lines in paragraph form.

SPEED: Type each line of 177-C twice and each line of 177-D three times.

This drill is especially good as a remedy for the typist who jams keys!

177-E-F. For your goal:

ACCURACY: Type 177-E three times and 177-F two times, typing the lines in paragraph form.

SPEED: Type each line of 177-E twice, each line of 177-F three times.

177-G. Filling in all the missing vowels (and don't mark the book!), type two copies. GOAL: To finish a copy without an error in 1 minute or less time.

177-H. Measure your growth by typing this paragraph in the same way you typed 176-B and 176-G. GOAL: To finish the copy within 3 minutes and 1 error.

SI 1.34—normal and fully alphabetic

46/47-D. Prepare a summary of manuscript enumerations

Using plain paper or workbook pages 61-64, type Manuscripts 5-8 as a four-page project to illustrate forms of enumerations. GOAL: To complete each manuscript in 10 minutes (3-4 to prepare for the assignment; 6-7 to produce it) or less, with *no* arrangement errors and 4 or fewer other errors.

Manuscript 5

ONE-PAGE REPORT
Paper: full sheet
Plan: by formula
Body: 117 words
SI: 1.45—high
    normal

ENUMERATIONS | A Report to Mr. Strang | By Jean L. Worth | 34

An enumeration is a series of steps or items whose exact sequence is shown by numbers, letters, alphabetic arrangement, or other means.   50   62   65

FOUR STYLES | Style 1 is illustrated by this and the following three paragraphs.   81   85

Style 2 is one in which numbers or letters are typed at the margin, with all other copy indented in one tabular step of either three or four spaces.   101   114   120

Style 3 is the outline form in which the copy is typed in tabular steps of four spaces each.   135   142

Style 4 is the kind used in book and article listings: alphabetic by last name of first author.   159   166

SPACING | Any of the four styles may be arranged either in single or in double spacing. | Balance line?   179   190

LISTED ENUMERATIONS   12

Manuscript 6

ENUMERATION
Paper: full sheet
Plan: center an
    exact copy
SI: 1.41—normal

13
14

1. Any series of numbered items may be classified as an "enumeration"; to most persons, however, the word means a displayed listing like this one, with numbers standing out at the left.   24   34   44   54   55

2. The numbers are typed at the margin. The word copy is aligned after the period and space that follow the number. A tab stop is set to help align the "run over" lines of copy.   65   76   86   95   96

CENTER ➜ 3. If most items take one line or less, they are single spaced with no blank lines left between them; one space follows the period.   106   116   124   125

4. If most listed items fill more than one line, all are single spaced with one blank line left between items; two spaces follow the period.   135   146   156   157

These are the basic rules; they are not applied to the unique displays of listings.

5. The periods must align. When the figures run to 10 or more, the typist must space in once before typing each figure, 1 through 9.   167   177   186

1 | 2 | 3 | 4 | 5 | 6 | 7 | 8 | 9 | 10

176-E. Type to your goal.

ACCURACY: Each group of lines, as a paragraph, three evenly paced times.

SPEED: Each line three rapid, consecutive times.

176-E. Improve control on adjacent-stroke preview words

14 UI linguistic UI squirt UI quills XC excellent XC exciting,
15 OP proportion OP people OP chop PO oppose PO ponder PO upon
16 AS sarcastic AS phrasing AS phrases AS basic AS case AS has
17 RT courtesy RT effort RT squirt RT effort RT start RT short

    1 | 2 | 3 | 4 | 5 | 6 | 7 | 8 | 9 | 10 | 11 | 12

18 IO injection IO proportion IO obvious IO millions IO idioms
19 ER shorter ER writer ER ponder ER expert ER wonder ER every
20 OU courtesy OU could OU proud OU hour OU your OU out OU our
21 RE create RE great RE fired RE read RE sure RE more RE core

176-F. Type three times, double spaced; or take three 1-minute writings.

GOAL: To finish the copy in 1 minute without error.

SI 1.00—very easy

176-F. Regain stride on very easy material

22 Pride in work is one thing that will make you like the   12
job you have now. To work so well that you can be proud of   24
what you do and what you turn out, you have to have all the   36
skill that you can use in the job. If you do not have what   48
it takes, you will not do work in which you can take pride.   60

    1 | 2 | 3 | 4 | 5 | 6 | 7 | 8 | 9 | 10 | 11 | 12

176-G. To mark progress and set your goal for Lesson 177, follow the same directions you did when you typed 176-B.

SI 1.39—normal and fully alphabetic

176-G. Now inventory your skill again

23 The core of the problem, one suspects, is the quantity of mail that   15
an office must handle. Mail has a clear habit of multiplying itself. It all   30
starts when a firm targets a broadside to stir up some more business;   44
back come replies, and these evoke replies in turn. And while the ex-   58
change of letters goes on, some zealot, stirred up by the success, if   72
such it be judged, of his prior effort, lets loose with new broadsides,   86
to start new spirals that overlap the first one and create a dizzy chaos   101
that makes the firm use lackluster letters as so many sandbags on the   115
dikes of correspondence. The man who protested that he didn't have   128
time to compose a shorter letter seems to have crystalized the basic   142
problem.   144

    1 | 2 | 3 | 4 | 5 | 6 | 7 | 8 | 9 | 10 | 11 | 12 | 13 | 14

177-A. Tune up by repeating 176-A

177-B. Improve control on opposite-finger preview words

177-B. Type to your goal, defined by 176-G score.

ACCURACY: Each group of lines, as a paragraph, three vigorous times.

SPEED: Each line three times individually.

24 OW flow ow slow ow now ow how WO wonders wo worked wo would
25 GH onslaught gh mighty gh light gh high NG change ng having
26 IC sarcastic ic ironic ic basic UR further ur turns ur sure

    1 | 2 | 3 | 4 | 5 | 6 | 7 | 8 | 9 | 10 | 11 | 12

27 TH whether th there th think th them th that th with th the
28 NT investments nt eloquently nt quantity nt ancient nt want
29 DI directions di dilute di didn't di idioms di dikes di did

10
12
15
16
26
37
46
48
52
53
62
73
83
94
104
113
123
134
142
144
148
149
160
170
181
190

Manuscript 7

OUTLINE
Paper: full sheet
Plan: center an
    exact copy
SI: 1.44—normal

I. MARGINS

    A. Set margin stops to center the average full line, allowing for the first roman numeral.

    B. Center the outline vertically. ↓3

II. INDENTIONS ↓2

    A. Steps are indented 4 spaces each.
       1. Set several tab stops 4 spaces apart.
       2. Indent similar parts in similar steps.

    B. Guide letters or numbers precede the steps.
       1. Follow each guide with a period.
       2. Space twice after the period.

    C. For roman numerals that take more than one space, use the margin release and backspace from the left margin stop.

III. SPACING

    A. Put 2 blank lines before an all-caps line.
    B. Put 1 blank line after an all-caps line.
    C. Single or double space all the other lines, but be consistent in which you use.

CENTER➤

Many typists follow this simple rule: Double space all lines in an outline except "run over" lines.

BIBLIOGRAPHY ↓3

7
9
16
36
41
57
70
89
104
112
114
126
137
150
161
177
184

Manuscript 8

BIBLIOGRAPHY
Paper: full sheet
Plan: center an
    exact copy
SI: 1.41—normal

A. Books ↓2

Book by 1 author
  Ames, James Hill. The Colonials, Rebels. Boston: Cole Press, 1962.

Book by 2 authors
  Barr, Ruth L.; and Blaine, Max H. Background of The Flag. New York: McGraw-Hill, 1963.

Government publication
  U. S. Bureau of the Census. Eighteenth Census of the United States, 1960. Washington: Government Printing Office, 1961. ↓3

B. Magazine Articles

Article by 1 author
  Hughes, Anne Mae. "Paul Revere, Man on a Horse," Newsweek (August 12, 1963), pp. 16-17.

Article by 3 authors
  Krell, John F.; Chan, Lee Ki; and Wilbert, Anne F. "John Adams Said So," Journal of History (June, 1962), pp. 216-232.

LINE: 60
TAB: 5
SPACING: DRILLS SINGLE,
    PARAGRAPHS DOUBLE
DRILLS: THREE TIMES
GOAL: BOOST SKILL FOR
    THREE MINUTES
STRESS: EVEN PACING,
    VIGOROUS STROKES

176-A. Each line three
times, or a half-minute
timing on each line.
Repeat in Lesson 177

176-A. Tune up on these review lines

1 Ken did pay for half the ham, but they paid for the turkey.
2 The day her film took a prize box, Jacqueline was very gay.
3 Type 3 and 6 and 9 and 12 and 15 and 18 and 21 [Continue to 60]

    1 | 2 | 3 | 4 | 5 | 6 | 7 | 8 | 9 | 10 | 11 | 12

176-B. Confirm 60-space
line, 5-tab indention,
and double spacing. The
lines should align.

To determine your goal
for this lesson, take a
3-minute writing or type
one copy (GOAL: Complete
a copy within 3 minutes
and within 1 or 0 error).

If you make 1 or 0 error,
your goal is speed. If
you make 2 or more errors,
your goal is accuracy.

SI 1.34—normal and
fully alphabetic

176-B. Inventory your present skill

4 When you think of how many letters are tossed into the nation's 14
mailbags each day and how many people compose them and read 26
them over, you would guess that by now we would be a nation of 38
mighty expert letter writers. Alas, such isn't the case at all. In spite of 54
high wages, great investments of time, the use of fine machines, and 68
the frenzied efforts of our better writers, a high proportion of our 82
letters are just linguistic junk. You cannot help but wonder whether a 96
bit of the lovely phrasing of olden days came, really, from the slowness 111
of the ancient scribe who worked with a quill. Having time to ponder 125
every nuance as he dipped his pen, he mixed a flow of his personal 138
courtesy with the flow of ink. 144

    1 | 2 | 3 | 4 | 5 | 6 | 7 | 8 | 9 | 10 | 11 | 12 | 13 | 14

176-C. Type to your goal.

ACCURACY: The lines as
a paragraph, three times.

SPEED: Each line three
times, individually.

176-C. Improve control on double-letter preview words

5 correspondents really, letters effort guess dizzy will seem
6 excellent slowness millions tossed cannot dipped still toss
7 correspondence stirred success office loose quill witty all

    1 | 2 | 3 | 4 | 5 | 6 | 7 | 8 | 9 | 10 | 11 | 12

176-D. Type to your goal.

ACCURACY: Lines 8-10 as
a paragraph, three times;
lines 11-13 as paragraph,
two slow-but-even times.

SPEED: Lines 8-10 twice
each; lines 11-13 three
speed-pickup times each.

176-D. Improve control on double-stroke preview words

8 MU multiply MU formula MU much MU must FR frenzied FR frank
9 EC suspects EC injection CE excellent CE success CE offices
10 JU adjust JU judge JU junk NU nuance UN junk UN gun NY many

    1 | 2 | 3 | 4 | 5 | 6 | 7 | 8 | 9 | 10 | 11 | 12

11 RR courtesy RT effort RT squirt RT expert RT short RT start
12 LO eloquent LO slowness LO tailor LO loose LO flow OL olden
13 ED frenzied ED worked ED tossed ED judged ED mixed ED fired

1 When did he go to the city and pay them for the world maps?
2 Max had a zest for quiet living and placed work before joy.
3 At 39:00 & 28:00 & 47:00 & 56:00 & 10:00 & (THEME) (ANNCR:)

48-B. Lines twice. Speed
up on each repetition. To
build confidence in number
control, force yourself to
keep your eyes on the copy!

48-B. Improve control of the number keys

4 we 23 or 94 to 59 up 70 ye 63 it 85 re 43 ow 92 pi 08 et 35
5 wee 233 you 697 try 546 pet 035 wit 285 our 974 tee 533 533
6 weep 2330 true 5473 wore 2943 type 5603 wipe 2803 purr 0744
7 wet 235 tie 583 out 975 yet 635 ore 943 pup 070 tot 595 595

48-C. Make an exact, line-
for-line copy of the letter,
without pausing or raising
your eyes a single time.

Or, take a 5-minute writing
on it; start with carriage
at right margin, ready to
pivot today's date. If you
finish before time is called,
double space and start
over (begin with date).

GOAL: A copy in 5 minutes,
with 4 or fewer errors.

48-C. Sustain your skill in production typing

                                        Current date   12

Mr. Wayne F. Potter   20
Potter & Vince, Inc.   see page   24
3910 Madison Avenue   57   28
New York, New York   10028   34

Dear Wayne: 37

We are pleased to approve your campaign plan for the next   50
radio series, but with the following two changes: 60

1. We wish to strengthen the commercial at the end of the   73
    tenth broadcast. We are enclosing a proposed revision. 85

2. We wish to drop the two Ohio stations from the plan,   98
    for we have no dealers in that state. The revised list 110
    of stations is also enclosed.   117

Please let me know when you have received this note. I   129
shall be eager to hear what you have to say about the new   141
script!   143

                        Sincerely yours,   149
                                                            152
                        Paul Ness Trent   157

urs   159
2 Enclosures   162

Letter 15

BLOCKED LETTER
WITH ENUMERATION
Paper: letterhead
Tab: 4 and center
Line: 4 inches
   (not as shown!)
Body: 92 words
SI: 1.33—fairly
   easy

When a letter has more
than one enclosure, use
correct number and
"Enclosures."

48/49-D. Speed up production of a letter and enclosure

Review letter typing, pages 57-58, then type Letter 15 on a workbook letterhead page. Review tabulation, pages 66-70; then type Table 10 on a full sheet of plain paper. Review enumerations, pages 78-79; then type Manuscript 9 on a full sheet, too.

GOAL: To complete each assignment within 4 errors and 5 minutes from when the paper is inserted.

8 SKILL BUILDING • DICTATED LETTERS
UNARRANGED TABLES • REPORTS

Table 10

4-COLUMN TABLE
Paper: plain, full sheet
Spacing: single,
with items in
3-line groups

THE MONARCH CAMPAIGN (REVISED)

First Quarter, 19--

Station	City	A. M.	P. M.	
WOK	Albany	7:15	6:30	18
WGS	Atlanta	7:30	7:00	32
WCA	Baltimore	6:59	7:30	34
WKB	Buffalo	7:20	7:30	51
WCS	Charleston	7:00	7:45	62
WGI	Greensboro	7:30	7:15	69
WDR	Hartford	6:45	6:45	77
KQV	Pittsburgh	7:00	6:55	85
WPR	Providence	7:45	6:45	93
WRV	Richmond	7:00	7:15	101
WTO	Savannah	6:55	7:05	110
WFB	Syracuse	7:00	7:00	118

CENTER➡

Leaving a blank line after
every three lines makes it
easier to read a long table.

Manuscript 9

RADIO SCRIPT
Paper: plain, full sheet
Spacing: double
Tab: 10 spaces in
from margin
Copies: one exact copy

SCRIPT 10 (REVISED) ↓3

Music	(Theme)	12
Anncr	Your typing tip for today—	13
Music	(Up and fade on theme)	16
Anncr	—from Monarch, the Portable for today!	24
Music	(Up and fade into . . .)	31
Mary	Ralph, get out the Monarch for me, will you?	41
Ralph	Sure, honey. (Sound) Here he is, Monnie,	48
	good old Monnie. (Sound of opening case)	60
Mary	Hey, don't take the machine out of the case!	70
	Just unhook the cover!	80
Ralph	Hey yourself! You SHOULD take any portable	91
	out of its case when you want to type!	97
Anncr	Ralph is right, Mary. Never leave your port-	108
	able in its carrying case. Remember:	117
	"To keep a portable from starting to skid,	128
	Take it out of the case and out of the lid!"	137
Music	(Theme)	146
		156
		160

CENTER➡

A script is an enumeration
by cues, isn't it! Options:
(1) The "cue keys" at the
margin may be in all caps,
and they may be followed
by colons. (2) The material
in parentheses may be
typed in all caps.

incoming letter, add-
ing all the necessary
notations.
Grade: box, page 270;
or panel, page 233
SI: 1.41—normal

October 25, 19—   36

                                                   44

Dr. Graham J. Goodman   50
Head, Department of Speech   55
Michigan State University   60
East Lansing, Michigan   48823   66
                                                   67

Dear Doctor Goodman: 72
                                                   73

I am pleased to tell you that our New York office has sent me   85
the official word that our network will be happy to sponsor   97
the appearance of William Newhouse as a speaker at your next   109
workshop for news broadcasters. This is the message: 120
                                                               121

    Mr. Newhouse will be available to you and to the   133
    University from May 3 through May 7. There will   143
    be no expense to the University; we are pleased to   155
    sponsor him as a service of the network. We are   165
    sure that Mr. Newhouse will wish the full details   176
    about the part he is to play in the program, how   177
    many talks he is to prepare and give, whether he   188
    will be housed on campus, and so on, just as soon   199
    as these matters are settled.   206
                                                               207

I believe, Doctor Goodman, that it would now be appropriate   219
for you to write directly to Mr. Newhouse and give him as many 231
details as you can. If the schedule is not yet fixed, you may 244
wish to note that Mr. Newhouse has Sunday broadcasts before   256
and after your program; so he is certain to be grateful if you 269
can stage him late on Monday and early on Friday.   279
                                                               280

If there is any way in which I can help with arrangements or   292
equipment for your workshop, please let me know.   302
                                                               303

                    Cordially yours,   308

                                                               317

                    Director, Department of   324
                    Service and Public Relations   332
EJLambert:TEK   Radio Station W L K O   339

Blocked Letter with Quotation Paragraph, Three-Line
Signer's Identification, and Signer's Name in Reference Position

PART SEVEN TEST   LESSON 175   272

Progress Test on Part Two

Test 2

Test 2-A

5-MINUTE WRITING
ON PARAGRAPHS
Paper: workbook
    page 71; or plain
Line: 60
Tab: paragraph
Spacing: double
Start: machine set,
    carriage at margin
Grade: box below
SI: 1.34—fairly easy

So you like to hike the trail, do you, and camp in the   12
woods and fish in the lakes and cook over open fires! Then   24
you are one of legions who have that idea. It's been esti-   36
mated that some five million families took such a "four for   48
the price of one" vacation last summer. The national parks   60
themselves had a total of more than thirty million campers.   72

One of the things that surprise us all over again each   84
year is the variety of shelters that vacation campers bring   96
with them, ranging from a simple pup tent to a big imported   108
camping trailer. The most popular type of tent is probably   120
the umbrella tent, with its four corner poles; at least, we   132
see more of this kind than of any other kind. The umbrella   144
comes in two sizes, the 10 by 10 for four people and the 12   156
by 12 for five people. It is easy to put up and even looks   168
nice, for it has a canopy that serves to roof a front porch   180
or kitchen for you. It is usually equipped with a floor of   192
canvas and screens for door and windows.   [START OVER] 200

1 | 2 | 3 | 4 | 5 | 6 | 7 | 8 | 9 | 10 | 11 | 12

5-MINUTE SPEED
WITHIN 4 ERRORS*

40-up wam . . . . . . A
35-39 wam . . . . . . B
25-34 wam C
20-24 wam . . . . . . D

* If more than 4 errors
are made, compute the
speed on what is typed
before the fifth error.

CARE OF THE MACHINE   12

                                           14

1. Daily: Clean the type faces by brushing them   24
    with a stiff brush or by using some commercial   34
    product made for the purpose.   41

2. Daily: Dust the machine carefully, using a   52
    long-handled brush to whisk out the inside and   62
    a soft cloth to wipe off the outside.   71

3. Daily: Wipe off the desk, being sure to wipe   82
    under the machine as well as around it.   91

4. Daily: Keep machine covered when not in use.   102

5. Weekly: Wipe the carriage rails with a soft   113
    cloth that has been dampened in oil. Do not   123
    put oil directly on any part of the machine.   133

6. Monthly: Wipe the cylinder with a soft cloth   144
    that has been dampened in alcohol. [START OVER]   152

1 | 2 | 3 | 4 | 5 | 6 | 7 | 8 | 9 | 10

**Test 2-B
(Manuscript 10)**

5-MINUTE WRITING
ON AN ENUMERATION
Paper: workbook
    page 72; or plain
Center exact copy
Tab: for overruns
Start: machine set,
    carriage centered
Grade: box above
SI: 1.31—fairly easy

Style: a bound page
Grade: box, page 270;
   or panel, page 233

Years	School	Place	Grad
59-60	Empire Bus. Col.	New York, New York	1960
55-59	East Side High School	Newark, New Jersey	1959

EXPERIENCE (Last first)			
Years	Company	Position	Salary
64---	Prudential Life	Secretary	$75
60-64	Paramount Corp.	Stenographer	68

Comments **Plans to take evening-school refresher course and then try test again. Almost passed on first attempt.**

Duplicated personnel card, 6 by 4 inches

SECRETARIAL DUTIES   Page 38

Table 43
How Secretaries Influence Purchases

Item	Percent	Rank
Adding machines	24%	10
Calculating machines	17%	11
Copyholders	39%	5
Desk pen sets	38%	6
Desk staplers	45%	4
Dictation machines	31%	8
Duplicating machines	27%	9
Electric typewriters	48%	1
Manual typewriters	47%	2
Office desks	32%	7
Posture chairs	46%	3
Photocopy equipment	16%	12
Average	**34%**	**—**

16
39
51
60
72
80
87
94
100
107
114
122
129
138
144
151
158
170
176
188

The secretarial influence in purchases of desk and office equipment should be recognized by salesmen. As shown by the figures in Table 43, above, a third of the secretaries say they influence the brand selection in purchases of the items listed.

The editor of the magazine made an interesting comment in her editorial remarks about the survey: ". . . apparently the employers trust their secretaries' judgment more in those things that secretaries themselves will use (45.5 percent) than in the things that will need to be shared with others on the office staff (21.0 percent)."[12]

199
207
215
223
232
241
249
256
265
274
282
291
300
310

12. Sally Browne, "A Survey Told Us So," *Modern Secretary*, Volume 59, No. 11 (July, 1964), page 19.

328
342

Paper: workbook 349
Data: abstract from
   following narrative
Grade: box, page 270;
   or panel, page 233

CARD 1. Robert F. Buckner, of 889 West Bend Street, Terre Haute, Indiana, applied yesterday for a job as accountant but was turned down because your company would not pay the $8,000 a year he requested. Born on May 1, 1932, Mr. Buckner graduated from Indiana University (Bloomington) in 1954 and from Muncie (Ind.) Senior High School in 1950. Since 1963 he has worked as an accountant with H. H. Harris, Inc., at $7,200 a year. Prior to that, he worked from 1959 until 1963 for the Illinois Central Railroad as an accountant at $6,600 a year; and from 1954 to 1959 for the Corning Glass Company as a junior accountant at $5,800 a year. Note: He has a standing offer to join our staff at $7,500 a year.

9
15
24
34
39
49
60
77
85
89
96
103
109
117
129

CARD 2. Harriet B. Stewart, of 177 Third Street, Terre Haute, applied yesterday for a stenographic job. She asked $70 a week, but there was no vacancy. She was born July 12, 1945, and attended Howe High School, in Indianapolis, graduating in 1962. She has worked as a stenographer at $60 a week for the Jackson-Keen Company since June, 1963; and prior to that was a receptionist at the same company at $50 in 1962 and 1963. Note: Miss Stewart should be contacted for the next vacancy.

8
15
30
41
56
71
79
82
89
95
100

If preferred, Tests 2-B, 2-C, and 2-D may each be centered on a page (time: 10 minutes each) and then checked for penalties (Penalty Scale); the total penalty then graded on the Grading Scale.

PENALTY SCALE

—3 for each major error (top margin, line length, line-spacing, general correctness of form, etc.)
—2 for each minor error (blocking, aligning, centering, indenting, etc., of individual parts of the job)
—1 for each typographical error

GRADING SCALE

0-1 PENALTY .... A
2-3 PENALTY .... B
4-6 PENALTY C
7-8 PENALTY .... D

BASIC RATING PLAN FOR TIMED WRITINGS
Five Minutes Within Four Errors

Speeds	Lesson 25	Lesson 50	Lesson 75	
				22
				43
15–19 wam	Fair	Under Par	Under Par	69
20–24 wam	Average	Fair	Under Par	81
25–29 wam	Average	Average	Fair	90
30–34 wam	Superior	Average	Average	99
35–39 wam	Excellent	Superior	Average	109
40–44 wam	Excellent	Excellent	Superior	120
45–49 wam	Excellent	Excellent	Excellent	131
50–up wam	Excellent	Excellent	Excellent	142
				152

[START OVER]

1 | 2 | 3 | 4 | 5 | 6 | 7 | 8 | 9 | 10 | 11

Test 2-C
Table 11

5-MINUTE WRITING ON A TABULATION
Paper: workbook page 73; or plain
Center the table
Spacing: double
Start: machine set, carriage centered
Grade: box below

5-MINUTE SPEED WITHIN 4 ERRORS*
40-up wam ...... A
35-39 wam ...... B
25-34 wam C
20-24 wam ...... D
* If more than 4 errors are made, compute the speed on what is typed before the fifth error.

Test 2-D
Letter 16

5-MINUTE WRITING ON A LETTER
Paper: workbook page 74; or plain
Style: blocked
Tabs: center, 4
Start: machine set, carriage ready to pivot the date
Caution: use correct line and spacing; need initials and enclosure note
Body: 98 words
Grading: box above
SI: 1.36—normal

Today's date 12

Mr. Carl S. Norman 20
The Norman Press, Inc. 24
3947 Fourth Street 29
Louisville, Kentucky   40201 34

Dear Mr. Norman: 39

Please let us know what you would charge to print the 51
two displays that I enclose. Details of these two jobs 62
are as follows: 65

1.   We require 5,000 copies of each job. 75

2.   The table should be set in type styles suitable for 88
display in a dark green ink on a light green card, 99
6 by 4. 101

3.   The listing would be set in a similar type size and 114
displayed in dark brown ink on a buff or a tan card, 124
6 by 4. 127

We would ask for assurance that the cards could be de- 139
livered before January 3. 144

Yours truly, 150

Dexter K. Lynch 158

Closing lines 162

[START OVER]

1 | 2 | 3 | 4 | 5 | 6 | 7 | 8 | 9 | 10 | 11

or 10 min. (1)
Grade: box below
SI: 1.37—easy-normal

first. Just about every person who knows that you can type has said 29
to you that he wishes that he, too, knew how to type; the person who is 43
a skilled typist is the envy of all his friends. One evidence that typing 58
is so popular is shown by the fact that more persons take courses in 72
typing than in anything else (except English, that is; but then, 85
English is a required course). Today it is not just the office trainee 100
who learns to type, although he must, of course; but everyone else 113
seems to be taking the course, too. I visited a college a short time ago 128
and found that the school had just taken a poll to find what purpose 142
the students had in mind when they signed up for typing. You might 155
be amazed at one finding of this poll: enrolled for the typing course 169
was at least one student from every department in the college! 182

It is natural to marvel and to wonder why so many persons desire 197
this skill. The answer is that almost all careers in modern life now 211
involve the use of much paper and require that you be able to express 225
yourself, whether what you wish to report is a new plan for packaging 239
snow, a new scheme for a sales campaign, a history of jazz, a formula 253
for splitting the atom, or a news account of life in Quebec. And the 267
simple truth is that what you write has to be typed. No editor worth 281
his salt would look at a penned manuscript these days; and the modern 295
employer would be aghast if one of his assistants handed him any note 309
of more than a dozen words that was handwritten; he wants them 322
typed! 323

The simple truth is that the typewriter has become an instrument 338
that is used in a great many trades. These would, of course, include 352
the office jobs of a thousand and one kinds, not only secretarial and 366
clerical posts but also the creative ones of editors and writers, and 380
so on. In addition, there are many positions in which the ability to 394
type is a plus value that helps a person meet competition. The field 408
salesman who can type his own reports is preferred to one who cannot. 422
The dental assistant who can type is preferred to one who cannot. An 436
assistant in a physics lab who can type the lab reports is preferred, 450
of course, to one who cannot. We seem to have approached a time 463
when just about everyone had jolly well better become an efficient 477
typist. 478

| 1 | 2 | 3 | 4 | 5 | 6 | 7 | 8 | 9 | 10 | 11 | 12 | 13 | 14 |

5-MINUTE SPEED
WITHIN 2 ERRORS

10-MINUTE SPEED
WITHIN 5 ERRORS

55-up . . . . A
50-54 . . . . B
40-49 C
35-39 . . . . D

If you make excessive
errors, base speed on
what you type prior to
first excessive error

3 SKILL BUILDING • CARDS AND LETTER
DISPLAY • FORMS • REPORTS

Design for a Table of Contents

Manuscripts 62, 63

CONTENTS AND COVER
Paper: plain, full
Style: as shown
Line: 50 spaces

CORRESPONDENCE MANUAL ⎤
                       | Center in
Prepared by | upper half
Charles R. Perkins   ⎦

TYPEWRITING III ⎤
                 | Center in
Miss Mary Bowers, Instructor | lower half
School of Business ⎦
October 10, 19—

Design for a Cover Page

(names show at bottom) and
flip up to reveal recorded data.

| Stevens, | Patrick | A. (Dr.) |
| LAST NAME | FIRST NAME | MIDDLE NAME OR INITIAL |

2. Address: 193 East Montauk Road
3.   Providence, Rhode Island
4.   02904
5. Post: Providence
6. Initiation: September 22, 19--
7. Service: Navy (Medical Corps)
8. Rank: Commander
9. Years Service: 3½
10. Occupation: Physician
11.

| LAST NAME | FIRST NAME | MIDDLE NAME OR INITIAL |
| Stevens, | Patrick | A. (Dr.) |

TYPIST PLEASE NOTE: THIS SCALE CORRESPONDS TO PICA SPACING. If your machine is elite, use the other side of this card. Set the paper guide so that the scale on your machine corresponds to the spacing on this scale. Set the left margin stop at the first arrow and tab stops at the other arrows. Fold back or remove this stub after typing card.

Index Card for a Visible-Index File

Form 70

TRANSFER SHEETS
Form: workbook 343

CORRESPONDENCE TRANSFER

FORWARDING INFORMATION	ORIGINATING INFORMATION
Date: October 12, 19--	Date: October 8, 19--
Dep't To: Sales	Writer: Mrs. Martha Culpepper
Dep't From: Credit	Manager, Ace TV Shop
	318 Multnomah Square
	Seattle, Wash. 98101

YOUR ATTENTION IS CALLED TO THE FOLLOWING, QUOTED FROM THE CITED CORRESPONDENCE:

One more thing, please: I do not think very highly of the
new window-display pieces that you sent us this fall. They
are drab and faded. They do not "pull in the customers
right off the street," as you had said they would. With
better support from your advertising department, maybe my
store could sell some JK sets and get some money to pay the
bill you have been sending me twice a week!

Correspondence Transfer Form

1. Transfer from Sales to Advertising a copy of paragraph
2, letter 77, page 245.

2. Transfer from E. R. Bigler, Accounting, to John Fleshman,
Credit Union, a copy of paragraph 3, Letter 85, page 258.

Unit 9. Skill Development

LINE: 60
TAB: 5
SPACING: SINGLE
DRILLS: THREE TIMES
 EACH
GOAL: TO BOOST BOTH
 SPEED AND CONTROL
STRESS: CORRECT
 POSTURE

51-A. Ripple through lines 1-3 three times each. Try to keep your palms low, but not touching the machine. Repeat in Lesson 52, too.

51-A. Tune up on these easy lines

1   duel rich town pale odor name melt lamb kept cork irks hang
2   Inez says Jack played a very quiet game of bridge with Rex.
3   Did the Halls move to 1028 39th Street or 3947 56th Street?

51-B. To define practice needs, type a double-spaced copy and then proofread it carefully.
 GOAL: To finish it in 3 minutes or less.

Should you make 4 or more typing errors, your goal in Lesson 51 is ACCURACY.

Should you make 3 or fewer typing errors, it is SPEED.

51-B. Measure and improve your skill

4   If you ever get a chance to observe the technique of a   12
truly expert typist, listen to the sound of his typing. It   24
is certain to have a steady flow that seems to waver within   36
a span of a dozen words a minute. When the going is rough,   48
which is to say that the copy is difficult, he drops to his   60
easy pace, which sounds like a jog trot; but when the going   72
is smooth and easy like this turn of words is, he speeds up   84
like a driver turning out to pass another car on a highway.   96
The trick lies in not speeding up or slowing down too much.   108
     1 | 2 | 3 | 4 | 5 | 6 | 7 | 8 | 9 | 10 | 11 | 12

51-C. Practice to achieve your improvement goal:

ACCURACY: The whole group of lines three times.

SPEED: Individually, each drill line three times.

SI 1.31—fairly easy

51-C. Improve control of A, B, C, D, E

5   aaa All aaa aid aaa alas aaa apart aaa salad aaa appeal aaa
6   bbb But fbf bit fbf blob fbf blurb fbf abbot fbf bubble bbb
7   ccc Can dcd cue dcd corn dcd clock dcd click dcd clinic ccc
8   ddd Did ddd dye ddd dude ddd dried ddd idled ddd muddle ddd
9   eee End ded eye ded heel ded elves ded tense ded eleven eee
10   When library books are due back, please take care that   12
they get back, because dedicated readers may be waiting for   24
their chance at them. Anyone can get a book back when due.   36
     1 | 2 | 3 | 4 | 5 | 6 | 7 | 8 | 9 | 10 | 11 | 12

51-D. Type to reach your skill-improvement goal:

ACCURACY: The whole group of lines three times.

SPEED: Each drill line, individually, three times.

SI 1.32—fairly easy

51-D. Improve control of F, G, H, I, J

11   fff For fff off fff buff fff fifth fff fifty fff affair fff
12   ggg Got fgf log fgf gong fgf going fgf soggy fgf groggy fgf
13   hhh Hot jhj the jhj high jhj which jhj hunch jhj higher jhj
14   iii Ink kik did kik Mimi kik visit kik mimic kik liquid kik
15   jjj Job jjj joy jjj just jjj major jjj jewel jjj justly jjj
16   Judge Joy may have just as much fun going to the fifth   12
annual affair as Major Hughes. Fifty to fifty-five mimics,   24
I hear, are going to join a gang of kids and serve liquids.   36
     1 | 2 | 3 | 4 | 5 | 6 | 7 | 8 | 9 | 10 | 11 | 12

LINE: 60
15
G: SINGLE
EE TIMES

three
, or half-minute
writings, to get back
your full typing pace.
Repeat in Lesson 174.

173-A. Tune up on these review lines

1 The chairman of the panel may wish to sign the audit forms.
2 My black ax just zipped through the fine wood quite evenly.
3 Reports #10, #28, and #39 were much harder than #47 or #56.

1 | 2 | 3 | 4 | 5 | 6 | 7 | 8 | 9 | 10 | 11 | 12

173-B. What's your goal?

ACCURACY: Lines 4-7 as
a paragraph, three times.

SPEED: Type each line
individually three times.

173-B. Boost skill by selective preview practice

4 abbreviation resulted United States follow three after body
5 punctuation distinct "close" option letter comma style form
6 expectation (except) pattern (line) common still block ends
7 salutation signature involve phrase commas looks other ones

1 | 2 | 3 | 4 | 5 | 6 | 7 | 8 | 9 | 10 | 11 | 12

173-C. Change machine to
50-space line (lines will
align), double spacing,
5-space tab indention.

Type one complete copy.

SI 1.44—upper normal

ALTERNATE PLAN:
1. Take a 5-minute timed
writing, resting for 10
seconds after each minute.

2. Take a 5-minute timed
writing without rests.

GOAL: To type 45 or more
wam within 2 errors.

173-C. Sustain skill on production copy

Part 3. Letter Punctuation Styles

The punctuation used in the *body* of a letter involves no option; 16
the demands of proper English must be met. But in the punctuation 29
that follows the ends of the *display lines* above and below the letter 48
body, there *is* option; and it has resulted in three distinct styles for 63
use with such lines. 67

A. Standard Style. This is the one in most common use. It re- 88
quires the salutation to end in a colon, the closing phrase to end in 102
a comma; no other punctuation, except for the period after an abbre- 116
viation, is used to end or to "close" any of the letter parts that precede 131
or follow the body. 135

B. Open Style. In this pattern, no display line—not even a 154
salutation or a closing phrase—ends with a punctuation mark. The 167
lone exception is a line that ends with an abbreviation; it will have a 182
period after it. When a letter is written in this style, it has a clean, 196
modern look to it. 202

C. Closed Style. This design, once in wide use in the United 222
States and still in wide use in other countries, requires some punc- 235
tuation at the end of every display line to "close" it. All the display 240
lines end with either a period or a comma except the salutation, which 254
ends with the colon. The comma is used to close each line of an inside 269
address (except the last line) and each line of a signature block (except 283
the last line); all other display lines must be closed with a final period. 299

1 | 2 | 3 | 4 | 5 | 6 | 7 | 8 | 9 | 10 | 11 | 12 | 13 | 14

173/174-D. Apply skill to production assignments

Manuscript 60

BOUND REPORT (10)
Include page heading
to identify this
material as page 10

Manuscript 61

PREFACE
Use 169-C, typed on
a 60-space line,
double spaced, be-
ginning on line 11

UNIT 28

51-E. Type to reach your skill-improvement goal:

ACCURACY: The whole group of lines three times.

SPEED: Each drill line, individually, three times.

SI 1.32—fairly easy

17 kkk Key kkk eke kkk kick kkk knick kkk knack kkk knocks kkk

18 lll Lay lll all lll will lll level lll allot lll little lll

19 mmm Map jmj jam jmj maim jmj mimic jmj madam jmj moment mmm

20 nnn Nay jnj nag jnj nine jnj inner jnj anent jnj winnow nnn

21 ooo Oak lol own lol odor lol motor lol moron lol follow ooo

22 Oliver King may not like lemons or lemons may not like   12

him, but my dollars will take even money that Mr. King will   24

not balk at eating lemon meringue pie like my mother makes.   36

   1 | 2 | 3 | 4 | 5 | 6 | 7 | 8 | 9 | 10 | 11 | 12

51-F. Make an interim progress check

51-F. To confirm progress in Lesson 51 and to set your goal for Lesson 52, repeat 51-B, page 85.

52-A. Learn to type on and center on a line

52-A. The numbers within parentheses refer to the numbered machine parts that are shown on pages 2-5. Machines vary; so:

(1) Type a solid line of underscores; how much space, if any, shows between the line and aligning scale?

(2) Check whether variable spacer on your machine (the button in the left cylinder knob) must be pressed in or, on some models, pulled out to adjust line of writing.

(3) Determine how to adjust the ribbon control so that the ribbon is disengaged (to set it for stencil). A typical arrangement:

STEP 1. Adjust the paper to place the line in the position that a line of underscores would occupy.

To loosen the paper while you adjust it, use the paper release (24).

To turn the paper slightly up or down, turn the left cylinder knob while the palm of your left hand presses the variable spacer (43, the button in the left cylinder knob).

To test the position of the line, type one *light* underscore stroke with the ribbon-control lever (35) set for stencil (disengaged).

<u>Too Low</u>
Too High
<u></u>
<u>Just Right</u>

STEP 2. Determine how many spaces to indent the typing from the start of the line: set the carriage at the start of the line; tap the space bar once for each space the typed line will fill; then (counting strokes) continue spacing to the end of the line to find how many spaces remain to be divided around the name.

<u>? John Jones ?</u>
<u>John Jones12345678</u>
<u>1234John Jones5678</u>

PRACTICE. Draw 10 straight lines, varying from 3 to 4 inches long, on a sheet of paper. Insert the paper and center your name on each line.

TOP
MIDDLE
BOTTOM
STENCIL

52-B. Improve control of P, Q, R, S, T

52-B. Type to your goal as redefined in 51-F, above.

ACCURACY: The whole group of lines three times.

SPEED: Each drill line, individually, three times.

SI 1.34—fairly easy

23 ppp Pay ;p; pen ;p; prop ;p; upper ;p; paper ;p; prompt ppp

24 qqq Que aqa qui aqa quit aqa quell aqa queen aqa quaint qqq

25 rrr Roy frf rug frf roar frf error frf carry frf repair rrr

26 sss Sue sws sis sws loss sws sales sws issue sws system sss

27 ttt Tom ftf tot ftf mutt ftf title ftf total ftf static ttt

28 Roy stated that he thought aqua paper was pretty. Sue   12

says statistics show that total sales of white paper do far   24

surpass aqua sales. Queen plans to get six quires of aqua.   36

   1 | 2 | 3 | 4 | 5 | 6 | 7 | 8 | 9 | 10 | 11 | 12

Manuscript 59
Table 49

BOUND REPORT (9)
Caution: Won't you
need some of the
material here to
fill out page 8?

                                                                       10
                                                                       14

Table 5

SOME CORRECT FORM(S) OF ENCLOSURE NOTATIONS   41
                                                                       52
                                                                       63
                                                                       73

One Enclosure	More than One	Enumerated
Enclosure	2 Enclosures	Enclosures:
Enc.	2 Encs.	Check
Encl.	2 Enc.	Invoice
1 Enc.	Enc. 2	
1 Enclosure	Enclosures (2)	Enclosures—
Check Enclosed	Enclosures: 3	1. #Check
Bill Enclosed	Enclosures—4	2. Bill

83
90
96
100
110
120
130
141
144

Make this quotation
No. 10 and cite this
page of this book as
the source for it. Is
there an appropriate
abbreviation you can
use? Review page 263.

5 ← Typing <u>Enclosure</u> or <u>3 Enclosures</u> is enough in most   160
← case, but "It is important to identify enclosures if any   172
is small, if any is valuable (as a check would be), or if   183
~~someone~~ other than the typist will seal and mail the letter."   197
¶ The only time when an enclosure notation can be omitted is   210
when a letter is formal (when the address is at the bottom)   222

N. The <u>Post Script</u> is a an extra paragraph added at the very bottom   244
of the letter and is ~~treated as such if it is~~ indented or ~~is~~   250
blocked as are the other paragraphs. The initials <u>PS.</u>, <u>PS:</u>,   263
<u>P. S.</u>, or <u>PS—</u> are typed at the start of the paragraph.   274

O. The "cc" <u>notation</u> is typed under the (enc) notation   295
to indicate to the addressee that carbon copies (hence "cc")   308
have been ~~are being~~ sent to the persons indicated. Samples of styles: 320

cc Miss Hall ← 6/# → cc JJH ← 6/# → cc: Hall   338
cc Mr. Lewis   cc FJL   Lewis   356

P. The "bcc" Notation indicates to   373
whom copies of the letter have been   379
sent without the addressee's know-   386
ing it. "Blind carbon copies" (hence   393
"bcc") are identified: 398

[Typist: Insert here the second
and third sentences, para. 7, page 246,   516
of the typewriting book.]

Make the quotation
No. 11. Don't forget
to footnote it!

52-C. Improve control of U, V, W, X, Y, Z

52-C. Practice to achieve
your improvement goal.

ACCURACY: The whole
group of lines three times.

SPEED: Each drill line,
individually, three times.

SI 1.51—fairly rough

29   uuu Use juj ups juj dual juj usual juj usury juj unused uuu
30   vvv Vow fvf vie fvf view fvf vivid fvf valve fvf velvet vvv
31   www Why sws two sws wavy sws which sws would sws wigwam www
32   xxx Six sxs box sxs next sxs taxis sxs index sxs extras xxx
33   yyy You jyj yet jyj year jyj yearn jyj yards jyj heyday yyy
34   zzz Zip aza zoo aza zone aza zeros aza azure aza zigzag zzz

35   Zimmy will amaze you, I know, with his unusually even,   12
speedy typing. Six or seven times every week, he types for   24
an extra hour or two to very even music, to improve rhythm.   36

   1 | 2 | 3 | 4 | 5 | 6 | 7 | 8 | 9 | 10 | 11 | 12

52-D. Speed up on downhill preview words

52-D. Type to your goal:
ACCURACY: The whole
group of lines three times.

SPEED: Each drill line,
individually, three times.

One-hand words:

"ed" words:

Double letters:

Alternate-hand words:

36   betters brash only zest seat upon were ever you at no be in
37   directed precede hailed raised failed pledge named tried ed
38   affectionate installed college recall issue guess good door
39   problem social worms right them duty than clan they own the

52-E. Measure your skill in sustained writing

52-E. To measure your
skill improvement, follow
either of these two
schedules: (1) Type
paragraph 40 two times.

GOAL: To finish either
copy within 5 or fewer
minutes and with not
more than 4 typing errors.

(2) Or, take two 5-minute
writings on the article.

GOAL: 35 or more words a
minute, within 4 errors.
(Record the better score.)

In either case, use a tab-
5 paragraph indention and
double space the copy.

SI 1.34—nearly normal

IDEA: Use both paragraphs
for stretching your skill,
not for testing your skill:

(1) Take a 5-minute timing
with a 10-second rest after
each of the minutes; then,

(2) Take a 5-minute timing
without rests but with the
minutes called off, so that
you can see whether or not
you are staying on pace.

40   When I was a college boy and a pledge to a fraternity,   12
the good brothers had a number of rules by which they tried   24
to acquaint us unworthy ones with the right paths of social   36
behavior. There was a rule, for example, that no one of us   48
worms, as we were affectionately named, should ever precede   60
one of our betters, and you can guess who were our betters,   72
through a doorway but rather were directed to open the door   84
and hold it open as a gesture of love and service. The one   96
who failed in this duty would be hailed before the tribunal   108
and instructed in manners with a justice and zest that went   120
at once to the heart, or the seat, of the problem. I still   132
tingle each time I hold the door open for my own fair lady.   144

41   Well, one day the college installed a lot of revolving   156
doors at its many entrances and exits. Can you imagine the   168
problem that this made for the fraternal clan? These doors   180
were very heavy, and it was next to impossible to push them   192
without going through them. If any of us worms had to open   204
the door by pushing it, he then had to precede his superior   216
through the doorway. Always a brash person, I was the worm   228
who raised the issue; and I spoke more eloquently about the   240
subject than a worm should, as I recall painfully.   250

   1 | 2 | 3 | 4 | 5 | 6 | 7 | 8 | 9 | 10 | 11 | 12

J. The attention line, ~~is~~ an extension of the inside ad-   20

dress, ~~and~~ is typed between the inside address and salutation.   32

It is _always_ precede^d and followed by (1) blank line. It is usually   46

blocked left but may be centered~~, too.~~ It may be arranged in   58

many different styles, as shown in Table 4, below.   68

½" #   71

Table ~~5~~ 4   77

← confirm this

STYLES OF ~~MODERN~~ ATTENTION AND SUBJECT LINES   100

112

| (Subject) Lines | (Attention) Lines | 122
|---|---|

133

| ATTENTION: CREDIT MANAGER | SUBJECT: SPECIAL SALE | 144
| Attention: Credit Manager | Subject: Special Sale | 172
| Attention of the President | Subject--Special Order | 200
| Attention of the President | Subject--Special ~~Sale~~ _Order_ | 216
| Attention Legal Department | Refer to File 158-6599 | 233
| ATTENTION Mr. ~~Jack Dennis~~ _John Parsons_ | RE: The Lewiston Case | 243
| Attention of Mr. Jack Dahl | In re Shaw vs. Shipley | 260

272

½" #   275

K. #The Subject Line is a preview of the message and so   357

is typed between the salutation and the body. It may _be_ ^cen-   369

tered; it may be blocked at the left. It _may_ ~~can~~ be arranged in   381

many different styles, as shown in Table 4 [Tell where it is].   391

Since the purpose of an attention line is to direct   286

the letter to a particular person in the company,   297

the inclusion of this line does not change the saluta-   309

tion. The letter is addressed to the firm; there-   323

fore, the salutation must be Gentlemen.8   337

L. The Company Signature is typed in all-capitals, a _letters_   414

double space below the complimentary closing. Illustrations   426

of its use are shown in Table 3, Page 6. It is often left   438

out, but ~~is sometimes~~ _may be_ required ." . . . when the letter in-   447

volves an obligation of the company rather than _of the_ ^signer."9   461

M. _The_ ^Enclosure Notations ~~are~~ _is a_ signal, like the ones shown in   485

Table 5, next page, to remind both ^_the_ sender and ^_the_ receiver ^_of a letter_ that   500

something is enclosed in the same envelope. The notation is   512

typed ~~one~~ _a_ or two lines below the ~~reference~~ initials.   521

Manuscript 58

BOUND REPORT (8)
Caution: You must determine where to end page 7 and to start page 8; do not forget heading at top of page 8.

QUOTATION REMINDERS

1. A quotation taking three or fewer lines of typing is displayed in quotation marks. Longer quotations are not put in quotation marks but are displayed in single spacing and indented 5 spaces on each margin.

2. Make and insert the footnote for quotation No. 8. It is from page 18 of the book by Gavin, previously mentioned (see page 261).

3. Make and insert the footnote for quotation No. 9. It is from page 97 of the book by Lloyd, previously mentioned (see pages 262, 263).

4. Ellipsis (. . .) indicates omission.

Skill Drive

LINE: 60
TAB: 5
SPACING: SINGLE
DRILLS: THREE TIMES
   EACH
GOAL: BOOST SKILL
STRESS: KEEPING
   BACKS OF HANDS
   FLAT

53-A. Set a smooth pace on line 1; then hold the pace on lines 2 and 3. Repeat this warmup in Lesson 54.

53-A. Tune up on these easy lines

1   paid firm born hand pair land burn busy form half soap sigh

2   Five or six dozen clubs may sign up with Karl for jonquils.

3   Did it happen on May 10, 1956; May 3, 1947; or May 1, 1928?

53-B. To define practice needs, type a double-spaced copy; then proofread it carefully. GOAL: To finish it in 3 minutes or less.

If you make 3 or more typing errors, your practice goal in Lesson 53 is ACCURACY.

If you make 2 or fewer typing errors, your goal is SPEED.

SI 1.37—normal

53-B. Measure and improve your skill

4   About the time when our parents were children, two out   12
of ten American citizens lived in a city. The others lived   24
on farms or in small towns where most people lived in homes   36
with lawns, knew each other well, and enjoyed an atmosphere   48
of quiet calm. The picture has changed today; seven out of   60
ten now live in cities or close to them, not because cities   72
are better places in which to live but because there exists   84
in the urban centers something that mechanization has taken   96
from the farm and the forest: the chance to make a living.   108

   1 | 2 | 3 | 4 | 5 | 6 | 7 | 8 | 9 | 10 | 11 | 12

53-C. Type to reach your practice goal, with special attention to keeping wrists from swinging in and out.

ACCURACY: The whole group of lines three times.

SPEED: Each drill line, individually, three times.

SI 1.54—difficult

53-C. Improve control of sideway motions

5   AFA affix afar ARA arrow rain ATA attic data AGA again saga

6   LJL jural jell LUL lucid dull LYL slyly duly LHL lathe hall

7   ABA papal baby AVA avail vain ZGZ graze gaze QTQ quiet quit

8   LNL banal only LML balms melt PHP graph soph PYP happy pure

9   The photographer tried an hour to get the baby to look   12
happy and sit quietly. He finally got a dull photograph of   24
the baby gazing stupidly, slyly, at an array of jelly jars.   36

   1 | 2 | 3 | 4 | 5 | 6 | 7 | 8 | 9 | 10 | 11 | 12

53-D. Type to reach your goal; keep hands quiet—don't let them bounce!

ACCURACY: The whole group of lines three times.

SPEED: Each drill line, individually, three times.

SI 1.30—fairly easy

53-D. Improve control of vertical motions

10   BTB baton tubs BRB bribe ribs CTC catch tact CRC crack rich

11   NYN money yank NUN nutty unit MYM maybe hymn MUM mummy bump

12   XEX vexed exit XWX waxen waxy ZEZ dozen maze BEB begin ebbs

13   NIN ninth nine NON north once MIM mimic rims MOM month some

14   Monty may bring a bunch of records to give as our door   12
prize on the ninth. At the next meeting, maybe someone can   24
bring us six extra boxes of candy or crackers or something.   36

   1 | 2 | 3 | 4 | 5 | 6 | 7 | 8 | 9 | 10 | 11 | 12

Manuscript 56
Table 47
BOUND REPORT (6)

CORRESPONDENCE MANUAL   Page 6   8
                                                                         10
                                                                         14
Table 3

SOME CORRECT ARRANGEMENTS FOR CLOSING LIN~E~S   42
                                                                         55
                                                                         64
Cordially yours,	Yours very truly,	66
2 #		
Vice-President	Vice-President, Research ~Personnel~	76
		87
Very sincerely yours,	Respectfully submitted,	98
2 #		100
Paul Todd, President	Secretary to Mr. Wilson	111
		123
Yours very truly,	Sincerely yours,	132
THE KERR CORPORATION	DOWN CONSTRUCTION COMPANY	144
2 #.		146
Harrison Dwyer	Richard Markham Graham	157
President	General Manager	166
		177
Yours truly,	Very cordially yours,	187
THE INTERNATIONAL COMPANY	S T Y L E , 3# I N C .	199
2 #		201
Parke Alexander	Mrs. Ruth Mann Osborne	211
Chairman of the Board	Advertising Department	221
		233

TECHNICAL NOTES:

1. Underscore rules are often used to divide long tables and displays.

2. For equal space above and below a line, single space before typing it and double space after it.

3. To save space, leave only two blank lines in each signature space.

4. For fast production, just copy the indentions in Column 1 by visual inspection; but do tabulate to start of Column 2.

236

move out to margin

THE SUPPLEMENTAL LETTER PARTS   244

_5_ In the course of many years *of business communication*, the business letter has   260

picked up a *number of* ~great many~ extra parts to serve particular   271

purposes. *While* None of these *parts are* ~is~ essential for getting a message   286

across to the addressee, ~but~ they do serve as aids to him,   297

or to the writer, *or to both,* or to their secretaries. ¶ Table 2, ~on~   311

Page 3, lists eight supplemental letter parts.   320

I # The Reference Line is used in businesses where (re   341

cords are kept in numerical files or *where* transactions are   353

handled by a very large staff. # It is a line, *like* When reply-   368

ing, Refer to, printed in the letterhead. The typist of   385

an out-going letter types the correct file number *beneath* ~alongside~   396

that reference guide. ¶ When replying to *a letter with* such a notation,   412

a ~the~ typist includes a subject line (in which he refers to   423

the same reference file number) in his letter of response.   435

Manuscript 57
Table 48
BOUND REPORT (7)

Caution: You must determine where to end page 6 and start page 7.

53-E. Type to reach your practice goal, with very special attention given to continuity—don't let the copy break your rhythm.

ACCURACY: The whole group of lines three times.

SPEED: Each drill line, individually, three times.

SI 1.32—fairly easy

53-F. Repeat 53-B, page 88, to confirm your progress and to pinpoint goals for Lesson 54.

54-A. Using the aligning scale to align insertions is important not only for inserting a missing letter but also in all kinds of corrections of work and in the use of all kinds of fill-in business forms.

Different typewriters vary in the precision of the placement of the aligning scale; this is why it is so important to note closely the position of the scale on any machine you use.

53-E. Improve control of one-hand words

15 effect minion after knoll zest only fear pool gab him at no

16 limply agreed hilly wages lion were puny safe you bad up be

17 feared lumpy, extra union gate milk fast lily car hop as in

18 pinion accede pylon trace junk fees link rate joy was no we

19 dreads nylon, cases join; ease pill test holy set ink as in

20 In my opinion, we were in bad after you set up a union   12

rate on wages. We feared a million ill effects. I dreaded   24

a union fee. I gave in only after you set up better rates.   36

      1 | 2 | 3 | 4 | 5 | 6 | 7 | 8 | 9 | 10 | 11 | 12

53-F. Make an interim progress check

54-A. Learn how to make typed insertions

The key to correct typed insertions is the alignment of your typing with your machine's aligning scale. Right now, type the alphabet on your machine and compare your typing and aligning scale with this illustration:

1. To align insertions *vertically*, you must know *exactly* how much space (if any) there is between the typing and the top of the aligning scale.

2. To align insertions horizontally, you must know *exactly* how nearly the markers on the scale come to the center of the letters (easiest to check:

i, l, m, I, T, period, colon).

PRACTICE 1. Type this name (with space left for the omitted letters) in four places on a sheet of paper:

M ss El a W ll amson

Remove the paper, reinsert it, and fill in the missing letters:

Wrong: Miss Ella Williamson
Right: Miss Ella Williamson

Use the variable spacer (in the left cylinder knob) for vertical adjustments of the paper. Use the paper release for horizontal adjustments.

PRACTICE 2. In four places on the paper, type FROM: and, under it, TO:. Remove the paper, reinsert and align it, and then type your name 2 or 3 spaces after each of the colons.

54-B. Improve control of double-letter words

54-B. Type to reach your goal, with special attention given to accenting second letter of the doubles as much as the first letter.

ACCURACY: Type the group of lines three times.

SPEED: Type each drill, individually, three times.

SI 1.42—normal

21 bb bubble cc accent dd middle ee needle ff suffer gg logger

22 ll bullet mm jammer nn dinner oo poodle pp dapper rr borrow

23 ss issues tt putter zz sizzle bb lubber cc accord dd puddle

24 ee keeper ff muffle gg rigger ll called mm hammer nn annoys

25 oo rooter pp supply rr mirror ss missed tt little zz puzzle

26 Bill Mazzle needs a bookkeeper and will see applicants   12

tomorrow. He will screen all who apply. He will arrange a   24

follow-up meeting for all who seem well fitted for the job.   36

      1 | 2 | 3 | 4 | 5 | 6 | 7 | 8 | 9 | 10 | 11 | 12

LINE: 60
TAB: 5
SPACING: SINGLE
DRILLS: THREE TIMES
GOAL: SUSTAIN SKILL
    IN STEADY TYPING
STRESS: EARNEST
    KEEP-GOING-NESS

171-A. Each line three times at a very steady, word-eating pace. Repeat 171-A in Lesson 172.

171-A. Tune up on these easy review lines

1 The men may fix their antique auto and go downtown with it.
2 Jack found the gravel camp six below zero quite a few days.
3 The 10's, 28's, 39's, 47's, and 56's make up pair patterns.

  1 | 2 | 3 | 4 | 5 | 6 | 7 | 8 | 9 | 10 | 11 | 12

171-B. Three copies at least, plus as many more as may be required for you to produce at least one copy without error. Repeat in Lesson 172.

SI 1.03—VERY easy

171-B. Restore full skill on very easy material

4 The men quit their work to run down the dock and catch   12
the light lines we threw from the deck of the big ship. In   24
no time at all, the men on the dock had pulled in the light   36
lines and the thick ropes we had tied to them. The men got   48
the end of each rope looped over a post, and then we turned   60
to the deck engines to take up the slack and so pull us in.   72

  1 | 2 | 3 | 4 | 5 | 6 | 7 | 8 | 9 | 10 | 11 | 12

171-C. Change machine to double spacing and check margins for 60-space line (lines will align) and a 5-space tab indention.

ACCURACY: Type each of the paragraphs once.

SPEED: Type any one of the paragraphs three or more consecutive times.

Repeat in Lesson 172.
SI 1.25—easy

171-C. Sustain full skill on easy alphabetic paragraphs

5 One of the smartest girls I know is one who sat beside me when   14
I took a course in typing. She was not the fastest typist in our class,   28
and modesty will not let me say who it was that acquired this honor;   42
but it was she who turned out the most and best work. It happened,   56
over and over. While the rest of us were still analyzing the problem,   70
that young lady would be poking keys. No job was too complex for   83
her.   84

6 One day I asked her how she did it. I expected her to say she had   99
acquired a key to the problems, like the one an instructor gets, and   112
that she simply studied the key before coming to class each day. Or,   126
I thought, perhaps she would say that she had taken the same course   140
somewhere else, even using the same book; that would justify her   153
success. But I was wrong; her answer left me amazed at her coy   166
craftiness.   168

7 She paused before giving her reply, and I pressed with more ques-   182
tions. No, she did not have a machine at home nor one she could   195
borrow. No, she did not have an answer book. I must have looked   208
exasperated or something, for she turned on a suspicious but dazzling   222
smile and asked whether I felt it unjust to study the book and solve   236
the problems ahead of time. No, I did not. A light dawned. What   250
I mean, smart!   253

  1 | 2 | 3 | 4 | 5 | 6 | 7 | 8 | 9 | 10 | 11 | 12 | 13 | 14

171-D. Before resuming work on the Manual, you would find it helpful to review information about footnotes given on pages 115, 116, 120.

171/172-D. Continue typing the Correspondence Manual

54-C. Improve control of alternate-hand words

54-C. Type to reach your goal, with special attention to striking keys so briskly these key-jammers don't!

ACCURACY: Type the whole group three times.

SPEED: Type each drill, individually, three times.

SI 1.12—very easy

27   apricot island visit their when rich town man and for go is
28   bicycle profit vigor field dish down kept dog the but an to
29   bushels laughs right works land fish girl sit pay bid so by
30   rituals eighty turns roams with firm lake eye big men do he
31   auditor icicle goals shape body auto both fit cut aid of it

32   Did the men make a visit to the auto firm in the city,   12
or did they go to the firm at the lake? If they got to the   24
lake, Bob may pay for the auto and also land a fish for us.   36
   1 | 2 | 3 | 4 | 5 | 6 | 7 | 8 | 9 | 10 | 11 | 12

54-D. Measure your skill in sustained writing

54-D. To measure your skill improvement, follow either schedule (use double spacing and a tab-5 indention):

(1) Type paragraph 33 twice. GOAL: To finish either copy within 5 minutes, with 4 or fewer typing mistakes.

(2) Or, take two 5-minute timings on the paragraphs; record your better score. GOAL: 35 or more words a minute, within 4 errors.

SI 1.31—fairly easy

33   Many years ago, when the Post Office asked that a zone   12
number be shown in city addresses as a means of speeding up   24
the handling of the mail, there was no problem about typing   36
the zone number; it was placed after the city, was followed   48
by a comma, and then was followed by the name of the state.   60
But when the Post Office brought ZIP numbers into being and   72
again asked that a change be made in the form of addressing   84
letters and cards, there was quite a problem: The scanning   96
machines could do their jobs only if the ZIP number was set   108
off from the rest of the address. So writers were asked to   120
shift the zone guide from after the city to after the state   132
and to leave some space between the state and the ZIP Code.   144

IDEA: To use the paragraphs for skill stretching instead of testing, (a) take a 5-minute writing; (b) type every line in which you made an error three times each; and (c) repeat the 5-minute timing to measure growth.

34   How much space? Pressed on this item, the Post Office   156
just said the space ought not to be less than two spaces or   168
more than six spaces on a pica typewriter. Translated into   180
elite spacing, that would be not less than three spaces and   192
not more than seven spaces. Wanting to come up with a firm   204
and single recommendation that would fit all machines best,   216
the authors of this book selected three spaces as the right   228
number on which to standardize, which explains why you will   240
frequently be reminded to space three times before you type   252
a ZIP number. You are told to do this both on the envelope   264
and in the inside address so that you will get the habit of   276
always ending any address with three spaces and a ZIP Code.   288
   1 | 2 | 3 | 4 | 5 | 6 | 7 | 8 | 9 | 10 | 11 | 12

In a display like this, center longest line and align others with it.

```
Mr. Clark Hess, Manager            15
Florida Fashion Company            22

Dr. Lawrence Coulter               28
Secretary—Treasurer                34

Miss Rowena G. Thompson            41
Manager, Seabeach Hotel            48
```

The factor that determines in which position the title should be [61] placed is the length of the lines, which should be kept as nearly [74] equal as possible. Rowe and his coauthors say, "Use the position [87] that best equalizes the lines of the address."[4] [97]

D. *The Salutation* is placed between the inside address and body. [119] It is typed at the left margin, always preceded and followed by a [132] blank line. It is almost always followed by the colon. One should [145] capitalize only the first word, any title, and any noun; thus, *Dear* [160] *Doctor Jones* vs. *My dear Doctor Jones.* [179]

E. *The Body* contains the message. It is most likely to be single [198] spaced with a blank line between paragraphs. If a letter is very short [212] (50 or fewer words) or if it is a report that is several pages long, it [226] may be double spaced. [231]

F. *The Complimentary Closing* is the signing-off phrase. It begins [257] at the left margin in some letter arrangements; but most commonly [270] it begins at, or near, the center. It almost always ends with a comma. [285] Only the first word is capitalized. [292]

G. *The Signer's Identification,* which is typed under the space [318] left for the handwritten signature, may be the name, or the title (or [332] department), or both, of the writer. Illustrations of various arrange- [346] ments and various combinations of the signer's identification are [359] given in Table 3, next page. [Page 265.] [365]

Three blank lines are ordinarily left for the penwritten signature, [380] but some leeway is allowed; the space may be "up to 6 blank lines"[5] [395] or "as few as 2 blank lines."[6] [402]

H. *The Reference Initials* include the initials of the letter dic- [426] tator (unless his name appears under the signature) and those of the [440] typist, separated by some kind of mark. The common forms are [452] *DIC:TYP* and *DIC/typ* when both sets are used and *TYP* and *typ* [472] when only the initials of the typist appear. [481]

The reference initials are typed at the left margin two lines below [496] the identification of the signer but can be typed higher or lower when [510] doing so will improve letter placement.[7]   [Continues on page 265] [520]

[526]

———————————

3. John L. Rowe, *et al., Gregg Typing, 191 Series, Book One* (New [555] York: McGraw-Hill, 1962), page 112. [562]

4. *Ibid.,* page 138.   6. *Loc. cit.* [576]
5. Lloyd, *op. cit.,* page 57.   7. *Loc. cit.* [593]

CAUTION!

1. Stop the page-4 text in time to get footnotes 3 and 4 on that page and still maintain the bottom margin of 1-1½ inches.

2. Provide the proper heading for page 5, too.

Manuscript 55

BOUND REPORT (5)

IN THE FOOTNOTES:

1. "Et al." means "and others."

2. "Ibid." means "same book as in the preceding footnote, but reference is on a different page."

3. "Op. cit." means "in the book by this author named in a previous (but not the preceding) footnote."

4. "Loc. cit." means "in the same place as the preceding footnote" (same book and same page).

5. Short footnotes may be typed beside or below one another, whichever is best for bottom margin.

Skill Drive

LINE: 60
TAB: 5
SPACING: SINGLE
DRILLS: EACH THREE
TIMES
GOAL: BOOST SKILL
ESPECIALLY NUMBER
CONTROL
STRESS: TOUCH
CONTROL

55-A. Alternate line 1 and line 2, line 1 and line 3, etc. Repeat in Lesson 56.

55-B. To define practice goals, make two double-spaced copies of paragraph 4; proofread your work.

GOAL: To complete the two copies within 3 minutes, without looking up once.

Your goal in Lesson 55 is ACCURACY if you make 3 or more errors.

Your goal is SPEED if you make 2 or fewer errors.

SI 1.25—easy (if you know your number keys well!)

55-C. Type to reach your skill-improvement goal.

ACCURACY: The whole group of lines three times.

SPEED: Each drill line, individually, three times.

SI 1.15—easy IF

55-D. Type to reach your skill-improvement goal.

ACCURACY: Type the whole group three times.

SPEED: Type each drill, individually, three times.

SI 1.12—easy IF

55-E. Type to your goal.

ACCURACY: Type the whole group three times.

SPEED: Type each drill, individually, three times.

SI 1.33—fairly easy IF

SUGGESTION: For certain number-key control, focus practice on 3, 6, and 9 until they are as automatic as ABC. If you do this, the numbers will be easy.

55-A. Tune up on these easy lines

1   town them when form down dock firm with girl work both they

2   Vi found Jack was right: Pam was being quite lazy and lax.

3   I plan to study pages 10, 28, 39, 47, and 56 for that test.

55-B. Measure and improve number-typing skill

4   He expects a special group of 180 to 195 to attend the   12

June 17 meeting. About 43 of these are due from St. Louis,   24

37 to 46 from Nashville, 28 or 29 from Louisville, 46 to 50   36

from Knoxville, plus about 25 or 30 local members, as well.   48

   1 | 2 | 3 | 4 | 5 | 6 | 7 | 8 | 9 | 10 | 11 | 12

55-C. Improve control of 1, 2, 3, 4

5   111 a1a1a a1a The 11 teams played 11 games with 11 players.

6   222 s2s2s s2s The 22 men got 22 tickets for the 2:22 train.

7   333 d3d3d d3d The 33 boys had 33 books with 33 stamps each.

8   444 f4f4f f4f The 44 dogs had 44 collars with 44 gold tags.

9   Try to get Order No. 31 out on the 12:43 train. Then,   12

if you can, get Order No. 42 out on the next train at 3:42.   24

   1 | 2 | 3 | 4 | 5 | 6 | 7 | 8 | 9 | 10 | 11 | 12

55-D. Improve control of 5, 6, ½, ¼

10   555 f5f5f f5f The 55 men checked 55 references in 55 books.

11   $\frac{1}{2}\frac{1}{2}\frac{1}{2}$;$\frac{1}{2}$;$\frac{1}{2}$; ;$\frac{1}{2}$; The 9$\frac{1}{2}$ size sells 1$\frac{1}{2}$ times as many as the 8$\frac{1}{2}$.

12   $\frac{1}{4}\frac{1}{4}\frac{1}{4}$;$\frac{1}{2}$;$\frac{1}{4}$; ;$\frac{1}{4}$; The first $\frac{1}{4}$ includes $\frac{1}{4}$ as many as the last $\frac{1}{4}$.

13   666 j6j6j j6j The 66 tests were for 66 girls in 66 classes.

14   Map 56 shows the steep climb between $\frac{1}{4}$ and $\frac{1}{2}$ mile east   12

of Point 66 and between $\frac{1}{4}$ and $\frac{1}{2}$ mile northwest of Point 55.   24

   1 | 2 | 3 | 4 | 5 | 6 | 7 | 8 | 9 | 10 | 11 | 12

55-E. Improve control of 7, 8, 9, 0

15   777 j7j7j j7j The 77 cars averaged 77.7 mph for 77 minutes.

16   888 k8k8k k8k The 88 pianists pounded 88 keys on 88 pianos.

17   999 19191 191 The 99th Regiment sent 99 men for 99 parades.

18   000 ;0;0; ;0; The 100 girls had scores between 100 and 110.

19   Most scores on Test 9 fell between 70.8 and 90.0, with   12

the mode at 78.9; the median at 79.8; and the mean at 78.0.   24

   1 | 2 | 3 | 4 | 5 | 6 | 7 | 8 | 9 | 10 | 11 | 12

Manuscript 53
Table 46
BOUND REPORT (3)

Table 2

PARTS OF THE BUSINESS LETTER

Basic Parts	Supplemental Parts
A. Letterhead	I. Reference Line
B. Date Line	J. Attention Line
C. Inside Address	K. Subject Line
D. Salutation	L. Company Signature
E. Body	M. Enclosure Notation
F. Complimentary Closing	N. Postscript
G. Signer's Identification	O. "cc" Notation
H. Reference Initials	P. "bcc" Notation

TECHNICAL REMINDERS:

1. Leave ½-inch space (3 lines) under table.

2. Leave TWO spaces after "A.," "B.," etc.

3. Italic printing is underscored when typed.

4. Any short display line is centered.

5. Footnote separation line is 2 inches long.

6. "Et al." in footnote means "and others" and is used when there are more than two authors.

7. In footnote, title of book is underscored but edition is not.

A. The Letterhead contains the name and address of the company, in print. Most letterheads are 1 3/4 inches deep, but they may be as shallow as 1 inch and as deep as 3 inches. When a letterhead is more than 2 inches deep, the date should be typed at least three lines below the bottom of the printing.[2]

B. *The Date Line* contains the month, day, and year the letter is typed. The month is never abbreviated in a business letter; a comma always separates the day and year:

October 9, 1967

The armed forces and some government bureaus (and many persons who have served in those forces or bureaus) prefer the "military" arrangement, with the day before the month:

9 October 1967

---

2. Alan C. Lloyd, et al., Gregg Typewriting for Colleges, Second Edition (New York: McGraw–Hill, 1964), page 260.

C. *The Inside Address* includes the identity and address of the addressee. These are normally typed above the body of a business letter; but as one authority notes, "Placing the inside address at the bottom, which is correct arrangement when writing to a public official, makes a letter formal."[3]

When the business title of an addressee is used in addition to his name, the title may be placed after the name, or on a line by itself, or at the start of the next line:

Manuscript 54
BOUND REPORT (4)

Display with quotation marks only a quotation that will fill three or fewer typewritten lines.

[Continues on next page]

55-F. Regain stride on these easy paragraphs

55-F. Type to your goal.

ACCURACY: Alternate 20 and 21 three times.

SPEED: Type 20 and 21, individually, three times.

SI 1.04—very easy

20   My goal is to make a big profit when I go down to work   12
for the rich man by the lake. If so, then I may aid Jan if   24
he kept the bicycle of the neighbor girl down by Coal Lane.   36
   1 | 2 | 3 | 4 | 5 | 6 | 7 | 8 | 9 | 10 | 11 | 12

21   When Jack said he might take six scouts to the zoo, he   48
did not know they would be so quick to take him up on it at   60
this time. He should have known that most boys would be in   72
the mood to go on just such a trip at the drop of your hat.   84

55-G. Make an interim progress check

55-G. To confirm progress in Lesson 55, repeat 55-B.

56-A. Learn how to make corrections

56-A. SPECIAL NOTES.

(1) Erase only when your instructor directs or gives you permission to do so. Erasing: a crutch learners should avoid leaning upon!

(2) One erasure crumb can disable a machine; this is why it is so important the carriage be moved aside.

(3) Never moisten an eraser. A damp eraser "scags" paper.

(4) On an electric machine, you must temporarily turn the pressure regulator (26) to 0 before typing over any erasure you have made.

ERASING. Turn paper up so error is on top of cylinder. Move carriage to extreme left or right (use margin release, 15) so erasure grit *can't* fall into machine. Keep paper from slipping as you erase by pressing it against cylinder with fingertips (but don't touch the typing!). Use an *ink* eraser in light, up-and-down, oval motions while blowing lightly and dryly to puff away erasure grit. Then restore paper to typing position and type—*lightly!*—the correction.

SQUEEZING. If an extra letter must be inserted, move all letters in the word a half space to the *left*:

Method 1. Before each stroke, press and hold down the half-space key—if your machine has one. On some makes, the space bar can be held down to half-space the carriage.

Method 2. Before each stroke, press and hold down the backspace key at an estimated halfway-down depth.

Method 3. Before each stroke, press against the left end of the carriage, pushing it back a half space.

Method 4. If only the correction is to be typed, use the paper release and shift the paper itself.

SPREADING. To make a correction fill an extra space, move the word a half space to the *right*, using any of the methods of carriage control.

PRACTICE. Make three *exact* copies of lines 22 and 23.

22   The firs step in any operation iss to review all the steps.
23   The first step in any operation is to review all the steps.

56-B. Improve control of punctuation marks

56-B. To define practice goals for Lesson 56, type a copy of paragraph 38 (on page 93); check your work.

Your goal in Lesson 56 is ACCURACY if you make 3 or more typing mistakes.

Your goal is SPEED if you make 2 or fewer errors.

Then type the 56-B drill lines to fit your goal.

ACCURACY: Type the whole group of lines three times.

SPEED: Type each drill, individually, three times.

"M" drill: manual machine.
"E" drill: electric machine.

24   ,,, k,k,k k,k Yes, it is, or may be, a help, or guide, too.
25   ... l.l.l l.l Dr. and Mrs. J. A. Mills, Jr., left at 1 p.m.
26   /// ;/;/; ;/; Ship it 4/1/64, but date it 4/2/64 or 4/3/64.
27   ??? ;/;?; ;?; Who is there? Is it Bill? What do you want?
28M   ''' k'k'k k'k It's Joe's car, isn't it? No, it's Wilbur's.
28E   ''' ;';'; ;'; It's Joe's car, isn't it? No, it's Wilbur's.
29   !!! ala!a a!a Look! Over there! It's Mr. Kerr! Call him!

30   Mr. and Mrs. Smith hoped to go on the afternoon train,   12
on or about 4/4/64. But it was two weeks later, wasn't it,   24
before they left? What a trip they had! It was wonderful!   36
   1 | 2 | 3 | 4 | 5 | 6 | 7 | 8 | 9 | 10 | 11 | 12

Manuscript 52

BOUND REPORT (2)
Shown: in elite
Paper: plain
SI: 1.48—fairly hard

SPECIAL NOTES
1. Listings are double indented (i.e., indented 10 spaces).
2. Periods after numbers and letters in listings and headings may be followed by either one or two spaces, uniformly. In this report, follow such periods by TWO spaces.
3. In a footnote, "ff" means "and following pages."

CORRESPONDENCE MANUAL   Page 2   8

                                                                         9

100 and 200 words, he builds a placement plan that will serve all such   23
average letters; then he stretches shorter letters and telescopes the   37
longer ones to make them, too, fit in the space of an average letter.   51
To stretch a short letter, he may: 58

        1. Allow extra space after the date.   68
        2. Divide letter into more paragraphs.   79
        3. Insert a company signature line.   89
        4. Allow extra space for signature.   98
        5. Lower the reference lines.   107

To telescope a long letter into less space, he may: 118

        1. Allow less space after the date.   129
        2. Divide letter into fewer paragraphs.   139
        3. Edge lines farther into right margin.   150
        4. Possibly omit the company signature.   160
        5. Allow less space for the signature.   171
        6. Raise the reference lines.   179

The point is that he makes every possible letter fit into the space of 194
an average one. Only for letters under 75 words or over 225 words does 208
he adjust margins or alter the date line.   217

                                                                        218

                   Part 2. Parts of a Letter   235

    A business letter may have as many as 16 different parts,[1] listed 250
in Table 2, next page. It is rare, of course, that any letter contains 264
all the possible parts.   269

                                                                        270

THE BASIC LETTER PARTS   275

    Every business letter has eight parts that are so basic that the   289
letter would be incomplete or unusual if any were omitted. These parts 303
are listed in Column 1, Table 2, next page.   312
                                                                        318
_____

    1. R. E. Gavin and E. L. Hutchinson, Reference Manual for Stenog- 344
raphers and Typists, Third Edition (New York: McGraw-Hill, 1961), pages 366
10 ff.   367

Continuation Page of a Formal Manuscript

56-C. Improve control of more punctuation marks

```
31    ;;; ;j;j; ;;; Make it blue, then; or red; or tan; or brown.
32    ::: ;:;:; ;;; Leaving at 1:10, he can get the 1:34 or 1:42.
33M   """ s2s"s s"s Sue divided the "report" into six "chapters."
33E   """ ;'";"; ;"; Sue divided the "report" into six "chapters."
34    ( ) 19(1 ;0); We need (1) time, (2) cash, and (3) guidance.
35M   ___ j6j_j j_j You simply must read The Gwen, by John White.
35E   ___ ;-;_; ;_; You simply must read The Gwen, by John White.
```

```
36    I found The Gwen (a new book by John White) to be top-      15
flight reading (I like "whodunits," you see); my one criti-       27
cism of it:  It takes too long to reach its "happy ending."       42
```
1 | 2 | 3 | 4 | 5 | 6 | 7 | 8 | 9 | 10 | 11 | 12

56-D. Regain stride on two easy paragraphs

56-E. To measure your skill improvement, follow either schedule (double space and use a tab-5 indention):

(1) Type paragraph 37 two times. GOAL: To complete either copy in 5 minutes, with 4 or fewer errors.

(2) Using paragraphs 37 and 38, take two 5-minute timings. GOAL: 35 or more words a minute, within 4 errors. Then, record the better of the two scores.

SI 1.35—nearly normal

56-E. Measure your skill in sustained writing

```
37    The ZIP numbers that are used on letters and envelopes       12
got their start in the spring of 1963, when the Post Office        24
introduced a "Zoning Improvement Plan" to speed up delivery        36
of the mail.  The plan of using five digits after the state        48
name caught on at once, for the Department took great pains         60
to "sell" the plan.  Firms were requested to show their new        72
numbers on their letterheads and envelopes and reply cards,        84
and most firms made that adjustment when they got new ones.        96
The Post Office in each zone told the public what the local       108
zone number was to be and asked people to include it in the       120
return address on their letters and envelopes.  So success-       132
ful was the promotion that most persons began using the new       146
numbers and have continued doing so up to the present time.       158
```

```
38    But for a long time we will expect to see many letters      170
with no zone mark at all, because writers will not know the       182
ZIP number of some folks to whom they write, or because the       194
address is in a country that has no ZIP numbers, or because       206
a writer may not bother to confirm the number.  We will see       218
for years to come letters with the old sequence of city and       230
zone and state, since office files are full of letters with       242
just that sequence shown on their letterheads and since all       255
mail to be sent abroad will be expected to show that style.       276
```
1 | 2 | 3 | 4 | 5 | 6 | 7 | 8 | 9 | 10 | 11 | 12

Manuscript 51

Table 45

BOUND REPORT (1)
Shown: in pica
Paper: plain
Line: 6 inches
Spacing: as shown
SI: 1.47—high normal

REVIEW: Formal manuscript arrangement, pages 113-114
REVIEW: Ruled table arrangement, pages 139-140

CORRESPONDENCE MANUAL

Part 1. Letter Placement

A letter should be so arranged that the margins serve as a white frame around the letter. In general, the arrangement should be in the same proportion as is the paper (longer than wide); the text centers within equal side margins. The bottom margin should be a little wider than either side margin.

Many plans for placement have been invented, but none is a set answer for all letters because the lengths of letters and sizes of letterheads vary so much. Table 1, below, shows the one plan that is used most widely; but even this plan is just a general guide and has to be adapted for many letters.

The veteran office typist does not use a formula. Knowing that a great majority of business letters contain between

Tables go at top or bottom of page, with a locational reference to them (such as "Table 1, below") in text.

Table 1

STANDARD LETTER–PLACEMENT PLAN

Letter Factor	Short	Average	Long
Words in the body	Under 100	100–200	Over 200
Position of date*	Line 15	Line 15	Line 15
Drop to address	5 lines	5 lines	5 lines
Length of line	4 inches	5 inches	6 inches

* On letterheads more than 2 inches deep, position the date
   three lines below the bottom of the letterhead printing.

First Page of a Formal Manuscript

LINE: 60
TAB: 5
SPACING: SINGLE
DRILLS: THREE TIMES
GOAL: LEARN NEW
  CORRESPONDENCE
  FORMS
STRESS: PREPLANNING

Unit 10. Correspondence

57-A. Tune up on these review lines

57-A. Lines 1-3 three or more times, with emphasis on pressureless effort. Repeat them in Lesson 58.

1 They may make a big profit if they work with the field men.

2 Jo saw six big packs of cards and very quietly seized them.

3 10 & 28 & 39 & 47 & 56 $10 and $28 and $39 and $47 and $56.

57-B. Build skill on these preview words

57-B. Instead of repeating lines individually, type all four lines as a group three times. Start slowly; speed up on repetitions.

4 AA answer BB blocked CC choice DD date EE prefer FF helpful

5 GG give HH which II like JJ judge KK pick LL letter MM most

6 NN one's OO others PP people QQ unique RR better SS persons

7 TT that UU use VV have WW what XX extreme YY yes ZZ bizarre

57-C. Build and measure skill in sustained writing

57-C. You should be able to type both paragraphs in 5 minutes or less, within 4 errors. See if you can!

If you have doubt about your speed, precede this effort by retyping line 1 three times. If you doubt your ability to meet the accuracy requirement, retype line 2 three times.

Swing quickly from this preliminary practice into the sustained typing.

SI 1.35—easy-normal

8 What is the best letter style? That question does not   12
have an answer, for preference in letter styles is a matter   24
of one's own taste. For example, some people like a letter   36
to be blocked; others may prefer it indented. Some like to   48
use a company name. Some prefer the date centered horizon—   60
tally. There is no way to judge what one form is the best,   72
but it is helpful to know what forms are most popular: the   84
blocked and semiblocked forms, the two of which are used in   96
around 95 percent of the letters typed in business offices.   108

9 The purpose of a letter might influence your choice of   120
style, too. For example, you might pick for an advertising   132
letter a bizarre form that would catch one's eye because it   144
is unique; but you would reject that same style for, say, a   156
letter of sympathy. Yes, these are extreme cases; but they   168
do show that the purpose of a letter might affect its form.   180

  1 | 2 | 3 | 4 | 5 | 6 | 7 | 8 | 9 | 10 | 11 | 12

57-D. Learn a shortcut for positioning a date line

57-D. The production word counts from here on will assume that you are using one or the other of these two positioning shortcuts.

Most letters today have the date at the right margin but the trend is to start it at the center.

In the letters you have typed this far, you have pivoted (backspaced from the right margin) to position the date. Slow, wasn't it! There are two popular shortcuts:

1. Estimate the starting point of the date, as many typists do. You have pivoted enough dates, now, to have good judgment. And, after all,

you can't go *far* wrong! The shortest date (May 1) takes 11 spaces; the longest (September 30) fills but 18.

2. Start the date at the center, thus aligning the date with the closing lines (it balances neatly). This method is very easy, very quick, and *the method you are to use* in the letters and cards in this part.

Unit 28. Manuscripts

LINE: 60
TAB: 5
SPACING: SINGLE
DRILLS: THREE TIMES
GOAL: SUSTAIN SKILL
 ON LONG MANUSCRIPT
STRESS: PRECISION

169-A. Each line three times. Use them to get your fingers flying! Repeat in Lesson 170.

169-A. Tune up on these easy review lines

1   Kane kept the key so he may paint the shelf ivory and blue.
2   Paul reviewed the subject before giving Max and Kay a quiz.
3   Pages 10, 28, 39, 47, and 56 were most interesting to them.
     1 | 2 | 3 | 4 | 5 | 6 | 7 | 8 | 9 | 10 | 11 | 12

169-B. Three copies—one of which is errorless— or more until you do one that IS errorless. Repeat this in Lesson 170, too.

SI 1.10—very easy

169-B. Restore full skill on very easy material

4   If you put some small stones and one or two big stones   12
in a bottle and shake it, the big ones will quickly rise to   24
the top. Turn the bottle upside down and shake it, and the   36
big stones are back at the top in no time flat. There is a   48
moral in that story, and it has to do with life. When life   60
is dull, no one rises; it takes a shake to find the leader.   72
     1 | 2 | 3 | 4 | 5 | 6 | 7 | 8 | 9 | 10 | 11 | 12

169-C. Change machine to double spacing and check margins for 60-space line (lines will align) and a 5-space tab indention.

NOTE: words in italic print must be underscored.

Type two copies (one in Lesson 169, one in 170); repeat extra paragraphs, if necessary, until each is typed without error.

Or, take a 5-minute writing with a 10-second rest at the end of each minute; and then another 5-minute writing without rests. GOAL: To finish the selection within 6 minutes and 2 mistakes.

SI 1.45—upper normal

169-C. Sustain skill on production material

PREFACE

This manual has been prepared to serve the writer as a sum-   13
mary of the technical details, large and small, involved in typing 25
business letters and formal reports. It is hoped that these pages   38
will serve as a reference source, as well.   47

Letters. Because so many different persons in so many different   64
kinds of work write letters for so many different reasons, it is natural 79
that there be, as there are, a great number of fine points, some of which 93
will pertain to all or most letters, but some of which concern only a   107
special few. Whether they concern a few or many letters, these   120
technical points are so many facts that the typist must have in mind. 134

Reports. Like letters, reports may be typed with many special   151
flairs or touches unique to the persons who prepare them; but, by and 165
large, there is a standard format for the formal report. The pages of 179
this handbook have been set up to illustrate the standard format,   192
complete with footnotes, quotations, tables, listings, headings of all 206
kinds, and so on, along with the right spacing—single, double, or   220
extra.   221

The authority for the statements in this manual is the textbook   235
by Lloyd, Rowe, and Winger: *Gregg Typewriting for Colleges*, Second 263
Edition, to which credit is herewith made.   275
     1 | 2 | 3 | 4 | 5 | 6 | 7 | 8 | 9 | 10 | 11 | 12 | 13 | 14

The production work of this unit is a 10-page Correspondence Manual. It will be easier to do if you precede it with the Learning Guide on workbook pages 337-338 and use the visual guide on workbook page 339.

169/170-D. Apply skill to typing a Correspondence Manual

57/58-E. Practice the production of postal cards

Study the illustrations and annotations below; then, using workbook pages 79-82 (or slips of paper 5½ by 3¼ inches), type Cards 1-6. Once the machine is set, you should *easily* produce each card within 5 minutes, with no errors or with not more than 1 error.

Card 1

POSTAL CARD
Shown: in pica
Line: 4½ inches
Spacing: single
Tabs: two

↓ MARGIN   TAB ↓   ↓ TAB   MARGIN ↓

Return address:
Blocked; started
on line 3, a half
inch from edge.
No personal title
unless it is Mrs.

Richard F. Carlson   4
Student Union Building   8
Reno, Nevada   89503 ↓6   13

⟨ THIS SIDE OF CARD IS FOR ADDRESS ⟩   18

Block address 3
lines below OF.
Double space a
3-line address;
single space a
longer one.

Mr. Donald W. Keane, Jr.   24
Apartment 3-C   27
1047 East Third Street   33
Reno, Nevada   89503   38

Production count
allows 8 words
to flip card.

   46

Start date at
center, on line 3.
Following blank
line is optional.

December 2, 19--   55
   56

Dear Mr. Keane: 60
   61

Margins ½ inch,
by estimate.

The next meeting of the Finance Committee of   70
the Alumni Association will be held at 8:30   78
p.m., Saturday, December 10, at the home of   87
John F. Elkins (1200 West 21 Street). The   96
agenda includes a study of the finance plan   105
for the Alumni House, a matter so important   113
that committee members are urged to attend.   124

   125

Leave room for
signature, if
needed; otherwise,
one blank line.

Richard F. Carlson   131
Executive Secretary   137

URS   138

Card measures
5½ x 3¼ inches.

Postal Card in Standard Arrangement

Letter 85

SEMIBLOCKED LETTER
WITH REPLY COUPON
Paper: plain
Line: 6 inches
SI: 1.51—fairly difficult

THE NATIONAL FEDERATION OF VETERANS ⌐

190 University Drive

Iowa City, Iowa   52241

Date

Dear fellow Member
of the National Federa-
tion of Veterans:

Do you feel that ~~our~~ *an* organization of more than 25,000 men
can build a National Head-quarters Building without having to
~~get~~ a bank ~~loan~~ and pay~~ing~~ interest on ~~borrowed~~ money?

(borrow money from)

OF COURSE WE CAN!

Our new building ~~will~~ *is going to* cost us about $100,000. Of this
amount, more than $65,000 has already been paid ~~over~~ to the
architect and builders. This money was drawn from the special
Building Fund ~~Account~~ into ~~what~~ *which* a share of Member('s) dues has
~~been~~ deposited every year for the past twelve years. We have
$10,000 that we can draw from our National treasury. That
leaves us with just $25,000 that we must raise. Can we do it?

OF COURSE WE CAN!)——————→

Our Constitution forbids ~~our~~ raising dues, but it doesn't
forbid our going straight to every Member of the Federation
and asking him, "How is about anteing up for the ~~Headquarters~~
Building Fund? That's the purpose of this letter. How about
it? How about anteing up for the building fund? All you ~~have
to~~ do is fill in the form below and mail ~~this letter~~ back ~~to
us~~ with your check for a ~~buck~~ *dollar* or more. Can we count on you?

OF COURSE WE CAN!

*Typist – Tell
Duplicating Dep't we
need 5,000 of these
by next Monday morning.
I will need to see the stencil
R.W.*

Roger Wilkins, Executive Secretary ~~and
Treasurer, Headquarters Building Fund~~

- ⌐

National Federation of Veterans
190 University Drive
Iowa City, Iowa   52241

Sure, you can count on ME! Here('s) my check for $ _____ for⌐
The NFV Headquarters Building Fund.

*(OK as corrected
R.W.)*

Name _____

Street _____

City, State, ZIP _____

Post _____

94
105
117
131
144
156
169
181
194
207
215
229
241
253
266
278
280
292
298
311
313
322
336
343
347
352
365
373
383
393
404
413

Draft of a Solicitation Circular Letter

Card 2
POSTAL CARD

From: Richard F. Carlson | Student Union Building | Reno,   10
Nevada   89503 | *To:* Reservations Department | Lake Tahoe   25
Lodge | 1200 Lake Place | Tahoe City, California   95730   35
| *Date* | Gentlemen: | I should like to reserve four double rooms   61
with bath, at $12 each, for a party of eight skiers for the week-   74
end of December 14-16. We shall arrive about seven o'clock on   87
Friday evening and depart in midafternoon on Sunday. I should   99
appreciate your sending me a confirmation of this reservation. 112
↓₃ | Richard F. Carlson | (*No initials*) 118

Card 3
POSTAL CARD

From: Richard F. Carlson | Student Union Building | Reno,   10
Nevada   89503 | *To:* Mr. Damon Struthers | Men's Suits   24
Department | Stacy's Department Store | 451 Vallejo Street | 35
Reno, Nevada   89501 | *Date* | Dear Mr. Struthers: | Thank   57
you for letting me know that the annual clearance sale of winter   70
suits is scheduled for the first week in January. If you have any   83
dark blue or gray 37-Longs, I should be grateful if you could set   96
them aside for me. I shall stop in to look at them on the first day 110
of the sale. Thanks for remembering me! | Dick Carlson | (*No* 118
initials) 122

Duplicated fill-in cards are often used for acknowledgments. Front is addressed as usual (but no return address). This side is filled in as is shown: date at center, salutation and initials aligned at margin, and amount centered in area.

ALUMNI ASSOCIATION - Student Union - Reno, Nevada   89503

December 3, 19--

Dear Mr. Kenilworth:

We should like to acknowledge your contribution of

$25.00

to the Alumni House Fund. We are confident that it
will not be long before we can begin construction.

                  Richard F. Carlson
                  Executive Secretary

URS

Cards 4-6
Forms 1-3

FORM POSTAL CARDS
Shown: in elite

Card 4. Acknowledge a contribution of $25.00 by Mr. Charles S.
Kenilworth | 4819 Heyer Avenue | Castro Valley, California   94541.   55
    Card 5. Acknowledge a contribution of $100.00 by Mr. Edwin G.
Bernhardt | 5620 North 58 Street | Portland, Oregon.   56
    Card 6. Acknowledge a contribution of $1,000.00 by Mr. and Mrs.
Fred W. Miller | 3328 Faircrest Drive | Anaheim, California   92804.   58

LINE: 60 SPACES
TAB: 10, 25, 56
DRILLS: THREE TIMES
GOAL: SKILLFUL TYPING
    BETWEEN RULES
STRESS: EYES ON COPY

167-A. Each line three
times, or two ½-minute
timed writings on it.
Repeat in Lesson 168.

167-A. Tune up on these review lines

1 The widow is kept busy with the field and turkeys she owns.
2 Jeff moved six dozen quilted coats at night by power truck.
3 The 56¢ and 47¢ toys sold before the 10¢, 28¢, or 39¢ ones.
   1 | 2 | 3 | 4 | 5 | 6 | 7 | 8 | 9 | 10 | 11 | 12

167-B. Change to double
spacing and confirm tab
stops: 10, 25, and 56
spaces from left margin.

Type each line, as shown,
three times. Then take
a 3-minute writing or
type one complete copy;
GOAL: an errorless
copy within 3 minutes.

SI 1.33—fairly easy if
you can manage tab and
numbers wholly by touch

167-B. Sustain skill on production material

CONTRIBUTIONS TO THE HEADQUARTERS BUILDING FUND

Date October 6, 19--		No. Contributors 4	7
Name	Address	Amount	8
Jason F Faucett	3521 85th St West		15
	Jackson Hts N Y 11372	5	22
Ruben L Edwards	138 Duquesne Rd		30
	Huntsville Ala 35801	15	38
E I Marshall	560 Park Ave		44
	Huntsville Ala 35801	25	52
Harmon L Hess	476 Imperial Ave		59
	Fresno Calif 93721	10	67
October 7, 19--			72
R E Clarke	10 So Lee St		78
	Waterbury Conn 06701	25	86
John Jay Shane	391 Hamilton Lane		94
	Macon Ga 31202	10	101
Park Van Nuys	729 E 13 St		107
	Flint Mich 48502	10	114
Alvin C Corey	1802 Lakeside Rd		121
	Green Bay Wis 54301	5	129
Max C McDuff	2731 Wisteria Av		136
	Newark N J 07102	25	144
Carl F Leigh	1592 Capitol St		151
	Wilmington Del 19899	5	159

Form 67

RULED REPORT FORMS
Forms: workbook 333
Directions: Prepare
    October 6 report
    and October 7 one
    separately
Style: space-saver
    abbreviating

Form 68

FILL-IN POSTAL CARDS
Cards: workbook 335
Directions: Prepare
    acknowledgment cards
    for the four checks
    arriving October 6

167/168-C. Apply skill to production output

Letter Typing

LINE: 60
TAB: 5
SPACING: SINGLE
DRILLS: THREE TIMES
GOAL: LEARN NEW
   CORRESPONDENCE
   TECHNICALITIES
STRESS: OUTPUT

59-A. Try to type these lines smoothly, as though keeping time to music. Repeat them in Lesson 60.

59-B. Type these lines the same as you would type a paragraph. Repeat this "paragraph" three times; speed up on repetitions.

59-C. You should be able to type both paragraphs within 5 minutes, with 4 or fewer errors. Can you?

If speed is a problem for you, retype line 1 three times before starting 59-C, to set a fast pace. But if accuracy is your problem, retype line 2 three times, for an intensive review of all the key reaches. Be sure to swing quickly from this preliminary practice to the sustained writing before the effect of the preliminary practice fades.

SI 1.37—normal

59-A. Tune up on these review lines

1 The goal of the rich man is to fix a bicycle for the girls.
2 A blazing jam quivered as the ax point struck flying blows.
3 Look for boxes #10, #28, #39, and #47; then search for #56.

59-B. Build skill on these preview words

4 AA paragraph BB back CC casual DD indented EE each FF flash
5 GG zigzag HH have II lines JJ just KK look LL all MM common
6 NN penned OO tone PP experts QQ quite RR address SS message
7 TT that UU build VV have WW writer XX extra YY style ZZ zip

59-C. Measure and build skill in sustained writing

8 Back in the days when a letter had to be penned by the 12
writer, it was not usual to leave extra space between parts 24
of a letter; the writer had to use indentions instead. The 36
start of each paragraph had to be indented. The lines of a 48
return address, of an inside address, and of the close were 60
all set up as a series of indentions, just like steps. The 72
result was that letters seemed to have quite a zigzag look. 84

9 Letters got a new look when the typewriter came along. 96
Because it is a lot faster to block than to indent lines on 108
a machine, a letter today is not likely to have many inden- 120
tions. The experts say you can build a "tone" for a letter 132
by the number of indentions you do or do not inject in your 144
letter. Many indentions make a letter look conservative; a 156
few make it seem casual; having none at all gives a message 168
a streamlined zip that is the equivalent of a modern touch. 180

1 | 2 | 3 | 4 | 5 | 6 | 7 | 8 | 9 | 10 | 11 | 12

Use the letterheads on workbook pages 85-94 for letters 17-21. If you have no workbook, use plain paper—but rule or type a line across the paper, a half inch from the top, to simulate the depth of a letterhead. Note that the letters require a 5-inch line: 50 pica; 60 elite.

59/60-D. Practice the production of letters

Type Letters 17-21, trying to finish each of these "average length" letters in 6 minutes, with 4 or fewer errors. Note that the letters feature these special display parts:

1. The attention line (page 98) precedes the salutation. It may be centered, but is usually blocked at the margin and underscored.

2. The subject line (page 100) follows the salutation. It may be typed at the margin, but is usually centered and underscored or all-capped.

3. A company signature is usually typed in all capitals a double space below (and aligned with) the complimentary closing. It is used when the letter involves an obligation of the company rather than of the signer.

4. A "cc" (carbon copy) note is added to the other reference symbols if someone gets a copy of the letter.

Form 64

MAILING LABELS
Forms: workbook 327
Directions: Address
a label to each of
the adjutants named
on Form 61

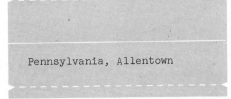

Addressing of Plain Labels on a Gummed, Perforated Sheet

| Mr. Daniel F. Shapiro
NFV Post Adjutant
169 Via Riviera
San Diego, Calif. 92101 | Mr. Nathan S. Graham
NFV Post Adjutant
4431 Vineyard Drive
San Jose, Calif. 95113 | Dr. Trayne W. Foster
NFV Post Adjutant
883 West 41 Street
Santa Ana, Calif. 92702 |
| Mr. Clifford S. Atkinson
NFV Post Adjutant
P. O. Box 198
San Francisco, Calif.
94101 | Mr. J. Kenneth Reladio
NFV Post Adjutant
3919 U. S. 101
San Mateo, Calif. 94401 | Mr. Harrison R. Hall
NFV Post Adjutant
395 Parkway East
Santa Barbara, Calif.
93102 |

To simulate sheet of labels, type hyphen row every six lines and divide page into thirds by vertical rulings.

Plain labels in sheets perforated for easy detachment are used for addressing packages, tubes, and oversize envelopes. Faster to address than are envelopes, the sheets are also used in mass mailings of envelopes for circulars, catalogs, and the like.

The typist uses all the labels in the first column, then those in the second, then those in the third.

The typing begins on the second line below the perforation, two or three spaces from the edge, blocked and single spaced. The postal ZIP number is typed *under* the state name if there is not room *after* it.

Form 65

FILE-FOLDER LABELS
Forms: workbook 329
Directions: Prepare
labels for folders
for a geographic
file of the data in
Form 61

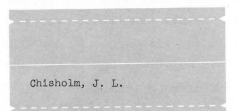

Chisholm, J. L.

File-Folder Label: Alphabetic

Pennsylvania, Allentown

File-Folder Label: Geographic

For identifying file folders, gummed labels are available in long rolls, perforated for easy detachment and grooved (narrow line in each illustration) for easy folding. The typing is begun three spaces from the left edge two lines below the groove, thus leaving a full blank line of space between the groove and the typing.

To simulate a label roll, on every fourth line of a page type alternating lines of underscores ("grooves") and of periods ("perforations"); then slice the page into three equal strips.

CARD 1. Bloomsburg Post owes October post schedule and the finance statement for quarter that began on July 1.

CARD 2. Wilkinsburg Post is overdue with initiation report for the July 1 quarter and its building-fund pledge.

CARD 3. Hazleton Post owes its log of August activities and its building-fund pledge.

NATIONAL FEDERATION OF VETERANS

190 University Drive   Iowa City, Iowa   52241

                                        October 5, 19--

Post Adjutant: This office has not yet received your—

___ Log of Post Activities for month of _____
 X Schedule of Post Activities for month of October _____
___ Register of Members, quarter beginning _____
___ Initiation Report, quarter beginning _____
___ Statement of Finance, quarter beginning _____
 X Other Post pledge for building fund _____

Please forward this information by return mail.

urs   OFFICE OF THE NATIONAL COMMANDER

Fill-in Notification Postal Card

Letter 17

BLOCKED LETTER
Shown: in pica
Body: 137 words
Line: 5 inches
Tab: center only
SI: 1.39—normal

JUDD-KANE, INC.

CABLE ADDRESS: JUDKANDEN

1410 GLENARM STREET • DENVER, COLORADO   80202 • TABOR 5-7500

December 4, 19--

REMEMBER:
Space three
times after
state before
typing postal
ZIP number.

Parke & Blake, Inc.
4728 La Junta Street
Pueblo, Colorado   81002

Attention of the President

Gentlemen:

Thank you for the letter in which you describe the
financial problems that you are having and request
us to extend for two months the date on which your
final payment on our building contract will be due.

We are happy to make the extension you wish, and we
enclose with this letter an agreement to cover the
added time. You will note that it simply involves
your continuing for two more months the same rate
of interest you have been paying on your balance.

Our Colorado Springs agent, Mr. Willis Crane, will
call you early next week to learn when you may wish
him to visit you and execute the papers. If there
is any help or counsel that he can provide, you may
be sure he will be happy to be of service to you.

Yours truly,

JUDD-KANE, INC.

Thomas J. Kane, Jr.
Executive Vice-President

urs
Enclosure
cc Mr. Judd
cc Mr. Crane

Business Letter in Blocked Style, with Attention Line,
Company Signature, and "cc" Notations

Form 61

MAILING LIST
Paper: workbook 325

PENNSYLVANIA ➔➔ 3

POST (CITY)	ADJUTANT	ADDRESS	ZIP CODE	4
Allentown	John L. Chisholm	4311 Eighth Avenue	18101	17
Altoona	Edward S. Venters	P. O. Box 449	16601	29
Bethlehem	John St. Vincent	1200 U. S. 22/ ~~Easton~~	18015	42
Bloomsburg	*Charles W. Foreman* ~~Albert Fitzsimmons~~	377 ~~822~~ Berwick Avenue	17815	56
Butler	Maurice Hopkins	1817 Kittaning Road	16001	68
Erie	C. C. Kenobski	14452 Euclid Avenue	16501	81
Harrisburg	Benjamin Wister	Manager, Pennwood Hotel	17105	95
Hazleton	*Victor Seligman* ~~Drew L. Voeckler~~	*861 Shenandoah Street* ~~P. O. Box 113, Pottsville~~	18201	109
Johnstown	Kirby J. Anderson	772 Reservoir Road	15901	122
Kane	Martin Corwin, Jr.	Camp Corwin, U. S. 6	16735	135
Lancaster	Harold Kloovoer	941 Susquehana Drive	17601	149
Lewiston	*Prentice E. Clover* ~~Wilbur F. Carmody~~	*157 West Water Street* ~~Bucknell Square West~~	17044	163
Mansfield	Barton D. Dixon	Tioga Motel, U. S. 15	16933	177
Philadelphia	F. Randolph Carr (Dr.)	2744 North Broad Street	19104	193
Mt. Lebanon, ~~Pittsburgh~~	James K. Zinsser	1250 Woodhaven Road	15228	207
Reading	Louis van Polk	R. D. 1, French Creek Road	19603	222
Scranton	Oliver R. Henderson	*900* ~~148~~ Tunkhannock Avenue	18503	236
Shippensburg	Thomas Vanderbilt	*148* ~~900~~ Caledonia Street	17257	251
Warren	Furston Lincoln	397 New Sheffield Road	16365	264
Wilkes-Barre	*Conrad Huxkley*	*3712 East Plymouth Street*	18701	279
Williamsport	Paul F. Tremaine	Tremaine Business College	17701	294
Wilkinsburg	*Franklin J. Kelly*	*37 Peebles Street*	*18701*	308

Forms 62-63

PLAIN INDEX CARDS
Paper: 5 x 3 cards or
slips of paper
Directions: make (a)
an annotated name
file and (b) a ZIP-
geographic file of
the Form 61 data

```
Chisholm, John L.
    4311 Eighth Avenue
    Allentown, Pennsylvania   18101


    Adjutant, Allentown Post
```

Card for alphabetic name file, with annotation
for further identification.

```
Pennsylvania   18101   Allentown

    Mr. John L. Chisholm
    Adjutant, Allentown Post
    4311 Eighth Avenue
    Allentown, Pennsylvania    18101
```

ZIP-geographic card (filed by state and ZIP)
used in circulation lists.

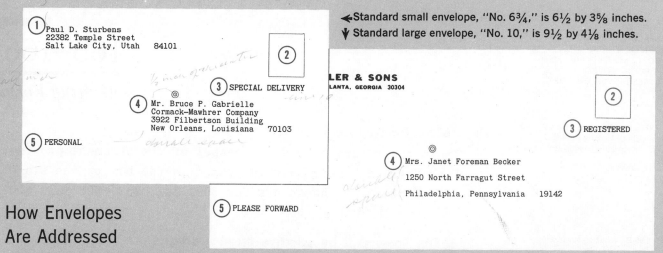

Standard small envelope, "No. 6¾," is 6½ by 3⅝ inches.
Standard large envelope, "No. 10," is 9½ by 4⅛ inches.

① Paul D. Sturbens
22382 Temple Street
Salt Lake City, Utah   84101

②

③ SPECIAL DELIVERY

④ Mr. Bruce P. Gabrielle
Cormack-Mawhrer Company
3922 Filbertson Building
New Orleans, Louisiana   70103

⑤ PERSONAL

LER & SONS
LANTA, GEORGIA 30304

②

③ REGISTERED

④ Mrs. Janet Foreman Becker
1250 North Farragut Street
Philadelphia, Pennsylvania   19142

⑤ PLEASE FORWARD

How Envelopes Are Addressed

1. Return address (if not printed) begins on line 3, single spaced and blocked ½ inch from edge. No personal title, except *Mrs.*, is used.

2. Stamp goes ½ inch from top and right.

3. Special mail service, if any, is typed on line 10, pivoted from right edge of stamp.

4. Name and address begin under and about ½ inch left of estimated center (*i.e.*, line 12 of small envelope; line 14 of large one), arranged in three double-spaced lines or in four or more single-spaced lines. In a United States address, type the ZIP number three spaces after the state. If you do not know the ZIP number, type the zone number between the city and state. In a foreign address, indicate the zone with the city, and type the country name in all caps on a separate line.

5. Special reminders (like "confidential" or "please forward" or "Attention of the Advertising Manager") are typed in all caps a double space under the address, ½ inch from the edge.

Letter 18

BLOCKED LETTER
Paper: letterhead
Body: 144 words
Line: 5 inches
Tab: center only
SI: 1.39—normal

A simulated envelope is printed on the back of each workbook letterhead; be sure to address it.

Current Date | Kerr, Bidell & Todd, Inc. | 1039 Statler Building | 18
Boston, Massachusetts   02103 | Attention Mr. Roger Todd | 39
Gentlemen: 41

We must find some way to move faster on the Boston building   54
project. I appreciate the fact that your best men are busy with   67
other commitments, but the simple truth is that we will not have   80
a building if we do not wrap up the final design in a few weeks.   93

As you know better than I, the cost of material and labor is 106
going up at a rapid rate; the tentative budget that you and we 119
estimated a year ago is already outdated. Credit is much tighter 132
and costlier, too. 136

Is there any chance of your having the plans ready within a 149
month or six weeks? Tell me frankly. My board members will be 162
pressing me for a report; and if I cannot say that we are getting 175
ready for bids, I fear that the entire project will be abandoned. 189

Yours truly, | JUDD-KANE, INC. | Willard Judd, President | urs 208
| cc Mr. Kane | cc Boston Office 213

LINE: 60
SPACING: SINGLE
DRILLS: THREE TIMES
GOAL: LEARN MAIL
    ROOM TYPING
STRESS: EYES ON COPY

165-A. Lines three times without looking up once! Repeat in Lesson 166.

165-A. Tune up on these review lines

1 It is their turn to rid the chapel of the ornament problem.
2 Five "wizards" very quickly jumped in the box on the stage.
3 The outstanding checks are for $56, $47, $39, $28, and $10.
    1 | 2 | 3 | 4 | 5 | 6 | 7 | 8 | 9 | 10 | 11 | 12

165-B. What's your goal?

ACCURACY: Type each group of lines like a paragraph, three times.

SPEED: Type each line individually three times.

165-B. Boost skill by selective preview practice

4 capitalization accountant secretaries quarterly junior copy
5 concentrating advertising grammatical worthless zigzag too;
6 transcribing corrections handwritten quotations select fact
    1 | 2 | 3 | 4 | 5 | 6 | 7 | 8 | 9 | 10 | 11 | 12
7 work with|very much|that are|from his|that is|done in|we do
8 must look|fact that|must not|must one|must be|able to|it is

165-C. Each paragraph two times, one of which must be perfect or contain not more than one error.

Use double spacing, a 70-space line (margins will align), and a tab indention of 5 spaces.

SI: 1.35—easy-normal

165-C. Boost skill on sustained alphabetic paragraphs

1 | 2 | 3 | 4 | 5 | 6 | 7 | 8 | 9 | 10 | 11 | 12 | 13 | 14

A lot of the typing that is done in a modern office is from copy 14
that is far from perfect. A copy expert in an advertising agency 27
may type from his own sketchy notes. A junior accountant may 39
prepare his quarterly reports from his own pencil work, complete 52
with corrections and erasures. The bill clerk types from handwritten 66
copy, too; while editors and their staff work with a stream of rough 80
drafts. And most secretaries spend many hours transcribing those 93
zigzag marks that are called shorthand. We do not work very much 106
with perfect copy matter. 111

Now all this adds up to the simple fact that a typist must learn 125
how to think while he is typing. He must be able to make grammat- 138
ical corrections; he must be able to manage capitalization and 151
quotations, read rough drafts, catch and fix wrong dates and names, 164
think through problems of word division at the ends of lines—and 178
all this thinking must be done in a quick flash of good judgment. 191
These skills require practice; the place to get it is not on the job 204
but in the classroom. Asked to select which one of these skills is 218
most worth concentrating on,we should pick out the use of the warning 231
bell. The other skills are worthless if one must look up at the end of 244
every line of typing. 251
1 | 2 | 3 | 4 | 5 | 6 | 7 | 8 | 9 | 10 | 11 | 12 | 13 | 14

ALTERNATE PLAN:

In Lesson 165, take a 3-minute writing with a 10-second rest after each minute; then follow up with a 3-minute writing without rests, trying to maintain the same pace. Goal: maximum speed with one or fewer mistakes.

In Lesson 166, repeat the same routine, using 5-minute efforts. Goal: maximum speed with two or fewer errors.

MARTIN MILLER & SONS

HEALY BUILDING

58 BROAD STREET   ATLANTA, GEORGIA   30303

Letter 19
Table 12

BLOCKED LETTER
Shown: in elite
Body: 109 words, plus
   table spacings
Line: 5 inches
Tabs: table only
SI: 1.39—normal

December 5, 19—   4

8

Mr. J. Stewart Young   12
National Federation of   17
   Sales Executives   21
1820 Trayne Building   25
Little Rock, Arkansas   72203   30

31

Dear Mr. Young: 34

Indent runover line 3 spaces.

35

SUBJECT: YOUR GEORGIA TRIP   52

53

When I let our Georgia NFSE chapters know that you might be   65
willing to speak at one of their dinners if they could plan   77
their meetings to fit your trip schedule, their response was   90
wonderful. Therefore, the following schedule has been set   101
up for you: 104

105

Before typing the letter, set three tabs for columns. For date and subject line, center carriage by hand. When ready to type the closing lines, clear table tabs; set one at center.

Date	City	Audience	
			118
			119
May 30	Atlanta	225	128
May 31	Athens	150	135
June 1	Macon	160	141
June 2	Columbus	175	148
June 3	Augusta	100	155
			156

If you approve this heavy schedule, Mr. Young, we will move   168
at once to make proper arrangements for your transportation   180
and hotels. I want you to know that we shall spread out the   192
welcome mat for you!   197

198

Cordially yours,   204

207

Humphrey N. Lambert   212
State NFSE Chairman   217

urs   218
cc Chapter Presidents   222
cc Martin Miller, Jr.   226

**Business Letter in Blocked Style, with Subject Line,
Tabulation Display, and "cc" Notation**

To Chainfeed Envelopes and Cards . . .

After typing first envelope or card, roll it back until only ½ inch or so is showing. Insert next envelope or card *from the front*, placing its bottom edge between the first envelope or card and the cylinder. Turn cylinder to back out the first envelope or card and to draw the second into position. Continue "feeding" the envelopes or cards in this manner (from the *front*) until all are done. The completed envelopes or cards stack up on the paper table in the same sequence in which they were typed.

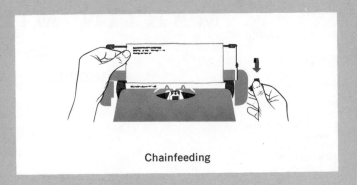

Chainfeeding

Form 59

PLAIN INDEX CARDS
Paper: use 5 x 3 cards or slips of paper
Directions: for each name on the Form 57 list, type a name and a geographic card

```
Stevens, Patrick K. (Dr.)

193 East Montauk Road

Providence, Rhode Island    02904
```

Name file

```
Rhode Island, Providence

  Stevens, Patrick K. (Dr.)
  193 East Montauk Road
  Providence, Rhode Island    02904
```

Geographic file

When typing on plain index cards:

1. Arrange the first line in index (filing) order. Omit *Mr.* and *Miss* but indicate all other personal titles (type them in parentheses).

2. Start in the third space of the second line.

3. Leave one blank line under the first (key) line. The other lines may be blocked or be indented, and either single or double spaced.

Form 60

FILL-IN INVOICES
Forms: workbook 323
Directions: for each name on the Form 57 list, prepare an appropriate invoice

NATIONAL FEDERATION OF VETERANS

190 UNIVERSITY DRIVE   IOWA CITY, IOWA   52241

October 1, 19--

Dr. Patrick K. Stevens
193 East Montauk Road
Providence, Rhode Island   02904

Initiation Fee $15.00

Membership Emblem 5.00

Dues until next December 31 .... 1.50

Total Amount Due 21.50

(Please return this statment with your remittance)

Fill-in printed invoice form

Date the four invoices for the first of next month and figure the dues (50 cents a month) to the end of the year. On each invoice, insert the amount of the dues and the total due.

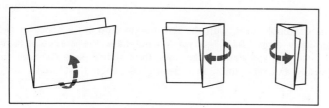

FOLDING A LETTER FOR A SMALL ENVELOPE

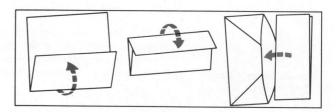

FOLDING A LETTER FOR A LARGE ENVELOPE

august 6

Letter 20

BLOCKED LETTER
Body: 131 words
Line: 5 inches
Tab: center only
SI: 1.44—normal

Current Date | Mr. Marvin N. Maxwell | 2839 Clary Street | Fort   18
Worth, Texas   76111 | Dear Mr. Maxwell: 27

SUBJECT: YOUR JOB APPLICATION   47

We have received and have noted with interest your letter of   60
application for a sales position with us.   69

At present we do not have a vacancy near Fort Worth, but we   82
do need a representative who would make his headquarters in or   94
near Lubbock and cover the northwestern part of the state. If   107
you would like to be considered for this opening, please fill in and   121
mail back to us the enclosed application form.   130

I shall be in Fort Worth near the end of the month to attend a   144
convention; while I am there, I should be pleased to talk with   156
you. If you are qualified for and truly interested in the position,   170
we might be able to settle the matter then and arrange the em-   182
ployment details. | Sincerely yours, | MARTIN MILLER & SONS | 198
Humphrey N. Lambert | General Sales Manager | urs | En-   213
closure | cc Personnel Department   219

Letter 21

BLOCKED LETTER
Body: 133
SI: 1.48—fairly
    difficult

fixin at
home

42
25
17

42
25
5
72

Date | Dr. James Kendall | School of Commerce | Lake Stone   17
College | Savannah, Georgia   31403 | Dear Doctor Kendall: 30

SUBJECT: CONFERENCE PLANS   47

I am writing to confirm our telephone conversation about   59
your taking part in our March 14 conference. It is most grat-   71
ifying to know you will join us.   78

The audience will consist of 75 men who represent our com-   90
pany in the southeastern states, plus 11 of our executives. These   104
men meet here in Atlanta two times a year to learn about our   116
new products and to advance in their knowledge of professional   129
selling.   131

We should like you to lead a session, to last about one and a   144
half hours, on "How to Help the Retailer Expand His Business."   157
We shall reimburse you for all expenses, plus your $250 fee.   169

Let me say again that we are very glad you will be with us. We   183
look forward to your program. | Yours sincerely, | MARTIN   198
MILLER & SONS | Humphrey N. Lambert | General Sales Man-   212
ager | urs | cc Mr. John Miller   218

Type the handwritten data on the workbook form, with the left margin stop set a space or two inside "Post" and a tab stop similarly after "Date." If you do not have the workbook form, copy the one shown here before inserting the data; make your form a full page (enough for ten names). List names alphabetically and type them in indexing sequence (last name first).

NATIONAL FEDERATION OF VETERANS

REPORT OF INITIATION OF NEW MEMBERS

Post *Nashville, Tennessee*   Initiation Date *October 1, 19—*   8

1. Name	Robert E. Perkins	Service	Navy	16
Address	103 Trinity Lane	Highest Rank	Ensign	22
	Nashville 38107	Years in Service	6	27
		Present Work	Dept. Store Buyer	31
2. Name	J. Thomas Perkins	Service	Air Corps	39
Address	103 Trinity Lane	Highest Rank	Staff Sergeant	46
	Nashville 38107	Years in Service	4	51
		Present Work	Lawyer	54
3. Name	Eugene L. Carr	Service	Army	60
Address	719 Cumberland Circle	Highest Rank	First Lieutenant	69
	Nashville 38114	Years in Service	3 ½	74
		Present Work	Owns Men's Store	78
4. Name	Oscar T. Moeller	Service	Air Corps	86
Address	2311 Highland Avenue	Highest Rank	Lt. Colonel	93
	Nashville 38105	Years in Service	3 ½	99
		Present Work	Minister	102

Form 58

FILL-IN INDEX CARDS
Paper: workbook 321
Directions: for each
  name on Form 57,
  fill in data on one
  fill-in index card

Card holders, UP . . . when
typing on cards or envelopes

Stevens, Patrick K. (Dr.)
LAST NAME   FIRST NAME   MIDDLE NAME OR INITIAL
Post .... Providence, Rhode Island
Initiation ... September 22, 19--
Address .... 193 East Montauk Road
             Providence, Rhode Island   02904

Service .... Navy (Medical Corps)
Rank ...... Commander
Years Service 3½
Occupation Physician

Fill-in printed index card

LINE: 60
TAB: 5
SPACING: SINGLE
DRILLS: THREE TIMES
GOAL: REVIEW LETTER
 DISPLAYS
STRESS: OUTPUT

61-A. Type as evenly as you can—refuse to falter on the figures in line 3. Repeat in Lesson 62.

61-A. Tune up on these review lines

1 He and I did work the eighth problem also, and it is right.
2 Zoe enjoys a Pym diving board, which is quick but flexible.
3 Those five divisions increased 10%, 28%, 39%, 47%, and 56%.

61-B. Type lines 4-9 three times each; then repeat three more times either lines 4-6 for an accuracy gain or lines 7-9 for an increase in your speed.

61-B. Build skill on preview words and phrases

4 average serves uphill extra cases only ever rare him are on
5 suggest squeeze assumes indeed office letter three will all
6 paragraphs adjusts trusts these cases there here, even rare

7 of the | or one | on the | is not | of two | in the | be one | or the one
8 two or | one or | and he | are to | and if | for it | and so | one or two
9 than body name then with when make such but and for the man

61-C. Read the copy (it gives information worth remembering). Then, copy paragraph 10 twice if you need a speed gain or both paragraphs once if you need to improve in accuracy.

Or, take a 5-minute timing (with a 10-second rest after each minute) in Lesson 61 and another 5-minute writing (without rests) in Lesson 62. GOAL: At least 35 words a minute, with 4 or fewer errors.

SI 1.35—nearly normal

61-C. Build skill in sustained writing

10   Most of the letters typed in offices are plain ones of   12
two or three straight paragraphs. Such letters are easy to   24
place on the page; the standard guide to line length serves   36
quite well. But now and then there comes a letter with one   48
or more special parts to be displayed, like a subject line,   60
an attention line, a company name to be shown in the signa-   72
ture, or even a table or listing. These special parts take   84
more room than the word count would suggest (a subject line   96
of four words, for example, will alter the placement of the   108
letter as much as would two dozen extra words in the body).   120

11   What to do about placement, then, if a letter includes   132
some parts to be displayed? In most cases, the typist does   144
nothing special. He trusts that he will be able to squeeze   156
or spread the closing lines enough to adjust the placement.   168
Only in a borderline case (when it is debatable whether the   180
letter ought to be considered a short vs. average one or an   192
average vs. long one) should the typist make any adjustment   204
for the display lines, and here he assumes the letter to be   216
the next larger size and adjusts the margins for that size.   228

    1 | 2 | 3 | 4 | 5 | 6 | 7 | 8 | 9 | 10 | 11 | 12

61-D. GOAL: To complete each letter within 6 or fewer minutes, with not more than 4 typing errors. All four letters may be typed with identical tab and margin settings.

61/62-D. Produce a summary of letters with displays

Type as a four-page project, on plain paper or workbook pages 95-98, the four versions of Letter 22, as directed on page 103. The table in the letter is centered with 6 spaces between columns. Set a tab stop for each column; do not confuse these tabs with the one you set at the center.

Unit 27. Printed Forms

LINE: 60
TAB: 5
SPACING: SINGLE
DRILLS: THREE TIMES
GOAL: KEEP SKILL
    FROM LAGGING
STRESS: WRISTS,
    SHOULDERS, ARMS

163-A. Each line three times, smooth as music! Repeat in Lesson 164.

163-A. Tune up on these review lines

1   The profit they make by it may pay for the downtown chapel.
2   I was quickly penalized five or six times by Major Higgins.
3   Please fill in blanks No. (10), (28), (39), (47), and (56).
      1 | 2 | 3 | 4 | 5 | 6 | 7 | 8 | 9 | 10 | 11 | 12

163-B. What's your goal?

ACCURACY: Type each group of lines like a paragraph, three times.

SPEED: Type each line individually three times. Repeat in Lesson 164.

163-B. Boost skill by selective preview practice

4   professional alternated constantly questions amateur wonder
5   instructions telephones conference shrewdest realize novice
6   officemates interrupted executives notepaper respect reveal
      1 | 2 | 3 | 4 | 5 | 6 | 7 | 8 | 9 | 10 | 11 | 12
7   know what|that they|does not|what the|like to|what he|if it
8   will make|will ever|with the|will not|wish to|sign of|so he

163-C. Each paragraph two times, one of which must be perfect or contain not more than one error. SI 1.35—normal

163-C. Boost skill on sustained alphabetic paragraphs

9   The typical beginning worker does not like to ask many   12
questions. His is a normal fear: he does not want to seem   24
a novice; he does not wish to reveal what he does not know.   36
So he hopefully goes ahead with the tasks that are assigned   48
him, praying that all comes out well. He does not realize,   60
of course, that any error he makes just because he does not   72
know what he is to do next will make his officemates wonder   84
why in the world the newcomer didn't ask a question or two.   96
      1 | 2 | 3 | 4 | 5 | 6 | 7 | 8 | 9 | 10 | 11 | 12

ALTERNATE PLAN: Take 2-minute timings on each paragraph until you can complete each in 2 minutes with one or no error. Then (a) take one 5-minute timing to see how rapidly you can type within two errors, or (b) type the selection completely, to see how nearly you can complete it in 6 minutes with not more than two errors.

10   To protect himself and at the same time to get clearly   108
in mind the exact details of a set of instructions, the new   120
worker should grab a pencil and jot down enough notes to be   132
certain he has every step itemized. If there is any detail   144
that is not clear, he should ask a question about it. What   156
the majority of young workers do not know is that they will   168
be interrupted constantly. Steps three, four, five are not   180
so easy when they are alternated with steps in another job!   192
      1 | 2 | 3 | 4 | 5 | 6 | 7 | 8 | 9 | 10 | 11 | 12

11   Jotting down notes or asking questions is not the sign   204
of an amateur but the mark of a professional. All the real   216
executives carry a pencil and notepaper in their pockets at   228
all times. They keep a pencil and pad by their telephones.   240
They never go to a conference without pen and pencil. They   252
are the shrewdest quiz masters and speediest answer writers   264
you will ever see in action. They have great respect for a   276
person who knows what to ask, and when to ask it, and asks!   288

SPECIAL ASSIGNMENT: To review the rules of alphabetic indexing, do the Learning Guide on workbook pages 315-318.

163/164-D. Apply skill to production forms typing

ASSIGNMENTS	ARRANGEMENTS	SPECIAL INSTRUCTIONS	WORDS
Letter 22	Blocked form	Type the letter shown below (set tab stops for table before starting to type).	196
Letter 23	Blocked form	Type the letter below, but add JUNIOR EXECUTIVE (as a company signature).	202
Letter 24	Blocked form	Type the letter below, but add Attention Mr. Frank L. Klein.	214
Letter 25	Blocked form	Type the letter below, but add SUBJECT: YOUR RATE INQUIRY.	215

Letter 22

BLOCKED LETTER
Shown: in elite
Paper: workbook
Body: 122 words
Tabs: 3 (center
    and table)
SI: 1.52—fairly
    difficult

December 10, 19— 4

8

Foote, Klein & Hughes, Inc. 14
1300 Rider Building 18
Trenton, New Jersey   08607 22
23

Gentlemen: 25
26

Thank you for your inquiry of December 5 concerning our rates 39
for space in JUNIOR EXECUTIVE magazine. We are enclosing our 51
standard rate card. You will note on it that the rates for 63
the space dimensions about which you specifically asked are 75
as follows: 78
79

Quarter page $125.00 85
One-half page   235.00 91
Complete page   400.00 98
99

Worth noting also is the 10% discount that you earn for four 111
or more reservations in one calendar year. We allow the usual 123
15% agency fee, of course. 129
130

If you wish to reserve space in our February issue, which is 142
the next one going to press, we should have your reservation 154
(and copy, if it is to be set) not later than December 28. 166
Thank you for your inquiry. 172
173

Yours very truly, 179

182

J. Paul Prescott 187
Business Manager 192
193

urs 194
Enclosure 196

Business Letter in Blocked Style, with Table

Letter 84

ORDER-FORM LETTER
Paper: plain
Carbons: 3
Position: center
SI: 1.49—fairly hard

Prepare four copies of this order-form letter, centered vertically and horizontally: the original to bear the fastened note to the Duplicating Department, two carbons for enclosing with Letters 82 and 83, and one carbon for Mr. Harris's Promotion Plans file. Indicate on his copy "cc's to Owen Johnson and Jim Blake; original to Duplicating on [date]."

Duplicating Department:
    500 copies by 4:00 p.m. tomorrow, please.
                            F. G. H.

		Fall
Judd—Kane, Inc.		~~Spring~~, 19--	10
1410 Glenarm Street			14
Denver, Colorado 80202			19

ATTENTION OF *Frank G. Harris* ~~THE SALES MANAGER~~   39

Gentlemen: 43

Please send me, *express* ~~postage~~ prepaid, the indicated quantities of the   57
~~the~~ following advertising aids for Judd—Kane Products: 67

Quantity	Item No.	Description *(center)* →]	
	WC7R (8)	Large window cards in which a J-K radio may	103
_8_		be *placed* ~~inset~~. ~~Approx~~. 4x4 feet. #←	109
	WC7T	Large window cards that may be used to frame	124
		a J-K television set. 5x6 feet.	133
	SC3R	Set cards to place beside a J-K radio. Hand	148
		on card points to dials. 18x8 inches.	158
	SC3T	Set cards to place *on* ~~atop~~ a J-k television set.	172
		Hands point to push buttons. 24x16 inches.	183
	Nm5R	News mat, for use in advertising any *J-K* ~~Judd-~~	197
		~~Kane~~ radio in newspaper.S 3x3 ~~feet.~~ *inches*	206
	Nm5T	News mat, for use in advertising any J-K	220
		television *set* in newspapers. ~~5x3~~ *out 3x3* inches.	231

I understand that these aids *will* come to me with ~~no~~ *out 3x3* charge and maybe   245
used or not ~~be~~ used as I may prefer.   254

Send to: 258

Person or Dept   271
Company Name .... _____   285
                                              299
Street Address .... _____   300

City, State, ZIP .... _____   313

OK as corrected
F. G. H.

Draft of an Order-Form Letter

Unit 11. Printed Forms

LINE: 60
TAB: 5
SPACING: SINGLE
DRILLS: THREE TIMES
GOAL: PRODUCE
   OFFICE MEMOS
STRESS: TOUCH
   OPERATION

63-A. Tune up on these review lines

63-A. Set an easy, steady pace on line 1; then try to maintain it on lines 2 and 3. Repeat in Lesson 64.

1 When is it the duty of the eight men to visit their island?
2 Mr. Black requested sixty jeeps for moving the prizes away.
3 10 28 39 47 56 we 23 up 70 out 975 wit 285 rue 473 yip 680.

63-B. Build skill via preview word practice

63-B. Type these preview lines as though they were a paragraph; then type the "paragraph" three times; speed up on repetitions.

4 AA any BB bills CC check DD don't EE need FF office GG good
5 HH help II its JJ adjust KK work LL likely MM memos NN many
6 OO once PP reports QQ quarter RR require SS less TT typists
7 UU cut VV involves WW whole XX example YY unlikely ZZ sizes

63-C. Build skill in sustained writing

63-C. Read the copy and silently rehearse reaches to the tabulator and the numbers; type a single-spaced copy (leaving a blank line between each of the paragraphs, of course) completely by touch and without pausing.

Or, take a 5-minute timing (with a short rest after every minute) in Lesson 63 and another 5-minute one (with no rests) in Lesson 64. GOAL: 35 or more words a minute, within 4 errors.

SI 1.35—nearly normal (if you indent by touch!)

One of the modern trends in office work is to use more   12
printed forms. There are many good reasons for this trend: 24

1. One reason is the fact that our government requires   37
many reports, all of which must be prepared on exact forms.   49

2. A second is the fact that the forms are so designed   62
that the typist is unlikely to leave out or to misplace any   74
important details; thus, accuracy is helped to some extent.   86

3. One value of forms is the way they get rid of prob-   99
lems of placement and arrangement; you don't have to adjust   111
margins for memos or bills of different sizes, for example.   123

4. The use of forms reduces the need for adjusting the   136
typewriter, too. Once a machine has its margin and its tab   148
stops set for a certain form, the typist can produce copies   160
of that form all day long without adjusting the typewriter.   172

5. Forms cut down the amount of typing required to say   185
what is to be said. A check, for instance, is a whole mes-   197
sage boiled down to its essence, which involves less than a   209
quarter of what would have to be said in a complete letter.   221

6. Studies show that using forms for routine work cuts   234
costs, because they increase output, with a higher quality.   246

1 | 2 | 3 | 4 | 5 | 6 | 7 | 8 | 9 | 10 | 11 | 12

63/64-D. Learn to type interoffice memoranda

63-D. It might be a good idea for you to repeat the two alignment drills in Lesson 54-A on page 89.

Study the illustrations on the next two pages; then see how many of the assignments you can complete within the time limits suggested.

LINE: 60
TAB: 5
SPACING: SINGLE
GOAL: APPLY SKILL
　TO PRODUCTION
DRILLS: THREE TIMES
STRESS: ATTENTION
　TO TECHNICALITIES

LESSONS
161–162

Order Letters

161-A. Each line three times. Repeat in 162.

161-A. Tune up on these review lines

1　Why not buy him the new cap and let him see you pay for it?

2　When did Professor Black give you a major quiz on the text?

3　The 10%, 28%, and 39% discounts remain; the 47% and 56% go.

　　1 | 2 | 3 | 4 | 5 | 6 | 7 | 8 | 9 | 10 | 11 | 12

161-B. Change to double spacing and a 70-space line (lines will align).

Type each paragraph (the letter body) twice; one copy, at least, must be typed with 0 or 1 error.
SI: 1.29—easy

161-B. Sustain skill on production copy

This letter is to Mr. Owen Johnson, Manager, Meyer TV-Radio Store, 1229 East　27
Ninth Street, White Plains, New York　10602. Provide a bcc copy for the Dealer　36
Service Dept. OPENING LINES.

4　Dear Mr. Johnson: I apologize for the delay in replying to　13　50
your recent letter in which you inquired whether we would have　26　63
new display pieces for our dealers this fall; we were working on　39　76
the announcement about them when your letter reached my　50　87
desk, and so I held up a reply until I could have a copy for you.　63　100
Well, the copy is enclosed; check off what you want, just as you　75　114
did last year, and send it back to me. I invite your attention to　90　128
the third item on the list; it is new, and it is a honey that will　103　141
pull in the customers right off the sidewalk! Thank you again　116　155
for writing. I hope you get excellent sales results. CLOSING LINES.　126　191

　　1 | 2 | 3 | 4 | 5 | 6 | 7 | 8 | 9 | 10 | 11 | 12　↓

Letter 82

BLOCKED LETTER
Paper: workbook 311
Carbons: ?
Paragraphs: 3
Enclosure: Letter 84
Body: 119 words
SI: 1.36—easy-normal

This letter is to James N. Blake, Manager, East Akron Music Store, 4273 West　28
Farm Park, Akron, Ohio　44309. Provide a bcc copy for the Dealer Service Dept.　34
OPENING LINES.

5　Dear Jim: As I promised you at the convention in White　138　47
Springs, I am sending to you an advance copy of the general　150　59
announcement about our new fall advertising aids, the one that　162　72
will be mailed out to the dealer list about the first of next month.　176　86
If you will send the list back to me by return mail, marked for　189　100
my attention, I will take steps to see that your requisition gets　202　113
to Akron in time for your big sale. The third item on the list is　216　126
the dandy I described at White Springs. If there's any hitch,　228　140
Jim, don't hesitate to wire or call me collect; I am just as eager　242　153
as you are to see you sell a thousand of our sets! CLOSING LINES.　252　189

　　1 | 2 | 3 | 4 | 5 | 6 | 7 | 8 | 9 | 10 | 11 | 12

Letter 83

BLOCKED LETTER
Paper: workbook 313
Carbons: ?
Paragraphs: ?
Enclosure: Letter 84
Body: 123 words
SI: 1.33—fairly easy

If you lack the workbook letterheads, use plain paper on which you show the depth of a letterhead by a ruled line or crease 1½ inches from the top.

161/162-C. Apply skill in letter production

An interoffice memo is a message from one person to another in the same firm, usually typed on a form with printed "guides" (like *To* and *Date*).

1. The forms are either full size (8½ by 11) or half size (8½ by 5½, or 5½ by 8½). Guide words may appear in any of many different arrangements.

2. Set left margin at the heading aligning point and right margin to equal the left (by estimate).

3. Begin insertions 2 or 3 spaces after the pertinent guides, aligned with them at the bottom.

4. Separate body and heading by 2 blank lines.

5. Ordinarily, use no salutation or closing.

6. Align the signature line (initials, name, or title, as writer prefers) with the date (set tab).

7. Use reference lines as you do in letters.

```
To:       Margaret Norton          December 12, 19--
          Millinery Department

From:     Frederick Lincoln
          Personnel Department

Subject:  Promotion for Jean Louise Young


We are pleased to approve your recommendation that Miss Young
be advanced to the position of Assistant Buyer and receive a
salary increase of an additional $100 a month.  The new posi-
tion will become effective on January 2.  Please extend our
sincere congratulations to Miss Young.

                                         F. L.

urs
cc Payroll Department
```

Memos may also be typed on plain paper. LINE: 60. TAB: 10 (to align heading details). TOP MARGIN: 1 inch. DATE: Pivoted. SIGNATURE: Aligned with date (tab).

Form 4

INTEROFFICE MEMO
Shown: in pica
Form: in workbook
SI: 1.30—fairly easy

Interoffice Memorandum

TO:	N. P. Montclaire	**DATE:** December 12, 19—	8
	Bureau of Personnel		12
			13
FROM:	Simon V. Johnston		17
	Vice-President		20
			21
SUBJECT:	Conference on New Kinds of Employment Tests▼3		29

```
                                                                    30
                                                                    31
          At some time in the near future, Nate, please try to      42
          set up a meeting at which you, Miss Benz, Mr. Clark,       53
          and I could spend an hour or two in conference with        63
          Dr. Mark Bjorgens, of Houlton College, to talk about       74
          the tests we give to job applicants.                       81
                                                                    82
          Doctor Bjorgens has just wound up a long study on the      93
          values of some new kinds of tests for predicting the      104
          success of new office workers.  From what I have been     114
          told, his findings should be of keen interest to us.      125
          We may ask him to review the tests we are now using.      136
                                                                    137
                              S. V. J.                              140
                                                                    141
     urs                                                            142
```

Standard Arrangement of an Interoffice Memorandum

Letter 79

BLOCKED LETTER
Paper: workbook 305
Carbons: two bcc's,
  two cc's, one file
Paragraphs: 3
Body: 119 words and
  attention line
SI: 1.40—normal

This letter is from Mr. Harris to Allied Carrier Group, Inc., 1800 First Trust Building, 1448   20
West Ninth Street, Phoenix, Arizona 85026, attention of Mr. J. T. Norge. Provide bcc   45
copies for the Roswell Factory and Mr. Hodges. Provide cc copies for Mr. Kearn and Mr.   49
Pierson. Identify the enclosure as "Silverman letter." Provide all missing elements.   57

This letter is to confirm our telephone call about the three damaged   74
TV sets delivered two days ago to the retail store of Silverman &   88
Brothers, Inc., in Albuquerque. Protection against this damage is our   102
Policy No. 88-3617 with you. As you will note from the letter enclosed,   117
we have asked the store to hold the damaged TV sets and the crates in   131
which they arrived until your agent can pick them up. We are also ask-   145
ing Mr. John Pierson, our own agent, to view these materials to see   159
what change, if any, ought to be made in our crates. When you are   173
ready to settle this case, please write our counsel, Mr. Ralph E. Kearn,   188
at this address. CLOSING LINES.   208

Letter 80

BLOCKED LETTER
Paper: workbook 307
Carbons: ?
Paragraphs: 3
Body: 149 words
SI: 1.36—easy-normal

This letter is to Mr. John F. Pierson, Field Service, Inc., 3274 West Desert Road, Tucson,   22
Arizona 85702. Provide bcc copies for Mr. Hodges and Mr. Kearn. Provide a cc copy for   24
the Roswell Factory. Identify the enclosure letters. Because Pierson and Harris are friends,   39
this is a "Dear Jack" letter. OPENING LINES.   41

As you will see from the enclosed carbon copies, we have one more   56
case of a damaged shipment to Silverman's, in Albuquerque—the   68
third case in two years. If you can, Jack, fly that Apache of yours over   84
to our factory in Roswell, to see the exact steps used in crating our TV   99
sets; then fly over for a look at the sets and crates at Silverman's   113
before the Allied agent picks them up. I know this is a great deal of   127
trouble for three little TV sets, but there may be more involved than   141
meets the eye. I shall be most interested in what you may find out.   156
Who is at fault? Our men at the factory, the truck driver, or someone   170
at the store? Although I am very anxious for your report, Jack, take   184
enough time to dig out the facts and tie them together for us. CLOSING.   212

Letter 81

BLOCKED LETTER
Paper: workbook 309
Carbons: ?
Paragraphs: 3
Body: 51 words
SI: 1.46—fairly hard

This letter is to the addressee of Letter 74, page 244. Provide a bcc copy to Jeannette   33
Rawlins, of Letter 75, with the annotation "Good! The kind man gave us a GO signal. Let's
move on the first newsletter, shall we?" Add a copy, including the bcc notation, to the
Letter 75 file. Provide all missing elements.

Thank you very much for your prompt reply to my letter of [*date of*   50
Letter 74]. Thank you even more for giving permission for us to quote   64
you in the newsletter we plan to publish soon for our dealers! I hope   79
that I may have an early chance to repay your kindness. CLOSING LINES.   117

INTEROFFICE MEMO

Date: December 13, 19--

From: Ewell Blackstone   **Ext.** 2182
Art Department

To: George McAdams   **Floor:** 5
Advertising Department

Subject: Art for the <u>McCalls</u> Advertisement

I am sorry to tell you that we sh~~~
be delayed a~ ~~~~

~~~ in <u>McCalls</u>.

Blackstone

urs

Memorandum

TO: Stephen R. Quinette   **FROM:** Inez C. Carpenter
Systems Division   Training Department

SUBJECT: Use of Printed Forms   **DATE:** December 12, 19--

When I attended a recent meeting of the National Office
Management Association, I was amazed to learn that--

1. Most of the other large firms in the city use many
more printed forms than we do.

2. Th~

      I. C. C.

urs
cc Mr. Thompson

Interoffice memorandum forms appear in many sizes, arrangements,
and styles; but the guide words make most of them "self-coaching."

Form 5

INTEROFFICE MEMO
Form: workbook (or
plain paper; see
page 105 example)
Goal: 5 minutes
SI: 1.43—normal

Memo to Paul W. Graham | Training Bureau | *From* Simon V.   15
Johnston | Vice-President | *on the subject of* Sending Someone to   24
Houston Conference | I noted in an article in <u>Junior Executive</u>   45
magazine that the University of Houston will conduct a con-   57
ference for a week this summer for directors of office training. It   71
seems to me that it might be wise for us to have you or a mem-   83
ber of your staff take part in this program. *New Paragraph.*   92
Please write to the University and obtain full details. When you   106
have them, please draft for me an estimate of what it would cost   119
for us to send someone. If possible, let me have your report well   132
before the first of March. | S. V. J. | urs | cc Mr. Montclaire   147

Form 6

INTEROFFICE MEMO
Form: workbook
Goal: 5 minutes
SI: 1.39—normal

Memo from George McAdams | *Extension* 2044 | Advertising   13
Department | *To* Ewell Blackstone | *Floor* 8 | Art Department   23
| *on the subject of* Art for the <u>McCalls</u> Advertisement | Thank   37
you for letting me know about the delay in getting the art ready   52
for the special <u>McCalls</u> campaign. I got in touch with the maga-   69
zine as soon as I received your note and found we could have an   79
extension of a week in the deadline. *New Paragraph.* Even so, we   90
shall have to move with dispatch in getting the art finished and   103
the plates made. I hope it will be possible for you and your staff   117
to place a high priority on the job for us. Thanks again for your   130
help. | McAdams | urs | cc Miss Patrick cc Mr. Benardo   144

Form 7

INTEROFFICE MEMO
Form: workbook
Goal: 10 minutes
SI: 1.36—normal

Memo to Inez C. Carpenter *of the* Training Department *from*   9
Stephen R. Quinette *of the* Systems Division *on the subject of* Use   19
of Printed Forms *dated today.* | You are correct in noting the   35
trend toward the increasing use of forms. There are many good   47
reasons for this trend: [*Continue with the six numbered para-*   52
graphs on page 104; arrange them in enumeration form, as on   294
page 80.] S. R. Q. | urs   298

Type "bcc" notation
after removing the
original and carbon
copies that are not
to carry this note.

September 22, 19—

Mr. Marti
Silverman
388 Buena
Albuquerq

Dear Mr.

Thank you
the marri
televisio
assure yo

I am havi
you. Plea
in which
you are v
Allied Ca
He will d
relieve y

Again let
inconvenie
you wish

urs
cc Allied
cc Mr. Pie

JUDD-KANE, INC.

CABLE ADDRESS: JUDKANDEN

1410 GLENARM STREET • DENVER, COLORADO   80202 • TABOR 5-7500

September 22, 19—   4

7

Please retype on full-size stationery

Mr. Martin T. Silverman   12
Silverman & Brothers, Inc.   17
388 Buena Vista Plaza   22
Albuquerque, New Mexico   87101   28

29

Dear Mr. Silverman: 33

34

Thank you very much for ^bringing ~~calling~~ our attention ~~to~~   44
the marring of the finish on three of the twelve   54
television sets that you recieved last week. I   64
assure you that your chagrin is matched by ours.   74

75

I am having three replacement sets expressed to   84
you.# Please ~~return~~ *keep* the damaged sets and the boxes   94
in which they came, if you still have them, until   104
you are visited within a week or ^so by an agent of   114
Allied Carrier Group, which insures our shipments.   125
He will decide on the disposition of the sets and   135
relieve you of them.   139

140

Again let me say that we are sorry you have been   150
inconvenienced. If there is any further action   159
you wish us to make, please let ~~us~~ *me* know.   168

169

Very sincerely yours,   174

176

Frank G. Harris   180
urs   Sales Manager   185
cc Allied Carrier   189
cc Mr. Pierson   192

Blocked Business Letter on Baronial Stationery, with CC and BCC notations

---

Letter 78

BLOCKED LETTER
Paper: workbook 303
Carbons: two cc's,
  two bcc's, one file
Body: 123 words
SI: 1.42—normal

Forms Typing

LINE: 60
TAB: 5
SPACING: SINGLE
DRILLS: THREE TIMES
GOAL: PRODUCE
INVOICES
STRESS: NUMBERS
BY TOUCH

65-A. Set an easy, smooth pace on line 1; then try to hold the same pace on lines 2 and 3. Repeat this warmup in Lesson 66.

65-B. Type lines 4-7 three times each: first, slowly and very evenly; then, steadily speeding up until you race across the line on your third typing of it.

65-C. Read the copy; then type and retype each of the paragraphs until you can complete each one in 3 minutes, within 3 errors.

Or, take a 3-minute timing on each paragraph, followed by a 5-minute timing on the two together.

GOAL: 40 or more wam with 4 or fewer errors.

SI 1.24—easy (fine for increasing your speed!)

If you can maintain the standard "waltz" tempo of 3 strokes a second, your speed is 36 words a minute!

If you do not have the workbook forms, perhaps you can rule some like those shown on page 108.

65-A. Tune up on these review lines

1 He paid the neighbor to make an ivory panel for the chapel.
2 Six or seven flashing new jet planes quickly zoomed by him.
3 He got 56 green ones @ .39; 47 blue @ .28; 10 purple @ .10.

65-B. Speed up on downhill preview words

4 glance, tricks forms ought make them with aid for the to be
5 weights sheets check judge gift then also yet the one if no
6 closing flinch would study know each time out all his or if
7 papers, typist whole first sure size that the aid may be on

65-C. Build skill in sustained writing

8 At first glance, some of the printed forms used in the   12
office might seem to be complex; but only a moment of study   24
is required to understand how to use most of them, for most 36
forms are simply letters. Take a bill or a check or a memo 48
or a telegram, for instance; each is just a letter with the 60
greeting and closing left out. Once you realize this fact, 72
forms begin to make sense. You can also see from this fact 84
how much time forms save; if you had to type a whole letter 96
instead of fill in a form each time you prepared a telegram 108
or bill or check, you would not get a quarter as much done. 120

9 One more aid that pays its way by saving time and that 132
is part of the equipment to be found in all desks is carbon 144
paper. If no one knew of carbon sheets, so that the typist 156
had to write one at a time all his extra copies of business 168
papers, and then someone came up with carbon paper as a new 180
thing, you sure would judge it to be the finest gift of all 192
time. Far from flinching from the use of carbons, a typist 204
ought to bless the lovely stuff and learn all the tricks of 216
using it. Yet few typists know much about the many colors, 228
sizes, and weights in which this magic aid may be obtained. 240

  1 | 2 | 3 | 4 | 5 | 6 | 7 | 8 | 9 | 10 | 11 | 12

65/66-D. Learn to type invoices and telegrams

Study the illustrations on the next two pages; then see how many of the assignments you can complete within 5 minutes and 4 errors each.

LINE: 60
TAB: 5
SPACING: SINGLE
GOALS: BUILD SKILL,
MASTER "BCC"
STRESS: STROKING FOR
CARBON COPIES

159-A. Tune up on these review lines

159-A. Each line three
or more times. Repeat
fully in Lesson 160.

1 You may ask her for the old oak box she had him get for us.

2 James lazily picked the big onyx rings off the woven quilt.

3 The five maple boards measured 10", 28", 39", 47", and 56".
   `  1  |  2  |  3  |  4  |  5  |  6  |  7  |  8  |  9  | 10  | 11  | 12`

159-B. Extend skill on copy of normal difficulty

159-B. Change to double
spacing. Confirm margin
settings for a 60-space
line (copy aligns if you
observe bell correctly).

Type each paragraph one
or more times—until it
is typed with no or only
one error. You may wish
to divide this practice
between 159 and 160.

SI 1.37—normal, average

`  1  |  2  |  3  |  4  |  5  |  6  |  7  |  8  |  9  | 10  | 11  | 12  | 13  | 14`

4 There are two kinds of carbon copy notations, and they are used   14
so frequently that the typist should know of both.   24

5 The first is the one that is typed below the reference symbols to   39
assure the addressee that other persons involved in the matter at   53
hand have been informed. If Mr. Harris is writing to Mr. Dole to   66
tell him that Mr. White will make an adjustment in a bill, Mr. Dole   79
will be reassured if he sees the expected "cc Mr. White" note at the   93
foot of the letter.   97

6 The second kind of note is the one that is made when a copy of a   112
letter is to go to a third party without the fact being told to the ad-   126
dressee of the letter. For example, if a customer writes you an angry   141
letter, you might answer him gently but hustle a copy of his letter   154
and of yours to your local agent with the request that he check into   168
the matter. Or, again, suppose your firm is worried about a flaw in   182
one of its products; you might have been asked to relay to some   195
department copies of all the correspondence about the item.   207

TOP OF PAGE:

bcc Accounting
bcc Miss Carr
bcc Mr. French

7 When a copy is to be sent without the knowledge of the addressee,   222
the fact should not be shown on the original, of course, but has to be   236
written on the copy itself and on the file copy. When the typist   249
finishes the letter and removes it from his machine, he peels off the   263
original copy and any others on which the notation is not to appear;   277
then he puts the rest of the carbon pack back into the machine and   291
types the notation at the left margin, about an inch from the top of   304
the paper. The notation consists of the letters "bcc"—blind carbon   318
copy—and the name of the department or person to whom the copy   331
is to be sent; if several copies are to be distributed, the letter may have   346
both "cc" and "bcc" notes.   353

BOTTOM OF PAGE:

cc Mr. Jones
cc Miss Smith
cc Lima Office

`  1  |  2  |  3  |  4  |  5  |  6  |  7  |  8  |  9  | 10  | 11  | 12  | 13  | 14`

159/160-C. Apply skill to an integrated letter series

If you lack the workbook
letterheads, use plain
paper on which you show
the depth of a letterhead
by a ruled line or crease
1½ inches from the top.

An invoice is a list of the charges for one delivery of goods or services, usually typed on a form with printed guide words for positioning heading details and ruled lines for positioning the columns.

1. Invoices come in an infinite variety of sizes, designs, and arrangements.

2. Number columns are aligned at the right, 2 or 3 spaces before the end of their column areas.

3. Word columns are aligned at the left, 2 or 3 spaces after the start of their column areas.

4. The left margin is set at the first column. Tab stops are set for additional columns.

5. To the extent possible, heading entries are aligned at the margin or tab stops of the body.

6. The words *Amount Due* are aligned (tab stop) at the start of the printed word, *Descriptions*.

7. The typist is responsible for *all* details.

```
              MEREDITH TYPING SERVICE

        305 Rosslyn Street - Los Angeles, California   90057

    To:        Mr. Chester L. Harris          December 14, 19--
               1039 West Eighth Avenue
               Los Angeles, California   90017

    Subject:  Invoice for Materials Delivered Herewith
    _____

               Chapter I of thesis:
    12         Pages of straight copy @ .30              3.60
     6         Pages involving unique display @ .50      3.00
     2         Pages involving tables @ .50              1.00
    40         Pages of carbon copies @ .05              2.00

               AMOUNT DUE                                9.60
```

Invoices may also be typed in memo style on plain paper. Return address is centered (not typed after From). LINE: 60. TABS: 10 and 56. TOP MARGIN: ½ inch. DATE: pivoted.

Form 8

INVOICE
Form: workbook (or plain paper, as shown above)
Word count: 121
Tabs: 4

MEREDITH TYPING SERVICE

305 ROSSLYN STREET · LOS ANGELES, CALIFORNIA   90057

TO: Mr. Chester L. Harris
       1039 West Eighth Avenue
       Los Angeles, California   90017

DATE: December 14, 19--   INVOICE

QUANTITY	DESCRIPTIONS	UNIT PRICE	AMOUNT
	Chapter II of thesis		
14	Pages of straight copy	.30	4.20
6	Pages including tables	.50	3.00
40	Pages of carbon copies	.05	2.00
	Chapter III of thesis		
24	Pages of straight copy	.30	7.20
2	Pages including tables	.50	1.00
52	Pages of carbon copies	.05	2.60
	AMOUNT DUE		20.00
	3% SALES TAX		.60
	TOTAL AMOUNT DUE		20.60

STANDARD INVOICE FORM

The bottom two lines would be omitted if no taxes were involved.

Form 9

INVOICE
Form: workbook

Prepare another invoice to Mr. Harris, above; compute all amounts. For Chapter IV of thesis: 30 Pages of straight copy @ .30 | 6 Pages including tables @ .50 | 72 Pages of carbon copies @ .05 || For Chapter V of thesis: 19 Pages of straight copy @ .30 | 13 Pages including tables @ .50 | 64 Pages of carbon copies @ .05. Check the "Amount Due" carefully and add on the 3% sales tax. The "Total Amount Due" should come to $31.93.

25
35
54
81
89
104
119
121

16

1851 Diversey Parkway   LINE 8   31

32

Chicago, Illinois   60614   LINE 10   49

52

Letter 77

COPY OF AN INCOMING
SEMIBLOCKED LETTER
Paper: plain, full
Copies: original for
   Letter 74 enc. plus
   carbon in 74 file,
   carbon as 75 enc.,
   carbon for 75 file
SI: 1.56—difficult

December 21, 19--   67

68

C O P Y   77

79

Mr. Frank G. Harris   83
Sales Manager   86
Judd-Kane, Inc.   89
1410 Glenarm Street   93
Denver, Colorado   80202   98

99

Dear Mr. Harris: 103

104

This is not the usual kind of letter in which   114
a dealer writes to protest about something. To the   124
contrary, it is a letter of appreciation.   133

134

We have now been handling Judd-Kane television   144
and radio sets for almost exactly one year. In that   155
time we have sold more than a thousand J-K products.   166
At no time have we had to wait for deliveries. At   176
no time have we suffered either loss or inconvenience   187
from shipping damages. At all times your firm moved   197
promptly and effectively to serve our needs.   206

207

So, this is just a quiet note to let you know   218
that at least one of your dealers truly appreciates   228
the service that Judd-Kane gives its dealers. It's   238
a real privilege, we feel, to carry the J-K sign on   249
our door and to represent you in Chicago.   257

258

Yours very sincerely,   265

266

UNITED APPLIANCES COMPANY   273

274

(SIGNED)   279

280

E. L. Houston, Manager   287

288

FTT/urs   295

Exact Copy of an Incoming Semiblocked Letter

Typist makes exact, line-for-line copy (even including errors, if any), adding
only the parts (shown here in color) that identify it as a copy, not original.

Prepare an invoice of the Manufacturers Institute to the Training Department | J. F. Belton Company | 3500 Riverside Road | Lincoln, Nebraska 68504 | for the following items: 21 (copies of) Rafael: Production Tooling @ 4.50 = 94.50 | 1 (copy of) Rafael: PT Instructor's Manual @ 5.50 = 5.50 | 70 Benkley: Modern Plant Safety @ 2.50 = 175.00 | 1 Benkley: MPS Instructor's Manual @ 3.50 = 3.50 | AMOUNT DUE = 278.50 | 10% MEMBER'S DISCOUNT = 27.85 | TOTAL AMOUNT DUE = 250.65.

18
25
43
56
71
87
105

Prepare another invoice of the Manufacturers Institute to Mr. Thomas S. Klauss | Training Department | Condon & Willhite, Inc. | 1700 Cimmaron Building | Tulsa, Oklahoma 74102 | for the following (compute all amounts): 10 Stephens: Dredges and Drills @ 4.00 | 1 Stephens: DD Instructor's Manual @ 7.50 | 20 Rafael: Production Tooling @ 4.50 | 1 Rafael: PT Instructor's Manual @ 5.50 | 1 Rafael: PT Filmstrip (Set) @ 65.00 | Compute AMOUNT DUE | Indicate 10% MEMBER'S DISCOUNT | TOTAL AMOUNT DUE should be 187.20.

17
30
39
54
72
89
108
124

TELEGRAM FORM

(1) Align left margin with box in which you type "X" to indicate desired service.

(2) Set a tab stop 2 or 3 spaces inside the charge box to align the name of the paying (sending) firm, the origin-date line, and the signature lines.

(3) Plan to leave equal space to balance right margin with left margin.

(4) Use blocked form and single spacing, as shown.

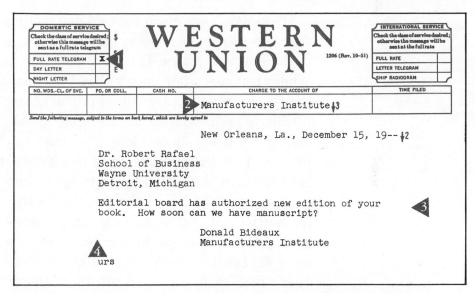

Telegram 1. Full rate | from Manufacturers Institute | New Orleans, La., current date | to Mr. Herbert F. Lewis | Starrett Engineering Co. | 15300 Euclid Avenue | Cleveland, Ohio | Pleased to accept your invitation to speak at May 9 convention. Thanks for the privilege. | Donald Bideaux | Manufacturers Institute | urs

14
28
38
51
64
70

Telegram 2. Full rate | from Manufacturers Institute | New Orleans, La., current date | to Dr. Maurice Trethaway | School of Business | University of Illinois | Champaign, Illinois | New Simpson edition delayed until May 1. Shall we fill order with present edition? | Donald Bideaux | Manufacturers Institute | urs

14
28
41
53
67
69

NOTE: Attach to each letter all the materials to be enclosed with it.

Letter 74

BLOCKED LETTER
Paper: workbook 297*
Paragraphs: 3
Carbons: file and
    letter 75 enclosure
Body: 113 words
Enclosures: original
    of Letter 77
SI: 1.45—average

*Or plain paper on which you rule or crease a line across the page 1½ inches from the top to represent the depth of a letterhead.

Letter 75

BLOCKED LETTER
Paper: workbook 299
Paragraphs: 5
Carbons: file only
Body: 181 words
Enclosures: copies of
    Letters 74, 77
SI: 1.40—average

Mr. Harris prefers numbered paragraphs to be displayed as shown on page 80.

Letter 76

BLOCKED LETTER
Paper: workbook 301
Paragraphs: 3
Carbons: file only
Body: 82 words
SI: 1.34—easy-normal

Mr. Harris permits use of company signature when it helps letter placement.

Your employer is Frank G. Harris, sales manager of Judd-Kane, Inc. He prefers the blocked form as illustrated on page 206. This letter is to Mr. E. L. Houston, Manager, United Appliances Company, 1851 Diversey Parkway, Chicago, Illinois 60614. Provide all missing elements. | 11 / 28 / 44

Last December you were kind enough to send us a fine letter concerning the services that Judd-Kane had extended to you during your first year as a Judd-Kane agency; I am enclosing a copy of your letter on the chance you may not have one at hand. If you still feel as enthusiastic about our services as you did when you sent that letter, we should like your permission to quote your last sentence in one of a series of promotion newsletters that we are planning to develop as an additional service to our dealer network. We should be very happy, Mr. Houston, to receive a letter of permission from you. CLOSING LINES. | 58 / 71 / 85 / 100 / 114 / 127 / 141 / 156 / 183

This letter is to Miss Jeannette Rawlins, Graham-Jacobs Agency, 5475 Bulwer Avenue, St. Louis, Missouri 63155. OPENING LINES. | 21 / 31

Thank you very much for bringing us up to date on the status of the plans you are developing for our campaign to recruit more dealers in the southern states. Let me answer the questions you raised: (1) While there are a few details that I should like to discuss with you, the general plan has the full approval of our Executive Committee. (2) I have reviewed a number of recent letters from our dealers to find one with a good "quotable quote" that might be suitable for your purpose. I am enclosing a copy of it. I have written to my correspondent to ask his permission for us to quote him; I am enclosing a copy of this letter. (3) Yes, I think we are ready to establish a schedule for putting the campaign in action; I should appreciate your suggesting one that would fit the design of your campaign. I expect to be in St. Louis in about two weeks. Do you think we could meet at your office then and iron out the final details of the campaign? CLOSING LINES. | 44 / 58 / 74 / 89 / 101 / 118 / 132 / 147 / 162 / 178 / 192 / 208 / 222 / 235 / 253

This letter, to be issued over your signature as "assistant to Mr. Harris," is to Reservations Manager, Sheraton-Jefferson Hotel, 415 North 12 Boulevard, St. Louis, Missouri 63155. OPENING LINES. | 19 / 36 / 39

Please make a reservation for Mr. Frank G. Harris, sales manager of this firm. Mr. Harris would like a single room, with either shower or bath, for five nights beginning [*insert date of second Sunday from now*]. He will arrive by air late in the day and is willing to make a deposit to assure that a room is held for him. Please let us have a confirmation of this reservation and let us know whether you wish us to make a deposit on the room. CLOSING LINES. | 53 / 68 / 80 / 92 / 107 / 120 / 138

LINE: 60
TAB: 5 AND CENTER
SPACING: SINGLE
DRILLS: THREE TIMES
GOAL: REVIEW FORMS
  AND LETTERS
STRESS: VIGOR

67-A. See whether you can type lines 1-3 four times in a minute. Repeat these lines in Lesson 68, too.

67-B. The vertical lines are simply to guide you in recognizing phrases; don't pause when you come to one. Start slowly and speed up on repetitions.

67-C. Take five 1-minute writings, with a pause after each minute; then take a straight 5-minute writing (with no rests). Try to equal the score you made in Lesson 65-C.

Or, type a copy of this letter, trying to finish it within 5 minutes and with 4 or fewer errors.

Note that the letter is shown here on a 55-space line; when you type it, however, use a 50- or 60-space line (whichever is correct for an average letter on your machine).

Letter 26

BLOCKED LETTER
Paper: workbook
Body: 146 words
SI: 1.35—the easy
  side of normal

NOTE: Reference initials (like "urs") may be typed either in small letters, as shown, or in all caps.

67-A. Tune up on these review lines

1 When did she go to the man and pay for the Oak Lake island?

2 We acquire jerky habits from having typed exercises lazily.

3 10 28 39 47 56 we 23 rot 495 pew 032 toy 596 rip 480 up 70.

67-B. Speed up on fluent preview phrases

4 with this|long list|this work|know that|been more|been true

5 you the|and the|has not|for you|for the|and for|and for you

6 of your|to know|of most|to work|we are|to our|of the|in the

7 list of|true of|most of|give us|you to|may we|and if|one of

67-C. Sustain your skill in production typing

8   *Current date*   4

                                                                    8

Mr. Chester L. Harris   12

1039 West Eighth Avenue   17

Los Angeles, California   90017   23

Dear Mr. Harris: 27

            SUBJECT: END OF THE JOB!   44

With this letter we are sending you the final parts of   56

your thesis: the last two chapters and the long list   67

of readings. We are also enclosing an invoice for this   78

work, which brings your balance to $45.   86

We should like you to know that typing this material has   99

been more than "just one more job" to our group of typ-   109

ists. All of us have found your writing to be extremely   121

interesting, a fact that has not been true of most of   132

the theses that we've typed in the past.   140

We are grateful to you for the many kind things you have   152

said about our work. May we quote from one of your let-   163

ters when next we compete for a contract? Please give   174

us permission, Mr. Harris; and give us also a chance to   186

work for and with you once more.   192

                    Very sincerely yours,   199

                    MEREDITH TYPING SERVICE   206

                                                                  209

                    Jean I. Meredith   213

urs   215

Enclosures   217

Unit 26. Correspondence

LINE: 60
TAB: 5
SPACING: SINGLE
GOALS: STABILIZE
  SKILL; MAKE COPIES
STRESS: SHARP,
  MULTICOPY STROKING

157-A. Each line three or more times. Repeat fully in Lesson 158.

157-A. Tune up on these review lines

1 Rod can use the new car and let Dad fix the old one for me.

2 Working quietly, Max alphabetized the census of vital jobs.

3 Pair patterns are typed like this: 10 & 28 & 39 & 47 & 56.

    1 | 2 | 3 | 4 | 5 | 6 | 7 | 8 | 9 | 10 | 11 | 12

157-B. Change to double spacing. Confirm margin settings for a 60-space line (copy aligns if you observe bell correctly).

Type paragraphs 4 and 5 in Lesson 157, paragraphs 6 and 7 in Lesson 158. Repeat each paragraph until it is typed with no or with only one error.

SI 1.42—normal, average.

157-B. Sustain skill on copy of normal difficulty

1 | 2 | 3 | 4 | 5 | 6 | 7 | 8 | 9 | 10 | 11 | 12 | 13 | 14

4 When a man has more mail to handle than he can manage, he hires 14
someone to help him with it. He expects to decide what is to be said 28
in each letter and then, having said it, to leave to the person he hired 42
the responsibility of doing whatever else has to be done to complete 56
the communication. 60

5 The boss assumes that his helper will check the dates, names, 76
addresses, amounts, times, and the like. He assumes that the helper 89
will provide the salutation and the closing phrase, or correct the ones 104
dictated if they are incorrect. He assumes that the helper will divide 118
the letter body into proper paragraphs, will give appropriate display 132
to subject and attention lines and body quotations or tables, and 145
will handle the carbon copies. These are what he is paid to do. 158

6 Making and handling the copies is more of a chore than one might 174
at first anticipate. To start with, there should be a copy for the files; 189
and this copy must bear a complete record of the distribution of all 203
copies of the letter. If the firm is large enough to be departmentalized, 218
a copy may be needed for another department. If the letter concerns 231
a third person, perhaps he should receive a copy. The typist must 245
plan his carbons with care lest he not have enough. A wise typist 258
always makes a spare copy or two, to play safe! 268

7 Sometimes the employer may wish to send someone a copy of a 282
letter he has received; he tells his secretary so. In large firms, the 296
secretary can make the copy in a second or two on a photocopying 309
machine. But if there is no machine, or if the one in that office is out 324
of order or is reserved for the work of someone else, then the helper 338
must know not only how to type the copy but also how to show it is 352
a copy and not the original letter. Sometimes the employer wishes to 366
send just part of a letter, copied from an incoming one, to another 379
department for a follow-up; the typist must know how a transfer 392
sheet is used for such purposes. The typist has to be very expert in 406
working with many kinds of copies. 413

1 | 2 | 3 | 4 | 5 | 6 | 7 | 8 | 9 | 10 | 11 | 12 | 13 | 14

ALTERNATE PLAN

1. Take a 3- or 5-minute writing. Type a full line of each word you missed.

2. Type three times each all the lines you typed in the timed effort, plus one more line of copy.

3. Repeat the first step to see whether you cover all the practiced copy in the same time but with no additional errors.

Carbon paper has a dull side and a glossy side that does the work.

Put glossy side against the paper on which the copy is to be made.

Check: You must have one more sheet of paper than of carbon paper.

Use both hands to get pack behind roll. You can see glossy sides.

Hold pack in left hand; turn roll with right. Dull sides show in front.

67/68-D. Apply your skill in a production review

Type Letter 26 (page 110) and Forms 14-16 below, each with one carbon. Time your work. GOAL: At least 35 words a minute production speed from time when machine is adjusted and paper is inserted, ready to type.

Form 14

INVOICE
Form: workbook (or plain paper, as shown on page 108)
Note: compute all extension figures

Invoice to Mr. Chester L. Harris | 1039 West Eighth Avenue | 9
Los Angeles, California   90017 | *for the following:* Chapter IX   29
of thesis: | 22 Pages of straight copy @ .30 | 3 Pages including   46
tables @ .50 | 50 Pages of carbon copies @ .05 || Chapter X of   66
thesis: | 10 Pages of straight copy @ .30 | 4 Pages including   83
tables @ .50 | 8 Pages of bibliography @ .50 | 44 Pages of car-   102
bon copies @ .05 || AMOUNT DUE | 3% SALES TAX | TOTAL   128
AMOUNT DUE 22.45   133

Form 15

INTEROFFICE MEMO
Form: workbook (or plain paper, as shown on page 105)

Memo to MTS Production Staff | MTS Service Staff | *From* Jean I.   7
Meredith | Manager | *on the subject of* The Next Big Job | *Date.*   24

    We have just been notified that we have been awarded the   38
big contract to prepare eight training manuals for the Air Force   51
Base in Fargo, North Dakota. The manuscript will begin to   62
flow to us on or about March 1 and will provide a sufficient   75
volume to keep us on full production for at least two months.   87

    Between now and March 1, therefore, we will wish to clean   100
up any small jobs that came to us but had to be deferred while   113
we were concentrating on the Harris job. We will also wish to   126
have all the equipment serviced; the Air Force job will consist   139
of our preparing many thousand Duplimat masters for offset   151
reproduction, and for this we need machines to be in perfect-   163
plus condition. | J. I. M. | urs   172

Form 16

TELEGRAM
Form: workbook
Caution: note that this is a day letter and not full rate

Day-letter *telegram from* Meredith Typing Service | Los An-   13
geles, Calif., *date* | *to* Senior Training Officer | Fargo Air Force   29
Base | Fargo, North Dakota | 34

    We look forward with pleasure to beginning work on Air   46
Force contract AFT17/64A-H on March 1. Suggest your repre-   58
sentative make first delivery of manuscript in person to set up   71
style manual for production. | Jean I. Meredith | Meredith   85
Typing Service | urs   90

156-B. Two copies with eyes rigidly on the copy or a 3-minute writing.

If you make two or more errors, your goal should be accuracy; fewer than two, the goal is speed.

156-A. Repeat the tune-up on page 241

156-B. Measure your skill on a technical paragraph

23   The men asked for a 15% increase across the board, but   12
they settled—if that is the word—for a 10% one. My raise   24
was for $12.50 a week, bringing me from $125.00 to $137.50,   36
which increased my annual salary to $6,500.00. When all my   48
deductions were out—about 18%—my take-home was $5,300.00.   60

   1 | 2 | 3 | 4 | 5 | 6 | 7 | 8 | 9 | 10 | 11 | 12

156-C-D-E Pattern:

ACCURACY: The one-line drills alternately three times (plus once more if you missed the symbol in 156-B), then the three-line paragraph twice.

SPEED: Each one-line drill twice (plus once more if you missed the symbol in 156-B), then the paragraph three times very steadily.

156-C. Improve control of the $ key

24   fff f4f f44 f4$ f$$ fff f4f f44 f4$ f$$ $4 $44 $444 $44.44.
25   They asked for $10 and $28 and $39 and $47 and $56 at once.
26   The 1903 dollar was $1,500 in 1962 and went up $30 one   12
year later, to $1,530. The 1898 mintings varied greatly in   24
cost after 1950: $300, $10, $6, $7, $38, and $350 in 1964.   36

   1 | 2 | 3 | 4 | 5 | 6 | 7 | 8 | 9 | 10 | 11 | 12

156-D. Improve control of % key

27   fff f5f f55 f5% f%% fff f5f f55 f5% f%% 5% 55% 555% 55.55%.
28   Our daily totals went from 10% to 28% to 39% to 47% to 56%.
29   My decision: freshmen, 15%; sophomores, 20%; juniors,   12
30%; and seniors, 35%. As it turned out, freshmen got 20%;   24
sophomores, 30%; and juniors and seniors received 25% each.   36

   1 | 2 | 3 | 4 | 5 | 6 | 7 | 8 | 9 | 10 | 11 | 12

156-E. Improve control of the hyphen key

30   ;;; ;-; ;— ;;; ;-; ;— ;;; ;-; ;— ;;; ;-; ;— ;;; ;-; ;—
31   These are some prefixes: for-, com-, pre-, con-, and mis-.
32   My in-laws own a sock-manufacturing firm; they concen-   12
trate on off-color two-tone patterns, like green-yellow and   24
orange-brown, or pink-red against slate-gray, and the like.   36

   1 | 2 | 3 | 4 | 5 | 6 | 7 | 8 | 9 | 10 | 11 | 12

156-F. Regain fluency by typing "we 23" combinations

33 we 23 22 21 two 529 528 527 rip 480 479 478 put 075 074 073
34 it 85 84 83 our 974 973 972 wet 235 234 233 eye 363 362 361
35 to 59 58 57 woo 299 298 297 rut 475 474 473 pie 083 082 081
36 up 70 69 68 rye 463 462 461 pep 030 029 028 too 599 598 597

   1 | 2 | 3 | 4 | 5 | 6 | 7 | 8 | 9 | 10 | 11 | 12

156-G. Repeat 156-B to measure your progress

Rough Drafts

Unit 12. Manuscripts

LINE: 60
TAB: 5
SPACING: SINGLE
GOAL: HOLD PACE ON
    REVISED COPY
STRESS: ATTENTIVENESS

69-A. Tune up on these review lines

69-A. Each line three times or for a minute each. Repeat all three drills when you do Lesson 70.

1 To make it to town, I paid a neighbor to sit with the girl.

2 Eliza quit her job, packed up six bags, and moved far away.

3 Type 1 and 2 and 3 and 4 and 5 and 6 and 7 and 8   [Continue to 50]

  1 | 2 | 3 | 4 | 5 | 6 | 7 | 8 | 9 | 10 | 11 | 12

69-B. Learn how revisions are indicated

69-B. To reinforce your mastery of the use and interpretation of these "rough draft" revision marks, do the exercises on workbook pages 115-6.

These are the markings used by writers, editors, and typists to indicate changes in all kinds of typed work when revising it for final retyping:

∧ Insert word	and⌃the
— Omit word	and so it
⁓ No, don't omit	and so it
＼ Omit stroke	and sob the
/ Make letter small	And so the
≋ Make capital	it may not
≡ Make all capitals	It may not
⟶ Move as indicated	and so the
// Line up, even up	and so the
≈ Line up, even up	TO: Mr. A.
SS⌈ Use single spacing ...	ss⌈ and so the
⌣ Turn around	and the so
ds⌈ Use double spacing ...	ds⌈ and so the
= Insert a hyphen	red= tipped
⑤ Indent 5 spaces	⑤ It may not

# Insert a space	andso the
⏐ Insert a space	andso the
⌒ Omit space	the a. m.
— Underscore this	It may be
⟋ Move as shown	it is not
⌒ Join to word	in search
— Change word	and if it
○ Make into period	or to it
◯ Don't abbreviate	Dr. Wilson
◯ Spell it out	① or ② who
¶ New paragraph	¶ We can try
∨ Raise above line	Halel says
+# More space here	It may not
-# Less space here	It may not
2# 2 linespaces here	It may not

69-C. Sustain a steady rate on revised material

69-C. Read the material on page 113 carefully, to be sure you can read it as fluently as would be the case if it were not in rough-draft form.

Then, beginning with paragraph 1, either copy all the material (GOAL: To finish in 7 minutes within 4 errors) or take a 5-minute writing on it (GOAL: 35 or more wam, within 4 mistakes).

SI 1.40—normal

69/70-D. Produce a two-page report (unbound form)

69-D. A ready-made visual guide appears in your workbook, page 117; use it for the production work in Lessons 69-74.

A visual guide is, of course, a summary of margin rules; compare the directions for this visual guide with rules given on pages 113-114.

A visual guide doesn't save much time on short reports, but saves time and assures consistency through a long report.

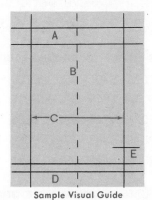

Sample Visual Guide

Study the technical information on pages 113-114; then type the material (make all the indicated revisions) as a formal, academic, two-page report.

It will be easier for you if you first make a "visual guide" on a plain sheet of 8½-by-11 paper:

A. Draw heavy lines 1 and 2 inches from the top.

B. Draw heavy centering line in the middle.

C. Draw margin lines for a 6-inch writing line.

D. Draw heavy lines 1½ and 1 inch from the foot.

E. Draw a short warning line 1 inch above (D).

Place this guide under the paper on which you will type; the lines will show through to guide you.

LINE: 60
TAB: 5
SPACING: SINGLE
DRILLS: AS DIRECTED
GOAL: BOOST CONTROL
OF FIGURE KEYS
STRESS: EYES ON COPY

155-A. Three times each. Repeat in Lesson 156.

155-A. Tune up on these easy review lines

1 Both the firm and city own half the lake and half the land.
2 Jo's brain is taxed with a very fine quiz on black pigment.
3 Type 1 and 2 and 3 and 4 and 5 and 6 and 7 and 8 [Continue to 50]

155-B. Two copies with eyes rigidly on copy, or a 3-minute writing.

155-B. Measure your skill on a technical paragraph

4 Congress certified the silver dollar on April 2, 1792.   12
The first one was minted in 1794. It weighed 416 grains of   24
silver, 892.4 fine. Mintage of dollars ceased between 1804   36
and 1836, 1873 and 1878, 1904 and 1921, and after 1935. In   48
all, 855,661,153 dollars were made in five different mints.   60
   1 | 2 | 3 | 4 | 5 | 6 | 7 | 8 | 9 | 10 | 11 | 12

155-C. Each line three times, plus twice more if the number is one which you mistyped in 155-B, plus twice more if you or anyone else catches you raising your eyes as you type each drill.

155-C. Improve control on individual number keys

5 aa 11 Of 111 teams, 11 were great, 11 poor, and 11 average.
6 ss 22 The 22 boys brought 22 gloves, 22 balls, and 22 bats.
7 dd 33 They gave me 33 boxes of the 33 kinds of No. 33 tape.
8 ff 44 Bingo game No. 44 had 44 players and paid 44 dollars.
9 ff 55 Car 55 comes out of the 55th Precinct on 55th Street.
   1 | 2 | 3 | 4 | 5 | 6 | 7 | 8 | 9 | 10 | 11 | 12
10 ;; 00 Figures like 010, 0010, and 00010 are just simply 10.
11 ll 99 When adding 9, 99, and 999, the sum can't be a 9,999.
12 kk 88 Club 88, on 88th, has 88 members paying 88 per month.
13 jj 77 No. 7 showed 77 times for No. 77 and for 777 dollars.
14 jj 66 I drove on Route 66 for 66 miles at 66 miles an hour.

155-D. If your allover basic need is for surer ACCURACY, type the three lines, as a paragraph, three times. But if your need is for SPEED, type each line three times.

155-D. Increase fluency by typing "we 23" combinations

15 we 23 24 25 two 529 530 531 rip 480 481 482 put 075 076 077
16 it 85 86 87 our 974 975 976 wet 235 236 237 eye 363 364 365
17 or 94 95 96 woo 299 300 301 rut 475 476 477 pie 083 084 085

155-E. Type two copies, earnestly trying to type at a steady, unbroken pace with your eyes kept rigidly on the copy.

155-E. Strengthen skill on cumulative-count groups

18 6701 8202 6303 7204 8705 9606 2707 1008 7409 8510 9311 8212
19 7613 6714 7015 6116 1017 5618 4919 3920 2821 1622 1723 1624
20 9725 8626 6727 5028 4729 3930 2831 7632 6733 6534 7435 1036
21 8737 1938 6739 9340 8241 7742 9843 9044 5645 4046 3947 2848
22 8049 3850 4851 2852 9453 5954 8955 9356 9857 9958 9059 4860

155-F. Repeat 155-B to measure your progress

Manuscript 11
Manuscript 12

2-PAGE REPORT IN
UNBOUND FORM
Shown: in pica
Paper: plain
Visual guide: work-
book page 117
SI: 1.40—normal

69-D

FORMAL MANUSCRIPTS

11

A Report for Typing I
By John E. Lake ↓3

27

38

Sally J. Kimball

69-C

The standard rules for typing a formal manuscript, such   12   53

as a term paper, are il*u*lstrated on this ~~or~~ *and* the next page. ↓3   24   65

   25   66

THE SPACING TO USE

29   70

<u>Single space</u> all special displays, such as headings that   46   87

take ② lines, quotations that ~~are sure to~~ *will* fill more than two   58   99

typed lines, foot notes, listings, and so forth.   67   108

<u>Double space</u> the body of the manuscript unless there is   84   125

a special reason for single spacing it (such as the need for   97   138

saving space ~~in~~ filing or saving materials ~~in~~ duplicating).   108   149

<u>Triple space</u> (that is, leave ② blank lines) after the   125   166

heading of any page and before any major sub heading.   135   176

¶ <u>Quadruple space</u> (leave three blank lines) to sep*a*erate a   154   195

table from the adjacent body of the manuscript. ↓3   163   204

  164   205

THE MARGINS TO USE

168   209

<u>The top margin</u> should be 2 inches deep on *the* first page and   187   228

1 inch deep on ~~all~~ the other pages. So, typing will begin on   199   240

Line 13 of the first page and on Line 7 of all ~~additional~~ *other* pages.   211   252

<u>The bottom m argin</u> should be at least ~~one~~ *1* inch deep and   229   270

may be up to 1½ inches deep. If the last page *of a manuscript* is short, ~~then~~   244   285

the bottom margin will, of course, be deeper.   253   294

| 1 | 2 | 3 | 4 | 5 | 6 | 7 | 8 | 9 | 10 | 11 | 12 |

Page 1 of a 2-Page Unbound Manuscript

154-A. Repeat the 153-A tune-up on page 238

154-B. Increase skill through selective sentence practice

154-B. Type to your goal.

ACCURACY: Lines 17-20
(as a paragraph) four
times; and lines 21-24
(as a paragraph) twice.

SPEED: Lines 17-20 two
times each; lines 21-24
four fast times each.

17 Clyde fixed quaint puzzles to give to John, Mark, and Webb.

18 Vick's big squad of experts clearly won three major prizes.

19 Jacques was amazed by Vi's skill and fixed her a good part.

20 Five or six big Zero planes sent by Mac to GHQ were junked.

1 | 2 | 3 | 4 | 5 | 6 | 7 | 8 | 9 | 10 | 11 | 12

21 Both the town and city may make the firm fix both big oaks.

22 They got paid for both the corn and fish but kept the hams.

23 Dick got both the land and auto but paid for half the lake.

24 When the busy man paid the men, the city got keys for them.

154-C. Sustain skill on developmental paragraphs

154-C. Type to your goal.

ACCURACY: Type entire
selection two times.

SPEED: Type individual
paragraphs twice each.

ALTERNATE PLAN: Take
1-minute writings on
paragraph 25 until you
set a new speed record
without error; then do
similarly on each of the
other paragraphs until
you equal on each the
paragraph 25 record.

25 Each time we plan to get out of town and buy some   11

house out where no one else is, I think of the old man   22

I know who had the same wish as we; each time he moved   33

out, the town caught up with him.   SI 1.00—very easy   40

26 The day that most dads dread most is the day when   11   51

junior is old enough to drive a car. On that day, one   22   62

man groaned, his son became tall enough to drive a car   33   73

but too short to pay for the gas.   SI 1.10—easy   40   80

27 If you live near a main road that leads to a lake   11   91

or seashore, you can tell when summer has come: Count   22   102

the autos that have a boat in tow. They swish by like   33   113

an avalanche of hopeful sunshine.   SI 1.20—easy   40   120

28 Loyalty to a team is a great thing, but I noticed   11   131

just recently that the sport screaming loudest for the   22   142

head of the coach of a losing team was the guy who had   33   153

cheered loudest in its victories.   SI 1.30—fairly easy   40   160

1 | 2 | 3 | 4 | 5 | 6 | 7 | 8 | 9 | 10 | 11

154-D. Strengthen skill by selective preview practice

154-D. Type to your goal.

ACCURACY: Lines 29-31, as
a paragraph, four times;
lines 32-34 two times.

SPEED: Lines 29-31 two
times each, lines 32-34
four fast times each.

29 harvesting nostrils crystal secured packed vapor steam drum

30 distillery planting extract growers you're stews piped tank

31 lucrative condenser pungent sunripe tramps acres mowed cars

1 | 2 | 3 | 4 | 5 | 6 | 7 | 8 | 9 | 10 | 11 | 12

32 just like |must find |that are |for the |is not |but it is |as if

33 that flow |from this |will you |all the |or add |and if it |or so

34 will find |that they |when the |and for |if you |are by it |to us

154-E. To measure your
progress over 153-B, take
a 5-minute writing from
page 239, starting at the
top of column 2; or copy
its first two paragraphs.

154-E. Measure your progress

5

The side margins should permit a 6-inch line of writing   24

(60 spaces pica, 70 spaces elite), centered ~~in~~ the ~~report~~ *if manuscript* is   37

not to be bound in a note book or binder but moved a quarter   49

inch to the right (giving a left margin of 1½ inches and right   62

margin of 1 inch) if the manuscript is to be so bound. ↓?   73

74

THE PLACEMENT OF Headings   79

The page-1 heading lines should be centered, the title   101

in all caps and other lines in capital and small letters.   112

¶ Major subheadings may be blocked at the margin (in which case   133

they are called "sideheadings") or be centered; They may be   145

typed in all caps, as in this manuscript, or be underscored.   157

paragraph headings are indented and underscored.   175

The page number is omitted on page 1; On other pages, it   187

is typed on line 7 at the right margin, with or without the   199

word "page," and is followed by ②blank line~~spaces~~.   209

LINE: 60
TAB: 5
SPACING: SINGLE
GOAL: USE FOOTNOTES
STRESS: THE DETAILS

Footnotes

71-A. Each drill for a minute or three times. Repeat in Lesson 72.

71-A. Tune up on these lines

1   The two old men set out the big red box and the boy saw it.
2   Because he was very lazy, Jack paid for six games and quit.
3   Type 1 for 2 for 3 for 4 for 5 for 6 for 7 for 8   [Continue to 50]
      1 | 2 | 3 | 4 | 5 | 6 | 7 | 8 | 9 | 10 | 11 | 12

71-B. Sustain a steady rate on revised material

71-B. Beginning with first paragraph, type the revised material on page 115 (GOAL: To finish in 8 minutes with 4 or less errors) or take 5-minute timing on it (GOAL: 35 or more wam within 4 or fewer mistakes). SI 1.60—difficult

71/72-C. Produce a two-page report (bound form)

Study the information on pages 115-116; then type a correct copy as a 2-page *bound* report (so: 1½-inch left margin and 1-inch right margin).

To end lines evenly, LINE: 60, TAB: 5.
Use double spacing. SI: 1.25—easy

1 | 2 | 3 | 4 | 5 | 6 | 7 | 8

MINTING GOLD FROM OIL

The next time you delight in the flavor 9
of peppermint, put in a word for Oregon, 17
won't you? It is likely that the mint you 26
enjoy came from there, because more mint 34
is raised in Oregon than anywhere else. 42
It just happens that Oregon, with its 50
rich soil and its frequent but light rains, 59
is one of the few places in the country 67
where mint can be grown as a crop, just as 75
other parts of the country grow sugar beets 84
or corn or what have you. For a long time, 93
mint was raised only in the middle valley 101
of the state; but now you can see and sniff 110
those green, beautiful fields all over the 119
state. 120

CULTIVATION

The mint plants are set out in the field 130
in rows about two feet apart, which allows 139
room for cultivating even when the little 147
plants have grown into bushes about a 155
foot and a half high. Mint has to be cared 164
for like a baby, for it is subject to many 172
diseases, most of which make the mint 180
plant wilt; and once a mint field has be- 188
come diseased, it will be many years before 197
the acreage will again produce a good and 205
pure crop. To ripen, the plants must have a 214
hot summer sun precisely like the one that 223
Oregon has on tap every summer. 229

Weeds are a bit of a minor problem, or 239
used to be, for they thrive on the same 247
things that mint needs; but someone found 256
that geese do not like mint but do enjoy 264
the kinds of weeds and grass that grow in 272
mint fields; so the sight of a flock of geese, 282
busy at the task of weeding out a field for 291
a farmer, is a common and welcome one 298
throughout the state. 303

PROCESSING

When it is sunripe and mature, the mint 313
crop is mowed, just like hay, and dried 321
for two or three days. Then it is fed into 330
a machine that chops the plants into little 338
pieces and flows them into trucks that are 347
tank cars. To pack the mint hay solidly in 356
the tank, teams of young workers tramp, 364
tramp, tramp the flow of hay until the tank 373
is packed full. 376

Off goes the tank truck to the mint 385
distillery. There a cover is secured on the 394
tank and live steam is piped into it for 402
about an hour and a half, cooking the hay. 411
The mint stews in the steam; a vapor of 419
mint oil and steam rises and is drawn 427
through a condenser, which separates the 435
water and mint oil. The mint oil that flows 444
into storage drums is as clear as crystal 452
and so pungent that it makes your nostrils 461
quiver even if you're a good half mile from 470
the distillery. 473

THE FINANCIAL PICTURE

There is not a mint of money in mint 483
growing, but it's still a lucrative business 492
for the top growers. One ton of mint hay 500
is the produce of some three acres. A drum 509
of oil is the extract of about three tons of 518
hay. A drum is worth about two thousand 526
dollars, take or add a little, according to 535
the market. This means a mint farmer can 543
earn about two hundred dollars an acre, 551
but from that he must take all the cost of 560
planting and raising and harvesting the 568
crop. Even so, there is a profit in a normal 577
year; and if you are able to count your 585
acres by the hundreds, you will find you 593
have struck oil, the golden kind, straight 602
from the Oregon mint. 606

Manuscript 13
Manuscript 14

2-PAGE REPORT
IN BOUND FORM
Shown: in elite
Paper: plain
Visual guide: work-
book page 118
SI: 1.58—difficult

To provide 1½-inch left margin and 1-inch right margin—
1. Use the visual guide on workbook page 118; or
2. Set stops for 6-inch line and then shift them 3 spaces to right; or
3. Set stops for 6-inch line and then shift paper guide ¼ inch to left.

FOOTNOTES IN MANUSCRIPTS

A Report for Typing I
By A. J. Wilson

The principal rules for typing footnotes in manuscripts are shown and explained on this and the next page. The works of Hutchinson,[1] of Gavin and Hutchinson,[2] and of others are authorities for the statements made in this brief report.

Purposes of Footnotes

1. Footnotes are used to identify references mentioned in the body of the manuscript; for example, the footnotes on this page identify the two references in the first paragraph.

2. Footnotes are used to give the source of a quotation cited in the manuscript. Examples: Footnotes 3 and 5.

3. Footnotes are used for an explanations of something mentioned in the body. Example: Footnote 4.

Styling of Footnotes

4. If a footnote refers to a book, the data are arranged as shown in the footnotes in this report: authorship, title, publishing source and date, and exact page if it is needed.

———————————————————

1. Lois Hutchinson, <u>Standard Handbook for Secretaries</u>, Seventh Edition (New York: McGraw-Hill, 1955).

2. Ruth E. Gavin and E. Lillian Hutchinson, <u>Reference Manual for Stenographers and Typists</u>, Third Edition (New York: McGraw-Hill, 1961).

| 1 | 2 | 3 | 4 | 5 | 6 | 7 | 8 | 9 | 10 | 11 | 12 | 13 | 14 |

Page 1 of a 2-Page Bound Manuscript, with Footnotes

LINE: 60
TAB: 5
SPACING: SINGLE
DRILLS: THREE TIMES
GOAL: BOOST SKILL
STRESS: MAINTAINING
  BRISK, EVEN STROKES

153-A. Each line three times, or a half-minute writing on each line. Repeat in Lesson 154.

153-A. Tune up on these review lines

1 Jane's neighbor kept the dog and also paid for the big pen.

2 Jacques picked five boxes of oranges while Diz stayed home.

3 Adding 10 and 28 and 39 and 47 and 56 gives a total of 180.
```
 1 | 2 | 3 | 4 | 5 | 6 | 7 | 8 | 9 | 10 | 11 | 12
```

153-B. A five-minute writing on page 239 or copy once the first two paragraphs. If you make 3 or more errors, your goal is accuracy; fewer, your goal is speed.

153-B. Confirm your present level of skill

153-C. Type to your goal.

ACCURACY: Type each group (as though it were a paragraph) three times.

SPEED: Type each line three consecutive times.

153-C. Speed up by practicing alternate-hand sentences

4 He and Jay may aid the man and cut the hay for the big cow.

5 He did fix the pen for the sow and may bid for the big tub.

6 The coal firm also paid them when they laid down rock jams.
```
 1 | 2 | 3 | 4 | 5 | 6 | 7 | 8 | 9 | 10 | 11 | 12
```
7 Rodney signs the eight forms when the usual audit is right.

8 The chairman of their panel may handle the problem of maps.

9 The duty they paid irks them when they work with such risk.

153-D. Type to your goal.

ACCURACY: Two copies.

SPEED: Each line as it is shown, two times. SI 1.16—easy

153-D. Sustain the new rate on an easy alphabetic paragraph

10 If you are like me, now and then you have to jog your— 12
self out of your rut to take a look at the world all around 24
you. It is easy, quite easy, to get lost in our work. One 36
way to wake yourself up someday, just for an example, is to 48
get up early enough to leave early enough to walk the first 60
mile or two on your way to school or office or wherever you 72
are going first thing that day. You will be amazed at what 84
there is for you to see and hear and sense; and the feeling 96
of being back in step with the world will buoy you all day! 108
```
 1 | 2 | 3 | 4 | 5 | 6 | 7 | 8 | 9 | 10 | 11 | 12
```

153-E. Type to your goal.

ACCURACY: Lines 11-13 four times each; lines 14-16 two times each.

SPEED: Lines 11-13 two times each; lines 14-16 four times each, fast.

153-E. Strengthen skill by selective preview practice

11 frequent country welcome allows seldom enjoy many grow long

12 diseased weeding machine almost Oregon cared crop mint wilt

13 anywhere subject acreage thrive raised truck tank once very
```
 1 | 2 | 3 | 4 | 5 | 6 | 7 | 8 | 9 | 10 | 11 | 12
```
14 course their field time with will like how sun the it as or

15 worker about there last been half into one has and at of to

16 summer sight these when from also this few you for by in is

153-F. Repeat 153-B to measure your progress.

153-F. Measure your progress in sustained typing

5. Each footnote is set up as a separate, single-spaced paragraph, 20
preceded by a blank line and indented five spaces. 30

6. Foot notes must be (clearly separated) from the body, or text, of 44
a manuscript. One book states: 51

Indent quotations
of three or more
lines 5 spaces
on each side.

     Separate the footnote from the text by a line of under- 65
scores 2 inches long. Single space before typing the line 78
and double space after typing it in order to leave one blank 91
space above and below.3 99

7. If the last page of the manuscript is short, ~~insert~~ extra space 113
above the separation line to make sure that the footnotes will appear 127
just above the *proper* ~~appropriate~~ bottom margin. 135

 136

<u>Numbering of Footnotes</u> 149

8. The references in a manuscript should be numbered in sequence. 164
for a reference
The footnote is given the identical number and must appear on the same 181
page as the references. 186

9. The number in the body must be superior[4] and follow, without a 201
a space, the reference or ~~the~~ (punctuation mark following) ~~it~~. 212

[10. The number in a footnote may be ⁄superior,⁀ separated "from 225
the first word of a footnote by one letter space,"5 or may be in ordi- 240
nary enumeration form as shown in this report.[6] 251

To know how much
space to leave here,
read paragraph 7.

"Et al." means "and others."
"Op. cit." means "the book
already mentioned." 259

_____

3. Alan C. Lloyd, <u>et al</u>., <u>Gregg Typewriting for Colleges</u>, Second 288
Edition (New York: McGraw-Hill, 1964), page 116. 298

 299

4. A "superior" number is one raised above the line, ~~by holding the~~ 311
~~cylinder turned part way while you type the number key~~. 311

 312

5. Gavin and Hutchinson, <u>op. cit</u>., page 146. 325

 326

6. Lloyd, <u>op. cit</u>., page 116. 336

Page 2 of 2-Page Bound Manuscript, with Footnotes

152-A. Repeat the 151-A tune-up on page 235

152-B. Increase skill through selective rhythm practice

152-B-C-D-E Drills:

ACCURACY: Type groups
of lines as though they
were paragraphs: Each
alphabetic group four
times, each alternate-
hand group two times.

SPEED: Type each line
by itself: alphabetic
lines twice, alternate-
hand lines four times.

18 was six big quo jam key cod pet zoo fin the run vim ask lot
19 five joke left quiz hump race taxi bows give boys went down
20 extra prove amaze jumbo squad right frank while climb young
     1 | 2 | 3 | 4 | 5 | 6 | 7 | 8 | 9 | 10 | 11 | 12
21 and dig for the she own but did man may big cut got pay six
22 lake work firm them name down busy with rich bowl when hand
23 visit forms their fight blame vigor girls turns sight vigor

152-C. Increase skill through selective word-line practice

24 penalize quickly models would fight jinx oven man but or is
25 extremes amazing follow block quiet jade very got his by up
26 figuring twelves behind quick jumps lazy left fix put or if
     1 | 2 | 3 | 4 | 5 | 6 | 7 | 8 | 9 | 10 | 11 | 12
27 neighbor bicycle profit gowns blame rock owns key dog is it
28 quantity problem handle shape docks town lamb hay cow or by
29 chairman torment island laugh throw soap turn men bit to do

152-D. Increase skill through selective sentence practice (1)

152-D-E. Alternate plan:

1. Take ½-minute timed
writings on line 33 until
you set a new record for
speed without an error.

2. Take 1-minute timed
writings on lines 33-35
together until you can
match the (1) record.

3. Take ½-minute timed
writings on line 30 until
you match same record.

4. Take 1-minute timed
writings on lines 30-32
together until you can
match the same record.

5. Repeat the same four
steps on lines 36-41.

30 Max realizes by now that Jack Paige worked quite fervently.
31 Judge Quick fined Buzz sixty dollars and waived his permit.
32 Dixie loves pizzas and got quite a few when Jary came back.
     1 | 2 | 3 | 4 | 5 | 6 | 7 | 8 | 9 | 10 | 11 | 12
33 Henry did cut the eye a bit and may go to the city for aid.
34 Alene got a giant fish for the dog and paid me for the box.
35 Dick paid their firm to handle the audit forms for the men.

152-E. Increase skill through selective sentence practice (2)

36 Jarve is quite lazy, but he expects to fix Gwen's darkroom.
37 Val and Diz requested that Jim Golfway keep the next batch.
38 Rex Flavick sings amazingly well and hopes for a quiet job.
     1 | 2 | 3 | 4 | 5 | 6 | 7 | 8 | 9 | 10 | 11 | 12
39 Six or eight maps go to the chairman of the downtown panel.
40 The profits for their work paid for eighty bushels of corn.
41 The neighbor may cut the hay for them if the land is right.

152-F. Measure your progress

152-F. To measure your
progress over 151-B, take
a 5-minute writing from
page 236, starting with
the third paragraph; or
copy paragraphs 3 and 4.

Review

LINE: 60
TAB: 5
SPACING: SINGLE
GOAL: REVIEW
   PRODUCTION
STRESS: SELF-RELIANCE

73-A. Ask a neighbor to pace you: He types line 1 evenly while you type lines 2 and 3 in step. Then reverse the roles. Repeat in Lesson 74.

73-A. Tune up on these lines

1 How can the two old men cut the big log you put out for us?
2 We promised Jackie eight dozen, but sixty equals only five.
3 Type 1 the 2 the 3 the 4 the 5 the 6 the 7 the 8 [Continue to 50]
   1 | 2 | 3 | 4 | 5 | 6 | 7 | 8 | 9 | 10 | 11 | 12

73-B. If you need to increase speed, type each line three times. If you need to sharpen accuracy, type the group of lines (as a paragraph) three times.

73-B. Sharpen control on an alphabetic preview

4 AA agent BB boxes CC concern DD December EE Peebles FF felt
5 GG Garage HH ship II did JJ judge KK spark LL line MM name,
6 NN Nebraska OO sorry PP plugs QQ requested RR Rural TT that
7 UU Route VV value WW went XX the XL line YY today ZZ the EZ

73-C. Adjust machine for 70-space line and for double spacing.

Read the copy; study the corrections before you begin any typing.

Type a complete copy, trying earnestly to do so without looking up even once. GOAL: To complete the copy in 5 minutes, within 4 errors.

Or, take a 5-minute writing with a pause to rest after every minute; follow this by a straight 5-minute writing without pauses. GOAL: 40 or more words a minute, with only 4 or fewer typing errors.

The copy will double block on 70-space line.

SI 1.42—normal

73-C. Sustain a steady rate on revised copy

	C	D
Send this message today to the Peebles Garage, on	11	11
Rural Route 2, in Harrison, (Neb)., attention of the pur-	23	31
chasing agent. ~~Dear Sirs~~: *Gentlemen*:	28	42
Your letter of (Dec) 24, concerning the order we de-	40	54
livered to you on December 18, arrived here this morn-	50	64
ing, as did the boxes of XL Spark Plugs that you did not	62	76
wish to receive and have returned to us.	70	84
When we send your order, we should have let you	81	95
know ~~that~~ *which* we sent the XL plugs instead of the EZ plugs	91	105
you had requested. You see, the firm that had been mak-	102	116
ing the EZ plugs recently went out of business. Because	114	128
our xl line is the nearest ~~thing~~ to the EZ in value and	124	138
quality, we have been shipping the XL plugs in all ~~or~~	134	148
orders that are for rush delivery.	140	154
We are ~~very~~ sorry you were not happy with the XL	150	164
shipment and felt it necessary to return the boxes to	161	175
us. We are crediting the four boxes to your account	171	185
and are enclosing a revised statement of the account.	182	196
Now, close the letter by telling him that we are	193	207
very truly his; insert our company name, The Carlin	203	217
Company; and give him my ~~standardized~~ Paul Alvin Wil-	213	225
son, Sales Manager; plus your initials, plus Enclosure.	224	233

1 | 2 | 3 | 4 | 5 | 6 | 7 | 8 | 9 | 10 | 11

73/74-D. Apply your skill in a production review

Following exactly the directions in the boxes, see whether you can turn out the production assignments within the cited time and error limits.

Letter 27

BLOCKED LETTER
Review: pages 97-100
Goal: within 6 minutes and 4 errors
Body: 152 words
Paper: letterhead
Tab: center only
SI: 1.44—normal

A trademark is often a picture, symbol, word, mark, or   12
figure used to make some product stand out from all others.   24
At first, pictures or symbols were used because most people   36
could not read or write. Do you recall the barber pole and   48
its red and white stripes? You really did not have to know   60

SI 1.20—
easy

how to read to know what it meant. The pole served as sign   72
of the fact that one seeking a barber could find him there.   84

In the early days, goods were purchased because of the   96
worker's reputation. If the craftsman was skilled with the   108
tools of his trade, he did not have to affix a tag or label   120
to the product he had made; folks knew him and knew that an   132
item he had made was good. But as others began to make and   144

SI 1.25—
easy

offer similar products, each man applied some kind of mark,   156
as a sign that the product was his and that he stood by it.   168

So long as firms were small and the buyers lived near,   12 180
control was not too much of a problem. But as machine-made   24 192
goods appeared and as the markets grew, customers would ask   36 204
for brands. At first, a man had to prove in court that his   48 216
was the first product of that nature so branded. Now, laws   60 228

SI 1.30—
fairly easy

permit anyone to register a trademark at the patent office.   72 240
This step taken, no such mark can be used on similar goods.   84 252

The stories of how makers first came to pick their own   96 264
trademarks would be fun to read. A study of the first ones   108 276
would show a trend toward pictures and common names; a very   120 288
good case in point is the popular cough drop that has never   132 300
had its whiskers trimmed. Some firms have created words to   144 312

SI 1.35—
fairly easy

depict their wares, and the public has added many a special   156 324
nickname. Symbols are becoming very popular as trademarks.   168 336

Many of our brands have been shown for decades without   180 348
basic changes in design. On the other hand, one large firm   192 360
just made its sixth change in four years. One popular mark   204 372
resulted from a schoolboy contest fifty years ago which led   216 384
to national favor. Still another has made such good use of   228 396

SI 1.40—
normal

color and design that the mark is displayed on every box of   240 408
this item. A study of trademarks should be most rewarding!   254 422

    1 | 2 | 3 | 4 | 5 | 6 | 7 | 8 | 9 | 10 | 11 | 12

Forms 17-18

INVOICES
Review: pages 108-109
Goal: within 4 minutes
and 3 errors
Forms: workbook (or
on plain paper as
shown on page 108)

Prepare the following invoices from the Manufacturers Institute:

1. No. 26173 to Mr. Clarence J. Markham | Training Depart- 14
ment | Shreveport Sugar, Inc. | 1600 Clark Street | Shreveport, 28
Louisiana   71006 *for the following:* 10 *(copies of)* Benkley: 40
Modern Plant Safety @ 2.50 = 25.00 | 1 *(copy of)* Benkley: MPS 52
Instructor's Manual @ 3.50 = 3.50 | 1 *(set of)* Benkley: MPS 65
Filmstrip (Set) @ 36.00 = 36.00 | AMOUNT DUE = 64.50 | 10% 82
MEMBER'S DISCOUNT = 6.45 | TOTAL AMOUNT DUE = 58.05 97

2. No. 26174 to Training Division | Nucleonics Corporation | 14
Mundo El Cortez Boulevard | San Diego, California   92108 27
| *for the following (compute all amounts):* 20 Rafael: Production 37
Tooling @ 4.50 | 1 Rafael: PT Instructor's Manual @ 5.50 | 20 56
Gavelin: Cost Estimating @ 4.00 | 1 Gavelin: CE Instructor's 74
Manual @ 5.00 | 20 Poe: Production Reporting @ 1.25 | 1 Poe: 94
PR Course Outline @ 2.00 | *Compute* AMOUNT DUE | *Indicate* 111
10% MEMBER'S DISCOUNT | TOTAL AMOUNT DUE *should be* $186.75 129

Manuscript 15
Manuscript 16

PAGE 1 OF REPORT
Review: pages 112-116
Goal: a copy within
8 minutes, 6 errors
Copy 1: arrange as
page 1 of UNBOUND
report; may use the
visual guide on
workbook page 117
Copy 2: arrange as
page 1 of a BOUND
report and under-
score sideheadings
instead of all caps;
use visual guide,
workbook page 118
SI: 1.48—fairly
difficult

HOW TO MAKE A CORRECTION 15

Double space all but the footnote

Center→ A Report for Typing I 29

Center→ By Ralph E. Young 42

+ # 44

¶ The purpose of this report is to review the techniques *involved* in 59
erasing and correcting errors in typed work. 70
+ #

TO ERASE ON THE ORIGINAL COPY 77

Turn up the paper so that the point of correction will 88
be on the top of the cylinder; move the carriage to one side, 101
far enough for eraser grit to fall outside the machine. 112

Press the paper against the roller with the *free* unoccupied 123
hand, to prevent slippage; *then,* 129

Blowing lightly to puff away all eraser grit and using a 141
typewriter (ink) eraser with a sharp point or narrow edge, 151
erase each letter that is to be deleted. 160
+ #

TO ERASE ON THE CARBON COPIES 167

Use a soft (pencil) eraser; erase the carbon copies one 179
at a time, starting at the top and ending *at* on the bottom. ¶ To 192
keep the erasing on any one page from marking the next, use a 204
stiff card; before erasing on a page, insert the card under 216
under the paper at the point of correction, between the paper 227
which is to be erased and the following sheet of carbon paper. 240
+ # 246

x x x x x

1. The procedures that are outlined in this brief report 256
are explained in great detail by Miss Ruth E. Gavin and Miss 266
E. Lillian Hutchinson in Reference Manual for Stenographers 292
and Typists, Third Edition (New York: #Gregg, 1961), pages 5–7. 310

McGraw-Hill

Unit 25. Skill Development

LINE: 60
TAB: 5
SPACING: SINGLE
DRILLS: THREE TIMES
GOAL: BOOST SKILL
STRESS: KEEPING HANDS
AND WRISTS QUIET

151-A. Tune up on these review lines

151-A. Each line three times, or a half-minute timing on each line. Repeat in Lesson 152.

1 Henry works with me and pays for the auto with the profits.
2 Mr. Pix was quick to admit frankly he gave Buzz the jewels.
3 Models 1028, 1039, 1047, and 1056 are all new for the year.
    1 | 2 | 3 | 4 | 5 | 6 | 7 | 8 | 9 | 10 | 11 | 12

151-B. Inventory your present skill

151-B. If you make more than 2 errors, your goal in Lessons 151-152 is ACCURACY. If you make 2 or fewer errors, your goal should be SPEED.

Take a 5-minute writing on page 236 (or copy the first two paragraphs; you should be able to complete them both in 4 minutes) to determine your practice goal for Lessons 151-152 and establish your present rate. The paragraphs are loaded with combinations like those drilled below.

151-C. Improve control on one-hand preview words

151-C-D-E-F Drills: Target on your goal.

ACCURACY: Type each group (as though it were a paragraph) three times.

SPEED: Type each line three consecutive times.

BOTH: Stress very smooth typing, accelerating very slowly and gradually.

4 decade only barber serve trade only area were was you at in
5 created look aware start look grew join read look red as on
6 based upon wares kill fact jump base bar him see hum red up

151-D. Improve control on double-letter preview words

7 success office accept recall added skill look keep soon all
8 shopper filled little common seeks goods well been sell see
9 applied looked appear really proof small tool book need too
    1 | 2 | 3 | 4 | 5 | 6 | 7 | 8 | 9 | 10 | 11 | 12

151-E. Improve control on vertical-reach preview words

Hold your wrists as motionless as you can; make your fingers do the up-down reaching.

10 control served design prove shown find some firm him one in
11 special permit symbol point often long from item con fun on
12 nickname picture hasn't buyers known man's know bent any no
13 employed because became nature brand sixth many very not be

151-F. Improve control on horizontal-motion preview words

14 changed similar market nature could early part have boy out
15 popular stories others patent meant cough what with ago had
16 register brands basics should shown white take that how his
17 shorted however taking barber which basis this show can day
    1 | 2 | 3 | 4 | 5 | 6 | 7 | 8 | 9 | 10 | 11 | 12

151-G. Repeat 151-B. to measure your progress

151-G. You should now be able to type faster and smoother, with fewer errors and hesitations.

Progress Test on Part Three

Test 3

Test 3-A

5-MINUTE WRITING
ON PARAGRAPHS
Paper: workbook page
125, or plain paper
Line: 60
Tab: paragraph 5
Spacing: double
Start: machine set,
carriage at margin
Grade: box below
SI: 1.39—normal

5-MINUTE SPEED
WITHIN 4 ERRORS*
45-up wam ...... A
40-44 wam ...... B
30-39 wam C
25-29 wam ...... D
* If more than 4 errors
are made, compute the
speed on what is typed
before the fifth error.

	A	B
Please send the following letter to Mr. Gerald Jordan,	12	12
Acme Drill Company, 383 Azure Street, Hartford, Connecticut	24	21
06107. At the correct point in the letter, center and type	36	23
in all capitals the subject line: Please Settle Your Bill.	48	41
Dear Mr. Jordan: We were pleased to extend to you the	60	53
rare privilege of buying from us on credit, although it has	72	65
long been our policy to require the payment of all invoices	84	77
in ten days. As you can see from the date on the duplicate	96	89
bill that I have enclosed, more than nine weeks have passed	108	101
since we delivered to you the merchandise that you ordered.	120	113
In all those many weeks, you have made no payment. We	132	126
do not like to press the matter, Mr. Jordan, but we feel it	144	138
is only fair for us to ask you to settle this bill at once.	156	150
The only way by which we can continue to offer the low	168	163
prices for which we are well known is to avoid the expenses	180	175
of a credit department. Mr. Jordan, we trust that you will	192	187
repay our courtesy by sending us your check by return mail.	204	199
Now, assure Mr. Jordan that we are sincerely his. Put	216	204
in our company name, Nelson Hardware Company, above my name	228	214
and title, Carlton Zoerner, general sales manager, plus the	240	224
usual initials and anything else that may need to be added.	252	227

```
1 | 2 | 3 | 4 | 5 | 6 | 7 | 8 | 9 | 10 | 11 | 12
```

Test 3-B

Letter 28

5-MINUTE WRITING
ON BLOCKED LETTER
Paper: workbook page
126 or plain paper
Tab: center only
Start: carriage set
at center tab
Body: 148 words
Grading: box above
SI: 1.39—normal

If preferred, Tests 3-B,
3-C, and 3-D may each be
typed on plain paper
(time: 15 minutes each,
maximum). Test 3-C
should then be arranged
in memo form (see
page 108), on a 70-space
line, with tabs in 9, 20,
54, and 64. Omit the
column headings. Check
each paper for penalties
and grade it on the
adjacent grading scale.

PENALTY SCALE

—3 for each major error (top margin, line length, line-spacing,
general correctness of form, etc.)
—2 for each minor error (blocking, aligning, centering, indenting, etc., of individual parts of the job)
—1 for each typographical error

GRADING SCALE

0-1 PENALTY .... A
2-3 PENALTY .... B
4-6 PENALTY C
7-8 PENALTY .... D

7 SKILL BUILDING • LETTER COPIES
RECORDS FORMS • 10-PAGE MANUAL

Test 3-C

Form 19

5-MINUTE WRITING
ON AN INVOICE
Form: workbook page 127
Spacing: single, with
  groupings as shown
Start: machine set;
  carriage positioned
  to type the address
Grade: box below

Invoice: Acme Drill Company │ 383 Azure Street │ Hartford, Connecticut   06107   14
Special: Type DUPLICATE *before* Invoice *and use* October 28, 19-- *date.*   29

QUANTITY	CAT. NO.	DESCRIPTION	UNIT PRICE	AMOUNT	
50	PD14	Electric power drills	4.00	200.00	45
50	PD399	Electric power drills	5.00	250.00	58
50	PD422	Electric power drills	6.00	300.00	71
100	WHO12	Hoses, 25' x 1", plastic	2.00	200.00	85
50	WHO38	Hoses, 40' x 3/4", plastic	3.00	150.00	99
25	WHO50	Hoses, 50' x 5/8", plastic	3.00	75.00	113
50	PDB11	Drill bits, kit sizes	.80	40.00	127
50	PDB32	Drill bits, kit sizes	1.00	50.00	140
100	PDB66	Drill bits, kit sizes	1.25	125.00	152
200	EX125	Electric cords, 5'	.10	20.00	166
150	EX135	Electric cords, 6'	.12	18.00	178
100	EX160	Electric cords, 9'	.20	20.00	190
		AMOUNT DUE		1,448.00	200
		DELIVERY		47.00	208
		TOTAL AMOUNT DUE		1,495.00	219

5-MINUTE SPEED
WITHIN 4 ERRORS*
  45-up wam ...... A
  40-44 wam ...... B
  30-39 wam C
  25-29 wam ...... D
* If more than 4 errors
are made, compute the
speed on what is typed
before the fifth error.

SHORT CUTS FOR USE IN FOOTNOTES   *double space all body but not footnotes*   18

center → A Report for Typing I   34
center → By J. N. Strong   45

When a ~~full~~ *complete* book reference is ~~cited~~ *given* in a footnote, much   61
data must be given: #the author or authors; the title of the   73
book, underscored or in capitals; the city, publishers, and   85
date of publication, typed in parentheses; and the page.1   98

ENTER THE SHORTCUTS   103

¶But footnotes may be shortened, when especially the ~~very~~ same   115
data are repeated, by using these 4 abbreviations:2   128

    Loc. cit. means "Exactly as in the preceding footnote."   143

    Ibid. means "same as the preceding footnote, but on a   157
different page, which is—." It is followed by a number.   168

    Op. cit. means "as in the previous footnote relating to   183
the same authorship." It is preceded by the last name   194
of the author or authors and is followed by a page number.   206

    Et al. means "and others" and is used only *when* ~~if~~ there are   220
three or more authors. Note that it is typed after the name   232
of the first author in place of the other authors' names.3   245

                                                                     250

    1. John L. Rowe, et al., Gregg Typing, 191 Series, Book 2   278
(New York: McGraw-Hill, 1963), page 246.   287

    2. Ibid., page 247.   295

    3. Loc. cit.   302

Test 3-D

Manuscript 17

5-MINUTE WRITING ON
UNBOUND MANUSCRIPT
Form: workbook page 128
Style: arrange as the
  first page of a long
  UNBOUND manuscript
Start: carriage set
  at center tab
Grade: box above
SI: 1.42—normal

Test 6-D

Manuscript 50

5-MINUTE WRITING
ON AN AGREEMENT
Paper: workbook 288
or plain, ruled
Spacing: double
Start: machine set,
carriage centered
Grade: box, page 231

If preferred, Tests 6-B, 6-C, and 6-D may be typed completely (maximum time for each: 15 minutes) and then be graded on this penalty basis:

PENALTY SCALE

—3 for each major error (top margin, line length, line-spacing, general correctness of form, etc.)
—2 for each minor error (blocking, aligning, centering, indenting, etc., of individual parts of the job)
—1 for each typographical error

GRADING SCALE

0-1 PENALTY . . . . A
2-3 PENALTY . . . . B
4-6 PENALTY C
7-8 PENALTY . . . . D

1-inch top margin

A G R E E M E N T 10

.... 12

THIS CONTRACT made and concluded this eleventh day of [*use next Monday*] 24

June, 1964, by and between the Charinge Precision Corporation, ... 37

of 315 Fourth Street, Terre Haute, Indiana, party of the first 49

part, and Charles L. Ferguson, 2828 Ruskin Street, Fort Worth, [*P. Clark, 402 Cochran Road, Pittsburgh,*] 61

Texas, party of the second part. [*Pennsylvania*] 69

Article 1. Services. The said party of the second 89

part covenants and agrees to and with the party of the first 101

part, to furnish his services *exclusively* to the said party of the first 116

part as special demonstrator and representative for the period [*advertising manager*] 124

of one year, or twelve (12) calendar months, beginning July 1, [*(start this beginning next month)*] 137

1964, and expiring June 30, 1965; and the said party of the sec- [*(date this a year later)*] 149

ond part covenants and agrees to perform faithfully all duties 162

incident to such employment. 168

Article 2. Wages. And the said party of the first 186

part covenants and agrees to pay the said party of the second 199

part, for the same, the sum of seven thousand two hundred dol- [*twelve*] 209

lars ($7,200.00), as follows: The sum of eight hundred dollars [*$12,000.00*] [*one thousand*] 221

($800.00) on July 31, 1964, and an equal sum on the last day of [*$1,000.00*] [*(use end of next month)*] 235

each succeeding calendar month until the period of one year 247

shall have expired. [*2# here*] 251

IN WITNESS WHEREOF, the parties to this Contract have 265

hereunto set their hands the day and year first above written. 277

.... 279

.... 293

_____   Bryant Gaynor, Vice-President 311
Charles L. Ferguson [*center*]
[*P. Clark*]
.... 313

_____   _____ 326
Witness to Signature [*center*]   Witness to Signature 343

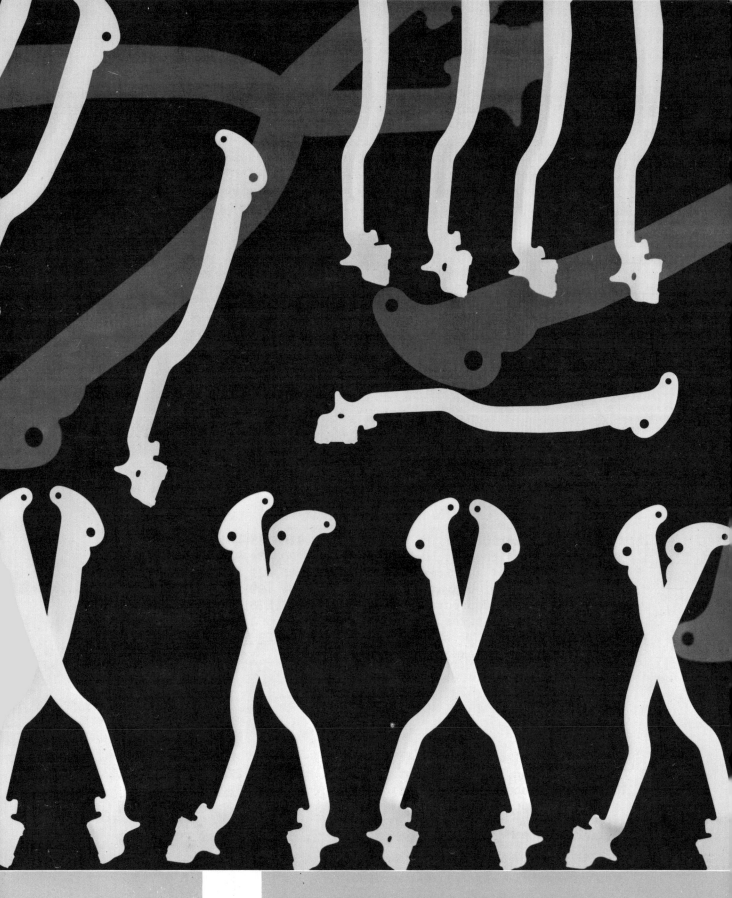

4 SKILL BUILDING • SEMIBLOCKED LETTERS
DISPLAY TABLES AND MANUSCRIPTS

Test 6-B

Letter 73

10-MINUTE WRITING
ON 2-PAGE LETTER
Paper: workbook 285
Style: blocked
Body: 400 words
Start: machine set,
   carriage at date
Grade: box, page 231
SI: 1.38—normal

SPECIAL DIRECTIONS: Type a copy of the "Mr. Wilson" letter, page 231, altering the salutation, wording, and closing as may be necessary, so that it is from Bryant L. Gaynor, Advertising Director, to Charles P. Clarke, 402 Cochran Road, Pittsburgh, Pennsylvania 15228. Insert a subject line, centered in all capitals: *Welcome to the Family!* If you use plain paper, type a line 15 lines from the top, clear across the page, to represent the depth of a first-page letterhead. The 6-B word count includes appropriate allowances for the inside address and other opening lines (40), second-page heading (26), and letter closing (22).

Test 6-C

Table 44

5-MINUTE WRITING ON
A FINANCIAL REPORT
Paper: workbook 287
Line: 70 spaces (not
  65, as shown below)
Start: machine set,
   carriage at center
Grade: box, page 231

STATEMENT OF OPERATIONS			14
For Nine Months Ended September 30, 19—			41
			43
Operating revenues		$77,763,296	63
Operating expenses:			68
Cost of materials	$25,135,401		80
Cost of services purchased	20,434,964		92
Maintenance of services	5,229,245		104
Amortization of conversion costs	199,697		116
Provision for depreciation	3,576,652		128
Federal income taxes	3,563,300		140
Other taxes	9,222,607		152
Total operating expenses		67,361,866	169
Operating income		$10,401,430	183
Other income		305,112	201
Gross income		$10,706,542	214
Nonoperational deductions:			221
Interest on long-term debt	$ 2,943,225		233
Miscellaneous other deductions	306,990		250
Total nonoperational deductions		3,250,215	267
Net income		$ 7,456,327	281
Dividends on preferred stock		618,751	299
Net income after preferred dividends ...		$ 6,837,576	312
Earnings per share of common stock		$1.34	335

Skill Drive

Unit 13. Skill Development

LINE: 60
TAB: 5
SPACING: SINGLE
DRILLS: THREE TIMES
GOAL: BOOST SKILL
STRESS: LOW WRISTS

76-A. Tune up on these reach-review lines

76-A. Each line three times very evenly (or a 1-minute timing on each). Repeat in Lesson 77. Keep the wrists low.

1   late dusk into dark long file jets came call eyes full size
2   Gary won five more prizes but quietly junked the xylophone.
3   Alll J777 S222 K888 D333 L999 F444 J666 F555 K800 S200 L900
      1 | 2 | 3 | 4 | 5 | 6 | 7 | 8 | 9 | 10 | 11 | 12

76-B. Measure and improve your skill

76-B. To define practice goals, type a double-spaced copy (GOAL: To type it in 3 minutes). Proofread carefully.

If you make 4 or more errors, your Lesson 76 goal is ACCURACY. If you make 3 or fewer errors, it is SPEED.

SI 1.24—easy

4   As the late dusk slowly faded into dark, Squadron Five   12
steamed on and on, a long file of shapes along the horizon.   24
Somewhere above us was the air escort; we heard the distant   36
whine of the jets above the throb of our own engines. From   48
the ship ahead came a gleam, a flicker, a signal to call up   60
extra hands and eyes for the night watch. The darkness was   72
tense, for it was a full job just to keep in station within   84
a squadron of such size. The con officer studied the radar   96
box on the bridge, waiting for the exact second of the next   108
quarter hour, when he must change course so as to zig or to   120
zag in cadence with the other blobs of light on the screen.   132
    1 | 2 | 3 | 4 | 5 | 6 | 7 | 8 | 9 | 10 | 11 | 12

76-C. Improve control of A, B, C, D

76-C. Type to your goal.

ACCURACY: The whole group of drills three times.

SPEED: Each drill, individually, three times.

SI 1.05—very easy

5   A Alma Alan Alamo aAa gala papa salad aAa alas aria canal A
6   B Bobo Baby Bobby fBf bomb blob blurb fBf bleb blab abbot B
7   C Coca Cola Chuck dCd crow cork clock dCd tick city check C
8   D Dude Dody Daddy dDd dyed odds dried dDd duds died dandy D
9   Dude hailed a cab and dashed back to the dark cabin on   12
the back beach. The dry sand squeaked as he raced from the   24
cab to the back door of the cabin. He called out to Chuck.   36
    1 | 2 | 3 | 4 | 5 | 6 | 7 | 8 | 9 | 10 | 11 | 12

76-D. Improve control of E, F, G, H, I

76-D. Type to your goal.

ACCURACY: The whole group three times.

SPEED: Each drill three times.

SI 1.21—easy

10   E Erne Edie Ethel dEd else jeep eerie dEd even meet level E
11   F Fifi Effy Guffy fFf buff doff fluff fFf tiff muff offer F
12   G Gene Gigi Gregg fGf gang gong going fGf glug grog aging G
13   H Hale Hope Heath jHj hash hath shush jHj hush hand hunch H
14   I Inez Ibis India kIk kiwi into livid kIk irks tips limit I
15   The eighteen fire rangers came by a night flight to be   12
with us by eight in the morning, to help fight the nine big   24
fires in the heights. They were mighty efficient fighters.   36
    1 | 2 | 3 | 4 | 5 | 6 | 7 | 8 | 9 | 10 | 11 | 12

Test 6-A

TIMED WRITINGS ON
PARAGRAPH COPY

Paper: workbook 283
Line: 70 spaces
Tab: paragraph 5
Spacing: double
Length: 5 minutes (2)
   or 10 minutes (1)
Grade: box below
SI: 1.34—easy-normal

Progress Test on Part Six

Test 6

| 1 | 2 | 3 | 4 | 5 | 6 | 7 | 8 | 9 | 10 | 11 | 12 | 13 | 6-A | 6-B |

Dear Mr. Wilson: We are pleased to learn that you have ac- 13 49
cepted our offer and that you will be joining our staff on the 25 61
first of next month. We know that you have a big contribution to 38 74
make to our sales effort, and all of us here in the home office 51 87
will be pleased to meet you again and to welcome you to a desk in 64 100
our Advertising Department. 70 106

We have made a few plans for your first weeks with us. You 83 120
will start, of course, by becoming familiar with the company or- 96 133
ganization, getting to know the persons with whom you will work, 109 146
and learning all you can about our products and our services. The 122 159
first two days, you will report to Personnel for the regular 134 171
orientation program in which you will learn a great deal not only 148 185
about the company but also about all our employee policies— 160 197
vacations, paydays, insurances, and so on. 169 206

Then, after you have been at your own desk long enough to 181 219
become familiar with the duties that will be yours, you will spend 195 233
two weeks making calls with one of our local salesmen. You will 208 246
meet customers and hear the questions they raise. You will see 220 258
what features of our products interest them and why. You will 233 271
have a chance to visit some workrooms of our present customers 246 284
and to see how these customers use our products; you will see 258 296
what our merchandising problems are. And, you will learn much 270 308
about the kinds of service we give our customers. 280 318

Our plans indicate that you will be busy with training for 293 332
quite some time before you come to grips with your main duties. 306 345
We believe that the training can be completed, however, several 319 358
weeks before the time when our next promotion campaign, which 331 370
will be your first major assignment, must get rolling. Thus, you 344 383
will have opportunity to get acquainted with all aspects of the 357 396
job before you start the campaign. 364 403

I am enclosing a contract for your position, Mr. Wilson. 377 442
Please note that it covers all the elements that we talked about. 390 455
We should like to have it back soon. If you would like help in 403 468
your search for your new home, all of us here would be pleased to 416 481
help. Let me state once again, Mr. Wilson, that we are pleased 429 494
to have you join us. All of us are looking forward to your work- 442 507
ing with us. Yours very truly, [START OVER] 448 531

| 1 | 2 | 3 | 4 | 5 | 6 | 7 | 8 | 9 | 10 | 11 | 12 | 13 |

5-MINUTE SPEED
WITHIN 3 ERRORS

10-MINUTE SPEED
WITHIN 6 ERRORS

55-up	A
50-54	B
40-49	C
35-39	D

If you make excessive
errors, base speed on
what you type prior to
first excessive error.

76-E. Improve control of J, K, L, M

16   J John Jojo Jerry jJj jury joys judge jJj jade just rajah J
17   K Kirk Kate Kenny kKk kink kick knock kKk kind bake knack K
18   L Lola Lois Lloyd lLl tall bill shall lLl dull toll allow L
19   M Mimi Emma Mammy jMj maim mums mimic jMj mama mums mamma M

20   Judge Kellock sent Jake Lamont to jail for a month for   12
taking money from the Lake James Motel last July. Old Jake   24
claimed Judge Kellock and the jurors had made unjust jokes.   36

   1 | 2 | 3 | 4 | 5 | 6 | 7 | 8 | 9 | 10 | 11 | 12

76-F. To confirm your progress in Lesson 76, type a double-spaced copy of paragraphs 21 and 22 (GOAL: Within 3 minutes, 3 errors) OR take one 3-minute writing (GOAL: 40 or more words a minute within 3 errors).

If you make 4 or more errors, your goal for Lesson 77 must be for ACCURACY. Otherwise, your goal is SPEED.

SI 1.32—fairly easy

76-F. Make an interim progress check

21   When we see in a newspaper a picture that, the caption   12
says, was taken by a camera from a jet flying a dozen or so   24
miles above the earth, most of us gape and marvel. For one   36
quick moment we think of one of the sad shots we have taken   48
with a box Brownie at ten feet, then we wonder what kind of   60
mystic camera can photo a hundred square miles at one shot.   72

22   Compared to what the shutterbug has, the aerial camera   84
seems to be a mystic tool, indeed. Its lens is so powerful   96
that even little details can be picked up from miles aloft.   108
In one test, an airplane took pictures of a city from eight   120
miles up; one shot was so clear that it showed a man in his   132
backyard, rocking in a rocking chair as he read his papers.   144

   1 | 2 | 3 | 4 | 5 | 6 | 7 | 8 | 9 | 10 | 11 | 12

77-A. Improve control of N, O, P, Q

23   N Mann Anne Ronny jNj none inns sunny jNj nine nuns inner N
24   O Oreo Olaf Orono lOl oboe cool solos lOl took foot odors O
25   P Paul Pepe Peppy ;P; prop pups happy ;P; plop pipe paper P
26   Q Quen Quad Queen aQa quit quid pique aQa quip quay quilt Q

27   On our Quebec trip we popped aboard a quaint old ship,   12
the Norse Queen, anchored on the quay. We poked around it,   24
quite happy, for a quiet noon hour and departed for Quebec.   36

   1 | 2 | 3 | 4 | 5 | 6 | 7 | 8 | 9 | 10 | 11 | 12

77-B. Improve control of R, S, T, U, V

28   R Ruth Raul Kerry fRf roar errs marry fRf purr burr error R
29   S Sirs Tess Susan sSs less sues socks sSs uses sits loses S
30   T Tora Etta Dotty fTf that trot truth fTf toot tote trout T
31   U Ulla Judy Trudy jUj used rule usual jUj tour true usury U
32   V Vera Vick David fVf very veil vivid fVf view even never V

33   Rusty never did trust Vic to touch our TV set while he   12
was a star student in his TV course; but after Vic wound up   24
his study, Rusty loved to have him visit us and our TV set.   36

   1 | 2 | 3 | 4 | 5 | 6 | 7 | 8 | 9 | 10 | 11 | 12

Manuscript 49

FIRST AND LAST PAGE
OF 8-PAGE CONTRACT
Paper: plain, ruled
Spacing: double
Tab: 10, center

Please double space

2" top margin — *center between rules*

A G R E E M E N T

2#

THIS AGREEMENT, made the fifth day of June, 19--,
by and between The Dwyer Construction Company, a corporation
under the laws of the state of California, located at 1938
Mills Road, Oakland, California, hereinafter called The Contractor, and The Black-Gray Company, 1396 Sutter Street, San
Francisco, California, hereinafter called The Owner.

WITNESSETH that the contractor and Owner, in consideration of the stipulations hereinafter named and made a
part hereof, agree as follows:

Subdivisions of a
legal document are
called "articles."
They are indented
to paragraph depth
and underscored.

Article 1. Scope of Work. The Contractor agrees to
furnish all the materials and to perform all the works indicated on the drawings and described in the Specifications, entitled "Specifications, with Accompanying Drawings, Describing
Materials to be Used and Labors to Be Performed in Constructing an Extension to the GARAGE of the Black-Gray Company at
1932-1934 Sutter Street, San Francisco, California," prepared
by Mortimer Bell, 209 Ninth St., Sacramento, California, and
referred to and acting as Architect in this Agreement, the
General Conditions of the Contract, the Specifications, and
the Drawings. *and referred to as such*

Article 2. Time for Completion. Work *which is* to be performed under this contract shall be commenced as soon as is
possible after the signing of this agreement.

2#   Page 1 of 8

1½" top margin

Assume this point
starts page 8 of
this agreement.

10] Article 8. The Contract Documents: The General Conditions of the Contract, the Specifications and Drawings,
together with this Agreement, constitute the Contract, and are
considered as much a part of the contract as if herein given.

2#

IN WITNESS WHEREOF, the parties hereto have executed
this Agreement, the day and year first above written.

2#

FOR THE BLACK-GRAY COMPANY   FOR DWYER CONSTRUCTION COMPANY

3#

Signature rules
divide page evenly,
with 2 or 3 spaces
left between them.
Center the titles
under the rules.

_____   _____
Executive Vice-President   President

3#

_____   _____
Witness for the Owner   Witness for the Contractor

2#

Page 8 of 8

77-C. Improve control of W, X, Y, Z

77-C. Type to your goal.
ACCURACY: The group of lines three times.
SPEED: Each drill, individually, three times.
SI 1.44—normal

34 W Will Owen Twila sWs wows whew which sWs away when where W
35 X Next Taxi X-ray sXs axis foxy sixes sXs axle oxen taxes X
36 Y Your Yule Daily jYj days many shyly jYj year duly slyly Y
37 Z Zola Zero Dizzy aZa hazy doze fizzy aZa zone zoom dozen Z

38   Citizens are always unhappy to pay taxes; yet you must   12
realize that a city the size of Wentz has extra expenses to   24
meet, which you pay by taxes and not by quizzing the mayor.   36
    1 | 2 | 3 | 4 | 5 | 6 | 7 | 8 | 9 | 10 | 11 | 12

77-D. Spot-check your weakest controls

77-E. Type to your goal.
ACCURACY: The group of lines three times.
SPEED: Each drill, individually, three times.

77-E. Confirm control on preview words

39 AA faces BB budgets CC chief DD desks EE executive FF false
40 GG agree HH high II item JJ junior KK desk LL tell MM small
41 NN only OO one's PP group QQ squirm RR trim SS such TT trim
42 UU bureau VV every WW wreathes XX except YY young ZZ sizzle

77-F. To measure your progress, follow either of these two schedules:
1. Type a complete copy of these paragraphs. GOAL: To do so within 6 minutes and 4 errors.
2. Take two 5-minute timings on the article (GOAL: 35 or more wam within 3 errors). Then, record the better score of the two on the chart on workbook page 131.
SI 1.32—fairly easy

77-F. Measure your skill in sustained writing

43   The bigger any organization is, the more meetings that   12
the men and women in the executive group must attend. This   24
is uniquely true in the business world. If you run a small   36
firm and are the one and only executive, you do not have to   48
go to any meetings at all; but if you are head of a depart-   60
ment or chief of a bureau, you must attend a dozen meetings   72
a month. At such meetings, all will agree that budgets and   84
salaries and sales are not high enough and that the expense   96
items of personnel and service costs must be trimmed in all   108
the major departments, except one's own, in the whole firm.   120

44   Once in a long, long while, a scheduled meeting has to   132
be postponed; this is the moment when you learn whether you   144
are a junior or a senior executive: No one tells the young   156
juniors that the meeting is called off, and so they show up   168
after all; they sizzle in their chairs for a while and then   180
squirm all the way back to their own desks, furious despite   192
a false smile that wreathes their faces. Once this happens   204
to you, and it will, you will make it a firm rule that your   216
secretary must confirm every meeting before you hike to it.   228
    1 | 2 | 3 | 4 | 5 | 6 | 7 | 8 | 9 | 10 | 11 | 12

Tables 41-43

FINANCIAL REPORTS
Paper: full, plain
Spacing: as shown
Position: center

From the letter below, lift the *Comparative Financial Results, January Through May* (modify the column headings) and type it in three styles:

TABLE 40. With *no* leaders after column 1. Review page 211.
TABLE 41. With *close* leaders, on a 50-space line. Review page 212.
TABLE 42. With *open* leaders, on a 60-space line. Review page 215.

Letter 72

BLOCKED LETTER WITH
FINANCIAL STATEMENT
Shown: in elite
Paper: workbook 279
Line: 6 inches

June 5, 19—   3

                     7

TO OUR STOCKHOLDERS: 11
                              12

There are shown below the financial results of our operation for the   26
five months ended May 31, with the corresponding figures for the same   40
five months of last year: 45

	This Year	Last Year
Gross Revenue	$34,559,388	$32,984,787
Operating Expenses	29,653,710	27,402,135
Net Income before Federal Income Taxes	$ 4,905,678	$ 5,582,652
Estimated Federal Income Taxes	2,616,667	3,005,247
Net Income	$ 2,289,011	$ 2,577,405
Earnings per Share (880,000 Shares)	2.60	2.93

In first column, note irregular linespacing, to keep the spacing consistent in the money columns.

Although the earnings figure is lower for the first five months than it   188
was last year, the operating expenses include several appropriations for   202
activities that will continue throughout the year. Accordingly, there   217
is reason to expect that earnings for the year will be equal, or nearly   231
equal, to the record earnings that we enjoyed last year.   243
                                                                 244

Very truly yours,   251

                           255

Chairman of the Board   262

Some executives wish their names to be typed in the reference position:

Vincent Young/URS   267

LINE: 60
TAB: 5
SPACING: SINGLE
DRILLS: AS DIRECTED
GOAL: RAISE SPEED,
   IMPROVE TECHNIQUE
STRESS: PURPOSE

Skill Drive

78-A. Lines three times or ask someone to pace you by typing line 1 while you type 2 and 3 in even cadence. Do again in Lesson 79.

78-A. Tune up on these reach-review lines

1   that just like this line when goal type make hazy rate grow
2   He quickly trained a dozen brown foxes to jump over a gate.
3   A1 A1 J7 J7 S2 S2 K8 K8 D3 D3 L9 L9 F4 F4 :0 :0 F5 F5 J6 J6
    1 | 2 | 3 | 4 | 5 | 6 | 7 | 8 | 9 | 10 | 11 | 12

78-B. To define practice goals, type a double-spaced copy (GOAL: To finish within 3 errors and 3 minutes). Check your work carefully.

If you make 4 or more errors, your Lesson 78 goal is ACCURACY.

If you make 3 or fewer errors, goal is SPEED.

SI 1.36—normal

78-B. Measure and improve your skill

4   How quickly can a typist increase his skill in typing?   12
It depends on the typist. Oh, his machine matters; and the   24
number of hours he practices matters; and the material that   36
he uses matters; but how much these things matter is rather   48
hazy. The major thing that marks the rate of growth of the   60
expert typist is what brainpower he invests in his efforts.   72

5   For example, just copying a line of drill, even a half   84
dozen copies, will not benefit your typing. It is when you   96
study a drill to see what it is for, when you set your goal   108
for squeezing out the practice juice, and when you type the   120
drill over and over until you make your goal that you grow.   132
    1 | 2 | 3 | 4 | 5 | 6 | 7 | 8 | 9 | 10 | 11 | 12

78-C-D-E. In each set, type toward your goal.

ACCURACY: Each group, like a paragraph, once for each error in 78-B (but at least three times).

SPEED: Each line once for each error in 78-B (but at least three times).

78-C. Eliminate all hesitation on the space bar

6   and dog gun not the elm may yes sow who our run nip pen nor
7   rue end dot two old due elf fly yen new way yet tub bar row
8   The U. S. A. has the U. S. N. and the U. S. M. C. together.

78-D. Eliminate all hesitation on one-hand words

9   hilly free join seat mill get oil saw pun car hum far my at
10   waste noon dear upon rate my; wax hip act mop bad pin as on
11   pylon fast only race hill was you far him see up; set in be

POINT TO CONFIRM: Between your body and the machine there is a handspan of space.

78-E. Eliminate all hesitation on double-letter words

12   wall less seem mass seek keep puff fill loss soon need dill
13   still loose error rooms sleet toddy yells snoop polls sassy
14   sizzle essays summer rubbed dinner really yellow wheel loop

78-F. Type paragraph 15 three times (GOAL: A perfect copy within 1 minute) or take three 1-minute timings to see how rapidly you can type without an error.

SI 1.00—very easy

78-F. Now speed up, on very easy copy, for a minute

15   If you wish to see your speed rate go up and up, first   12
you must give the speed a big push through the use of lines   24
like these, so full of short words that you will be sure to   36
type them at a high speed, like a race you run down a hill.   48
    1 | 2 | 3 | 4 | 5 | 6 | 7 | 8 | 9 | 10 | 11 | 12

To end lines evenly:
LINE: 70   TAB: 5
SI: 1.33—fairly easy

148-C. Sustain skill on easy, fluent paragraphs

| 1 | 2 | 3 | 4 | 5 | 6 | 7 | 8 |

In a day and age when most of our men 9
of science are looking far beyond the skies 17
into the heavens of space, it is interesting 26
to know that other men of science are 34
looking in the opposite direction, down 42
into the earth itself, to see what our world 51
is made of. Men already know more about 59
the space that surrounds our globe than 67
they do about what is in it. We know how 76
to hurtle a mortal hundreds of miles into 84
space; but the deepest hole we have made 92
in the earth is one oil well five miles deep, 101
and the deepest mining shaft is only two 110
miles deep. 112

There is much speculation about the 121
nature of the globe on which we live, most 130
of it based on where the echoes of earth- 138
quakes show up, plus what has been learned 147
from the study of volcanoes, all of which, 155
taken together, is something less than what 164
you could learn about the elephant by 172
studying a flea bite on the tip of its tail. 181
We know the earth is not a solid chunk of 189
rock, for example, because quake echoes 197
do not run through the globe the way they 206
would through a solid rock. We know, 213
similarly, that there must be liquid and 221
heat and tremendous pressure under our 229
shoes, for volcanic action and lava require 238
these. Putting such scant evidences to- 246
gether, the scientists built a theory. 254

The current thought is that the earth 263
is an iron ball surrounded by three layers 272
or shells, each made up of a different ma- 280
terial. The iron ball, which is known as the 289
inner core, is about fifteen hundred miles 298
thick. Around this ball is the outer core, a 307

mixture of nickel and iron so hot and under 316
such pressure that it is liquid; geologists 325
say they think that this layer is about 333
fourteen hundred miles thick. 339

The next layer is the big one, called the 349
mantle, which is about eighteen hundred 357
miles thick. The mantle is made of basalt, 366
the lava rock; and judging from the heat 374
of running lava, the mantle must have a 382
temperature of at least five thousand de- 390
grees. Basalt is so heavy, even in the oozing 400
stage, that mere granite practically floats 409
on it. 410

The final layer of the earth is the out- 420
side, known as the crust, made up of a thin 429
skin of light rocks, if you do not mind 437
thinking of the Rockies and Alps and other 445
granite mountains as being light. The depth 454
of this skin ranges from three miles under 463
some parts of oceans to some forty miles in 472
the highest, thickest parts of the continents. 481

Now, to get to the point of the matter, 491
what the scientists hope to do is to learn 500
whether their speculation is right. To this 509
end, a project has been started by the Na- 517
tional Science Foundation to locate one of 526
those thin places where it may occur with- 534
in two or three miles of the surface of the 543
sea; and having found it, to drill down 551
through the crust at the sea bottom into 559
the mantle with a pipe drill that is two or 568
three inches across—and seven or more 575
miles long! It will be a dazzling triumph 584
when the first mantle rock reaches Science's 593
hand. 594

To think of it puts perspective on our 604
own efforts, does it not?   [START OVER] 609

| 1 | 2 | 3 | 4 | 5 | 6 | 7 | 8 |

148/149-D. Review the production problems of this part

78-G. Each sentence two times; then a complete copy (GOAL: Within 2 minutes and 2 errors) or a 2-minute timing. (GOAL: Highest speed within 2 mistakes). SI 1.00—very easy

78-H. Repeat 78-B to confirm your progress in Lesson 78 and set goals for Lesson 79.

If you make 4 or more errors, your goal for Lesson 79 must be ACCURACY. Otherwise your goal is SPEED.

78-G. Now hold your speed on easy copy for 2 minutes

16 Both men said they would like to make the trip for us.   12
She lost those keys and found them when she looked in here.   24
You will hear from him when he gets down to the lake shore.   36
She said that she did not wish to work with them this year.   48

17 If he wants to see us, please tell him to let us know.   60
I said that we might hear from them by the end of the week.   72
The men do as well as they can with the time they have off.   84
The six men took the old boat down to the side of the lake.   96
    1 | 2 | 3 | 4 | 5 | 6 | 7 | 8 | 9 | 10 | 11 | 12

78-H. Make an interim progress check

79-A. Renew your new speed on common words

79-A. Type to your goal.
ACCURACY: The group of lines three times.
SPEED: Each drill, individually, three times.

18 days feel just call here deal came file help keep came fill
19 give knew hear high back does find glad know bank done pace
20 hold last gone been five good home come each hope left bill
21 coal girl lent half goal land paid down form both keys hand
    1 | 2 | 3 | 4 | 5 | 6 | 7 | 8 | 9 | 10 | 11 | 12

79-B. Hold your new speed on easy copy for 5 minutes

79-B. Type two copies (GOAL: A copy within 5 minutes, 3 errors).

Or, a 1-minute timing on each paragraph and a 5-minute writing on the whole selection (GOAL: Highest speed within three errors).

SI 1.00—very easy

22 If you wish to see your speed rate go up and up, first   12
you must give the speed a big push through the use of lines   24
like these, so full of short words that you will be sure to   36
type them at a high speed, like a race you run down a hill.   48

23 Once you get the feel of the new rate for a short time   60
on a few smooth drill lines of short words, you should then   72
move on to what you know the next step must be: to keep up   84
the new speed for more time and on more lines of new words.   96

24 When you first start to type at a new speed, you sense   108
that you are not sure of some of the keys you hit; but when   120
you have typed a lot of lines of speed words, you feel much   132
less ill at ease with the new pace; you get the feel of it.   144

25 Now you know, of course, that the speed you have built   156
is one that you can hold just on lines that are full of the   168
kind of words you have found in the smooth drills; what you   180
do next is to shift to drills with more long or hard words.   192

26 This does not mean that you should turn to drills that   204
are full of long and hard words; it means that you now must   216
turn to drills with a few of them, then to drills with more   228
of them, and then to lines with a fair share of such words.   240
    1 | 2 | 3 | 4 | 5 | 6 | 7 | 8 | 9 | 10 | 11 | 12

PROFESSIONAL HINT:

When typing very easy copy like this, don't press for speed (let the ease of the copy bring the speed) but rather press for a steady, unabating pace that is as even as you can hold on the copy.

[handwritten annotations: "1-inch top margin", "29" above the 8, circled elements]

[handwritten: "2 # here"]

          [handwritten: "Wallace"]

    Mrs. Pavlue reported that the material for the mailing to
dealers was now on press and that an investment of $970 would
be lost if the mailing were not made. Mr. Perkins pointed out
that calconning space in Premium would bring our year's space
in that magazine under the minimum for the special reates that
we have been enjoying. Miss Clarke reported that nearly all
mechanicals, art work, and engravings have allready been made
for our present advertising schedule and would have to be done
over, at an estimated cost of $1,500, if the space dimensions
were reduced in our advertisements in other magazines. The
committee decided to eliminate spcae in the next three issues
of Premium, with Mr. Perkins demurring,

          [handwritten: "Wallace"]

                         Respectfully submitted,

                         Marguerite Powell, Secretary

Distribution:
    Vice-Presidents
    Committee Members
    Permanent File

LINE: 60
SPACING: SINGLE
DRILLS: THREE EACH
GOAL: APPLY SKILL
  IN REVIEW
STRESS: ACCURACY

LESSONS
148–149
Review

148-A. Each line three times or two ½-minute timings on each line. Repeat in Lesson 149.

148-A. Tune up on these review lines

1 Those girls think their dress sales might bring extra cash.
2 Jacqueline was glad her family took five or six big prizes.
3 we 23 22 23 24 it 85 84 85 86 to 59 58 59 60 ur 74 73 74 75
   1 | 2 | 3 | 4 | 5 | 6 | 7 | 8 | 9 | 10 | 11 | 12

148-B. Type to goal. ACCURACY: Each set three times, as a paragraph. SPEED: Each line three times, successively.

148-B. Increase skill on selective preview drills

4 AA age BB bit CC core DD down EE earth FF far GG get HH hot
5 II oil JJ just KK rock LL lava MM may NN one OO most PP pit
6 QQ quake RR our SS is TT two UU run VV five WW we ZZ dazzle
7 earthquake tremendous direction volcanoes opposite surround
8 science require deepest mixture mortal hurtle theory liquid
9 shaft chunk globe layer crust flea bite big one of it do so

148-C. Same routine as in 144-C, page 219.

27   When you work on lines that are just a bit harder than   12
the copy on which you built your new speed, you have to put   24
pressure on yourself to keep up the pace, even though to do   36
so may mean that you may have to risk a couple more errors.   48

   1 | 2 | 3 | 4 | 5 | 6 | 7 | 8 | 9 | 10 | 11 | 12

79-D. Stabilize your rhythm on these quiet-hand drills

28   all led ask tea ill dad ail red if; fed pal lad old lea was
29   desk risk sold tall told tusk will gold held leak mask fold
30   rocks leaks scold sells speak tiles rules males ricks pleas

79-E. Hold your new speed on still harder copy

31   You should not expect to equal the new speed the first   12
time you tackle a harder selection. If you did achieve the   24
proper feel for the new pace, however, you should find that   36
you accomplish it on the second or third time that you try.   48

   1 | 2 | 3 | 4 | 5 | 6 | 7 | 8 | 9 | 10 | 11 | 12

79-F. Now measure your skill on normal, sustained typing

32   When speaking of speed building, it would not be right   12
to overlook the matter of accuracy; speed without accuracy,   24
of course, is worth nothing at all. It takes a half minute   36
to erase on an original and about a quarter minute or so to   48
erase on each carbon. If you are typing something with two   60
carbon copies, it takes just a little more than a minute to   72
make a correction; so you can recognize why making an error   84
a minute would give you exactly a zero, or less, in output.   96

33   There are four major elements that solve the questions   108
about accuracy. First of all, you must intend to type with   120
few or no errors; you must make a conscious effort to avoid   132
running down the hill so fast that you trip. Secondly, you   144
must maintain good posture; if you squirm around and change   156
posture, so that you also change the angle at which fingers   168
jump up and down the keyboard steps, then the errors occur.   180
Thirdly, you need exact control of the keys; the importance   192
of this is confirmed by the great number of drills you have   204
noted in this book. Finally, you must be sure that you use   216
easy copy when you drive to increase speed; only when a new   228
rate has been achieved should you then turn to normal copy.   240

   1 | 2 | 3 | 4 | 5 | 6 | 7 | 8 | 9 | 10 | 11 | 12

79-C. Type paragraph 27 three times (GOAL: To finish it within 1 minute and 1 error) or take two 2-minute races on it (GOAL: To equal your best 79-B speed, but within 2 errors).

SI 1.14—easy

79-D. Type to your goal.

ACCURACY: The whole group three times.

SPEED: Each drill, three times.

79-E. Type paragraph 31 three times (GOAL: To finish it within 1 minute and 1 error) or take two 2-minute races on it (GOAL: To equal your best 79-C speed, but within 2 errors).

SI 1.28—fairly easy

79-F. To measure your progress, follow either of these two schedules:

1. Type a complete copy of these paragraphs. (GOAL: To do so within 6 minutes, 4 errors).

2. Take two 5-minute timings on the article (GOAL: 40 or more wam within 3 errors). Then record the better score of the two on the chart on workbook page 131.

SI 1.37—normal

PROFESSIONAL HINT:

Drill lines 28-30 are especially useful. Each line is of same-length words and therefore a fine aid for rhythm. Each word results in your hands' return to the home-key position; so the drills are fine practice for retaining the home-key position, for keeping the wrists low, and for keeping the hands very quiet.

Manuscripts 47-48

MINUTES OF MEETING
Paper: plain
Copies: two styles
1. Single spaced
2. Double spaced

These minutes illustrate the correct arrangement for minutes; they are usually single spaced to save space in the permanent file of minutes. These minutes also show the proper sequence for reporting what transpired, whether or not events took place in the order that is shown.

2-inch top margin

Of the Advertising Committee

MINUTES OF THE MONTHLY MEETING

May ~~18~~ 29, 19--

1½-inch margin

1-inch margin

ATTENDANCE:

The regular monthly meeting of the Advertising Committee was held in the office of Mr. Larimore, Advertising Director, who presided at the meeting. The following were present:

Mr. J. Carty	Mr. Fisher	Miss Powell
Miss Clarke	Mr. Larimore	Mr. Stark
Miss Clooney	Mrs. Pavlu	Mr. Wallace
	Mr. Perkins	

put names in 2 columns

The meeting began at two o'clock and adjourned at ~~4:00~~.

OLD BUSINESS:

The secretary ~~Miss Powell~~ read the minutes of the last meeting. They were approved as read.

Mr. Stark reported that the show-case cards ~~which~~ *that* had been prepared for dealer's use *have* ~~had~~ proved notably successful. His follow-up survey among 250 dealers indicated:

5 [Dealers wanting additional cards .... 230 (92%)] 5
Dealers using the cards 180 (72%)
Dealers reporting sales increases 215 (86%)

NEW BUSINESS:

Mr. Larimore reported that the Department has been directed to curtail its advertising expenditures by $2,500.00 for the coming quarter. Discussion hinged on ~~these~~ *three* possibilities:

(1. Eliminat~~e~~ *ion of* the June Mailing to dealers; *and/or*
  2. Elimination of the space in <u>Premium</u> magazine; *or*
  3. Reduction of space in all magazine ads.

1 to 1½-inch bottom margin

(CONTINUED ON NEXT PAGE.)

Skill Drive

LINE: 60
TAB: 5
SPACING: SINGLE
DRILLS: AS DIRECTED
GOAL: NUMBER
  CONTROL
STRESS: EYES ON COPY

80-A. Tune up on these reach-review lines

80-A. Each line three times or for 1 minute. Stress steady, even stroking. Repeat in Lesson 81.

1 The profit they make by their fight may pay for the chapel.
2 Jasper quietly viewed the fox, zebra, kangaroo, and camels.
3 A161 J767 S262 K868 D363 L969 F464 :060 F464 J666 S234 L987
     1 | 2 | 3 | 4 | 5 | 6 | 7 | 8 | 9 | 10 | 11 | 12

80-B. Measure your skill on these numeric sentences

80-B. Type a complete copy (GOAL: Within 3 minutes and 3 errors) or take a 3-minute timing (GOAL: Highest speed within 3 errors).

If you make 4 or more errors, your Lesson 80 goal is ACCURACY.

If you make 3 or fewer errors, goal is SPEED.

4 I phoned rooms 10, 28, 39, and 47 before he called room 56.
5 Did the Halls move to 1028 39th Street or 3947 56th Street?
6 Read pages 10 and 28, then 39 and 47, and finally page 156.
7 Ask for 10 to 28 men, 39 to 47 women, and 56 boys or girls.
8 We put guests in rooms 10, 28, 39, and 47, then in room 56.
9 The dates on pages 10, 28, and 39 match those on 47 and 56.
10 We emptied boxes 10, 28, and 39; box 47 still has 156 left.
11 Is the room 10 by 28, 10 by 39, 10 by 47, or 10 by 56 feet?
     1 | 2 | 3 | 4 | 5 | 6 | 7 | 8 | 9 | 10 | 11 | 12

80-C. Strengthen your control of number keys

80-C. Preliminary step: Put a light pencil mark before each line in 4-11 in which you made any error in 80-B. For each number incorrectly typed in 80-B, put a mark in front of the matching number drill in 12-21.

ACCURACY: (1) Type three copies of each drill, 4-21, before which you have put a pencil mark. (2) Type a complete copy of drills 4-21.

SPEED: (1) Type a copy of each drill in 4-21 before which you have a mark; then (2) type drills 4-21, each line typed twice as a consecutive pair.

12 1 a q 1 a q 1 a 1 or 1 and 11 and 111 and 1,111 and 11,111.
   1 a q 1 Albert said that 111 is 1 less than 1,111, I think.

13 2 s w 2 s w 2 s 2 or 2 and 22 and 222 and 2,222 and 22,222.
   2 s w 2 Steven said that 222 is 2 less than 2,222, I think.

14 3 d e 3 d e 3 d 3 or 3 and 33 and 333 and 3,333 and 33,333.
   3 d e 3 Deidre said that 333 is 3 less than 3,333, I think.

15 4 f r 4 f r 4 f 4 or 4 and 44 and 444 and 4,444 and 44,444.
   4 f r 4 Flavia said that 444 is 4 less than 4,444, I think.

16 5 f 5 f 5 f 5 f 5 or 5 and 55 and 555 and 5,555 and 55,555.
   5 f 5 5 Foster said that 555 is 5 less than 5,555, I think.

17 6 j y 6 j y 6 j 6 or 6 and 66 and 666 and 6,666 and 66,666.
   6 j y 6 Johnny said that 666 is 6 less than 6,666, I think.

18 7 j u 7 j u 7 j 7 or 7 and 77 and 777 and 7,777 and 77,777.
   7 j u 7 Joanne said that 777 is 7 less than 7,777, I think.

19 8 k i 8 k i 8 k 8 or 8 and 88 and 888 and 8,888 and 88,888.
   8 k i 8 Kathie said that 888 is 8 less than 8,888, I think.

20 9 l o 9 l o 9 l 9 or 9 and 99 and 999 and 9,999 and 99,999.
   9 l o 9 Leslie said that 999 is 9 less than 9,999, I think.

21 0 ; p 0 ; p 0 ; 0 or 0 and 10 and 100 and 1,000 and 10,000.
   0 ; p 0 Philip said that 100 is 0 less than 1,000, I think.

80-D. Measure your progress in controlling numbers

80-D. Repeat 80-B to measure your progress.

Manuscript 45

RESOLUTION

Paper: plain
Spacing: double
Line: 60
Position: center

JOHN HERBERT KAUFMANN

WHEREAS John (H.) Kaufmann is retiring from his post [position]
as Secretary-Treasurer of this firm, having served it and his
associates for more than (35) years; and

WHEREAS, he devoted all his skill and knowledge
to the development and expansion of this company,
its products, its services, its facilities, and its
staff, to the end that today this company is the
largest and most successful in its field of
business enterprise; and

WHEREAS he has given generously of himself in the
encouragement, inspiration, and assistance of ~~everyone~~ [all those] who
~~was~~ [were] fortunate enough to work with him personally, to the end
that virtually all the Executives of [this] ~~his~~ company have, in
effect, been ~~taught~~ [schooled] by this wise and gentle teacher; and

Whereas he has proved himself a generous leader, a
(thoughtful and warm) associate, and a man endowed as much with
openness of heart and hand as with ~~a spirit of justice and~~
wisdom, so that his name is a legend in this industry and ~~so~~
that he is loved for what he is even more than for what he
has done: Therefore, be it ~~hereby~~

RESOLVED, That the Officers, the Members of the
Board of Directors, and the Entire Personnel of The Hayes
Manufacturing Company do commend, for his ~~dedication~~ [devotion] to them
and his [unstinting] loyalty, JOHN HERBERT KAUFMANN [and leadership in their behalf]

center, triple
space below

Manuscript 46

RESOLUTION

Paper: plain
Spacing: single
Line: 50
Position: center

81-A. Type a complete copy (GOAL: To finish within 3 minutes and 3 errors) or take one 3-minute writing on it (GOAL: Highest speed within 3 errors).

SI 1.39—normal, if you are master of top row

NOTE: In this book, word counts credit you with triple strokes for each underscored word and 5 strokes for each use of the tabulator mechanism (as, in indenting).

81-A. Measure your skill in technical typing

22 There are three sure keys to expert typing of numbers: 12

  1. Type <u>many</u> numbers (this is why there are so many of 26
them in the production jobs and drill groups in this book). 38

  2. Force yourself <u>always</u> to use correct fingering (the 52
"we 23" and other basic drills are designed for this need). 64

  3. Automatize the numbers in pairs for use as pegs for 76
quick control of the numeral keys (this is the objective of 88
drills like "10 and 28 and 39 and 47 and 56" in this book). 100

  1 | 2 | 3 | 4 | 5 | 6 | 7 | 8 | 9 | 10 | 11 | 12

81-B. "M" drills are for manual machines; "E," for electrics.

Each drill twice plus once more if you erred on the related symbol key when typing 81-A.

81-B. Practice the punctuation symbol keys

23M k8k k'k k8k k'k That isn't Bob's dog. I'm sure it's Joe's.
23E ;'; ;'; ;'; ;'; That isn't Bob's dog. I'm sure it's Joe's.

24M s2s s"s s2s s"s I said, "Hey, there." He growled, "Hello."
24E ;'; ;"; ;'; ;"; I said, "Hey, there." He growled, "Hello."

25 ;-; ;-; ;-; ;-; My in-laws are the stay-away-from-you type.
26 191 1(1 ;0; ;); Tell them (1) what, (2) why, and (3) where.

27M j6j j_j j6j j_j Well, I <u>told</u> him to read <u>Ask the West Wind</u>.
27E ;-; ;_; ;-; ;_; Well, I <u>told</u> him to read <u>Ask the West Wind</u>.

81-C. In all "we 23" drills, the word cues you to the fingering of the next number.

1. Each line twice.
2. Repeat lines 28-33 twice more, omitting all the "cue words."

81-C. Speed up your typing of numbers

28 wet 235 tie 583 rye 463 pet 035 you 697 owe 923 wit 285 285
29 tow 592 rip 480 roe 493 our 974 pie 083 yet 635 too 599 599
30 ire 843 pup 070 ere 343 ewe 323 toe 593 eye 363 yew 632 632

31 weep 2330 tour 5974 type 5603 pity 0856 wept 2305 rope 4903
32 riot 4895 pipe 0803 wore 2943 your 6974 wire 2843 toot 5995
33 wiry 2846 true 5473 poor 0994 rout 4975 prow 0492 trip 5480

81-D. Drill on typing solid, cumulative numbers

34 1601 1602 1603 1604 1605 1606 1607 1608 1609 1610 1611 1612
35 1513 1514 1515 1516 1517 1518 1519 1520 1521 1522 1523 1524
36 1925 1926 1927 1928 1929 1930 1931 1932 1933 1934 1935 1936

81-E. Type the paragraph twice without stopping. GOAL: To surpass your pretest score in 81-A.

Or, take one 3-minute writing on the paragraph (GOAL: Highest score within 3 errors).

SI 1.17—fairly easy

81-E. Remeasure your skill in technical typing

37 When our club was at 39 28th Street, it was called the 12
"3928 Club." Now that we've moved to 47 56th Street, it is 24
called the "4756 Club." The club is growing since we moved 36
(last June 10), for 100 to 110 <u>more</u> men have now joined us. 50

  1 | 2 | 3 | 4 | 5 | 6 | 7 | 8 | 9 | 10 | 11 | 12

146-C. Type one copy in Lesson 146 and another in Lesson 147; or, take these practice steps:

1. Read the material.

2. Practice the three hardest words you see in each paragraph.

3. Take a 5-minute timed writing with a 10-second rest after each minute.

4. Practice words with which you had trouble.

5. Take a final 5-minute writing without rests.

GOAL: Maximum speed within 3-error limit.

SI 1.25—easy if you can respond to warning bell!

146-C. Stretch your skill on easy straight copy

The error into which most of us fall is in thinking that we will 14
get a new lease on life whenever we decide to do so. We coast along, 28
telling ourselves that, when our big chance comes along, one worth an 42
effort, we will then stretch and make good. There is no mistake that 56
is worse than this. Once you get the habit of coasting, it's too bad 70
for you. The habit gets you and keeps you coasting; and there's only 84
one direction you can coast. To build muscles, you have to use them. 98

Ambition is seldom wholly dead in any of us; most of us long for 112
the good things that are out of our reach at the moment. But the way 126
to get them is not to give up and let go; rather, it's to take a leaf 140
from the story of the old warrior whose son complained that his spear 154
was too short. The boy's father said, "Then step closer to the foe." 168

All this is worth talking about because you will soon be in your 182
first position; and the work in any first position is usually so easy 196
for you, since no one expects much of you as a beginner, that you can 210
get the idea that you can relax on the job and stop growing. If that 224
happens, you start coasting, which takes you back down the hills that 238
you climbed to get where you are. If your work is easy, then that is 252
the time to push, and push hard while the pushing is easy. Don't let 266
yourself coast nor stand still; get your muscles ready for the climb. 281

The climb is not easy, which is a good thing for you; if it were 295
easy, the ladder would be full of people ahead of you. Sometimes the 309
ladder of advancement shakes and trembles, and you with it; some- 321
times the rungs seem mighty far apart. But it's when the stretching 335
is the hardest and the climbing the toughest that your strength and 349
will and heart enable you to reach the next rung that others could not 363
attain. The relaxing and coasting is for those who lack the drive to 377
succeed. 379

146/147-D. Apply skill to legal-styled typing—perhaps

Such legal-*looking* touches as deep indentions, all-caps, vertical rules, and so on, are often used in other manuscripts (whether or not legality is involved) for the sake of dramatic formality. The following minutes and resolution are illustrations. Alternative assignments may, however, be more helpful to you:

DEVELOPMENTAL SKILL DRILL

If increasing speed or accuracy is more important, repeat the drills on pages 125-127.

SUSTAINED PRODUCTION OUTPUT

If maintaining steady production is more important, produce a magazine article on "What's What about Horizontal Centering" (pages 194, 197) for a journal that uses a 45-space line, 3-space paragraph indention, and subheadings that are centered and underscored.

Suggestion: Make three carbon copies of each of these manuscripts.

Unit 14. Correspondence

LINE: 60
TAB: 5 AND CENTER
SPACING: SINGLE
DRILLS: AS DIRECTED
GOAL: PRODUCTION OF
CORRESPONDENCE
STRESS: CONTINUITY

82-A. Tune up on these review lines

82-A. Lines three or more times or a 1-minute timing on each line. Repeat in Lesson 83.

1 They got a giant of a man to make the panel for the chapel.
2 Jumping quickly from the taxi, Hazel brushed a woven chair.
3 He called "10," then "28," then "39," then "47," then "56."

   1 | 2 | 3 | 4 | 5 | 6 | 7 | 8 | 9 | 10 | 11 | 12

82-B. Boost skill on these preview words

82-B. For speed boost, each line three times. For accuracy boost, the group of lines three times. Try to hold a steady pace, speeding up a little on each line.

4 particularly conference products familiar plastic thank wax
5 combination scheduling pamphlet hallways covering about two
6 application durability described designed traffic which one
7 protective properties engineers airtight familiar heavy but

82-C. Build skill on production material

82-C. Type a double-spaced copy, line for line (GOAL: To finish within 5 minutes and 3 errors) or take one 5-minute writing on it (GOAL: At least 40 wam within 3 errors).

SI 1.38—normal

If time permits, take a 5-minute writing in Lesson 82, with a 10-second rest at the end of each minute; then repeat in Lesson 83, without any pauses.

8 Dear Mr. Jeffers: 4

        Thank you for your inquiry about Floor Guard, our   15
   fine new kind of protective floor covering. I enclose   26
   a pamphlet that describes this new product, which is a   37
   combination of liquid plastic and wax, with the finest   48
   properties of each: the ease of application and shine   59
   of wax and the high durability of strong plastic film.   70

9   Although Floor Guard was designed to serve in the   81
   home, particularly in the kitchen and in hallways that   92
   bear heavy traffic, there is no reason why Floor Guard   103
   should not be used in the case that you described; the   114
   wax won't yellow, and the plastic is an airtight bond.   125

10   One of our engineers is scheduling a trip to your   136
   city in about two weeks. He is familiar not only with   147
   Floor Guard but also with our other floor products; if   158
   you would like him to visit you for a conference about   169
   your problem, please tell us within the next few days.   180

   TAB ➤ TAB ➤   Sincerely yours,   185

   1 | 2 | 3 | 4 | 5 | 6 | 7 | 8 | 9 | 10 | 11

82/83-D. Practice the production of semiblocked letters

Analyze the arrangement of the letter on page 131; then type it and the letters assigned on page 132. GOAL: To type each letter within 6 minutes, with 3 or fewer errors.

LETTER GUIDE

Date 15
Address .. 20
—100 .... 4"
100-200 ... 5"
200+ .... 6"

Manuscript 44

POWER OF ATTORNEY
Paper: plain, ruled
Spacing: double
Position: centered
vertically

Remember: Double
line should fall
1½ inches from
left; single line,
½ inch from right.

P O W E R   O F   A T T O R N E Y   *please double space & center*

← 2 #

KNOW ALL MEN BY THESE PRESENCE: TS

       THAT I, JOHN R. APPLEMAN, of the city of Elizabeth,
County of Union, state of New Jersey, have made, constituted,
and appointed, and by these presents do make, constitute, and
appoint Mr. (Fred) N. Bold, of this City, County, and State, my
true and lawful Attorney for me and in my name, place, and
stead to act as my agent in the management of my property, an
apartment house situated at 1811 Bergen Road, of this City,
County, and State, giving and granting unto my *said* attorney full
power and authority to do and perform all and every act and
thing whatsoever requisite and necessary to be done in the
said management as fully, to all intents and purposes, as I
might or would do if personally present, with full power of
substitution and revocation, hereby ratifying and confirming
all that my said attorney or his substitute shall lawfully do
or shall cause to be done by virtue hereof.

    IN WITNESS WHEREOF, I have hereunto set my hand and seal
this twenty-eighth day of May, 19—. 2↓
   (center this line)   2 # _____ (L. S.)
  → Signed and affirmed in the presence of 2↓
             and _____
          make equal

41
53
65
78
90
107
114
127
139
151
163
175
187
200
207

221
228
239
265
279

LINE: 60
SPACING: SINGLE
GOAL: MORE ABOUT
LEGAL TYPING
DRILLS: THREE TIMES
STRESS: CONTINUITY

146-A. Type lines 2, 3
in cadence with someone
who sets a sharp, even
pace on the first line.
Or, each three times.

146-B. Type to your goal.

ACCURACY: Each pair
three times, as a
paragraph.

SPEED: Each line three
times successively.

In all cases, emphasize
smooth, continuous work.

146-A. Tune up on these review lines

1 Did you see the big new axe her dad had her get out for me?
2 Queen Judy gave my boy an exciting gold prize for his work.
3 Give us a quick report on (10), (28), (39), (47), and (56).
    1 | 2 | 3 | 4 | 5 | 6 | 7 | 8 | 9 | 10 | 11 | 12

146-B. Increase skill on patterned preview drills

4 coasting thinking climbing relaxing growing pushing talking
5 Sometimes Ambition Don't There Once All But The To If We Or
6 so. you. are. them. this. good. easy. short. coast.
7 position; coasting; effort, rather, still; "then" easy; go;
8 beginner warrior attain still; effort error hills fall; too
9 usually happens telling succeed ladder good, will, soon all

SEMIBLOCKED LETTER STYLE

Date and Closing Lines Start at Center • Paragraphs Indented 5 Spaces

Letter 29

SEMIBLOCKED LETTER
Shown: in pica
Body: 152 words
Line: 5 inches
Tab: 5 and center
Paper: letterhead
SI: 1.44—normal

January 4, 19-- ▼5   4

                                                                      8

Miss Lee Anne Sloane   12
The Graham Company   16
2847 West Yates Street   21
Billings, Montana   59103   25
                                                                      26
Dear Miss Sloane: 29
                                                                      30

REMEMBER:
After typing
state name,
space three
times before
typing postal
ZIP number.

    I am happy to answer your questions about the   41
details of our letter patterns. The answers are,   51
I believe, illustrated by this letter.   59
                                                                      60

    This is a semiblocked letter, which is simply   74
a blocked letter with the paragraphs indented. As   84
a rule, indentions are for five spaces; but it is   94
not uncommon to indent ten or even more spaces.   104
                                                                     105

    In this letter style, the date line is typed   115
either to end at the right margin or, as shown in   125
this letter, to start at the center; and the group   135
of closing lines is blocked at the center, too.   145
                                                                     146

    This letter also shows how and where a typist   156
indicates that he is enclosing something with the   166
letter: To serve as a reminder to himself and his   177
addressee, he types Enclosure or Enclosures on the   194
line below the reference initials.   202
                                                                     203

                    Sincerely yours, ▼4   207

A woman is assumed to be
Miss unless Mrs. is either
typed as shown here or
included parenthetically in
the penned signature.   210

                    Mrs. Ruth Leeds Murphy   216
                    Training Department   221
                                                                     222
urs   224
Enclosure

If you take a timed writing on
production copy and end with an
incomplete line, count 1 word
credit for each 5 strokes and
for each use of the tabulator
in that final incomplete line.

Business Letter in Semiblocked Style

IN WITNESS WHEREOF, I have hereunto set my hand and
seal the twenty-first day of May in the year one thousand nine
hundred and sixty-four. ↓2

_____ (L.S.)
↓2
(L.S.) means "place
of the seal." It is
typed without a space.

Sealed and Delivered
in the Presence of

_____ ↓3

Page 2 of 2

Continuation page has
1½-inch top margin (so
start on line 10). Top
margin is deep because
legal papers are bound
together at the top.

Signature line begins
at center. Witness
line runs from margin
to center of area.

Final page number is
typed a triple space
under body, not at
bottom of the page.

Form 55

BILL OF SALE
Form: workbook 275
Data: as shown

Form 56

BILL OF SALE
Form: workbook 277
Data: Manuscript 42

BILL OF SALE

𝔎now all 𝔐en by these 𝔓resents,

That I, John Edward Foster, of 936 Forest Avenue, Chicago, Cook County,
State of Illinois, --of the first part,

for and in consideration of the sum of One Thousand Dollars ($1,000) --------------

lawful money of the United States, to me ----in hand paid, at or before the ensealing and delivery of
these presents by Martin Miller & Sons, of 58 Broad Street, Atlanta, Fulton
County, State of Georgia, --------------------------------------
of the second part, the receipt whereof is hereby acknowledged, have bargained and sold, and by these
presents do sell, grant and convey unto the said part y - of the second part, its --- executors,
administrators and assigns my design and working model of a machine to simplify
the fastening of key caps to key bars in typewriters. ----------------

To have and to hold the same unto the said party -- of the second part, its ---executors,
administrators and assigns forever. And I do for me and my -----heirs, executors and administrators, covenant and agree, to and with the said party -- of the second part, to warrant and defend
the sale of the aforesaid design and machine ------------hereby sold unto the said part y -
of the second part, its --executors, administrators and assigns, against all and every person and
persons whomsoever.

In Witness Whereof, I have hereunto set my -hand -- and seal - the twenty-
first --day of May ----------in the year one thousand nine hundred and sixty-four.

Sealed and Delivered in the presence of

_____   _____ [L.S.]

Legal Document on Fill-in Printed Form (Reduced)

Letter 30

SEMIBLOCKED LETTER
Body: 175 words
Line: 5 inches
Tabs: 5 and center
Paper: letterhead
SI: 1.42—normal

Lack the workbook
letterheads? Then
use plain paper on
which you crease or
rule a line across
the paper 1½ inches
from the top, to
represent the depth
of a letterhead.

Letter 31

SEMIBLOCKED LETTER
Body: 166 words
Paper: letterhead
SI: 1.42—normal

Letter 32

SEMIBLOCKED LETTER
Body: 176 words
Paper: letterhead
SI: 1.46—fairly hard

Current Date | Dr. Edward L. Prall | Dean of Instruction | The Park Place School | Lincoln, Neb.   68504 | Dear Dean Prall: 17 / 30

Thank you for your letter inquiring about the training program we have developed for new employees. I am pleased to tell you about its three phases.   43 / 56 / 62

For the first week, each new employee learns about the company, its policies, and its products.   76 / 84

In the second week, each new employee studies the style manual used by all our office employees. This concerns our letter style, the forms used to requisition supplies, telephoning, and so on.   97 / 110 / 123 / 125

During the next few weeks, the new employees work in a production pool from which they are sent to cover the desks of absent workers or help with rush assignments. As we have vacancies, then, the trainees are ready for quick placement.   139 / 151 / 163 / 175

We are quite pleased with the success of this training program, Dean Prall. We should be happy to have you visit us and observe the program. | Sincerely yours, | Mrs. Ruth Leeds Murphy | Training Department | *Initials?*   188 / 201 / 220 / 228

Current Date | Mr. Carl W. Vance | Vance Service Center | 1028 Kearney Street | Hastings, Neb.   68901 | Dear Mr. Vance: 17 / 30

Your letter asking about our new Floor Guard protective floor covering arrived on the same day that we mailed to you and all our other dealers a complete report on this wonderful new product. On the chance that your copy is delayed, however, let me answer the questions you asked in your letter.   43 / 55 / 67 / 78 / 91

Yes, our advertising campaign for Floor Guard will begin next month in the national magazines.   105 / 112

No, we did not authorize the article you saw in Runyon's column; because his comments echo what we say in our first ads, we guess that one of the magazines tipped him off about our advertisement.   126 / 138 / 150 / 154

Yes, Floor Guard is in full production, ready to deliver to dealers who rush their orders to us. Window display units and store banners will go out with the first Floor Guard shipment to each dealer. | [*Complimentary Closing:*] Get your order in! | Howard T. Blackstone | District Sales Manager | *Initials?*   167 / 180 / 193 / 203 / 217

Current Date | Mr. Kenneth M. Jeffers | Supervising Engineer | Hotel Mann Lodge | Omaha, Neb.   68104 | Dear Mr. Jeffers: 17 / 29

[*The body and closing of this letter are on page 130.*] Howard T. Blackstone | District Sales Manager | urs | Enclosure   233 / 246

BILL OF SALE

BILL OF SALE

Top margin of first page should be 2 inches (start on line 13). If document will fit within one page, either center the typing or start it on line 7.

Title of document should be spread-centered. The center point is ½ inch to right of usual midpoint.

Manuscripts 42-43
BILL OF SALE
Paper: 8½ by 11 (draw margin-guide rules)
Copy 1: double space on 2 pages, as shown
Copy 2: single space on 1 page, centered
SI: 1.57—difficult

Spacing may be single but is usually double. Indent the paragraphs 10 spaces.

Bottom margin should be 1 to 1½ inches. Page is numbered as shown here: expressed cumulatively, centered between rules, three lines below body.

B I L L   O F   S A L E   14

16

KNOW ALL MEN BY THESE PRESENTS: 22

THAT I, Robert Dale Hetrick, of 138 Duquesne Street,   34
Concord, Merrimack County, State of New Hampshire, of the first   47
part, for and in consideration of the sum of Two Thousand Dol-   59
lars ($2,000) lawful money of the United States, to me in hand   71
paid, at or before the ensealing and delivery of these presents   84
by Atlas Victor Company, of 380 West Sixth Street, Camden,   96
Gloucester County, State of New Jersey, of the second part, the   109
receipt whereof is hereby acknowledged, have bargained and sold,   122
and by these presents do sell, grant and convey unto the said   134
party of the second part, its executors, administrators and as-   146
signs my design and working model of the Type-Meter, an instru-   159
ment to indicate the speed at which a typewriter is operated.   171

TO HAVE AND TO HOLD the same unto the said party of   183
the second part, its executors, administrators and assigns for-   195
ever. And I do for me and my heirs, executors, and adminis-   207
trators, covenant and agree, to and with the said party of the   220
second part, to warrant and defend the sale of the aforesaid   232
design and machine hereby sold unto the said party of the sec-   244
ond part, its executors, administrators and assigns, against all   257
and every person and persons whomsoever.   265

267

Page 1 of 2   276

(CONTINUED ON NEXT PAGE)

Legal Document on Ruled Stationery (Reduced)

Stationery is 8½ by 11, 13, or 14 inches. Margin stops are set a space or two inside double rule 1½ inches from left and single rule ½ inch from right edge.

Letter Typing

LINE: 60
TAB: 5 AND CENTER
SPACING: SINGLE
DRILLS: AS DIRECTED
GOAL: SPEEDUP IN
  PRODUCTION
STRESS: POSTURE

84-A. Each line three or more times (or 1-minute timing on each line).

Repeat in Lesson 85.

84-A. Tune up on these review lines

1   The name of the firm they own is to the right of the forms.

2   Six jumbo elephants quickly moved the wagon from the blaze.

3   The sum of "47" and "56" is more than "10," "28," and "39."

    1 | 2 | 3 | 4 | 5 | 6 | 7 | 8 | 9 | 10 | 11 | 12

84-B. For speed boost, each line three times; or, for an accuracy boost, the group of lines three times. Start each line slowly and evenly, and gradually accelerate.

84-B. Boost skill on these preview words

4   toastmaster Saturday whether consult annual honor hope that

5   invitation sincerely evening Council should voice find time

6   selection designate schedule helping please today then will

7   earnestly committee selected banquet notify heard know sure

84-C. Type a double-spaced copy, line for line (GOAL: To finish within 5 minutes and 3 errors or take one 5-minute writing on it). (GOAL: At least 40 wam, within 3 errors).

SI 1.29—fairly easy

84-C. Build skill on production material

8   Dear Judge Young: 4

     I am writing to confirm that the annual dinner to   15

honor our "Man of the Year" will be held on a Saturday   26

evening in April and to ask you whether we might count   37

on your helping the Council, as you did in each of the   48

past six years, by serving as the banquet toastmaster.   59

If time permits, take a 5-minute writing in Lesson 84, with a 10-second rest at the end of each minute; repeat in Lesson 85, without any pauses.

9   As a member of the selection committee, you know,   70

of course, that Fred Hughes is The Man; I have written   81

to him today to notify him and to ask him to designate   92

the date of the banquet. As soon as I have heard from   103

him, which should be within a few days, I shall inform   114

you of the date he has selected; then you will be able   125

to consult your own schedule and let us know for sure.   136

PROFESSIONAL HINT:

Whenever you can, precede the start of a timed writing by special drilling, as:

(1) To sharpen your concentration, type a line or two backwards.

(2) To reduce errors, practice any unique stroking combinations (like the quotation marks in paragraph 8).

(3) To increase speed, race through two or three copies of a very easy sentence, like line 1.

10   The invitation to serve as toastmaster comes from   147

all of us on the committee, of course. But please let   158

me add my own voice: busy though you are, I earnestly   169

hope that you can find the time to help us once again.   180

             Yours very sincerely,   186

    1 | 2 | 3 | 4 | 5 | 6 | 7 | 8 | 9 | 10 | 11

84/85-D. Practice the production of semiblocked letters

Study the arrangement of Letter 33; then see whether you can type it and Letters 34-36 within 6 minutes and 3 errors each.

To end lines evenly:
LINE: 70 spaces
INDENTIONS: 10 spaces
SI: 1.30—fairly easy

Dear Mr. Jones:

        Thank you for r
than we had expected

KNOW ALL MEN BY THES

        That I, Ro

Concord, Merrimack C

part, for and in con

o the said part ies -of the
    I do for me and my ---
the said part ies -of the s
invention -------------
dministrators and assigns,

hereunto set my - hand --
 the year one thousand nir

Willi

144-C. Increase skill on easy alphabetic paragraphs

1 | 2 | 3 | 4 | 5 | 6 | 7 | 8 | 9 | 10 | 11 | 12 | 13 | 14

Most of us have great respect for the law, for we feel that it   14
is complex and full of fine points that might trip us in some way. As   28
a result, there is a tradition, or what amounts to one, that legal   41
typing is very hard. Nothing could be further from the truth. Legal   55
jobs are quite easy to type, much easier, come to think of it, than a   69
majority of the jobs that are typed day in and day out in the office.   83

After all, such documents are nothing more or less than the   97
routine kind of manuscript with some fancy touches to impress people.   112
One such touch is the flair of indenting paragraphs ten spaces rather   126
than the standard five spaces. One more such flair is the antiquated   139
wording that is used time and again, such as "executors and heirs and   153
assigns forever." A wise typist just smiles, knowing that such terms   167
become easy to type when they are typed often enough. After a while,   181
the typist learns how to zip off such turns of words in nothing flat.   195

An extra legal touch in most states is using vertical lines   209
to show you where to set the margin stops. The lines are in color in   223
most cases, giving a bright but stern and official look to the papers   237
on which they appear. What is typed on the paper is supposed to stay   251
between the ruled lines without touching either of them; so the smart   265
typist adjusts the margin stops so they will be a space or two inside   279
the lines, and that is that. When you realize how much time is saved   293
by such guides, you can't help but wish we had them for letters, too!   308

One more unique thing in typing legal documents is that the   322
pages are bound at the top instead of at the side, which means that a   336
continuation page has to have an extra half inch of space at the top;   350
so you leave nine blank lines at the top of such pages instead of the   364
six lines that you leave on the continuation pages of manuscripts and   378
reports. In law offices and in the legal departments of major firms,   392
covers are made for legal documents that have many pages. The covers   406
are trimmed a little larger than the size of the paper, and the upper   420
half inch is folded over; the typed pages are jounced into the pocket   434
thus made, and the entire packet is fastened by two or three staples.   448

But the splendor of this lavish treatment of manuscripts is   462
dimming. One can find most of these papers in printed form at a dime   476
a dozen in any stationery shop, and one just inserts a few words here   490
and there on the form. Gone are the rows of shouting capitals. Gone   504
are the deep bows at the starts of the paragraphs. Gone are the firm   518
but colorful rules that fenced in the majestic words. And to replace   532
them, what have we? We have a printed form, a form full of holes and   546
gaps in which we insert a word, a name, a date, an amount. We do not   560
even display these things; we put each as near the start of its space   574
as we can, then dump in stuttering hyphens to fill up any extra room.   588
A fine day it is, when a document is no more challenging than a bill!   602

1 | 2 | 3 | 4 | 5 | 6 | 7 | 8 | 9 | 10 | 11 | 12 | 13 | 14

Letter 33

SEMIBLOCKED LETTER
IN FORMAL DISPLAY
Shown: in elite
Body: 170 words
Line: 5 inches
Tab: 5 and center
Paper: letterhead
SI: 1.43—normal

February 9, 19— ↓5   4

                                                            8

Dear Mr. Hughes: 12
                                                            13
      Each spring the members of the Madison Business Council   25
select and honor at a dinner the member of the Legislature   37
who has done the most to promote the growth of business in   48
our state. I am privileged to inform you that you have been   61
awarded this honor for this year. We should like to invite   73
you to attend and to speak at the dinner in your honor.   84
                                                            85
      We should like to hold the dinner on a Saturday evening   97
in April. If you would let us know which date would be most   109
convenient for you, we could then proceed to make the arrange-   121
ments for the dinner.   126
                                                            127
      Will you help us keep this news confidential? From past   139
years you probably know that we seek to withhold the news of   152
our selection until the moment it is announced at the dinner.   164
Only the selection committee and a few of those involved in   176
the dinner program will know who is our "Man of the Year."   188
                                                            189
                    Yours very sincerely, ↓4   197

                                                            200

                    Executive Secretary ↓3 or 4   206
                                                            207
                                                            208
The Honorable Fred Hughes   213
Member of the Legislature   218
The Wisconsin State House   223
Madison, Wisconsin   53702   227

Use no reference
symbols when an
address is typed
below the letter.

Typing the address at the
bottom of any letter makes
it "formal" or "official."
Letters to dignitaries are
given this special display.

Formal or Official Letter in Semiblocked Style

LINE: 60
SPACING: SINGLE
GOAL: LEARN ABOUT
LEGAL TYPING
DRILLS: THREE TIMES
STRESS: WARINESS IN
PRODUCTION

Unit 24. Manuscripts

144-A. Tune up on these review lines

144-A. Type lines 2, 3
in cadence with someone
who sets a crisp but
even pace on line 1;
then, exchange roles.

1 Sue said that they will have your gray suit back next week.

2 Vick did put a dozen tiny jugs from Iraq on the waxy table.

3 Type page 10 or 28, page 39 or 47, and page 56 or 100, Joe.

  1 | 2 | 3 | 4 | 5 | 6 | 7 | 8 | 9 | 10 | 11 | 12

144-B. Build skill on selective preview drills

144-B. Type to your need.

ACCURACY: Lines 4-7 like
a paragraph three times;
lines 8-11, twice; then
lines 4-7 once more.

SPEED: Type each line, 4
through 11, three times.

In all cases, emphasize
the elimination of arm,
elbow, and hand motion;
stress finger action.

4 paragraphs result papers easier truth heirs hard how for   2-3

5 blanks, black; small, hands, canal lack fans can and man   2-1

6 supposed further either appear people flair just are way   2-3

7 between become bounce unique worn upon more come ten now   1-3

8 very hard|less than|with some|than most|form that will   4&4

9 and his|the law|zip off|the use|off the|you can|but for   3&3

10 is too|by the|to one|is the|in any|on the|all of|if you   2&3

11 of us|of it|is to|up to|to be|to it|to do so|if it is so   2&2

144-C. Build skill on easy alphabetic paragraphs

144-C. Make a complete
copy of page 220, doing
half of it in Lesson 144
and half in Lesson 145.
Or, follow these steps:

1. Read the material.

2. Practice the three
hardest words you see
in each paragraph, 1-3.

3. Take a 5-minute timed
writing with a 10-second
rest after each minute.

4. Practice words with
which you have trouble.

5. Take a final 5-minute
writing without rests.

In Lesson 145, use these
steps on paragraphs 4-5.

SI 1.30—fairly easy

For surer understanding
of legal typing, do the
special learning guide
on workbook pages 273-4.

The paragraphs are on the next page. Note that you are to use a 70-space line for it and (in preparation for the legal documents that follow) a *10-space* paragraph indention. The selection is long enough that, if you wish, you could test your skill on a 7- or 10-minute writing—the kind you would be given in an employment test.

144/145-D. Apply skill to legal typing—perhaps

The legality of a document is based on its contents and signatories, not on how it is typed; but certain conventions have been established which must be observed by typists:

1. Documents are equally legal whether typed in full or on a form.

2. Erasures on *key* details, such as names and amounts and dates, are forbidden in most states (the page must be retyped or be initialed by all signers of the document).

3. The mechanical elements are illustrated and discussed on the next three pages; study them analytically.

The legal-typing assignments on pages 221-222 are interesting and valuable experiences, but it is possible that alternative practice may be more helpful to your growth:

DEVELOPMENT SKILL DRILL

If you cannot yet type 40 wam for 5 minutes with 3 or fewer errors, you may wish to omit the legal assignments and repeat the sequence of skill drills on pages 122-124.

SUSTAINED MANUSCRIPT TYPING

Or, you may wish to substitute for the legal typing the production of a magazine article by you, "What's What about Carbon Paper" (pages 158 and 161), for a magazine that uses a 45-stroke line and 3-space paragraph indentions (review page 150).

Current Date | Dear Judge Young: | [*The body and closing of this* 202
letter are on page 133] | Yours very sincerely, | Executive Secre- 214
tary ↓ 3 or 4 | The Honorable John Young | Judge of Superior 226
Court | Federal Court Building | Madison, Wisconsin   53702 237

Current Date | Dear Mr. Blaine: | The Madison Business 16
Council, which is a civic group in this city, wishes to ask and to 30
urge you to support House Bill 3301. This is the bill that would 42
give the owners of retail stores the right, such as owners of fac- 55
tories now have, for an early tax write-off for new equipment. 68

As you may know, the Madison Business Council is made up 79
of top management of nearly 400 Madison firms (only a quarter 91
of which are retail outlets) which employ some 18,500 persons. 104
The members of the Council believe firmly not only that this 116
bill is fair and just but also that it is long overdue. 127

Mr. Blaine, our whole city would benefit from tax relief for 142
our retail stores, for it would save some stores and encourage 154
others to modernize, thus helping all the supporting trades and 167
bringing new life to our downtown business center. We urge 179
you to do all you can to support H. B. 3301 and bring its 191
benefits to your constituents. | Respectfully yours, | MADISON 209
BUSINESS COUNCIL | Executive Secretary | The Honorable Paul 225
S. Blaine | Representative from Wisconsin | The House of Rep- 236
resentatives | Washington, D. C.   20025 | *Initials?* 242

Current Date | Mr. Harvey F. Hall, Manager | The Hilton 16
Motor Lodge | 211 Atwood Street | Madison, Wis.   53704 27
| Dear Mr. Hall: 31

The Madison Business Council plans to hold its annual 44
spring banquet on some Saturday evening in April. We esti- 56
mate that attendance will be between 200 and 250 persons and 68
that the affair will run from six to ten o'clock. 78

Please let us know for what Saturday evenings, if any, your 92
main ballroom could be reserved for us and what menus can be 104
offered at $7.50 and $10.00 per plate. 112

Please phone or write us so that we may hear from you not 126
later than the first of next month. | Sincerely yours, | Executive 146
Secretary | MJB | urs 149

Current Date | Mr. Fairleigh Lee Graham | Manager, Madison 16
Hotel | 1800 Eighth Street | Madison, Wisconsin   53701 | 27
Dear Mr. Graham: [*Prepare the same message.*] 149

Table 40

LEADER TABLE, BOXED
Center exact copy,
paper sideways in
machine. Available
lines: 8½ x 6 = 51

For review of
"boxed" table,
turn to pages
142 and 143.

DISTRIBUTION OF SALES INCOME

(Prepared by the Department of Research and Statistics)

How Our Sales Dollar Was Distributed	This Year		Last Year	
	Amount	Ratio	Amount	Ratio
Materials, Services from Others	$512,236,000	54.2%	$456,367,000	53.8%
Wages, Salaries	298,289,000	31.6%	281,769,000	33.2%
Pensions, Social Security, Insurance, Other Benefits	19,938,000	2.1%	18,470,000	2.2%
Depreciation, Amortization	17,314,000	1.8%	15,174,000	1.8%
Interest on Long-Term Debts	4,875,000	.5%	4,595,000	.5%
Taxes on Income and Property	47,772,000	5.0%	41,657,000	4.9%
Dividends Declared for the Year	22,052,000	2.3%	19,963,000	2.3%
Extra Dividend Last Quarter	4,284,000	.5%	—	—
Reinvested in the Business	18,480,000	2.0%	10,769,000	1.3%
TOTALS	$945,240,000	100.0%	$848,764,000	100.0%

LINE
9
10
11
12
13
14
15
16
17
18
19
20
21
22
23
24
25
26
27
28
29
30
31
32
33
34
35
36
37
38
39
40
41

Letter Review

LINE: 60
TAB: 5
SPACING: SINGLE
DRILLS: AS DIRECTED
GOAL: SPEEDUP IN
    LETTER TYPING
STRESS: DETAILS

86-A. Each line twice; then repeat three more times whichever one fits your objective. Repeat in Lesson 87.

86-A. Tune up on these review lines

1 If the men do their work by six, they may go to the social.

2 Hal was quick to give us extra pizza and juice for my boys.

3 I need number signs for: (10), (28), (39), (47), and (56).

    1 | 2 | 3 | 4 | 5 | 6 | 7 | 8 | 9 | 10 | 11 | 12

86-B. For speed boost, each line three times; or, for an accuracy boost, the solid group, like a paragraph, three times. Type without pausing.

86-B. Revive speed on fluent preview phrases

4 his use of the|than it is to|or how they|one of the|what to

5 will always be|how they will|and if they|just a bit|when he

6 in the same way|in the world|who has the|is the one|most of

    1 | 2 | 3 | 4 | 5 | 6 | 7 | 8 | 9 | 10 | 11 | 12

86-C. Type a double-spaced copy (GOAL: To finish within a limit of 5 minutes and 3 errors) or take one 5-minute writing to see whether you can type 40 or more wam, with 3 or fewer errors.

SI 1.30—fairly easy

86-C. Sustain speed on fluent paragraph material

7   One of the most difficult things in the world for most   12
of us is to be consistent, yet the habit of being so is the   24
jewel in the crown of success. He who is consistent is the   36
person who has the respect of his fellow citizens, for they   48
know what to expect of him, right or wrong. The people who   60
do not always act the same way are the ones of whom most of   72
us are suspicious; our not being able quite to predict what   84
they will do or how they will act or what decision they may   96
make leaves us wary and just a bit uncomfortable with them. 108

Letter typing requires so much attention to detail that you might be tempted to cut your pace; these paragraphs should help to restore your best momentum.

8   The knack of being consistent is more important to the 120
typist than it is to most persons. When he is grinding out 132
page after page of a long report, for example, the touch of 144
quality comes from his use of the same margins and the same 156
heading styles on each page. When he is turning out tables 168
that summarize what the department has just done this month 180
or quarter, they must match the style and design of reports 192
of prior periods in order that the same data will always be 204
found at a glance at the same point. And what is accuracy, 216
you know, but always hitting the same keys in the same way? 228

    1 | 2 | 3 | 4 | 5 | 6 | 7 | 8 | 9 | 10 | 11 | 12

86-D. Special notes: To give you a broad review of the display of feature lines in a letter, Letter 38 is shown with far more different displays than you are likely to see in a business letter. Rarely is an attention line used in a letter with a subject line.

If you were to make a carbon of each letter, you could mark up the carbon with reminders about the arrangement for the next letter.

86/87-D. Produce a summary project of display letters

Type as a four-page project on plain paper or workbook pages 155-158 the four versions of Letter 38, as directed on page 137. The table in the letter is to be centered with 6 spaces between columns; preset a tab stop for each column. Use a 60-space line for each letter.

LINE: 60
TAB: 5, 10, 30, 42
SPACING: SINGLE
GOAL: AUTHORITATIVE
 PRODUCTION OUTPUT
STRESS: WARINESS

142-A. To develop a skill momentum that will carry through the production, take two 1-minute timings on each sentence.

NOTE: Italicized words must be underscored when they are typed.

142-B. If you have not yet reached 50 or more wam within 3 errors for 5 minutes, use 140-B on page 213 and the steps at the foot of the page. Otherwise, these steps:

1. Analyze this letter.

2. Practice every line containing any numbers.

3. Take a 5-minute timed writing with a 10-second rest after each minute, or type a copy with a rest for each paragraph.

4. Take a 5-minute timed writing or type one copy without pausing to rest.

GOAL: 50 or more wam, with 3 or fewer errors.

SI 1.44—normal

142-A. Tune up on these review lines

1   The men held a social to pay for their visit to the chapel.

2   The expert quickly noted five bad jewels among the zircons.

3   Report *Monday* on Sections (10), (28), (39), (47), and (56).

    1 | 2 | 3 | 4 | 5 | 6 | 7 | 8 | 9 | 10 | 11 | 12

142-B. Sustain skill on production copy

```
4                                            Current Date   4
    and Mrs.
Mr. ^ J. W. Swensen                                         13
Apartment 9-J West                                          17
35-53 187th Street                                          21
Flushing, New York   11351                                  26
(Salutation)                                                34
            happy      reply to
We are always glad to answer questions from our             46
             for        the
stockholders. Our report ^ our operations in this last      58
            now    will
quarter, which is now being printed ^ and is to be          71
mailed in about two weeks, will show that our Net           83
Earnings are $5.04 a share, which is better than            95
           the              figures
average for this time of year. These are the data:          96
```

```
Gross Revenue ....................[21]... $55,999,275.00      107
Net Income before Federal Income                            114
   Taxes .......................    9,339,180.00            125
Estimated Fed. Income Taxes .......    4,905,227.00         136
Net Income ........................    4,433,953.00         148
Earnings per share ...............          5.04            159
                                                            160
```

```
             strong
We expect a great increase in our sales for the next        172
             shall
quarter, for we will be launching Vita-shine, the fine      185
                working on
new product we have been developing for more than           197
two years; if Vita-shine lives up to our forecasts,         209
                               very
which are based on a careful market                         221
          survey
study, then our sales and profits will show sharp           233
                                   margin
gains, putting us far ahead of any previous profit          234
We                   information                there are
we have enjoyed. I trust that this analysis is what         247
you wished. If you have other details that you              258
would like to have, we should be very happy to send         264
them along to you.                                          
                        Yours very truly,                   272
                                                            275
                        Mr. Orville L. Mitchell             282
                        Aide to the president               289
urs                                                         290
```

142-C. Apply skill to leadered production problems

Table 39

PIVOT-LEADER DRILL
Paper: half sheets
Copies: make three
Leaders: open
Spacing: double
Line: 40, 60, 50

Letter 71

BLOCKED LETTER WITH LEADERED TABULATION
Paper: workbook 271
Line: 60, as shown
Body: 180 words
SI: 1.44—normal

ASSIGNMENTS	ARRANGEMENTS	SPECIAL DIRECTIONS	WORDS
Letter 38	Semiblocked, in business display	Use 60-space line. Copy as shown but indent paragraphs 15 spaces and omit the subject line.	236
Letter 39	Semiblocked, in business display	Use 60-space line. Copy as shown, with paragraphs indented 10 spaces; but omit attention line.	237
Letter 40	Semiblocked, in formal display, as on page 134	Use 60-space line, date at right margin. Convert attention line to first line of inside address, with "Dear Mr." salutation. Omit subject line and indent paragraphs only 5 spaces.	225
Letter 41	Blocked, as shown on page 98	Use 60-space line, paragraphs NOT indented. Omit subject line and the company signature.	232

                                        February 11, 19---↓5   4

                                                                                     8

Southern Speakers Bureau   13
1250 College Park Place   18
Knoxville, Tennessee   37912   24

Attention of Mr. Clark T. Krane   43

Gentlemen: 47

                    SUBJECT: TRIP FOR DOCTOR MAHR   67

        We are pleased to report that we have been able to   79
make final plans with four Kiwanis groups for the West Coast   91
trip of your client, Dr. Charles Mahr: 99

                    May 6   San Diego   106
                    May 7   Los Angeles   113
                    May 8   (Travel)   119
                    May 9   San Francisco   126
                    May 10   (Travel)   132
                    May 11   Portland   138

        As we said in our prior letter, the Kiwanis groups   150
will pay all of Doctor Mahr's expenses and his speaker's fee   163
of $150 each time he gives his "Give Him a Break" talk.   174

        We hope that you will let us know at once that the   186
plans meet with your and Doctor Mahr's approval in order that   199
we may complete the contract with Kiwanis. Please tell us,   211
also, whether Doctor Mahr would like our help in making his   223
hotel and his travel arrangements for the trip.   232

                                Yours very truly,   240

                                THE WEST COAST LYCEUM   248

                                                                                   251

                                The College Division   259

MFS/urs   260
cc Kiwanis Clubs   264

Letter 38
Table 13

SEMIBLOCKED LETTER
Paper: letterhead
Body: 141 words
SI: 1.43—normal

Semiblocked Business Letter with Special Features

the vertical spacing of each half, adding or deleting blank lines so as to make both halves end evenly.

4. Divide the heading lines to embrace both pages. The section on the first page is pivoted from the right margin; the section on the second page begins with the left margin.

5. Use the same length of line on each half; if necessary, spread the data to fill the line. The display on each page *may* be centered, but the total display will look better if the margins are narrower on the sides where the pages will adjoin.

6. Tape the pages together on the *back* side, fastening them with two or three 1-inch strips of tape.

LINE		
14	A c m e C o r p o r a t i o n	
15		
16	S H E E T	
17		
18	December 31, 19——	
19		
20		
21	L I A B I L I T I E S	
22		
23	Legal Reserve for Life and Annuity	
24	Contracts	$302,514,963.00
25		
26	Reserve for Disability Policies	2,257,617.00
27		
28	Reserve for Epidemics and	
29	Mortality Fluctuations	2,500,000.00
30		
31	Reserve for Investment Fluctuations	5,000,000.00
32		
33	Reserve for Policy Claims in	
34	Process of Adjustment	1,459,619.00
35		
36	Gross Premiums and Interest Paid	
37	in Advance	1,768,036.00
38		
39	Taxes Accrued but Not Yet Due	2,078,495.00
40		
41	Agents' Bond Deposits (Field Employees) . .	683,764.21
42		
43	Commissions Accrued to Agents,	
44	and Miscellaneous Items	936,106.60
45		
46	Total Liabilities Other Than	
47	Capital and Surplus	$319,198,600.81
48		
49	Capital and Surplus	28,667,592.10
50		
51	TOTAL LIABILITIES	$347,866,192.91
52		

Table 38

BALANCE SHEET
(PAGE 2 OF 2)
Line: 60, with 1-inch
left margin
Leaders: open

Unit 15. Tabulation

LINE: 60
TAB: EVERY 9 SPACES
SPACING: SINGLE
DRILLS: THREE TIMES
GOAL: MASTER
  RULED TABLES
STRESS: EFFICIENCIES

88-A. Maintain perfect rhythm—including the tabulating in line 2—if you possibly can.

88-A. Tune up on these review lines

1 cab ade fag ham aim jar kay lax pan oat qua was vat tap zag

2 one   six   two   ten   two   six   eight

3 Flight 47 leaves at 10:28, while Flight 56 leaves at 10:39.

88-B. To gain speed, type each line three times. To gain accuracy, type the group of lines, as a paragraph, three times. Try for rhythm without trying to speed up.

88-B. Sustain rhythm on these preview words

4 horizontal centering shortcut writing crease let's even six

5 adjustment backspace checking someone anyhow quite back out

6 arithmetic advancing vertical realize square paper once for

88-C. In Lesson 88, type one complete copy, being sure to type as evenly as you can and to rest after finishing each paragraph. Then, in Lesson 89, warm up by typing, three times each, every line in which you had an error the first time you copied this; and type four copies of the last paragraph (GOAL: To type the four copies in 5 minutes, with not more than 3 errors, without looking up even once!).

Or, take a 5-minute writing in Lesson 88, with a 10-second pause after each minute; and take a 5-minute timing without rests in Lesson 89 (GOAL: 40 or more wam, within 3 errors).

Use double spacing, a 5-space paragraph tab indention, and listen for the bell. If you respond correctly to the bell, all lines will end even at the margin.

SI 1.31—fairly easy

88-C. Sustain speed on fluent alphabetic paragraphs

7   Just about the time that we think we know all there is to   12
know about our work, along will come someone with a fine   23
shortcut that is new to us. I ran into such a plan five or six   36
months ago. It is a plan for taking the arithmetic out of verti-   48
cal centering. What you have to do is to back down from the   60
center of the paper, just like we back up from the middle of the   73
paper for horizontal centering. You will not quite realize how   86
easy it is until you try it for yourself.   95

8   But first you have to learn how to locate the vertical center   108
of the paper when it is in the machine. Let's learn to do this   121
right now. Fold a sheet of paper from bottom to top and crease   134
it horizontally. Next, open and insert this sheet in the machine,   147
advancing the paper until the top and bottom come even when   159
you press them back against the paper table, the way you do   171
anyhow when you are checking that the paper is straight. Now,   184
count how many lines you must turn up the paper to bring the   196
crease to the writing point; this will be four to six lines. Re-   208
member the number. From here on you can insert paper and   220
advance it until the bottom and top square up, then make the   232
adjustment of the extra lines, whose number you know, to get   244
to the exact vertical center.   250

9   Now you can guess how the plan works. You insert your   262
paper to its exact center; then, looking at the lines to be   274
centered, back out the page one line for every two lines of space   287
the copy will require, just as you backspace once for each pair   300
of spaces when you center something horizontally.   310

1 | 2 | 3 | 4 | 5 | 6 | 7 | 8 | 9 | 10 | 11 | 12 | 13

NOTES ON TYPING "OPEN" LEADERS

"Open" or "spread" leaders (alternate periods and spaces) are slower to type than "close" leaders (page 212) but look better when a table includes many blank lines between the typed lines.

Begin the first leader line with one space (note below the space between *Loans* and the first period). Note whether the periods fall in the odd- or even-number spaces on the scale; use this fact when you start each subsequent leader line. You will often need to space twice at the start of a leader (see the two spaces after *Owned* in the sixth leader) to enable you to keep all the periods aligned.

NOTES ON TYPING TWO-PAGE TABLES

1. Two-page tables are usually planned so that the two pages may be taped in adjacent positions.

2. Divide the data into equal or logical halves.

3. Use the same top margin on both pages. Check

Table 37

BALANCE SHEET
(PAGE 1 OF 2)
Line: 60, with 1-inch
 right margin
Leaders: open

	LINE
The Providence—	14
	15
B A L A N C E	16
	17
For the Year Ending	18
	19
	20
A S S E T S	21
	22
Real Estate Loans $162,587,305.68	23
	24
Bonds Owned:	25
Government Bonds $45,507,650.33	26
Railroad Bonds 4,508,135.65	27
Public Utility Bonds . . 62,449,231.34	28
Industrial Bonds 26,878,473.54	29
	30
Total Bonds Owned 139,343,490.86	31
	32
Stocks Owned (Basic Industries	33
with Dividend Records) 13,129,036.89	34
	35
Policy Loans Made to Policyholders 11,862,942.16	36
	37
Net Unpaid and Deferred Premiums	38
(Being Collected) 7,099,713.61	39
	40
Cash in Banks and Offices 6,340,534.93	41
	42
Real Estate Owned (Including	43
Home Office Building) 5,980,846.78	44
	45
Interest Due and Accrued	46
on Bonds and Mortgages 1,412,662.00	47
	48
Collateral Loans (First Mortgages Only) . . 109,660.00	49
	50
TOTAL ASSETS $347,866,192.91	51
	52

88-D. Review the production of open tables

Line		Words
1	ADVERTISING RATIOS	11
2		12
3	January, 19—	21
4		22
5		23

Line	Insertion Order No.	Number of Readers	Cost per Thousand	Words
6	Insertion	Number of	Cost per	41
7	Order No.	Readers	Thousand	58
8				59
9	➤ 4,534	2,000,000	$4.00	68
10	4,535	1,550,000	3.50	77
11	4,536	675,000	3.75	83
12	4,537	1,125,000	4.00	89
13	4,538	1,725,000	4.25	95
14	4,539	1,265,000	6.00	109
15				110
16	AVERAGE	1,390,000	$4.25	118

Review, on page 66, the basic steps in typing a table and, on page 69, the procedure for a table that includes column headings.

NOTES: When a table has an averages or totals line: (1) underscore the columns concerned; (2) precede the line by 1 blank line; (3) type the word *Average* [or *Total*, whichever is appropriate] in all capitals at the left edge of the table; and (4) if the line includes a $ sign, align it with the one above it.

PRACTICE. Type Table 14. GOAL: To be ready within 3 minutes and to type a copy within 3 minutes and 3 errors.

Table 14

OPEN TABLE
Paper: full sheet

88-E. Learn how to type tables in ruled form

Line	Insertion Order No.	Number of Readers	Cost per Thousand	Words
1	ADVERTISING RATIOS			11
2				12
3	January, 19—			21
4	_____			29
5				30
6	Insertion	Number of	Cost per	38
7	Order No.	Readers	Thousand	45
8	_____			53
9				54
10	➤ 4,534	2,000,000	$4.00	63
11	4,535	1,550,000	3.50	72
12	4,536	675,000	3.75	78
13	4,537	1,125,000	4.00	84
14	4,538	1,725,000	4.25	90
15	4,539	1,265,000	6.00	96
16	_____			108
17				109
18	AVERAGE	1,390,000	$4.25	116
19	_____			124

As Table 15 illustrates, tables are often prepared with ruled lines of underscores to separate the parts of the table. Note that: (1) *one* blank line is left above and below each ruled line; (2) column heads are *not* underscored; but (3) in other regards a ruled table is arranged just like an open-form table.

Two helpful cautions: (1) Complete all machine adjustments and compute the top margin *before* inserting the paper; and (2) be sure to extend the rules to the full width of the table.

PRACTICE. Type Table 15. GOAL: To be ready within 3 minutes and to type a copy within 3 minutes and 3 errors.

Table 15

RULED TABLE
Paper: full sheet

89-F. Produce tables (next page) in ruled form

Table 36

BALANCE SHEET
WITH LEADERS
Shown: in elite
Line: 60 spaces

The Providence–Acme Corporation

B A L A N C E   S H E E T

For the Year Ending December 31, 19--

A S S E T S

Real Estate Loans		$162,587,305.68
Bonds Owned:		
Government Bonds	$45,507,650.33	
Railroad Bonds	4,508,135.65	
Public Utility Bonds	62,449,231.34	
Industrial Bonds	26,878,473.54	
Total Bonds Owned		139,343,490.86
Stocks Owned (Basic Industries		
with Dividend Records)		13,129,036.89
Policy Loans Made to Policyholders		11,862,942.16
Net Unpaid and Deferred Premiums		
(Being Collected)		7,099,713.61
Cash in Banks and Offices		6,340,534.93
Real Estate Owned (Including		
Home Office Building)		5,980,846.78
Interest Due and Accrued		
on Bonds and Mortgages		1,412,662.00
Collateral Loans (First Mortgages Only) ...		109,660.00
TOTAL ASSETS		$347,866,192.91

L I A B I L I T I E S

Legal Reserve for Life and Annuity	
Contracts	$302,514,963.00
Reserve for Disability Policies	2,257,617.00
Reserve for Epidemics and	
Mortality Fluctuations	2,500,000.00
Reserve for Investment Fluctuations	5,000,000.00
Reserve for Policy Claims in	
Process of Adjustment	1,459,619.00
Gross Premiums and Interest Paid	
in Advance	1,768,036.00
Taxes Accrued but Not Yet Due	2,078,495.00
Agents' Bond Deposits (Field Employees) ...	683,754.21
Commissions Accrued to Agents,	
and Miscellaneous Items	936,106.60
Total Liabilities Other Than	
Capital and Surplus	$319,198,590.81
Capital and Surplus	28,667,602.10
TOTAL LIABILITIES	$347,866,192.91

Side notes:

To facilitate your copying, paper-clip to the page a line guide (envelope or paper) you can slide down the page as you begin each line.

Leaders carried through column area end evenly with the column.

Long items are doubled up if fewer than 3 leaders would be left. Basis of doubling up is clarity for the reader.

Principal totals in a balance sheet are preceded and followed by one blank linespace.

Consistent steps of any size (2, 3, 5, 10, etc.) may be used for runover lines.

Capitalization and phrasing patterns are optional, but they must be consistent.

Table 16

RULED TABLE
Paper: full sheet

SPECIAL NOTES:
1. Arrangement here is alphabetic.
2. $ signs at bottom and top must align.
3. One blank line precedes and follows each underscore line.

AMENDED SALES QUOTAS

Fourth Quarter, 19—

Name	Quota	Headquarters
Allerton, Fred	$ 7,500	Chicago
Cox, Francis	9,000	New York
Farley, Harold	6,000	Mobile
Jordan, Thomas	8,000	Seattle
Maxwell, Joe	6,500	Las Vegas
Paulson, Henry	7,500	Emporia
Teacher, Leo	8,000	Nashville
TOTAL	$52,000	. . . .

12
13
25
35
36
43
52
53
64
72
79
87
97
105
115
124
125
132
141

Table 17

RULED TABLE
Paper: full sheet

Arrangement here is by sales amounts.

REPORT OF SALES

Fourth Quarter, 19—

Rank	Name	Sales	Quota
1	Jordan, Thomas	$10,000	$ 8,000
2	Cox, Francis	8,500	9,000
3	Paulson, Henry	6,750	7,500
4	Teacher, Leo	6,000	8,000
5	Maxwell, Joe	5,200	6,500
6	Farley, Harold	4,980	6,000
7	Allerton, Fred	4,500	7,500
TOTAL	. . . .	$45,930	$52,000

9
10
23
33
43
52
61
70
80
90
100
109
118
128
140
149

Table 18

RULED TABLE
Paper: full sheet

Arrangement here is by percentages. The percent sign must be repeated; it is not omitted as the $ sign usually is.

ANALYSIS OF SALES PERFORMANCE

Fourth Quarter, 19—

Rank	Name	Quota	Sales	Ratio
1	Jordan, Thomas	$ 8,000	$10,000	125%
2	Cox, Francis	9,000	8,500	94%
3	Paulson, Henry	7,500	6,750	90%
4	Farley, Harold	6,000	4,980	83%
5	Maxwell, Joe	6,500	5,200	80%
6	Teacher, Leo	8,000	6,000	75%
7	Allerton, Fred	7,500	4,500	60%
TOTAL	. . . .	$52,000	$45,930	87%

18
32
41
52
61
74
85
96
107
117
128
139
148
160
169

LINE: 60
TAB: 5
SPACING: DOUBLE
GOAL: MASTERY OF
   LEADERED TABLES
STRESS: PERSONAL
   EFFICIENCY

140-A. Whisk through each line three times.

140-B. These alphabetic paragraphs are fluent and easy (SI 1.22), just the thing to enable you to withstand the "drag" effect of the leadered tables you are typing.

GOAL: You ought to be able to complete each paragraph within 2 minutes and 1 error.

Before you type each table in Lessons 140 and 141, type at least one of these paragraphs within 1 error; attach the paragraph to the table to show you have paid your premium on your "skill insurance."

SI 1.22—easy

140-A. Repeat the warmup on page 210, then—

140-B. Revive typing fluency on this easy copy

1 | 2 | 3 | 4 | 5 | 6 | 7 | 8 | 9 | 10 | 11 | 12

1   When I take a business trip, I stay in good hotels. I   12
do not like to stay in private homes. Now and then someone   24
will urge me to stay at his home; but I know that the offer   36
is likely to be just a show of goodwill and that the friend   48
is holding his breath, not quite sure how he can explain to   60
his wife the importance of having this guest. I always let   72
my host off the hook at once, for I am by no means eager to   84
forego a long shower and half hour of reading before I turn   96
out the light and curl up for a long sleep. No, thank you.   108

2   When you stay at a hotel, you can do as you wish. You   120
can order up a late snack, take a quick nap if you have the   132
urge to do so, repack the luggage, walk around in your bare   144
feet, write a report, or read all night if the book is that   156
good. You can make a phone call home to see whether Junior   168
brought home his report card. If you prefer, you can relax   180
as long as you wish in a tub or snooze through a TV program   192
or two that you cannot get at home. By contrast, what's it   204
like when you get trapped into staying all night in a home?   216

3   In the first place, you have trouble finding the home.   228
Your host cannot take you, of course, because he has to zip   240
home ahead of you. If he lives in town, it is in an apart-   252
ment that your taxi driver cannot locate. If he lives in a   264
suburb, which is quite likely, the train he suggests is one   276
that, it turns out, runs just on Sundays. So you catch the   288
bus; and, of course, the directions he gave you for getting   300
from the station do not serve to get you from the bus stop.   312
When you do arrive, the host has hopefully given up on you.   324

4   The family has eaten, of course; but it is no trouble,   336
no trouble at all, to fix up something for you. So you eat   348
cold food that squelches such appetite as you brought along   360
while the family sits there and watches each jiggle of your   372
fork. Then your hostess, after a suspiciously long session   384
of dishwashing, packs the little ones off to bed. But they   396
do not fall asleep; they have been shuffled to create a bed   408
vacancy. Thus you waste all evening, trying resolutely not   420
to think of the lazy ease you would be enjoying in a hotel.   432

1 | 2 | 3 | 4 | 5 | 6 | 7 | 8 | 9 | 10 | 11 | 12

140/141-C. Apply typing skill to financial statements

NOTE: These paragraphs are also excellent for increasing your skill:

1. Read the material.

2. Practice the three hardest words you see in each paragraph.

3. Take a 5-minute timed writing with a 10-second rest after each minute.

4. Practice words with which you had trouble.

5. Take a final 5-minute writing, without rests.

LINE: 60
TABS: EVERY 9 SPACES
SPACING: SINGLE
DRILLS: THREE TIMES
GOAL: LEARN TO TYPE
  BOXED TABLES
STRESS: TOUCH
  TABULATION

90-A. Maintain perfect rhythm—including the tabulating in line 2—if you possibly can.

90-A. Tune up on these review lines

1 eat ice vex few bye jet keg elm row pen que set ode the zoo
2 $10 $28 $39 $47 $56 $10 $1000
3 We had 1,039 employees in 1947 and 2,847 employees in 1956.

90-B. To gain speed, type each line three or more times. To gain accuracy, type the group of lines (like a paragraph) three times.

90-B. Maintain rhythm on these preview words

4 model plane being seize every ahead prize quest tasks quota
5 true test drug shop jugs desk keep beat only dull need dare
6 job day new lab fix try way who one not can for old any par

90-C. In Lesson 90, first take a 2-minute writing or make one copy of paragraph 7 (SI 1.13—very easy), trying to complete it in 2 minutes. Then, practice paragraph 8 (SI 1.28—fairly easy) in the same manner; and, finally, practice paragraph 9 (SI 1.44—normal) similarly.

Then, in Lesson 91, take a 5-minute timing on the three paragraphs together or make one copy, trying to finish it in 6 minutes or less.

SI 1.27 allover—fairly easy when practiced.

Use double spacing, a 50-space line, and the usual tab-5 indention.

90-C. Sustain speed on fluent alphabetic paragraphs

7   Much of the work in any kind of job is about   10
the same, day in and day out. This is as true in   20
the clouds where you test a new model of a plane,   30
or in a lab where you work with a new drug, or in   40
a shop where you design new ways to fix up broken   50
jugs as it is at an office desk. The way to keep   60
from being bored is to seize every chance to beat   70
the record, to try the unique, and to find better   80
ways to do all the things you have to do somehow.   90

8   The only sure way to get ahead in most kinds   100
of work is to gain a reputation for doing good or   110
better work. If you are the only person who does   120
a certain job, no one knows whether you deserve a   130
prize or not. Only in the routine tasks that you   140
do in common with other people can what you do be   150
compared. Only in these things can others recog-   160
nize that your work excels. If you want success,   170
your quest should be for skill in doing the dull.   180

9   But there is one hazard about which most new   190
workers have to be cautioned, and that is the old   200
danger that the new worker does not know what has   210
already been tried and rejected by the older mem-   220
bers of the firm. A quota of natural mistakes in   230
judgment is permitted to any newcomer; but trying   240
to tell more experienced workers what they should   250
be doing is not included in the newcomer's quota.   260
One has to reach par before he dare coach others.   270

1 | 2 | 3 | 4 | 5 | 6 | 7 | 8 | 9 | 10

RECONCILIATION
WITH LEADERS
1. Single spaced on
   60-space line
2. Double spaced on
   56-space line

Jos. Cooper & Sons

BANK RECONCILIATION STATEMENT

Month Ending April 30, 19—

Bank balance, March 31 .... $10,722.58

Deposit, April 4 .... 2,750.00

Deposit, April 11 .... 2,750.00

Deposit, April 18 .... 2,750.00

Deposit, April 25 .... 3,000.00

Total deposits and balance $21,972.58

Checks cleared since March 31 ...... $ 9,633.75

Check Apl4 outstanding 525.25

Check Apl78 outstanding 100.00

Total checks drawn 10,259.00

Corrected bank balance $11,713.58

Checkbook balance $11,713.58

These are "close" or "solid" leaders;
compare with "open" ones, page 115

$10,722.58¹² $21,972.58

Open space at
start and end
of leader line

Leaders end at
same point

To arrange table
on an assigned
length of line,
pivot from right
to set tabs for
money columns*

* Tab stops help only in locating the
first entry in each money column.
The other entries and leaders are
aligned visually—you have to look.

P&L STATEMENT
WITH LEADERS
1. May, 60 spaces,
   single spaced
2. June, 56 spaces,
   double spaced

Lincoln & Packer, Inc.

SUMMARY STATEMENT OF PROFIT AND LOSS

For the Month Ending May 31, 19--

— June 30

SALES		$27,453.28	*$26,943.35*
COST OF MERCHANDISE			
Starting inventory	$15,267.00		*$12,613.50*
Inventory purchases	8,476.50		*18,732.90*
Total available	$23,743.50		*$31,346.40*
Closing inventory	12,613.50		*19,290.60*
Cost of merchandise sold		11,130.00	*12,055.80*
GROSS PROFIT ON SALES		$16,323.28	*$14,887.55*
EXPENSES			
Selling expense	$ 5,425.85		*$ 5,109.20*
Rent expense	2,500.00		*2,500.00*
Heat and light	620.43		*481.30*
Depreciation of equipment	1,000.00		*1,000.00*
Total expenses		9,546.28	*9,090.50*
NET PROFIT, BEFORE TAXES		$ 6,777.00	*$ 5,797.05*

Compare with
Table 30 for
capitalization
and phrasing.

Table 19

RULED TABLE
Paper: full, plain
Spacing: single

National Motor Company

POSITION IN THE AUTO INDUSTRY

(In Thousands of Units)

Year	Industry	Number We Made	Percent We Made
1955	6,666	1,555	23.2%
1957	5,433	1,166	21.4%
1959	4,312	1,003	23.3%
1961	6,117	1,541	25.2%
1963	5,559	1,688	30.4%
1965	7,908	2,238	28.3%

In ruled table, lines are typed as underscores.

13
14
33
34
49
58
59
65
74
83
84
98
106
113
121
129
136
145

90-D. Produce tables in "boxed" form

A *boxed* table is one with both vertical and horizontal ruled lines. The lines divide the columns and headings but do not close in the sides. The typist types the table as usual, *omitting all the rules but leaving space for them,* and then draws the lines by pen or pencil and ruler. Fine points:

1. The horizontal lines should extend a quarter inch beyond the two sides of the typed table.

2. The vertical lines should be centered within the 6 blank spaces left between the columns.

3. It is acceptable to type the horizontal lines and draw the vertical ones; but it is preferable to draw all the lines so they match each other.

Compare Tables 19 and 20. They are to be done alike except that all the rules in Table 20 are to be drawn in after the table has been typed.

Table 20

BOXED TABLE
Paper: full, plain
Spacing: single

National Motor Company

POSITION IN THE AUTO INDUSTRY

(In Thousands of Units)

Year	Industry	Number We Made	Percent We Made
1955	6,666	1,555	23.2%
1957	5,433	1,166	21.4%
1959	4,312	1,003	23.3%
1961	6,117	1,541	25.2%
1963	5,559	1,688	30.4%
1965	7,908	2,238	28.3%

In boxed table, lines are drawn after the table has been typed.

138-D. Apply typing skill to financial statements

RECONCILIATION
Paper: plain, 8½ x 11
1. Single spacing
2. Double spacing

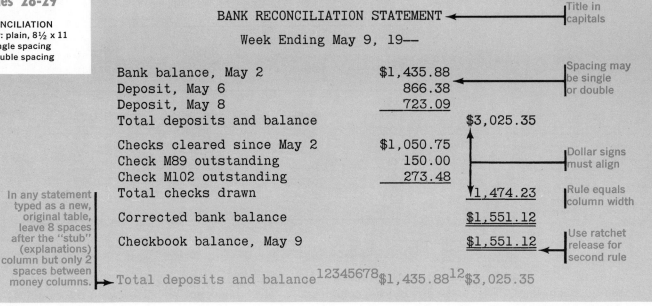

Business Service Company

BANK RECONCILIATION STATEMENT ← Title in capitals

Week Ending May 9, 19—

Bank balance, May 2	$1,435.88	← Spacing may be single or double
Deposit, May 6	866.38	
Deposit, May 8	723.09	
Total deposits and balance		$3,025.35
Checks cleared since May 2	$1,050.75	Dollar signs must align
Check M89 outstanding	150.00	
Check M102 outstanding	273.48	
Total checks drawn		1,474.23	Rule equals column width
Corrected bank balance		$1,551.12	
Checkbook balance, May 9		$1,551.12	← Use ratchet release for second rule

In any statement typed as a new, original table, leave 8 spaces after the "stub" (explanations) column but only 2 spaces between money columns. →

Total deposits and balance¹²³⁴⁵⁶⁷⁸$1,435.88¹²$3,025.35

Before typing Tables 28-31, read 138-C carefully—doing so can save you much time, particularly in Table 31.

Tables 30-31

P&L STATEMENT
1. February
2. March

The Winslow-Halpin Company

SUMMARY STATEMENT OF PROFIT AND LOSS

Month Ending February 28, 19--

			March 31
SALES		$48,431	$49,651
DEDUCT COST OF MERCHANDISE SOLD:			
Merchandise Inventory, February 1	$16,401		$16,512
Merchandise Purchases	35,208		33,147
Total Available for Sale	$51,609		$49,659
Merchandise Inventory, February 28	16,512		14,185
Total Cost of Merchandise Sold		35,097	35,474
GROSS PROFITS ON SALES		$13,334	$14,177
DEDUCT EXPENSES:			
Selling Expense	$ 4,131		$ 4,273
Rent Expense	1,024		1,194
Heat and Light	261		273
Depreciation of Equipment	500		480
Total Expenses		5,916	6,220
NET PROFIT, BEFORE TAXES		$ 7,418	$ 7,957

91-E. Produce boxed tables with "braced" headings

A *braced* heading identifies and is centered above two or more columns (example: *Men Employees* in Table 21). Technical fine points:

1. Omit the braced heading (but leave appropriate space for it) until the line under the braced heading has been typed; then, turn back the paper and carefully insert the braced heading.

2. Easiest way to center the braced heading over its columns: count the spaces in the columns' area (including the spaces between the columns) and the spaces in the braced heading; then, from the start of the first column, indent the braced heading half the difference in the two counts (drop any fraction). Thus, *Men Employees* (13) takes 6 spaces less than *Number*+6+*Percent* (19) and so is indented 3 spaces from the start of the *Number* column.

3. Use of a braced heading in a table requires the use of the *boxed*-table arrangement.

Table 21

BOXED TABLE WITH
BRACED HEADINGS

Table 1

SUMMARY OF OFFICE EMPLOYEES ↓3

Year	Men Employees		Women Employees ↓3		Total ↓3
	Number	Percent	Number	Percent	
1940	32	40.0%	48	60.0%	80
1945	35	38.8%	55	61.2%	90
1950	40	38.1%	65	61.9%	105
1955	40	32.0%	85	68.0%	125
1960	45	31.2%	99	68.8%	144
1965	37	38.1%	60	61.9%	97

(line numbers at left: 1–18; at right: 4, 5, 23, 24, 25, 34, 35, 36, 49, 50, 51, 73, 83, 93, 103, 114, 124)

Table 22

BOXED TABLE WITH
BRACED HEADING

Note that the number of a table, if it has one, is centered above the title line.

Table 2

TENURE OF PRESENT EMPLOYEES

Years	Numbers			Percent
	Men	Women	Total	
0- 1	20	33	53	8.3%
2- 5	32	194	226	35.3%
6-10	67	119	186	29.0%
11-15	45	24	69	10.8%
16-20	35	19	54	8.4%
21-25	22	18	40	6.2%
26 up	8	5	13	2.0%
TOTAL	229	412	641	100.0%

(line numbers at right: 4, 22, 29, 41, 61, 69, 78, 87, 96, 105, 113, 124)

LINE: 60
SPACING: SINGLE
DRILLS: THREE EACH
GOAL: MASTERY OF
  LEADERED TABLES
STRESS: PRECISION

Unit 23. Tabulation

138-A. Tune up on these review lines

138-A. Lines three or more times; type lines 2 and 3 in cadence with someone who sets even pace by typing line 1. Then, reverse roles.

1 They will seek some more work when they have done your job.
2 The banquet speaker, James Boxell, analyzed a few carvings.
3 we 23 25 27 29 ow 92 94 96 98 to 59 57 55 53 up 70 68 66 64
   1 | 2 | 3 | 4 | 5 | 6 | 7 | 8 | 9 | 10 | 11 | 12

138-B. Increase skill on an acceleration preview

138-B. Target on goal.

ACCURACY: Three copies of lines 4-6 as though they were a paragraph.

SPEED: Three copies of each, consecutively.

4 backspacing example, easiest columns tables size you get it
5 explanation whatever squared special method type not six or
6 statements financial quarter project hazard sign the end of

138-C. Sustain skill on technical, alphabetic paragraphs

138-C. Adjust machine: 50-space line, double spacing, and a tab-5.

Type one complete copy in Lesson 138; repeat in Lesson 139. GOAL: a copy in six minutes or less, with three or fewer typing errors.

Or, take one 5-minute writing, with a short rest after each minute, in Lesson 138; and one similar writing, but without any rests, as a Lesson 139 follow-up.

SI 1.29—fairly easy

7 Of all the forms of tables, the ones easiest   10
to set up are financial statements. They are al-   20
ways in the same form, month after month, quarter   30
after quarter. The right way to set up a new one   40
is to copy the old one; that is, you get from the   50
files the last statement of the same type, insert   60
it in the machine, and set up your margin and tab   70
stops by eye. If there is none to copy, however,   80
you can plan it just as you would any other kind,   90
size, or form of table: simply backspace to cen-   100
ter it. There is even a special method, based on   110
the fact that the explanations column can be wide   120
or narrow, as you may wish. You set your margins   130
for whatever line length you wish; you pivot from   140
the right margin, backspacing through your amount   150
columns and setting tab stops for them. Then you   160
use whatever space is left for your first column.   170

SPECIAL NOTE: On pages 267-270 of your workbook is a powerhouse of drills to strengthen your grip of the keyboard. If the numbers in the tables on the following pages give you trouble, concentrate on workbook page 269!

8 There are some things you must keep in mind.   180
For example, all dollar marks in a column must be   190
squared up; and you might forget that the longest   200
number, which makes the dollar sign project most,   210
may be the one at the bottom of the column. Note   220
that you do not put six spaces between columns in   230
a statement; instead, put two spaces between your   240
money columns and eight spaces between the state-   250
ment column and the following money column. When   260
you type lines of leaders, watch one more hazard: 270
you must not forget to leave one blank space both   280
at the start and at the end of a line of leaders.   290
   1 | 2 | 3 | 4 | 5 | 6 | 7 | 8 | 9 | 10

LINE: 60
TAB: EVERY 9 SPACES
SPACING: SINGLE
GOAL: REVIEW TABLE
   PRODUCTION
STRESS: ATTENTION
   TO DETAILS

92-A. Each drill three or more times. Do the special extra-spacing drill (No. 3) wholly by touch, alternating the pair of lines.

92-B. For an accuracy gain, type the drills four times as a paragraph; for a speed gain, type each line four times.

92-C. Type a complete copy (GOAL: Finish it within 6 minutes and within 3 errors).

Or, in Lesson 92, take a 5-minute timing with a 10-second rest after each minute; and, then, in Lesson 93, take a 5-minute writing with no pauses to rest.

Adjust the machine for double spacing, a 55-space line, and a 5-space tab indention.

SI 1.33—fairly easy

92-A. Tune up on these lines

1 aid ice jig kin rip sir wit zip bit fix him via qui oil yip
2 I asked discounts of 47% and 56% but got 10%, 28%, and 39%.
3 100   280   390   470   560   100   10.00
    47   56   39   28   10   1000   100.00

92-B. Regain rhythm on these fluent preview words

4 which table often three first model which shown other lines
5 must know this form when they have many most will have been
6 can use the one for its use and can set off any but has not
7 is to be if we to do so or is he to do or be to us am or by

92-C. Sustain your rate on this fairly easy copy

8   It is not often that the typist has to select the   11
   style in which to arrange a table, for the patterns to   22
   be used are usually determined by the character of the   33
   table or the occasion for its use; but the typist must   44
   know he can set up any table in at least three styles,   55
   which are shown by the three model tables that follow.   66

9   First of all, he can set up the table in the open   77
   form; this form requires no ruled lines other than the   88
   underscores that set off the column headings and total   99
   lines if and when they are used. This style is picked   110
   for very short tables and for tables in letter bodies.   121

10   Secondly, he can display the table in ruled form,   132
   which uses horizontal lines of underscores to mark off   143
   the main parts of the table. This is the normal style   154
   for use in tables in formal papers and reports and for   165
   tables that are wide or have many very narrow columns.   176

11   Thirdly, he can use the boxed form for the table;   187
   in this form the columns and headings and footings are   198
   set apart by both vertical and horizontal lines, which   209
   most commonly are drawn on the table after it has been   220
   typed. This form is the one that must be used where a   231
   braced column heading is involved or when a table will   242
   be very long or has many columns or is fairly complex.   253

    1 | 2 | 3 | 4 | 5 | 6 | 7 | 8 | 9 | 10 | 11

Manuscript 18

CENTERED DISPLAY
Paper: workbook
   page 161 or plain
Directions: center
   a double-spaced copy
   of 92-C on the full
   page. Entitle it
   THREE WAYS TO
   TYPE ANY TABLE

92/93-D. Produce a project that reviews table styles

Using workbook pages 161-164 or four sheets of plain paper, center Manuscript 18 and Tables 23-25 according to the directions. GOAL: To complete each of the four assignments within 7 minutes and 4 errors.

<table>
<tr><td>

Letter 68

BLOCKED TWO-PAGE
BUSINESS LETTER
</td><td>

Paper: standard, with 2½-
inch deep letterhead, on
workbook page 263
Paragraphs: 6
Body: 308 words
SI: 1.38—average
</td></tr>
</table>

Mr. Nelson B. Pierce, Director of Research, Pearson and Pierce, Inc., 829 East Ninth Street, Tulsa, Oklahoma 74111 (*Salutation*) SUBJECT: REQUEST FOR YOUR REPORT   13 21 29 49 53

It is our hope that you will soon be able to finish the study you are making of our garage operation and to let us have your report. A number of recent developments have occurred which make it urgent that we have your report soon; here are four: 63 71 79 87 95 104

First, there has been no decrease in the number of complaints that we are getting from our customers; if anything, we note a slight increase in the number. We do not dare delay action very much longer. Second, our loss from the operation of the garage is still mounting; again, we feel we must take some action. Even as we wait for your report and findings, our balance sheet gets worse and worse.   113 121 129 138 148 157 165 173 180 186

Third, the workmen at the garage have become more and more apprehensive about the work of your team and of the possible results of their study. Rumors of every kind are flying, as you would imagine. The men are showing the strain. We lost a foreman last week, and today a group of six workmen began talking about quitting. Fourth, the agent of the firm that has sounded us out about buying the property tells us that his customer seems to have lost interest and is looking at several other garages. The agent may or may not be trying to force us to a lower figure, but his pressure does enter the story.   195 203 211 220 229 238 246 255 264 272 281 290 298 307 310

We would not wish you to neglect any part of the study which is vital, of course; but the members of the board and company officers are no less eager to learn your findings than are the men in the garage. All of us hope, therefore, that you will find it practical to give us your report within the next three weeks and will tell us when we may expect to receive it. (*Complimentary closing*)   343 352 359 367 375 384 393 401 409 414

GRISTMEYER BROTHERS Senior Vice-President, JKE:URS   428 431

<table>
<tr><td>

Letter 69

BLOCKED TWO-PAGE
BUSINESS LETTER
</td><td>

Paper: baronial, 5½ x 8½,
on workbook page 265
Paragraphs: 5
Body: 254 words
SI: 1.37—average
</td></tr>
</table>

Repeat the same letter, with these modifications: (1) Delete the *fourth* reason given in the letter and change the ending of the first paragraph to "here are three:"; (2) change the inside address by deleting Mr. Pierce's name and title, and make the corresponding changes in the salutation and closing.

<table>
<tr><td>

Letter 70

BLOCKED LETTER
</td><td>

Paper: baronial, 5½ x 8½,
on workbook page 265
Paragraphs: 3
Body: 85 words
SI: 1.34—fairly easy
</td></tr>
</table>

Miss Dorrie Anne Barr, whose address you have [Letter 67]. (*Salutation*)   14 29

Thank you for replying so promptly to my request for permission to tell about your fire fighting with Flameproof Fabrics. We do understand and honor your reasons for not wishing your name or that of your firm to be linked to the story. We assure you that such use as we may make of the incident will involve no names. We are grateful to you for reporting the matter to us; if we can repay your favor in the future, please let us do so. (*Complimentary closing, etc.*)   38 46 55 64 72 81 89 98 106 116 125 138

1 | 2 | 3 | 4 | 5 | 6 | 7 | 8

Table 23

OPEN TABLE
Paper: workbook
    page 162 or plain
Special: double
    space the body

Table 3

AGES OF OFFICE EMPLOYEES

Range	Men	Women	Total
To 25	43	150	193
26-35	70	68	138
36-45	53	81	134
46-55	39	69	108
56-65	22	38	60
66 up	2	6	8
TOTAL	229	412	641

Table 24

RULED TABLE
Paper: workbook
    page 163 or plain
Special: insert
    today's date as a
    subtitle line

Table 3

AGES OF OFFICE EMPLOYEES

Range	Men	Women	Total
To 25	43	150	193
26-35	70	68	138
36-45	53	81	134
46-55	39	69	108
56-65	22	38	60
66 up	2	6	8
TOTAL	229	412	641

Table 25

BOXED TABLE WITH
BRACED HEADINGS
Paper: workbook
    page 164 or plain
Special: condense
    table as shown*

* Condense this table
in these two ways:
1. For each ruled line
double space instead
of triple spacing (as
you did in Table 21).
2. Instead of leaving
the standard 6 spaces
between columns, leave
only 4 spaces.

Table 3

AGES OF OFFICE EMPLOYEES ↓2

Range	Men		Women ↓2	
	No.	Percent	No.	Percent ↓2
To 25	43	18.8%	150	36.4%
26–35	70	30.6%	68	16.5%
36–45	53	23.1%	81	19.7%
46–55	39	17.0%	69	16.7%
56–65	22	9.6%	38	9.2%
66 up	2	0.9%	6	1.5% ↓2
TOTAL	229	100.0%	412	100.0%

136/137-D. Learn and apply rules about letter technicalities

LETTER SALUTATIONS

1. Use the last name of the addressee if it is known, preceded by *Dear* and a title, thus:

Dear Mr. Lench: *Dear Prof. Grant:*
Dear Miss Barr: *Dear Doctor Hall:*

2. Whenever a letter is addressed to a firm or department instead of to a person by name or title, and always after an attention line, use *Gentlemen:*.

3. If a letter is addressed to a person by his business title (as, *Personnel Director*) without the use of his name, use *Dear Sir:* as the salutation.

4. Use a first name (as, *Dear Jack:*) only when it is dictated or was used in previous letters.

5. Plural salutations are quite acceptable:

Dear Mr. and Mrs. Jones: (both)
Dear Mr. and Mrs. Jones: (either)
Dear Miss Hall and Mr. Williams:
Dear Committee Members:
Dear Friends: or *Ladies and Gentlemen:*

6. Professional titles like *Doctor, Professor,* and *Captain* may be spelled out or abbreviated.

LETTER COMPLIMENTARY CLOSINGS

7. A closing means the same no matter in what sequence words appear or whether *very* is used. Thus, *Cordially yours, Very cordially yours,* and *Yours very cordially,* all mean the same.

8. Use a "truly" closing (*a*) whenever a letter is frosty or formal and (*b*) whenever *Gentlemen:* or *Dear Sir:* is used as the salutation.

9. Use a "cordially" or "sincerely" closing if the letter is casual, friendly, or sales-slanted *and* if the addressee is named in the salutation.

10. Use a "respectfully" closing in a letter to anyone to whom great respect is due, such as a churchman, public official, or elderly person.

11. Use an informal closing (like *See you soon!*) only when it is specifically dictated.

12. In case of doubt, use a "truly" closing.

LETTER PARAGRAPHING

13. Letters should have at least two paragraphs.

14. Paragraphs should reflect the letter parts.

15. No paragraph should exceed ten lines.

Letter 66

BLOCKED LETTER
Paper: baronial, workbook 261
Body: 101 words
Paragraphs: 3
SI: 1.39—normal

This letter is to Mr. John K. Lench *of* Young & Wilde, Inc., *whose* 15
address is 4422 East 81 Street *in* Akron, Ohio   44309. (*Salutation*) 27

Your inquiry about the use of Flameproof Fabrics for drapes in a 40
business office has been forwarded from our Akron branch. Flameproof 55
Fabrics were developed to meet the need of offices for a drape material 69
that would conform to Fire Code standards for buildings that were to 83
be insured as fireproof structures. You will find, on page 11 of the en- 98
closed booklet, precise details on the resistance value of each of our 112
four grades of Flameproof Fabrics. If you need a statement to show 126
to your insurance agent, the branch at which you made the purchase 140
will issue one to you. (*Complimentary closing*) 150

From Paul F. Clarke, Jr., Service Manager. (*Reference lines*) 164

Letter 67

BLOCKED LETTER
Paper: baronial, workbook 261
Body: 110 words
Paragraphs: 3
SI: 1.34—fairly easy

This letter is to Miss Dorrie Anne Barr, *of* Watts and Sons Company 16
at 3502 Sixth Street *in* Fort Worth, Texas   76101. (*Salutation*) 29

Thank you for all those kind things you said about our Flameproof 43
Fabrics in the letter you wrote us on May 12. Although we have received 59
letters in the past which gave tribute to the colors and patterns built 73
into our fabrics, we have never before received one that described so 87
vividly how a drape was torn down and used to smother a fire that had 101
started. Miss Barr, you certainly thought quickly! Your letter was so 117
novel that it has been shown to most of our executive staff, all of whom 131
wondered whether you might permit us to tell your story in our ad- 144
vertising. May we have your permission? 153

Close in the same way you did Letter 66. 170

Unit 16. Manuscripts

LINE: 60
TAB: 5
SPACING: SINGLE
GOAL: LEARN ABOUT
  NEWS RELEASES
STRESS: FULL POWER
  IN PRODUCTION

94-A. Lines three times. If possible, have a classmate type line 1 to set a cadence for you to match while typing lines 2 and 3.

94-A. Tune up on these review lines

1 oar zoo box quo cod boy woe son fog mop how vox oil oak jot

2 If the SHIFT LOCK is depressed, New York IS typed NEW YORK.

3 On March 10, 1928 and 1939; and on April 28, 1947 and 1956.

94-B. To gain speed, type each line three or more times. To gain accuracy, type the group of lines (like a paragraph) three times.

94-B. Stabilize rhythm on these preview words

4 large first steps would could green prize sound quite short

5 made fine then wish must find what kind will sell best when

6 new one for box let use you buy out to do so or if it is so

94-C. Type two complete copies (one in Lesson 94, one in Lesson 95). GOAL: To finish each copy within 5 minutes and within 3 errors.

Or, take a 5-minute writing in Lesson 94 with 10-second rests after each minute; then, take a 5-minute writing in Lesson 95 without rests. GOAL: 40 or more wam with 3 or fewer errors.

Use double spacing, a 5-space indention.

SI 1.20—easy (good for increasing speed)

94-C. Sustain speed on fluent alphabetic paragraphs

7   If you made a fine new product that you wished to sell   12
to the public at large, one of your first steps would be to   24
find what kind of package for your product would appeal the   36
most to your customers. If you learned that you could sell   48
it best in a green cake box with a prize thrown in for good   60
measure, you would use a green cake box with a prize, would   72
you not? Your sound judgment would require that you do so.   84

8   That theme is quite important to the typist. When you   96
type a manuscript that you hope to have published, the work   108
you turn out is the product; and the person who receives it   120
and reads it and passes judgment on it is, let us hope, the   132
customer. If you really do wish to sell your product, then   144
you must find out in what kind of package he is most likely   156
to buy your product. An editor of a magazine, for example,   168
is more likely to buy your article or one you type for your   180
employer if it is typed with wide margins; so of course you   192
use a short line. You know: green cake box, with a prize.   204

  1 | 2 | 3 | 4 | 5 | 6 | 7 | 8 | 9 | 10 | 11 | 12

If you do not have the news releases on workbook pages 165 and 167, type only Manuscripts 19 and 22, arranging both like Manuscript 19.

94/95-D. Apply your skill to producing news releases

Review the use of revision symbols, page 112; then, type the news releases that follow. GOAL: Each within 7 minutes and 3 errors.

LINE: 60
TAB: 5
SPACING: SINGLE
DRILLS: THREE EACH
GOAL: MASTER LETTER
    TECHNICALITIES
STRESS: ATTENTION
    TO FINE DETAILS

136-A. Each line three times or two ½-minute timings on each line. Repeat in Lesson 137.

136-B. Type to your goal.

ACCURACY: Three copies of lines 4-7 as though they were a paragraph.

SPEED: Three copies of each line consecutively.

136-A. Tune up on these review lines

1   The two men who had had the car got the gas and oil for us.

2   Jack's man found exactly a quarter in the woven zipper bag.

3   we 23 22 21 20 to 59 58 57 56 or 94 93 92 91 it 85 84 83 82
    1 | 2 | 3 | 4 | 5 | 6 | 7 | 8 | 9 | 10 | 11 | 12

136-B. Increase skill on an acceleration preview

4   paragraphs graciously sentences question, proposal message:

5   factors typical writing obvious divide finale allows single

6   break serve parts first right when must that each will then

7   how may two has try the out and now but any ten it is so be

136-C. Sustain skill on fairly easy production copy

136-C. Change to double spacing. Follow steps:

1. Read the material.

2. Practice the rapid insertion of an extra line, followed by the all-capital sideheadings.

3. Take a 5-minute timed writing, pausing for a 10-second rest after each minute; or type one copy, pausing to rest after every 5 or 6 full lines.

4. Take a 5-minute timed writing, without pauses; or type a copy without pausing a single time.

GOAL: To finish the copy within 5 minutes and with 3 or fewer errors.

SI 1.28—fairly easy

8   When the typist must decide how to break a letter into   12
paragraphs, he may count on two factors to serve as guides.   24

OUTLINE OF THE LETTER   29
    The typical letter has three parts. Try to divide the   41
letter so that each of these parts stands out very clearly.   53

    The first part tells who is writing the letter, why he   65
is writing, and how he happens to be writing right now; but   77
a typist can, of course, leave out things that are obvious.   89

    The second part is the main message: the details, the   101
facts of the matter, the proposal, the question, and so on.   113

    The third part is the grand finale in which the writer   125
states what he demands or hopes that the reader will do and   137
then bows out as graciously as the tone of the note allows.   149

LENGTH OF A PARAGRAPH   155
    The second clue to the typist is the hope that he will   167
be able to keep his paragraphs down to eight or fewer lines   179
of typing; ten lines is a top limit for a single paragraph.   191

    It is easy to keep the first and last parts within the   203
desired number of lines; each of these parts is a paragraph   215
that will contain only one or two sentences, in most cases.   227
If there is a problem, and there may not be, it will appear   239
in the middle part of the letter, where the writer may have   251
more to say than he can fit within ten lines. He will then   263
need to split the part into two or more smaller paragraphs.   275
    1 | 2 | 3 | 4 | 5 | 6 | 7 | 8 | 9 | 10 | 11 | 12

SPECIAL:
From now on, you will need to divide letters into their paragraphs and to provide missing salutations and closing phrases. So, read 136-C and 136-D very closely; and, then, reinforce your knowledge by doing the Learning Guide given on workbook pages 259-260.

NEWS RELEASE   From James M. Donald   10
                                          Press Syndicate   14
Manuscript 19

NEWS RELEASE
Shown: in pica
Line: 6 inches
Tabs: 5, center
Top: 1 inch
SI: 1.41—normal
                                          390 West 44 Street   19
                                          New York, New York   10036 25
                                                                      26
                                          Release February 17, 19-- ↓₃ 31
                                                                      32
                                                                      33
          A TYPIST CAN WRECK A NEWS RELEASE ⊙ ↓₃   54
                                                                      55
          DATELINE   56
                                                           expert
     NEW YORK CITY, Feb. 17--Many a publicity ~~writer~~ works up   68
a fine press release ~~release~~ only to have his typist spoil any   79
chance of its getting ~~any~~ attention on an editor's desk, for   91
                                    just as   as
how a news release looks is ~~more~~ important ~~than~~ what it says. 104
                                                                      105
     That is what James M. Donald, ~~distinguished~~ chief wire   114
editor for the Press Syndicate, told members of the New York   126
                                                    editors
Publicity club at their annual luncheon for news~~hawks~~, which   137
                                            Hilton Statler
was attended by 200 publicists at the ~~Savoy Plaza~~ today.   150
                                                                      151
     "We Editors receive news releases by the ~~dozen~~ in every   163
                                             score
mail," he said, "telling us about the great talent of a stage   176
star or the unsurpassed merits of some new dog food# We ought   188
                           e
to read each hand-~~f~~out with great care, I know. But an editor   200
          busy
is so ~~lazy~~ that he is likely to use first whichever release   212
will require the least change and so can be put on the press   224
or on the wire circuit ~~most~~ easily. If you are ~~savvy~~, you'll 237
                                                    wise
make your releases easy for the editor to use⊙" ~~he said~~.   246
                                                                      247
                   six
Donald gave ~~seven~~ guides for "easy to use" releases: 259
                                                                      260
   2. In the heading, indicate who vouches for the facts.   272
                                                                      273
   3. Give a clear title, telling the story in one glance.   285
                                                                      286
   4. Start the story with a date line: city and date.   298
                                                    Errors make editors 299
   1.4. Be sure the typing is correct. ~~If we spot an error,~~   311
~~we~~ wonder whether the release is reliable.   319
                                                                      320
   5. Use a 5- or 6-inch line of typing, never longer.   332
                                                                      333
                                                      Double
   6. Keep the story down to one page if you can. ~~We like~~   345
          is fine
~~double~~ spacing, but if you must single space, then do so.   357

                         Draft of a News Release
       (arranged as it would be typed or duplicated on plain or colored paper)

LETTER 62

United Cooperative Association

1243 Canal Street · New Orleans · Louisiana

May 4, 19—

Mr. Edward L. Kingsport
The J. K. Hauser Company
7376 Grant Avenue
Cleveland, Ohio   44102

Dear Mr. Kingsport:

We should like to invite an estimate for production
of 10,000 copies of our next price list. A copy of
our present list is enclosed to illustrate the size
and mechanical features of the publication.

We shall have the manuscript and pictures ready for
the new price list by the first of June. We require
delivery of the new edition prior to September 15.
We assure prompt handling of all proofs. Your cost
estimate should include the costs for all printing,
composition, engraving, paper, and delivery to us.

We hope that you will let us know that we may look
forward to receiving an estimate from you within a
week or ten days.

Sincerely yours,

Albert A. Arden
Advertising Manager

urs
Enclosure

LETTER 62: OFFICIAL stationery, the government size . . . 8 by 10½ inches . . . accommodates letters on 4-, 5-, and 6-inch line, like standard stationery, but center is ¼ inch to left . . . date on line 14 . . . address 5 lines lower.

LETTER 63

THE DARRIS COMPANY

3674 NORRAND BOULEVARD, ST. LOUIS, MISSOURI

May 4, 19—

Mr. Edward L. Kingsport
The J. K. Hauser Company
7376 Grant Avenue
Cleveland, Ohio   44102

Dear Mr. Kingsport:

We should like to invite an estimate for production
of 10,000 copies of our next price list. A copy of
our present list is enclosed to illustrate the size
and mechanical features of the publication.

We shall have the manuscript and pictures ready for
the new price list by the first of June. We require
delivery of the new edition prior to September 15.
We assure prompt handling of all proofs. Your cost
estimate should include the costs for all printing,
composition, engraving, paper, and delivery to us.

We hope that you will let us know that we may look
forward to receiving an estimate from you within a
week or ten days.

Sincerely yours,

Albert A. Arden
Advertising Manager

urs
Enclosure

LETTER 63: LEFT-WEIGHTED standard stationery . . . 8½ by 11 inches . . . center is moved ½ inch to right, but otherwise placement is standard: 4-, 5-, or 6-inch line, with date on line 15 and address begun 5 lines lower.

LETTER 64

CHARINGE

PRECISION CORPORATION
INDUSTRIAL DEVELOPMENT DEPARTMENT

TERRE HAUTE, INDIANA

May 4, 19—

Mr. Edward L. Kingsport
The J. K. Hauser Company
7376 Grant Avenue
Cleveland, Ohio   44102

Dear Mr. Kingsport:

We should like to invite an estimate for production
of 10,000 copies of our next price list. A copy of
our present list is enclosed to illustrate the size
and mechanical features of the publication.

We shall have the manuscript and pictures ready for
the new price list by the first of June. We require
delivery of the new edition prior to September 15.
We assure prompt handling of all proofs. Your cost
estimate should include the costs for all printing,
composition, engraving, paper, and delivery to us.

We hope that you will let us know that we may look
forward to receiving an estimate from you within a
week or ten days.

Sincerely yours,

Albert A. Arden
Advertising Manager

urs
Enclosure

LETTER 64: DEEP-LETTERHEAD standard stationery . . . 8½ by 11 inches . . . letterhead more than 2 inches deep . . . uses 4-, 5-, or 6-inch line . . . date goes at right, 3 lines below letterhead . . . address only 3 lines below.

LETTER 65

American Paper Company

ROCK ISLAND, ILLINOIS

Los Angeles · New York · Rock Island

Mr. Edward L. Kingsport   May 4, 19—
The J. K. Hauser Company
7376 Grant Avenue
Cleveland, Ohio   44102

Dear Mr. Kingsport:

We should like to invite an estimate for production
of 10,000 copies of our next price list. A copy of
our present list is enclosed to illustrate the size
and mechanical features of the publication.

We shall have the manuscript and pictures ready for
the new price list by the first of June. We require
delivery of the new edition prior to September 15.
We assure prompt handling of all proofs. Your cost
estimate should include the costs for all printing,
composition, engraving, paper, and delivery to us.

We hope that you will let us know that we may look
forward to receiving an estimate from you within a
week or ten days.

Sincerely yours,

Albert A. Arden
Advertising Manager

urs
Enclosure

LETTER 65: Standard WINDOW stationery . . . for use with window envelope . . . center address in cornered area . . . placement otherwise normal: date on line 15, salutation on line 25 (as though address were in normal position).

NEWS RELEASE

MARTIN MILLER and SONS
58 BROAD STREET
ATLANTA, GEORGIA   30303

RELEASE: February 18, 19—   4

FROM: William V. Miller ↓3   8

Manuscript 20

NEWS RELEASE
Shown: in elite
Form: workbook
Spacing: double
SI: 1.47—fairly difficult

NEW USE OF COLOR INCREASE~~S~~ PRODUCTION RATES ↓3   35

37

ATLANTA, ~~Georgia,~~ *Ga.,* Feb. 18—Painting the work~~ing~~ spaces in offices   50

and factories ~~with~~ the right color can ~~bring about~~ *result in* much higher produc-   64

tion rates, according to the results of a practical test ~~which has just~~ *recently*   77

~~been~~ completed by the Research department of Martin Miller & Sons, of   90

this city.   92

"Using the bright color," said Richard Miller, director of the   106

MM&S research *program,* "does not make the machinery go ~~any~~ faster or the mechanics   121

work any harder.# But the right color reduces eye strain; and ~~that~~ *this* means   135

much less fatigue, and fewer accidents, and a lessening of tension ~~in~~ *among*   149

workers. ~~Boosts~~ *Increases* in production rates are a natural result."   162

The ~~test~~ of "color dynamics" was made in several departments of   176

the Clover Mills Company, Wilmington, Delaware. The results credited   189

color with reducing absenteeism by hundreds of hours and allover *with* pro-   204

duction ~~boosts~~ *increases* of 7 per cent in the factory and 9% in the offices.   220

The color is applied to walls, to machinery, and to work areas,--   233

~~including~~ *even* floors. The plan tested at Clover reduced ~~inside~~ *from outside* glare and,   247

at the same time, provided eye-rest areas that lessened eye strain and   261

the tensions to which ~~this~~ *it* usually leads. The paints used, especially   275

manufactured (for the purpose by MM&S), *are* ~~is~~ nonreflective and gloss free.   289

Draft of a News Release
(arranged as it would be typed or duplicated on a news release form)

Manuscript 21 NEWS RELEASE	Retype Manuscript 19 on a news release form (workbook). Use single spacing.	**Manuscript 22** NEWS RELEASE

Retype Manuscript 20 on plain paper, as shown on page 147. Use double spacing.

LETTER 60: BARONIAL stationery . . . 5½ by 8½ inches . . . accommodates up to 125 words on 4-inch line only . . . longer letters require second page . . . date goes on line 9 or 10 . . . address begins 4 lines below the date.

LETTER 61: MONARCH stationery . . . 7¼ by 10½ inches . . . accommodates up to 150 words on 4-inch line, 250 words on 5-inch line . . . longer letters require second page . . . date goes on line 14 . . . address begins 5 lines below.

Letters 60-65

BLOCKED LETTERS ON PROBLEM STATIONERY
Body: 120 words
SI: 1.42—normal

SPECIAL DIRECTIONS: Type this letter six times—once on each of the six kinds or sizes of stationery illustrated above and on page 206. Use workbook pages 253-258 or plain paper on which you mark lines to simulate the proportions and arrangements of the six letterheads.

Mr. Edward L. Kingsport ǀ The J. K. Hauser Company ǀ 7376	18
Grant Ave. ǀ Cleveland, Ohio 44102 ǀ Dear Mr. Kingsport: ǀ	30

Thank you for sending us so quickly your estimate for producing 10,000 copies of our price list. We are more than pleased by the promptness with which you replied.

We are equally pleased by the figures you supplied, but they are so much lower than we had anticipated that we wonder whether you might have left out some cost factor. There is no mention, for example, of our use of a second color; is it included in the press charges, or is it an oversight?

We are ready to accept your bid but feel you should have a chance to confirm it or correct it before we issue a contract on it. May we expect to hear from you soon?

Sincerely yours,   Albert A. Arden   Advertising Manager ǀ *urs*

43
56
64
77
88
101
114
123
136
149
158
175

1 ǀ 2 ǀ 3 ǀ 4 ǀ 5 ǀ 6 ǀ 7 ǀ 8 ǀ 9 ǀ 10 ǀ 11 ǀ 12 ǀ 13

Publishing

LINE: 60 TAB: 5
SPACING: SINGLE
GOAL: LEARN TO TYPE
   FOR PUBLICATION
STRESS: POSTURE,
   SUSTAINED TYPING

96-A. Lines three times. If possible, have a classmate type line 1 to set a cadence for you to match as you type lines 2 and 3.

96-A. Tune up on these review lines

1 buzz vous quit must jury crux sunk cuff pour laud huge lure
2 we 23 up 70 or 94 et 35 pi 08 to 59 it 85 ow 92 ep 30 we 23
3 Names of "stores" (like Gimbel's) have to be "capitalized."

96-B. To gain speed, type each line three or more times, speeding up as you repeat it. To gain in accuracy, type the whole group of lines three or more times, trying to hold your pace constant.

96-B. Stabilize rhythm on these preview words

4 guide sheet which heavy lines zones other place under quick
5 this task each time mark that will type same page sure that
6 one for all who odd job use off and any set all you can new

96-C. Type two complete copies, one in Lesson 96 and one in Lesson 97. GOAL: To finish a copy within 5 minutes and within 3 errors. Or, take a 5-minute writing in Lesson 96 with a 10-second rest after each minute; and, take a 5-minute timing in Lesson 97 with no rest after each minute. GOAL: 40 or more words a minute within 3 or fewer errors.

SI 1.28—fairly easy

96-C. Sustain speed on fluent alphabetic paragraphs

7 One of the best tricks of the typing trade, a trick to   12
be recommended for all who frequently have to type some odd   24
kind of typing task, is the use of a visual guide. This is   36
just a sheet of paper on which you draw heavy lines to mark   48
off the margin zones, center point, and any other factor in   60
the arrangement of that odd task. Then, each time you must   72
do that task, you simply place the guide under the paper on   84
which you will type; the lines show through to guide you as   96
you set the margins, and so on, for doing that special job.   108

8 For example, suppose that the man for whom you work is   120
the author of a column in a journal or a magazine. All the   132
manuscripts you type for him should be set up alike, always   144
with the same margins, same display of headings, same posi-   156
tion for page numbers, and so on. Rather than try to memo-   168
rize the settings, design a visual guide that shows all the   180
details; then you can be ready to type a new installment in   192
one quick minute or less, sure that the form is consistent.   204

   1 | 2 | 3 | 4 | 5 | 6 | 7 | 8 | 9 | 10 | 11 | 12

IDEA: For experience, why not make a visual guide for Manuscripts 23-24 or Manuscript 25, or both? Doing so will make typing easier.

96-D. Apply your skill to typing publication manuscripts

Analyze closely the assignments on the next two pages; then, type them. GOAL: To type Manuscripts 23-24 within 5 minutes and 3 errors each, and Manuscript 25 within 10 minutes and 5 errors.

LINE: 60
TAB: 5
SPACING: SINGLE
DRILLS: THREE EACH
GOAL: MASTERY OF
 STATIONERY
STRESS: ALERTNESS
 TO DIRECTIONS

134-A. Lines three times
or two ½-minute timings
on each line. Repeat in
Lesson 135, as well.

134-A. Tune up on these easy review lines

1 He paid the widow for the enamel emblem he got for his pal.

2 Jack quietly gave some dog owners most of his prize boxers.

3 we 23 24 25 26 up 70 71 72 73 or 94 95 96 97 it 85 86 87 88

   1 | 2 | 3 | 4 | 5 | 6 | 7 | 8 | 9 | 10 | 11 | 12

134-B. Type to your goal.

ACCURACY: Three copies
of lines 4-7 as though
they were a paragraph.

SPEED: Three copies of
each line consecutively.

134-B. Increase skill on an acceleration preview

4 "standard" different measures quarter expert (and) that may

5 "official" tailoring smallest shallow length width work for

6 stationery "monarch" printing offices adjust sizes five and

7 "baronial" longways; balanced inches; eleven eight half off

134-C. Change to double
spacing; follow steps:

  1. Scan the material.

  2. Select the hardest
line in paragraphs 8,
9, and 10; type those
three lines three times.

  3. Take a 5-minute timed
writing, pausing for a
10-second rest after each
minute; or, type one copy,
pausing to rest after you
finish each paragraph.

  4. Take a 5-minute timed
writing, without rests;
or, type a copy without
pausing for any rests.

GOAL: To finish the copy
within 5 minutes and
with 3 or fewer errors.

SI: 1.33—fairly easy

134-C. Increase skill on developmental paragraphs

8   The person who wants to be a true expert in the typing   12
of letters has to learn how to adjust his placement plan to   24
fit the kinds of stationery with which he may need to work.   36

9   There are four sizes of stationery. The one used most   48
widely is the "standard" one, eight and a half inches wide,   60
eleven inches long. Trim a half inch off the width and the   72
length of that size, to get a sheet that is eight inches by   84
ten and a half inches, and you get the "official" size used   96
by most government offices and the armed forces. Trim down 108
that width to seven and a quarter inches; now what you have 120
is called "monarch" size. The smallest sheet is "baronial" 132
size, which is half a standard sheet turned longways. This 144
measures five and a half inches by eight and a half inches. 156

10   Adding to the problem is the fact that the printing on 168
the paper may be in many different designs. The letterhead 180
may be shallow or may be deep; it may be loaded on one side 192
or balanced in the middle. Even a standard sheet has to be 204
treated as a narrow one if it has a long list of offices or 216
something else taking an inch or more of space on one side. 228

11   So the typist must (and will, if he is as wise as you) 240
learn all he can about tailoring letters to his stationery! 252

   1 | 2 | 3 | 4 | 5 | 6 | 7 | 8 | 9 | 10 | 11 | 12

134-D. The six letters
will make a booklet if
you use workbook pages
253-258 or paper marked
and cut to simulate the
illustrated stationery.

134/135-D. Learn how to tailor letters to stationery

Read the next two pages; then type the problem letter correctly for each
of the six letterheads described. GOAL: to produce each copy within 4 minutes
and 3 errors after the machine is adjusted.

Manuscripts 23-24

TWO-PAGE ARTICLE
Paper: plain
Carbon copies: 1
Line: 40 spaces
Tab: paragraph (3
    spaces in), center
Top: 2" on page 1,
    1" on page 2
SI: 1.59—Difficult

MANUSCRIPTS WITH SALESMANSHIP   18

    19

By Kenneth B. Willhite   34

Formerly, Associate Editor   52

<u>Today's Secretary</u> ▼2   71

    72

(44 Lines of 40 Spaces) ▼3   88

    90

THE TYPING of a manuscript can help or   99

hinder its publication. An editor is a   107

busy person who reads many manuscripts,   115

many more than he can publish. It is   123

(Continue in column one, below.)

natural that he should be prejudiced in   8
favor of material that looks as though he   16
had written it himself.   21

There lies the secret of selling any maga-   31
zine article: Convince the editor that the   39
article was written especially for him by   48
one who knows his magazine.   54

\#   56

IT IS NOT enough to tell the editor that   64
such is the case. The typist must prove the   73
point by the form of the manuscript. It   81
must look professional. My advice: 89

1. Type the article with the same length   98
of line as that used in the columns of the   107
magazine. Type 10 lines from a copy of the   116
magazine. Determine the average line   141
length—and use it. Do not exceed that   149
line length by more than two spaces on any   158
one line.   160

2. Precede the page number on every   168
page by the author's name.   174

3. Indicate how many lines your manu-   182
script will fill in the magazine.   189

4. Double space the manuscript. If it   198
divides into sections, like this one does,   207
type a number sign in the middle of the   215
blank line, to indicate "insert 1 blank line."   225
It counts as a whole line.   230

5. Use only 8½- by 11-inch paper.   238

6. Use touches of the magazine's own   247
style. If it uses sideheads, use them; if it   256
uses short paragraphs, use them; if it uses   265
footnotes, so should you. If it—whatever   274
it does, so should you.   279

\#   281

MY, WHAT a lot of trouble! Yes, but not   289
as much trouble as it is to write an article   298
and have it rejected because it did not look   307
professional—did not seem to belong in the   316
magazine.   318

(END)   323

Continuation pages of a magazine manuscript:
A. Use same line length as on page 1.
B. Type heading (author's last name, a dash, and the page number) on line 7 at the right margin.
C. Triple space before resuming the text.

Mr. John Reed Carr
Page 2
May 3, 19—

7. The page-2 heading is begun on line 7, leaving 6 lines in
the top margin. Two blank lines are left between the heading
and the material that follows it.

8. The second page of an interoffice memo addressed to one
or two persons is given a heading like that of a letter; but
if there are more addressees, give the <u>subject</u> of the message
(as, <u>Personnel Order No. 8</u>) instead of listing all the names.

I hope that this information resolves your problem, Mr. Carr.
Is there any other help I can offer?

                         Yours very sincerely,

                         William R. Rice
                         Training Consultant

    urs

328
329
332
334
346
358
365
366
378
401
413
426
427
439
447
448
453
455
459
464
465
466

Second Page of a Two-Page Business Letter in Blocked Form

Letter 58

LETTER, PAGE TWO
Paper: plain
Words: 113

Arrange the page-2 material above in the alternate form shown in the illustration below.

Letter 59

MEMO, PAGE TWO
Paper: plain
Words: 90

Arrange the material above (delete closing paragraph) as page 2 of a memo, as illustrated below.

Mr. John Reed Carr   Page 2   May 3, 19—

7. The page-2 heading is begun on line 7, leaving 6 lines in
the top margin. Two blank lines are left between the heading
and the material that follows it.

8. The second page of an interoffice memo addressed to one
or two persons is given a heading like that of a letter; but
if there are more addressees, give the <u>subject</u> of the message
(as, <u>Personnel Order No. 8</u>) instead of listing all the names.

I hope that this information resolves your problem, Mr. Carr.
Is there any other help I can offer?

                Yours very sincerely,

                William R. Rice
                Training Consultant

urs

Personnel Order No. 8
Page 2
May 3, 19—

7. The page-2 heading is begun on line 7, leaving 6 lines in
the top margin. Two blank lines are left between the heading
and the material that follows it.

8. The second page of an interoffice memo addressed to one
or two persons is given a heading like that of a letter; but
if there are more addressees, give the <u>subject</u> of the message
(as, <u>Personnel Order No. 8</u>) instead of listing all the names.

                William R. Rice

urs

Page-2 letter heading, alternate style

Page 2 of a memo, with subject heading line

UNIT 22   LESSON 133   203

Manuscript 25

BOOK MANUSCRIPT
Shown: elite draft
Paper: plain
Carbon copies: 1
Tab: 5, 10
SI: 1.44—fairly difficult

NOTES ABOUT BOOK MANUSCRIPTS
1. They are typed in standard "bound manuscript" form. Review page 114.
2. Listings are single spaced and "double indented" 10 spaces.
3. The title of the book or chapter is identified in a "running head," typed in all-caps at the left margin, on a line with the page number.

AUTHORS GUIDE   *Page 21* ↓3   8
                                                                                           9

but whether to use st, d, th, etc., after street numbers will depend on   34

local preference; they are omitted more and more. ↓3   44
                                                                                 45
2#
17. Most Common Uses of Capitals: 64

H We apply some rules about the use of capitals so often that we do not   79
                     them as
even think of ~~their being~~ rules. Every ~~writer~~ knows, ~~we trust,~~ to use   94
                                         author
a capital letter—   98

Indent   1) to start a proper name   107
10 spaces.   2) to start any sentence   114
                  3) to start a direct quotation   123
                  4) to start each line in an outline or poem   135

The first rule is used ~~the~~ most often, for there are so many different   150

~~different~~ kinds of names. We must use a capital for names of—   162

                  1) deity, like <u>God</u> and <u>Holy Spirit</u>   179
In material to be 2) people, like <u>Joe Brown</u> and <u>Ann Smith</u>   197
published, italic 3) geographic places, like <u>Los Angeles</u>   211
type is indicated 4) companies, like <u>Gimbel Bros</u>.   225
by underscoring. 5 6) trade names, like <u>Ivory Soap</u> and <u>Wheaties</u>   243
                  6 7) days of the week; months; holidays   253

Any word substituted for a name begins with a capital, too; like <u>Windy</u>   271

<u>City</u> for <u>Chicago</u>, <u>Honest Abe</u> for <u>Lincoln</u>, etc.   291
                                overlooked
     One rule that is often ~~forgotten~~ is this: Use capitals for family   306

titles that are used as names but are <u>not</u> preceded by a possessive pro-   320
                             would
noun. Thus: "My aunt ~~will~~ be glad to tell Mother, but I shall ask   333

Father to speak to my mother first."   341

     When a title is used with a name in a sentence, capitalize the title   356

if it precedes the name <u>but not if it follows the name</u>. Thus: "There is 371

Governor Smith with Tom Lake, mayor of our town." Exceptions: <u>Always</u>   387
                                                           such
capitalize the title of any high government official, as: "Mr. Reed, Sec-   402

retary of Commerce."   406

Draft of a Manuscript for a Book

Two-Page Letter

IN THE VERY, VERY FLEXIBLE

Blocked Style

Arranged in Paragraph-Enumeration Form

Letter 57

TWO PAGES, BLOCKED
Shown: in pica
Paper: workbook 251
SI: 1.33—fairly easy

May 3, 19--   4

8

Mr. John Reed Carr   12
Director of Training   16
Parke and Wells, Inc.   21
1209 Washington Avenue   25
St. Louis, Missouri   63158   31

32

Dear Mr. Carr: 35

36

This two-page letter illustrates the guidelines for letters   49
that take more than one page: 55

56

1. The line length and top margin are the same as for a long   69
letter. The typist uses a 6-inch line of writing; types the   81
date on line 15 or 2 lines below the letterhead, whichever   93
is lower; and drops 5 lines to begin the inside address.   104

105

2. The bottom margin of page 1 should be 7 or 8 lines deep,   117
so that it will be slightly broader than either side margin;   129
but it can be as many as 10 lines deep or as few as 5.   141

142

3. At least two lines of a paragraph should be typed at the   154
foot of page 1 and at the top of page 2. If a paragraph has   166
three lines, they should all appear on one or the other page.   179

180

4. Page 1 is typed on a letterhead; page 2 is typed on plain   192
paper of the same quality as that used for the letterhead.   204

205

5. Page 2 and each additional page should have a heading so   217
complete that it would identify the page if it were detached   229
from the rest of the letter. The heading should include the   242
name of the addressee, the page number, and the date.   253

254

6. The usual arrangement of the page-2 heading is to arrange   266
the name, page number, and date in three lines blocked at the   278
left margin. The three items may, however, be displayed in   300
one line across the page, with the name at the left, the date   313
at the right, and the page number centered between them.   324

First Page of a Two-Page Business Letter in Blocked Form

LINE: 60
SPACING: SINGLE
GOAL: REVIEW PART
   FOUR TECHNICALITIES
STRESS: FOLLOWING
   DIRECTIONS EXACTLY

98-A. Copy each line for a full minute. Repeat in Lesson 99.

98-A. Tune up on these review lines

1 Let the two men get out the box and rip off the lid for us.
2 busy city edgy fray hazy joys quay yank yelp wavy waxy yams
3 Use the quotation (") for inches: 10", 28", 39", 47", 56".

98-B. To gain speed, each line three or more times. To gain accuracy, the group of lines (like a paragraph) three times.

98-B. Boost Accuracy on these preview words

4 AA paces BB about CC cares DD dictation EE speed FF offices
5 GG good HH thing II time JJ judge KK talk LL slow MM matter
6 NN number OO short PP speak QQ frequently RR rapid SS story
7 TT tenth UU unless VV very WW who XX exact YY you ZZ zigzag

98-C. Type a complete copy in each lesson (GOAL: To finish it within 5 minutes and within 3 errors).

Or, take a 5-minute timing in Lesson 98 with a 10-second rest after each minute; then, in Lesson 99, take another 5-minute timing, this time with no end-of-minute rest. GOAL: 40 or more words a minute within 3 or fewer typing errors.

Adjust the machine for double spacing, a 50-space line, and a 5-space tab indention.

SI 1.42—normal

98-C. Sustain your rate on alphabetic paragraphs

8   One of the topics frequently talked about by   10
all who work in offices is the rate of dictation.   20
Most men feel that they dictate at a modest pace,   30
while most secretaries say that the dictators ac-   40
tually talk much faster than they realize. It is   50
hard to judge the exact speed of dictation unless   60
you have, and use, special devices to measure it.   70

9   A short time ago, a man who cares about this   80
matter made such a machine and measured the speed   90
of dictation as it was going on in a great number   100
of offices. When he analyzed the results, he had   110
quite a good picture of dictation and the jolting   120
news that no one has such a thing as an "average"   130
rate of expressing himself. His speaking varies.   140

10   He found that businessmen have four paces of   150
speaking. About a sixth of the dictation is very   160
slow, about half is fairly fast, about a third is   170
fluent, and about a tenth is very rapid. He also   180
found that there is no routine pattern; dictation   190
speed is jumbled. It zigzags from fast to rapid,   200
from slow to extreme speed. It is quite a story.   210

   1 | 2 | 3 | 4 | 5 | 6 | 7 | 8 | 9 | 10

This review will get you completely ready for the end-of-part test in Lesson 100.

98/99-D. Review the production work of Part Four

Type the four assignments indicated on the next page, preceding each by the indicated review. GOAL: To do each within 10 minutes and 3 errors.

Unit 22. Correspondence

LINE: 50
TAB: 5
SPACING: SINGLE, BUT
  DOUBLE IN 132-C
GOAL: APPLY SKILL TO
  TWO-PAGE LETTERS
STRESS: CONTINUITY
DRILLS: THREE EACH

132-A. Recall skill by taking two ½-minute timings on each line. Repeat in Lesson 133

132-A. Tune up on these easy review lines

1 The man who got the job said you did not <u>want</u> it.
2 Quietly pack the crate with five dozen gum boxes.
3 Take 10 and 28 and 39 from 47 and 56 to get what?

  1 | 2 | 3 | 4 | 5 | 6 | 7 | 8 | 9 | 10

132-B. Type to your goal:

ACCURACY: Three copies of lines 4-7 as though they were a paragraph.

SPEED: Three copies of each line, consecutively.

132-B. Increase skill on an acceleration preview

4 justify squeeze second signer person chance extra
5 sheet paper dozen trap; let's most fall long page
6 more pack does into each look now and one two any
7 has who one the his get had our or so it if to us

132-C. Steps to take for developmental effort:

1. Scan the copy, just to see what it says.

2. Select the hardest line in each paragraph; type them three times.

3. Take a 5-minute timed writing, pausing for a 10-second rest after each minute; or, type one copy, pausing to rest after you finish each paragraph.

4. Take a 5-minute timed writing, without rests; or, type one copy, without pausing for any rests.

GOAL: To finish the copy within 5 minutes and with 3 or fewer errors.

SI 1.34—fairly easy

132-C. Sustain skill on alphabetic paragraphs

8   Most of us fall into the trap, now and then, 10
of trying to squeeze on one page a letter that is 20
long enough to justify using two pages. Somehow, 30
we begrudge the extra sheet of paper or the dozen 40
or so seconds involved in inserting one more pack 50
of paper and typing a heading on the second page. 60

9   Well, let us not fall into any trap; rather, 70
let's look for each chance to stretch our letters 80
into two pages. Think of the person who gets the 90
letter. In one hand he holds a letter that is so 100
filled that the signer had to squeeze his name to 110
get it in. In the other hand he holds our letter 120
that has generous margin space and that runs over 130
to an extra page. Which letter will impress him, 140
will please him, will make him feel that the sub- 150
ject of the letter merits his thoughtful reading? 160

10   "When I see a letter that is squeezed," said 170
a business acquaintance of mine, "I get a feeling 180
that the writer is going to put a squeeze on me." 190
This is mere hokum, of course; but it does reveal 200
that the allover appearance of a letter does make 210
a general impression that can prejudice, for good 220
or for bad, the mind of the reader even before he 230
starts to read. The investment of an extra page, 240
plus a few seconds, can pay rich dividends to us. 250

  1 | 2 | 3 | 4 | 5 | 6 | 7 | 8 | 9 | 10

132-D. Type Letter 57 on workbook page 251. Use plain paper for the continuation pages.

132/133-D. Apply skill to two-page letters

Study Letter 57 carefully, then type it and Letters 58-59.

Letter 42

SEMIBLOCKED LETTER
Body: 157
Paper: letterhead
Review: page 131
Tab: 5, center
SI: 1.59—difficult

Editor, Executive Weekly | 505 Elm Street | Dallas, Texas 75202 | Dear Sir:

Most of your readers are, I know, executives who have secretaries and who give dictation regularly. I believe that your readers might be interested in an article that discusses the dictation rates and habits of businessmen and ends with a number of suggestions for increasing dictation skill.

I have prepared such an article. I enclose the first part and a table from the manuscript. The entire article includes 438 lines and four tables. The article is based on a fine study conducted a few years ago at the University of Pittsburgh by Dr. H. H. Green and on several recent studies that confirm his findings and enlarge on them to some degree.

I should appreciate learning from you whether you would wish me to submit the entire manuscript for your review.

Yours very truly, | Thomas Young | English Department | *Initials? | Other reference notations?*

Table 26

RULED TABLE
Paper: plain
Spacing: double
Review: page 139

EVERY DICTATOR'S CHANGES OF PACE		
Dictator's Manner	Dictation Pattern	Percent of Time
Groping	Very slow	15.0%
Thoughtful	Steady	45.0%
Confident	Fluent	30.0%
Sprinting	Very fast	10.0%
TOTAL	- - - - - - -	100.0%

Manuscript 26

2-PAGE ARTICLE

Manuscript 27

BOOK MANUSCRIPT

Using the page-1 heading shown below and a 40-space line, type 98-C as a magazine article. Use plain paper. Make 1 carbon copy of each page.

HOW BUSINESSMEN DICTATE
By Thomas Young
Arizona State University
Tempe, Arizona

Using a 6-inch line (shifted to the right to provide space for inserting the page in a three-ring binder) and double spacing, type 98-C as *Page 43* of a book on *Executive Dictation*. Use plain paper. Make 1 carbon copy of the page. NOTE: Between the first and second paragraph, insert an underscored side-heading, *Study of Dictators' Rate of Speaking.*

131-A. Measure your skill on this technical paragraph

131-A. After tuning up by repeating 130-A, do drills 24-25, below, once or twice, so you can make brackets expertly. Then type a double-spaced copy of this exercise on a 50-space line; try to finish the copy in 2 minutes or less. If you make more than two errors, your next goal is to be ACCURACY; otherwise, it's SPEED.

SI 1.39—normal

NOTE: Constructing the bracket counts the same as typing 3 words.

TWO FRACTION FACTS

(1) If a sentence contains a number of fractions, one of which has to be built because it is
not on the machine, then build all the fractions.

(2) If a mixed number contains a built fraction /like 48 3/5/, leave one blank space between
the whole number and the fraction that you built.

131-B. Improve your control of symbol keys

131-B. Type to your goal.

Reset your machine for a 60-space line and for single spacing. You'll have to look up when you construct the brackets.

ACCURACY: Type each pair of lines, as pairs, two times; and then once more if they focus on a symbol with which you had trouble in 131-A.

SPEED: Type each line two times consecutively, and once more if it is focused on a symbol key with which you had any difficulty in 131-A.

20 ;/; /// 1/3 and/or 1/5 and/or 1/6 and/or 1/7 and/or 18 1/9.
21 We gave 1/3 of it to John, 1/6 to Ralph, and 1/2 to Edward.
22 _ _ tea rub arc end off lug ash ink awl arm won too sip our
23 You must get around very soon to reading Call of the Yukon.
24 Left: / _ / / / ¯ / / / / Right: _ / / / ¯ / / / / / /
25 /bracket/ /one/ /two/ /three/ /four/ /five/ /seven/ /eight/
26 191 1(1 ;0; ;); (parentheses) (one) (two) (three) (sixteen)
27 Try to type (1) rapidly, (2) accurately, and (3) correctly.

131-C. Regain stride on an easy paragraph

131-C. Type three copies (or, take three 1-minute writings). GOAL: To finish within 1 minute and within 1 error.

SI 1.00—very easy

28 Now and then the best of us find that we get tired of,
or bored with, the chores we have to do day in and day out.
Right then, when we are tired or bored, is the time when we
must dig in and work so much the more, just to show that we
can, if we must, take it on the chin and stand to the test.

131-D. Stabilize your skill via selective practice

131-D. Type to your goal.

ACCURACY: Lines 29-31 four times each; then, lines 32-34 twice each.

SPEED: Lines 29-31 two times each, then lines 32-34 four times each.

Or, take 1-minute timed writings (lines 29-31, for accuracy; and lines 32-34, for speed gain).

131-E. Repeat 131-A.

29 Zeke quietly placed five jumping hares in the new grey box.
30 Six reports were quickly given the amazed audience by Jeff.
31 Liza quit her new job, packed six bags, and moved far away.
32 I am to go to work for the audit firm by the eighth of May.
33 Lena is busy with the big signs for the social; so is Jane.
34 The girls may make a big profit for the chapel by the lake.

131-E. Confirm and boost your progress

Progress Test on Part Four

Test 4

Test 4-A

5-MINUTE WRITING ON PARAGRAPHS
Paper: workbook page 177 or plain paper
Line: 50
Tab: paragraph 5
Spacing: double
Start: machine set, carriage at margin
Grade: box below
SI: 1.33—easy-normal

5-MINUTE SPEED WITHIN 3 ERRORS*

45-up wam	A
40-44 wam	B
30-39 wam	C
25-29 wam	D

* If more than 3 errors are made, compute the speed on what is typed before the fourth error.

Test 4-B

Manuscript 28

5-MINUTE WRITING ON NEWS RELEASE
Paper: workbook page 178 or plain paper
Start: machine set, carriage at margin
Grade: box above
SI: 1.37—normal

		4-B
N E W S R E L E A S E	From William L. Miller	10
	Martin Miller & Sons	16
	58 Broad Street	20
	Atlanta, Georgia 30304	26
	Release February 22, 19—	32
		34
PAINT FIRM TO OPEN SCHOOL		50
		52
ATLANTA, Ga., Feb. 22—		58

	4-A	
The first special school for engineers to be	10	68
trained in how to use color to help production in	20	78
plants and offices will open here within the next	30	88
six weeks. The new school will be sponsored by a	40	98
local paint firm that has set the pace in the new	50	108
field of color dynamics. Head of the school will	60	118
be the company's color expert, Dr. Lauren Martin.	70	128
Announcement of plans for the new school was	80	138
made by Martin Miller, head of the firm of Martin	90	148
Miller & Sons, who pointed out that the company's	100	158
research in the use of color not only had created	110	168
a new field of study but also had led to requests	120	178
for experts who could serve as color consultants.	130	188
Only by setting up the new school could the local	140	198
firm assure its patrons the counsel they request.	150	208
Men enrolled for the training will be put on	160	218
the MM&S payroll in return for a pledge to remain	170	228
with the firm for two years. They must be twenty	180	238
or older, must be single, and must have completed	190	248
two or more years of college. The training is to	200	258
be a six-month program in the "color kitchens" of	210	268
the firm's new plant in the suburbs of this city.	220	278

1 | 2 | 3 | 4 | 5 | 6 | 7 | 8 | 9 | 10

LINE: 60
TAB: 5
SPACING: SINGLE
DRILLS: THREE TIMES
STRESS: KEEPING
  EYES ON THE COPY
GOAL: BOOST SKILL
  ON THE TOP ROW

130-A. Each line three times, or a half-minute writing on each line. Repeat in Lesson 131.

130-A. Tune up on these reach-review lines

1 The rifleman got eight big ducks at the lake for the girls.

2 Five or six new jet planes quickly zoomed by the big tower.

3 The 10's and 56's are harder to type than 28's, 39's, 47's.

  1 | 2 | 3 | 4 | 5 | 6 | 7 | 8 | 9 | 10 | 11 | 12

130-B. Type one copy in 2 minutes or less time. If you make more than 2 errors, your goal is accuracy; 2 or fewer, your goal is speed.

When you proofread, make a list of every number you mistype.

SI 1.41—normal, with all digits and letters

130-B. Measure your skill on this technical paragraph

4   The Post Office Department of each region includes 250   12
zones, with 250 zone branches. Each region has 148 special   24
men trained to handle lost parcels and 63 more who are kept   36
busy with dead letters. The 1964 annual report showed that   48
22,737,478 letters and 906,437 packages had been delivered.   60
These figures scored quite a jump, about 8.83 percent, over   72
those of 1960, which had been exactly the same as for 1955.   84

  1 | 2 | 3 | 4 | 5 | 6 | 7 | 8 | 9 | 10 | 11 | 12

130-C. Type to your goal:

ACCURACY: The lines as a group three times, then repeat once more lines that concentrate on a number you missed.

SPEED: Each line three times, plus once more if it concentrates on a number key you missed.

130-C. Improve your control of the number keys

5 3 9 33 39 93 99 333 339 393 399 933 939 993 999 3,939 9,393

6 2 8 22 28 82 88 222 228 282 288 822 828 882 888 2,828 8,282

7 4 7 44 47 74 77 444 447 474 477 744 747 774 777 4,747 7,474

8 5 6 55 56 65 66 555 556 565 566 655 656 665 666 5,656 6,565

9 1 0 00 01 10 11 001 010 011 100 101 110 111 101 1,010 1,110

130-D. Type to your goal:

ACCURACY: The group of lines three times.

SPEED: Each line three times consecutively.

130-D. Improve fluency in typing numbers

10 we 23 24 25 26 27 28 up 70 71 72 73 74 or 94 95 96 97 98 99

11 ow 92 93 94 95 96 97 it 85 86 87 88 89 ye 63 64 65 66 67 68

12 wet 235 236 237 238 tie 583 584 585 586 rip 480 481 482 483

13 out 975 976 977 978 ere 343 344 345 346 wry 246 247 248 249

130-E. Type to your goal as you did in 130-D.

130-E. Speed up with pair-pattern sentences

14 You should be able to type 10, 28, 39, 47, and 56 fluently.

15 Cars 10 and 28 raced at 1:00; Cars 39 and 47 raced at 1:56.

16 Joe sold 1028 clips, 3947 pens, and 5610 tablets yesterday.

17 They won the games 56 to 47, then 39 to 28, then 100 to 56.

18 I filled Order No. 1028, Order No. 3947, and Order No. 566.

  1 | 2 | 3 | 4 | 5 | 6 | 7 | 8 | 9 | 10 | 11 | 12

130-F. Precede retyping the paragraph in 130-B by typing twice every line in which you made an error the first time.

130-F. Repeat 130-B to measure your progress

PENALTY SCALE

—3 for each major error (top margin, line length, line-spacing, general correctness of form, etc.)
—2 for each minor error (blocking, aligning, centering, indenting, etc., of individual parts of the job)
—1 for each typographical error

GRADING SCALE

0-1 PENALTY . . . . A
2-3 PENALTY . . . . B
4-6 PENALTY C
7-8 PENALTY . . . . D

Test 4-C

Letter 43

5-MINUTE WRITING ON SEMIBLOCKED LETTER
Paper: workbook page 179 or plain paper
Body: 166 words
Start: machine set, carriage centered
Grade: box below
SI: 1.41—normal

5-MINUTE SPEED WITHIN 3 ERRORS*

45-up wam . . . . . . A
40-44 wam . . . . . . B
30-39 wam C
25-29 wam . . . . . . D

* If more than 3 errors are made, compute the speed on what is typed before the fourth error.

Test 4-D

Table 27

5-MINUTE WRITING ON A RULED TABLE
Paper: workbook page 180 or plain paper
Start: machine set, carriage centered
Grade: box above

Today's date | The Pelham Assurance Company | 19 South | 15
Wabash Street | Chicago, Illinois   60603 | Gentlemen: | 25

We believe that it is time for a review of the insurance rates | 40
that we are paying you in behalf of our six main plants. | 51

The contract rates we now pay were set in 1944 on the basis of | 66
our accident record for a period of four years that began in | 78
January, 1940. An earnest campaign for safety since that time | 91
has slashed the number of accidents and the extent of damage so | 103
much that we feel a lower rate is due us. | 112

I have enclosed a table that gives the accident figures for | 126
the six factories that are covered under our contract with you. | 139
All the accidents that have involved damages are, of course, al- | 152
ready in your own records. The details are a matter of record, | 164
which we shall be pleased to place at your disposal. | 175

We hope that you will ask your underwriters to study our | 189
rates and that we may expect a reduction in the rates by the | 201
start of the next quarter. | Yours very truly, | SOUTHERN STATES | 219
CORPORATION | C. D. Ferry, Treasurer | *reference notations?* | 235

AVERAGE NUMBER ACCIDENTS PER MONTH | 21
Southern States Corporation | 39
| 50

# Factory Locations	1940 to 1949	1950 to 1959	1960 to Date	
Chattanooga, Tennessee	18.3	16.5	10.8 ~~12.4~~	98
Forth Worth, Texas	12.4	10.3	8.7 ~~9.2~~	108
Greensboro, (N. C.)	31.7	24.6	18.7 ~~20.8~~	119
Little Rock, Arkansas	15.0	12.1	10.3 ~~10.9~~	129
Memphis, Tennessee	9.1	6.4 ~~6.5~~	6.3 ~~6.5~~	139
Montgomery, Alabama	....	4.5	3.4 ~~3.8~~	149
				162
~~TOTALS~~ AVERAGES	17.3	12.4	9.7 ~~10.6~~	169
				182

Triple space and start over | 192

129-A. Increase skill via weighted sentences

129-A. Type to your goal.
ACCURACY: each line two times, then repeat lines 19-21 two more times. SPEED: each line two times; then, repeat lines 22-24 two more times. Don't let the one-hand runs in 19-21 make you break rhythm, and don't let the rhythm of 22-24 speed you up so much that you make a lot of errors!

19 You were off base, in my opinion, when you gave Lou a pony.
20 Philip drove my car carefully uphill but sloppily downhill.
21 Dad gave Molly a fat pumpkin at breakfast, as a funny joke.

   1 | 2 | 3 | 4 | 5 | 6 | 7 | 8 | 9 | 10 | 11 | 12

22 Joe's squad never quits until their sales reach their goal.
23 How soon will your boys come back here from that long trip?
24 Why did the boy cut the top off the new box you got for us?

129-B. Concentrate via a half-space centering drill

129-B. These drills would be very easy to do on a machine with a half-space key; but you might not always have a machine with such a key—so "do it the hard way," as it is described here. Half-spacing is worth the effort only when the display is brief or the paper is very important. See paragraph 5, page 197.

To type a character in half-space position, (1) set the carriage at the following full space; (2) press the left end of the carriage until the printing-point indicator is at half position; then, (3) tap the appropriate key with the free right hand.

Practice on this numbers exercise and then copy the adjacent display.

```
ONE
FOUR
THREE
FIVE
ELEVEN
```

```
THE
FOUR
MINSTRELS
APPEAR
NIGHTLY

DON'T
MISS
THEIR SHOW
TONIGHT!
```

129-C. Increase skill on patterned word drills

129-C. Type to your goal. ACCURACY: type the seven lines, as though they were a paragraph, three times. SPEED: type each twice, then repeat lines 28-31 twice more each. Don't let the one-hand words in 25-27 make you slow down or sway, and don't let the ease of the alternate-hand words in 28-31 speed you up so much you jam your keys!

25 ages hymn sags jump drag kink fads look grab hulk drag junk
26 quart plump sweat plunk eases hilly reset phony tread jolly
27 crazed limply extras oniony exceeds opinion dredger million

   1 | 2 | 3 | 4 | 5 | 6 | 7 | 8 | 9 | 10 | 11 | 12

28 quantity element island panel girls quake blend shake works
29 sight ivory tight bland fight chair eight furor right cocoa
30 also both city dusk end, fuel goal hand isle jams keys name
31 oaks pair quay risk such tick urns vial when six, flay doz.

129-D. Increase skill on patterned sentences

129-D. Type to your goal. ACCURACY: type the three alphabetic sentences in 32-34 three times each and the alternate-hand sentences twice. SPEED: all lines twice, and then repeat 35-37 twice more.

32 Why did Professor Black give you a quiz on the major taxes?
33 Bill gave a quick jump as the zebra and lynx fought wildly.
34 Jacqueline was very glad the day her film took a prize box.

   1 | 2 | 3 | 4 | 5 | 6 | 7 | 8 | 9 | 10 | 11 | 12

35 Keith may wish to make oak handles for the six giant signs.
36 She is so busy with big problems that she might not aid us.
37 If the girl makes a sign for them, it is their duty to pay.

129-E. Measure your skill improvement

129-E. GOAL: Maximum speed within 3 errors. Remember to listen for the end-of-line bell.

Type the last two paragraphs on page 197 (or take a 5-minute timing on the last three paragraphs) to measure your improvement.

5 SKILL BUILDING • LETTER STYLING •
BILLING, PAYROLL FORMS • DISPLAYS

Lines end evenly
on a 70-space line.
See also page 194.

COUNTING

METHOD

Most of the times when you must center something, you can do the · · · 14
centering with the backspace key or the space bar; but there are some · · 28
occasions when you will find it easier, in the long run, to count the · · 42
characters and spaces in the problem and solve it by easy arithmetic. · · 56

LESSON1234
ASSIGNMENT
LESSON
ASSIGNMENT

If a column heading is four spaces narrower than its column, for · · 70
example, you do not have to use the backspace key or the space bar to · · 84
determine that the heading should be indented two spaces; in any such · · 98
situation, it is easier to count the spaces and split whatever is the · · 112
difference than it is to avoid the simple bit of arithmetic involved. · · 126

THREE

SHORTCUTS

With so much centering to be done even in routine work, it is no · · 140
surprise that typists have invented shortcuts and rules of thumb that · · 154
speed up the task of centering in some cases. Here are some of them. · · 168

The most common aid to centering is adjusting the paper guide so · · 182
the center of the paper will fall at a point that is easy to remember · · 196
and is easy to locate. If you are one of those who has set his paper · · 210
guide so that the center of your paper will fall at 50, you would not · · 224
even know that this is a shortcut. But there are millions of typists · · 238

who still set the paper guide to align with zero on the linescale, so · · 252
that the midpoint of their paper falls at an odd number like 42 or 43 · · 266
or 51, which do not appear as numbers on the scale and so are readily · · 280
confused with 37 and 38 and 49, and which are difficult to add to and · · 294
subtract from when planning margins. Using 50 or 60 as the centering · · 308
point is a great deal surer and faster; so it is a shortcut, you see. · · 322

One of the awkward problems is what to do with a two-line column · · 336
heading when one line is only one space shorter than the other. Now, · · 350
if each line is centered separately, sometimes the left-over space is · · 364
on one side and sometimes it is on the other, depending on the number · · 378
of strokes in the two lines; but most typists now ignore this trivial · · 392
difference, saving time by centering the longer one and then blocking · · 406
the shorter line with the start of the longer one. Worth mentioning, · · 420
however, is the fact that some machines now have a half-space key for · · 434
use if the work must be dressed up. If you hold down this key as you · · 448
tap a letter key, the letter appears half a space to the right. This · · 462
key permits exact centering that is grand to see but very slow to do. · · 476

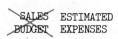

In a similar vein, typists now use the dollar sign as a flexible · · 490
point in centering a money column under its heading. If counting the · · 504
dollar sign as a part of the column width will make centering easier, · · 518
then count it; otherwise, do not count the dollar sign in the column. · · 532
This is a shortcut that will save time in every money table you type! · · 546

LINE: 60
TAB: 5
SPACING: SINGLE
DRILLS: THREE TIMES
STRESS: CORRECT
 TECHNIQUES
GOAL: BOOST SKILL

Unit 17. Skill Development

101-A. Lines three or more times, or a half-minute writing on each line.

101-B. Proofread your work carefully, to set your Lesson 101 goal: If you make 4 or more errors, your goal is ACCURACY. Type each set of drills like a paragraph three times and once more if assigned. If you make three or fewer errors, your goal is SPEED. Type each drill three consecutive times, plus an additional time if so indicated.

101-C. Type as directed in 101-B. Add an extra repetition if you had any raised capitals in the 101-B writing.

101-D. Type as directed in 101-B. Add an extra repetition if you left out a word in 101-B.

101-E. Type as directed in 101-B. Add an extra repetition if you find any very light or very dark letters in 101-B.

101-F. Type as directed in 101-B. Add an extra repetition if you made any error in, or jammed keys in, a one-hand word in the 101-B copy.

101-G. To confirm your progress, repeat 101-B.

101-A. Tune up on these reach-review lines

1 If it is their turn to go, they may find the work cut down.
2 The six zebras very quickly jumped out of the winter glare.
3 He assigned us pages 10, 28, 39, 47, and 56 for our lesson.
   1 | 2 | 3 | 4 | 5 | 6 | 7 | 8 | 9 | 10 | 11 | 12

101-B. Inventory your operating techniques

Type the first four paragraphs on 101-H (or take a 5-minute writing on it), pressing your skill to its utmost: type rapidly but with good control, relentlessly keeping eyes on the copy and forcing yourself to continue the way you would if you worked in an office and if your employer gave you five minutes to get the job done!

101-C. Improve your capital-shifting technique

4 Ted Lou Red Ima Dan Joe Sam Lil Eve Jim Cal Kip Val Ina Wes
5 Alf Ken Don Kay Rue Ned Wyn May Bob Yve Guy Hal Bud Pam Son
6 Dana Nora Stan John Carl Lila Fred Mike Sara Joel Drew Hope
7 Ruth Mary Alan Jack Cora Paul Vick Pats Dora Hank Will Oren
8 Joe told Bob, Tom, and Red to bring Peg, Jen, Eve, and Gay.
9 We elected Bill Hamm, Anne Toll, Lynn Rodd, and Bobby Gill.
10 They drove to Akron, Cleveland, Buffalo, and Niagara Falls.
   1 | 2 | 3 | 4 | 5 | 6 | 7 | 8 | 9 | 10 | 11 | 12

101-D. Improve your eyes-on-copy technique

11 down. cut work the find may they go, to turn their is it If◄
12 .eralg retniw eht fo tuo depmuj ylkciuq yrev sarbez xis ehT◄
13 H- qu-ckl- tr--ned a d-z-n br-wn f-x-s t- j-mp -v-r a g-te.

101-E. Improve the evenness of your stroking

14 one some knows what end long would work big like sheet with
15 had five typed each out need times both who made which side
16 ink thin stock more wax used pound make six four eight know

101-F. Improve control of one-hand words

17 My case was deferred after John agreed on greater tax fees.
18 In my opinion, Lynn was dazed after severe stress in water.
19 Phillip was my best pupil after we defeated Joplin in polo.
20 You gave Johnny a great scare after you faced a grave test.

101-G. Measure your progress in sustained writing

LINE: 70
TAB: 5
SPACING: SINGLE
DRILLS: THREE TIMES
STRESS: ELBOWS IN
   AND WRISTS DOWN
GOAL: BOOST SKILL,
   IMPROVE CENTERING

128-A. Each line three times, or a half-minute writing on each line. Repeat in Lesson 129.

128-B. If you make 3 or more errors, your goal in Lessons 128-129 is ACCURACY; otherwise your goal is SPEED.

128-C. Type to your goal. ACCURACY: The group of lines three times. SPEED: Each line three times. Try to avoid pausing at the thin vertical lines.

128-D. Clear tabs. Set one every 13 spaces. Copy the "typewritten" lines; then, center under each word the entry given in regular print. Use the arithmetic method (paragraph 2, page 197), ignoring all fractions.

128-E. Type to your goal, just as you did in 128-C. Type slowly (even lazily) the first time through, but then speed up; hold rhythm constant, even.

128-F. Type three lines consisting of 20, 19, and 18 underscores and repeat a triple space below; then, center the names of the months as shown, above and below.

128-G. Type to your goal. ACCURACY: The group of lines three times. SPEED: Each line three times. Don't pause; keep going as smoothly as you can!

128-A. Tune up on these reach-review lines

1 She said that Kent told them both that they must work hard.
2 Jim knew the buzzing talk could vex my quiet old professor.
3 The pair patterns of 10, 28, 39, 47, and 56 will total 180.

  1 | 2 | 3 | 4 | 5 | 6 | 7 | 8 | 9 | 10 | 11 | 12

128-B. Inventory your present rate of skill

Type the first three paragraphs on page 197 (or take a 5-minute writing on the page), pressing your skill to its utmost—as though you were in a speed-and-accuracy contest and were ahead of the others.

128-C. Increase skill on runs of two-letter words

4 report on it which of us have to do when it is to one of us
5 expect to be since it is much as we have to be at see if it
6 wonder if it would he be sent to us most of it is can it be

128-D. Concentrate via a special centering drill

EXPENSE	AMOUNTS	MANAGER	BUREAUS	PERCENT
10%	10.00	Jones	Eastern	19.1%
DIVISION	LOSS	NUMBERS	PROFIT	TOTAL
Budget	$1,000	41,200	(None)*	381.14
BRANCHES	SALES	TERRITORY	DATE DUE	RESULTS
Chicago	$1,477	Southern	May 2	-137

128-E. Increase skill on runs of three-letter words

10 filled the one think you are which may not went out for the
11 looked for his tried the new since the one must ask him why
12 better for our which our men write out the will you get our

128-F. Concentrate via a special centering drill

January	February	March
April	May	June
July	August	September
October	November	December

128-G. Build skill on one-hand-run preview words

15 difference remember however shorter easier faster only fact
16 characters millions dressed similar spaces common easy case
17 separately subtract readily awkward column locate link bars
18 determines planning exactly started simple center sets upon

128-H. Repeat 128-B to measure your progress

101-H. Build skill in sustained typing

WHAT'S WHAT ABOUT CARBON PAPER

1 | 2 | 3 | 4 | 5 | 6 | 7 | 8

No one knows who invented carbon   7
sheets, for the event happened long ago,   15
even before the typewriter was invented;   23
but whoever it was deserves to be honored   32
by a big monument in the middle of Wall   40
Street or some other business street.   47

Can you imagine what office work would   57
be like with no carbon paper? On the aver-   65
age, business uses five copies of what-   73
ever is typed; if each copy had to be typed   82
separately, business would need five times   90
as many typists, which would be the end of   99
business, or typists, or both. Out of honest   108
respect to the person who made office work   117
possible through his invention, let's review   126
what we ought to know about it.   134

QUALITY IN CARBONS

A carbon paper is a sheet of thin, strong   145
paper coated on one side with a solution of   154
ink and wax. The quality of the sheet   161
depends on the quality of the paper and   169
coatings.   172

The thickness, or weight, of the paper   182
used in carbons is one factor to check. The   191
thinner the sheet is, the more copies you   199
can make at one typing, but the sooner the   207
sheet wears out. If you normally make from   216
four to seven copies, as most typists do,   225
then you should stock the middle weight of   233
carbon, the six pound. If you commonly   241
make more copies than seven, then you use   250
a thinner weight, such as the four pound;   258
or, if you normally make four or fewer   266
copies of what you type, then you would   274
get more value from heavier paper, such as   282
the eight pound. But, six pound is almost   291
standard.   293

A second main factor of carbon paper   302
that every typist should know is the hard-   310

ness, or finish, of the coating. In general,   320
a hard finish gives more uses of the carbon   328
sheet; but each copy is lighter. On the other   338
hand, a soft finish gives darker copies; but   347
the sheet cannot be used as often. If you   355
have a noiseless machine or a light touch,   364
you ought to use a soft finish. If you have   373
an electric machine or a heavy touch, then   381
you should use a hard finish. For normal of-   390
fice work on a manual machine, the best   398
finish is medium.   402

PLUS EXTRA FEATURES

Putting together what you have just   411
noted about finish and weight, you can   419
understand why most orders for boxes of   427
carbon sheets seem to be for "a medium   435
six, if you please."   439

But, makers of carbon papers are always   449
looking for new ways to make their prod-   459
uct better than that made by others; as a   465
result, some brands feature things that   473
others do not.   477

You can get carbon paper, for example,   486
that is given a special coat that will   494
prevent curling. You can get carbon   501
sheets with clipped corners, for easy sepa-   510
ration of a sheaf of papers and carbons.   518
You can get carbons edged in white, for   526
clean handling; and some carbons even   534
have a line count printed on the white edge,   543
so you know how far you are from the   551
bottom. All such features increase the price   560
of carbon paper, of course; but they are   568
worth the extra few pennies.   574

But, whether or not you use carbon   583
paper with such plus features, be sure to   591
include a word of thanks to the person who   600
began it all, the next time you reach for a   608
medium six.   [START OVER]   611

1 | 2 | 3 | 4 | 5 | 6 | 7 | 8

127-A. Build skill on bounce-back preview words

127-A. Type to your goal.
ACCURACY: The group of
lines three times. SPEED:
Each line three times.

127-A. Build skill on bounce-back preview words

13   ava available exe exercise ele element olo follow eve never

14   ici efficient ara separate wkw awkward ete letter pap paper

15   ara character ivi dividing ese reserve ata attain ere where

127-B. Concentrate via a special centering drill

CENTERING SHORTCUT

Midpoint of ruled line or open area: Average (add; then, divide by 2) scale points where area starts and ends; as, $10+70=80 \div 2=40$. If there is a fraction, count it a whole; as, $10+75=85 \div 2=42\frac{1}{2}$ $=43$, centering point.

PRACTICE 1. Type six periods, one under another, at 20 and 60. Then center the indicated items, using the space bar (see paragraph 4, on page 194).

PRACTICE 2. Type six periods, one under another, at 20 and 70. Then center the same items by backspacing from the midpoint (see box in column at left).

> · *Center your name* ·
> · *Your instructor's name* ·
> · *Name of your school* ·
> · *Your class period* ·
> · *Your city and state* ·
> · *Today's date* ·

127-C. Type to your goal.
ACCURACY: The group of
lines three times. SPEED:
Each line three times.
· Stress an even pace.

127-C. Build skill on preview words ending in -ING

16   ing operating ing dividing ing tapping ing heading ing ings

17   ing beginning ing counting ing calling ing marking ing ings

18   ing centering ing starting ing spacing ing finding ing ings

127-D. Since what you do
here is quite similar to
what you did in 127-B,
you should be able to do
these two exercises in
2 minutes or less each.

127-D. Concentrate via a special centering drill

PRACTICE 3. Type six underscore lines, double spaced, from 25 to 75. Center on these lines the data in 127-B. Use the space-bar method (paragraph 4, page 194).

PRACTICE 4. Type six underscore lines, double spaced, from 5 to 50. Center the same data on these lines by the backspace method (see box in directions column again).

127-E. Type to your goal.
ACCURACY: The group of
lines three times. SPEED:
Each line three times.
Type evenly; avoid any
stalls and any spurts.

127-E. Build skill on compound preview words

19   avail able available available; short cut shortcut shortcut

20   some times sometimes sometimes; mid point midpoint midpoint

21   back space backspace backspace; left over leftover leftover

127-F. Type to your goal,
as you did in 127-E. Do
your utmost to hold your
rhythm constantly steady.

127-F. Build skill on double-letter preview words

22   LL horizontally CC occasions LL followed PP tapping EE need

23   TT typewritten FF efficient NN beginning LL calling SS less

24   NN unnecessary LL especially RR carriage EE proceed LL fill

127-G. Type to your goal,
as in the preceding
exercises. Do not let
yourself falter or slow
down on the double-reach
combinations or words.

127-G. Build skill on double-reach preview words

25   HN techniques ED proceed RG margin FT after MU must NY many

26   RT shortcut UN unequal RV reserve RT expert CE once HU thus

27   DE indented CE practice TR strokes LO below FT left MU much

127-H. GOAL: Maximum
speed within 3 errors.
Remember to listen for
the end-of-line bell.

127-H. Measure your skill improvement

Type the last two paragraphs on page 194 (or take a 5-minute timing on the last three paragraphs) to measure your improvement.

102-A. Set your practice goals for Lesson 102

Review the errors you made in Lesson 101 to see which of the following mistakes you made *two or more* times (indicate by light checkmark).

☐ Misstroke on bottom-row key   ☐ Misstroke on the space bar
☐ Misstroke on home-row key   ☐ Misstroke on an adjacent key,
☐ Misstroke on third-row key   like typing *w* for *e*, or *n* for *m*

102-B. Improve control on bottom-row keys

21   azaza ;/;/; sxsxs l.l.l dcdcd k,k,k fvfvf jmjmj fbfbf jnjnj
22   lazy, hazy, daze, maze, dozen vixen next, fixes mixes main.
23   f.o.b. c.o.d. a.m. blame bane cane vane came name balm calm
24   cab, dab, gab, jab, lab, nab, mob, sob, cob, nob, fox, fix.

102-C. Improve control on home-row keys

25   lad load road clad glad glade all gall call ball hall shall
26   ash dash hash mash lash flash ale gale kale dale hale shale
27   alk balk talk walk calk chalk ask bask cask mask task flask
28   ade fade jade made wade spade ail hail jail mail sail snail

102-D. Improve control on third-row keys

29   aqaqa ;p;p; swsws lolol deded kikik frfrf jujuj ftftf jyjyj
30   quirt quilt quits quips quirk apply apple paper piper papas
31   fully gully dully sully truly power tower lower bower cower
32   scows shows slows snows stows tried fried cried pried shied

102-E. Improve control on the space bar

33   a b c d e f g h i j k l m n o p q r s t u v w x y z . , ; ?
34   thinner recent trial less see element typing guest they yes
35   Mr. J. D. said the C. O. D. shipment got here about 2 P. M.

102-F. Improve control on adjacent keys

36   EWE ewer fewer ERE here beret RTR trim earth UYU yule buyer
37   UIU ruin juice IOI join prior OPO rope spout ASA sash basal
38   SDS aids sides DFD daft doffs FGF gaff flags JHJ jury rajah
39   JKJ jack jokes KLK balk ankle CVC cave civic NMN mint enemy

102-G. Restore momentum on easy sentences

40   You know that they will help them when they need some help.
41   The last plan that they said they made does seem very fine.
42   We may ask the new man for the big dog she got for her son.
43   He and the boy got the car and had the two men fix the top.

     1 | 2 | 3 | 4 | 5 | 6 | 7 | 8 | 9 | 10 | 11 | 12

102-H. Confirm your progress in sustained writing

Sidebar:

102-A. Continue same goal and practice plan you used in Lesson 101:

ACCURACY: Consider each set of drills a paragraph; type the paragraph three times.

SPEED: Type each line three times consecutively.

102-B. Type as directed in 102-A. Add an extra repetition if you had 2 or more bottom-row errors in your Lesson 101 work.

102-C. Type as directed in 102-A. Add an extra repetition if you had 2 or more home-row errors in your Lesson 101 work.

102-D. Type as directed in 102-A. Add an extra repetition if you had 2 or more third-row errors in your Lesson 101 work.

102-E. Type as directed in 102-A. Add an extra repetition if you had 2 or more space-bar errors in your Lesson 101 work.

102-F. Type as directed in 102-A. Add an extra repetition if you had 2 or more errors involving adjacent keys in your typing in Lesson 101.

102-G. Type as directed in 102-A. Focus on even, rhythmic typing. Do not push hard for speed; let the ease and evenness of the copy boost your rate.

102-H. Type final four paragraphs of 101-H, or take another 5-minute writing on page 158.

HORIZONTAL CENTERING

Of all the techniques that help a typist turn out a lot of work, especially when the work involves any display, the most useful one is centering; this technique is also the one that you will find the most dangerous, for nothing stands out so clearly as the mark of an office amateur as a word or line that should be centered but is not. Expert centering, therefore, is an art that merits a great deal of practice.

The standard steps by which a typist may center a line or a word horizontally are, of course, well known: You set the carriage at the midpoint of the paper, you press the backspace key once for every two characters or spaces in what you must center, and thus you attain the starting point for typing the line or word. The one caution you must exercise is what you do when you have a single letter left over after backspacing for the pairs: You must not backspace for such a letter.

Once in a while the words to be centered must also be spread; in instances of this nature, you separate letters by one blank space and separate words by three blank spaces. To center such a line, you may proceed in the basic way if you wish, calling off a space after every character that you name in calling the pairs of strokes for which you backspace; but it will dawn on you that naming the space each time is unnecessary, and after that you will use the shortcut: You will just backspace once for each stroke, except the last letter, that the line normally would fill if it were not spread. The last letter has to be excepted, for it's not followed by the space it needs to make a pair.

But there is another way to center which is very useful and will sometimes work better than the basic way. What you do is to set your carriage at the beginning of the space in which you are to center the material; tap the space bar once for each stroke in the words you are centering; and continue tapping the space bar to the end of the space available, counting the strokes to see how many spaces are left over. Dividing your leftovers in half tells you how much the copy has to be indented if it is to be centered within the space you have available.

This method may be used on many occasions. It is efficient, for example, if you must center a heading or title between two margins of unequal width, or a column within a ruled space, or a title below the typewritten name at the end of a letter, or names below the rules for signatures on a legal paper, and so on. If your backspace key is not operating correctly, you can always use this method as a reserve one.

14
28
42
56
70
84
98
112
126
140
154
168
182
196
210
224
238
252
266
280
294
308
322
336
350
364
378
392
406
420
434
448
462
476
490
504
518

Lines end evenly on a 70-space line. See also page 197.

BACKSPACING METHOD

CENTERING
꜀꜀꜀꜀

THE MENU
꜀꜀꜀꜀꜀
THE MENU

SPACE BAR METHOD

JOHN HALE123456

123JOHN HALE456

John Hale

NAME
John Hale
Tom Smith

| | AFFIDAVIT | |

John Hale
Vice-President

SI 1.35—easy-normal

103–104

Skill drive

LINE: 60
TAB: 5
SPACING: SINGLE
DRILLS: THREE TIMES
STRESS: WRISTS KEPT
    CLOSE TOGETHER
GOAL: BOOST SKILL

103-A. Lines three times or a 1-minute sprint on each line. Be sure to repeat these in Lesson 104.

103-B. Type first third of 103-H, on next page (or, take a 5-minute writing on it) to set your practice goals: ACCURACY, if you make over 3 errors; SPEED if you make 3 or fewer.

103-C. Each couplet three times (for accuracy) or each line three times (for speed). Or, take 1-minute timings on couplets (for accuracy) or lines (for speed).

SI 1.08—very easy

103-D. Type three copies (or three 2-minute writings), pausing to type correctly a line of each word mistyped in preceding effort.

SI 1.25—fairly easy

103-E. The triplet three times (for accuracy) or each line three times (for speed). Or, take half-minute timings.

103-F. The foursome three times (for accuracy) or each line three times (to focus on speed).

103-G. Type the second third of 103-H (or a 5-minute writing) to confirm your progress.

103-A. Tune up on these reach-review lines

The profit of eighty bushels of corn may pay for the panel.
Max worked quietly, alphabetizing the cards for vital jobs.
See pages 28, 39, and 47 in Manual No. 1056 for new models.

  1 | 2 | 3 | 4 | 5 | 6 | 7 | 8 | 9 | 10 | 11 | 12

103-B. Confirm your present level of skill

103-C. Boost your rate on rhythmic one-line sentences

He may yet see how the two men dug out the old log for him.
An old man may ask you how you got the red cap she had hid.

The boys know that they must read more when they come here.
Why must they stay here when they like your home much more?

Your older folks often speak about their never being tired.
Jake hoped these women would stamp these brown forms first.

  1 | 2 | 3 | 4 | 5 | 6 | 7 | 8 | 9 | 10 | 11 | 12

103-D. Sustain the new rate on an alphabetic paragraph

The person who wishes to get ahead in the world has to   12
realize that he is going to be compared. He will be judged   24
not so much by what he does that others do not do as by how   36
much better he does the things that the others also do. He   48
must excel in those common, frequent things that provide an   60
honest yardstick by which all may be measured and compared.   72

  1 | 2 | 3 | 4 | 5 | 6 | 7 | 8 | 9 | 10 | 11 | 12

103-E. Sharpen your concentration ability

captain edward harris is now major edward harris.
there are mr. and mrs. frank toll, of pittsburgh.
tom carr invited lou pyle to visit bob at easter.

  1 | 2 | 3 | 4 | 5 | 6 | 7 | 8 | 9 | 10

Capitalize six words in each line.

103-F. Practice patterned preview words

illustrate between appeal button called press need good all
normally treeing offices attack common sheet worry toss off
creases in my extra on up great only tree jump save you few
problem handle shake turns works such make snap both end it

103-G. Measure your progress in sustained writing

LESSONS 103-104

Unit 21. Skill Development

LINE: 70
TAB: 5, CENTER
SPACING: SINGLE
DRILLS: THREE TIMES
STRESS: MAINTAINING
  HAND POSITION
GOAL: BOOST SKILL AND
  IMPROVE CENTERING

126-A. Each line three times, or a half-minute writing on each line Repeat in Lesson 127.

126-A. Tune up on these reach-review lines

1 The boy did not see the two big men who hid the box for us.
2 Vic quickly mixed the frozen strawberries with grape juice.
3 The 10's, 28's, 39's, 47's, and 56's are the pair patterns.

  1 | 2 | 3 | 4 | 5 | 6 | 7 | 8 | 9 | 10 | 11 | 12

126-B. If you make more than 3 errors, your goal in Lessons 126-127 is ACCURACY. If you make fewer errors, then your goal should be SPEED.

126-B. Inventory your present rate of skill

Type the first two paragraphs on page 194 (or take a 5-minute writing on them), pressing your skill to its utmost—as though your employer were standing behind you, listening and watching you.

126-C. Type to your goal. ACCURACY: the group of lines three times. SPEED: each line three times.

126-C. Increase skill via alternate-hand words

4 lament throw sight soaps their usual whale throe gowns goal
5 eighty girls blend fight firms forms sighs usury angle with
6 usurps throb right ivory lairs giant gland towns blend pals

126-D. If you do this correctly, a "white stripe" will appear down the center. First, however, read paragraph 2, page 194.

126-D. Concentrate via a touch-centering drill

Tab the carriage to the center, then type three copies of this display *without raising your eyes.* Use the tabulator to reposition the carriage for backspace-centering each line.

THE ERA OF GOOD HUMOR	21
A New Novel	33
by John Harris	49
Just Off	58
Press Today	70

126-E. Type to your goal. ACCURACY: the group of lines three times. SPEED: each line three times.

126-E. Increase skill via downhill run of preview words

7 especially technique standard display expert paper also the
8 characters dangerous midpoint nothing stands known what you
9 therefore, backspace starting caution spaces every when the

126-F. If you do this correctly, the letter D in each line will align. First, however, read paragraph 3, page 194. NOTE: Italicized words must be underscored when they are copied.

126-F. Concentrate via a touch spread-centering drill

Tab the carriage to the center, then type three copies of this display *without raising your eyes.* Be sure to spread-center each line.

FORDHAM	8
WEST DENVER	22
SAN DIEGO	33
STANDMONT	45

126-G. Type to your goal. ACCURACY: the group of lines three times. SPEED: each line three times. Try to avoid pausing at the vertical lines.

126-G. Increase skill via preview phrase drills

10 that help|will find|turn out|you must|when the|all the|is a
11 line that|each time|also the|and thus|that you|tap the|do a
12 must also|left over|once for|yet this|must not|the one|or a

126-H. Repeat 126-B to measure your progress

103-H. Build skill in sustained typing

WHAT'S WHAT ABOUT CARBON PAPER, Continued

1 | 2 | 3 | 4 | 5 | 6 | 7 | 8

CHALLENGE TO CARBONS

There is one main worry for the spirit of the inventor of carbon paper. This is the thought that science may come forth with some easy way to make extra copies without using carbons, a problem in which science is making some headway. 9 18 26 34 42 48

To illustrate: In most large offices there is already a copying machine; if you need a few more copies of a typed page, you slip the page and some special copying paper into the machine, push a button, and reach for the copy that the device turns out in a few seconds at a cost of a few cents. 58 67 75 83 92 101 109

Along another line of attack, science has come up with chemical coatings for paper. As you type on one sheet, you press the chemical from the back of that page onto and into the chemical on the front of the next page; the result is a copy of what you typed. The method works like magic but is costly, and erasures are next to impossible. Such paper is called NCR since it makes a copy with "No Carbon Required." 119 128 136 144 152 161 169 177 186 194

SNAP-OUT CARBON PACKS

But what gain has been made in the effort to eliminate carbon paper has been more than balanced by the great gains for using a lot more of it, particularly through snap-outs. 203 211 220 229 231

A snap-out is a ready-made carbon pack. When you have used one, you hold it at the bound end and snap your wrist; like magic, the papers and carbons separate, or "snap out." You toss away the used carbons; that is how cheap they are. 241 250 259 267 275 281

Snap-outs come in all sizes. They come both plain and with printing on some or all papers. The papers may be any color, 291 299 307

in any sequence, you might wish. The pack may be as lean as two pages or as thick as a dozen, whatever you wish to order. And order them people do! There are a number of companies now that do nothing but print snap-outs to order. Their appeal is obvious: They are easy and clean to handle and save a great deal of time for the typist, and they give perfect alignment on any snap-outs that are a printed form. 316 324 332 340 348 356 364 372 381 389 390

CARBON-PAPER EFFICIENCIES

Despite the trend toward using snap-outs, most typists will have frequent use for individual sheets of carbon paper and need to know the common efficiencies in their use. For example, always insert a carbon pack slowly, to prevent the pages from slithering; and always press the paper release a time or two, to avoid creasing or treeing the carbon paper. 399 408 416 424 432 440 449 458 463

Typists who use single sheets of carbon paper normally cut off the corners of the sheets; then, to separate papers from carbons, the typist holds the pack at one corner as he shakes the pack gently; the carbon sheets slide out easily. Typists should turn carbons, top to bottom, for each reuse. 473 481 489 498 507 515 523 526

To insert a thick carbon pack, first insert a sheet of paper and run it up until only an inch remains on the paper table; if you put the carbon pack between the paper and the cylinder, the pack will go in easily. Some typists like to insert the paper slightly, then to interleaf their carbons. 537 545 554 562 571 578 587

Using carbon paper is part of every good typist's job. 596 600

[START OVER]

1 | 2 | 3 | 4 | 5 | 6 | 7 | 8

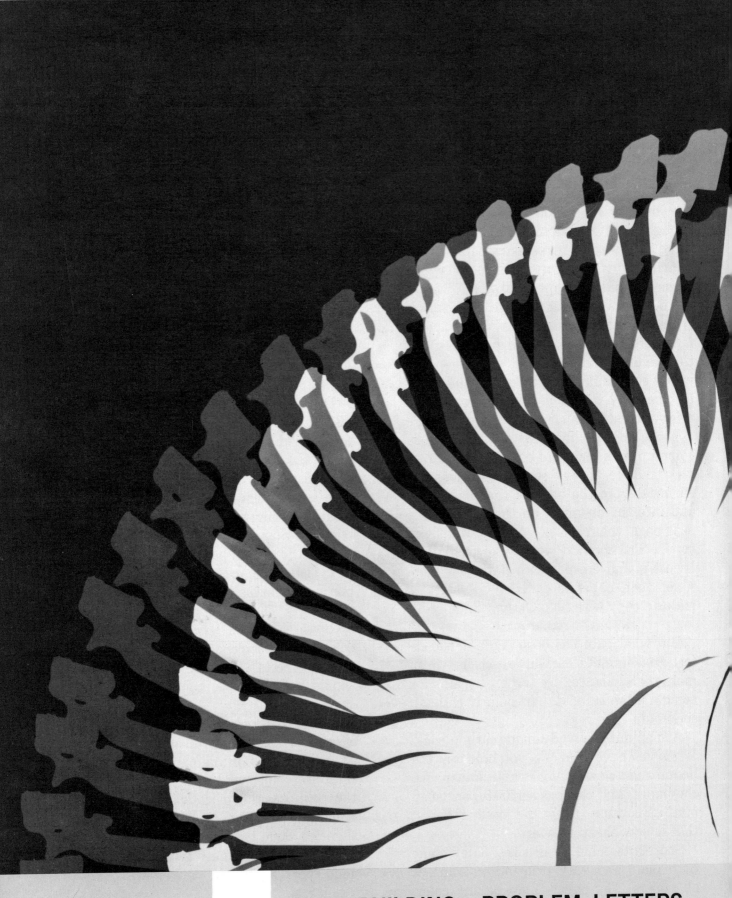

6 SKILL BUILDING • PROBLEM LETTERS • FINANCIAL TABLES • LEGAL PAPERS

104-A. Inventory your keyboard control

104-A. Your goal for Lesson 104 should be ACCURACY if you make 4 or more errors; be sure to type sets of drills as paragraphs.

Your goal is SPEED if you make 3 or fewer errors; repeat drill lines individually.

Without pausing, type seven copies of the alphabetic sentence below; then, check your work to find in which controls you erred *two or more* times:

☐ First finger, left hand   ☐ First finger, right hand
☐ Second finger, left hand   ☐ Second finger, right hand
☐ Third finger, left hand   ☐ Third finger, right hand
☐ Fourth finger, left hand   ☐ Fourth finger, right hand

18   Jeff quickly amazed the audience by giving six new reports.

104-B. Strengthen control of your forefingers

104-B-C-D-E. Type each set of lines (accuracy) or separate lines (speed) once for every whole 10 words a minute you typed in your last long timed writing. (Example: if you typed 37 wam, do these drills three times.)

When you finish 104-E, repeat two times (on one line) each half-line drill for the fingers you checked off in 104-A.

LEFT HAND   RIGHT HAND
19   frf fry fret frog fruit front|juj jut jury just judge jumpy
20   ftf aft tuft heft shaft after|jyj joy July duty jiffy juicy
21   fgf fag gaff guff foggy fight|jhj hub hunt hurt truth hurry
22   fbf fib buff flub bluff abaft|jnj Jan junk June funny runty
23   fvf vat five give favor fiver|jmj jam jump hums tummy gummy

104-C. Strengthen control of your second fingers

24   deded dee deed feed reed heed|kikik kid kind kick dike like
25   dcdcd cod dock duct cold cord|k,k,k ok, ink, irk, kip, ilk,
26   dedcd ace cede deck dice peck|kik,k pi, phi, chi, psi, Ali,

104-D. Strengthen control of your third fingers

27   swsws sew sews news swam wows|lolol low loll roll cool wool
28   sxsxs sex axes oxes exit next|l.l.l lb. Col. bbl. Del. Ill.
29   swsxs wax waxy wash taxi swab|lol.l so. too. ago. woo. Leo.

104-E. Strengthen control of your small fingers

30   aqaqa qua aqua quit quip quay|;p;p; pep prop pulp prep pump
31   azaza zag lazy hazy jazz raze|;/;/; a/b four/five nor/never
32   aqaza equalize quiz quizzical|;p;/; up; prep/prop step/stop

104-F. Now regain stride on easy paragraphs

104-F. Each paragraph two times (or, take a 1-minute timing on it).

GOALS: To set a record on very easy paragraph 33 (SI 1.00) with 1 or no error; then, to do equally well on easy paragraph 34 (SI 1.16) and on fairly easy paragraph 35 (SI 1.32).

33   Of all the things that tell a thief that a home has no   12
one there and so is ripe for a raid, it seems that the main   24
clue is on the steps out front: the milk you did not stop.   36

34   To learn more about the way that hearing works, a team   12
is making a study of the bat, which the team thinks is able   24
to see in the dark with its ears rather than with its eyes.   36

35   In case you are annoyed by the imperative ring of your   12
home telephone, you can have a chime installed, one you can   24
adjust to any pitch or volume that you just happen to like.   36

    1 | 2 | 3 | 4 | 5 | 6 | 7 | 8 | 9 | 10 | 11 | 12

104-G. Confirm your progress in sustained writing

104-G. Type the final third of 103-H, page 161, or take a 5-minute writing on that part.

PENALTY SCALE

—3 for each major error (top margin, line length, line-spacing, general correctness of form, etc.)
—2 for each minor error (blocking, aligning, centering, indenting, etc., of individual parts of the job)
—1 for each typographical error

GRADING SCALE

0-1 PENALTY .... A
2-3 PENALTY .... B
4-6 PENALTY C
7-8 PENALTY .... D

Test 5-C
Letter 56

SEMIBLOCKED LETTER WITH SPECIAL DISPLAY
Paper: workbook 243
Body (with postscript): 184 words, plus centered subject line
Tab: paragraph 10, Date, closing: as in Illus. 10, page 172
Start: machine set, carriage at the date
Grade: box below
SI: 1.43—normal

Miss Jeanette F. Baur | Weston's Department Store | 1300   19
Stonewall Street | Macon, Georgia   31202 | Dear Miss Baur: | 31
[*subject line:*] IT'S TIME TO PLAN FOR HAWAII! | 52

Are you going to be one of the 1,000 members of the National   66
Retail League who come to Hawaii for the convention in August?   79
We hope you are! Hawaii is beautiful at any time of the year, but   92
in August it simply shines with flowers and sunlight and splashing   105
whitecaps off Waikiki—a perfect place for holidays, and a perfect   119
place for conventions, also.   125

If you wish to be at The Lanai Waikiki, where your conven-   138
tion is to be held, you need to reserve your room long in advance.   152
Hawaii is a busy place in the summer, with few rooms available   165
(with a view of Diamond Head, that is!). We should be pleased to   178
reserve one for you now, if you wish; the enclosed leaflet gives   191
you the details about room sizes, the rates, the deposit, and so   204
on.   218

Cordially yours,   218

THE LANAI WAIKIKI   242
Ruth Soong Ki, Reservations   263

Notations   266

P. S. Most visitors who come here find Hawaii so lovely   279
that they stay over for a longer holiday. Should you decide to do   293
so, we should be pleased to assure you the same low rates you will   306
enjoy during your convention stay.   313

1 | 2 | 3 | 4 | 5 | 6 | 7 | 8 | 9 | 10 | 11 | 12 | 13

5-MINUTE SPEED WITHIN 3 ERRORS*

50-up wam ...... A
45-49 wam ...... B
35-44 wam C
30-34 wam ...... D

* If more than 3 errors are made, compute the speed on what is typed before the fourth error.

Test 5-D
Forms 50-54

5-MINUTE TIMING ON PAYROLL VOUCHER CHECKS
Forms: workbook 244-246
Start: machine set, form inserted to first entry
Grade, errorless copies:
5 forms done .... A
4 forms done .... B
3 forms done C
2 forms done .... D

PAYROLL REGISTER

NO.	NAME	INCOME TAX EXEMPTION	GROSS PAY		DEDUCTIONS						TOTAL		NET PAY	
					I.T.W.		F.I.C.A.		GROUP INSURANCE	MISC.				
1	Caswell, Ruppert G.	3	151	30	13	20	6	05	2 18		21	43	129	87
2	Fordyce, J. Elliot	1	124	55	18	10	4	98	83	1 94	25	85	98	70
3	Gordon, Elizabeth D.	1	142	50	20	90	5	70	1 50		28	10	114	40
4	Klein, Mark L.	2	110	70	10	70	4	43	57	1 94	17	64	93	06
5	Preston, Henry K.	2	165	00	20	60	6	60	1 80		29	00	136	00
6														
7														
8														
9														
10														

Use above data for payroll voucher checks J162-J166 for these five persons.

LINE: 60
TAB: 5
SPACING: SINGLE
GOAL: NUMBER
CONTROL
STRESS: EYES ON COPY
DRILLS: AS DIRECTED

105-A. Each line three or more times—press for smooth, steady typing. Repeat in Lesson 106.

105-B. As a pretest, type a copy without pausing or looking up once. Proofread. For each number that you type incorrectly, put a light pencil mark before the matching drill in lines 5-14.

SI 1.42—normal, with all digits and letters

105-C. Each line three times, plus an additional time if the drill is for a number that you typed incorrectly in 105-B.

When you finish typing drill 14, check your work (lines 5-14) very carefully: If there is any drill for which you have not typed at least one perfect copy, retype that drill until you do have a perfect copy.

105-D. Type each line three times, with at least one perfect copy of it. Do not type the underscores.

105-E. Type each line three times, with at least one perfect copy of it.

105-F. Repeat 105-B.

105-A. Tune up on these reach-review lines

1 Rickey did not wish to pay the usual duty for the fur pelt.
2 My fine black ax just zipped through the wood quite evenly.
3 3 and 6 and 9 and 12 and 15 and 18 and 21 and 22 [Continue to 60]

105-B. Measure your skill on this numeric paragraph

4 John's company now has 56 stores, located in 30 cities 12
in the West. They employ 147 girls and 138 men, or a total 24
of 285 workers, in these stores. The various products they 36
sell are supplied by some 90 different firms, located in 26 48
states. These figures are pretty exciting when you realize 60
that this unique firm did not get into business until 1947. 72

1 | 2 | 3 | 4 | 5 | 6 | 7 | 8 | 9 | 10 | 11 | 12

105-C. Improve your control of the number keys

5 ll ala Of the 111 men, 11 were too tall, 11 were too short.
6 22 s2s Each of the 22 men got 2 copies of the 22-page book.
7 33 d3d The 33 boys in Camp 3 got 3 daily meals for 33 days.
8 44 f4f Of the 4,444 men, 44 bought seats on the 4:44 train.
9 55 f5f The 55 men in Squadron 5 had accrued 55 days' leave.
10 66 j6j Project 666 was done by 66 men in each of 6 classes.
11 77 j7j They need 77 coats, 77 hats, and 77 kits in Camp 77.
12 88 k8k The 8th Group bought 888 boxes of No. 88 ammunition.
13 99 l9l You will never get 9,999 by adding 9 and 99 and 999.
14 00 ;0; They saw 10 or more on Islands No. 10, 100, and 110.

105-D. Increase fluency in typing numbers

15 we 23 23 23 wey 236 236 236 tip 580 580 580 our 974 974 974
16 up 70 70 70 you 697 697 697 wit 285 285 285 ire 843 843 843
17 or 94 94 94 yet 635 635 635 rip 480 480 480 owe 923 923 923
18 to 59 59 59 wry 246 246 246 put 075 075 075 tie 583 583 583

1 | 2 | 3 | 4 | 5 | 6 | 7 | 8 | 9 | 10 | 11 | 12

105-E. Speed up with pair-pattern numbers

19 She scored 28, 39, 47, 56, and 100 on that series of tests.
20 Trunk No. 10 is in Room 47, No. 28 in 56, and No. 39 in 10.
21 Check in closets 10, 28, and 56 for boxes number 39 and 47.

1 | 2 | 3 | 4 | 5 | 6 | 7 | 8 | 9 | 10 | 11 | 12

105-F. Confirm your progress in number control

Progress Test on Part Five

Test 5

Test 5-A

5-MINUTE WRITING
ON PARAGRAPHS
Paper: workbook 241
Line: 55 spaces
Tab: paragraph 5
Spacing: double
Start: machine set,
   carriage at margin
Grade: box below
SI: 1.36—normal

5-MINUTE SPEED
WITHIN 3 ERRORS*

50-up wam	A
45-49 wam	B
35-44 wam	C
30-34 wam	D

* If more than 3 errors
are made, compute the
speed on what is typed
before the fourth error.

Test 5-B

Manuscript 41

5-MINUTE WRITING
ON COMMITTEE REPORT
Paper: workbook 242
Spacing: SINGLE
Line: 6 inches
Top margin: 8 lines
Start: machine set,
   carriage centered
Grade: box above
SI: 1.42—normal

POLICY ON REPETITION OF ADS

     The experts in the field of advertising find that one question comes up time and again: Is it better to repeat a good advertisement or to keep showing new ads to the public? Our committee was asked to see whether there is a reply to this question which would apply to the basic products that we promote in our advertising.

RESEARCH

     We found that a great many studies have been made on this subject. We were able to review nine studies. We regret to report that no study deals with a problem quite like ours; each is concerned with some one phase of the problem, and in no case is that phase quite the same as any of those we face in our promotion program.

     But put together, the studies add up to some help for us. There is an interesting study on the best use of color, for example. There is one on the space size and two on the page position. There are other studies dealing with the special problems of special products, but there is none dealing with our repetition problem.

RECOMMENDATIONS

     On the basis of our own researches and experience in recent years, we should like to suggest that future displays for our main products include these features:

     1. Let us standardize on the color that we use in all ads that involve the use of color; the color to be selected should also be used in our product packaging.

     2. Let us design and use a uniform signature line for all our ads, no matter where they appear, in order that we may pound home our name and our new trademark.

     In other regards (including when to repeat an ad, when to write a new one, and so on), we feel that members of the promotion team should be left a free hand.

Harold Harms (Sales); Martha Holder (Production); George Blane (Promotion); John Hess (Agency), Chairman

1 | 2 | 3 | 4 | 5 | 6 | 7 | 8 | 9 | 10 | 11

106-A. Measure your skill on a paragraph with symbols

106-A. As a pretest, type a copy without pausing or looking up once. Proofread. For each symbol that you typed incorrectly, put a light pencil mark before the matching drill in lines 24-28.

SI 1.36—normal

22   If you use a dash to show a break in thought, like "We   12
know--well, we think--we passed the test," make the dash of   26
two hyphens without a space before, between, or after them.   38
23   But when you wish to use a dash to indicate a span, as   52
in "about 10 - 20% off" or "about 10-20% off," use a single   64
hyphen, either with one space on each side of it or with no   76
space on either side of it; "about 10--20%" would be wrong.   88

      1 | 2 | 3 | 4 | 5 | 6 | 7 | 8 | 9 | 10 | 11 | 12

106-B. Improve mastery of these symbol keys

106-B. Each line three times, plus an extra time if the drill is for a symbol you got wrong in the pretest.

The "M" lines are for manual typists; the "E" lines are for the electric machines.

24M   k8k k'k }
24E   ;'; ;'; } It's a good day, isn't it?   John's dad won a prize!

25   ;p- ;-; My in-laws are cordial--well, reasonably so--to me.

26M   j6j j_j }
26E   ;-; ;_; } Stop reading The Call of the Wild and listen to me!

27   f5f f%f It may be typed 10% to 28%, or 10 - 28%, or 10-28%.

28M   s2s s"s }
28E   ;'; ;"; } "Well," he said, "so long."   We begged, "Don't go!"

106-C. Increase fluency in typing numbers

106-C. Type each line three times, with at least one perfect copy of it. Do not type the underscores.

Note that this drill differs from 105-D.

29   we 23 24 25 wey 236 237 238 tip 580 581 582 our 974 975 976
30   up 70 71 72 you 697 698 699 wit 285 286 287 ire 843 844 845
31   or 94 95 96 yet 635 636 637 rip 480 481 482 owe 923 924 925
32   to 59 60 61 wry 246 247 248 put 075 076 077 tie 583 584 585

      1 | 2 | 3 | 4 | 5 | 6 | 7 | 8 | 9 | 10 | 11 | 12

106-D. Regain stride on an easy paragraph

106-D. Type three copies (or take three one-minute writings), with this GOAL: To finish a copy within 1 minute and no errors whatsoever!

SI 1.11—very easy

33   I stood by the door of the cabin and looked at a vista   12
that seemed to stretch on and up to the rim of the world, a   24
deep cut of a valley that the snow had made as white as the   36
finest piece of china you may ever have held in your hands.   48

      1 | 2 | 3 | 4 | 5 | 6 | 7 | 8 | 9 | 10 | 11 | 12

106-E. Confirm and push your progress

106-E. As a post-test, make two attempts to complete this loaded paragraph within 2 minutes, with only 2 or fewer errors. Note that the word count gives triple credit for underscored words.

SI 1.59—difficult

34   "If you've a series of words to be underscored," Ralph   12
said, "underscore them solidly unless there is some special   27
reason why they must be stressed separately. For 90-95% of   41
the cases, you'll type the line with no breaks for spaces."   54
      I asked, "What about marks of punctuation?"   64
      He said, "You will--of course--underscore them if they   76
occur in a solid group; in other cases, it doesn't matter."   88

      1 | 2 | 3 | 4 | 5 | 6 | 7 | 8 | 9 | 10 | 11 | 12

Manuscript 40

PERSONAL DATA
RESUME
Paper: plain, full
Shown: in elite
Placement: center
Option: Prepare your
own personal resume

Applicant: RICHARD E. JORDAN

Address: 1041 West 22 Street
                  Oak Park, Ill.   60301

Telephone: TAlcott 1-4526

Applying for: Junior Accountant

Date: March 21, 19—

A. PERSONAL DATA
1. Age: 22. I was born March 3, 19—.
2. Height: 5 feet 10 inches. Weight: 160 pounds.
3. Military status: Served 3 years in the Navy.
4. Marital status: Single, but engaged.
5. Residence: Live with parents.

B. PERTINENT EXPERIENCE RECORD
1. Maintained storekeeper records and payroll records during $1\frac{1}{2}$ years of Navy duty.
2. Was cashier at Carson's (Chicago) on Saturdays and some evenings during last year of high school.
3. Was bookkeeper for a Junior Achievement Group during my first year at Central City College.

C. EDUCATIONAL RECORD
1. Graduated from Oak Park High School, May 29, 19—, after completing a college-preparatory course.
2. Will graduate from Central College on June 3, after completing the two-year accounting program.
3. Academic and skill achievement—
   a. Accounting: 15 semester hours, honor grades.
   b. Business machines: Can use all calculators.
   c. Typewriting: 60 words a minute (10-minute test).
   d. Filing and Systems: Completed 50-hour course.
4. Have ranked on Dean's list throughout college program.
5. Extracurricular activities—
   a. Served as business manager for college newspaper.
   b. Treasurer of my church's Youth Group.

D. REFERENCES
1. Dr. John K. Younger, Dean of Men, Central College, 6 North Michigan Boulevard, Chicago, Illinois   60607.
2. Mr. Richard Forbes, Manager, Men's Suit Department, Carson's, 1 South State Street, Chicago, Ill.   60607.
3. Mr. Adam Gerhold, Director, Oak Park Youth Guild, DeCook Court, Oak Park, Illinois   60301.

Form 49

JOB APPLICATION

Pages 237-238 of your workbook are a replica of a genuine employment application form. Fill it in completely with your personal data, as though you were applying for an office job.

Unit 18. Correspondence

LINE: 50
TAB: 5, CENTER
SPACING: SINGLE
GOAL: LEARN ABOUT
LETTER DESIGNS
DRILLS: 3 EACH
STRESS: APPLY FULL
SKILL TO LETTERS

107-A. Tune up on these easy review lines

107-A. Recall skill by taking two ½-minute timings on each line. Repeat in Lesson 108.

1 Jip has two men who can fix the old car you have.
2 He quickly extinguished the most dangerous blaze.
3 It began at 10:28 in Room 47, was in 56 by 10:39.

107-B. Build skill via developmental sustained writing

107-B. Steps to take:

1. Scan the copy, just to see what is said.

2. Select the hardest word in each line and type a line of it.

3. Take a 5-minute timed writing, pausing for a 10-second rest at the end of each minute. Or, type a copy, pausing to rest after you complete each paragraph.

4. Take a 5-minute timed writing without rests. Or, type a copy without pausing a single time. GOAL: Best possible rate within 3-error ceiling.

SI 1.43—normal

4   FOREWORD

AT FIRST THOUGHT, it might seem desirable for all letters to be standardized, to be arranged alike. Certainly it would make the production of letters quite easy for the typist. Imagine: No problems in placement, in line lengths, in the arrangement of the inside address and closing, in any of many other points of form that now concern the typist.

But the plain truth is that no one wants his letters to look exactly like those of other writers. Like a football player who wishes a uniform like that of his teammates but wants a number all his own, each writer wants his letters to be like other letters in general, but in some way unique.

And so business letters appear in many forms that, like the football uniforms, are quite alike and yet can be distinguished by some unique point of arrangement. These forms are called "styles." Two styles, the blocked and the semiblocked, bear the burden of traffic in nine out of ten letters; and other styles share the remaining tenth. As a review and a guide, the following pages present a gallery of the modern styles of business letters.

Insert day's date   Pivot your name

Manuscript 29

CENTERED FOREWORD
Paper: workbook page 183 or plain paper
Spacing: single
Arrangement: unbound
SI: 1.43—normal

Note: If you use plain paper for the letters, draw or type a line 1½ inches from the top, to represent the depth of a letterhead. Then, type in the blank letterhead space the caption that appears on the model illustration of the style you are to use in each letter.

107/108-C. Become an expert in letter design

Center Manuscript 29 on plain paper or on workbook page 183; then type Letters 44-47 on plain paper or workbook pages 185-192. Work carefully, for these five assignments may be used as the start of a *Letter Styles Book* that you can develop from the assignments in Unit 18.

LINE: 60
TAB: CENTER
SPACING: SINGLE
DRILLS: THREE TIMES
GOAL: PRACTICE ON
APPLICATION PAPERS
STRESS: LOW WRISTS

123-A. Each line three times—consecutively, for a speed increase; but alternately, for a gain in your accuracy. Repeat in Lesson 124.

123-B. Note the changes in the letter. Adjust margins to make them suitable for a "long" letter. Skim the letter and type, three times, each capitalized word and each number. Insert clean paper, dropping to the proper starting line. Then follow one of these two routines:

1. See whether you can produce a correct copy of the letter within 6 minutes and 3 errors. You may try twice. If you succeed, lo! you have typed Letter 55.

2. Take two 5-minute timings, trying for 46 or more words a minute within 3 errors. Save your papers; you may be able to count one as your letter 55!

SI 1.50—fairly hard, especially in the form of a rough draft copy!

Letter 55

PERSONAL-BUSINESS BLOCKED LETTER
Paper: plain, full
Body: 187 words (and an attention line)
Review: page 61
Caution: line length shown is not right for pica or elite!

UNIT 20

123-A. Tune up on these review lines

1   It is your turn to shape the emblem and pay the man for it.
2   John very quietly picked the six razors from the woven bag.
3   The checks outstanding are for $10, $28, $39, $47, and $56.

  1 | 2 | 3 | 4 | 5 | 6 | 7 | 8 | 9 | 10 | 11 | 12

123-B. Sustain your skill on production copy

4   *1041 West 22 Street* ~~931 East Graham Street~~   5
    Oak Park ~~Evanston, Illinois 60204~~   11
    Today's date ~~March 22, 19~~ *60301*   15
                                                             16

~~The National Company~~ *Martin + Stevens, Inc.*   21
~~6 North Michigan Avenue~~ *4652 Chase Street*   24
Chicago, Illinois   60607   30

ATTENTION OF THE PERSONNEL DEPARTMENT   38

Gentlemen: 42

I should like to apply for the position of *junior accountant* ~~secretary~~, 55
as advertised in this morning's ~~Gazette~~, *Times*.   65

I was pleased to see your advertisement. I was among   77
the group of seniors from Central College conducted   87
on a tour of your offices a few weeks ago; ever since   98
then, I have hoped that a vacancy might occur for   108
which I might qualify. I shall graduate ~~on May 30~~ *June 3*; 118
my class schedule, however, is such that I could work   129
afternoons from now until that date.   137

For this vacancy, you require someone who is both in-   148
terested in the work and qualified for it. The fact   159
that I am *in accounting* ~~a secretarial~~ major at Central College is 169
evidence of my interest in this work and the training   180
that I can bring to it.   185

With this letter I enclose a personal data sheet that   197
gives my qualifications in more detail. Won't you   207
please review it? If you will be kind enough to ~~tell~~   217
~~me on the enclosed postal card~~ when I might be given   230
a personal interview, I shall be grateful for the op-   241
portunity to apply for the position in person.   250

telephone me at TAlcott 1-4526   Sincerely yours, 256
to let me know

                                               Richard E. Jordan
                                               ~~Pauline W. Lambert~~ 262

2 Enclosure*s*   264

LESSONS 123-124   188

Full-Blocked
VIGOROUS, AGGRESSIVE
Letter Style

With a subject line and open punctuation

March 6, 19—

Mr. Roger S. Patterson
Western Life Company
2867 East Fourth Street
Cincinnati, Ohio   45202

Dear Mr. Patterson

Subject: Form of a Full-Blocked Letter

This letter is set up in the full-blocked style, in which every line begins at the left margin. A few companies modify it by moving the date to the right, but most firms use it as shown here. Because this style is the fastest to type, it is considered very modern. It is natural, although not necessary, to use "open" punctuation with this style of letter.

This letter also illustrates one arrangement of the subject line, which may be used with any style of letter. Like an attention line, a subject line may be typed with underscores or capitals. In a full-blocked letter, it must be blocked; in other letter styles, it may be blocked or centered. It always appears after the salutation and before the body, for it is considered a part of the body.

Legal firms and the legal departments of companies sometimes prefer to use the Latin terms Re or In Re instead of the English word Subject.

Yours very sincerely

Mary Ellen Smith

Mary Ellen Smith
Reference Department

urs

Simplified
THE EFFICIENCY EXPERT'S
Letter Style

With open punctuation and full-blocked design

March 6, 19—

Mr. Richard W. Parker, Jr.
Humphrey Lumber Company
520 Southwest Park Avenue
Portland, Oregon   97208

A WORD ABOUT THE SIMPLIFIED LETTER

Several years ago, Mr. Parker, the National Office Management Association designed a new letter form that they called the "NOMA Simplified Letter." It is illustrated by this letter.

1 It uses the efficient full-blocked form and "open" form of punctuation. It even omits periods in enumerations.

2 It contains no salutation or closing. (NOMA believes such expressions to be meaningless.)

3 It displays a subject line in all capitals, both preceded and followed by two blank lines.

4 It identifies the signer by an all-capitals line that is preceded by three blank lines and is followed by one.

5 It seeks to maintain a brisk but friendly tone, partly by using the addressee's name at least in the first sentence.

Despite obvious merits, Mr. Parker, this style has not proved popular except among those to whom efficiency is especially important. Perhaps, as some say, this form does not really look like a business letter; but its efficiency suggests that this style is worth a trial where output must be increased.

Ralph E. Jones

RALPH E. JONES, TRAINING CONSULTANT

urs

1. FULL-BLOCKED STYLE . . . so efficient it seems youthful, aggressive . . . every line starts at left margin . . . shown here with a subject line, too . . . and "open" punctuation (no salutation colon, no closing comma).

2. SIMPLIFIED FULL-BLOCKED . . . efficiency expert's dream: no insincere salutation or complimentary closing . . . no indentions . . . open punctuation . . . display of what reader wants most to know: what? from whom?

Letter 44

FULL-BLOCKED LETTER
Paper: workbook page 185, or plain paper
Body: 143 words
Directions: arrange like Letter 1 above
SI: 1.43—normal

Letter 45

"SIMPLIFIED" LETTER
Paper: workbook page 187, or plain paper
Body: 143 words
Directions: arrange like Letter 2 above
SI: 1.42—normal

Letter 44   45

Date | Mr. Charles T. Elkins | 1216 Academy Drive | Colorado   18   18
Springs, Colo.   80901 | Dear Mr. Elkins   27   23

Subject: Reference for John Walcutt   50   30

Mr. John Walcutt has given us your name, Mr. Elkins, as that   63   44
of someone who can attest his character and experience in store   76   57
management. We are considering him for the post of assistant   88   69
manager of the branch store we will open in your city next month.   101   83
Might you be kind enough to advise us?   109   91

1. Does Mr. Walcutt have the character required for handling   124   106
large amounts of cash?   129   110

2. Does Mr. Walcutt have the ability to direct the work of   144   125
nine or ten other persons?   149   130

3. Does Mr. Walcutt have the creative touch and the strong   164   145
sense of duty that are so important in running a large store?   178   158

If you will answer these questions, Mr. Elkins, and the few   191   171
others asked on the enclosed printed form, we shall be most   203   183
grateful to you. Your statements will, of course, be held in strict   216   197
confidence.   219   200

Sincerely yours | J. Walt Flynn | Personnel Manager | urs | 233   211
Enclosure   235   213

1 | 2 | 3 | 4 | 5 | 6 | 7 | 8 | 9 | 10 | 11 | 12 | 13

Manuscript 39

DISPLAY REPORT
Placement: center
Paper: plain, full
Line: 72 spaces
Tab: in 3, 39, 42
Shown: in elite

For added mastery of the rules
for number expression, use the
Learning Guide, workbook 235.

THE EXPRESSION OF NUMBERS

A Summary by Your Name

WRITE IN WORDS--

a. Ten and the numbers below it:
   The plane has four jet engines.
   I found five dogs and two cats.

b. Round numbers, in general:
   About ten thousand should vote.
   I expect nearly twelve hundred.

c. Numbers that start a sentence:
   Twenty-eight players took part.
   Two hundred twelve were needed.

d. Indefinite amounts of money:
   They gave thousands of dollars.
   He had several hundred dollars.

e. Numbers that are ordinals:
   It is their second anniversary.
   It's his twenty-first birthday.

f. Ages and years, when general:
   He must be seventeen years old.
   He worked here for eight years.

g. Names of centuries, decades:
   Back in the nineteenth century.
   He told about the gay nineties.

h. Street names, ten and below:
   The store is near Fifth Avenue.
   She lives at 191 Second Avenue.

i. Time, informal and o'clock:
   Come over about quarter to ten.
   My plane leaves at ten o'clock.

j. Military, political divisions:
   With the Forty-second Regiment.
   The Fortieth Election District.

WRITE IN FIGURES--

a. Exact numbers above ten:
   The airplane had 36 passengers.
   He has 367 or 368 Irish stamps.

b. Round numbers in advertising:
   We have sold over 10,000 books.
   We get nearly 500 orders a day.

c. Numbers in a series:
   Get 8 bags, 4 boxes, 28 crates.
   I saw 6 men, 11 boys, 14 women.

d. Exact amounts of money:
   They gave $1,500 to the school.
   He had either $1,500 or $2,500.

e. Numbers used with percentages:
   No discount is over 10 percent.
   Sales: shoes, 16%; coats, 14%.

f. Ages and years, when exact:
   John is 17 years 11 months old.
   He worked 21 years and 3 weeks.

g. Graduation, historical years:
   He belongs to the class of '56.
   The fine spirit of '76 and '98.

h. Street names above ten:*
   The store is near 188th Street.
   He lives at 919 East 22 Street.

i. Time with minutes, a.m., p.m.:
   I expect Ralph at 9:45 tonight.
   The plane departs at 10:35 p.m.

j. Dimensions and measurements:
   The back room is 14 by 25 feet.
   The pail holds 2 quarts 1 pint.

---

* Whether to use st, d, rd, or th after street-name numbers (like 22
  Street) depends on local preference. More and more businessmen prefer not to use them, particularly when a word separates the building
  and street numbers, as in 919 East 22 Street or 199 South 147 Avenue.

Illustration of a Display Report

Square-Blocked
THE EFFICIENT SPACE-SAVER
Letter Style   With subject line and "corner fillers"

Mrs. Truda Tracy George   March 7, 19—
President, Pi Omega Pi
California State College
San Diego, California 92101

Dear Mrs. George:

        SUBJECT: THE SQUARE-BLOCKED LETTER

A square-blocked letter like this one is simply the familiar
full-blocked letter with (1) the date moved to the right and
typed on the same line with the start of the inside address,
to "square off" that corner; and (2) the reference symbols
also shifted to the right, to "square off" that corner.

This arrangement has many advantages. It is almost as quick
to type as the full-blocked style. Because it saves lines of
space that are otherwise given to the drop after the date and
below the signer's identification, you can get seven or eight
additional lines of typing on a page; you can see why this is
popular among secretaries whose employers dictate rather long
letters! Any letter looks shorter when typed in this style.
It permits any kind of display, either centered or blocked.

This letter style does have one disadvantage. If your letter
is very short, the date and inside address might run into one
another; so most persons who use this letter style make it a
rule not to use less than a 50-space line. For an ordinary
letter, where you do not need to save space, you must remind
yourself to start two or three lines lower on the page, lest
your letter look too high on the stationery.

Incidentally, one reminder: A married woman should indicate
her "Mrs." in either her penned or her typed identification.

Fraternally yours,

Elsie Frost

Mrs. Elsie Dodds Frost   urs
                                             2 Enc.

Semiblocked
CONSERVATIVE, EXECUTIVE
Letter Style   With attention line and cc notation

                                 March 7, 19—

Savard, Foster & Company
171 Westminster Street
Providence, Rhode Island 02904

        ATTENTION TRAINING DIRECTOR

Gentlemen:

        For a letter design that is both standard
and distinctive, try this style: semiblocked (one
of the two most popular styles) with the paragraphs
indented ten spaces (instead of the usual five).

        This letter also shows you an alternative
arrangement for the attention line: centered, in
all capitals (instead of being blocked at the left
margin and underscored). In two regards, however,
the use of the attention line here is standard: It
is accompanied, as it should be, by the salutation
"Gentlemen"; and it is typed above the salutation.

        Worth noting also in this letter are the
following: (1) positioning the date at the margin,
as an alternative to starting it at the center; (2)
the use of "standard" punctuation, which calls for
a colon after the salutation and a comma after the
complimentary closing; and (3) the use of the "cc"
notations at the bottom to indicate to whom carbon
copies of the letter are being sent.

        Yours very truly,

        (Mrs.) *Elsie Frost*
        Elsie D. Frost, Director

URS
cc Miss Filene
cc Dr. Young

3. SQUARE-BLOCKED . . . greatest space-saver, can get an extra hundred words on page . . . for date is lowered to square up top right corner . . . and reference symbols are moved up and over to square off bottom right corner.

4. SEMIBLOCKED . . . the restrained, cordial look that top executives like . . . shown here with an attention line . . . deep 10-space paragraph indentation, just for distinctiveness . . . and carbon-copy notations, too.

Letter 46

SQUARE-BLOCKED
LETTER
Paper: workbook page
  189, or plain paper
Body: 170 words
Punctuation: standard
Directions: arrange
  like Letter 3 above
SI: 1.34—normal

Letter 47

SEMIBLOCKED LETTER
Paper: workbook page
  191, or plain paper
Body: 170 words
Punctuation: standard
Directions: arrange
  like Letter 4 above
SI: 1.34—normal

	Letter 46	47
Date	Employees Credit Union	The Lehigh Corporation	1800	24	18
Farm Center Building	Little Rock, Arkansas 72201	*In*	34	28
Letter 46: SUBJECT: CREDIT UNION STOCKS *but in Letter 47:* ATTEN-	38	34
TION HOWARD KLING	Gentlemen:	57	49

At the suggestion of the League of Credit Unions, to which your — 71 — 64
group belongs, we have made a survey to learn to what extent the — 84 — 77
funds of credit unions are now invested in stocks. — 95 — 88

The survey has been completed. A report has been published as a — 109 — 103
64-page booklet. If you wish, one of our staff members will bring — 122 — 116
you copies of this report and discuss its details with you. — 134 — 128

Our findings show that, of the 320 groups that took part in the — 148 — 143
survey, 274 groups now hold stocks and 30 more groups are plan- — 160 — 155
ning to purchase them; thus, 304 of the 320 groups, or 95 percent of — 174 — 169
them, will hold stocks by the end of this year. — 184 — 179

The complete report indicates what stocks have been bought and — 198 — 193
what stocks will be purchased, according to the present plans of — 211 — 206
the 320 groups in the study. If you would like us to help you — 223 — 219
review the report and shape a plan of future action, just return — 236 — 232
the card that is enclosed. | Yours very truly, | Robert E. Splane | — 252 — 252
Vice-President | *reference symbols?* — 261 — 259

1 | 2 | 3 | 4 | 5 | 6 | 7 | 8 | 9 | 10 | 11 | 12 | 13

PERSONAL TITLES IN BUSINESS LETTERS

The committee appointed by Mr. Wilhelms to study the use of personal titles in business letters found that the subject is amply treated in many sources, most of which concur.

DEFINITION

This report deals with personal titles that are commonly used in _business_ letters, like Professor, Reverend, Doctor, Dean, Miss, Mr., Mrs., and so on. This report does not concern social letters or titles of rank, job, or position.

FINDINGS

1. A personal title of some kind should always be used before a personal name that occurs in any part of a business letter other than in the signer's typed identification, which most often does not include a personal title.

2. Two titles, Mr. and Mrs., are always abbreviated.

3. _In addresses_, personal titles other than Mr. and Mrs. are written in full only when the last name is given alone, with neither a first name nor an initial; if either is given, the title is abbreviated (if it is one that can be).

4. _In a salutation_, personal titles other than Mr. and Mrs. may be either abbreviated or typed in full, as a writer may prefer. The trend is toward the short form.

5. _In the body_, personal titles other than Mr. and Mrs. should be abbreviated if either a first name or initial is given with the last name; if neither is given, the title may be abbreviated or typed in full, as the writer may prefer.

6. _In the typed signature_, a man does not indicate his personal title unless his first name could be confused with that of a woman. An unmarried woman does not indicate _Miss_ unless her first name could be confused with that of a man. A married woman may (and some authorities say _should_) have the personal title, Mrs., typed before her name.

Chairman's name may
be first, last, or
in alphabetic order.

Thomas F. Allerton
Virginia Saxon
Your Name, Chairman

	21
	23
	36
	48
	59
	61
	63
	77
	92
	104
	116
	118
	120
	132
	145
	157
	166
	179
	197
	209
	222
	233
	252
	264
	274
	291
	303
	315
	327
	349
	361
	375
	387
	401
	411
	418
	423
	429

Illustration of a Committee Report, Single Spaced

LINE: 60
TAB: 5
SPACING: SINGLE
DRILLS: THREE EACH
GOAL: LEARN MORE
LETTER DESIGNS
STRESS: SKILL WITH
AGGRESSIVENESS

109-A. Tune up on these review lines

109-A. Recall skill by taking two ½-minute timings on each line. Repeat in Lesson 108.

1   They may end the big fight by the lake by the usual signal.

2   Jack quietly moved up front and seized the big ball of wax.

3   On April 10, 1928, their firm moved to 3947 East 56 Street.

    1 | 2 | 3 | 4 | 5 | 6 | 7 | 8 | 9 | 10 | 11 | 12

109-B. Build skill via developmental sustained typing

109-B. Steps to take:

1. Scan the copy; solve the revision markings.*

2. Select a hard word in each line; practice it.

3. Take a 5-minute timed writing, pausing for a few-seconds rest at the end of each minute. Or, type one copy, pausing to rest when you finish typing each paragraph.

4. Take a 5-minute timed writing without a rest. Or, type a copy without pausing even one time.

SI 1.29—fairly easy, if you know revision marks.

4   If you have to answer a letter which is signed by Jean   12
Holt White, should you send your answer to Mr. Smith, or to   24
Miss Smith, or Mrs. Smith? Unless you happened to see that   36
the handwriting clearly is that of man, there is no way out   48
of your dilemma, the person who puts you in such a spot is   60
is discourteous. When writing to stranger, it is the height   72
of bad taste not to clearly show what title one should use.   84

    A married woman is expected to show her Mrs. either in   96
parenthesis as part of her penned signature or, without the   108
parenteses in the typed name line under her handwriting. A   120
lady who shows no Mrs. is, or may be assumed to be, a Miss.   132

    Should the Mr. or Miss never be typed? Yes, whenever   144
the sex of the name is mistakeable. The name Marion, as an   156
example, is as often given to a boy as to a girl; a stranger   168
could not know. The bearer of any such name, man or woman,   180
has to indicate the Mr. or Miss; and these are shown in the   192
same way which Mrs. is shown: in or under the signature, it.   204

    Such rules do not apply, of curse, to any person who is   216
a notable or to letters betwixt people who know each other.   228

    1 | 2 | 3 | 4 | 5 | 6 | 7 | 8 | 9 | 10 | 11 | 12

Manuscript 30

CENTERED DISPLAY
Paper: plain
Spacing: double
Line: 60 spaces
Heading: "The Title of Your Name"
SI: 1.29—fairly easy

109/110-C. Continue production of letters in new designs

Type Letters 48-51 on plain paper or workbook pages 193-200, then type Manuscript 30 (entitle it *The Title of Your Name*) on a plain sheet for possible inclusion at the end of your *Letter Style Book*. Note that the new styles in these letters require *very* careful attention to your consistent use of the tabulator.

* Uncertain of meanings of the revision markings? Then review, on page 112, the table that explains these markings.

UNIT 18

LINE: 60
TAB: 5
SPACING: DOUBLE
DRILLS: THREE EACH
GOAL: APPLY SKILL
   TO TYPED REPORTS
STRESS: EYES ON COPY

121-A. Each line three times, or take a half-minute writing on each. GOAL: Flawless rhythm. Repeat in Lesson 122.

121-A. Tune up on these review lines

1 He may wish to visit the rock chapel with us on the eighth.

2 Vicky placed a dozen jugs from Iraq on the waxy table tops.

3 Discounts of 10%, 28%, 39%, 47%, and 56% are quite unusual.

    1 | 2 | 3 | 4 | 5 | 6 | 7 | 8 | 9 | 10 | 11 | 12

121-B. To increase your progress, follow either of these schedules.

1. Read the copy, type a full line of each of a half dozen words that are worth prepracticing. Then, type a copy of each paragraph; GOAL: To complete either within 3 minutes and 2 errors.

2. Read the copy, type a full line of each of a half dozen words that merit prepracticing, and then take two 5-minute writings, the first with rest after each minute and the second with full fluency but no rests. GOAL: 46 or more words a minute within 3 errors.

SI 1.31—fairly easy

121-B. Boost skill on fluent alphabetic paragraphs

4   It is said that each worker supports a dozen or so who   12
live on the circulation of his money. There is the man who   24
sells him his clothing, the one who delivers his groceries,   36
the one who fixes his shoes, the boy who cuts his lawn, the   48
teacher who instructs his children, and all the many others   60
to whom his earnings are relayed. If his income stops, be-   72
cause his hands are no longer purchased for farm or forest,   84
for mine or mill, all these others feel the pinch, too; the   96
worker who leaves is a leak in the local economy. If other   108
workers leave with him, those who exist on serving them are   120
not long in following; and thus the leak may quickly become   132
a break, and the break a flood that sweeps into our cities.   144

5   Now, cities are big and they grow fast; but there is a   156
limit to how rapidly they can expand before they feel grow-   168
ing pains. All our cities are suffering adjustments today.   180
People are moving in faster than new homes can be built for   192
them; so they must crowd into smaller quarters or move to a   204
suburb. People bring their cars, too, faster than the city   216
can widen streets to bear them or make places to park them.   228
People also bring their children with them, faster than the   240
city can build schools to seat them or parks in which these   252
new city citizens may play and let off their animal energy.   264
The problems are huge, but so are the talents and resources   276
that a city can join in firm efforts to solve its problems.   288

    1 | 2 | 3 | 4 | 5 | 6 | 7 | 8 | 9 | 10 | 11 | 12

If you have wondered how many carbons you could produce at one time, or if you have wanted to type a duplicating stencil or master, Manuscript 39 would be a good one to use—it merits multicopy production!

121/122-C. Apply skill to production typing

Manuscripts 37-39 require the longest sustained effort yet; GOAL: See whether you can finish each within 12 minutes and 4 errors.

5. INDENTED STYLE . . . conservative, or European, look . . . has even, five-space indentation steps . . . shown here with closed punctuation (each heading and closing line is "closed" by some kind of punctuation mark).

6. DOUBLE-SPACED INDENTED . . . great letter-stretcher . . . permits even a brief message to look man-size . . . often used for simple acknowledgments . . . typist must remember to double body-length estimate for placement.

Letter 48

INDENTED LETTER
Paper: workbook page 193 or plain paper
Body: 106 words
Spacing: single
Punctuation: closed
Directions: arrange like Letter 5 above
SI: 1.39—normal

	Letter 48	49

LETTER 48 | *Date* | Lynch and Forbes, Inc. | 2228 South Port Street | 18 | .. |
| Detroit, Michigan   48233 | Attention of the Personnel Department | 47 / 52 | .. / .. |

    Gentlemen: You will recall that a young man on your staff came   68   38
to our school to meet and talk with several of our seniors just be-   81   51
fore their graduation last year. As a result, your firm was able to   95   65
obtain a number of fine young employees.   104   74

    Do you wish to conduct a similar schedule of interviews this   118   88
spring? If you do, please fill in and return to us by May 1 the   131   101
planning form that accompanies this letter.   140   110

    You will note that the planning form asks you to choose two alter-   155   125
nate dates; we hope that having a choice will help us reduce the   168   138
number of conflicts in appointments. | Yours very truly,   183   153

    COLLEGE OF COMMERCE | Dean of Women | SEV:URS | *Others?*   208   165

1 | 2 | 3 | 4 | 5 | 6 | 7 | 8 | 9 | 10 | 11 | 12 | 13

Letter 49

INDENTED LETTER
Paper: workbook page 195 or plain paper
Body: 106 words
Spacing: double
Punctuation: standard
Directions: arrange like Letter 6 above
SI: 1.39—normal

LETTER 49 | *Let's send a copy of that letter also to* Davis & Wilson, Inc.   ..   11
| *They're down on* South Port, *too, at* 1318, *same zone and so on.* | *I*   ..   22
should like to see how the letter would look in double *spacing, with
ordinary,* standard *punctuation. I am afraid the letter might stretch
out a great deal, so omit the attention line and our school name.*

Manuscript 35

MENU
Paper: plain
Line: 60 spaces

Center each line /B - G   C O M P A N Y   C A F E T E R I A

Menu for Thursday, March ~~1120~~ *1#* *2#*

APPETIZERS *1#*

Tomato Soup or Clam Chowder (cup) .... .15
Fresh orange or Grapefruit Juice .... .10

LUNCHEON PLATES

Salmon Salad with French Dressing, Cucumber Slices,
    Tomato quarters, and Potato Waffles .... .60
Stuffed Braised Ribs of Beef, Jumbo Pears and Carrots,
    ~~Cold Slaw~~, and Mashed Potatoes .... .75
Coleslaw

SANDWICHES *2#* *1#*

Grilled American Cheese, with tomato Slices .... .35]
Tomato, Lettuce, and Bacon (on Rolls) .... .35
[Chipped Ham Saute on Large Bun *or on. toast* .... ~~20~~ 25
Swiss Cheese and Tomato on Fresh rye Bread, ... , ~~20~~ 35

DESSERTS *2#* *1#*

Chocolate or Butterscotch Sundae on Chocolate Ice Cream . .20
Apple, Cherry, Banana Cream, ~~and~~ *or* Peach Pie .... .15
Chocolate layer *or* Angel Food Cakes .... .15

BEVERAGES *2#* *1#*

Milk (Individual Bottle) .... .12
~~Hot~~ Tea or Coffee .... .10

Manuscript 36

ITINERARY
Paper: plain
Line: 70 spaces

SCHEDULE FOR DETROIT TRIP
March 21-23, *year* *# #*

MONDAY	March 21		*4/6*
~~9:35~~ 8:00 a.m.	~~You will~~ leave Chicago on Flight AA~~214~~		Confirmed
~~10:15~~ *9:45* a.m.	~~You~~ arrive Detroit, ~~are~~ met by Mr. Graham		Assumed
11:00 a.m. *4#*	Register ~~for room~~ at Book-Cadillac *Hotel*		Confirmed
11:45 a.m. ←	Luncheon with Mr. Montrose, ~~of~~ Ford Motors		Confirmed
3:00 p.m.	Appointment with Mr. Young, Fordyce+Valve		Tentative
6:00 p.m.	Dinner at ~~the~~ hotel with ~~Doctor~~ *Dr.* Sampson		Confirmed

TUESDAY	March 22 *+ #*		
9:00 a.m.	Appointment with Mr. Stahl, Oldsmobile, ~~GM~~		Promised
10:15 a.m.	Appointment with ~~Fred~~ *Mr.* Reed, ~~of~~ Pontiac, ~~GM~~		Tentative *confirmed*
~~11:45 a.m.~~ 12:00 noon	Luncheon with Mrs. Flower, of Ford-Mercury		~~Tentative~~
]3:00 p.m.	Appointment with Mr. Milton, Fisher Body		Unconfirmed
7:00 p.m.	Dinner ~~for and~~ with Dr. and Mrs. Pfeiffer		Tentative

Wednesday	March 23 *+ #*		
8:50 a.m.	Leave Detroit on AA 57 for Chicago		Confirmed
9:45 a.m.	Arrive O'Hare, return to office		Confirmed

LESSON 120

184

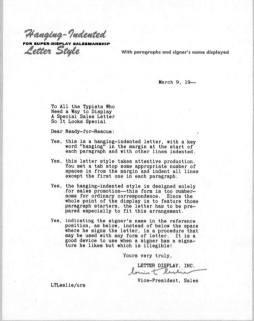

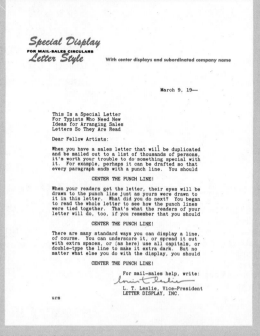

7. HANGING-INDENTED . . . for razzle-dazzle sales letters with catch-words "hanging" in left margin . . . all body lines are indented except the first in each paragraph . . . shown here with signer's name in reference position.

8. DISPLAY BLOCKED . . . another mail-sales design . . . hinges on use of paragraph-ending "punch lines" . . . shown here with company name under signer's title . . . Note here and in No. 7 the bizarre "inside address" form.

Here's a sales letter I've written to mail to all the seniors of the local colleges. Would it look better in hanging-indented form or in center-display form? I don't know; draft it both ways, please. And, to make reading easy, use a short line—say, a 50-space line. Better experiment a bit, first!

	Letter 50	51
Date	To Every Young Person	Who Wants to Become	A Business Executive	Dear Ambitious Friend:	18 / 26	18 / 26
If you could serve as apprentice to anyone whom you might pick, whom would you pick? The errand boy? Of course not! You would select some top businessman, one who could show you what an executive is. If you want to pick a man like that, you must do something about it!	41 / 55 / 69 / 84 / 87	39 / 52 / 64 / 83 / 92
If you want to work with an executive, you must be able to do something that will make him want you as his apprentice. Do you possess fine secretarial skills? Are you an accounting expert? If you have knowledge or skills to sell, you can do something about it!	102 / 116 / 131 / 146	105 / 118 / 132 / 157
If you want to do something about it, see us. Our business is helping top executives find the assistants they need. It does not cost you anything—the men pay us to find you. Now's the time to do something about it!	For example, visit:	WHITE COLLARS, INC.	Richard F. Benkley	District Manager	*reference symbols?*	161 / 175 / 190 / 210 / 226	170 / 184 / 197 / 225 / 233

1 | 2 | 3 | 4 | 5 | 6 | 7 | 8 | 9 | 10 | 11 | 12 | 13

119/120-D. Apply your skill to production typing

After typing Manuscript 32, page 182, as a quick recall of basic centering, type Manuscripts 33-36, following closely the helpful directions. You will need to look up often; CAUTION: *be careful not to omit any lines!* Your GOAL: To finish each manuscript within 10 minutes and 3 errors.

Manuscript 33

DISPLAY PROGRAM
Paper: plain, full
Spacing: double, extra
  line between "days"
Line: 51 spaces
Tab: center, 52
Caution: pivot lines
  with speakers' names

C O N F E R E N C E   P R O G R A M   *←1#*

Always put 3 spaces between spread-out words. Review page 70.

March 8–12, (year)   *←2#*

Monday: PUBLIC RELATIONS AND ADVERTISING
          Discussion Led by Harvey P. May   *←PIVOT*

Tuesday: INCENTIVE WAGE PROBLEMS
           Discussion led by Emil H. Bender   *Hale*

WEDNESDAY Morning: USING SALESMEN'S REPORTS   *M*
          Discussion Led by William J. Noran

Wednesday afternoon: Luncheon and Excursion

Thursday: ADMINISTERING JOB EVALUATIONS
            Discussion Led by Joseph Strong   *k.*

Friday: OUR WORK-SIMPLIFICATION PROGRAM
          Discussion Led by John Z. Duncan

Manuscript 34

DISPLAY PROGRAM
Paper: plain, full
Spacing: single
Line: 61 spaces
Tab: 10, center, 62

THE B-G FOUNDER'S DAY FESTIVAL

Center each line

Saturday, March 13
at
The Golden Bridge Club   *2#*

BANQUET .... 6:30 to 8:30   *←PIVOT*

A once-in-a-lifetime *big* charcoal-grilled   *←1#*
10# → steak dinner, complete from soup to nuts,
speaking of which reminds me *us* to mention--   *←2#*

THE SPEAKERS .... 8:30 to 9:00

Toastmaster Harold Freeman is bringing his *an*   *←1#*
alarm clock to make sure that no speakers
talk more than ⑤ minutes; we want to--   *←2#*

TRIP "THE LIGHT FANTASTIC" .... 9 10:00 to 12:30

The music is that of Dave Elliott and his   *←1#*
famous band, with vocals by Dora Deevers.

LINE: 60
SPACING: SINGLE
DRILLS: THREE EACH
GOAL: COMPLETE
  STYLE MANUAL
STRESS: COMPLETE
  TOUCH OPERATION

111-A. Recall skill by typing lines 2 and 3 in cadence with someone who types only line 1.

111-B. Readjust machine for double spacing, 50-space line, 5-space tab indention. Then follow this practice routine:

1. Scan the copy to be sure you can read it.

2. Select and practice any half-dozen words.

3. Take a 5-minute timed writing, pausing for a few-seconds rest at the end of each minute. (Or, type one copy, pausing to rest when you finish typing each paragraph.)

4. Take a 5-minute timed writing without a rest. (Or, type a copy without pausing even one time.)

SI 1.42—normal, if you can read the writing!

Manuscript 31

CENTERED DISPLAY
Paper: plain
Spacing: double
Line: 50 spaces
Heading: "Letter Placement"
SI: 1.42—normal

NOTE: 111-B will double block on a 50-space line. When you type it as Manuscript 31, copy from either the writing or your 111-B copy of it.

UNIT 18

111-A. Tune up on these review lines

1 They will find some more work when they have done your job.
2 The banquet speaker, James Carvings, analyzed a few hoaxes.
3 They have been at 3947 East 56 Street since April 10, 1928.

111-B. Sustain your skill on handwritten copy

4 Judging whether a letter is long or short or average is a problem to the novice, but it is not one to the experienced office typist. Except for a few very short or very long letters, the expert treats all letters as average ones, trusting that he will be able to stretch or squeeze the closing lines enough to balance the letter placement. In most cases he can do so, too, simply by adjusting the signature space from the standard three lines of open space to as few as two or as many as six.

5 The notations at the end of the letter are a point of easy expanding and squeezing. These may begin as high as level with the identification of the signer or may begin two or three lines below; and these lines may be single spaced, to conserve space, or be double spaced, to spread the letter. The enclosure notation is very useful in juggling letter length, for the items to be enclosed might or might not be listed, depending on space needs. Almost any letter other than one that's very long or very short can be treated as "average" length.

111/112-C. Continue production of letters in new designs

Type Letters 52-53 on plain paper or workbook pages 201 and 203, then type Manuscript 31 (entitle it *Letter Placement*) by centering it on a full page. Then assemble your complete *Letter Style Book*.

Unit 20. Manuscripts

LINE: 50
TAB: 5
SPACING: DOUBLE
DRILLS: THREE EACH
GOAL: APPLY PIVOTING
   TO MANUSCRIPT
   WORK
STRESS: POSTURE

119-A. Each line three
times, or take a half-
minute writing on it.
GOAL: No hesitations.

119-A. Tune up on these review lines

1 Why did you not get the new job you said you got?
2 Quickly pack the box with five dozen modern jugs.
3 Price these items at 10¢, 28¢, 39¢, 47¢, and 56¢.

   1 | 2 | 3 | 4 | 5 | 6 | 7 | 8 | 9 | 10

119-B. Boost skill on fluent alphabetic paragraphs

119-B. A complete copy
within 5 minutes and 3
errors, plus a retyping
three times of any line
you type with an error.

Or, take two 5-minute
writings; the first with
a rest at the end of
each minute, the second
with no rests at all.
GOAL: 45 or more words
a minute within 3 or
fewer typing mistakes.

SI 1.32—fairly easy

4   The person who wants to get ahead on the job   10
has to learn how to use common sense. It is fine   20
to know and to be able to quote the rules, but it   30
is better to know when the exact rule ought to be   40
set aside. You have to analyze the situation. A   50
report can be set up in manuscript style, for ex-   60
ample; but if you have to duplicate it, you might   70
be smarter to use single spacing so that you will   80
get the report on fewer stencil or master sheets.   90

5   On the other hand, the saving of paper might   100
not be as important as making a better impression   110
on the executives to whom you will send copies of   120
the report; you must use your judgment. You must   130
choose between the quick shortcuts and the longer   140
methods that give a more attractive product. You   150
must realize that there is a right time for each.   160

6   Good judgment in such matters might not come   170
until you have risked a few mistakes. You should   180
repeat some of your jobs, when time permits, try-   190
ing to arrange them in a different way, or trying   200
to fit them on a smaller size of paper, or taking   210
other liberties with the exact directions. True,   220
you must be quick to do what you are told to do——   230
but you must nurture your judgment skill as well.   240

   1 | 2 | 3 | 4 | 5 | 6 | 7 | 8 | 9 | 10

119-C. Review the technique of backspace pivoting

Manuscript 32

BASIC DISPLAY
Paper: plain
Spacing: double
Placement: center
Title: "Rules Versus
  Judgment"
SI: 1.32—fairly easy

Review pivoting, page
56; then, type the two
exercises shown here:
center the title, then
align the other lines
with the start and end
of the centered title.
Note leaders. Each row
of periods has a space
before and after it,
and all rows end at an
identical point.

PRACTICE 1

THE HIGHWAY CAVALIER

Chapter	Page
I	1
II	37
III	89
IV	166

PRACTICE 2

THE MYSTERY OF THE GLOVE

Chapter	Page
I. We Buy It	1
II. We Lose It	59
III. It Shows Up	138
IV. It Is Taken	203

March 10, 19—
REGISTERED

Mr. Philippe Vargos, Gerente
El Aguila, S. A.
1242 Avenida Insurgentes
Mexico D. F.
MEXICO

Dear Mr. Vargos:

It is current practice in American business letters
to display price quotations and similar special data
in a special paragraph, like this:

    The paragraph is indented five spaces on
    both sides and is preceded and followed
    by one ordinary blank linespace.

    If it is necessary to use more paragraphs
    for the quotation, then a standard single
    blank line is left between paragraphs.

We indicate the mail service (a double space below
the date) only if we are sending the correspondence
by some special service, such as "special delivery"
or "registered"; and we do so only to get the fact
indicated on our file copy of the correspondence.

Yours very sincerely,
Nora Suez Carlton
Assistant Director
Bureau of Information
and Public Relations

DIC/urs

P. S. We treat postscripts in the same way that we
treat other paragraphs, except that we precede each
postscript by "PS:" or "PS—" or "P. S."

10 March 19—

Mrs. Elizabeth Carr, Chairman
Committee on Standardization
The Hotel Winston-Salem
Winston-Salem, N. C.   27101

Dear Mrs. Carr:

There is no doubt that the blocked letter style is
the one most commonly used in business today. But
there is no reason why any company could not modify
the basic blocked design to incorporate some special
point of letter distinction. For example:

1. You might adopt the "military date" shown above,
   with the day preceding the name of the month.

2. You might devise a special arrangement for the
   closing lines, perhaps like the display below.

3. You might establish a policy that enclosures
   should always, or usually, be enumerated.

With a little ingenuity, you should easily be able
to develop a letter arrangement that would give you
the look of a standard business letter, along with
the efficiency of the blocked arrangement and some
special touch of unique individuality.

Cordially yours,

CORRESPONDENCE COUNSELORS
Harry L. Silverman
Regional Director

HIS/urs
Enclosures:
1. Booklet
2. Reply Card

9. BLOCKED LETTER . . . shown here with mail-service reminder under date . . . foreign address, country name on separate, all-capped line . . . set-off paragraphs . . . long signer's identification . . . and a postscript.

10. BLOCKED LETTER . . . most nearly "standard" form but often individualized by, as here: inverting date into armed-services style . . . centering closing lines on one another . . . listing enclosures in an enumeration.

Letter 52

BLOCKED LETTER
Paper: workbook page
   201 or plain paper
Body: 182 (with P.S.)
Line: 60 spaces
Directions: arrange
   like Letter 9 above
SI: 1.48—high-normal

Letter 53

BLOCKED LETTER
Paper: workbook page
   203 or plain paper
Body: 160 words
Line: 60 spaces
Directions: arrange
   like Letter 10 above
SI: 1.43—normal

	Letter 52	53
Date | OVERSEAS AIRMAIL | Dr. and Mrs. Foster T. West | Arabian	18	..
American Oil Company | Abu Hadriya Refinery | SAUDI ARABIA	29	..
We have found the Boston home you wanted. I am enclosing six	48	56
photographs and a floor plan. Here are the main details:	60	69
The house has ten rooms—four bedrooms (and three baths)	74	83
upstairs, four rooms (and powder room) on the first floor, and	88	96
a utility room and a playroom (and lavatory) in the basement—	101	100
and a double garage.	106	114
The house is five years old and in very good condition. It	120	127
has thermostat controls both for heating (oil) and for air-conditioning, although the latter has never been installed. The	132	141
conditioning, although the latter has never been installed. The	146	151
house will need to be painted (about $1,500).	157	165
The asking price is $45,000, but I believe we could get the	172	179
home for about $42,500. It has a mortgage; the purchase could	185	186
be financed with 20 percent down.	192	199
This home seems to come close to the description you gave in defining what you wished. Other realtors are looking at it, too; so	206	213
fining what you wished. Other realtors are looking at it, too; so	219	229
we should move swiftly if you wish to purchase it. | What is your	235	244
pleasure? | David D. Davis Agent | urs | Enclosures | P. S.	250	249
Since you may be en route to the United States, I am writing to you	264	..
also at your Maryland address.	270	..
LETTER 53 | *Address Dr. and Mrs. West* | at 3211 West Drummond	..	17
Drive, | Silver Spring, Maryland 20907. | *Delete the postscript.* |	..	25
Enumerate the enclosures. | *Number the three display paragraphs.*	..	44

VOUCHER CHECK

JUNIPER SALES SPECIALTY COMPANY
3399 MADISON AVENUE

NEW ORLEANS, LOUISIANA ___ March 19, 19 ___ No. 2118

1-785
266

PAY
TO THE
ORDER OF William Zaner _____ $ 318.50

Three hundred eighteen and 50/100 ─────────── DOLLARS

JUNIPER SALES SPECIALTY COMPANY

WARRANTY NATIONAL TRUST COMPANY
NEW ORLEANS. LOUISIANA

_____
AUTHORIZED SIGNATURE

DETACH AND RETAIN THIS STATEMENT

THE ATTACHED CHECK IS IN PAYMENT OF ITEMS DESCRIBED BELOW
IF NOT CORRECT PLEASE NOTIFY US PROMPTLY. NO RECEIPT DESIRED

Payment of expenses on trip to New Orleans, March 1-7, 19--

Mr. William Zaner
411 Packer Street
Green Bay, Wisconsin   54301

VOUCHER CHECK is regular check with detachable
stub (on any side) for address and explanation.

PROMISSORY NOTE

$ 625.85 _____ March 19, 19 --

Thirty days ─ ─ ─ ─ ─ ─ ─ ─ ─ ─ ─ ─ after date we promise to pay to

the order of Juniper Sales Specialty Company ─ ─ ─ ─ ─ ─ ─ ─

Six hundred twenty-five and 85/100 ─ ─ ─ ─ ─ ─ ─ ─ ─ ─ Dollars

at Louisiana National Bank, New Orleans, Louisiana ─ ─ ─ ─ ─ ─

Value received   ROGERS WHOLESALE COMPANY

No. 183 Due April 18, 19--

PROMISSORY NOTE . . . rules in underline position . . .
leaders (hyphens and spaces) fill in alterable spaces.

FILL-IN CARD

THE CENTURY INSURANCE COMPANY   *Buffalo, New York*

March 19, 19--

Dear Mr. Quinette:

We have received your request for a copy of:

"How Much Insurance Should I Have?"

We are sending it today, with our compliments. We hope that it will
prove to be of interest and value and that we may have the pleasure of
serving you again.

SERVICE MANAGER

urs

FILL-IN CARD has insertions that are
aligned vertically and horizontally.

LABELS

THE CENTURY INSURANCE COMPANY
255 Broadway • Buffalo, New York   14205

Mr. Charles L. Quinette
2839 Fairfield Avenue
Fort Wayne, Indiana   46802

THE CENTURY INSURANCE COMPANY
255 Broadway • Buffalo, New York   14205

Mrs. Katherine Newman
Apartment 12-K
475 Halledon Avenue
Corpus Christi, Texas   78401

LABELS . . . block the addresses, use
single spacing for more than 3 lines.

Forms 44-45

PROMISSORY NOTES
Forms: workbook 233

FORM 44. *Promissory Note No. 183:* The Rodgers Wholesale Company promises to pay $625.85 to the order of the Juniper Sales Specialty Company, at the Louisiana National Bank, New Orleans, 30 days from today.

FORM 45. *Promissory Note No. 184:* The Ford-Bart Corporation promises to pay $900.00 to the order of the Juniper Sales Specialty Company, at the Union National Bank, Bakersfield, California, 60 days from today.

Forms 46-47
Cards 7-8

ACKNOWLEDGMENT
CARDS
Forms: workbook 221

FORM 46 / CARD 7. Acknowledge a request for "How Much Insurance Should I Have?" from Mr. Charles L. Quinette, 2839 Fairfield Avenue, Fort Wayne, Indiana   46802.

FORM 47 / CARD 8. Acknowledge a request for "A College Education for Your Child!" from Mrs. Katherine Newman, Apartment 12-K, 475 Halledon Avenue, Corpus Christi, Texas   78401.

Form 48

SHIPMENT LABELS
Forms: workbook 233

LABEL NO. 1. To Mr. Quinette, address above.

LABEL NO. 2. To Mrs. Newman, address above.

LABEL NO. 3. To Dr. Edward Svensen, Central City Hospital, 3618 North Ridgewood Avenue, Worcester, Massachusetts   01601.

LABEL NO. 4. To Sr. [Senhor] Almyr Guimaraes, Caixa Postal 2360, Rio de Janeiro, BRAZIL.

Unit 19. Printed Forms

LINE: 60
TAB: 5
SPACING: SINGLE
DRILLS: THREE EACH
GOAL: INTELLIGENT
WORK ON FORMS
STRESS: NUMBERS
ONLY BY TOUCH

113-A. Each line three times, holding on lines 2 and 3 the high pace you set on easy line 1. Repeat in Lesson 114.

113-A. Tune up on these review lines

1 I am to go to work for the audit firm by the eighth of May.

2 Beckwith just managed to verify his extremely popular quiz.

3 Pages 10, 28, 39, 47, and 56 were most interesting to them.

   1 | 2 | 3 | 4 | 5 | 6 | 7 | 8 | 9 | 10 | 11 | 12

113-B. Each line three times, for speed gain; or the whole group of lines three times, for gain in accuracy, too. Type steadily; do not pause at vertical bars.

113-B. Regain fluency on these easy phrases

4 who will|firm that|each part|they use|all the|but it|is the

5 the form|that most|have once|that you|who use|one of|if you

6 and then|that save|time will|form for|day and|set up|to use

   1 | 2 | 3 | 4 | 5 | 6 | 7 | 8 | 9 | 10 | 11 | 12

113-C. Type a complete copy in Lesson 113 and another in Lesson 114; GOAL: Finish the copy within 6 minutes, with 3 or fewer errors.

Or, take one 5-minute writing in Lesson 113, with a 10-second rest after each minute; and one 5-minute writing in Lesson 114 without pausing for any rest. GOAL: 45 or more words a minute within 3 or fewer typing errors.

Use double spacing and 5-space tab indention.

SI 1.29—fairly easy

113-C. Hold stride on fairly easy alphabetic paragraphs

7   One of the most thriving kinds of business in this day   12
and age is the business of designing business forms. True,   24
almost all stationers have standard forms on their shelves;   36
but it is true, too, that most big firms bring in an expert   48
who will analyze all the forms they use and then design new   60
ones that are easier to use and that save time for the per-   72
sons who use them. You would not suppose a firm that sells   84
jars of medicine would use the same billhead as a firm that   96
sells steel axles. In the same sense, the requisition form   108
for office supplies would not serve the needs of a factory.   120

8   Each form is organized on principles that good typists   132
should know. Here are some examples: All forms should use   144
standard typewriter spacing; you should never have to shift   156
a tab stop, squeeze a number, or adjust the variable spacer   168
after you have once set up the machine. A form should have   180
guide words or signals to show what should be typed in each   192
part of the form; you should not have to guess. Every form   204
must resemble a letter; that is, you should be able to type   216
the entries on the form in almost exactly the same sequence   228
that you would if you were typing them in a regular letter.   240

   1 | 2 | 3 | 4 | 5 | 6 | 7 | 8 | 9 | 10 | 11 | 12

If you lack workbook forms, type Lesson 113-114 assignments either in typed memo form (see page 108) or as blocked business letters, with all the data given in proper, complete sentence form.

113/114-D. Apply production skill to billing forms

Study the six illustrations that follow; then, type Forms 20-31 on workbook pages 207-218. Although these tasks are varied, they are so easy you should type them without error easily in five minutes each.

LINE: 60
TAB: 5
SPACING: SINGLE
DRILLS: THREE EACH
GOAL: CONFIDENT
    FORM PRODUCTION
STRESS: GO-POWER

117-A. Recall skill by half-minute writings on each line. Repeat these drills in Lesson 118.

117-A. Tune up on these review lines

1   Their men wish to blame me for both of their big work jams.
2   Rex amazed Jack by pointing quickly to five of the answers.
3   The data on pages 10, 28, and 39 are repeated on 47 and 56.
    1 | 2 | 3 | 4 | 5 | 6 | 7 | 8 | 9 | 10 | 11 | 12

117-B. Each three times (consecutively, for a speed gain; alternately, for an accuracy gain).

117-B. Sharpen your control of capitals

4   Wisconsin Terrific Packer Street Sales Zaner Green Dear Bay
5   Enclosure Manager William Alfred Stahl Sales Yours Bill But

117-C. Adjust machine for double spacing and copy line for line.

1. Scan the copy.

2. Make an exact copy in each lesson, trying to complete it within 5 minutes and 3 errors. Or, take a 5-minute writing twice—once with a rest after each minute and, then, once without any such rests. GOAL: Maximum speed within 3-error limit.

SI 1.32—fairly easy

117-C. Increase your skill on production copy

		(C)	(D)

6   Good morning. Please take this letter to William   11   10
Zaner, at 411 West Packer Street, Green Bay, Wisconsin   22   21
54301. Dear Bill: 26   25

     When we have an account to square up, all we need   37   36
to do is issue a voucher check; we do not even need to   48   47
write a letter, because the stub on the check explains   59   59
quite clearly what payment we are making. I have been   70   70
told, indeed, that the reason we use such checks is to   81   81
eliminate the need for having a letter of explanation.   92   92

     But when a speaker has come the distance that you   103 103
did and has performed the service that you did for our   114 114
sales staff, he deserves a letter, too, that tells him   125 125
that he was terrific; so this is why I am writing you.   136 136

     Bill, you were terrific. <u>Terrific!</u>   148 148

     The check for your expenses is enclosed, complete   159 159
with a voucher that reminds you what the check is for;   170 170
the stub does not say you were terrific, but you were.   181 181

     Yours very sincerely, and the usual Alfred Stahl,   192 195
Sales Manager; and be certain that you <u>do</u> make out and   204 197
enclose the voucher check. If you forgot it after all   215 200
I have said about it, he would never let <u>me</u> forget it!   227 ...
    1 | 2 | 3 | 4 | 5 | 6 | 7 | 8 | 9 | 10 | 11

Letter 54

FULL-BLOCKED LETTER
Review: page 166
Paper: workbook 229
Punctuation: open
Body: 141 words
SI: 1.34—near-normal

117/118-D. Apply your skill to production typing

     FORM 42. *Voucher Check No. 2118.* Pay $318.50 to Mr. Zaner for "Payment of expenses on trip to New Orleans, March 1-7, 19—."
     FORM 43. *Voucher Check No. 2119.* Pay $150.00 to yourself for "Payment for services as technical advisor, March 6, 19—."

Forms 42-43

VOUCHER CHECKS
Forms: workbook 231
Illustration: page 181

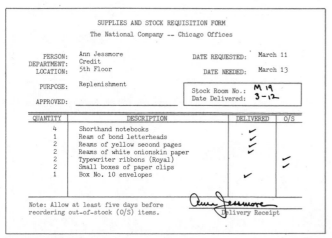

SUPPLIES AND STOCK REQUISITION FORM

The National Company -- Chicago Offices

PERSON: Ann Jessmore   DATE REQUESTED: March 11
DEPARTMENT: Credit
LOCATION: 5th Floor   DATE NEEDED: March 13

PURPOSE: Replenishment

APPROVED: _____   Stock Room No.: M 19
     Date Delivered: 3-12

QUANTITY	DESCRIPTION	DELIVERED	O/S
4	Shorthand notebooks		
1	Ream of bond letterheads	✓	
2	Reams of yellow second pages	✓	
2	Reams of white onionskin paper	✓	
2	Typewriter ribbons (Royal)		✓
2	Small boxes of paper clips		
1	Box No. 10 envelopes	✓	

Note: Allow at least five days before
reordering out-of-stock (O/S) items.

Ann Jessmore
Delivery Receipt

Purchase Requisition No. 2516

The National Company • 6 North Michigan Ave. • Chicago, Illinois 60607

DEPARTMENT: Sales Promotion   DATE OF REQUEST: 3/11/--
LOCATION: Room 416   DATE WANTED: 4/1/--
PERSON: T. M. Winters

REASON: Office furnishings for new employee

APPROVALS: *TMW*   *Ellwood Perkins*
     Signature of Department Head   Other Signature Required

QUANTITY	DESCRIPTION	SUGGESTED PURCHASE SOURCE
2	Steel file cabinets, 4-drawer, 13 inches, gray	MM&Sons 58 Broad Street Atlanta 30303
1	Steel desk, executive, gray	
1	Steel desk chair, executive, gray	
2	Steel chairs, guest, arm, gray	

PURCHASING DEPARTMENT INFORMATION

Ordered from: Martin Miller & Sons   Purchase Order Number: 6377
     58 Broad Street   Date Ordered: 3/12/19--
     Atlanta, Georgia 30303   Date Received: 3/28/19--

STOCK REQUISITION is used to draw everyday supplies from a storeroom. Forms vary (depending on company inventory control) and may be either printed or (above) duplicated.

PURCHASE REQUISITION is used to ask Purchasing Department to buy something, such as replacement of warehouse stock (above), furniture, and so on. Forms are usually printed.

Forms 20-21

STOCK REQUISITIONS
Forms: workbook 207
Directions: arrange
as shown above, left

FORM 20. Ann Jessmore, a Credit Department secretary, 5th Floor, needs these desk replenishments by next Friday: . . . 4 shorthand notebooks . . . 1 ream of bond letterheads . . . 2 reams of yellow second pages . . . 2 reams of white onionskin paper . . . 2 typewriter ribbons (Royal) . . . 2 small boxes of paper clips . . . 1 box No. 10 envelopes.   11 / 32 / 47 / 61 / 73

FORM 21. John Deer, Shipping Department, 1st Floor, needs (by Monday of next week) routine replenishment of: . . . 6 rolls No. 14 twine . . . 5,000 shipping tags (5 x 3, oaktag) . . . 300 No. 7 cardboard cartons . . . 200 No. 11 cardboard cartons . . . 5 rolls No. 17H (heavy duty) stapler wire . . . 10 rolls 3-inch paper binding tape.   19 / 32 / 47 / 61 / 73

Forms 22-23

PURCHASE
REQUISITIONS
Forms: workbook 209
Directions: arrange
as shown above, right

FORM 22. Mr. T. M. Winters, head of Sales Promotion, Room 416, wants office furnishings for a new employee, due the first of next month: . . . 2 steel file cabinets, 4 drawer, 13-inch width, in gray . . . a steel desk, executive type, in gray . . . a steel desk chair, executive type, in gray . . . and two steel guest chairs, with armrests on them, in gray.   15 / 25 / 43 / 55 / 63

Mr. Winter suggests that these be purchased from Martin Miller & Sons, at 58 Broad Street, Atlanta, Georgia 30303.   66 / 77

FORM 23. Mr. Aloysius Vincent, Stores-Supplies Department, 18th Street Annex, needs to replenish his paper stocks by the first of next month: . . . 500 reams NatCo letterheads, 8½ by 11 . . . 100 reams NatCo letterheads, 8 by 10½ . . . 300 boxes NatCo No. 10 envelopes (500 per box), third class (open-end flap) . . . 300 boxes NatCo No. 10 envelopes (500 per box), first class (standard flap) . . . 100 boxes NatCo No. 6¾ envelopes (500 per box), first class (standard flap).   12 / 24 / 42 / 57 / 72 / 88 / 102

Mr. Vincent mentions that these items are all available under Contract 61-332 with Walsh & Weir, Printers, of Cleveland.   104 / 114

An earnings record is kept for each employee. It must match corresponding payroll registers and is brought up to date at end of each payroll period.

EARNINGS RECORD OF _____ Benjamin F. CROSLEY
                                                    NAME

ADDRESS 1340 North Pike Street   SOCIAL SECURITY NO. 144-60-3928

_____ Ortonville, Minnesota _____   MARRIED ___X___   SINGLE _____

TELEPHONE 131-2208   NO. INCOME TAX EXEMPTIONS ___3___

DATE PERIOD ENDED	AMOUNT EARNED	I.T.W.	F.I.C.A.	GROUP INS.	MISC.	NET PAY
1/14	246 20	30 30	9 85	2 46	18 75	184 84
1/28	246 20	30 30	9 85	2 46		203 59
2-11	246 20	30 30	9 85	2 46	18 75	184 84
2-25	246 20	30 30	9 85	2 46		203 59
3-11	246 20	30 30	9 85	2 46	18 75	184 84
3-25	246 20	30 30	9 85	2 46		203 59

Forms 37-38

EARNINGS RECORDS
Forms: workbook 225
Copy 1: Mr. Crosley
Copy 2: Mr. Danderson

FORM 38. For the same six payroll periods as in Form 37, prepare the earnings record of Frederick L. Danderson, who lives at 908 North Elm Street in Ortonville. His phone is 131-7736. His Social Security number is 273-38-4707. He is married and has 4 income tax dependents. He has no miscellaneous deductions. Each line of his record will, therefore, read the same: Date ... Amount Earned, $218.40 ... Income Tax Withheld, $18.90 ... F.I.C.A., $2.31 ... Group Insurance, $1.14 ... Net Pay: $196.05.

W-2 Income Tax form is summary of employee's earnings record and tax withholdings for the previous calendar year. Fifth column is used if a state income tax has been withheld. Form is prepared with enough carbons to serve firm, agencies, and employee.

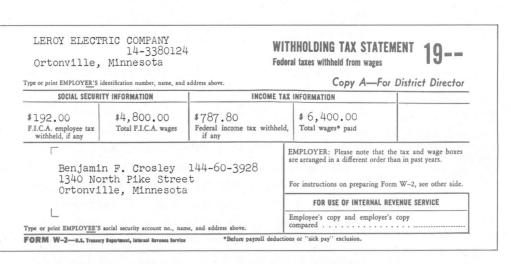

LEROY ELECTRIC COMPANY
                14-3380124
Ortonville, Minnesota

WITHHOLDING TAX STATEMENT 19--
Federal taxes withheld from wages

Type or print EMPLOYER'S identification number, name, and address above.

Copy A—For District Director

SOCIAL SECURITY INFORMATION		INCOME TAX INFORMATION	
$192.00	$4,800.00	$787.80	$6,400.00
F.I.C.A. employee tax withheld, if any	Total F.I.C.A. wages	Federal income tax withheld, if any	Total wages* paid

Benjamin F. Crosley   144-60-3928
1340 North Pike Street
Ortonville, Minnesota

EMPLOYER: Please note that the tax and wage boxes are arranged in a different order than in past years.

For instructions on preparing Form W-2, see other side.

FOR USE OF INTERNAL REVENUE SERVICE

Employee's copy and employer's copy compared ....

Type or print EMPLOYEE'S social security account no., name, and address above.

FORM W-2—U.S. Treasury Department, Internal Revenue Service   *Before payroll deductions or "sick pay" exclusion.

Forms 39-41

W-2 INCOME TAX FORMS
Forms: workbook 227
Copy 1: Mr. Crosley
Copy 2: Mr. Danderson
Copy 3: Mr. Parkleigh

FORM 40. Prepare the W-2 form for Mr. Danderson (Form 38). His figures should read: $4,800.00 ... $120.00 ... $5,680.00 ... $491.40.

FORM 41. Prepare the W-2 form for a fellow employee of Mr. Danderson's, Stephen L. Parkleigh, whose Social Security number is 088-36-4414. He lives at 1392 South Oak Street, in Ortonville. His figures: $4,800.00 ... $120.00 ... $6,000.00 ... $522.50.

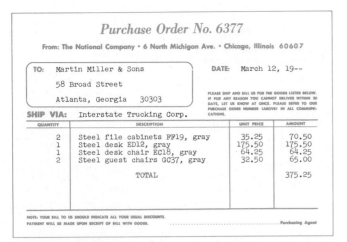

<table>
<tr><td colspan="3">Purchase Order No. 6377</td></tr>
</table>

Purchase Order No. 6377

From: The National Company • 6 North Michigan Ave. • Chicago, Illinois 60607

TO: Martin Miller & Sons

58 Broad Street

Atlanta, Georgia   30303

DATE: March 12, 19--

PLEASE SHIP AND BILL US FOR THE GOODS LISTED BELOW. IF FOR ANY REASON YOU CANNOT DELIVER WITHIN 30 DAYS, LET US KNOW AT ONCE. PLEASE REFER TO OUR PURCHASE ORDER NUMBER (ABOVE) IN ALL COMMUNICATIONS.

SHIP VIA: Interstate Trucking Corp.

QUANTITY	DESCRIPTION	UNIT PRICE	AMOUNT
2	Steel file cabinets FF19, gray	35.25	70.50
1	Steel desk ED12, gray	175.50	175.50
1	Steel desk chair EC18, gray	64.25	64.25
2	Steel guest chairs GC37, gray	32.50	65.00
	TOTAL		375.25

NOTE: YOUR BILL TO US SHOULD INDICATE ALL YOUR USUAL DISCOUNTS.
PAYMENT WILL BE MADE UPON RECEIPT OF BILL WITH GOODS. .... Purchasing Agent

MARTIN MILLER & SONS
58 BROAD STREET   ATLANTA, GEORGIA 30303

INVOICE

CUSTOMER'S ORDER NO.   6377   DATE   March 26, 19--   3122

SOLD TO   SHIP TO

The National Company   Same
6 North Michigan Avenue
Chicago, Illinois   60607

SHIPPED VIA   Collect Interstate Trucking Corp.

QUANTITY	DESCRIPTION	CAT. NO.	UNIT PRICE	TOTAL
2	Steel file cabinets	FF19	35 25	70 50
1	Steel desk	ED12	175 50	175 50
1	Steel desk chair	EC18	64 25	64 25
3	Steel guest chairs	GC37	32 50	97 50
	TOTAL			407 75
	LESS 10% TRADE DISCOUNT			40 77
	TOTAL AMOUNT DUE			366 98

PURCHASE ORDER is an official order form from a Purchasing Department to any outside supplier of goods or services. It may be any size from half page (above) to many pages.

INVOICE is a form, different in different businesses, for listing the charges for one delivery of services or goods. Omission of decimals (above) is emerging trend.

Forms 24-25

PURCHASE ORDERS
Forms: workbook 211
Directions: arrange
   as shown above, left

FORM 24. Martin Miller & Sons [58 Broad Street, Atlanta, Georgia 30303], please ship via Interstate Trucking Corp. the following: . . . . . . two steel file cabinets FF19, gray @ $35.25 . . . a steel desk ED12, gray @ 175.50 . . . a steel desk chair EC18, gray @ 64.25 . . . two steel guest chairs GC37, gray @ 32.50. Please double-check the total.   16 24 41 61 78

FORM 25. Walsh & Weir, Printers [1200 Broad Street, Cleveland, Ohio 44101], please ship via C&C Express, Inc., the following items, priced by our Contract 61-332: . . . 500 reams NatCo letterheads, 8½ by 11 @ $2.75 . . . 100 reams NatCo letterheads, 8 by 10½ @ 2.63 . . . 300 boxes NatCo No. 10 envelopes (500 per box), third class (open-end flap) @ 3.15 . . . 300 boxes NatCo No. 10 envelopes (500 per box), first class (standard flap) @ 3.50 . . . 100 boxes NatCo No. 6¾ envelopes (500 per box), first class (standard flap) @ 2.75. Confirm the total.   17 31 41 62 76 95 112 133

Forms 26-27

STANDARD INVOICES
Forms: workbook 213
Directions: arrange
   as shown above, right

FORM 26. Invoice No. 3122 from Martin Miller & Sons to The National Company [6 North Michigan Avenue, Chicago, Illinois   60607] for a shipment, collect via Interstate Trucking Corp., for: . . . two steel file cabinets, catalog FF19 @ $35.25, for $70.50 . . . one steel desk, catalog ED12 @ 175.50, for 175.50 . . . one steel desk chair, catalog EC18 @ 64.25, for 64.25 . . . and 3 steel guest chairs, catalog GC37 @ 32.50, for 97.50. Total bill, 407.75, less 10% trade discount 40.77, for the total amount due: $366.98. Confirm the total.   12 25 39 51 65 79 100 109

FORM 27. Invoice No. M-321 from Walsh & Weir, Printers, to The National Company [6 North Michigan Avenue, Chicago, Illinois   60607] for a collect shipment via C&C Express, Inc.: [Compute extensions] 500 reams NatCo letterheads, 8½ by 11 @ $2.75 . . . 100 reams NatCo letterheads, 8 by 10½ @ 2.63 . . . 300 boxes NatCo No. 10 envelopes, third class @ 3.15 . . . 300 boxes NatCo No. 10 envelopes, first class @ 3.50 . . . 100 Boxes NatCo No. 6¾ envelopes, first class @ 2.75. Add 3 percent sales tax.   1 21 30 50 67 84 104 130

PAYROLL REGISTER

NO.	NAME	INCOME TAX EXEMP-TION	GROSS PAY		DEDUCTIONS												NET PAY	
					I.T.W.		F.I.C.A.		GROUP INSURANCE		MISC.		TOTAL					
1	Bobbitt, Robert C.	4	131	50	4	90	5	46		80			11	16			120	34
2	Devine, William F.	2	165	00	20	60	4	12	1	80			26	52			138	48
3	Harrison, Joanne C.	1	103	40	13	90	2	58		50			16	98			86	42
4	Johnson, Charles K.	3	151	30	13	20	3	78	2	18			19	16			132	14
5	Masters, Helene L.	1	124	55	18	10	4	98		83	1	94	25	85			98	70
6	Norton, V. Russell	1	142	50	20	90	5	70	1	50			28	10			114	40
7	Romanoff, Jerome	2	110	70	10	70	4	43		57	1	94	17	64			93	06
8	Thomas, Robert G.	1	148	60	22	40	5	94	1	50	1	94	31	78			116	82
9																		

Form 34

PAYROLL REGISTER
Form: workbook 221

In some companies the permanent payroll register is a typed copy of a draft that is first made in handwriting from employees' timecards and related records.

1. When typing *between* a series of horizontal lines, center (approximately, by estimate) the typing vertically between the pairs of lines.

2. When typing amounts in a column with a vertical line to separate dollars from cents, adjust the paper so the decimal (which is *not* typed) would, if typed, fall exactly on the separation line.

[Most forms are designed for elite spacing; on a pica machine you will need to adjust the carriage, retarding it by hand, in order to insert some cents figures correctly in the space assigned them.]

3. When typing *on* a single ruled line, adjust the paper so the line is in the underscore position.

4. When typing amounts after a $ sign, position the figures so close to the $ sign that no figure could be inserted between the $ and the number.

5. To fill in a line with leaders, use hyphens and spaces alternately.

Forms 35-36

VOUCHER CHECKS
Form: workbook 223
Copy 1: Check for
 Robert G. Thomas
Copy 2: Check for
 Jerome Romanoff

A payroll check is usually (as here) a "voucher check" with a stub on which may be explained the origin of the amount of the check (copied from a payroll register or a similar payroll record).

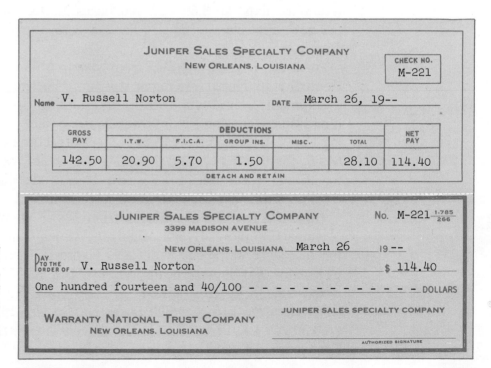

JUNIPER SALES SPECIALTY COMPANY
NEW ORLEANS. LOUISIANA

CHECK NO.
M-221

Name V. Russell Norton   DATE March 26, 19--

GROSS PAY	DEDUCTIONS					NET PAY
	I.T.W.	F.I.C.A.	GROUP INS.	MISC.	TOTAL	
142.50	20.90	5.70	1.50		28.10	114.40

DETACH AND RETAIN

JUNIPER SALES SPECIALTY COMPANY   No. M-221 $\frac{1-785}{266}$
3399 MADISON AVENUE

NEW ORLEANS. LOUISIANA   March 26   19--

PAY TO THE ORDER OF V. Russell Norton $ 114.40

One hundred fourteen and 40/100 - - - - - - - - - - - - - - - DOLLARS

WARRANTY NATIONAL TRUST COMPANY   JUNIPER SALES SPECIALTY COMPANY
NEW ORLEANS. LOUISIANA

AUTHORIZED SIGNATURE

MARTIN MILLER & SONS
58 BROAD STREET   ATLANTA, GEORGIA 30303

Credit Memorandum

TO   The National Company   DATE   March 28, 19--
     6 North Michigan Avenue   CREDIT MEMO NO. 2435
     Chicago, Illinois   60607   ORDER NO.   3122

YOUR ACCOUNT HAS BEEN CREDITED AS FOLLOWS:

QUANTITY	DESCRIPTION	CAT. NO.	UNIT PRICE	TOTAL
1	Steel guest chair, in excess of order	GC37	32 50	32 50
	TOTAL			32 50
	LESS 10% TRADE DISCOUNT			3 25
	TOTAL			29 25
	PLUS DELIVERY CHARGE			2 60
	TOTAL AMOUNT CREDITED			31 85

MARTIN MILLER & SONS
58 BROAD STREET   ATLANTA, GEORGIA 30303

Statement of Account

WITH   DATE March 30, 19--

The National Company
6 North Michigan Avenue
Chicago, Illinois   60607

AMOUNT ENCLOSED $ ....

PLEASE RETURN THIS STUB WITH YOUR CHECK

DATE	REFERENCE	CHARGES	CREDITS	BALANCE
Mar 1	Brought forward			130 00
Mar 5	Payment on account		95 00	35 00
Mar 19	Invoice No. 2913	255 05		290 05
Mar 23	Payment on account		35 00	255 05
Mar 26	Invoice No. 3122	366 98		622 03
Mar 28	Credit Memo No. 2435		31 85	590 18
Mar 29	Payment on account		255 05	335 13

PAY LAST AMOUNT IN THIS COLUMN

CREDIT MEMORANDUM is a fairly standard form used to let a customer know that a change has been made (usually but not always in his favor) in his account balance.

STATEMENT OF ACCOUNT is a periodic (usually monthly) summary of transactions with a customer, showing charges and credits and the cumulative balance right up to date.

Forms 28-29

CREDIT MEMOS
Forms: workbook 215
Directions: arrange
as shown above, left

FORM 28. Martin Miller & Sons issues Credit Memorandum No. 2435 5
to The National Company [6 North Michigan Avenue, Chicago, Illinois 18
60607] to correct an error in the shipment for which Invoice No. 3122 21
had been issued: For 1 steel guest chair in excess of order, catalog GC37 40
@ $32.50 for a total of 32.50. From this amount, however, must be 53
deducted the 10 percent [3.25] trade discount; then to the amount must 70
be added the allowance for the two-way delivery charges for the chair [2.60]. 89

FORM 29. Walsh & Weir, Printers issues Credit Memorandum No. 1421 7
to National [address above] to correct a shortage in the shipment for 21
which Invoice No. M-321 had been issued: For 200 reams NatCo letter- 39
heads, 8½ by 11, shortage in delivery, @ $2.75. Include 3 percent tax 63
refund, too. 73

Forms 30-31

MONTHLY STATEMENTS
Forms: workbook 217
Directions: arrange
as shown above, right

FORM 30. Monthly statement from Martin Miller & Sons recapitulates 5
the firm's transactions with The National Company for March: 19

Mar 1 Brought forward (from February)	......	......	130 00	35
Mar 5 Payment on account (credit)	......	95 00	35 00	47
Mar 19 Invoice No. 2913 (charge)	255 05	......	290 05	57
Mar 23 Payment on account (credit)	......	35 00	255 05	68
Mar 26 Invoice No. 3122 (charge)	366 98	......	622 03	78
Mar 28 Credit Memo No. 2435 (credit)	......	31 85	590 18	90
Mar 29 Payment on account (credit)	......	255 05	335 13	102

FORM 31. Monthly statement from Walsh & Weir, Printers recapit- 5
ulates the firm's transactions with The National Company for March: 19

Mar 1 Brought forward (from February)	......	......	000 00	36
Mar 26 Invoice No. M-321 (charge)	4025 24	......	4025 24	48
Mar 27 Payment on account (credit)	......	3000 00	?	61
Mar 28 Credit Memo No. 1421 (credit)	......	566 50	?	73

LINE: 60
SPACING: SINGLE
DRILLS: THREE EACH
GOAL: LEARN TO TYPE
ON RULED FORMS
STRESS: TOUCH
CONTROL ON
NUMBERS

115-A. Recall skill by half-minute writings on each line. Repeat these lines in Lesson 116.

115-A. Tune up on these review lines

1 She may wish to pay them if and when they go to work for us.

2 To jeopardize and hit six of the brigades, we moved quickly.

3 She assigned pages *10, 28, 39, 47, and 56* for the next week.

1 | 2 | 3 | 4 | 5 | 6 | 7 | 8 | 9 | 10 | 11 | 12

115-B. Readjust machine for double spacing, 50-space line, and tabs at 10 and 20. Then, steps:

1. Scan the copy, to be sure you can read it, and note use of tabulator.

2. Select and practice any half-dozen words

3. Take a 5-minute timed writing, pausing for a few-seconds rest at the end of each minute. (Or, type one copy, pausing to rest at each "double-double" spacing point.)

4. Take a 5-minute timed writing without pauses. (Or, type a copy without pausing even one time.) SI 1.40—normal, if you can tabulate by touch!

115-B. Sustain your skill on production copy

4	Date:	*March 16, 19 —*	6
To:	John K. Speare, Head, Payroll Section	16
From:	Ruth N. North, Personnel	23
Subject:	Adding New Employee to the Payroll ↓4	33
		34

5 The following has been processed by Personnel and   44

may now be added to the payroll.   Data you need: ↓4   54

		55
6	Full name:	*Mr. Ralph Hale Carr*	63
Local address:	*1321 West Sixth Avenue*	72
Phone:	*392–4141*	77
Soc. Sec. No.:	*343–28–6102*	84
Marital status:	*Married*	90
No. dependents:	*Self and one*	97
Savings bonds:	*$50 per month*	104
Section assigned:	*Stores and Supply*	113
Effective date:	*March 24, 19 —*	121
Starting rate:	*$5200 per year* ↓4	128
		129

7 If there are other data you need, the file of this   139

new employee will be available in this department. ↓4   150

Holly Anne Graham   157
For Ruth N. North   163

Forms 32–33

FILL-IN MEMORANDUMS
Paper: workbook page 219 or plain paper
Copy 1: data shown here
Copy 2: your personal data, as a $75-a-week secretary in Sales

If you lack workbook forms, type the Lesson 115-116 assignments as memos or as tables, to the extent that they can be so arranged.

115-C. Learn to type payroll forms

The payroll forms used in different businesses vary considerably both in their arrangement and in the extent to which they *are* typewritten. Typical *typewriting* problems involved in typing on such forms include: